Good People Evil Society

A Philosophical and Moral Inquiry

Brynne VanHettinga,
J.D., M.P.A., Ph.D.

Printed in the United States

First Edition

ISBN: 978-1-7322856-5-1

Questions, comments, or requests to the author for speaking engagements, email **books4thinkers@gmail.com**

For more by this author visit: **https://www.books4thinkers.com**

Other Books by this Author

Full Length Books

The Great Jobs Deception: Why More Workforce Education Will Not Solve the Problem of Inadequate Jobs (2018)

Why Assholes Rule the World (2019)

EBooks

The REAL History of Labor Day and the War on American Workers

Campaign Finance Reform: The Shifting and Ambiguous Line Between Where Money Talks and Speech is Free

Survival in the Gig Economy or get it **Free** by visiting www.books4thinkers.com

Table of Contents

Prelude 1

Introduction 5

Part I: The Good Society

Introduction to Part I 21

Section One: What Makes a Good Society? 27

Section Two: Radical Individualism and Loss of A Moral Commonwealth 53

Section Three: The Role of Religion. 73

Part II: The Nature of Human Morality

Introduction to Part II 103

Section One: The Evolution of Moral Codes 107

Section Two: "Us" Versus "Them" and the Moralization of Immorality 125

Section Three: Power, Privilege, and Antisocial Pathology 151

Section Four: Obeying Orders: When Good People Go Bad . . . 171

Section Five: Administrative Evil: When Systems Go Bad 187

Part III: How Societies Become Evil

Introduction to Ponerology. 213

Section One: Individual Psychopathy 223

Section Two: The Hysteroidal Cycle and Ponerogenic Process. . 253

Section Three: Pathocracy 281

Part IV: How Ponerization and Pathocracy Manifest Today

Introduction to Part IV 311

Section One: Our Livelihoods: Work Isn't Working For Us 325

Section Two: The Economy: Extreme Inequality Harms
More Than Our Bank Accounts 353

Section Three: The Government: Democracy Under Siege 381

Section Four: The Media: Fake News and Manufactured Reality 411

Section Five: Generalized Signs of Hystericized Thinking 437

Part V: Is A Good Society Possible?

Interlude 467

Section One: What Will Be the Future? 483

Section Two: What Are We To Do? 505

Postlude 535

Bibliography 543

Prelude

On March 3, 1991, four LAPD officers arrested a Black man by the name of Rodney King following a high-speed chase along I-210. King—who had a history of alcohol abuse and other run-ins with the law—was obviously inebriated at the time of his arrest. But instead of simply arresting King and transporting him to the drunk tank, the officers brutally kicked and beat King for a full 15 minutes, while about a dozen additional officers stood by and watched. As a result, King suffered multiple skull fractures, broken bones and teeth, and permanent brain damage. Unknown to the officers at the time, the beating was captured on video by an amateur videographer—a technological development that has since come to cast doubt on the usual instant credibility given to police (and other representatives of the establishment) in such matters.

Based on the video, the four officers were charged with assault and excessive use of force. Following a three-month trial, a mostly white jury acquitted the officers of all charges on April 29, 1992. Within hours, violent protests erupted in South Central Los Angeles. These were not mere protests, but included looting and burning of small and minority-owned businesses. At first, the violence was limited to the area around Florence and Normandie, but it quickly spread to other areas throughout Los Angeles. Mayor Tom Bradly declared a state of emergency, and California Governor Pete Wilson sent 2,000 National Guard Troops into the city. On May 1, 1992, during the third day of rioting, King made his now famous plea:

Can't we all just get along?

Almost 30 years later, we are again urgently asking the same question. The news cycle is again filled with protests against police brutality and murder of Black citizens. Some of us wanted to believe that we were now in a post-racial society, having witnessed the first Black American President who was elected to two terms. Yet this apparent sign of progress has seemed to aggravate a divisiveness that might never have really been on the wane. While most of the current protests are peaceful when compared to the King verdict riots, they are occurring against a backdrop of not only a resurgence of visible racism, but a society that is characterized by a hypercompetitive dog-eat-dog, everyone-for-himself ethos that seems to have destroyed any sense of community and created a hate-filled war of all against all.

Most of us are not hateful people, nor are we overt racists. At the same time, we sense that something is happening which seems to make us view the world cynically and quick to take offense at the slightest provocation. Our society is becoming increasingly authoritarian, with even ordinary people (i.e., non-elites) calling for increased social control and abridgement of freedoms. Systemic racism is embedded in an economy that creates obscene wealth for a few while precariatizing the many. We live in a culture that values image over substance. "Disruption" is celebrated by those who can position themselves in a network of opportunities while the rest of us struggle to navigate the externalized chaos. Even as we turn to our faith traditions in search of answers to building a more cohesive society, we find another form of us-versus-them division. All of these things operate to change us—and not for the better.

We like to believe that we are masters of our own free will, consciously deciding how we will behave in the moment. We also like to believe that individuals are either good or bad, and behavior is an expression of some combination of inherited personality traits and childhood upbringing. However, research suggests that even good people can go horribly bad when presented with certain situations or environments. The most famous of these studies are Stanley Milgram's electroshock and Philip Zimbardo's Stanford prison experiments, which we will fully analyze herein. We will also explore why some people might be more susceptible to these negative influences while others are more able to resist them.

The purpose of this book is not to excuse someone who consciously commits a bad act. It is also not a book about racism *per se,* although it does address the behavioral dynamics (evolutionary psychology and sociology) of why we tend to divide the world into "us-versus-them" and the cooperation-competition dichotomy.

Additionally, there are segments of society who benefit from keeping the majority of us divided—either based on immutable physical characteristics such as race, gender, and national origin or on group membership of personal choice such as religion, political party, unionized workers, or public servants. While some of these differences are manufactured and manipulated (because stirring up resentment increases loyalty, serves as distraction, or promotes revenue-producing engagement behaviors), the most salient—and toxic—source of social difference is that which is based on differentials of power and privilege.

When we look past the differences that seem to be so acute at the present moment, most of us have the same fundamental life goals. We want to have enough to meet our needs for today and not be unduly worried about how we will meet our needs tomorrow. We want to have the opportunity to reach our full potential—to find and develop our God-given abilities and natural talents and use these to help make the world a better place. We want to be seen and heard, along with the ability to influence the people, places and events that impact our lives. We want the same for our children and grandchildren, along with a sense of hope for the future. On some fundamental level, most of us acknowledge that we should also want all these things for everyone else, since it is the only way that we can rightfully claim them for ourselves.

When we acknowledge our common humanity, we join Rodney King in asking why we can't all get along. Herein, we will indulge in a deep dive of exploration and inquiry, assisted by thinkers and researchers in psychology, sociology, politics, government, law, economics, philosophy, and religion, as we also ask a more complex question:

Who are "We" and why does it matter?

Introduction

I do not understand my own actions. For I do not do the good I want, but the evil I do not want.

Romans: 7:15

Even before the coronavirus pandemic and the recent Black Lives Matter protests, our world was in turmoil. People were not necessarily rioting in the streets, but our politics had become increasingly divisive, and our social life seemed fractured. On top of this, most of us had been working harder for less for decades, even as Wall Street was booming. There was a sense of frantic running in place while going nowhere, yet few were questioning it because this was assumed to be part of "progress."

When we generally think about good and evil, we tend to focus on individual behavior, dividing the world into "good guys" and "bad guys." Most of our understanding about good and evil comes from our faith or religious traditions. Because faith is a personal matter of free will, the teachings focus on what we need to do to be (or become) good people. Here in America, with our cultural tradition of individualism, we like to think that good behavior is simply a matter of individual choice.

Advancements in secular science have provided us a greater understanding of human behavior. Research in psychology and genetics has found that there is a subset of individuals who are predisposed to bad behavior—either because of inherited antisocial personality traits or dysfunctional upbringing. We also like to think that such antisocial individuals are readily identifiable, and that the rest of us can take appropriate measures to ensure that these individuals do not attain positions of power where they can adversely affect society as a whole. While science allows us a greater understanding of the causes of bad behavior, this approach also tends to focus on individuals and their immediate environment.

More so than a random collection of individuals, complex societies are made of institutions, or systems of rules and social ordering. These systems of rules, procedures and practices do not arise by themselves, but are in some sense collectively constructed. They may be so constructed with the input of all of us or input from only a few of us. Indeed, most of these systems are designed by those who occupy higher positions in the social hierarchy (i.e., elites) or those with particular technical expertise. Most of the time, these systems and institutions are designed with prosocial intentions—mutual protection, efficient allocation of resources, the development of human talent and potential, and the inculcation of moral and cultural values. Even in cases where a system has the potential for authoritarian overreach, the objective is the maintenance of social order and preservation of safety.

This book asks the question whether societies can become evil, even if the majority of persons living within them are basically good. It is not a question that lends itself to a simple yes-or-no-answer. Because, if the answer is yes, the next line of inquiry is how could this be possible? And how would we even recognize such a thing if it happened?

New studies in both sociology/anthropology and neuroscience have found that social systems and cultures can have as much influence on who we are as our inherited genetics. This should ***not*** be construed as a "the devil made me do it" excuse for bad behavior, but an analysis of how systemic processes affect behavior independent of individual personality traits. That is, we do not have a simple good-bad switch that we can turn on and off by the operation of free will. In addition to our own personality characteristics, we have also inherited various genetic triggers, which can change our behavior in response to certain environmental conditions. Most of us have heard of the "fight or flight" response to imminent physical threats, but what happens when we are under lower levels of chronic anxiety (will we be able to pay the bills or even have a job next month)? Such low-grade yet inexorable conditions can actually "rewire" us, shifting our neurochemical responses and even our ability to regulate our own behavior.

It is both unfortunate and telling that the majority of research on institutional culture today is conducted on behalf of corporations—for the purpose of inculcating a manufactured social solidarity in order to enhance the bottom line. Culture is something that is collectively (and organically) created over time, not something that is imposed from the top down for purposes of narrow and predetermined objectives. History suggests that culture is often defined and determined by those who occupy higher social positions. We might recall from our classes in history learning about kings, rulers, generals, popes, scientists, and various intellectuals, but we probably didn't learn much about what life was like for ordinary people—particularly their inner life.

In ***Good People, Evil Society,*** we will analyze how a culture can be corrupted, as well as how this adversely affects the inner life of the people living within it. While the corruption of culture often begins with too much (unaccountable) power in too few hands, it is much more complex than the rise of a "bad guy" into a dictatorship position. The process may be so incremental that it is barely noticed, but one sure sign is when antisocial and malevolent worldviews become assimilated into the mainstream, usually couched in seemingly prosocial frameworks such as efficiency, meritocracy, law and order, prosperity, or freedom. This is more easily accomplished when the majority of people are living under conditions of (even low-level) constant fear, stress or anxiety. It is often accompanied by evidence of a "dumbing down" or lack of critical thinking.

In order to understand the institutionalization of corruption, we must also understand institutions themselves: government, law, economics, education, religion, etc. Bruce Malina distinguishes four broad basic social institutions: kinship, politics, religion, and economics.[1] Ideally, these institutions should operate in some kind of balance, although in most complex societies one or two of them tend to predominate. In biblical societies, the primary institutions were kinship and politics. Although people did worship, "religion" was described in terms of covenant and law, and was expressed in terms of belonging (kinship/tribe) and power (politics). There was no vocabulary to describe market economies nor the abstract reasoning of formal religion. This is what makes modern biblical interpretations—particularly those that apply to economic issues--difficult and ambiguous.

In modern times, kinship-dominant systems are represented by Latin America and most Mediterranean countries. While these countries are predominantly Catholic, "theology is…rooted in the practical attempt to dislodge economics from kinship and embed it in politics," and society is ruled by "well-born" persons who have a sense of *noblesse oblige.*[2] Countries who are politics-dominant belong to those defined as "applied Marxist"—the former Soviet Union and the People's Republic of China. Here, political institutions govern the rules of kinship, religion, and economics. Most Islamic republics today are religion-dominant, where sharia law determines the norms of kinship, economics, and politics. (This was also the case in medieval Christianity).

In the U.S.—and "to a far lesser extent in Western Europe"—economics is dominant.[3] How this has affected our social norms will become apparent in Section IV. However, we can readily observe how an economics-dominant culture has affected the other systems: Kinship becomes "networking," religion promotes Prosperity Gospel, and the dominance of money in politics is a subject that itself is too extensive to be covered here. Even our view of human nature is colored by economics. We describe human behavior in the language of *homo economicus,* or the enlightenment idealized "rational man." Rational man makes all decisions on the basis of a calculated self-interest. In theory, the rational man is not purely selfish, because his calculations include how his actions are going to impact others (e.g., they may discontinue doing business with him if they find out he is cheating them). Yet, the rational man model excludes the possibility of an interest in the betterment of society or any other form of higher purpose.

America is known as being a highly individualist society. It was settled by peoples who came from elsewhere looking for opportunity outside the constraints of more socially integrated societies. Although it is easy to believe that Americans are characteristically more selfish than other cultures, there are a number of studies that find an overwhelming majority of Americans agree that we should find ways to help the less fortunate and insure that everyone has the opportunity to succeed.[4] Even here in America, where our culture of individualism and suspicion of government place primary responsibility on individual effort, we also acknowledge that sometimes random bad stuff happens and that "we" (collective society) have to step in to insure the welfare of others. Yet, as we will address at greater length herein, our culture itself induces tendencies (both natural and not) to selfishness and competition, which operates to frustrate the creation of any kind of commonwealth, moral or otherwise. At its extreme, hyper-meritocratic individualism can segue into a war-of-all-against-all.

In 1990, James L. Perry and Lois Wise proposed a way to measure a construct they termed Public Service Motivation, or PSM.[5] This research followed a decade of tax revolts, public austerity, and bureaucrat bashing. Consequently, federal agencies (as well as many state governments) were concerned about recruiting the next generation of public servants to replace an aging workforce. Perry's model was proposed to suggest that certain individuals are motivated by a desire to serve the public—to "make a difference"—in contrast to the utility-maximizing, self-interest-seeking *homo economicus* that represented the cultural establishment behavioral model of humanity. Perry's objective was to find a different way to attract new people into public service, since money and status/respect (as well as the job security and benefits which were often the only inducements government employment had to offer) simply were not likely to be available. Subsequent research expanded the notion of PSM, parsing it into subtypes, as well as examining correlates with other personal characteristics such as religious attendance and income.

While PSM is something that is measured at the individual level—and indeed it varies along a continuum between individuals—it can also be affected by institutional factors. That is, while each individual has a hard-wired propensity for either a high, middle, or low level of PSM, this level can be boosted upward or pushed downward based on situational factors. Later research has identified three forms of what it terms "social value orientations." The first type is the cooperative, or pro-social orientation.[6] These are the folks who value the needs of others as much as their own, and often look for equality of outcomes. Cooperatives are the employees who will spend extra time to help a customer or client even if their own personal rewards are based on numbers and efficiency. The second type is the individualistic orientation.[7] The individualist is focused on promoting their own self-interest and is largely indifferent to the outcomes for others. The third group are those with a competitive orientation.[8] Competitors are concerned with comparisons of their own outcomes with the outcomes of others, and they will choose options that maximize their relative, rather than their absolute, reward. One study found that some 46% of people are cooperators, 38% are individualists, and 12% are competitors.[9]

A recent study of police officers analyzed social value orientation in 102 police officers actively serving in the Israeli national police.[10] Police officers are public servants, and—like military soldiers—often put their own lives at risk in order to perform their duty. As such, we would expect police officers to have a higher level of PSM or social value orientation. Conversely, other research has suggested that persons who choose "hierarchy-enhancing" professions like law enforcement or military also have a higher degree of Social Dominance Orientation (SDO, generally regarded as anti-social) and authoritarianism.[11] However, the point of this particular study was not to examine the differences between police officers and the general public, but to look at changes in social value orientation between the officers' on-duty and off-duty activities. The researchers found a significant negative difference in social value orientation between the officers' on-duty and off-duty lives. They also found a negative correlation between years of service and social value orientation—suggesting that social value orientation decreased with length of time on the job.

The obvious conclusion is that the work environment had a negative impact on any pre-existing level of social value orientation. The authors suggest several explanations for their findings. One is that "conflicts between immediate self-interests and longer-term collective interests are so pervasive in everyday life," that successfully managing these conflicts is "the most challenging task [faced by] governments and public service organizations."[12] They also suggest (citing other research) that high demands in the form of work stress, rules, complexity, and a rigid hierarchy can attenuate social value orientation. Finally, they address the effects of New Public Management, or running government more like a business. The imposition of competitive-based rewards and punishments can serve to "crowd out" pro-social motivations, because people are viewed as "cases" rather than citizens, and the focus is on the numbers. Although this is only one study and the authors themselves admit that the findings cannot be generalized to other public service occupations, the bottom line is that work environment can have an effect on pro-social or anti-social behavior above and beyond an individual's natural predisposition.

Lawyers are frequently pointed to as representatives of corruption that is facilitated by the system. However, many people would be surprised at how active the legal profession is in advocating for the public interest. Most State Bar associations do a lot of work to improve the profession as a whole, and engage in proactive campaigns to encourage prosocial behavior among attorney-members. Bar associations and their officers constantly exhort their members to participate in pro bono (providing free legal services to the poor) and public service activities. Awards and attention are showered upon members who donate money and time to pro bono representation and service to the bar itself as well as to the legal profession generally. To look at most bar association publications, one would not believe that attorneys are publicly recognized for how much money they make or how many cases they win among their own, but rather for what they give back.

Most bar associations also acknowledge the everyday stresses faced by attorneys—particularly those in solo and small practices that constitute the majority—and provide bar-sponsored programs to assist with everything from drug and alcohol dependence, anxiety, depression, and office management resources to improve efficiency. Unlike the urgent exhortations to increase production and work harder that typifies most workplaces, the approach taken by State Bar associations to improve the well-being of individual attorneys is surprisingly humane. Bar associations are thus organizational models for the promotion of prosocial behavior as well as for realistic compassion in a culture that is generally workaholic. Although these State Bars work hard to encourage prosocial behavior among their ranks, they are not immune from dysfunctions operating in the larger society.

Rather than disparage attorneys as greedy ambulance-chasing barratrists, we should commend the majority of attorneys who spend countless unpaid hours working to improve the legal profession and insuring that lower-income citizens have access to the courts. Most of the attorneys who involve themselves in bar association work are sincere in their noble objectives. Indeed, many people come into law school with the goal of "making a difference" and improving the lives of underserved populations in some way. Yet, notwithstanding these good intentions, many attorneys—including those who hold leadership positions in bar organizations—end up working for large national and global law firms who generally represent the interests of corporations and the wealthy against everyone else—workers, consumers, the environment, etc.

This schizoid dichotomy is not perceived by those who participate in it because it is essentially masked by business as usual—the fish who does not see the water in which it swims because the fish is surrounded by it. In any given Bar association publication, one is likely to see a group of smiling, suited men and women passing a giant check (with a large number on it) to some non-profit or public interest organization. The attorneys often work for some large corporate firm and are patting themselves on the back because they are helping to fund a cure for cancer or have won a case for a disabled child. But no one makes the connection that the same firm may have represented a company who was poisoning the environment with carcinogens, or paying workers too little to afford medical care, or opposing rights of the disabled for the purpose of reducing costs.

An illustration of this paradox can be found in the December 2019 issue of the *Texas Bar Journal.* Here we find a letter of accolade from the Executive Director, praising Texas attorneys for donating millions to legal aid organizations, establishing free or low-cost clinics for veterans and survivors of domestic violence, and other "stories of big-heartedness" and public service. This is juxtaposed with the featured legal subject of the month, "International Law." Here we find articles about "key issues and clauses to consider" in your next international outsourcing deal, Asian mergers and acquisitions, managing global supply chains, and advice for businesses on how to exploit the new Trade Promotion

Authority/Free Trade Agreement. Apparently, no one has considered how any of this might contribute to increasing populations of persons moving across borders in search of livelihoods and subsistence.

The same pattern is repeated in the November 2020 issue: One article touts the newly founded Texas Poverty Law Project, which attempts to address the problems that keep people in the "poverty trap." The remaining articles feature "compliance issues" facing white collar criminal defense attorneys and corporate compliance officers. The problem here is framed as "managing environments with a high risk of corruption," along with the "intensifying enforcement activity," especially involving the Foreign Corrupt Practices Act. There is practically no discussion about moral degradation or even how such activities harm the public at large, but rather the objective is to keep the company out of costly trouble. In essence, by serving the system, attorneys are working on one end to create the problems that they are working so hard on the other end (through their bar association) to fix.

The December 2019 *Texas Bar Journal* also gives an example of the paradox that is experienced by the individual attorneys themselves. One article addresses tips and techniques for new working parents to make their lives less stressful. Another page displays a letter from the President of the Texas Young Lawyers that urges attorneys to practice kindness, prayer, and gratitude, while an article on the facing page urges attorneys to be "deliberate and relentless in the pursuit of your goals." This is tantamount to the irony one sees in popular magazines that contain articles on weight loss juxtaposed with photos and recipes that seem designed to make one hungry and test one's willpower.

It is hard to believe—even in these conspiracy-crazed times—that these paradoxical placements of information are deliberately calculated to make us crazy. Rather, most people are simply blind to the paradox. Law students go to law school with high hopes of becoming champions of justice, only to end up working for corporate firms because they need to pay their law school loans and have something left over to buy a home or start a family. Their (paid) legal work helps companies avoid laws designed to pay people a living wage, provide safe workplaces, or prevent environmental toxicity, but they can assuage themselves by spending their own time or money helping persons who are harmed by the behaviors they are enabling. Indeed, many of them may not even see the connection, because it is usually indirect and complex. They champion "access to justice" while serving a system that is inherently unjust. In their own lives, they may squeeze in a mindfulness class between leaving the office late and dashing off to a networking event. They may profess the importance of family and community, but work (billable hours, a lucrative client, partnership track) will always come first.

The foregoing description is not intended as lawyer-bashing, but rather as an example of basically good and decent people who simply choose the path of least resistance in a corrupted system. Which returns us to the central question herein: how can a system (a corporation, a government, a nation, a society) become corrupt if the majority of persons living and working within it are basically good? This is not to say that most of us are saints, but neither are most of us sociopaths. We all have the capacity to do the right thing or the wrong thing, and our propensity to choose one or the other depends both on our inherited traits of personality as well as our environment. The "system," therefore, can operate to either encourage or discourage prosocial or antisocial behaviors.

The creation of a good society involves more than dictate. Telling everyone to love their neighbor or just say no to drugs will not *ipso facto* make it so. Nor will instituting a system of hyper-rationalized and stringent regulation. The bigger question is how to design a society/system that encourages our better natures rather than our selfish ones. Our religious traditions are important, but they tend to be overly focused on matters of individual faith and authoritarian proscriptions. They also tend to create an "us versus them" division between believers and non-believers, which can destroy the social cohesion necessary to create a good society. Critical thinking—or enlightenment-style scientific rationality—is also important, but it tends to neglect necessary matters of the human spirit. Moreover, as more recent philosophers have proposed, technocratic rationality taken to extremes contains the potential for macrosocial evil when it is not counter-balanced by moral considerations.

We will begin our inquiry in Part I by asking what a good society would look like. Not just how do we get there, but basic things like what do we measure and what do we value. We next examine the good society in the context of a moral commonwealth. We ask the question whether our society may be too focused on the rights of individuals such that we have lost any sense of civic duty or obligation to the larger community. We then look at the role of religion, both as a system of rules and law and as a cultural phenomenon. We examine similarities and differences among and between the world's major religions, particularly what they have to say about right relations, human suffering, and evil.

In Part II, we turn to the science of human behavior. We see how moral codes evolved through the institutions of religion and government. We also look at the evolutionary purposes of both competitive and cooperative behavior, particularly how cooperative behavior allowed humans to develop complex societies. However, increasingly complex social structures created hierarchies of power and privilege, which tend to bring out more of our competitive dark side. We then look at modern behavioral research on how good people can go bad, specifically Stanley Milgram's electroshock experiments and Philip Zimbardo's Stanford prison experiment.

In Part III, we thoroughly analyze the work of Dr. Andrew Lobaszewsky. Lobaszewsky was a traditionally-trained psychiatrist who studied the behavioral degradation of the Polish population during occupation by first the Nazis and then the Soviet communists. Unlike most other documentaries of fascism—which either focus on the personalities of individual leaders or political-historical context, Lobaszewsky studied how the thinking and behavior of ordinary persons was affected by oppressive systems. Although Lobaszewsky's work was for the most part ignored during his lifetime, it provides a detailed description of the dynamics between an evil system and the psychological functioning of otherwise normal individuals. Lobaszewsky calls this new science ***ponerology***, or the study of evil that affects culture and systems.

In Part IV, we will apply Lobaszewsky's theory to what is happening in our society today, specifically in the United States in the latter twentieth and early twenty-first centuries, although we are seeing many of these phenomena globally. We first document the degradation of our work life. This is ironically where most of us are going to be exposed to (often) low-grade ponerizing influences such that we are barely able to recognize it. Our degraded work life is a consequence of extreme and growing inequality, which has created an unnatural oligarchy and plutonomy. An increasing concentration of wealth and power has in turn resulted in a form of pseudo-democracy, which retains the functional forms of voting and citizen free speech, yet the ability to effect systemic change is controlled by a small number of elite individuals.

In order to reduce the possibility of citizen revolt, information is also controlled rather than outright censored. As mass media and information technology platforms become concentrated in fewer hands, citizens are either kept distracted with celebrity glamor or kept enraged by inflammatory factoids which may or may not be true. The beginnings of a rudimentary pathocracy are already observable, as those who rise to positions of power do so more because of privilege and connections rather than inclination or ability to serve. These are individuals who are motivated primarily by self-interest. Their ultimate objective is to preserve the system (as well as their own privilege) and not to serve the people. Finally, we look at how all of this has negatively impacted our own worldview and behavior—including our ability to think critically and consult our own moral compass.

In the final Part V, we ask the critical question: What will be our future? We are poised at a period in time when the continuing degradation of society may ultimately result in the end of the human race. Alternatively, such things tend to be cyclical, in that normal decent people will eventually become sufficiently frustrated with the way things are and find the fortitude within themselves to reverse the current course. If we truly want to see change, we must confront our own dark side as well as work toward the common good. We also propose some practical suggestions.

It is my hope that this book will encourage people to both think harder and pray harder. Yes, there is also work to be done, but it cannot be the joyless, soul-sucking work in which most of us now spend too much time in exchange for purposeless subsistence. Moreover, this is not the type of work where you have a finish point and can say you are done. We have built the current system, which means that we can also build something else. But before we begin the work of rebuilding, we must first set our own moral compass. The work of creating a moral commonwealth—where all of us can thrive, where human decency is acknowledged, and where everyone, no matter who they are or where they come from, is treated with respect—is a job for all of us.

Notes

---

[1] Malina, B. (1987, October). Wealth and poverty in the New Testament World. *Interpretation 41*(4), 354-66. Also in M.L. Stackhouse, D.P. McCann, S.J. Roles, and P.N. Williams, Eds. *On Moral Business.* (1995). Grand Rapids, MI: Wm B. Eerdmans Publishing Co. at pp. 88-93.

[2] *Id.* at p. 91.

[3] *Id.*

[4] Sachs, J.D. (2011). *The price of civilization: Reawakening American virtue and prosperity.* New York, NY: Penguin Random House LLC.

[5] Perry, J.L., & Wise, L. (1990). The motivational bases of public service. *Public Administration Review 50*: 367-373.

[6] Chirumbolo, A., Leone, L., & Desimoni, M. (2016). The interpersonal roots of politics: Social value orientation, socio-political attitudes and prejudice. *Personality and Individual Differences, 91,* 144-53.

[7] Murphy, R.O., & Ackermann, K.A. (2014). Social value orientation: Theoretical and measurement issues in the study of social preferences. *Personality and Social Psychology Review, 18*(1), 13-41.

[8] Balliet, D., Parks, C., & Joireman, J. (2009). Social value orientation and cooperation in social dilemmas: A meta-analysis. *Group Process and Intergroup Relations, 12*(4), 533-47.

[9] Au, W.T., & Kwong, J.Y.Y. (2004). Measurement and effects of social value orientation in social dilemmas: A review. In *Contemporary Psychological Research on Social Dilemmas. (*R. Suleiman, D.V. Budescu, I. Fischer, & D.M. Messick, Eds.). Cambridge: Cambridge University Press at pp. 71-98.

[10] Cohen, N., & Hertz, U. (2020). Street-level bureaucrats social value orientation on and off duty. *Public Administration Review, 80*(3), 442-453.

[11] Pratto, F., Sidanius, J., Stallworth, L., & Malle, B. (1994). Social dominance orientation: A personality variable predicting social and political attitudes. *Journal of Personality and Social Psychology, 4*(67), 741-763, at p. 754.

[12] Cohen and Hertz, *supra* at p. 450.

Part I

The Good Society

Introduction to Part I
The Good Society

Liberty can no more exist without virtue...than the body can live and move without a soul.

John Adams

*

What we are confronted with is the realization that we live in an increasingly interdependent society where individual good is not possible outside the context of common good. It makes no sense to separate moral principles from institutional behavior, political power from economic influence, and environmental values from material rewards. To do so is to divorce the social system from its basic element, the human being, who does not behave in a fragmented manner.

S. Prakash Sethi[1]

*

Justice has a vital part to play, not only in the bare survival of moral systems, but in their flourishing as well. The struggle for justice has its own dynamic and reaches well beyond restraint of domination. Justice affirms the moral worth of individuals; sustains autonomy and self-respect; domesticates authority; and establishes a framework for moral discourse on public matters...If we reduce justice to a negative virtue or to a way of achieving minimal cooperation, we lost a great deal of its resonance and promise.

Phillip Selznick[2]

As modern thinking about society has grown more technocratic, researchers have attempted to find ways to quantify the quality of society. One way has been to measure subjective life satisfaction, which is sometimes called "happiness."[3] Individual happiness can serve as an indicator of the effectiveness of social policies because it is socially determined by the position of individuals and groups in a society's opportunity structure.[4] This suggests that if most of the individuals within a particular society are happy, it is probably a good one (or at least not a bad one). But it is not this simple; as we can intuitively sense that simply catering to everyone's hedonic gratifications will not necessarily lead us to a good society. We are seeing the paradox of this in twenty-first century modern societies today, where we have access to technological marvels and levels of material comfort that would have been undreamed of by our grandparents, yet we are seeing increased signs of angst in the form of stress, anxiety, addiction and suicide.[5]

While individual well-being and social well-being are linked, they are not necessarily the same. However, there appears to be a few recurring themes common to the welfare of both individuals and society as a whole. First, most people would have enough. They would not necessarily be wealthy, but they would have enough to meet their subsistence needs, as well as the ability to discover and develop their fullest potential. The second commonality is agency, or the ability to have meaningful input into the rules governing society at large that affect people directly. Indeed, some form of "democracy" is almost *de rigueur* in any version of a good society. The third requirement is community, or a network of reciprocal relationships which bind individuals to each other as well as to the larger society. A fourth, and more esoteric, requirement is a sense of a moral commonwealth. A moral commonwealth is often found among communities of religious faith and practices. However, the irony here is that, in a pluralistic society, a plethora of various faiths can destroy any sense of community or larger moral commonwealth. Hence the fifth requirement, which is institutions and procedures designed to deal with conflict in a fair and impartial manner (i.e., both substantive and procedural justice).

We will examine the role of religion in more depth in Section Three. For our purposes now, we will state that the teaching of most religions is directed at individual behaviors and not social structures. The choice to believe or not is an act of individual free will or a blessing of divine grace. The individual is solely responsible for his or her own behavior and eventually will be required to answer to a higher power. In the teachings of most faith traditions, the social structures in which their followers find themselves embedded apparently are regarded as irrelevant with respect to any issues of good and evil.

Faith communities themselves can be conflicted about their relationship to secular society. The early Jews viewed themselves as separate from the larger society, which was necessary to maintain their distinct culture and practices. Throughout history, members of various religious sects and orders have cloistered themselves in monasteries and other isolated communities to prevent entanglement with the corrupting effects of politics and society. There are churches today that favor the separation of church and state on the argument that this is the only way to preserve the purity of the faith. Conversely, many followers of various faiths believe that they have a duty to bring the love/Kingdom of God, the "good news," the "truth and the way," and other forms of moral teachings and practices to what is perceived to be a corrupt and fallen world.

The bigger social problem created by churches and religious communities is that, in spite of their own internal cohesion and moral commonwealth, many of them tend to divide the world into "us" (the elect, the chosen) and "them" (the infidels, the unbelievers, the damned). We will explore the psycho-social history of this "us versus them" dichotomy in Part II, Section Two. However, our premise is that religion (in a general sense) has an important role to play in the creation of a good society—***particularly in the prevention of macrosocial evil***—so long as its members (at least some of them) are able to transcend exclusionary and authoritarian tendencies.

In the first section, we ask the question, "What makes a good society?" i.e., how would we know it or recognize it? We analyze the research on human happiness, to include the complex relationship between income and happiness. Economists have found ways to correlate an inverse of happiness (sometimes referred to as a "misery index") with unemployment and inflation. Research by the epidemiologists Richard Wilson and Kate Pickett has found that inequality also correlates with symptoms of anxiety, distrust, and other forms of social breakdown. We then visit research on differences between cultural values (e.g., traditional/religious versus rational/secular and survival versus self-expression), and how these affect the well-being of the larger society.

In Section Two, we next ask whether a culture of hyper-individualism has completely subverted the possibility of finding or creating a moral commonwealth. In the final section, we briefly review the historical foundations of the world's major religions and their relationships with secular institutions. Here we also explore what the major religions have to say about human suffering and the nature of good and evil.

Notes

---

[1] Sethi, S. P. (1985, Summer). The righteous and the powerful: Differing paths to social goals. *Business and Society Review 54,* 37-44. Also in M.L. Stackhouse, D.P. McCann, S.J. Roels, & P.N. Williams, Eds. *On Moral Business: Classic and Contemporary Resources for Ethics in Economic Life.* Grand Rapids, MI: William B. Eerdmans Publishing Company.

[2] Selznick, P. (1992). *The moral commonwealth: Social theory and the promise of community.* Los Angeles, CA: University of California Press, p. 431.

[3] Jefferson's Enlightenment natural rights of "life, liberty and the pursuit of happiness" that we find in the American Declaration of Independence.

[4] Veenhoven, R. (2008). Healthy happiness: Effects of happiness on physical health and the consequences for preventive health care. *Journal of Happiness Studies 9*(3), 449-469.

[5] Case, A., & Deaton, A. (2020). *Deaths of despair and the future of capitalism.* Princeton, NJ: Princeton University Press. Full access available here: https://muse.jhu.edu/book/72589

Section One
What Makes A Good Society?

The whole is more than the sum of its parts.

Aristotle

*

Is…improvement in the circumstances of the lower ranks of the people to be regarded as an advantage or as an inconvenience to society?…What improves the circumstances of the greater part can never be regarded as an inconveniency to the whole. No society can surely be flourishing and happy, of which the far greater part of the members are poor and miserable.

Adam Smith, *The Wealth of Nations*, 1776

*

We ought to consider what is the end of government before we determine its best form. Upon this point all speculative politicians will agree that the happiness of society is the end of government, as all divines and moral philosophers will agree that the happiness of the individual is the end of man….All sober inquirers after truth, ancient and modern, pagan and Christian, have declared that the happiness of man, as well as his dignity, consists in virtue.

John Adams, *Thoughts on Government,* 1776

*

...the most numerous part of populations, whose talents are near average...generally accepts its modest social position...as long as the position fulfills the indispensable requirements of proper social adjustment and guarantees an equitable way of life no matter at what level of society the individual finds their proper fit.

Dr. Andrew Lobaszewsky

What does a good society look like? There is no shortage of historical philosophers who wrestle with describing what such a society would be like. The earliest of these in the Western tradition were the Greek moral philosophers; Plato (429 B.C), Socrates (399 B.C.) and Aristotle (384 B.C.).[1] In the West, our modern philosophies are based on foundations provided by Enlightenment thinkers: John Locke, Charles Montesquieu, Jean-Jacques Rousseau, Voltaire, and the Scottish political-economist Adam Smith. The age of Enlightenment arose as Europe was emerging from feudalism, and its emphasis was on reason (including the challenge of traditional authority), science, religious tolerance, and the "natural rights" of life, liberty and property. Here in the West (Western Europe and the countries that were founded by its colonists—the United States, Canada and Australia)—the concept of a good society tends to focus on individual rights and freedoms. Some contemporary philosophers make the argument that we have so fixed on individualism that we have lost any sense of commonwealth,[2] a subject that will be further explored in the following section.

We are better able to describe a good person than to describe a good society. While our ideas of what a good *individual* should be like share traditional, religious, and rational-philosophical roots, our ideas of what a good *society* should be like tend to be addressed solely by the rational-philosophical schools. Many of us obtain a prescription for what a good person should be like from our immediate family, from our faith tradition, or a combination of both. As we enter school, we become socialized through interaction with peers and learn about specific codes of behavior. Many of these early-learned behavioral rules involve submission to authority—to parents, to schoolteachers, to coaches and work bosses. A good person is someone who follows rules and respects others. This of course, assumes that "the rules" themselves are good, which most of the time is presumed as a given. As we enter adulthood, we might join professions or organizations with their own code of ethics, above and beyond civil laws and the Ten Commandments.

In addition to rules which generally operate to constrain behavior, we also learn about things such as freedom and democracy. This creates the first paradox: while obeying the law/rules is generally considered "good," the countervailing value of freedom proposes that individuals should not be unduly coerced by the collective. That is, at some point an overemphasis on rules can stifle free will and creativity and even segue into authoritarianism. In a purportedly "good" society, individuals should be free to pursue their own interests and agenda to the extent that these do not harm or infringe on the rights of others. The second paradox revolves around the question of whether or not the rules themselves are "good." This can be especially problematic when rules either create or presume privileges that apply to some groups or individuals but not to others. Thus, a system whereby everyone has a voice in creation of rules under which everyone is subject—what we know as democracy—becomes a necessary feature of a good society.

Here in America, we consider ourselves the paragon of freedom and democracy. Our first government was formed on the foundation of Enlightenment philosophies, and it became the model for most of Western Europe. Even those countries who maintain hereditary monarchies have established republican-style governments with institutions such as Parliaments, National Assemblies and elected representatives. America was also the model that other colonial nations (particularly in Africa) looked to in their own struggle for independence. Yet, democracy is not simply an all or nothing proposition: most countries operate along a continuum, where they may have some democratic features and institutions, but not others.

The Economist Intelligence Unit annually ranks 167 countries on a democracy index, measuring things such as free and fair elections, checks and balances, citizen participation and inclusion, and freedom of expression/civil liberties. In 2017, the United States dropped from being a "full democracy" to a "flawed democracy," coming in behind Uruguay, Malta, and South Korea.[3] Moreover, the *Economist*'s data suggests that democracy is decreasing globally.[4] Indeed, in the most recent (2020) democracy index, the *Economist* found a decline in democracy scores among 70% of the countries covered, with the global average score the lowest since this started to be measured in 2006. While the report suggests the global coronavirus pandemic may have played a part in this, the United States remained in the "flawed democracy" category at the rank of 25. The U.S. also saw an increase in "political participation and engagement" (generally a good thing), which was more than offset in the negative direction by a "collapse of social cohesion" and political polarization.[5]

Although most of us receive instruction on how to be a good person, our ideas about a good society (if we even think about it at all) tend to be more abstract. The rational-philosophical schools that concerned themselves with a good society (including the classical philosophers) were usually members of the educated elites and not the common people who struggled for everyday survival. Even today, subjects like civics education, government, law and political science are reserved for students attending elite colleges and graduate schools, while the ordinary working masses are channeled into "jobs," often with little or no understanding of the political and economic systems that govern their everyday lives. Today, the "good life" is described in terms of material standard of living or career advancement rather than more esoteric concepts like purpose and meaningfulness.

However, both the Greek and Enlightenment philosophers believed that the welfare of the common man was a primary objective of the good society. The foundations of democracy presume that the people ought to govern themselves, as they know their own needs better than anyone else. The American founders were also concerned about the possibility of tyranny of the majority, or the imposition of institutionalized inferiority on minority groups.

Although today we question how they could have been so blind to the perniciousness of slavery and the exclusion of women from citizenship, the idea that a small group of elites should not be making decisions for everyone else was heretical in a society that was emerging from feudalism and hereditary monarchy. Indeed, the subject of "justice" is frequently addressed in Enlightenment writings—a justice that involves more than the equal application of laws and rules, but an expanded concept of fundamental fairness.

Most descriptions (even historical ones) of a good society describe it in aspirational terms, rather than as a description of an actual reality. None of us have ever actually witnessed or experienced a truly good society. One can make a credible argument that such a thing may not even be possible, given the fallibility of human nature. But it is also human nature—at least for some of us—to strive to create a good society even as we recognize that a perfect utopia may be impossible. Various utopian societies have come and gone over time, and most proved to be unworkable. So, perhaps our good society need not be perfect. However, it must maintain institutions systems, and culture that are able to correct—rather than encourage— the inevitable manifestations of the darker side of human nature.

What do we Measure?

Perhaps the biggest difficulty in determining whether or not a society is good is deciding what we are going to measure. Modern societies typically judge their success primarily based on measures of economic output. One logical reason for this is that it is relatively easy to measure GDP. Yes, it involves significant effort in data collection and computational logistics, but the objective is simply to add up the value of all the goods and services produced in the relevant jurisdiction (the city, the county, the state, the nation). Other measurement problems arise when even true and accurate numbers don't serve as a sufficient descriptor of reality—a phenomenon we will next address.

We are now going to take a short detour for an exercise in practical statistics. For those of you who hate math, I hope to make this more interesting than what you might remember from the last time you were in a math class. For example, I am a fairly short person, barely over five-foot tall. Many basketball players are over six feet tall, often close to and sometimes even over seven feet tall. The "average" height between a five-foot tall person and a seven-foot tall person is six feet. It is relatively easy to intuit (without crunching any numbers) that the greater the difference between the very shortest and the very tallest, the less likely the "average" is going to fit any particular individual.

Now, assume that we must create something (a product, a law, a program, etc.) to accommodate the most people. A likely scenario is that we are probably going to design our project to accommodate the "average" six-foot tall person. This means that the shorter people will have to reach or stretch beyond their comfort zone to use the item or program, and the taller people will have to stoop or bend to use it. Metaphorically speaking, people who are of average height, or close to it, will find that the system or program suits their needs, while the outliers (those on both ends of the curve) will find the program to be less useful because they must make greater effort to accommodate themselves to it.

For purposes so far, we have assumed that this "something" is based on physical height (just like the people are). Hypothetically, it can also represent something about the way society is structured—rules, rewards, values—which can operate as either barriers or bridges, depending on how closely one conforms to the "ideal" that is presumed. Now let's take our hypothetical a step further. Assume that the tall people (all those above six feet) have more influence in what gets decided and what gets done. Now the structures and systems are more likely to accommodate those over six feet, while everyone else has to stretch and strain a bit further.

Here we will do some math (just a little bit, I promise). Take the following series of ten numbers: 5, 4, 5, 3, 6, 5, 7, 5, 6, 4. The average (or mathematical mean) of these numbers is five. The median, or middle is the point where half of the numbers are lower and half are higher. The mode is the number that occurs the most often. In this case, the median and the mode are also five. Now let's look at a second set of ten numbers: 2, 5, 3, 5, 63, 5, 40, 2, 9, 4. Here, the average is now 13.8, but the median and the mode are still 5. In the first example, a policy that uses the "average" as its baseline to make decisions is likely to be accommodating to the majority. In the second case, the "average" is skewed high compared to where most of the numbers actually are.

It is not hard to imagine how this plays out with respect to something like income. Our society measures its own progress in terms of wealth, more specifically economic growth and GDP. The presumption is that as long as these numbers are rising, all is well. As we have seen from our rudimentary exercise in statistics, averages can indeed rise—even quite significantly—at the same time making little difference to the "average" person or even to the majority of people. That is, all manner of dysfunction could be present at the same time we are happily patting ourselves on the back because the outcome we are measuring looks good.

The Complex Relation Between Income and Happiness

Most modern nations evaluate their success based on economic output, which is usually measured in money units of gross national or gross domestic product (GDP). This somewhat simplistic measure presumes that rising GDP benefits society as a whole (the "rising tide lifts all boats" argument), although the evidence is mixed as to whether the benefits of economic growth result in universal social benefit.[6] This worldview also assumes a direct correlation between increasing income and increasing well-being. Yet, recent research suggests that the relationship between income and happiness is not absolute. Additionally, even when aggregate income (or GDP) is rising rapidly, if it is also creating the skewness that we saw in our numbers exercise, it can actually result in dysfunction and social corrosion.

The focus of traditional economics is on decisional utility. That is, people make decisions based solely on the calculus of self-interest, which is usually presumed to be rational. Moreover, income (or wealth) is much easier to measure than the fuzzier concept of happiness. Some research also suggests that measures of subjective well-being can serve as proxies for utility.[7] Other research warns about the potential for bias, or the confounding of cause and effect. For example, people who are engaged in volunteer work report greater life satisfaction, but people who volunteer are also more likely to be extraverts. The question then becomes whether it is the activity of volunteering or the extraverted personality trait that results in higher life satisfaction.[8] Another theory suggests that happier people work harder and are more enterprising, and so they tend to earn more (an inverse causation correlation—happiness increases income rather than the other way around). However, studies of lottery winners and people receiving an inheritance have found that these individuals reported similar higher well-being the following year,[9] suggesting that it is the increase in income rather than individual personality traits creating the increase in well-being.

Research has suggested that money does "buy" happiness—but only up to a point. That is, once people have enough to meet their basic needs (including enough to feel relatively secure), more money does not necessarily make them happier.[10] Even some economists are beginning to recognize that economic growth does not always correlate with increasing well-being. In 1974, Richard Easterlin, then an economist at the University of Pennsylvania, made the surprising discovery that, while levels of income and happiness correlate at a specific point in time, happiness does not continue to rise at the same rate as increases in income, but rather tends to taper off over time.[11] This phenomenon came to be known as the "Easterlin paradox," and it has been corroborated by subsequent research on the connection between income and happiness over time. However, the traditional positivist view continues to dominate economics, and this line of research is not without its critics.

Consequently, some researchers have begun to take a broader view of whether or not things are working for most people using measures other than traditional income and GDP. New schools of thought have proposed that we can better determine the quality of society by measuring subjective life satisfaction, which is sometimes called "happiness."[12] The Happiness Institute is a research think tank in Copenhagen, Denmark, whose mission is to find ways to measure well-being that are not limited solely to income and wealth. The Happiness Institute employs a team of experts in not just economics, but also psychology, anthropology, political science, philosophy and physics, and it defines happiness in terms of subjective well-being, rather than the more short-term hedonic variety associated with attraction to fun and pleasure.

While individual well-being and social well-being are linked, they are not the same. However, individual happiness can serve as an indicator of the effectiveness of social policies because it is socially determined by the position of individuals and groups in a society's opportunity structure.[13] Some researchers have designed a model of Social Quality that measures a society across four domains: economic security (people have enough to meet their daily needs, enjoy a dignified lifestyle, and partake fully in the advantages of citizenship); social cohesion (the extent individuals are bound to their society and the degree of trust at the individual level); social inclusion (the degree to which people are integrated into institutions, organizations and systems); and social empowerment (the degree of agency and access to opportunity).[14] Applying this model across 27 countries in Europe (the U.S. was not included), the three countries that scored the highest were Denmark (1), Finland (2), and Sweden (3). The lowest scores were in Latvia, Lithuania, and Bulgaria (two are former republics of the old Soviet Union).

Because we are unable to measure happiness (or individual well-being) directly, we often have to turn to research to identify proxies, or a collection of things we can measure which have been correlated with the thing we are actually trying to measure. Happiness researchers generally measure it over three dimensions—cognitive (overall satisfaction with life), affective (are daily emotions characterized by peace, joy, worry or stress), and eudemonic (purpose and meaning, sometimes referred to as "blessedness."). When reliable measures of well-being become sufficiently established among researchers, mathematical correlations can then be done to test it against measures of income or other social and economic conditions.

The primary measurement of individual well-being is the Satisfaction With Life Scale.[15] The Satisfaction with Life Scale (SWLS) was developed to assess an individual's satisfaction with her/his life as a whole and so does not address specific life domains such as health or finances. Tests of the SWLS have found it to have high internal consistency and reliability. Scores on the SWLS correlate moderately to highly with other measures of subjective well-being, and also correlate predictably with specific personality characteristics.

The SWLS presents five questions, which respondents rate on a scale of 1 (strongly disagree) to 7 (strongly agree). The numbers are then tallied to produce a combined score indicating whether the individual is extremely satisfied (31-35) or extremely dissatisfied (5-9).

In most ways, my life is close to my ideal
The conditions of my life are excellent
I am satisfied with my life
So far I have gotten the important things I want in life
If I could live my life over, I would change almost nothing

A second "happiness" test used by researchers is the Positive and Negative Affect Schedule. The Positive and Negative Affect Schedule (PANAS)[16] is a self-report on various emotions experienced by an individual over the prior week. There is a 60-item and shorter 20-item version, in which individuals are asked to rate a particular emotion on a five-point Likert-type scale ranging from very little or not at all to extremely. The test totals separate scores on positive emotions (e.g., interested, enthusiastic, inspired) and negative emotions (e.g., distressed, irritable, ashamed). While the PANAS has been found to have good internal reliability, it is also subject to fluctuations in mood.[17]

No one disagrees that there is a robust and statistically significant correlation between income and happiness. What happens to distort this is something economists call diminishing marginal utility, or the observation that additional income does not result in a corresponding increase in well-being past a certain point. Here again, the issue is more complex than the attainment of a minimum standard of material well-being and personal security. Increases in individual income are much less likely to result in increased well-being if everyone else's income is also increased, thus leaving everyone better off but in the same relative social position.

This idea of "positional goods" was first proposed by Thorsten Veblen in his 1899 *Theory of the Leisure Class*. That is, a certain amount of consumption is not intended to meet immediate needs or even necessarily fulfill internal wants, but to announce the superiority of one's social position. This theory of conspicuous consumption was expanded upon by Harvard economist James Duesenberry, who proposed the relative income hypothesis: Individual attitudes toward consumption and saving are driven more by comparative incomes rather than some abstract standard of living. Because people look upward when making comparisons, the wealthy tend to exert a negative external effect on poor people, inducing them to spend more than they can afford, but the poor exert no such corresponding effect on the wealthy.[18] Although Duesenberry's theory has been all but abandoned in the contemporary teaching of economics, it has been found to have "substantial empirical credibility" in more recent research.[19]

Recent research (based in psychology rather than economics) has also identified a phenomenon called hedonic adaptation, or the hedonic treadmill.[20] When an individual's income is first increased (e.g., as with a job promotion, or a money prize), happiness increases. Yet, after a certain period of time, the individual's happiness returns to the previous level. The explanation is that because wants are insatiable, the individual continuously adjusts aspirations upwards, eventually becoming unsatisfied no matter how comfortable his current status. Hedonic adaptation theory also proposes that most people maintain a happiness "set point," or baseline, which is at least partially determined by genetics. This baseline can be disrupted either upward or downward by life events (such as winning the lottery or becoming disabled by illness or accident), but over time, happiness for the majority of individuals will return more or less to their baseline level.[21] We can see the phenomenon graphically in Figure *X.* As GDP rose consistently between 1978 and 1999, life satisfaction rose briefly in the middle 1980s, but generally declined throughout the period.

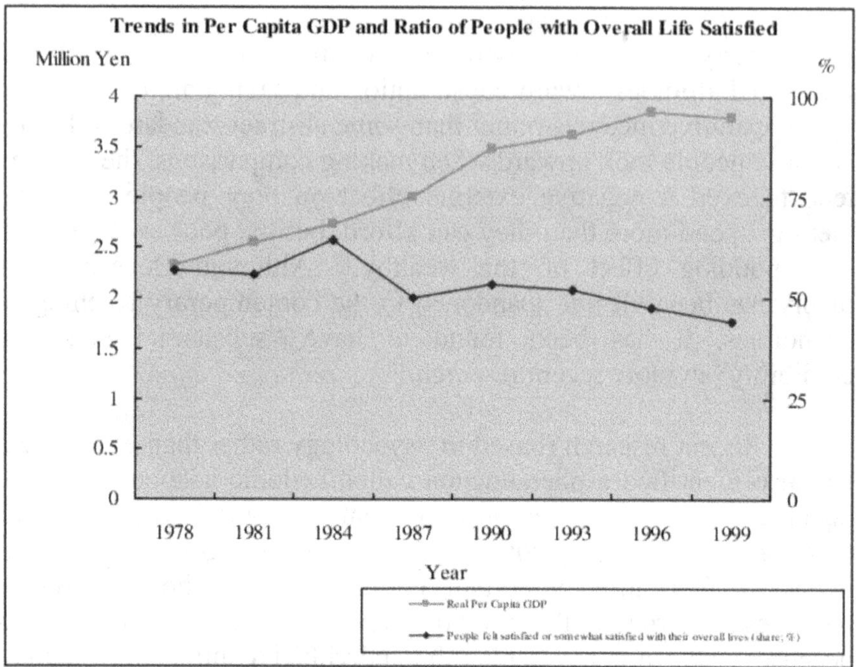

Graph from Takayoshi Kusago, Potential use of well-being indicators for community development in Japan.[22]

Institutional Factors that Affect Happiness

Correlating the research on money and happiness, the Happiness Institute researchers find that societies with high happiness scores tend to be economically developed countries with modern democracies. That is, wealthier societies are happier not only because they have more money, but because they are able to create stable governments that guarantee political, economic and personal freedoms. Yet the countries who score highest—Denmark, Norway, Finland and Sweden—are not the wealthiest. In addition to a minimal level of material wealth, happier countries also have a high level of social trust and a strong social safety net. People living in happier societies thus have a sense that society as a whole will take care of its members, and they do not view others in their community as personal threats or competitors.

Most of us can intuit that things such as justice, freedom and trust are necessary to a good society. Not surprisingly, freedom and democracy are also necessary features of societies with high happiness scores. Freedom, however, is broader than the litany of individual rights we normally associate with democracies, but includes agency (the ability to control outcomes that affect one's own life) and access to opportunity, regardless of one's position in the socio-economic structure. In happy societies, democratic processes allow average citizens influence in and access to decision-making processes equal to that of the more powerful and affluent. Such a system should ideally also include transparency as well as accountability mechanisms that permit popular correction in case of corruption or other breach of the public trust. According to the happiness researchers, voter participation rates and civic engagement are usually signs of a healthy and functioning democracy.[23]

Studies on the effect of unemployment further illustrate the complexity of the income-happiness equation. Unemployment decreases well-being more than any other single characteristic (such as divorce), and this effect is above and beyond the loss of income.[24] Being productively employed creates feelings of agency and social inclusion in addition to income which may be necessary for subsistence. This study also found that happiness levels were lower for women and Blacks, suggesting discrimination effects. However, the negative effects of unemployment fell harder on men, particularly men who were in their career prime. The suggested explanation is that unemployment creates a loss of self-esteem as well as corresponding social stigma above and beyond loss of income. Paradoxically, unemployment decreases well-being less if the unemployment rate is high overall, suggesting that when unemployment is more widespread, it mitigates social disapproval and stigma associated with self-blame.[25]

Inflation has also been found to correlate with decreased life satisfaction.[26] This has added a new dimension to economists' perennial quest to balance the trade-offs between inflation and unemployment. The research finds that higher unemployment benefits are associated with higher national well-being—that is, they mitigate the negative effects that unemployment has on well-being generally, even if this only addresses loss of income and not corresponding loss of esteem and social stigma.[27] Indeed, economists are now able to construct a misery index that includes both unemployment and inflation, although such models are likely to attribute too little weight to the effect of unemployment relative to inflation.[28]

In modern times, perhaps our biggest disconnect with a good society is in the way we earn our livelihoods. We will address more fully how modern work is failing to serve us—both as individuals and as a society—in Part IV, Section One. Our happiness researchers say that our work must fulfill a number of requirements for us: it must pay us enough to cover a minimally decent livelihood, however that is defined in our community; work must be in balance with our commitments to our families, friends, and other obligations in the community; and finally, our work must provide us purpose, meaning, identity, and connection to others.

Unfortunately, many of us working here in early 21st century America are either overworked, underemployed, insecure or impoverished. More than 50% of persons who receive public assistance are working, either because the jobs don't pay enough or because they are unstable.[29] A person who is working multiple part-time jobs to make ends meet is both underemployed (with respect to income) and overemployed (with respect to hours). At higher ends of the pay scale—where workers are more likely to be exempt from overtime regulations—overwork is a bigger problem. The institutions that employ professional and managerial workers are driven either by profit maximization or austerity dictates to constantly shed employees. The survivors of these downsizing and layoff exercises are then driven to work longer and harder, covering for now absent co-workers yet faced with the same (or increasing) amount of work. The victims of the downsizing often have to accept work that pays less and uses less of their skills and education.[30]

One major requirement of a good society that most modern work is lacking is a sense of meaning. Lower-level workers are nothing more than fungible production drones, while higher level workers deal in abstract information often without being aware of its ultimate purpose. In most workplaces, the only obvious objective is to make money for owners, shareholders, and those in the C-suites.

Most workers thus view their jobs as nothing more than a means to an end—a way to pay the bills so they can live their "real" lives outside of work. In earlier times, one may not have necessary loved to work, but the purpose of one's work was usually clear (e.g., the butcher, the baker, the shoemaker, the small shopkeeper, the family farmer). Moreover, work often served to bind one to the community rather than separate one from it. Today, many people must commute long distances to work (which takes even more time and energy away from family and community activities). Alternatively, they may work remotely, which saves the commute, but thwarts fuller development of professional and career relationships. However, work in ever larger and more impersonal bureaucracies involves something even darker than a lack of purpose, but has created a sense of what Dr. Michael Lerner terms surplus powerlessness.[31] Most modern work relationships are based on a system of inferiorization, which serves to keep workers from challenging the system that oppresses them. This has obvious negative implications for agency and democratic participation.

Inequality

A good society is not necessarily strictly egalitarian, but rather avoids extremes of inequality that operate to destroy other important elements of a good society, namely trust and community. This is sometimes expressed as the objective to provide equality of opportunity but not equality of outcomes. Here, we are not referring to everyday-type inequalities in which a neighbor or a co-worker has a bigger paycheck or a bigger home. Rather, we are concerned with inequalities that create entirely separate worlds in which individuals live—a bigger house is not a second floor or a couple hundred square feet, but several globe-spanning homes that rival the square footage of a super Walmart, complete with a backyard helipad or private jet runway. In societies where inequality is extreme, opportunity is often dictated by one's position in the social hierarchy, and so where one ends up is often more dependent on where one starts out (as a statistical matter—there are always individual exceptions) rather than on individual hard work or intelligence.

In 2009, the very British Webb Memorial Trust made a decision to "spend out" the remainder of its resources in exploring new and different ways of looking at poverty. This initiative came at the end of the global Great Recession, culminating in launch of a book about *Rethinking Poverty* by the fund's Barry Knight at the London School of Economics on September 13, 2017.[32] The premise behind *Rethinking Poverty* is that we need to stop viewing it as a problem to be solved, ostensibly by the imposition of technocratic programs (i.e., the welfare state), but rather start from a vision of what we want our society to look like. The argument is that alienation, poverty, inequality and powerlessness are "baked into" society, yet the traditional approach assumes that something or someone is blameworthy (often applied to the poor themselves). The new paradigm instead asks what people can do rather than what "should" be done for them and to them.

As part of the project, Webb conducted a survey of 10,112 people. The survey first asked what were important factors of a good society. The top factors were fairness and compassion (94% each), followed closely by freedom and security (93% each), with the absence of poverty coming in at 90%. The next question asked to what degree contemporary society was fulfilling these factors. Fairness and compassion did poorly, at 36% each. Freedom and security did a little better, at 68% and 62% respectively. However, absence of poverty was the most unfulfilled, at 24%.

Deeper questioning revealed that security mattered more than wealth. People weren't looking to get rich, but instead wanted to avoid the stress of constant worry about financial matters, which then had a negative impact on their personal relationships. The British economist Guy Standing has described a new (and growing) class of persons he calls the precariat—individuals across a wide range of demographics and occupations yet who share unpredictable work, fragmented careers, a short-term view of relationships, meaninglessness, and a constant fear that they must conform themselves to the dictates of the system or risk becoming losers.[33] This need for a minimum level of stability is consistent with research on happiness that finds once people reach a certain level of material subsistence and security, more money does not make them happier—unless by having more money they are now able to give more away.

Inequality, especially if it is extreme, is more damaging to the social fabric than basic unfairness. Public health researchers Richard Wilkinson and Kate Pickett have documented a plethora of negative social effects that are directly correlated with levels of social and economic inequality: mental illness and drug use, violence, crime and incarceration rates, decreasing educational performance, teenage births, lower life expectancy, and even something as seemingly unrelated as obesity rates.[34] Moreover, these negative externalities (as a matter of statistics) apply to everyone in society, and not just those at the bottom. Unequal societies are characterized by decreased trust and social cohesion. When people grow up in a more unequal society, it affects their assumptions about human nature, aggravating status competition and decreasing empathy. Extravagant consumption by the rich reduces the satisfaction of everyone else, and the scramble for ever-increasing levels of consumption threatens the very sustainability of the planet. Whether extreme inequality is a cause or a consequence of a dysfunctional (and thus less happy) society is yet to be determined, but this research suggests that deliberate efforts to decrease current levels of inequality has the potential to mitigate many other social problems.

Values

A discussion about a good society would not be complete without a discussion about cultural values. What does a good society value—and how are these values inculcated? The World Values Survey (WVS) is a global network of social scientists (political scientists, sociologists, psychologists, anthropologists and economists) who have been conducting periodic rigorous international surveys since 1981 in order to understand changing values and their impact on social and political life. The purpose of these studies is to analyze how the primary values in a society (expressed as an average) impact economic development, democratic institutions, and effective government; i.e., the connection between individual values and good society.

The WVS is headquartered in Vienna, Austria and they are currently in the process of collecting the seventh wave of survey data. This latest round of data collection began in 2017 and is anticipated to continue until 2020. The WVS has expanded the number of countries it covers from 60 to 80. The WVS web page has a moving graphic that shows how these values have shifted over the past six waves of surveys, beginning with the first survey in 1981 and occurring approximately every five years since 1990.[35]

The WVS plots national cultural values on two scales: survival (horizontal low) versus self-expression (horizontal high) and traditional (vertical low) versus secular-rational (vertical high). Countries that score low on the first axis are primarily concerned with physical and economic security. These countries include Latvia, Lithuania, and Bulgaria as well as Ukraine, Tunisia, Morocco, Azerbaijan, Jordan, Iraq and Palestine. Countries scoring highest in self-expression are Sweden, Norway, Denmark, Iceland and Canada. The U.S. comes in close behind Finland, Netherlands and Switzerland.

Countries that are traditional emphasize religious and family values, as well as deference to authority. High-traditional countries are primarily African Islamic and Latin American. Countries high in secular-rational values (i.e., Enlightenment-based) focus on individual rights, freedom, science and logic, and democratic participation. These include the countries of Protestant Europe (Sweden, Norway, Finland and Denmark) as well as Japan, Hong Kong, Taiwan and South Korea (Confucianism). The United States sits more in the middle, being neither (or equally both) secular-rational nor traditional. The graph shows a diagonal of extremes, with survivalist-traditional African-Islamic countries in the lower left quadrant and the self-expressive, secular-rational countries of Protestant Europe in the upper right. Countries that more or less occupy the middle are identified as Catholic Europe: Greece, Spain, Portugal, Croatia, and Slovakia.

By comparing happiness research with the World Values Survey, we see a connection between Enlightenment values, economic success and social well-being. One theory suggests that a certain level of material security permits democratic forms of governance to emerge. Only when people are freed from subsistence concerns can they then turn attention to higher-order needs such as individual rights and self-expression. Another theory suggests that more traditional societies also tend to be more authoritarian, some even deliberately believing that keeping order and stability is a preferable trade-off to creativity and change.

The WVS has identified a subset of self-expression values which it calls emancipative values. Emancipative values emphasize freedom of choice, equality of opportunity, lifestyle liberty, gender equality, personal autonomy and the "voice of the people." Emancipative values are a key cultural component in a larger process of human empowerment, which includes the broadening of democratic rights, the fostering of trust toward out-groups and a cosmopolitan worldview (acceptance of differences). Emancipative values do not necessarily increase the desire for democracy but rather emphasize democracy's empowering features rather than its bread-and-butter, law-and-order features. Emancipative values encourage non-violent protests, even in the face of repression, and citizens with stronger emancipative values tend to under-rate rather than over-rate their country's democratic performance. Thus, emancipative values operate to challenge authority and potentially create social conflict.

Community and Commonwealth

Perhaps the most salient feature of a good society is a sense of community, or a belief that we are all in this together. In a mobile and pluralistic society, how do we define the "community" and identity a collection of common interests? Most of us think of "community" in geopolitical terms: our nation, our state, our hometown or county of residence. Yet, even within our own communities we can want different things; e.g., some want to encourage a corporate relocation because they believe it will bring jobs and add to the tax base, while others fear increased traffic, pollution, and the rise of their own property taxes. We all also belong to a plethora of overlapping "communities" beyond our immediate neighborhoods: our college or university alma mater, our church (both our local congregation and the national or worldwide "church"), our workplace, various occupational or professional organizations, military veterans, sports and hobby groups, civic and charitable organizations such as Boy Scouts or League of Women Voters. These fragmented identities can make us feel like we at once belong everywhere and nowhere. We might even exhibit different sides of our personalities depending on whether we are at work, at church, or playing in a local softball league. While this is not necessarily a bad thing in and of itself (it broadens our horizons and might even help us to be more tolerant of differences), it can serve to disconnect us from a sense of more general community.

Faith communities represent a form of moral commonwealth, in that its members share common behavioral norms and culture. Faith communities generally also offer their members a source of material support and social refuge vis-à-vis the larger society. The issue that faith communities present to larger civil society is to what extent their members can integrate within it. From Jesus' admonishment to "render unto Caesar that which is Caesar's and to God that which is God's"[36] (people had a duty to both pay their taxes and do God's work) to the American founders' separation of church and state, citizenship and faith were very different things.

Faith communities themselves range widely with respect to their involvement in secular society. At one end we have communities like the Amish, who keep themselves almost totally separate from the rest of society. At the other end, we have evangelical communities whose leaders exhort their members to get involved in politics, even telling them how to vote (which can sometimes violate the democratic norms of the larger society). While religious communities can and should contribute to civic debate, it can result in dysfunctional hostility when issues are framed in terms of "us-versus-them" and "they" are viewed as evil. A position which itself often violates the words of the faith's own prophets which urge the faithful to peacefully coexist. Jesus tells Christians to love your neighbor[37] as well as your enemies.[38] The Qur'an urges Muslims to behave in a "just and equitable manner" with nonbelievers, as well as to "love and forgive your enemies."

Shared Reality

A more difficult to describe feature of a good society is one in which attention takes priority over distraction. That is, people are aware of the reality that surrounds them and make a conscious effort to avoid denial mechanisms. Our modern society is characterized by what researchers have called "alienated attention,"[39] the result of an energy-drained and anxious workforce who is unable to concentrate on anything for very long or plan for the long term.[40] The activities that once served to refresh and rejuvenate—vacations, family dinners, a night out with friends—have been largely abandoned because they are deemed detrimental to economic competition. A "withdrawal of responsible attention has spread throughout American society," coupled with a "pattern of self-seeking indifference."[41] In essence, everyone is busy and distracted, but few are actually paying attention.

In 1996, the economist Ravi Batra lamented that hardly anyone was paying attention to the fact that—in spite of an economy that appeared to be booming—wages had been stagnating for over two decades, accusing mainstream economists of having been "caught napping in their ivory towers."[42] Many of the problems and issues addressed herein—inequality, underemployment, the erosion of democracy—are hardly (if at all) ever addressed by the mainstream media, which always seems to be playing "catch up" to reality. We are presented with a glamorized model of freedom, equality of opportunity, democracy, and prosperity, thus anyone who feels unfree, unprosperous, unequal, or diminished is likely to experience cognitive dissonance as well as a sense of pessimistic futility. In our distracted inattention, we are bombarded with jingoistic ballyhoo (usually promoted by those in power to justify the way they are running society) that presents a society that is working better than it is. So…we either assume that our own anxious angst is attributable to our own defects (leading to despair), or we search for a convenient scapegoat.

Thus, we come up with the final requirement for a good society: the acknowledgement of truth. A society that attempts to influence decisions and behavior or otherwise disempowers its citizens' legitimate urges for change on the basis of hype, spin, and propaganda that does not accurately reflect reality cannot be a good one. We will explore this specific dysfunction further in Part IV, Section Four.

Notes

---

[1] Because the focus of this work is the United States, we do not cover the earlier Chinese philosopher Confucius (551-479 B.C.), who had similar ideas regarding personal and governmental morality, justice, right relationships, and sincerity.

[2] Bellah, R.N., Madsen, R., Sullivan, W.M., Seidler, A., & Tipton, S.W. (1991). *The good society.* New York, NY: Vintage Books/Random House, Inc. Also by same authors: *Habits of the Heart,* originally published in 1985, with later editions in 1996 and 2008.

[3]https://www.businessinsider.com/economist-intelligence-unit-2017-democracy-index-best-countries-2018-1#16-mauritius-822-16. One cannot accuse the Brits of too much bias, as their own country ranked at number 14—behind the major countries of Northern and Western Europe.

[4] Democracy Index 2018. https://www.eiu.com/topic/democracy-index.
See also *Freedom in the World 2019* at
https://freedomhouse.org/sites/default/files/Feb2019_FH_FITW_2019_Report_ForWeb-compressed.pdf

[5] *The Economist* Intelligence Unit. Democracy Index 2020. In sickness and in health? pp. 43-44.

[6] Lee, N. & Clarke, S. (2017, July). A rising tide lifts all boats? Resolution Foundation Report.
https://www.resolutionfoundation.org/app/uploads/2017/07/A-rising-tide-lifts-all-boats.pdf. Hines, J.R., Hoynes, H, & Krueger, A.B. (2001, July). Another look at whether a rising tide lifts all boats. Russell Sage Foundation.
https://gspp.berkeley.edu/assets/uploads/research/pdf/hhk-final.pdf

[7] Lucas, R.E., Diener, E., & Suh, E. (1996). Discriminant validity of well-being measures. *Journal of Personality and Social Psychology, 71*(3), 616-628.

[8] Frey, B.S. & Stutzer, A. (2002, June). What can economists learn from happiness research? *Journal of Economic Literature,* 402-435 at p. 407.

[9] Gardner, J., and Oswald, A.J. (2006, July). Money and mental well-being: A longitudinal study of medium-sized lottery wins. IZA Discussion Paper 2233. http://ftp.iza.org/dp2233.pdf; Gardner J. & Oswald, A.J. (2002, January). Does money buy happiness? A longitudinal study using data on windfalls.
https://www.researchgate.net/publication/4892491_Does_Money_Buy_Happiness_A_Longitudinal_Study_Using_Data_on_Windfalls

---

[10] Jebb, A.T., Tay, L., Diener, E., & Shigehiro, O. (2018). Happiness, income satiation, and turning points around the world. *Nature Human Behavior, 2*, 33-38. https://gspp.berkeley.edu/assets/uploads/research/pdf/hhk-final.pdf

[11] Easterlin, R. (1974). Does economic growth improve the human lot? Some empirical evidence. In P.A. David and M.A. Reder (Eds.). *Nations and households in economic growth: Essays in honor of Moses Abramovitz.* New York, NY: Academic Press, Inc. pp. 89-125. http://graphics8.nytimes.com/images/2008/04/16/business/Easterlin1974.pdf

[12] Jefferson's Enlightenment natural rights of "life, liberty and the pursuit of happiness" that we find in the American Declaration of Independence.

[13] Veenhoven, R. (2008). Healthy happiness: Effects of happiness on physical health and the consequences for preventive health care. *Journal of Happiness Studies 9*(3), 449-469.

[14] Abbott, P., & Wallace, C. (2012). Social quality: A way to measure the quality of society. *Social Indicators Research, 108,* 153-167.

[15] Diener, E., Emmons, R.A., Larsen, R.J., & Griffin, S. (1985). The satisfaction with life scale. *Journal of Personality Assessment, 49*(1), 71-75. https://www.tandfonline.com/doi/abs/10.1207/s15327752jpa4901_13

[16] https://ogg.osu.edu/media/documents/MB%20Stream/PANAS.pdf

[17] Magyar-Moe, J.L. (2009). *Therapists guide to positive psychological interventions.* American Psychological Association: Elsevier Academic Press. https://psycnet.apa.org/record/2011-00745-000

[18] Duesenberry, J.S. (1949). *Income, saving and the theory of consumer behavior.* Cambridge, MA: Harvard University Press.

[19] Sanders, S. (2010, July-September). A model of the relative income hypothesis. *The Journal of Economic Education, 41*(3), 292-305.

[20] Brickman, C. (1971). Hedonic relativism and planning the good society. In M.H. Apley, (Ed.), *Adaptation level theory: A symposium* at pp. 287-302.

[21] Fujita, F., & Diener, E. (2005). Life satisfaction set point: Stability and change. *Journal of Personality and Social Psychology, 88*(1), 158-164.

[22] https://www.researchgate.net/publication/255637222_Potential_Use_of_Well-being_Indicators_for_Community_Development_in_Japan

[23] This premise does not hold true in authoritarian regimes where voting is mandatory.

[24] Blanchflower, D.G., & Oswald, A.J. (2000, January). Well-being over time in Britain and the USA. NBER Working Paper No. 7487. https://www.nber.org/papers/w7487

[25] Frey, B.S., & Stutzer, A. (2002). *Supra* at pp. 420-421.

[26] Di Tella, R., MacCulloch, R., & Oswald, A.J. (2001, October). The macroeconomics of happiness. University of Bonn ZEI Working Paper No. B3. https://papers.ssrn.com/sol3/papers.cfm?abstract_id=285918

[27] An alternative explanation is that the social stigma of unemployment is less acute in societies that provide more generous unemployment benefits.

[28] Frey, B., & Stutzer, A. (2002), *Supra* at p. 422).

[29] Cole, N.L. (2019, September 28). Nine surprising facts about welfare recipients. https://www.thoughtco.com/who-really-receives-welfare-4126592

[30] For a fuller discussion of underemployment, see VanHettinga (2018) *The Great Jobs Deception.*

[31] Lerner, M. (1991). *Surplus powerlessness: The psychodynamics of everyday life and the psychology of individual and social transformation.* Atlantic Highlands, NJ: Humanities Press International, Inc.

[32] To read about the Rethinking Poverty project and access the book and related videos: https://www.rethinkingpoverty.org.uk/home-page/book-rethinking-poverty/

[33] Standing, G. (2011). *The precariat: The new dangerous class.* London: Bloomsbury Publishing. Available free at: https://www.researchgate.net/publication/256485856_Guy_Standing_2011_The_Precariat_The_New_Dangerous_Class_London_Bloomsbury_Academic_1999_pp_198_pbk and https://www.researchgate.net/publication/273739745_The_precariat

[34] Wilkinson, R., & Pickett, K. (2009). *The spirit level: Why greater equality makes societies stronger.* New York, NY: Bloomsbury Press.

---

[35] http://www.worldvaluessurvey.org/WVSContents.jsp Search for Finding and Insights, Live Cultural Map—WVS 1981-2015.

[36] Matthew 22:21.

[37] Matthew 22: 32

[38] Matthew 5:44.

[39] Bellah, R.N., Madsen, R., Sullivan, W.M., Seidler, A., & Tipton, S.W. (1991). *The good society.* New York, NY: Vintage Books/Random House, Inc. at p. 255.

[40] *Id.* at pp. 260-261.

[41] *Id.* at p. 277.

[42] Batra, R. (1996). *The great American deception.* Batra correctly predicted the stock market crash of 1987 and the fall of Soviet communism in 1990. His 1999 *The Crash of the Millennium* was wrong only in that he saw it would be cause by inflationary depression rather than the dot com bubble.

Section Two
Radical Individualism and Loss of a Moral Commonwealth

...the mere speculative conviction that it was our interest to be completely virtuous, was not sufficient to prevent our slipping and that the contrary habits must be broken and good ones acquired and established, before we can have any dependence on a steady uniform rectitude of conduct.

Benjamin Franklin[1]

*

Character is an attribute of institutions and communities as well as of persons....Character is, to a large extent, a product of personal and social history. It is composed of habits, dependencies, interest, and values—all, for the most part, unconsciously developed and embraced.

Philip Selznick[2]

*

...most people, even in the age of globalization and the Internet, live parochial lives. They are neither atomized individuals nor part of a great undifferentiated mass of the public. What's in front of them are the groups they belong to and the institutions they can see and touch: the schools that educate their children, their local governments, the places where they pray, their trade association, their ethnic organization, their political movements. Those are the means of protecting themselves, of improving their condition, of addressing their needs as they define them.

Nicholas Lemann[3]

*

The modern conservative is not even especially modern. He is engaged, on the contrary, in one of man's oldest, best financed, most applauded, and, on the whole, least successful exercises in moral philosophy. That is the search for a superior moral justification for selfishness.

John Kenneth Galbraith[4]

*

American cultural traditions define personality, achievement, and the purpose of human life in ways that leave the individual suspended in glorious, but terrifying, isolation.

From *Habits of the Heart*

Philosophers have been wrestling with how to define and express virtue for centuries. Most people intend to behave rightly and do good, but often fall short. We are tempted by the exigencies of an immediate situation, or even our own fatigue and inattention. That is, there are factors other than our own free will and good conscience that cause us to violate our own behavioral norms. Thus, the way to improve the odds that one would behave virtuously (most philosophers, including Franklin, acknowledged that perfection was impossible, but one could always improve) was to consciously develop virtuous habits: courage, humility, integrity, responsibility, respect, perseverance, frugality, and temperance (moderation). Moderation is necessary, because any virtue, when expressed to extremes could become a vice. For example, while too little courage results in cowardice, too much can result in foolhardiness. Likewise, lack of respect for authority can result in irresponsibility or anarchy, but too much of it can become blind obedience to power—a subject which we will expand upon in Part II, Section Four.

While philosophical prescriptions for virtuous behavior focused on the individual, they also included the concept of civic virtue. Civic virtue revolves around the responsibilities of citizenship, and it often focuses on justice. In the United States, civic virtue has been defined by classical republicanism—a blend of the classical and enlightenment philosophers. In addition to defense of the republic from outside threats, classical republicans were equally concerned about internal threats, particularly "overthrow of republican institutions by ambitious authoritarian elites."[5] In order that no one person or group dominate any other, a just republic must have a robust rule of law, as well as a sufficient number of informed and engaged citizens to both keep watch over public officials and be willing to serve in such capacity themselves. Such citizen activism and involvement is necessary because once political apathy sets in, "constitutional safeguards alone will not be sufficient."[6] Thus, a successful republic required governance by rule of law, political inclusiveness (to avoid the concentration of power and the dominance of a small elite), and a system of moderation and restraint to resolve competing factional claims and grievances.

The one thing that both classical and republican philosophers agreed on was the necessity of citizen engagement in public affairs. This presumes that citizens have both the inclination and the means to participate, and that participation is equally available to all groups. Today, we see troubling trends of both political apathy (or non-participation) as well as deliberate attempts to disenfranchise particular groups. People who work for a living do not have the time or the energy to stay informed and may not even have time to vote—or if they do vote it is only to select a candidate based on personality or party and then ignore politics and governance until the next election. Those who are most involved with politics are those who have the resources to be absent from a workplace, as well as travel to party conventions or visit officials in their distant offices. Because the participation of elites dominates the affairs of politics and governance, policy outcomes favor elites at the expense of the majority, which further disengages the average citizen from the political process.[7]

If virtue is determined by habits, what then determines our habits? Outside of our immediate families, most of us develop our moral beliefs and practices from institutions—school, church, work and popular culture. While institutions mediate the relationship between the self and the larger society, they often develop their own identity independent of the collective identities of the individuals who operate in them. However, institutions are harder to study than individuals, and they are less subject to moral control.[8] One can study a single school, church, or business, but it won't tell us enough about the institutions of education, religion, or the economy. Moreover, we are just now beginning to understand how these institutions affect individual behavior, which was once believed to be solely a matter of individual choice and free will. Yet these systems "appear to have an objective givenness that puts them beyond question," and failure or refusal to adapt to them can condemn the individual to permanent outsider status.[9]

Perhaps the most troublesome question is whether or not people believe that seeking the common good is even a worthwhile objective. Many find themselves busy and overwhelmed with making ends meet or managing their personal affairs (disengagement as practical). Others see the discord and corruption in politics and consciously decide it is better to focus on matters over which they can have a positive impact (disengagement as psychic survival). Yet others—those who occupy the "wrong" side of the social status-sorting curve—believe that their own voices and concerns won't make a difference (disengagement as powerlessness). On top of the various (logical) reasons for disengagement, our culture emphasizes rugged individualism and self-reliance. Public life, or "citizenship" thus becomes an afterthought—something we might think about during an election but otherwise ignore.

Historical Foundation of Individualism in America

Alexis de Tocqueville (1805-1859), the son of a French Normandy count, traveled to the new republic of the United States of America to document this new experiment in democratic government. As a member of the French aristocracy, Tocqueville was at first skeptical of this new form of governing, but he approached his task with an open mind and a sense of adventure. Tocqueville's travels resulted in the lengthy four-volume *Democracy in America* (1835-1840), in which he expresses deep admiration for the new American republic—a dynamic and open society in which a new political form had the potential to transform governance and become the model of the future. Democracy broadens the mind, encourages citizen responsibility, fosters pluralism, and promotes a spirit of equality and a healthy skepticism of power.

However, Tocqueville also noted a potential negative side—perhaps not so much as to democracy itself, but as an aspect of the American character. He observed that, "The whole philosophical method of democracy is pragmatic, centred on the effort of individuals to make sense of their world by harnessing their own individual understanding of things. Even in matters of religion, everyone shuts himself up tightly within himself and insists upon judging the world from there." In a place where people were "neither rich nor powerful enough to have much hold over others, but who nevertheless had enough to take care of themselves," Tocqueville predicted they "...would form the habit of thinking of themselves in isolation."[10] He used the term "individualism" to define this characteristic, which he thought of as an offshoot of egoism. Tocqueville also noted the paradox of a restlessness in the midst of prosperity—a shadow of sadness cast over the good life because one is always aware of what one does not have."[11]

In the mobile and egalitarian society of America (as opposed to the more rigid social structures of Europe), people were freer to define themselves on their own terms and even create their own social identities. Without a rigid class structure, people could meet and interact with others—including those who were different from themselves—more easily, but the ties between them were more likely to be casual and transient. American cultural iconic heroes also tended to be rugged individualists: pioneers, cowboys, officers of the law (small-town sheriffs or private detectives); i.e., lone wolf but morally impeccable individuals who dispense vigilante justice and generally operate outside the corrupting influence of society, especially that of bureaucratic organizations.[12]

In early America, the most ubiquitous form of socializing influence revolved around the small town, which was characterized by a "pattern of decentralized egalitarian democracy...anchored in the ethos and institutions of the face-to-face community..."[13] The small town created a community of memory linking the destiny of its citizens with their ancestors and descendants, and "...the moral imagination of Americans was nurtured by practices of commitment in the interlocking social, economic, and political life of strong and independent small towns....the moral language of the town father was the dominant language of the era Tocqueville described..."[14]

The small town was not only the focus of moral foundation, most of its citizens were bound to the town in other ways as well. The typical citizen was a self-employed producer of goods and services—the family farmer, craftsman, or independent retailer—people for whom the demands of work, family and community involvement converged with their involvement with the town.[15] Because the individual's welfare was inextricable from town life, citizens may have been initially motivated to participate in civic affairs based on self-interest. However, the experience of self-governance and the formation of civic associations gave them an understanding of civic affairs, as well as a sense of responsibility for the public good that grew to transcend self-interest.[16]

The small town citizen who was able to both earn a livelihood and participate in town governance mirrored the Jeffersonian ideal of the independent farmer who could also serve as an elected official. This way of life produced a generalized equality of citizens and status—an equality that allowed institutions such as democratic governance and the "free market" to operate according to their ideals. Our American founders were aware that power tended to follow wealth, and so they believed that "a rough equality of property...to be one of the prerequisites of a democratic republic."
However, even in the largely agrarian society of early America, Jefferson expressed concern that urbanization and manufacturing would "bring great inequalities of class and corrupt the morals of a free people."[17]

The classical republicans believed that there was a positive correlation between equality, civic virtue and a successful republic. Inequality undermines civic virtue because it undermines respect for the law (corruption) and creates factionalism,[18] an "us-versus-them worldview that undermines social cohesiveness. While classical republicans recognized the danger of extreme inequality, they differed on how to prevent it, as well as the appropriate role of commerce in a well-ordered republic. Some believed that an emphasis on luxury and consumption would divert citizen attention from public affairs, while others believed that material wealth could provide a foundation for generosity and liberality.[19] This philosophical split manifests in modern research on the complex relationship between money and happiness, which we analyzed in the previous section. Thus, a good society would not necessarily eliminate inequality, but it would be concerned with reducing it, along with guaranteeing a minimum of welfare for all its members.

In addition to the risks presented by an extremely individualistic culture, Tocqueville also predicted that an emerging "new industrial and financial aristocracy" would "continue the form but not the substance of democracy."[20] In spite of a proud tradition of democratic governance, this new form of unfreedom would not be resisted because the individualistic American would know of no way to collectively organize against it. Citizens of a democracy in name only, Americans would thus be subject to a form of "soft despotism," where power grows unchecked, creating an "orderly, gentle, and peaceful slavery."[21]

A group of modern social scientists today are making arguments that mirror Tocqueville's concern about radical individualism, proposing that we may have lost our ability to even define the common good, let alone find practical solutions. Because we can no longer articulate or imagine a common good, we are unable to organize opposition to the dark forces of concentrated power, or even the lesser threat of technocratic rationality, because all of our freedoms end with ourselves. Tocqueville made some observations about the then-emerging American society that are eerily prescient today: As he observed the beginnings of industry in the 1830s, Tocqueville (who could not have imagined the modern corporate state) "warned...[of] the creation of a new kind of aristocracy...an economic royalism...a new kind of feudalism fundamentally incompatible with democratic equality."[22]

<u>The Tradeoff Between Community and Autonomy</u>

The salient factor with "community" is how one defines it; i.e., the boundaries between members and non-members. Although most of us would agree that the larger society is too diverse and fragmented to have anything approaching "community," many of us can think of micro-communities that exist within the larger one. For example, members of a church congregation (communities of faith) or residents of a small town (where everyone knows everyone else). Yes, parochial feuds and jealousies arise in these venues as they do anywhere else, but the members usually find ways to contain these darker sides in the interest of preserving general harmony in the whole. Some of these communities may even be considered microcosms of the good society—with another example being a church who is active in broader social justice issues outside of itself (faith values are transformed into worldly action).

Amitai Etzioni is a sociologist who has spent most of his career researching and writing about the connections between community (the common good), democracy, and moral order. He defines community as a combination of a web of relationships (as opposed to one-on-one "chain-like" individual relationships) and commitment to a shared set of values, norms and meanings. Etzioni advocates for creation of structures/mechanisms of regular moral dialogue, which permits members of a society to continually revisit whether its own moral values are good or bad, and to integrate new values into the moral culture. Such a process can include looking at local consensus and traditions, worldwide parallelism, the opinions of ethicists, as well as a sense that certain values are self-evident. Etzioni admits that this process will often be "disjointed, emotive, repetitive and meandering," which puts it at odds with a society that values efficiency above all else.

A good society not only has regular dialogues about values, it makes a genuine effort to include everyone. According to Etzioni, the extent that power structures prevent the participation of significant numbers of its members in "megalogues" (society-wide dialogue on its common values), it cannot be a good society. The obvious danger is that a group of elites that is disconnected from the majority can come to view its own values as the only "good" ones. Etzioni argues that technological innovations such as the Internet and social media have the potential to support such large-scale megalogues. Alternatively, when popular media and "big tech" become monopolies where power and control is concentrated, the voice of the public can be shut out, even as millions may be "connecting" as consumers. Thus, Etzioni also argues that large media concentrates should be under public control and not dominated by oligopolies, due to the potential for moral corruption.

While old-style small town and church communities provided a form of moral commonwealth and social cohesion, they were often also restrictive, provincial, and even oppressive.[23] Indeed, a normative defect of all communities is that they divide the world between members and non-members. A totally cohesive society can become authoritarian (e.g., cults, gangs, and some fundamentalist religions). Here in America, some of us may recollect images of Chinese communists in the 1960s, toiling away in the fields and the factories in their drab uniform Mao jackets. We fear becoming a Borg-like pre-programmed automaton, where our individuality is subsumed into an authoritarian collective. Yet, when we withdraw into ourselves (to prevent assimilation), we ironically lose the collective voice that may be necessary to confront authoritarianism.

A good society would find the proper balance between individual autonomy (a focus on rights) and civic responsibility (a focus on social duty). Individual freedom is one of America's broadest and deepest values. However, what this often means in practice is the right to be left alone—to be free of arbitrary authority and not have other people's values, ideas or lifestyles forced upon you. Because everyone else has corresponding rights to be free of the demands of others, social bonds can thus be viewed as a form of restrictions that create obligations and impinge on freedoms. The fear that interdependence could lead to dependence and loss of freedom creates a healthy suspicion of concentrated power, but it also creates resistance to most forms of collective action in furtherance of the common welfare.

Our moral sociologists and authors of *Habits of the Heart*[24] found widespread and strong identification with the United States as a national community, yet "government" and "politics" had negative connotations. Citizens are skeptical of politics, which they view as an exercise of adversarial power struggles and interest bargaining among too many diverse communities with conflicting interests.[25] Alternatively, Americans tend to think about politics in terms of a consensual community of autonomous, but essentially similar individuals, and it is to such a conception that they turn for the cure of present ills.[26] When the real work of citizenship is discovered to be more challenging because the ideal of consensus does not exist, people are inclined to abandon the effort. We live in the paradox of a highly individualistic culture that values diversity and pluralism, yet when differences are acute and "almost impossible to adjudicate, interest politics must inevitably break down into coercion and fraud."[27]

One sign of declining values is an increased emphasis on laws, regulations and sanctions. Etzioni argues that a "high reliance on law enforcement for value fortification does not make for a good society."[28] Our Habits of the Heart authors suggest that "since there is no way to discuss or evaluate the relative merits of values and lifestyles in the culture of individualism, a generalized tolerance, dependent on strict adherence to procedural rules, is the best that can be expected."[29] Thus we are presented with a situation where—in order to preserve the rights and autonomy of individuals—we must turn to ever-stricter rules and regulations because we have no way to otherwise resolve our differences. Citizens increasingly come to view the sole purpose of government as protecting their rights and providing the means to pursue their private ends.[30]

Indeed, it may be impossible to have any sense of community in the diverse and pluralistic society that exists in the 21st century USA. Early philosophers like Plato and Aristotle favored small republics, or city-states, because the only way reason and virtue could prevail was through the personal relationships of the citizenry. Many of the American founders also favored federalism because the states were closer in scale to the classical ideal. Alternatively, James Madison proposed the counterargument that larger republics were better able to protect democracy because their natural political diversity would prevent the formation of factions—groups who were "actuated by some common impulse of passion or interest adverse to the rights of other citizens." Conversely, the modern political scientist Pippa Norris suggests that countries as large as the United States can suffer a "democratic deficit" of citizens who are less involved in politics, and are more likely to believe that their voice doesn't matter.[31]

Most any state is going to have active separatist movements, and the United States is no exception. There are active secessionist movements in formerly independent states such as Alaska, Hawaii and Puerto Rico, as well as more traditionally assimilated states (the Republic of Texas and the Vermont Republic), race/ethnic-based movements (the Republics of Lakotah and New Afrika, Aryan Nation) and even the former Confederate States of America. While these movements have currently active members, they are not necessarily taking specific political action to secede (with the possible exception of Puerto Rico). There are obvious benefits to living in an empire, particularly economic and military advantages, if not necessarily democratic ones. Unfortunately, the specific benefits of largeness also play into the will to power—the desire to simply win, to crush the opposition—which conflicts with everyone else's pursuit of happiness.

The (often) Invisible Influence of Institutions

We view ourselves as independent, self-directed individuals and tend to regard institutions as something that operates over our heads—controlled by experts and technocratic administration. So long as we have a reasonable amount of control and material security in our own lives, we ignore the fact that our institutions often operate without a common moral grounding. It is not that they are necessarily evil or even immoral, but rather amoral. Our primary institutions have also grown larger, more opaque and fragmented, making it more difficult to subject them to public oversight and control. Such a situation presents an obvious moral hazard, yet we continue to think of morality as being matters of individual choice.

Many of us also imagine society as a marketplace of fair competition among roughly equal competitors, even if we have a disquieting notion that this image is more idealized than reality. We maintain a healthy distrust of large and powerful institutions—especially when they are able to dominate whole sectors of the market, influence consumer choice through massive advertising, and are able to manipulate regulators to avoid scrutiny of their own claims on the public treasury. Yet, administrative centralization is now an integral part of American life and will likely remain so in the foreseeable future.

Our *Habits of the Heart* authors warn that we must understand institutions and how they affect our lives. As much as we would like to profess our independence, Americans have become increasingly dependent on large bureaucratic institutions for their security, autonomy and well-being. Two particular institutions—the federal government and the corporation—are the most powerful structures in our society. They affect everything else, including our culture and our character.[32] Our institutions have become "defined" without serious public discussion, as "... educational and occupational systems appear to have an objective givenness that puts them beyond question."[33] Failure or refusal to adopt to these technocratic systems can result in the deprivation of opportunity and social ostracization.

The increasing power and influence of institutions has been aided and abetted by the rise of professionalism. Professionals comprise a cadre of technocratic experts whose priorities are tied to the corporate administrative state. These professionals are inculcated into a culture of constant mobility, where professional life begins by leaving home to attend university, then graduate or professional school, then through various places of career advancement. Where professionals in the past once were the voice of morality and ethical philosophy, they have now become consumed by the ethos of individual success—which requires that one constantly separate and distance oneself to stand out from the crowd. Professionals view their duties through the lens of administration—keeping order and control over the vast machinery that determines life outcomes for the rest of us. Even when such objectives are benevolent, one can see the obvious foundation for authoritarianism.

Our politics have thus become privatized, where "individual achievement in the quest for wealth and power is elevated above the collective effort of communities to determine common destinies. Yet it is this antipolitical system that decides most important matters for us—where we work, where we can live, even how we can live—
and competes with political parties, and government itself for our allegiance and support."[34] The administered state only tightens "the hold of corporate business on our collective life" which results in the administrative despotism that Tocqueville warned against. Even the vision of economic democracy—the seemingly futile attempt to

bring the corporate economy under democratic control—is subject to dependence on technocratic experts and administrative hierarchies.[35] Yet, we refuse to recognize that "an interdependent national society has replaced the moral fiction of a world of independent individuals linked only by market exchange."[36] Americans are in denial, a conscious obliviousness fed by a "stubborn fear of acknowledging structures of power and interdependence."[37] We cling to the belief that our individual conscience is strong enough to keep us free from the darker influences of the corporate administrative state.

The Dangers of Extreme Individualism

Today, the public good is defined in terms of a utilitarian individualism. For the classic utilitarian individualist, there is no such thing as a social contract. The only valid contract is one based on negotiation between individuals acting in their own self-interest—an expression of free choices which is also free to be abandoned when it no longer serves the contracting parties. The freely contracting individual thus requires no binding obligations nor wider social understanding to justify the relationship.[38] Likewise, the public good also arises naturally as if by an invisible hand—out of the spontaneous interplay among rational and self-interested individuals.[39]

However, utilitarian individualism essentially abandons any claim to morality, instead justifying itself on the basis of rationality. The *Habits of the Heart* authors argue that, "…in the absence of any objectifiable criteria of right and wrong, good or evil, the self and its feelings become our only moral guide…Separated from family, religion, and calling as a source of authority, duty and moral example, the self first seeks to work out its own form of action by autonomously pursuing happiness and satisfying its wants…[I]ndividualism offers us only the cost-benefit analysis of external success, and the intuition of feeling inwardly more or less free, comfortable, and authentic on which to ground self-approval. Ideas of the self's inner expansion reveal nothing of the shape moral character should take, the limits it should respect, and the community it should serve."[40]

Our *Habits of the Heart* authors do not advocate abandoning individualism—it is indeed one of the strongest and deepest features of American identity—but propose that earlier forms of individualism were placed in a context of moral and religious obligations (i.e., limits) which have been abandoned. They rather advocate for the creation of "an American philosophy less trapped in the clichés of rugged individualism and more open to an invigorating, fulfilling sense of social responsibility."[41] Their bigger argument is that—taken to extremes—individualism can undermine the values that we intend for it to foster—values like democracy, mutual respect, and equality. As an example of this, they propose that well-meaning efforts to promote diversity and inclusion can operate to undermine pluralism because it elevates the assertion of one's own identity above the common good.[42]

As radical individualism has served to separate us from each other, our lives have become increasingly fragmented in other ways as well. This process of fragmentation began with early industrialization in the late nineteenth century, which accelerated in the twentieth. It began by separating the home and workplace, along with work and leisure. Family—the core of the private realm—is no longer an integral part of a larger moral ecology tying the individual to community, church, and nation.[43] The goal of family life today is not to link individuals to the public world, but to provide refuge and isolate them from it.[44] As the domination of bureaucratic consumer capitalism replaced older forms of integrated economic and civic life, moral culture devolved into an "untrammeled pursuit of wealth." However, fragmentation—along with these new cultural norms—"suited the needs of the industrial corporations."[45]

Fragmentation was not limited to working class families, but extended into the professional/managerial classes. Professionals and academics are becoming increasingly specialized, developing expertise in ever-narrower specialties and sub-specialties. Education is no longer about producing informed and responsible citizens, but has become "a means to advancement in an ever more complex educational system, itself a function of an ever more complex industrial and postindustrial division of labor."[46] Even the social sciences have become "empiricist, reductionist, and relativistic, viewing individuals as atomistic self-interested maximizers."[47] The rise of the research university and the ascendency of economic theory and analysis—with its emphasis on productivity and cost-effectiveness—are now applied to non-profit institutions, including colleges and universities.[48] Thus, even those privileged with higher education are losing the ability to conceptualize in terms of higher purpose or common good.

As the federal government has grown larger, it too has become balkanized. Politics is characterized by competing interest groups and special interest constituencies, which political parties attempt to placate depending on who makes the most noise (or has the most to offer in campaign contributions). There is no structure or platform for political parties (or anyone else) to discuss and debate the larger problems of society or to create a new vision of how to respond.[49] Politics is dominated by competing (or collusive) private interests because it has never formulated a vision of the common good.[50]

The institution of the law—which (with the possible exception of religion) has probably done the most to address contemporary social problems—also focuses its attention on the expansion of individual rights rather than addressing the "fundamental social and moral questions about the nature of a good society."[51] State Bar Associations make concerted efforts to inculcate a spirit of public service by encouraging members to provide pro bono service to indigent clients as well as to serve in professional organizations. Awards are given to attorneys for participation in pro bono and public service activities and not—as is the case in society at large—for obtaining huge sums of money or celebrity status. A lot of people like to disparage lawyers—and even lawyers themselves tend to complain that Bar associations focus on big firm lawyers (who generally defend corporations and wealthy individuals) at the expense of small firm and solo attorneys—yet bar associations are one of the few institutions in our society that promote the ideal of public service. Indeed, many of them also sponsor civics education programs in the community to encourage democratic participation and good citizenship behaviors.

Just as fragmentation has split work from home and family and public from private, society has been split into a business class and a working class "with the former dominant and the latter in many ways excluded from full participation in community life."[52] This dominant class has imposed its own values of calculating managerialism into areas of our lives (such as family and community) that once were governed by the norms of a moral ecology.[53] The "good life" is now defined in terms of economic growth and competitive success.[54] Liberty is equated with the spirit of enterprise and the right to amass wealth and power for oneself.[55] Because most of us will never become masters-of-the-universe billionaires, we have reduced our aspirations to finding some combination of occupation and "lifestyle" that is economically workable and psychically tolerable.[56]

Today we are faced with a growing level of inequality that further threatens social cohesion beyond the previously discussed forms of fragmentation. In *The Spirit Level*, Richard Wilkinson and Kate Pickett have made the best documented case against the harmfulness of extreme inequality.[57] *Habits of the Heart* authors also argue that class difference is morally wrong for the same reason that slavery is wrong, because it "deprives millions of people of the ability to participate fully in society and to realize themselves as individuals."[58] Yet we live in a society that presumes itself to be comprised of an egalitarian collection of autonomous middle-class individuals. Those who do not meet this criteria are excluded from social membership in "a way unknown in a hierarchical society" because "it is difficult to give moral meaning to differences considered fundamentally illegitimate."[59] The dysfunctional consequences of a delusion of equality amidst the reality of extreme inequality will be further explored in Part IV, Section Two.

Radical individualism is not only an ineffective defense against authoritarianism, it can even help facilitate it. The loneliness that results from such isolation may precipitate the hunger for order and group cohesiveness upon which authoritarian groups base their promises.[60] However, when individualism takes priority over any sense of social solidarity, people have no way to organize a collective resistance against the abuse of authority.[61] Our *Habits of the Heart* authors lament that, "A movement of enlightenment and liberation that was to have freed us from superstition and tyranny has led in the twentieth century to a world in which ideological fanaticism and political oppression have reached extremes unknown in previous history."[62]

Notes

[1] Excerpt from Franklin's reconstructed autobiography *The Private Life of the Late Benjamin Franklin, LL.D.*, 1793.

[2] Selznick, P. (1992). *The moral commonwealth: Social theory and the promise of community.* Berkeley, CA: University of California Press at p. 35.

[3] Lemann, N. (2019). *Transaction man: Rise of the deal and decline of the American dream.* New York, NY: Farrar, Straus and Giroux at p. 268.

[4] From a speech entitled "Wealth and Poverty" given before the National Policy Committee on Pockets of Poverty, December 13, 1963. Full quote at https://wist.info/galbraith-john-kenneth/7463/

[5] Lovett, F. (2015). Civic virtue. In *The Encyclopedia of Political Thought,* 1st Ed. New York, NY": John Wiley and Sons, at p. 2.

[6] *Id.* at p. 3.

[7]Gilens, M., & Page, B.I. (2014, September) Testing theories of American politics: Elites, interest groups, and average citizens. *Perspectives on Politics 12*(3), 564-581. https://www.cambridge.org/core/journals/perspectives-on-politics/article/testing-theories-of-american-politics-elites-interest-groups-and-average-citizens/62327F513959D0A304D4893B382B992B A majority of people believe that ordinary citizens would do a better job of solving problems than elected officials. https://www.people-press.org/2015/11/23/8-perceptions-of-the-publics-voice-in-government-and-politics/

[8] Bellah, R., Madsen, R., Sullivan, W., Swidler, A., & Tipton, S. (1991). *The good society.* New York, NY: Vintage Books/Random House, Inc. at p. 296.

[9] *Id.* at p. 43

---

[10] Bellah, R. N., Madsen, R., Sullivan, W.M., Swidler, A., & Tipton, S.W. (2008). *Habits of the heart.* Berkeley, CA: University of California Press at p. 37.

[11] *Id. a*t p. 117.

[12] *Id.* at p. 149

[13] *Id.* at pp. 38-39.

[14] *Id.* at p. 169.

[15] *Id.*

[16] *Id.* at p. 168.

[17] *Id.* at p. 30.

[18] Lovett, F. (2015). Civic virtue. In *The Encyclopedia of Political Thought,* 1st Ed. New York, NY: John Wiley and Sons at p. 5.

[19] *Id.* at pp. 4-5.

[20] Bellah, R. N., Madsen, R., Sullivan, W.M., Swidler, A., & Tipton, S.W. (2008). *Habits of the heart.* Berkeley, CA: University of California Press at p. ix.

[21] *Id.*

[22] Bellah, R., Madsen, R., Sullivan, W., Swidler, A., & Tipton, S. (1991). *The good society.* New York, NY: Vintage Books/Random House, Inc. at p. 99.

[23] Bellah, R.N., Madsen, R., Sullivan, W.M., Swidler, A., & Tipton, S.W. (2008). *Habits of the heart.* Berkeley, CA: University of California Press at p. 83.

[24] *Id. See also: The good society. (1991).*

[25] *Id.* at p. 201.

[26] *Id.* at p. 206.

[27] *Id.*

[28] Etzioni, A. (2002). The good society. *Seattle Journal of Social Justice 1*(1), p. 90. https://digitalcommons.law.seattleu.edu/sjsj/vol1/iss1/7/

---

[29] Bellah, R.N., Madsen, R., Sullivan, W.M., Swidler, A., & Tipton, S.W. (2008). *Habits of the heart.* Berkeley, CA: University of California Press.

[30] *Id.* at p. 265.

[31] Norris, P. (2011). *Democratic deficit: Critical citizens revisited.* New York, NY: Cambridge University Press.

[32] Bellah, R.N., Madsen, R., Sullivan, W.M., Swidler, A., & Tipton, S.W. (2008). *Habits of the heart.* Berkeley, CA: University of California Press at p. 275.

[33] Bellah, R., Madsen, R., Sullivan, W., Swidler, A., & Tipton, S. (1991). *The good society.* New York, NY: Vintage Books/Random House, Inc. at p. 43.

[34] Bellah, R.N., Madsen, R., Sullivan, W.M., Swidler, A., & Tipton, S.W. (2008). *Habits of the heart.* Berkeley, CA: University of California Press at p. 214.

[35] *Id.* at p. 270.

[36] Bellah, R., Madsen, R., Sullivan, W., Swidler, A., & Tipton, S. (1991). *The good society.* New York, NY: Vintage Books/Random House, Inc. at p. 125.

[37] Bellah, R.N., Madsen, R., Sullivan, W.M., Swidler, A., & Tipton, S.W. (2008). *Habits of the heart.* Berkeley, CA: University of California Press at p. 25.

[38] *Id.* at p. 107.

[39] *Id.* at p. 188.

[40] *Id.* at pp. 76-79.

[41] Bellah, R., Madsen, R., Sullivan, W., Swidler, A., & Tipton, S. (1991). *The good society.* New York, NY: Vintage Books/Random House, Inc. at p. 15.

[42] *Id.* at p. 304-305.

[43] Bellah, R.N., Madsen, R., Sullivan, W.M., Swidler, A., & Tipton, S.W. (2008). *Habits of the heart.* Berkeley, CA: University of California Press at p. 112.

[44] *Id.* at p. 107.

[45] *Id.* at p. 43.

[46] Bellah, R., Madsen, R., Sullivan, W., Swidler, A., & Tipton, S. (1991). *The good society.* New York, NY: Vintage Books/Random House, Inc. at p. 156.

[47] *Id.* at p. 163.

[48] *Id.* at p. 169.

[49] *Id.* at p. 112.

[50] *Id.* at p. 131.

[51] *Id.* at p. 124.

[52] Bellah, R.N., Madsen, R., Sullivan, W.M., Swidler, A., & Tipton, S.W. (2008). *Habits of the heart.* Berkeley, CA: University of California Press at p. 48.

[53] *Id.*

[54] Bellah, R., Madsen, R., Sullivan, W., Swidler, A., & Tipton, S. (1991). *The good society.* New York, NY: Vintage Books/Random House, Inc. at p. 296.

[55] *Id.* at. p. 58-61.

[56] *Id.* at p. 47.

[57] Wilkinson, R., & Pickett, K. (2009). *The spirit level: Why greater equality makes societies stronger.* New York, NY: Bloomsbury Press.

[58] Bellah, R.N., Madsen, R., Sullivan, W.M., Swidler, A., & Tipton, S.W. (2008). *Habits of the heart.* Berkeley, CA: University of California Press at p. xi.

[59] *Id.* at p. 206.

[60] *Id.* at p. 162.

[61] *Id.* at p. 240.

[62] *Id.* at p. 280.

Section Three
The Role of Religion in a Good Society

Do not impose on others what you do not wish for yourself.

Confucius

*

This is the sum of duty; do naught unto others what you would not have them do unto you.

Mahabharata 5:1517

*

Treat others with respect. How you treat others will be how they treat you.

Buddha

*

You shall not take vengeance or bear a grudge against any of your people, but you shall love your neighbor as yourself.

Leviticus 19:18

*

Jesus said, "You shall love the Lord you God with all your heart, and with all your soul, and with all your mind. This is the greatest and first commandment. And a second is like it: You shall love your neighbor as yourself.

Matthew 22: 37-39.

*

None of you believes until he wishes for his brother what he wishes for himself.

An-Nawawi's Forty Hadith 13

The teachings of nearly every religion contain some version of the Golden Rule, or a moral dictum of reciprocity. This involves both a matter of behavior and "doing unto" others as well as a mindset of "loving your neighbor/brother as yourself." Most religious interpreters also tell us that who is our neighbor or brother should be interpreted expansively, and not limited to only those who are literally members of our own tribe or family. Although almost everyone can point to real-world examples of bad behavior committed in the name of religion (the Israeli occupation of Palestine, the Christian Crusades, Islamic terrorism), these examples are contrary to the teachings of the respective prophets. Yet, faith traditions are more than simply another form of codified social rules that would be great if everyone followed them but—like all other systems—are sometimes ineffectual in the face of human fallibility.

Our faith traditions hold the promise of guidance toward a good society when technical rationality fails us. They do more than simply command us to follow rules and obey orders, but call us to a higher self that regards other human beings—including those who are not like us—as having equal claims to dignity and personal worth. That is, there is something more metaphysical about the notions of "good" and "evil" that extends beyond whether rules are being followed or a particular system or program is working. However, all religions or faith traditions are also products of the societies in which they arose. Religious philosophies and practices both influence the society in which they emerge as they are also influenced by it. As we will see from our visit through multi-faith history, a faith tradition can be spread when it attaches itself to an expansionary worldly power, where proselytization and conversion are accomplished with brute force rather than the power of love and example that the prophets profess.

What all moral systems do is establish a set of generalized rules to guide us in right relations. Both theistic religions and moralistic traditions like Confucianism thus contain many overlapping similarities, generally proscribing harmful behavior toward others and sometimes even to animals and the earth itself. Most of them focus on the development of personal morality as a means to achieving right personal relations, with little (or only tangential) concern for institutional relations. Although some of the later theistic religions do briefly address specific issues regarding relations with the state/empire[1] or even economics,[2] the focus of most religious and moral systems is on individual behavior.

Although religious doctrines have much to teach us about good and evil, they tend to have gaps, particularly with respect to practical implementation. The first, and obvious question is whose God or prophet is the "right" one? In a pluralistic society, we are not going to have a spirit of community solely based on religious membership. The alternative—theocracy—may appear to get everyone on the same page with respect to common values, but since many people are likely to resist (even if quietly and surreptitiously), any sense of common good is probably going to be perverted in some way. Moreover, the foundation of true faith is individual free will, thus an enforced submission to a religion that is not freely chosen violates some of its fundamental tenets.

Perhaps—like the near universal Golden Rule—we can distill some basic truths from the teachings of all religions and major belief systems. Of utmost salience for this analysis is establishing a framework for the discussion of good and evil. The major theistic religions all concern themselves with questions about the source and cause of evil. Evil is generally defined as something that causes human suffering, particularly if the suffering is undeserved.[3] A fundamental question among all of the theistic religions is the paradox of the existence of evil when God is purportedly all-good and omnipotent. That is, a good God would theoretically not create evil, and if evil exists then God would be sufficiently powerful to prevent it.

Thus, a number of theories were developed to explain this paradox. First, when God gave humanity free will and man disobeyed God, this created the condition of original sin, which exists in humanity as a permanent condition. However, this cannot explain suffering caused by natural disasters such as flooding and earthquakes, or sickness and disease—things which are totally outside the control of humanity. A corollary to creation theory is that an evil (i.e., disobedient) creature who is less powerful than God but more powerful than man exists in opposition to God. Satan (*aka* the devil) either creates evil on his own or alternatively tempts humanity into disobedience and sin. We will address this further later in this section, but [spoiler alert] no one has found the right answer to the cause of evil and suffering, and theologians of all the major religions continue to wrestle with these questions.

If the ultimate objective of a good society is the happiness and wellbeing of its citizens, religion presents a paradox. The countries with the highest happiness scores are the secular-rational countries of Protestant Europe, which tend to have lower rates of religious affiliation. Yet, a January 2019 global study by the Pew Research Center found that actively religious people tend to be happier than the "inactively religious" (they identify with a church but do not attend regularly) and the religiously unaffiliated.[4] A follow-up Pew survey in 2020 found that, across 34 countries, a plurality of 45% said that a belief in God was necessary to have good moral values, with 61% reporting that God played an important role in their own lives. The same survey also found that countries with higher per capita GDP and higher levels of education were ***less*** likely to think that a belief in God is necessary to be moral.[5] The data thus suggest that, while religion might not be necessary to the development of moral values, it can be conducive to and correlated with morality. That is, if religion is the only way for some people to define morality and behave prosocially, it should not be ignored by technocratic policy makers.

Other studies have found that the actively religious are more likely to be civically engaged, joining other types of (nonreligious) organizations and being more likely to vote. One theory is that persons who regularly participate in regular religious services tend to develop what Harvard University Professor Robert Putnam calls "social capital." Social capital is a network of relationships in which people can count on each other for support when experiencing life challenges, as well as pathways to jobs and opportunity. Additionally, actively religious people also tend to abstain from risky behaviors such as smoking, alcohol, illegal drugs and promiscuous sex, which increases health and longevity.[6] However, whether faith drives happiness, pro-sociality, and civic engagement or whether people who are more extraverted are also happier—and thus tend to be more socially active as well as more actively religious—has not been definitively determined. Other theories are that religion encourages behaviors and attitudes such as forgiveness, hope, and helping others, which serve to reduce conflict and stress. But perhaps the greatest contribution of religion is to encourage its adherents to acknowledge the universality of the human condition. A little more empathy and understanding could go a long way to curing many of the ills of modern technocratic society.

To give us a universal grounding, we will take a brief tour through the world's major religions, which comprise approximately three-quarters of the world's population. Some 14-15% of the global population can be categorized as secular/atheist/agnostic; that is, they do not practice or believe the tenets of any religion. Another approximately 9-10% of people belong to what is broadly categorized as traditional, or ethnic religions, generally based on smaller, tribal systems (e.g., native Americans). Among the world's main religions, they can be divided into two main categories: the Eastern religions (Confucianism, Hinduism, and Buddhism), and the monotheistic, Abrahamic religions (Judaism, Christianity, and Islam).

Here I will also divulge that I am Christian. Therefore, I am more familiar with Christian history and beliefs than the others, so it might seem that I may be favoring Christianity or attempting to proselytize. However, my purpose here is to explore how these various faith practices are similar—including their common historical roots—as well as how they are different. While no single religion has all the right answers, all of them have something useful to teach us. I have borrowed data from the PEW research center 2012 report showing geographic and demographic information about where the various religious populations are distributed.[7]

Confucianism. Confucianism is not a religion *per se,* but a form of scholarly tradition governing societal relationships. Confucius himself lived during the 6th to 5th centuries B.C., and was primarily responsible for recording and transmitting wisdom which had developed over the prior centuries, beginning with the Shang dynasty (18th to 12th centuries B.C). Although Confucianism originated in China, its influence extended to modern-day Korea, Japan, and Vietnam. Confucianism involved itself with social relations, ethics, politics, and philosophy, and occasionally addressed concepts such as heaven. Confucianism concerned itself with right relations; both relations between individuals and relationships between individuals and the state or their rulers.

The Confucian tradition is based on a lifelong process of education and self-realization. As with so many other moral traditions, Confucianism changed over time, as it was adopted by later thinkers and advocates. During the Tang dynasty (618-907), China was dominated by Buddhism, although Confucianism—which does not require a specific profession of faith—never really died out. Many people in China and East Asia continue to practice Confucian-based traditions, even as they declare themselves to be practicing members of other religions (like Buddhism or Christianity).

Hinduism. Hinduism is considered to be the world's oldest formal religion. It is believed that Hinduism started somewhere in the Indus valley between 2300 and 1500 B.C. Today, Hindus comprise about 15% of the world's population, and some 95% of the world's Hindus live in India. Hinduism does not have a "founder," but it does have sacred texts such as the Vedas, the Upanishads, the Bhagavad Gita, and others. Hindus believe that their sacred texts do not have a specific origin, but have existed since the beginning of time. Hindus recognize many gods and goddesses, who have various jurisdictions. The primary God is Brahma, who is responsible for the creation of the world and all living things, although many Hindus are followers of various combinations of the many different gods and goddesses.

Hindus believe in reincarnation (the cycle of birth, death, and rebirth) and karma (the universal law of cause and effect). A fundamental principle is that thoughts and actions in the present affect both one's current and future lives. Hindu's may worship at a temple or at shrines to specific gods or goddesses in their homes. They consider all living creatures sacred—most do not eat beef or pork, and many are vegetarians. The highest objective of a Hindu is to achieve dharma, or a state of moral uprightness and good living.

A feature of Hinduism that is incompatible with an egalitarian society is the caste system. People are born into the caste that they then occupy for the rest of their lives—there is no way to move up or out. The justification is that one's place in the hierarchy is determined by one's deeds in previous lifetimes. In this system, society is divided into four main castes, with the highest being the Brahmin, or intellectual and spiritual leaders. The remainder of society is divided (in descending order) into protectors and public servants (military and government), skilled labor/merchants, and unskilled labor/artisans. The so-called "untouchables" are traditionally assigned work that is considered too "impure" to be performed by everyone else. Untouchables, or Dalits, reside in segregated communities in which the state deliberately often fails to provide basic services, such as electricity and sanitation systems (i.e., the larger society guarantees their continued impurity). Although discrimination against untouchables was constitutionally abolished when India gained its independence, many of the old practices continue.

Buddhism. The historical founder of Buddhism is Siddhartha Gautama, who lived during the 5th century B.C. in present-day Nepal. Although Gautama was born into a wealthy family, he was concerned about human suffering and took a vow of poverty. He came to realize that voluntary self-impoverishment did nothing to solve the problems of the world, and so he began a quest for enlightenment. It is believed that Gautama found enlightenment while meditating under a Bodhi tree, and he began to teach the virtues of wisdom, kindness, patience, generosity, and compassion as paths to enlightenment that others could follow.

As Gautama gained followers, his teachings spread throughout India and into Tibet, China, Cambodia, Mongolia, Laos, Taiwan, Korea, Vietnam, and Japan. Today, about 6-7% of the world's population are practicing Buddhists, and they reside primarily in the Asian-Pacific area. Buddhists live by five moral precepts which prohibit killing, stealing, sexual misconduct, lying, and using drugs or alcohol, as well as four "noble truths" about human suffering. Buddhism does not recognize a deity, although its teachings are considered sacred texts. Rather, the focus is on achieving enlightenment through right practices.

Like Confucianism, Buddhism is sometimes considered to be more like a spiritual tradition than a religion *per se.* Like Hinduism, Buddhists recognize the concepts of both reincarnation and karma. They are also able to worship either in temples or at shrines in their own homes. Buddhism encourages its followers to find the "middle way" between the extremes of self-indulgence and self-denial. Many people—including those in Western countries—are adopting Buddhist philosophies and practices (e.g., meditation and mindfulness) without necessarily "converting" to Buddhism.

The three monotheistic Abrahamic religions—Judaism, Christianity, and Islam—derive from common roots, and collectively comprise over half of the world's population. While the news is often dominated by geopolitical conflicts based on a people's membership in one of these religions, they all share belief in a single deity who is responsible for creation (YHWH, or Elohim in Hebrew, God as Father or Trinity--Father, Son and Holy Ghost--for Christians, and the Muslim Allah). All three also recognize the same lineage of prophets and share much of the same foundational holy text—which is attributed to be the Word of God as pronounced through the prophets. In these religions we see the incorporation of descriptions of "creation" before the rise of humans, predictions of an apocalyptic "end times" (which we will discuss in more detail in Part V), and the concepts of sin and evil.

Judaism. Judaism is the oldest monotheistic religion, and it is the foundation of the two later religions which have become the faith majority today. It is believed that the God of Creation appeared to a Semitic/Hebrew nomad named Abraham around 2000 BC. God made a covenant with Abraham, promising him that a great nation would arise from Abraham's descendants in return for loyalty to the "one true God." Abraham's descendants took the name Israel and became known as the Israelites. During this time, the Israelites were a kinship-based society (as opposed to a more political society like the Greeks or Romans), as well as patriarchal. The holy texts of Judaism include the Torah (the law), the Ne'vim (the prophets), the Ketuvim (the writings, e.g., Psalms and Proverbs), as well as a collection of rabbinical teachings called the Talmud. Much of the Hebrew holy text was incorporated into the Old Testament of the Christian Bible. The Jewish holy text describes creation, the origins of humanity (including original sin), God's covenant with Abraham, and then follows the lineage of Abraham in detail.

Some centuries later, Solomon, the son of King David (who made Jerusalem the center of the 12 tribes) built the holy temple in Jerusalem, which became the central place of worship for all Jews. Between 600 and 500 B.C., the Babylonians invaded Jerusalem, destroyed the temple and scattered the Jews. Jews that were able shifted to worshipping in local synagogues. Some of them were enslaved in Egypt, where they were subsequently led to freedom by the prophet Moses. During their wandering back to their homeland, Moses encountered God on a mountain, where God inscribed the Ten Commandments on a stone tablet. These Commandments mirror some of the Buddhist proscriptions against murder, stealing, adultery and lying. However, one major difference was the command to be obedient to God, and to have "no other Gods."

The goal of Jews was the re-creation of a great Jewish nation that would have global influence. The actual nation of Israel was realized in 1948, although it came to be amidst conflict that continues today. Israel is one of only two nation states in North Africa and the Middle East with a liberal democracy and OECD membership. In 2019, there were approximately 9 million persons living in Israel, over 74% of them identifying as Hebrew/practicing Judaism. However, the state seems to be in a constant state of war, as other peoples (most notably Palestinian Arabs) claim rights to some of the territory. The capital, Jerusalem, contains holy historical sites for Jews, Christians, and Muslims, and so endures a history of recurring partition, political conflict and war. Today, Jews comprise less than 1% of the world's population, and they live primarily in Israel, or the U.S. and Canada.

Christianity. The foundation of Christianity is the life and teachings of Jesus, a Jew from the lineage of David (Abraham). Jesus was the product of virgin conception and believed to be the "son of God," the Savior/Messiah that was promised to the Jews in the Old Testament. Thus, the Christian holy text incorporates both the Hebrew Old Testament and then the story of Jesus as told by his apostles in the New Testament. It further includes letters that were written by the apostles Paul, Peter, James and John, as they spread and established the nascent Christian faith. It also includes the Book of Revelation, which we will cover in more detail in Part V.

Unlike the jealous and punitive God of the Old Testament,[8] the New Testament God allowed his own son to be born into human flesh, to live among humans and to suffer with them. The New Testament God himself seems to have transformed into something more compassionate, as the mission of Jesus was to preach the gospel of love and anchor this energy into humanity. Because Jesus was not about worldly power—and his arrival did not coincide with the establishment of a Jewish nation— many Jews continue to await the arrival of the promised Messiah.

What makes Jesus different from earlier prophets is that he was crucified and resurrected by God on the third day. Although there were stories of persons being raised from the dead in both the Old Testament (by the prophet Elijah and his successor Elisha) and New Testament (resurrections performed by Jesus himself), each of these persons lived out the remainder of their lives and eventually died naturally. Jesus is the only human being to have not only arisen from the dead, but ascend to eternal life. His message was that anyone who "believed in Him" could also do the same thing—rise to some form of ascended status after death.

In addition to the promise of resurrected life-after-death, Jesus also brought a new theology of right relations based on love—love of God, love of self (obviously without the sin of pride and hubris), and love of neighbor. While the Old Testament was full of behavioral and dietary prescriptions to achieve atonement, Jesus' message was that following the spirit of the law was more important than the letter of it: It was not sinful to heal the sick and feed the hungry on the Sabbath,[9] welcoming people had priority over fasting or abstaining from fellowship with sinners.[10] While Jesus preached that a pure heart was preferable to strict adherence to rules and regulations, he also advised people to obey the laws of earthly rulers, even if the rulers were non-believers.[11]

Christianity was initially spread by Jesus' chosen apostles, who were accustomed to traveling into towns where they were strangers with their message. Early Roman emperors were hostile to

Christianity, as they viewed it a challenge to their power. However, in 313, the emperor Constantine lifted the ban on Christianity and himself converted, which was a turning point in Christian history. By 380 A.D., Christianity was the official religion of the Roman Empire, and its church was established in Rome. The Pope, or Bishop of Rome, served as head of the Church, and he took the name of Peter, the apostle that Jesus anointed as the "rock [upon which] I will build my church."[12]

As experienced by most other religions, Christianity had its ups and downs, waxing and waning through historical shifts. It nonetheless continued to spread, although it has split into three main branches: Catholic, Orthodox, and Protestant. As Christianity grew and spread, it bifurcated into a church associated with the former Roman empire (the Catholic Church), and what is known as an Eastern (or Greek) Orthodox church. The original Christian "church" formally split when a "great schism" (sometime between 1054 and 1204, the period of the Crusades) arose due to cultural differences between East and West, as well as political conflicts. Today, the Catholic church is governed at the top by a Pope, who is based in Vatican City, a small independent territory located within the city of Rome. The Orthodox church doesn't have a Pope, but is governed by Patriarchs, who are elected by ecumenical councils or Synods. These Synods are located in Rome, Constantinople, Alexandria, Antioch and Jerusalem. Both Catholic and Orthodox churches claim to be keepers of the original apostolic traditions as directly transmitted by Jesus.

A larger and more abrupt split in Christianity occurred in 1517, when Martin Luther nailed his 95 Theses to the door of the church, founding the Protestant Reformation. The radical proposition of Luther's reformation was the so-called "priesthood of the people," or that individual believers did not have to go through a religious authority for salvation. This occurred during a period of corruption in the Catholic church, where popes and priests would demand payment (indulgences) for the forgiveness of sins. Protestantism itself has since further splintered into at least 20 distinct denominations, each with differing biblical interpretations and worship traditions. Perhaps it is this adaptability that has allowed Christianity to become the world's dominant religion, with

Christians comprising some 29-31% of the world's population. While countries like the United States, Canada and Australia are majority Christian, the greatest number of Christians (primarily Catholic) live in Mexico and South America.

Islam. The distinctive belief of Islam is that Muhammad is the last prophet of God. Like Jesus, Muhammad is also a descendant of Abraham, but through his son Ishmael. Ishmael was born of Hagar, a slave/servant of Abraham's wife, Sara. Sara allowed the conception because she was unable to have children, until God blessed her much later in life with the birth of Isaac,[13] who became the "father" of Israel, and its descendant Christianity. Muhammad (April 22, 571 to June 8, 632), was born to a single mother (his father had died before he was born) as a member of the Quraish, the most powerful and successful of the Arabic merchant tribes of the day. When he was about the age of 40, Muhammad began having visions and revelations, receiving messages from the Archangel Gabriel. Gabriel's revelations told of the existence of a single God (the current culture was polytheistic), as well as the basis of the Muslim holy book, the Qur'an.

At the time of the revelations, Muhammad was a resident of the Arab city of Mecca. Also at that time, Mecca was an important city, being a primary place of pilgrimage for Arab tribes as well as a place of trading. Thus, Islam was influenced by Arab philosophy, as well as emerging understandings of mathematics, science, and commerce. It was spread throughout the Middle East, North Africa, and Central Asia, reaching as far as Spain in the west to India in the East. Islam spread rapidly due to a combination of its incorporation of religion into a social community, Sufi (mystics) missionary activity, and its connection with the Arab trade system, which reached into Indonesia, Malaya and China. Today, Islam comprises some 23-24% of the world's population, who primarily reside in the Middle East and Africa.

Islam believes in one God (they reject the Christian Trinity and view Jesus as a legitimate prophet of God, but not the son of God), who brought the world into existence by the command "Be." The Muslim God combines the attributes of power, justice and mercy, and so in many ways is similar to the God of the Jews and

Christians. Theologically, the universe is viewed as being autonomous, but not autocratic. That is, everything in creation has its own definite nature which can be described as a pattern. This pattern has been set by God and is not limitless, but has been "created according to measure." The Five Pillars of Islam are to give to the poor, to fast during the month of Ramadan, to pray daily (ideally five times per day), make at least one pilgrimage to Mecca, and profess that there is no other God but Allah. Muslims follow a lunar calendar, which has only 354 or 355 days, which is why their holidays rotate from year to year. In the year 2020, the Muslim year is 1441, turning to 1442 sometime in August.

The Muslim holy text is the Qur'an, and it was originally written in Arabic. It incorporates the narrative of Adam, Abraham, Moses, and Jesus, and recognizes them as divinely inspired Prophets. All of the prophets (including Muhammad and Jesus) are not divine themselves, but they are the most perfect of humans who can receive revelations from God. The Qur'an also includes hadiths and sunna, or written practices and traditions of Muhammad along with scholarly commentary. Islam recognizes the fall of Adam, but in Islam God forgives Adam, so there is no "original sin." Although humans are born sinless, human nature is frail and faltering, given to pride and the belief in human self-sufficiency. The Qur'an, describes the creation of a parallel species of creatures called jinn, who are—like humanity—endowed with reason and free will, but are more prone to evil. The Qur'an also recognizes Satan, a being who fell from divine grace when he disobeyed God by refusing to "honor" Adam. In Islam, the purpose of the human soul is to witness the unity and grace of God, and the purpose of the prophets is to call humanity back to God.

Unlike Christianity and Judaism, which developed divisions and offshoots as they evolved over time, Islam was fractured soon after the death of Muhammad. This schism had nothing to do with matters of faith—all Muslims treat the Qur'an as holy text and profess the Five Pillars of faith—but rather the result of a dispute about who should be Muhammad's successor. The Sunnis, who comprise the majority (85%), believe that any faithful Muslim could be elected to leadership, and they chose Abu Bakr, who is sometimes described as Muhammad's father-in-law and sometimes as

Muhammad's friend. Shi'ites (the minority, or about 15%) believe that the Muslim leader should be a descendant of Muhammad. The Shi'ites looked to Muhammad's son-in-law and cousin, Ali bin Abu Talib. When Ali's only surviving son, al-Hussein, was killed by Sunnis in the Battle of Karbala (Iraq) in 680, this created a rift in Islam that continues to this day, with Shi'ites often viewing themselves as an oppressed minority. Iran and Iraq are majority Shi'ite countries (although Northern Iraq has a large and growing number of Sunnis), while Saudi Arabia, Afghanistan and most other Arab countries are majority Sunni.

Although we can define five major modern religious traditions, these are quite diverse, with some branches bordering on heterodox. Outside of the basic fundamentals, there is no one-size-fits all description of beliefs and practices that apply to every Christian, Jew, Muslim, Buddhist, or Hindu. For example, most Hindus are vegetarians, but many of them abstain only from beef and pork. Some Christians are concerned about the environment (pursuant to God's mandate to be good stewards of creation), while others focus on the Old Testament concept of "dominion" and believe that humans are entitled to "dominate" nature. None of the Abrahamic religions currently exist as a monolithic whole, where all adherents believe the same things with respect to the details of everyday life, nor is there even universal agreement on how to interpret the holy texts.

In Judaism, the major branches can generically be described as Orthodox, Conservative, Reform, Reconstructionist and Humanistic. As we have already seen, Christians can be Catholic, Orthodox or Protestant/Reform, and there are over 20 distinct Protestant denominations. Because Islam is a newer religion, it has not evolved into the same level of diversity, although some versions have incorporated Western philosophers (Plato, Aristotle), while others have attempted to incorporate Christian-style mysticism. While all members of a major religion profess the core fundamental beliefs, they vary in the extent to which sacred texts are to be interpreted literally, how much of salvation is dependent on faith as well as on works, and how to manage relationships with both secular states as well as other religions. There are Christian Zionists, who support the nation of Israel, as well as Jews for Jesus. Even within specific branches and denominations, there can be wide variation in the beliefs and practices between individual congregations, and even between individual faith practitioners. This means that, even among practitioners of the same faith, there may be no universal agreement on what is right or wrong in specific instances.

The Abrahamic religions have not always had hostile relations with each other, as they have common origins. Early Christians did not necessarily view themselves as distinct from Jews (since Jesus was also a Jew), although there are Christians even today who blame Jews for the death of Jesus.[14] Christianity did not became a distinct and separate formal "church" until it was incorporated into the Roman Empire, and the holy text was translated from Hebrew into Latin. Early Muslims also considered Jews and Christians to be "people of the book." Because Christians and Jews followed the same God as Islam (Islam arose in a polytheistic Arab culture), they were allowed a great degree of religious autonomy.

One primary driver of hostility between Jews, Christians and Muslims seems to be in how each of them interprets God's covenant to create a mighty nation from the descendants of Abraham. For Jews, this revolves around the nation of Israel and its global status. For Christians, the "nation" is considered to be the church itself, and not a political entity—which is why there are periodic efforts to advance a Protestant-Catholic reconciliation. Like Christians, Muslims do not perceive the great nation promised to Abraham's descendants as a specific place, but rather the incorporation of Islamic beliefs and practices (i.e., sharia law) into the affairs of government. However, the authority and the jurisdiction of the caliph (Muslim spiritual leader) over worldly or political affairs has shifted—and continues to shift.[15]

We have also seen that religious fortunes have waxed and waned depending on various political alliances and connections with empire-building. Thus, conflict is not always so much about differences of faith as it is about worldly power. It is also not hard to imagine how faith doctrine can be used to justify claims for one's own piece of land—or even the survival of one's own people. Jews, Christians, and Muslims have at various times and places been either subject to persecution or themselves be the oppressors. As we will explore in later sections herein, one's philosophy and worldview is greatly dependent on where one stands in the social hierarchy—whether one is part of the dominant system or is viewed as an outsider. These experiences of outsider-ship have served to incorporate more compassion into religious teachings. Yet—at various times in history—including today—members of every faith tradition have chosen to ignore the more compassionate words of their own prophets and holy teachings when it suits their purposes. Every religion thus experiences shifting ideologies that range from labeling any dissent as blasphemous heresy, to expansive toleration of not only dissidents within the faith, but members of other faiths as well.

For purposes of our analysis herein, we are going to look at what the various religious traditions have to say about the causes of human suffering, the relationship of the individual to worldly institutions, and the prevention of evil. Our argument here is that most religious teachings focus on changing individuals—how they behave, how and what they think, and how they treat others. However, we will attempt to make the more tenuous connection of how religious teachings can help us when faced with administrative or macrosocial evil that cannot necessarily be traced to the bad behavior of specific individuals.

<u>The Cause of Human Suffering</u>

The Four Noble Truths of Buddhism all involve human suffering: (1) it is an inevitable part of the human condition, (2) it is caused by ignorance and karma, (3) it can be eliminated by extinguishing ignorance and karma (a state known as Nirvana), and (4) the way to end suffering is through the Noble Eight-Fold Path: right views, right thoughts, right speech, right conduct, right livelihood (to earn our living in a way that avoids evil consequences),[16] right effort, right mindfulness, and right meditation. Thus, Buddhists do not regard suffering as something to be avoided or remedied, but managed. Humans have the capacity to achieve a higher state that is removed from suffering by a comprehensive system of individual right practices. However, by ascribing all suffering to the inevitable operation of karma, it absolves the individual from attempts to change social structures that may be the root of injustice (e.g., the caste system).

In the Hebrew Old Testament Book of Job, we see the first comprehensive analysis of suffering as explained in a monotheistic worldview. That is, if God is both good and all powerful, why does God allow suffering? The character of Job we are told is wealthy and successful, as well as "blameless and upright." Satan challenged God with the proposition that Job was only obedient because God had blessed him, and that without all his wealth, family and position, Job would turn away from God. God gave Satan permission to test Job, but Satan was not allowed to take Job's life. Satan then proceeded to take away Job's livestock, servants and children, and then afflicted Job with a serious health condition (from the biblical description, it sounds like leprosy). Job cursed the day he was born, but—even when urged to do so by his wife—Job did not curse God.

Three of Job's friends came to visit and support him in his grief. The remainder of the story involves a somewhat lengthy and convoluted dialogue between Job and his friends about why his suffering has come about. His friends all accuse Job of some bad deed for which he has not come clean. When Job disavows this, the theories turn to possible bad deeds of Job's children or his ancestors. Job finally admits that he may never understand the reason for his punishment, and lamented God's injustice. God finally "appears" in a whirlwind and questions Job, who admits that human knowledge is limited, while God's power is unlimited. God is pleased with this answer, restores Job's wealth to twice what is had been previously, along with 140 more years of life and four generations of grandchildren. Here we are beginning to see a shift away from the theory of karma—along with its blame-the-victim explanation for suffering—to an acknowledgement that bad stuff can happen to good people and there is not always a convenient explanation for it.

In the Christian tradition, we see Jesus demonstrating the power of God by restoring the sight of a blind man,[17] healing the sick,[18] raising the dead,[19] and feeding 5,000 people with five loaves and two fishes.[20] Jesus' ministry thus demonstrates a "hands on" ethic of responsibility to alleviate the suffering of others. Yet, Jesus is unable to prevent his own persecution and crucifixion. However,

Jesus' suffering had a holy purpose: he served as the sacrificial "lamb," a practice by Jews of slaughtering a lamb at the temple in order to atone for their sins and receive God's forgiveness. Indeed, God had once asked Abraham to sacrifice his son Isaac, which Abraham actually was prepared to do until God called it off, claiming it was a test of Abraham's faith.[21] Here, the sacrifice of Jesus atoned for all of the sins of humanity—past, present, and future. Now, humans could rid themselves of original sin by "believing" in Jesus without the necessity of a blood sacrifice. Jesus has now elevated suffering to a level of holiness. God himself has partaken of blameless suffering.

Islam has also struggled with the problem of human evil and suffering. Muhammad was ostracized for his profession of a single God in a polytheistic society, and he was driven from his hometown of Mecca to Medina (which marks the first year of the Islamic calendar). However, Muhammad was able to build an ever-growing community around his new faith and was eventually able to return to Mecca. Here, Muhammad was purportedly led by the angel Gabriel into both Heaven and Hell, where he came face-to-face with God and then returned to live out his natural life. Thus, we have no stories about personal suffering as we do for Jesus, rather Islam builds its theology of suffering from the story of Job.

Although this is probably an over-simplification of the theology, it appears that Muslims believe suffering to be a form of test and/or pathway to spiritual growth. There is a story of a housewife boiling chickpeas, and as a chickpea arises in the water to ask why it is being boiled and requests the housewife to relieve its suffering, the housewife tells the chickpea to "boil nicely" because "this affliction of yours is not on account of you being despised." Similar to both the theory of karma and the story of Job, Islam does not view suffering as a problem to be solved, but rather as a part of human experience—an experience that is necessary for human spiritual development as well as the actualization of God's ultimate plan.[22]

Relationships with Secular Institutions

The early Jews were a band of wandering tribes, having no land of their own. Their history is one of keeping their culture separate from the ruling one: the Babylonians, the Egyptians, the Romans. Christianity was incorporated into the Roman Empire and then became corrupted by it. The period between the 5th and 15th centuries is sometimes referred to as the "Dark Ages," or the period between the fall of Rome and the emergence of the Western European empires. During this time, there was a series of Rome-backed "holy wars" to regain territory lost to Islamic dominion known as the Crusades (1096-1271). The time of Martin Luther's reformation (1517-1648) coincided with the so-called "Enlightenment" period of Western Europe—a period of cultural ascendance that included an appreciation of reason, knowledge, science and tolerance, while religion was generally regarded with skepticism. Enlightenment ideals of constitutional government, democracy, and the ability (even necessity) of ordinary people to challenge authority formed the basis for the American Revolution.

Although we associate the separation of church and state with the American revolution, we see evidence of this basic philosophy during the time of Jesus and early Christianity. When asked about whether they should pay taxes, Jesus tells his followers to "render under Caesar what is Caesar's and unto God what is God's."[23] Christians are also instructed to submit to the governing authorities, purportedly because the authorities would not exist unless God has allowed (the biblical words are "instituted" or "established") it.[24] Thus civic duty is supposed to be separate from spiritual duty because they serve separate interests. This also suggests that we are to support the governing authorities, whether we agree with them or not. Of course, the bigger question is whether Jesus was speaking specifically about the Roman Empire (knowing that same would play a later part in spread of the Christian Church) or whether this admonishment applied to all rulers generally. We do know of one instance where Jesus directly defied authority—the scene where he drove the moneychangers from the temple and overturned their tables.[25] As a Christian, it is difficult to imagine that Jesus would ***not*** want us to oppose someone like Hitler or Stalin.

All of us can think of instances of authoritarian evil exercised under the color of state legitimacy. This goes beyond our (usually selfish) reasoning about not wanting to pay taxes or submit to other rules and regulations that cost us something or cause us inconvenience. Rather, we see authoritarian evil when it commands some of us to kill innocent others (e.g., the Jews under Hitler), commits genocide or other ethnic purges of human beings, infringes on freedoms for selfish purposes or otherwise without justification (slavery, forced migration of Native Americans, and the internment of Japanese Americans during World War II), or engages in violent suppression of legitimate grievances (various labor and civil rights protests throughout history, more recently the Black Lives Matter protests). Ideally, our faith teachings should motivate us to call out injustice that is perpetrated in the name of secular law and power.

There is a valid argument that the so-called "separation of church and state" is not expressly written in the constitution. The doctrine more likely developed from a concern among the American founders about the establishment of a singular state church like the Church of England, rather than about any danger from religious values generally informing government policy. As human history has demonstrated time and again, authoritarian evil perpetrated by kings, dictators and governments is especially pernicious when it is supported by religious authority. The problem the founding fathers attempted to address was how to prevent the dual corruption of church ***and*** state, not necessarily to remove all matters of faith from the public square. Today, even some religious leaders are ambiguous about whether the separation of church and state is good or bad. While they bemoan the loss of a moral foundation in matters of public governance, they also acknowledge the corrupting power of earthly authority. That is, keeping the church separate from government may be necessary to maintain its own spiritual purity, as well as its ability to serve as a countervailing force against state evil.

As the youngest of the major religions which arose in a culture that revolved around trade and mercantilism, Islam probably has the most to teach us about the relationship between faith values and economics. The Islamic ideals of *khalifah* (universal brotherhood) and *adalah* (justice) require that all economic activity—including the accumulation of wealth—must be used for the good of society as a whole.[26] Although Islam does not forbid profit and the accumulation of wealth, Muslims are prohibited from acquiring wealth by means of cheating, fraud, gambling, hoarding, or any form of gain that does not involve work or risk sharing (*riba*). Contemporary Islam today continues to debate whether the prohibition of *riba* means that banks cannot charge interest or whether they are only prohibited from charging usurious interest. As a practical matter, banks in Muslim countries are able to get around this by means of Islam-authorized creative financing structures such as venture capital and partnership models.[27] It is not difficult to see how the Islamic belief that all property belongs to God and man is only a steward of it—as well as specific prohibitions on accumulation—creates an obvious moral conflict with Western-style rentier and finance capitalism.[28]

In a free, post-enlightenment democracy, the structure and governance of religious communities are often viewed as incompatible with modern society. They can be conformist and authoritarian, which is antithetical to the values of individualism and democracy. Yet specific religions—as well as individual churches—vary widely in how they govern themselves. There certainly are the hierarchical, patriarchal varieties, in which a small group of men dictate the rules to everyone else (i.e., a Pope or a Patriarch). Others operate more like a moral commonwealth, where the members keep everyone else in line, although these can be even more oppressive than a traditional patriarchy (think cults, or extreme evangelicals, who are quick to harass, excommunicate, or purge anyone who doesn't conform). There are also those faith communities who operate more like deliberative democracies (Quakers, Congregationalists, Unitarian-Universalists), who engage in robust discussion and debate about matters of faith as well as what constitutes right behavior in the larger world.

The Prevention of Evil

The Abrahamic religions explain evil as the result of what is known as "the fall." In the Biblical Book of Genesis, the "original" human was Adam, who then was given a female mate by God named Eve. Adam and Eve lived in the "garden of Eden," where they were happy and wanted for nothing because they were in full communion with God. Adam and Eve were allowed to eat anything they could find within the Garden, except that God forbade them from eating from "the tree of knowledge of good and evil." However, the creature Satan, in the form of a serpent, tempted first Eve, who then tempted Adam to eat of the forbidden fruit—claiming that the fruit would give them knowledge and wisdom that would "make them like God." After eating the fruit, the bible tells us that "the eyes of both were opened, and they knew that they were naked."[29]

When God discovered this, Adam and Eve were expelled from the Garden. From here forward, human life would be a struggle—"by the sweat of your face you shall eat bread"—and the woman was further punished by pain during childbirth. Here we see a vindictive God who punishes disobedience by creating suffering for humans. In some interpretations, the "unfallen" Adam and Eve were incapable of sin, while the fallen ones were incapable of sufficient purification to be acceptable to God without specific acts or professions. The Jews thus were concerned with following laws, while the Christians believed that faith and acceptance of Jesus as personal savior would be sufficient. There is also the puzzling connection between knowledge and sin, although most theological interpretations revolve around disobedience. We will explore a secular explanation for the "fall" that addresses this connection in the next section.

Another subject that comes up in religious discussions of good versus evil is the concept of free will. One feature of most religions is that they view personal relationship with God and "salvation" as an individual choice. God has given each of us free will to choose to be in relationship (and hence, obey God's commands) or not. This begs the obvious question as to what God's will is, as this too seems to change over time or otherwise be subject to interpretation. Moreover, none of us has the authority to impose God's will on another, since everyone else must also be allowed to exercise the free will that God has given them. Although God has the power to impose His own will on all of creation, God opted to take a risk with humanity and allow us a degree of co-determination. That is, although God is the original creator, at any given time, the world is continually being co-created through the individual wills of humans.

We can see something like this here in America, where we have created a society based on the autonomous choices of free and independent individuals. We therefore also think of "good and evil" as individual choices, without a framework that expands this to community. Thus, whether a community, organization, institution, or culture is good or evil can thus be reduced to a formulaic calculus of how many people are "good" (law-abiding, God-fearing citizens that help their neighbor in need) versus how many others are "bad." As good Christians (or Hindus, Buddhists, Jews, Muslims, or other persons who obey God or the voice of their own prophet), the options we have to increase the good are to either set a good example ourselves and hope that others follow, or engage in a campaign of proselytization and conversion—which can backfire by making the target individual hostile, thus defeating our objective.

An example from my own experience serves to illustrate a version of this conundrum. Long before global climate change became a prominent political issue, I believed that the Earth was already straining and taxed from the burden of overpopulation and pollution. Perhaps this came about because, as a member of the baby-boom generation, our school classrooms were overcrowded and bursting, the environmental movement was just getting started (Rachael Carson's *Silent Spring* was published in 1962, the first Earth Day was celebrated in 1970), and I spent a good part of my young adulthood waiting in long lines to apply for jobs. Because I am a responsible person (or so I like to believe), I deliberately chose not to bear children and thus contribute to something I viewed as a major problem.[30] Fortunately, I was blessed with stepchildren, so this was not a major sacrifice on my part.

However, I have a libertarian streak that also believes reproductive choices are individual matters. I do not impose my own decision on others. Although I can pat myself on the back for not contributing to overpopulation, what is my duty to help solve the problem? I can make the argument that I already did my part and so I am not responsible for doing anything more. Yet, I must live in the same overcrowded, dirtier, and more desperate world as everyone else. The problem does not go away—neither for me, neither for the Earth, and neither for anyone else living upon it. Paradoxically (and perhaps hypocritically on some level), I rejoice with a friend or family that welcomes a new baby—even if this is their third, fourth, or fifth child. Thus, even the moral imperative to "value life" can find itself conflicted and troublesome.

Relying on personal relationships with God creates the same kind of dilemma. Most of us go through life expecting that other people are going to obey the law, their own God/prophet, or (hopefully) both. This mindset says that as long as we ourselves are right with God and do the right thing (as our individual morality sees it), we owe nothing else to society at large. As we are going to see in Part III, this let-everyone-follow-their-own-path philosophy breaks down when the society itself becomes evil, or it is taken over by individuals without moral compunction. Indeed, the church (if there is a primary church that dominates the larger society) may itself be co-opted, adapting its doctrines to justify the existing power hierarchy and subverting legitimate dissent. Moreover, as more of the selfish and ego-driven individuals assume positions of power, they have greater ability to affect cultural norms—including religious ones. In a corrupted society, it may become more difficult for regular people to find and follow their own moral compass, yet they will not be aware of these often subtle and incremental changes.

Regardless of how one views a good society or how one thinks we should get there, a significant—yet often unacknowledged—common denominator is that we ***presume that everyone else wants to live in a good society.*** Thus, such exercises usually focus on defining aspirational "goods" such as freedom, justice, democracy, community, autonomy, material sufficiency. Yet, we seldom address the inverse question as to whether such a society might also have a corresponding duty to mitigate evil, or undeserved suffering. We might think that anything "evil" would be obvious, or we define it as a problem or condition to be solved (e.g., war, poverty, slavery, dictatorship). Moreover, evil is something we usually associate with individual choice, or relegate to the mysticism of religion. It is not something that "happens" to an entire society.

But what if there exist individuals who don't share our basic premise that a good society (however it is defined or envisioned) is a worthy objective in and of itself? That is, in their view a good society is one that serves only them—either with vast material wealth, totalitarian power, or both—and the fate of everyone else is irrelevant. In the psychological worldview of such persons, concern either for individual others or society as a whole is viewed as an aberration. Moreover, what happens when such individuals gain positions of power,[31] from which they are then able to shape and direct the values and culture of the society at large? We might think that we would be on immediate notice of this and therefore do something to prevent it from happening. But such things might not manifest (especially immediately) as something that captures our attention or motivates us to take action. We instead see a gradual erosion of values—the breakdown of social cohesion and trust, a fragmentation of society, an erosion of democratic ideals as well as practical democracy.

Confronted with evidence of moral degradation, most of us will lay the blame on factors such as politics, a new generation, or the inevitable collateral damage that accompanies technological change. We will not call it evil, because evil is something we only talk about in church. However, our current society increasingly promotes behaviors such as narcissism[32] and a greed-is-good, winner-take-all, dog-eat-dog ethos that runs contrary to our religious teachings and moral traditions against pride, greed, selfishness, and hubris. Most of us know something is wrong, and—even as we can point to specific events or bad acts—have the uneasy realization that the problem is bigger than individual acts of crime, corruption, or social breakdown. The argument here is that any discussion about what is happening to us that is limited to individual behavior, or rationalized, technocratic (or even scientific-behavioral) language, frameworks and paradigms is, on some level, missing the fundamental essence of the problem. So, we might have to turn to religious traditions for a fuller understanding of the causes and effects of evil in a complex and interdependent society.

Notes

[1] Jesus tells the Pharisees that they must pay taxes to the Roman empire. Matthew 22: 15-22.

[2] The prohibition against charging interest in Shar'ia law, which falls under more general prohibitions against hoarding, gambling, cheating, fraud, and deceptive practices is analogous to many modern laws against "white-collar" crimes.

[3] The alternative explanation is that the suffering is deserved, even if it was precipitated by "the sins of the fathers" (Exodus Chapters 20:5 and 34:6-7), or karma from a previous lifetime.

[4] https://www.pewforum.org/2019/01/31/religions-relationship-to-happiness-civic-engagement-and-health-around-the-world/

[5] Tamir, C., Connaughton, A., & Salazar, A. M. (2020, July 20). The global God divide: People's thoughts on whether belief in God is necessary to be moral vary by economic development, education and age. Pew Research Center. https://www.pewresearch.org/global/2020/07/20/the-global-god-divide/

[6] The relationship between religious activism and health is not absolute. While the unaffiliated are more likely to smoke and consume alcohol, they are also more likely to exercise and less likely to be obese. Maybe it's all those church pot lucks!

[7] https://assets.pewresearch.org/wp-content/uploads/sites/11/2014/01/global-religion-full.pdf

[8] Exodus 20: 4-5; 24: 13-15. Indeed, much of the historical Hebrews' wandering and exile was explained to be a result from God's anger at their disloyalty and disobedience.

[9] Mark 2: 23-28.

[10] Mark 2: 15-21.

[11] Romans Chapter 13 suggests that government authorities have been "instituted by God" and should be obeyed the same as one would obey God. This passage, along with Matthew 22: 15-22, suggests that good Christians are also obligated to pay their taxes.

[12] Matthew 16: 15-19.

[13] Abraham was purportedly 86 years old when Ishmael was born, and 100 years old at the birth of Isaac. Sara purportedly lived to the age of 127, after which Abraham took a second wife, Keturah, who bore him six other children. Abraham purportedly died at the ripe old age of 175.

[14] Jesus was crucified under the orders of Pontius Pilate, the Roman Governor of the territory at that time. However, Pilate gave the order at the urging of Jewish religious leaders, who accused Jesus of blasphemy. It is ironic that a later reconciliation and partnership with the Roman Empire is what facilitated the spread of Christianity.

[15] The Sunni caliph—unlike the Christian Pope—has no authority to either define dogma nor to legislate. His primary function was to uphold and protect the faith by maintaining conditions under which people could live as good Muslims.

[16] We will analyze how our modern work relations make this nearly impossible in Part IV, Section 1.

[17] John 9: 1-12.

[18] Mark 5: 35-43; John 9: 1-41; Matthew 8: 1-4; Mark 1: 40-45; Luke 5: 12-16.

[19] John 11: 1-44; Luke 7: 11-15; Luke 8: 41-55.

[20] John 6: 1-15.

[21] Genesis 22: 1-18.

[22] Rouzati, N. (2018, February). Evil and human suffering in Islamic thought—towards a mystical theodicy. Religious Studies Department, Manhattan College, Riverdale, NY. https://www.mdpi.com/2077-1444/9/2/47

[23] Matthew 22:21).

[24] Romans 13:1

[25] Matthew 21: 12.

[26] Al-Omar, F., & Abdel-Haq, M. (1996). Islamic Banking: Theory, Practice and Challenges, xvi.

---

[27] Sharawy, H.M. (2000). Understanding the Islamic prohibition of interest: A guide to economic cooperation between the Islamic and Western worlds. GA. J. International Law, *29*, 153-179.

[28] A conflict which has been successfully exploited by Islamic terrorist recruiters.

[29] Genesis 3: 1-7.

[30] The carbon footprint of even the "greenest" American is more than double the global average.
https://www.sciencedaily.com/releases/2008/04/080428120658.htm

[31] In *Why Assholes Rule the World* (2019), I analyzed how individuals with antisocial personality traits often seek to dominate more than others in the society and find ways to gain power (bullying or manipulation). Many of us acquiesce to antisocial personalities in positions of power as a result of behavioral phenomena social scientists call just world theory, system justification, or (an older term) false consciousness. That is, we think things are OK simply because it is the way they are.

[32] Twenge, J.M., & Campbell, W.K. (2009). *The narcissism epidemic*. New York, NY: Free Press.

Part II

The Nature of Human Morality

Introduction to Part II
The Nature of Human Morality

We want to believe in the essential, unchanging goodness of people. In their power to resist external pressures, in their rational appraisal and then rejection of situational temptations. We invest human nature with God-like qualities, with moral and rational faculties that make us both just and wise. We simplify the complexity of human experience by erecting a seemingly impermeable boundary between Good and Evil…Paradoxically, by creating this myth of invulnerability to situational forces, we set ourselves up for a fall…

Phillip Zimbardo[1]

In Part II, we look at our evolutionary hard-wired tendency to divide the world into "us" and "them," as well as how this impacts our moral and civic institutions. While both moral and legal codes of behavior have common roots (thou shall not kill, thou shall not steal, thou shall not bear false witness), religious and politico-legal institutions have evolved into different (and sometimes competing) cultural establishments. Although—particularly in the United States of America—we tend to frame our reality in terms of individual choice and freedom, these institutions exert a significant influence on our culture—which in turn impacts who "we" are both collectively and individually.

In Section One, we look at what evolutionary and neurobiological science tell us about the dichotomy of cooperative and competitive human behavior. We also look at secular views of morality and "original sin," specifically Steve Taylor's theory in *The Fall* and Michael Shermer's *Science of Good and Evil.* We then trace how essential morality (both religious and philosophical) was incorporated into theories of political rights and personal liberty. We also address the difficulty of defining a moral commonwealth in a pluralistic and individualistic society.

In Section Two, we delve deeper into the dynamics of "us-versus-them" social divisions, particularly in the context of theories of moral development. As a forewarning, we face head-on discussions about religion and politics, which some of us remember being admonished to never engage in polite company. Our purpose here is not to convert or proselytize, but to better understand. Here we analyze Os Guinness' theories on the conflict between religious fundamentalism and secularism, along with the continuing debate regarding the separation of church and state. We then turn to Johnathan Haidt's theories on moral foundations: the neurobehavioral tendency of individuals to variously focus on moral issues related to care/harm, fairness/cheating, loyalty/betrayal, sanctity/degradation, or authority/subversion, and how this impacts political decision-making.

Section Three examines recent research on power and privilege—particularly the work of Paul Piff--and its connection to antisocial behaviors such as narcissism, greed, and selfishness. Attitudes of superiority/inferiority manifest both at the individual ("I am better than you") and group ("we are better than them") levels. Such antisocial worldviews are aggravated by the hierarchical social structures that characterize many of our large organizations in a modern society. They are also affected by prevailing cultural values, particularly those that glorify wealth, status, and celebrity.

In Section Four we begin to see how perverted cultural values can adversely impact individual behavior. We visit the story of John Demjanjuk, an individual who lived the majority of his adult life as a hard-working, religious family man and good neighbor, but who was convicted of participating in Nazi atrocities near the end of his life. We then look at more controlled scientific experiments designed to determine whether or not basically good people can be induced to perform bad acts, specifically Stanley Milgram's electroshock experiments in the 1960s (obedience to evil orders) and Philip Zimbardo's Stanford prison experiment in 1971 (conformity with evil environment).

Section Five investigates the emerging concept of administrative evil—a situation in which institutional perversion operates to subvert prosocial outcomes. This often operates at a level that evades detection, due to the complex and diffuse nature of modern organizations. That is, good people don't even necessarily have to commit bad acts, but can facilitate evil by simply doing their jobs and following the rules. We analyze the work of Guy Adams and Danny Balfour, who trace former Nazi influence at NASA (the recruitment of Nazi rocket scientists in Operation Paperclip) to the gradual perversion of culture that resulted in the space shuttle Challenger explosion on January 28, 1986. We also revisit Philip Zimbardo and his testimony at hearings on Abu Ghraib. Here we see that there is not always a direct and immediate connection between an evil order and an evil act, but rather a slow and often undetectable corruption that accumulates over a period of time. Thus, the process by which good people go "bad" is complex, and likely not to be remedied by pointing the finger of blame at individuals—particularly those that are lower in the hierarchy.

Notes

[1] Zimbardo, P. (2007). *The Lucifer effect.* New York, NY: Random House Publishing Group at p. 211.

Section One
The Evolution of Moral Codes

How selfish soever man may be supposed, there are evidently some principles in his nature, which interest him in the fortune of others, and render their happiness necessary to him, though he derives nothing from it except the pleasure of seeing it.

Adam Smith
The Theory of Moral Sentiments, 1759

*

Humans are, by nature, moral and immoral, good and evil, altruistic and selfish, cooperative and competitive, peaceful and bellicose, virtuous and nonvirtuous. Such moral traits vary within individuals as well as within and between groups…Most people, most of the time in most circumstances are good and do the right thing for themselves and for others. But some people some of the time in some circumstances are bad and do the wrong thing for themselves and for others. The codification of moral principles out of the psychology of the moral traits evolved as a form of social control to ensure the survival of individuals within groups and the survival of human groups themselves.

Michael Shermer
The Science of Good and Evil, 2004

Many have wrestled with the question whether human beings are fundamentally good or fundamentally evil. The traditional religious view was that human beings are mired in "original sin," which can only be overcome by regular acts of purification and/or unquestioning faith. Yet we see a lot of people—including those who aren't particularly religious—doing good in the world. This suggests that if we can discover what makes people "good" (or perform acts that benefit others), we can create the foundations of a "good" society. Conversely, we have historical evidence where entire societies have engaged in evil acts (generally exemplified by acts of unprovoked war, torture, and genocide), yet the majority of the persons living within these societies were not necessarily what we would consider evil. This paradox—that individuals who are either good or evil do not necessarily represent whether the society as a whole is good or evil, is the fundamental premise to be explored herein.

In this chapter we will analyze human nature from the standpoint of evolutionary biology and the development of morality from the standpoint of secular social sciences (anthropology, sociology and psychology). We have no intention of leaving God and religion out of any inquiry which involves good and evil. However, for purposes of this section, we are going to focus on what we know about human morality according to science. Indeed, moral codes often developed alongside religious beliefs and practices, and there tends to be a large degree of overlap. Religious commandments such as "thou shalt not kill" and "thou shalt not steal" have counterparts in most modern criminal statutes. Both secular codes and religious proscriptions intended to enforce prosocial behavior that would enhance the order and cohesiveness of the community. Such rules also served to create a distinctive social identity that separated its citizens/adherents from other groups or from society at large.

Secular Theory of Original Sin

Steve Taylor is a British writer and researcher in psychology at Leeds Beckett University. In *The Fall,*[1] Taylor gives a secular version of the Genesis story by analyzing historical and anthropological records. According to Taylor, primitive (i.e., "unfallen") Neolithic peoples enjoyed a sense of connection to a "spirit force" that infuses creation and animates all things. This universal life or spirit force is what connected them to nature/creation (including animals that they ate) as well as to each other. Consequently, pre-Fall peoples were generally peaceful (conflict was limited and ritualized), and they strived to live in harmony with their environment. That is not to say their lives were free of conflict, but conflict resolution rituals were non-violent because the objective was to maintain relationship.

Sometime around 6,000 years ago (4,000 B.C.E.), the area Taylor calls Saharasia (North Africa and the Middle East)—which had previously been green and fertile—began to become more desert-like due to climate change. The disappearance of fertility resulted in increased survival pressures on the people living in the area. The people at the center of this shift were Semites (the ancestors of modern Jews and Arabs) and Indo-European peoples. Taylor cites historical and anthropological records to trace the development and spread of what he calls "post-Fall" cultures, which gradually superseded the relatively peaceful pre-existing Neolithic cultures. Not all of the pre-existing cultures were hunter-gathering nomads, as a few of them had settled into permanent horticulture-based communities. Thus, settlement into towns and cities was not *ipso facto* the cause of this change, although it did tend to correlate with it.

The need to respond to a more challenging environment forced the Saharasians to develop higher levels of strategic thinking and logic, which also gave them a survival advantage. Taylor contrasts post-Fall behavior patterns with those of modern "unfallen" peoples, generally folks most of us would consider primitive. While primitive/neolithic peoples also told stories and made music, the cognitive changes of the Fall allowed the development of more complex forms such as novels and symphonies—in addition to the obvious advances in technology and more complex social structures. This increased reasoning ability also resulted in an increasing tendency of post-fall peoples to view themselves as separate—separate from other people, separate from nature, and even separate from their own bodies. However, the most salient change was what Taylor terms an "ego explosion." This was not so much a genetic or evolutionary change, but a psycho-behavioral shift that implicated changes in culture.

In the post-Fall mind, the body—particularly functions related to sex and reproduction—was considered unclean, in contrast to the purity of the mind and spirit. This led to both a dysfunctional attitude toward sex (e.g., shame associated with nakedness) as well as misogynist practices like suttee and social banishment during menstruation. Here we also see the beginnings of patriarchy, and the view that women were less "pure" because of their connection to reproduction (as well as the view of women as "temptresses"). Although women were also affected by the ego explosion, men were affected to a much higher degree, presumably because women retained some reproductive connection with nature. Other behavioral differences between fallen and unfallen peoples are a preoccupation with linear time (Taylor cites the example of Native Americans' ability to wait patiently without agitation) and a less controlling attitude toward children.

While some unfallen peoples recognized a creator God, this entity was remote and not involved in the day-to-day life of humans. Taylor describes how the rudiments of formal religion started with polytheism. Here, the animating universal "life force" was anthropomorphized into gods, spirits, or other beings who exercised control over specific domains. The work of these spirits was how earlier peoples explained natural phenomena before the advent of scientific reasoning (which Taylor argues is a characteristic of "fallen" peoples). While the purpose of religion was to reconnect humanity with creation, Taylor argues that most religions fail to accomplish this because they themselves are the products of flawed, post-Fall peoples.

Taylor reserves his highest criticism for the Abrahamic religions which came forth through the Semites: the God of the Israelites is jealous, vengeful, patriarchal and authoritarian. Here there was only one God, and He (whereas earlier divine beings could be of either or no gender) was punitive and jealous—at least in the earliest descriptions. This (now) patriarchal God of creation was separate from humans and only able to communicate with them through specific (chosen) individuals. This God at various times demanded obedience or, alternatively granted humans free will, although there would be consequences if one made the wrong choice. Taylor also proposes that the concept of an afterlife was developed to ensure continuation of the ego after death of the body.

The fallen individual who was no longer connected to the animating force of creation now viewed himself in opposition to it. Taylor traces the roots of increased competitiveness, a desire for wealth and power (materialism), and striving for status characteristic of individuals in fallen cultures. The post-Fall egoic personality was also characterized by a will to dominate other people and the environment. The disconnected, egoic individual has essentially lost what Taylor terms "primal empathy," or a quality of compassion that allows us to respond to the needs of others. Taylor alleges that this resulted in the modern "evils" of dominator culture, which manifest as war, patriarchy, and social inequality. Thus, Taylor's theory both tracks the biblical foundation of fallenness/evil as well as describes the individualistic, dominator culture that forms the foundation of much of the macrosocial evil we describe herein. We will cover the subject of lack of empathy in greater detail in our discussion of psychopathy in Section III, Part One.

The Cooperation/Competition Dichotomy

Michael Shermer was once a born-again Christian, but later became the founder of the Skeptics Society and a writer for *Scientific American.* Shermer is an atheist, so he does not equate God with good and the absence of God with evil. He points to his mother, one of the most decent, moral people he knows, who had no belief in God, and saw "no reason to foist a pretense of belief."[2] Shermer argues that some of most heinous acts have been done in the name of God. Even Hitler was not an atheist, writing about his faith in *Mein Kampf,* and proclaiming that he was doing the "Lord's work" by "warding off the Jews" in his 1938 speech to the Reichstag.[3] Moreover, Shermer argues that pure "evil" is a myth that suggests a supernatural explanation for bad behavior, and calling someone "evil" does nothing to help us understand the causes of the bad behavior.[4]

Using a logical syllogism, Shermer argues that if God is omnipotent, He can prevent evil, and if God is good, He will not allow evil to happen. If evil exists, then it is because God is either not omnipotent or not good. Religious adherents will counter-argue that this proposition does not address the issue of free will. That is, we are not pre-programmed automatons who automatically do what God commands of us, but rather have the free choice to decide for ourselves which behavioral road to follow—unless we have been overcome (or "possessed") by Satan. However, as we will see in later sections, our individual choices are not always completely "free," but are impacted and influenced by external situations, social roles, cultural constructions, and even sometimes how we are wired.

While Shermer does not believe in God, he nonetheless believes that religion developed to serve a useful social purpose. Shermer, who is also a libertarian, proposes the "rational choice theory of religion," in which religion evolved as a form of exchange relationship between humans and God or gods, especially in societies where resources were scarce. Religious rituals, miracles and mystical experience reinforced confidence that the deity(ies) would provide.[5] While many religions attribute bad acts of individuals to "sin," or "the work of the devil," Sherman argues that this does not adequately explain the existence of macrosocial evil, or evil that operates independently of individual human choice. The problem of this larger evil that exists independently of "bad" individuals will be further explored in Part III.

Although Shermer does not believe in God—or even that God is necessary for humans to be moral, he has done a lot of research into the nature of ethics and morality. According to Shermer, there are evolutionary pressures that induce both selfish and altruistic (or cooperative) behavior. Individuals are driven by the necessity for survival, and so the urge is to gain control over resources (to eat and be safe today) and selection of mates (to carry one's own genetic code into the future). From the perspective of individual survival, competition (dominance) insured that one had enough to eat, the ability to keep enemies subdued, and to perpetuate oneself through procreation. However, while competition (or selfishness) was good for individual survival, it was counterproductive among groups.

Early humans tended to organize themselves into small bands or tribes. Here, cooperative behavior better insured survival of the group as a whole. The collection of humans provided greater protection than an individual could provide for himself. The group provided protection not just from external enemies, but also from the vagaries of fortune and misfortune. Not every hunter was successful every day. A hunter who was successful today shared his bounty with the group, because this insured that he would also eat on those days he was unsuccessful. Likewise for protection: Sometimes an individual had to give up his own life in order to protect the group—which probably included his own descendants. Thus, while individuals who were selfish might have gained a temporary survival advantage, groups who were cooperative had a more sustainable advantage, and were able to grow beyond survival. As these small tribes gained greater stability and security, they were able to learn and develop higher-level cooperative skills. Indeed, the evolution of cooperative behavior was what permitted humans to attain greater intellectual progress and technological achievement.

Later theories suggested that competitive (or dominant) behavior was not so much about individual survival as it was about genetics. Individuals who were both better able to facilitate the reproduction of their own genetic code (competition) and assist other members of their group to do the same (kin or reciprocal altruism) were more likely to appear in greater numbers over time.[6] That is, competitive survival and reproductive strategies were incorporated into prosocial behavior.[7] An example of this is where one gains access to resources or mates through the formation of alliances or building of coalitions. This required evolved capacities for language, symbolic communication, imagination, planning, and creative thinking.

Yet, the competitive urge did not disappear, even within the relatively cohesive tribal groups. As human communities grew larger and more settled, the competition versus cooperation dichotomy had greater implications for social rank, or status. Although rank within a dominance hierarchy is determined by aggression between two competing individuals, in more complex societies, status is at least partly determined by alliances, which requires cooperative behavior. For example, in some hunting societies, it is considered taboo for hunters to consume their kills before sharing with the rest of the group or to brag about their hunting skills.[8] Although hunting skill is usually a determinative factor in male social status, one can easily lose coalitional support or disrupt the stability of the group with too much bragging and self-promotion. However, as human communities grew even larger, more materially stable, and more impersonal, the competitive urge morphed again to accommodate psychosocial needs rather than the exigencies of physical survival. Now competition was more about "impression management," or the need to keep from feeling inferior, marginalized, or to minimize loneliness, depression and status anxiety.[9]

In early human societies, informal rules to encourage moral behavior existed prior to the development of religion and government. Shermer argues that a form of "moral naturalism"—moral sentiments and an evolved moral sense that produced positive emotion from acts that helped others—arose through the process of natural selection. Individuals learned which behaviors were "good" and which behaviors were "bad" based on the reactions of others in the group. Shermer proposes that this type of informal moral instruction is effective in groups up to about 150 individuals. When groups began to exceed this size, more formal codification of behavioral norms was required.[10]

Moral Evolution and Neuroscience

Shermer has also developed a bio-cultural evolutionary pyramid, which has features similar to the hierarchy of needs developed by psychologist Abraham Maslow.[11] At the lower levels, behavioral control is imposed by the family and extended family. These discrete social units provided models of bonding, acceptance, affiliation, and kin altruism. As communities grew larger, the concept of reciprocal altruism emerged. This represented sharing beyond one's immediate group (with the anticipation that the other group would share something else) and early forms of trading. The next evolutionary step was indirect, or blind altruism, which included the broader concept of social justice. Toward the top of the pyramid Shermer places the concepts of species altruism and bio-altruism, which are concerned with the avoidance of extinction and the preservation of the environment. At these levels, morality is as much culturally determined as it is codified by law.

The dichotomy of human nature combined with evolved intelligence creates the potential for either great progress or great destruction. Humans have insights into the consequences of their behavior that most lower-level animals do not, as well as varying degrees of ability to inhibit our most harmful impulses (e.g. greed and aggression). Although survival strategies such as dominance and aggression exist in other species, they do not possess the same capacity for viciousness and cruelty. While an animal will kill to eat, protect itself, or eliminate a rival for a mate, only humans engage in torture, slavery, or are entertained by watching others suffer. Alternatively, we have developed various forms of religions and other philosophies whose objective is to combat our darker nature, treat others with compassion, and work for peaceful relations.

Research in neuroscience suggests that there are biological bases for moral (i.e., prosocial) behavior. The amygdala is a structure deep within our brain and is part of the limbic system. The limbic system is a more primitive part of our brain that is responsible for the fight-or-flight response. That is, it tends to switch on and off automatically rather than responding to conscious, deliberate thought. Medical imaging studies have found that the amygdala becomes activated if we consciously violate a social norm. That is, we have an expectation of punishment, which (for most people) serves as a deterrent. How neurotransmitters and various regions of the brain are involved in behavior will be covered in more detail in Part III, Section One (when we address psychopathy). Here, we will say that, while much of behavior is the result of conscious choice, predispositions to particular behaviors (i.e., prosocial, antisocial, and even the ability to regulate emotion) are also dependent on genetically coded switches.

Although it is unusual, a couple of mathematicians (associated with the London Mathematical Laboratory and the Santa Fe Institute) have propounded an economic argument for the development of cooperative behavior.[12] The authors first describe the biological evolution of the pooling and sharing of resources beginning with the formation of multi-cellular organisms, to pack animals and families sharing food, to the formation of firms and nations. They then ask the question why a better-off entity would choose to cooperate because it stands to suffer an immediate net loss.

They also lament that we haven't seen attempts to develop models of cooperation from economists, because "the basic message from mainstream economics seems to be that optimal, rational, sensible behavior would shun cooperation."[13]

The authors of this paper propose that more recent developments in mathematics allowed them to develop the necessary equations to describe resource outcomes in cooperating versus non-cooperating entities. The authors then proceed to develop a mathematical model of how and why cooperation evolves: As societies become more complex, any entity could find itself either better or worse off at any particular point in time. The net effect of these fluctuations on the time-average overall growth rate is negative. By pooling and sharing resources, these fluctuations are reduced, which results in better outcomes for the group as a whole. The authors demonstrate the "solution" to their equations in the form of a graph, which displays the obvious growth-rate differentials between cooperating and non-cooperating entities. As the authors conclude, "In many ways we see cooperation in the world despite, not because of, economic theory."

As human societies grew larger and settled into fixed places, the need for cooperation increased. At the same time as societies grew both larger and more permanent, the informal personal-based behavioral regulators (i.e., social approval or disapproval) became attenuated. Shermer proposes that both religion and government arose as socially constructed institutions for the purpose of encouraging cooperative/altruistic behaviors and discouraging selfish/competitive behaviors.[14] Thus, morality itself evolved along with increasing social complexity. In small tribal groups, cooperation was "enforced" ad hoc by others in the group. As tribal groups expanded, religion evolved as a social structure to regulate behavior, with God providing the ultimate punishment for violation of the social contract. Religion codified moral and social norms, and this process of formal rule codification was later adopted by those with power over large groups: The Code of Urukagina (one of the first rulers of a city-state in Mesopotamia, 24th century B.C.), the Code of Hammurabi (Mesopotamia, 1754 B.C.), the Draconian Constitution (Athens, 620 B.C.), the Twelve Tables of Roman Law (450 B.C.), the Magna Carta (King John of England, 1215).

The Concept of Political Rights and Personal Liberty

Many of these newer, more rights-based codifications were founded upon earlier religious laws: "The concept of belief in freedom of the human will and a consequent ability and duty of the normal individual to choose between good and evil is a core concept that is universal and persistent in mature systems of law."[15] Thus we see that the evolution of both law and religion often reinforced each other, with each containing foundations for the concept of both individual rights and social duties. As societies grew ever larger and more complex, law (and/or government) and religion split into separate institutions, often with different kinds of leaders and different internal cultures.

While religious rules tended to focus on individual behavioral do's and don'ts, the secular codes focused more on the establishment of broader social rights. For example, the purpose of the Draconian Constitution was to remedy the unequal access to legal knowledge between the aristocracy and everyone else, although it is better known for the imposition of severe (i.e., Draconian) punishment. The Code of Urukagina limited the power of priests and large property owners, and proscribed a number of behaviors (e.g., usury, seizure of property for payment of debt) often used by the powerful to exploit the less powerful. Indeed, we see this same intent to prevent the accumulation and misuse of power in our American Constitution, which represents a continuation of "modern" social justice thinking that began with the Enlightenment. In the words of John Rawls, "In a just society, the liberties of equal citizenship are taken as settled; the rights secured by justice are not subject to political bargaining or to the calculus of social interests."[16]

The Enlightenment, otherwise known as the Age of Reason, was a period of time generally described as occurring between the late 17th to the late 18th century. Enlightenment values generally involved reason, science, and skepticism, particularly with respect to the mysticism of religion. This period also saw the birth and development of "natural rights" concepts such as life, liberty and property, along with the value of the individual. Well-known thinkers and writers during this period were Thomas Hobbes (1588-1679), John Locke (1632-1704), Charles Montesquieu (1689-1755), and Jean-Jacques Rousseau (1712-1778, considered somewhat of a reactionary to the rule of science and logic). Enlightenment thinkers developed ideas around the sovereignty of the people (rather than kings or rulers) and separation of church and state—thinking which provided much of the foundation for the American revolution.

Shermer further elaborates on the concept of individual liberty as a social right:

> "For many millennia, the concept of liberty for all members of the state lay dormant, suppressed by the selfish and competitive drives of the political and religious leaders who held the reins of power. Even the occasional enlightened societies that set up quasi-representative bodies to protect the interests of the citizens at large restricted liberty to a narrow class of land-owning or power-wielding males. Only in the last couple of centuries have we witnessed the worldwide spread of liberty as a concept that applies to all peoples everywhere, regardless of their rank or social and political status in the power hierarchy."[17]

Shermer goes on to argue that liberty is most constrained in states that are theocracies, especially those that encourage intolerance. From an evolutionary standpoint, Shermer suggests that we are hardwired to cooperate with those we consider part of our group and we are hardwired to compete with those we consider part of an outgroup. This is especially so when resources are scarce. In Shermer's view, the biggest threat to social cooperation is intolerance, particularly religious intolerance, with its propensity to label those in the outgroup as "evil." Indeed, it is this impetus for outgroup intolerance that drives much of what can be considered immoral behavior—which is paradoxically justified on moral grounds.

Is a Universal Moral Code Possible?

With so many "us versus them" dichotomies, it may be impossible to find some universal moral code that everyone can agree on. Shermer proposes that "although cultures differ on what they define as right and wrong, the moral ***feelings*** of doing right (virtuous) or wrong (guilt) are universal to all humans."[18] He points to cognitive neuroscience, where brain scans physically demonstrate a positive connection between moral emotions and social exchange.[19] He also argues that we tend to focus on extreme acts of immorality and ignore the tens of thousands of acts of kindness daily that go unnoticed, repeating the standard idiom that bad acts dominate headlines precisely because they are unusual and hence newsworthy.[20]

So, this leads us to the larger question of what exactly constitutes moral behavior? Are there some universal moral principles that everyone can agree on? Most researchers in moral psychology define morality as "prescriptive judgments of justice, rights, and welfare pertaining to how people ought to relate to each other."[21] Shermer lists various (and sometimes contradictory) processes of determining what behavior is moral: Consequentialism (the outcome determines whether the behavior is good or bad), contractarianism (based on individual and social agreements), deontology (based on duty), emotivism (does the behavior make you feel good or bad), moral isolationism (moral issues are determined by one's immediate in-group), ethical egoism (which assumes all behavior is self-interested), natural law theory (does the behavior violate the "natural order of things"), and nihilism (which assumes that there is no absolute truth, everything is relative).[22] Notwithstanding all of these different theoretical foundations for determining morality, Shermer points to various forms of the "Golden Rule" that have appeared in "countless texts throughout recorded history and from around the world."[23]

Most of us agree that acts such as killing, stealing, lying and cheating are immoral. But even such a list may not be applicable to all acts in all circumstances. What about killing in self-defense? More specifically, are the tens of thousands of veterans who either risked their own lives or sacrificed themselves serving in a war zone evil or immoral because they have killed others? In America, we refer to the September 11th attacks as the evil work of terrorists. However, the "terrorists" were actually operating pursuant to a form of perverted morality. The Muslim people in countries which are controlled by U.S. interests view the United States as an evil, secular empire that is dominated by military and financial elites who are destroying traditional life and livelihoods, particularly those based on Muslim faith. Anti-abortion extremists who bomb women's clinics and kill doctors who perform abortions are another example of individuals who commit bad acts in what they believe is a higher cause. The old adage that one person's terrorist is another person's freedom fighter is certainly applicable, which suggests that the determination of whether any specific act is either "good" or "bad" depends on which side you are on.

Many of us have wrestled with moral ambiguities on a more personal scale. For example, most of us agree that lying is wrong. But what happens when a friend asks us if a new outfit she purchased looks good on her and (in our opinion) any one of the color, cut, fit, shape, and drape do not look good. Maybe our friend is recovering from some trauma (divorce, illness, job loss) and purchased the outfit to help lift her spirits. We don't want to hurt our friend or encourage her to beat herself up for a bad decision. So we don't tell her what we really think about the outfit (unless perhaps she is planning to wear it to a job interview or someplace where she is likely to be judged). We might even rationalize to ourselves that taste in clothes is highly subjective, the outfit might look good to *someone,* we ourselves just don't like the color, etc. In essence, we find ourselves conflicted because in order to do the "right" thing under one standard of morality (truthfulness) we would have to violate another standard of morality (don't hurt a friend unnecessarily, especially one who may be recovering or healing).

Moving beyond the triviality of white lies, a more difficult question is when we might have to break the law to do the right thing. Conscientious objectors to war who refuse a legal requirement of military service are one example of this. This type of moral dilemma is also a classic one faced by whistleblowers: An employee who has inside information knows that the company s/he works for is engaged in activity that harms the public (toxic pollution, dangerous products, insider trading, etc.). While there are internal routes of reporting wrongdoing, the employee knows that doing so will result in either termination from the job or demotion/ostracization. Once isolated, the employee would no longer have access to the information needed for "evidence." Moreover, such evidence would likely then be destroyed, meaning that it would be impossible for anyone (a regulatory agency, a watchdog organization, or a journalist) to document the problem. To make matters even worse, the law itself often requires whistleblowers to report the bad behavior internally before they are afforded statutory protection. On top of this are company rules against "stealing" company information or disclosing trade secrets. The whistleblower is thus faced with a Hobson's choice of likely losing his/her livelihood and the trust of his/her co-workers or protecting the larger public. In essence, the whistleblower must be willing to betray his/her company and co-workers (violating the social norms of the organization) because it is less morally distasteful than "living with the corrupted self"[24] by violating the norms of the larger society.

Shermer argues that human morality falls along a continuum. While humans "evolved to be moral animals," morality exists along a continuum and can be influenced by "historical contingencies" and the "cascading consequences of their decisions."[25] That is, most people are not completely moral nor completely immoral, but exhibit behaviors of each depending upon the situation. Because there are no moral absolutes, Shermer proposes the adoption of what he terms a "fuzzy logic" which assigns probabilistic fractions to moral answers rather than an either-or choice.[26] Like science itself, moral claims are not true or false in an absolute sense, but can be assigned a probability of whether they are true or false. Obviously, this means decision-making will be more complex and murkier, but it can also avoid the moral absolutism that can sometimes result in immoral outcomes.

In support of his argument that most people are good most of the time, Shermer argues that the Holocaust was not perpetrated by "ordinary" Germans but by a small minority under "extraordinary circumstances and conditions."[27] The small minority of individuals associated with Nazi atrocities (Hitler, Göring, Goebbels) were not exceptional personalities, but rather had three characteristics: overweening ambition, low ethical standards, and a strongly developed nationalism, combined with an opportunity to seize power.[28] Shermer thus suggests that we can prevent macrosocial evil by preventing the wrong individuals from attaining positions of power. Yet, as we shall see in Part III, there are often broader, less obvious phenomena that create macrosocial evil beyond a small group of antisocial individuals with power.

In answer to the practical question of "what shall we do," Shermer suggests a few simple rules to live by. First, before you "do unto" someone, ask that person if it is OK with them, rather than assume that the person is OK with it because you yourself are OK with it. The second principle is that when you are in pursuit of happiness and liberty that you always do so with the happiness and liberty of someone else in mind, and that you ***never*** seek such things if it leads to someone's else's unhappiness or loss of liberty. The third principle is that extremism in the defense of anything is no virtue and moderation in the protection of everything is no vice. Shermer's essence of morality thus seems to be summarized as a requirement to think about the rights and needs of others before making a decision, and to be willing to act outside the dictates of proscribed behavior when necessary.

Most of us also think that we know intuitively what behavior is moral and what is not. However, we also can likely think of situations in which the "right answer" is not conclusively apparent, particularly when we must choose an action that requires us to violate one moral norm in order to preserve a different one. Shermer recommends adopting what he terms a provisional morality. Provisional morality is somewhere in between absolute morality (enforced by strict and rigid codes of right and wrong) and the complete subjectivity of situational ethics. According to Shermer, the problem with systems of absolute morality is that a small minority sets themselves up as the final arbiters of truth. The world is then divided into good and evil, right and wrong, true believers and heretics. There is no allowance for questioning the rules or the status quo, effectively eliminating critical thinking.[29]

Shermer may indeed be correct in his assertion that most people are good most of the time. He is also likely correct in his arguments that morality constitutes a "fuzzy logic" from which we cannot distill some absolute, universal law. His proposition that out-group intolerance—although it is genetically hard-wired into our behavior systems—constitutes a threat to inter-group moral behavior and species survival also rings true. However, his argument that the

Nazi Holocaust was the result of a simple historical confluence of a couple of bad guys with the presence of opportunity ignores the reality of situational stressors as well as the complexity of societal corruption.

Notes

[1] Taylor, S. (2005). *The fall: The evidence for a Golden Age, 6,000 years of insanity, and the dawning of a new era.* New York, NY: O-Books/John Hunt Publishing, Ltd.

[2] Shermer, M. (2004). *The science of good and evil.* New York, NY: Henry Holt and Company, at p. 158.

[3] *Id.* at p. 153.

[4] *Id.* at p. 69.

[5] *Id.* at p. 35.

[6] Dawkins, R. (1978). *The selfish gene.* London: Paladin.

[7] Hardy, C.L., & Van Vugt, M. (2006). Nice guys finish first: the competitive altruism hypothesis. *Personality and Social Psychology Bulletin, 32,* 1402-1413.

[8] The Ache of Paraguay and Hadza of Tanzania.

[9] Gilbert, P., & Basran, J. (2019, June). The evolution of prosocial and antisocial competitive behavior and the emergence of prosocial and antisocial leadership styles. *Frontiers in Psychology*, 10, 1-19 at p. 9.

[10] "Sociologists know that once groups exceed 200 people, a hierarchical structure is needed to enforce the rules of cooperation and to deal with offenders, who in the smaller group could be dealt with through informal personal contracts and social pressure." Shermer, *supra* at p. 41.

[11] Shermer, *supra* at p. 48.

[12] Peters, O., & Adamou, A. (2015, June 10). The evolutionary advantage of cooperation. https://pdfs.semanticscholar.org/2719/f6a8e55d9a7bc892d6abf9d0f889cab36585.pdf

[13] *Id.* at p. 2.

[14] Shermer, *supra* at p. 7.

[15] *Id.* p. 119.

[16] Rawls, J. (1971). *A theory of justice.* Cambridge, MA: Belknap/Harvard University Press.

[17] Shermer, *supra* at pp. 189-190. We will challenge the suggestion that all humans possess universal feelings of virtue and guilt in Part III.

[18] *Id.* at p. 251.

[19] *Id.* at p. 257.

[20] *Id.* at p. 75.

[21] Turiel, E. (1983). *The development of social knowledge: Morality and convention.* Cambridge, UK: Cambridge University Press.

[22] Shermer, *supra* at p. 165.

[23] *Id.* at pp. 25-26.

[24] Alford, C.F. (2001). *Whistleblowers: Broken lives and organizational power.* Ithaca, NY: Cornell University Press.

[25] Shermer, *supra.*

[26] *Id.* at p. 159.

[27] *Id.* at p. 70.

[28] *Id.* at p. 74.

[29] *Id.* at p. 158.

Section Two
"Us-Versus-Them" and the Moralization of Immorality

Nothing is more characteristic of humankind than the natural and inescapable drive toward meaning and belonging, toward making sense of life and finding community in the world. As fundamental and precious as life itself, this "will to meaning" finds expression in ultimate beliefs, whether theistic or nontheistic, transcendent or naturalistic, and these beliefs are most our own when a matter of conviction rather than coercion.

Os Guinness[1]

*

Empathy is an antidote to righteousness, although it's very difficult to empathize across a moral divide.

Johnathan Haidt[2]

*

In the absence of any true control over their lives, people cling to identity as to a life raft—desperately, instinctively, driven by the impulse to save self, kith and kin rather than with regard or respect for the whole. Life rafts are useful, particularly in emergencies, but they will never be as good as a functioning boat.

Gary Younge[3]

We have seen that human beings have evolutionary behavioral roots for both competition and cooperation. As evolving humans discovered the benefits of cooperation—for both individuals and societies as a whole—the competitive urge was turned to those who were not members of our own tribe. Moreover, as we began to develop and codify moral behavior (thou shalt not steal, thou shalt not kill), this created ambiguities in how we were supposed to deal with outgroups. That is, while we prohibited stealing from or killing our neighbors, these proscriptions did not necessarily apply to rival tribes (or nations) who were competing with us for resources.

The formation of tribes or other human collectives thus morphed the competitive instinct from everyone-for-himself to a form of "us-versus-them." Moreover, this us-versus-them has a biological basis as well as a cultural one. Neuroscience research has found that the hormone oxytocin has prosocial effects (people become more cooperative, trusting, and generous) when dealing with members of their own group. However, its effects are the opposite when dealing with members of outgroups. Neuroimaging studies have shown activation of the amygdala (which is associated with more primitive emotions) even with a fleeting view of the face of an "other" long before the activation of higher-level cortical regions.[4]

The "us-versus-them" dichotomy also has implications for moral reasoning. Lawrence Kohlberg (1927-1987) was an academic psychologist who proposed a theory in which moral development progresses in stages as an individual matures.[5] At the earliest (preconvention) level, the individual conforms to rules imposed by authority figures in order to avoid punishment. At the second (conventional, or good person) level, conformity to social rules is still important, but the objective shifts to social approval rather than avoidance of punishment. Just beyond the third level (postconventional) is the beginning of abstract principles and generalized values. That is, one begins to seek or formulate guidelines that one can apply to all situations rather than a series of rules for specific circumstances. The fourth (law and order) and fifth (social contract) stages represent the development of more universal social rules (i.e., not based on individual relationships or exchanges). It is at these levels we see the creation of codified rules (law) that are intended to improve society as a whole, and the concept of individual rights. The sixth stage (universal ethical principle) is when the individual applies self-chosen abstract and universal principles to everyone who might be affected by the decision or action. In essence, the evolution of morality begins with doing the right thing with respect to our family and close relations, then our tribe (in-group), and gradually expanded to include all stakeholders, then everyone in the world today, and ultimately, future generations.

At the lower levels of moral development, we make different moral decisions depending on whether we are dealing with a member of an in-group or an out-group. Out-groups could sometimes be identified by physical (skin and hair color) or cultural (clothing, dietary preferences) differences. This identification of "us" or "not-us" also operates at the neurobiological level. Robert Sapolsky, a neuroendocrinologist and professor of neurological sciences at Stanford, has conducted studies using the Implicit Association Test. Individuals are presented with pictures of persons belonging to either ingroups or outgroups, which are then paired with words that have either positive or negative connotations. When reaction times were measured, there was a significant delay in processing "discordant pairings" (i.e., negative words with ingroups and positive words with outgroups). Sapolsky suggests that such reactions operate at the unconscious level—that is, people do not have time to "think" about discriminatory justifications.[6]

Sapolsky has identified various forms of "them," depending on the emotions being activated. The most common negative emotion associated with "them" is fear-based—the other is seen as threatening, angry or untrustworthy. For example, Whites judge Black faces to be angrier, and if an angry face is racially ambiguous, will categorize it as some other race. A second negative emotion associated with "them" is disgust. This is the response most of us associate when we smell something rotten, and its evolutionary purpose was to prevent us from eating something that was poisonous. Neuroscience studies have shown that this sensory disgust response activates the insula as well as the amygdala. This view of the other as somehow "unclean" also has historical roots, since disease was often carried into a community by visiting outsiders or those who were traveling through.

Sapolsky describes one experiment where a "staged" fan in distress at a sporting event received help from fans supporting the same team (as evidenced by team colors in clothing), but not from the opposition.[7] This experiment brings to mind the parable of the Good Samaritan, where the proper moral response is to offer assistance regardless of who the person is or which team/tribe they are with. Of course, while offering assistance would seem to be the most prosocial thing to do, failure to do so does not necessarily amount to a bad act. Yet, research suggests that this "us versus them" split manifests in a number of different ways. One is what Sapolsky calls essentialism, which is applying universal attributes to the "other," while allowing for circumstantial and situational explanations for those like us (i.e., people are viewed as individuals).

This essentialism is often expressed as stereotyping; e.g., slaves (or Negroes) are too simple-minded to handle independence, women are too emotional to govern, all Muslims are terrorists, etc. These stereotypes are often accepted even by the outgroup. By way of example, Sapolsky cites the "doll studies" done in the 1940s by Kenneth and Mamie Clark. Both Black and White children preferred playing with White dolls over Black ones, and ascribed more positive attributes (nice, pretty) to them.[8] This effect among Black children was even stronger in segregated schools, a fact that was cited in *Brown versus Board of Education.*

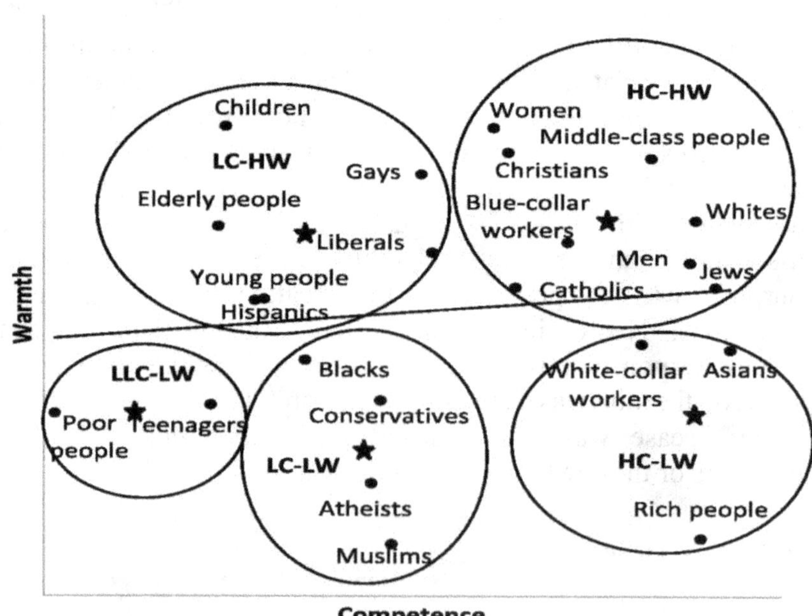

The us-versus-them dichotomy is not limited to the usual suspects of race, gender, and nationality, but also applies to how the rich and the poor view each other (i.e., class-based distinctions). Research by Susan Fiske, a Professor of Psychology and Public Affairs at Princeton demonstrates how status affects perception of competence and personal warmth (e.g., someone is likeable and easy to get along with).[9] In this study, participants were asked to assess an individual on competence and warmth after being "primed" with cues about the person's status. The ratings were plotted on something researchers call a bias map, or "stereotype content model."

Such mapping has even been applied to occupations:

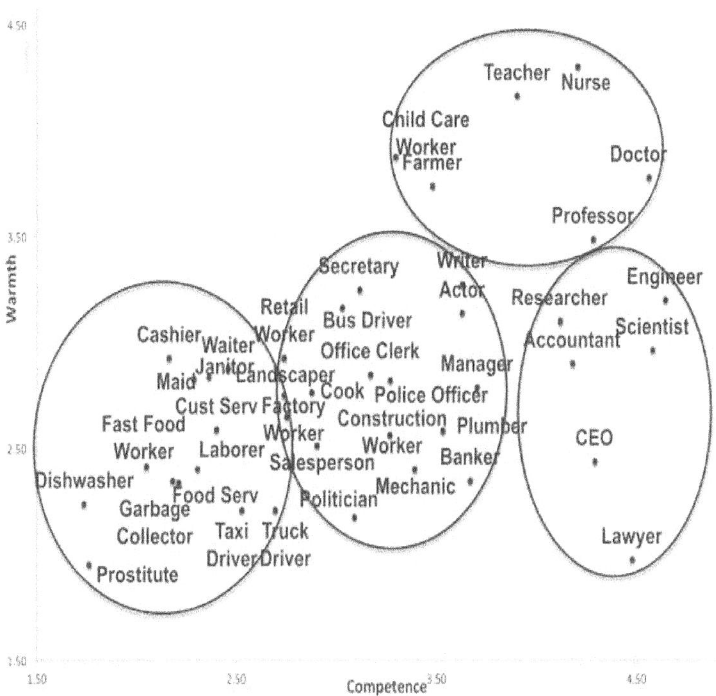

Socio-economic bias happens when the rich view the poor as low competence but high warmth (dumb and happy) and the poor view the rich as high competence but low warmth (i.e., the typical asshole who nevertheless is able to get things done). What also happens is that we usually rate those who are like "us" as HH (high in both warmth and competence). In America, "us" can include Christians, African-American professionals (even for White people) and the middle class. Pride is the typical emotion associated with HH ratings, because it is also associated with "us." Persons typically rated HL (high warmth, low competence) include the mentally disabled, handicapped and frail elderly. The emotion most associated with HL persons is pity. However, our most hostile emotions are directed at LLs (homeless persons and addicts, which triggers disgust) and LHs (low warmth and high competence, which is less a judgment of specific skill than the ability to achieve one's own goals). The emotion associated with LHs is envy and resentment—it is the way many minority Americans view Whites. Sapolsky says these emotions are backed up by neuroscience, with LL individuals activating the disgust reaction (amygdala and insula), while LHs and HLs activate the frontal cortex.

In addition to racial, gender, and class divisions, the us-versus-them dichotomy is sometimes even more acute in modern society with respect to religion and politics. Religion (or spirituality) is how many of us determine the rules for right living at the individual level. It includes our relationship to the creator/creation as well as with our family and immediate neighbors. Politics is about the rules we have for living within the broader society; i.e., the town, county, state, national, and even global levels. The irony is that when religion, politics, or both are defined by an us-versus-them framework, it makes it nearly impossible for constructive dialogue required to address pressing issues. We need no further evidence of this than the current state of national politics in the United States.

Religious Us Versus Them

According to Os Guinness, the religious divide is defined not so much as between Religion A versus Religion B as it is about religious fundamentalism versus secularism. In *The Case for Civility and Why Our Future Depends on It,* Guinness argues that attempts to exclude religion from what he calls "the public square" in the name of preserving religious freedom actually operates to destroy it. The so-called "culture wars" have led to the collapse of public life and a common vision of the common good. As a proposed solution, he offers the Williamsburg Charter[10] as a way of interpreting the First

Amendment to resolve the tensions between constitutional protection of the free exercise of religion and its prohibitions against government establishment of religion.

Guinness begins his argument with the history and rationale behind the Establishment and Free Exercises clauses. The Constitutional separation of church and state was never intended to banish matters of faith from the public square. Rather, its intent was to prevent the kind of "totalizing ideology" that existed in England and France, with their incestuous relationships between kings and clerics. Guinness then traces the divergent histories of England (which still has a state church) and France (which is almost completely secular),[11] followed by the story of what made America different, and thus successful in allowing faith to flourish in the absence of an official church.

By separating church and state, religious diversity was allowed to flourish, a process Guinness compares to the spread of free market capitalism, which the First Amendment predated by about 100 years. Religious "disestablishment" thus operated like de-monopolization by creating open competition and a level playing field.[12] In its early years, America was able to maintain the unique balance of a clear disestablishment of state religion which at the same time allowed the incorporation of individual faith and conscience into public discourse. Religion actually flourished in America not in spite of disestablishment, but because of it, as matters of conscience were "liberated to be a matter of free, voluntary, independent choice."[13]

Guinness argues that this was possible in early America because, although there were a plethora of unique denominations, the majority of them were Protestant. However, "the story of America is the story of an ever-expanding pluralism."[14] Early signs of fracture appeared when John F. Kennedy, a Catholic became President. Many expressed concern that Kennedy's loyalty would favor the Vatican over America. At some point, Catholicism versus Protestantism became integrated into public life, but then religious diversity expanded beyond different varieties of Christianity. Jews slowly became integrated into a broader Christian pluralism based on common roots of scripture, as did more recent offshoots like

Mormonism. As people of ever-expanding and diverse faiths (Muslims, Buddhists, New Agers, atheists) entered workplaces and public offices—around the same time that women and people of color were gaining rights—the culture wars heated up.

As religious diversity expanded, it created conflict in the public square. Whose prayer is to be prayed? This question has resulted in an ongoing litigious clash over prayer in the public schools. If a school enforces Christian prayer, it ignores diversity and "scandalizes" those who do not share the faith. Conversely, attempting to formulate a neutralized form of prayer secularizes faith at the same time it offends those who reject public prayer of any kind.[15] Guinness sides with the secularists in proposing that public schools are not the place to have official prayers—both for constitutional and religious reasons. At the same time, he asserts that students should be free to pray alone at any time, or even in after-school groups.[16]

The crux of Guinness's argument is that the original concept of "separation of church and state" was based on the idea of a single church and a single state as a monolithic arbiter of matters of conscience, rather than an absolute separation of government and religion more generally. Additionally, Guinness argues that the institutions of both government and religion have changed substantially over the course of two hundred years, perhaps making earlier interpretations anachronistic: In the early days of America, religion played a primary role in social life and the role of government was relatively minor. Today, these roles have been reversed.[17]

However, neither religious nor secular fundamentalists have the right answer. Rather, the vehemence of the warfare between them has ironically made each side a prime example of why it should be rejected: "One side's excesses have become the other side's arguments: one side's extremists the other side's recruiters. The danger is that, as the ideological warfare becomes self-perpetuating, more serious issues and broader national interest will be forgotten and the bitterness deepened."[18] Religious fundamentalists want to dominate the public square and establish an authoritarian theocracy. Alternatively, secularists want to banish religion from the public square altogether, which results in positivist and technocratic approaches to public policy that ignore moral implications. Although most of us can see the danger of religious fundamentalism (an extreme form of us-versus-them), the danger of a purely secularized (i.e., "rational") public square might be less obvious, but no less dangerous.

Guinness first turns his criticism toward religious fundamentalists. By politicizing faith, they have inadvertently equated it with a political party, which is the antithesis of true religious liberty's association with individual conscience. That is, the Christian faith becomes subservient to political agendas and not a foundation to inform political positions. However, the Christian Right's politicization of faith has resulted in "a double loss of independence," because it seeks "to find political solutions for problems that are essentially cultural and prepolitical."[19]

Guinness chastises Christian fundamentalists when they portray themselves as victims—a religious minority who is persecuted by liberal elites. Christians are actually a majority in America, and can hardly claim "persecution" when compared to the treatment of Christians in places like China and North Korea.[20] The actions of fundamentalists in the public square are distinctly theocratic and coercive, making it "the best argument for its worst opponents, the most powerful factor in its own rejection, and a prime reason for the repudiation of religion in contemporary America."[21] Moreover, in spite of its claim to moral superiority, the religious right has failed to articulate any common vision for the public good.

Guinness' complaints about the secularists are somewhat more theoretical. His first argument is that there is no real secular-based foundation for the concept of human rights. In the secular worldview, humans are simply a more highly evolved animal, so that human rights are "a form of ungrounded species chauvinism," which is a prejudice akin to ethnocentrism: "'Human rights' are only a late-Enlightenment Western ideology—high-sounding ideals that are the weapons with which the West promotes its power agenda."[22]

Moreover, secular extremism has become a "religion" of reason, with its adherents as blindly trusting and irrational as any fundamentalist. Secular intolerance extends not just to the religious extremist (which might have some basis for justification), but also to religious moderates who are accused of being enablers.[23] Conversely, toleration becomes a form of condescension by "those who consider themselves enlightened to those they consider ignorant."[24] This results in a strict separationist interpretation of the First Amendment, relegating all religious believers of any faith to "the segregated margins of private life on behalf of their self-interested liberal myth of a neutral public square."[25]

As a thought exercise, let's say the fundamentalists win, and we now have a "Christian" public square. The delusion is that now we will be able to get political things done because we are subject to a unifying "Christian" moral framework. Yet, this will not necessarily be the case: As a Christian myself, I can say that not all Christians stand together on every issue. While we might (and even this is not absolute) be on the same page with respect to Jesus, we may have completely different ideas about how to prevent war, solve climate change, or end homelessness. Thus, religious unity (especially if it is enforced) will not guarantee a unified polity.

The one thing that might be easier (for Christians, but not for others under an "official" Christianity) is persuasion and influence. If I am arguing before a judge or a member of Congress in a Christian theocracy, I can appeal to scripture and the teachings of Jesus to argue the moral foundations of my positions. Conversely in Guinness' religiously diverse public square, I may have to persuade a Jew, a Muslim, or even an atheist. If I am diligent, I will learn something about these other faith (or non-faith) moral philosophies to make my argument. The value of this is that learning about someone else's moral foundations will not adversely affect my own faith, but at the same time it re-incorporates moral considerations into policy discussions.

Next we imagine what happens if the secularists win, where any and all religion is banished from the public square. Decisions about the common welfare will then be reduced to technocratic rationality without any corresponding consideration of moral issues.

An example of this is a decision by former U.S. Supreme Court Justice Antonin Scalia, who ironically often touted his devout Catholicism. In the 1993 case of *Herrera v. Collins*,[26] an inmate on death row had his conviction overturned on the basis of the confession of the real murderer. Although the fact that new evidence had shown this individual was "actually innocent," in Scalia's opinion, execution would not constitute cruel and unusual punishment so long as the original trial had been free of identifiable error. Scalia then went on to disparage the fact that the dissenters claimed that such results "shocked [their] consciousness," implying that moral considerations had no place in the determination of justice. It is this kind of technocratic rationality—where efficiency concerns trump both Constitutional rights and fundamental justice—that results when any semblance of moral thinking is banished from legal and political forums.

Guinness suggests that "the way forward is to search for a means of coexistence rather than consensus."[27] First: Genuine religious freedom must be extended to all faiths, not just the majority, or "chosen" one. Freedom of faith is both a right and a reciprocity. Second: While all are free to exercise their conscience, the public square is not the place to debate the truth or untruth of various faiths. "Too much interference by the state above (i.e., totalitarianism or political correctness) or too much indifference (or alienation due to exaggerated, yet trivial differences) from the citizens below, and civil society will be cramped from above or cut off from its oxygen supply from below. The outcome in either case will be a deficit of freedom, as well as of human giving, caring, and engagement."[28] Third: ***Tolerance in the name of political correctness can lead to complacency in the face of true evil***—a phenomenon we will explore in much greater detail in Part III.

Political Us Versus Them

Politics, or the way we develop rules about how to live with each other in larger society, arose from the same systems of moral codes that gave rise to religion. Thus, religion and politics have common roots, and—as we have seen in Guinness' foregoing argument—there is no way to absolutely "separate" religion and politics (i.e., church and state) in a general sense without losing some part of who we are. We need only look at our own legal system: thou shalt not kill became laws against murder, thou shalt not steal became laws against theft. However, because both religion and politics touch upon foundational value systems, they are often prime culprits in fomenting an us-versus-them worldview. Many of us can recall being admonished to never discuss religion or politics in polite company. While this unwritten social code may serve to keep the peace, it also thwarts our ability to have necessary, yet painful, discussions about how we are to deal with intractable social problems.

For all the ballyhoo about the separation of church and state, recent research has established a connection between moral and political psychology. This so-called moral foundations theory[29] suggests that moral intuitions are based on neuro-bio-chemical hard wiring as much as on cultural influences. For example, biological and psychological differences manifest in policy preferences that we ascribe to the political left and the political right. One study found that between 20% and 40% of variability in political attitudes can be attributed to genetics.[30] More recent studies have been able to predict political views by measuring autonomic responses (startle, blinks, skin conductivity) to threatening images (e.g., conservatives are more reactive to threats).[31] These innate moral intuitions have also been found to predict positions on divisive policy issues over and above the "usual suspects" of political ideology, age, gender, education, and religious attendance.[32] However, even these hard-wired moral intuitions are not impervious to change.[33]

One proponent of moral foundation theory is Johnathan Haidt, a social psychologist and currently a professor of Ethical Leadership at New York University Stern School of Business. Haidt is also the author of *The Righteous Mind: Why Good People are Divided By Politics and Religion.*[34] Professor Haidt has spent most of his professional life studying the psychology of morality, and has given talks in a variety of forums about his research.[35] As a lifelong liberal who is also concerned about the breakdown of civility in our public discourse, Haidt set out to understand the conservative mind. In *The Righteous Mind,* he analyzes the different moral foundations of the political left and the political right, while also identifying the strengths and deficiencies of each. *The Righteous Mind* has received mostly positive reception across the political spectrum, as it avoids the usual demonization that often accompanies such a polarizing topic.

The essence of Professor Haidt's theory is that people are hard-wired to prefer varying degrees of different moral foundations, which then are revised by experience and culture. He describes an early recognition that his own moral framework was not universal when he traveled to India on a Fulbright fellowship. He reports feelings of "shock and dissonance" when dining with male colleagues whose wives served them in silence and then retreated to the kitchen, as well as when his hosts advised him to be stricter with the servants. However, his unease dissipated over time as he developed relationships with his hosts, who also assisted him with his research. "Rather than automatically rejecting the men as sexist oppressors and pitying women, children and servants as helpless victims, I began to see a moral world in which families, not individuals, are the basic unit of society, and the members of each extended family (including its servants) are intensely interdependent."[36]

When humans are born, they are genetically predisposed to varying levels of reactivity to certain threats. Australian scientists have found differences in serotonin glutamate levels between liberals and conservatives, which corroborates other research finding that conservatives are more reactive to threats of danger, including contamination and even low-level threats such as noise. Research by the political scientist John Jost finds that liberals tend to be more open to experience and seek novelty, while conservatives have greater needs for order, stability and structure. Thus, in addition to the effects of us-versus-them evolutionary neurobiology, we start out already with pre-wired psycho-behavioral differences.

Professor Haidt reviewed the academic literature and found that there are five basic foundations of morality (independent of religious beliefs):

Care/Harm: The care foundation involves concerns for the suffering of others and the virtues of caring and compassion. It is manifested in our tendency to look out for the vulnerable among us, usually children, elderly and disabled. Its evolutionary roots are obviously tied to species survival. The converse of this is the desire to punish anyone who causes harm to individuals or the group as a whole.

Fairness/Cheating. The fairness foundation is concerned about inequality and more abstract notions of justice. This is also the moral foundation that is the basis of the Golden Rule, as well as sharing and reciprocity. This "do unto others" is a near-universal moral code not only for most religions, but also for secularists, naturalists and atheists. While almost everyone subscribes to the fairness foundation, it manifests differently between liberals and conservatives, especially with respect to deservingness. Liberals tend to focus on systemic sources of unfairness, while conservatives lean more toward faith in the law of karma (you get what you deserve) and are more likely to blame sufferers for unfair outcomes.

Loyalty/Betrayal. The loyalty foundation focuses on the obligations of group membership, self-sacrifice, and vigilance against betrayal. Loyalty to groups outside of one's immediate kinship is what helped humans to develop advanced levels of cooperative behavior. Loyalty's modern manifestation appears in sports fans (who wear team colors, chant and move together) and military drill exercises, all of which have been proven to increase cooperative behavior and team spirit. While this moral foundation has obvious evolutionary benefits for group cohesion, its dark side is extreme forms of tribalism or partisanship. To attempt to befriend—or even simply understand—the "other" is an act of disloyalty that could result in one being excommunicated from the group.

Sanctity/Degradation. The sanctity foundation concerns itself with virtues such as chastity, wholesomeness, and control of desire. The sanctity (or purity) foundation likely arose in response to health concerns. We see this in Jewish dietary laws about keeping kosher as well as various cleanliness rituals and taboos in both Jewish and Muslim traditions. In some cases, the "other" is considered to be so impure as to require segregation from normal "decent" society. Examples of this are the low-caste Hindus called "untouchables" in India, and laws against inter-racial marriage that existed here in the U.S. until they were found to be unconstitutional in 1967. Again, this moral foundation has a liberal-conservative split, with conservatives defining impurity around behavior involving sex or illegal drugs, while liberal concerns about impurity involve food or environmental toxins. In its extreme form, the sanctity foundation can result in genocide, when the only way "we" can ensure our own purity is by eliminating "them."

Authority/Subversion. This is the law-and-order foundation, with its concerns about the social order and hierarchical relationships. The objective of this form of morality is to enforce prosocial behavior as well as to punish antisocial, or selfish behavior. It is usually associated with benevolent hierarchies, in which the higher-level individuals assume responsibility for the lower ones in exchange for deference and respect. Examples are parent-child, professor-student, master-servant, pastors, military officers, councils of "wise men," or ancestor worship. In earlier times, even kings and other royalty were presumed to have a duty to protect their subjects and ensure their welfare, a term referred to as *noblesse oblige.*

Liberty/Oppression. The dark side of authority is that it can result in oppression. Haidt argues that this sixth moral foundation arose later than the first five, as humans began to settle into larger permanent communities. Haidt does not know how this later foundation arose (the others all have traceable evolutionary roots), but at some point there arose a form of group resistance to attempted domination. While the leader who benefits the group must be respected, this respect is also tempered by vigilance for signs of self-aggrandizement and tyranny. Indeed, this liberty-based morality served as the basis for the American Declaration of Independence. Ironically, the extreme version, or Libertarianism, is also associated with both the extreme right (advocating the abolishment of government and regulation) and the extreme left (anarchists).

Moral differences between liberals and conservatives go beyond the nuanced variations in how they respond to the individual moral foundations. According to Professor Haidt's research, liberals generally score high on the care and fairness foundations, which results in them being concerned for social justice and those lower in the hierarchy. However, they tend to score low on the other three, viewing loyalty as tribalism or xenophobia, authority as authoritarianism, and purity as puritanism. Conversely conservatives tend to score about equally on all five of the basic foundations. Haidt argues that this gives conservatives a political advantage because they can appeal to a broader range of morality, as well as know how to push the right moral hot buttons when framing political issues.

Other researchers who have explored the differences in moral foundations between liberals and conservatives argue that conservatives are "developmentally stagnated" at Kohlberg's fourth stage—defining morality in terms of law-and-order and obedience to authority, where liberals are more likely to have evolved to stage 5 (social contract).[37] These differences in moral foundations have been attributed to the fact that liberals tend to have an optimistic view of human nature (perfectibility, or humans are basically good so long as they are not corrupted by external forces), [38] where conservatives have a pessimistic view of human nature (it is mired in original sin and must be subject to the constraints of authority, institutions and traditions).[39] In addition to differences in individual personality and worldview are the contextual and situational circumstances (the behaviorist view) in which one finds oneself. For example, those who consider themselves system "outsiders" would have a tendency to call for change (liberals) and those who are insiders, or otherwise are privileged by the existing system, would prefer the status quo (conservatives).

Another study argues that liberals and conservatives are not that different, at least when the question is framed around who (from a list of individuals identified as influential) they view as a moral exemplar rather than around specific issues (which could be more polarizing).[40] In this study, the researchers analyzed choices between a group of university professors as well as another group of "folk raters" (to compensate for the fact that university professors are not representative of the general population). In the group of professors, the top- rated moral individuals for liberals were Nelson Mandela, Mohandas Gandhi, and Martin Luther King, Jr. For conservatives, the list was Mother Teresa, Ronald Reagan, and Pope John Paul II. In the "folk rater" group, the top-rated moral individuals for liberals were Mohandas Gandhi, Martin Luther King, Jr. and Rosa Parks. For conservatives, this list was Mother Teresa, Ronald Reagan, and Mohandas Gandhi. Although the researchers found that Ronald

Reagan, Billy Graham, and Harvey Milk were polarizing figures, seven (professors) or nine (folk raters) individuals were found in the chosen top 15 on both lists. For the most part, "one partisan's hero was rarely the other's villain."[41]

These researchers also found some differences from Professor Haidt's analysis of liberal-versus-conservative moral foundations. In this study, moral judgments of personalities revolved around care, fairness, and purity on both sides. Loyalty was not a moral predictor on either side. The exception (the main source of difference) was authority. For conservatives, authority was neither a virtue nor a vice, where it was definitely a vice for liberals. This difference is what made the affable Reagan—with "his defense of authority structures against dissidents and his economic policies that increased social hierarchy"[42]—polarizing to liberals.

Professor Haidt argues that the evolution of morality—particularly as it is expressed in the form of religion—served a useful function in creating social cohesiveness around sacred practices. He cites the research of Richard Sosis, who studied two hundred cooperative communities in the 19th century. These communes required sacrifices from their members both in the form of resources (donated property or labor) and behavior (such as abstaining from tobacco or alcohol). What Sosis found was that these sacrifices enhanced the cohesion of religious communes but not secular ones. Haidt argues that religions create communities with shared norms and institutions that suppress selfishness by influencing both values and behavior.[43] However, the downside to this "bind" of cohesion is that it "blinds" its adherents to logic and rationality. Here, Haidt's argument mirrors that of Guinness, in that matters of faith—particularly those associated with fundamentalism—sometimes require the rejection of science and its insistence on empirical evidence, thus creating a religious/secular moral divide.

Haidt introduces the concept of moral capital. This is different from human capital (which is based on knowledge, skills and experience) and social capital (which is based on access to social networks and sources of influence), but instead is represented by the level of trust and cohesion within a group or community. He gives the example of small towns, where people leave their doors unlocked and allow children to roam unsupervised, which no one would think of doing in a big city. He argues that conservatives are more interested in preserving moral capital, while liberals tend to overlook how moral capital can be adversely affected by social change. While he primarily chastises liberals, Haidt also makes the argument that diverse political views are necessary for a healthy political life. Too much change and you have chaos, too much order and stability and you have stagnation. Haidt proposes that even both left and right-wing libertarianism have a place, mainly to prevent tyranny of the powerful (i.e., either corporations or government) against ordinary people. So, we are back to the necessity of finding ways to have civil discussions between and among persons or groups with vastly different neurochemical wiring, behavioral triggers, and moral foundations.

Perhaps the biggest and thorniest paradox is when moral righteousness is used to justify evil acts against a purportedly evil "other." We have seen that atrocities such as genocide are often based on the argument that "we" must ensure our own purity (or even survival) by eliminating "them." Our researchers have provided some suggestions for overcoming the us-versus-them dichotomy. Sapolsky argues that all of us have multiple "us-es," and we can sometimes overcome someone else's "them" by finding a shared "us." He gives two separate wartime examples; one in the Battle of Gettysburg and another during World War II, where a wounded soldier was able to save himself by establishing an "us" with his enemy captor. In the Civil War case, a mortally wounded Confederate general gave a secret Masonic sign to a Union officer, who had him transported to a field hospital. In World War II, a German general who was captured by the British recited an ode by Horace, and was joined in his recitation by the British commander. Recognizing that they had something in common, the two men remained in touch with each other after the war.

Sapolsky recommends that the way to reduce this cognitive division is to increase contact between individuals (the groups can see individual variations in the "other") in a situation where each side has approximately equal numbers and status. The best way to do this is involve them in a common goal. When people work together, they get to know one another as individuals, perhaps discovering some common "us" (a sports team, a hobby, or a favorite restaurant). Sapolsky also recommends that we learn to recognize and call out implicit biases, or alternatively foster empathy by putting yourself in the shoes of a "them."

Sapolsky also recommends flatter hierarchies. This is something that I also recommended in *Why Assholes Rule the World.* Flattening hierarchies not only reduces social distance (which tends to create an us-versus-them divide), it also minimizes the potential for dominance behaviors generally. Hierarchical social structures, particularly when they are institutionalized (imposed from the top down rather than agreed to by the group), tend to encourage antisocial behavior and can create toxic (or corrupt) organizations.[44] The science behind antisocial power dynamics is discussed in greater depth in *Assholes* than it is here. However, we will briefly analyze the connection between power, privilege and anti-social behavior in the following section.

For now, we will engage in a thought exercise on how to have a constructive dialogue across a moral divide. We are going to use as an example a fringe group who has beliefs and behaviors that many of us would consider moral and others that many of us would consider immoral. We will attempt to apply some of the lessons from Guinness, and Haidt, and (spoiler alert) we will see how intractable some of these issues can be, even when we start with the best of intentions.

Most of us normally think of environmentalists as a movement of the left. However, we are seeing the rise of so-called "eco-fascists," or neo-Nazi groups who are also sincere environmentalists.[45] These individuals often make their living on small farms, where they supply fresh produce and home-processed goods to local farmers markets and restaurants. (There may be some crossover with these individuals and others who are sometimes called "survivalists.") These individuals are almost apocalyptic in their concern for environmental and social collapse, which they blame on overpopulation—specifically overpopulation of the poor and non-White. Their moral foundation appears to be a yearning for purity in both the environmental and racial context.

In a perverted form of "lifeboat ethics," eco-fascists argue that a certain number of "them" must be permitted to die so that there will be enough resources for "us." Although eco-fascists have justifiable arguments against modern lifestyles (particularly urbanism and capitalism), their proposed "solution" involves strict controls over reproduction and immigration, as well as a return to pre-industrial life. Moreover, ecofascists ignore the fact that most environmental degradation is being caused by large-scale organizations, or individuals with much larger carbon footprints (frequent motor vehicle and airplane travel, multiple homes over 10,000 square feet, etc.) than the people who are their targets.

So, using our suggested techniques for the engagement of rational discussion, one way we could open a dialogue is to acknowledge an eco-fascist's concerns about overpopulation and environmental degradation. We can probably assume that we are dealing with genuine fear, a fear that is rooted in concerns about individual and even species survival. The fear of conflict over resources is backed up by a 2003 study from the Pentagon, which predicts that inability to adapt to rapid climate change (mainly in poorer countries) is likely to result in mass migrations as people search in desperate need of water, food, and energy, posing a threat to U.S. national security.[46] Once we acknowledge the legitimacy of their concerns, we can also express admiration for their commitment to living a greener lifestyle. That is, we can see the good in someone who walks their own talk by making lifestyle changes in pursuit of a prosocial objective.

Our ultimate goal in this exercise, however, is to persuade an eco-fascist to help us brainstorm more productive ways to deal with mass migrations caused by climate change that do not infringe on the rights of others. Once we have acknowledged their genuine concerns, we could then make the case that all of "us" are inhabitants of planet Earth, we all have a stake in the outcome, but most importantly, no specific person(s) or group(s) has a greater right to Earth's resources. Again, the common bottom line seems to be that no person or group should have greater rights (to survival, to a voice, to basic dignity) than any other person or group. Perhaps we could create a common bond by allowing an eco-fascist to view "the other" occupying a similar lifestyle of simple living off the land, and not as the rootless, urbanized go-getters (which they see in Jews) that they despise.

As much as we might attempt to sympathize with an eco-fascist, for some of us there will always be reservations about the potential for evil. We might be willing to work with a group who mainly exhibits a passive-aggressive philosophy of "let people die" toward those who are forced refugees of climate change, so long as they do not actively engage in harmful behavior. We may even be willing to excuse a negative attitude because these folks are doing more than most everyone else to address the fundamental problem. Yet, at what point does a "let them die" attitude become demonization of the "other," that is, anyone who does not look like, live like, pray like, vote like, or think like "us." At what point do such attitudes segue into potential genocide?

Which brings us to our trickiest challenge when discussing moral issues across a moral divide: How do you convince someone that eugenics, or allowing certain groups to decide who lives and who dies without input from those affected, is not the right answer? Most of us might agree that genocide (which some of these folks are advocating in the name of their own survival) is evil, or even in Shermer's "fuzzy logic" is likely to be assigned a near-zero probability of morality. So, the really big question is at what point—in a situation where the general rule is to be tolerant, empathetic, and hear everyone out—might there be some divergence so great that tolerance itself is no longer the proper choice, and if so, how will we know it?

By now, some of you may be thinking that eco-fascists are a small, fringe group unlikely to have major influence on policy decisions. But people do not develop their ideologies in a vacuum. Whatever you yourself might think about climate change, the majority of nations (including their military and national security apparatus), as well as insurance companies and other industries that analyze risk probabilities, are making contingency plans for unprecedented increases in both natural disasters and humanitarian crises. We already know that genocide was allowed to happen in Nazi Germany on the basis of wounded national pride. Therefore, what can we expect when the motivating force becomes survival itself? In a secularized public square, we may have even lost our capacity to discuss evil in a serious manner without being thought of as a fundamentalist zealot. Yet, how do we determine when a situation is sufficiently critical that some of us must abandon tolerance, stand our moral ground, and call something evil?

Notes

[1] From The Williamsburg Charter. Also found in *The Case for Civility and Why Our Future Depends on It* at p. 179.

[2] From *The Righteous Mind: Why Good People are Divided by Politics and Religion* at p. 49.

[3] Younge, G. (2011). *Who are we—and should it matter in the 21st century.* New York, NY: Nation Books/Perseus.

[4] Sapolksy, R. (2017, June 22). Why your brain hates other people and how to make it think differently. https://www.scribd.com/article/367297672/Why-Your-Brain-Hates-Other-People-And-How-To-Make-It-Think-Differently

[5] Kohlberg, L. (1980). *The meaning and measurement of moral development.* Worcester, MA: Clark University Press.

[6] Sapolsky, *supra.*

[7] Sapolsky, R. (2017). *Behave: The biology of humans at our best and worst.* New York, NY: Penguin Random House, LLC.

[8] The "doll studies" were instrumental in the Supreme Court reasoning overturning the "separate but equal" doctrine in *Brown v. Board of Education.* https://www.naacpldf.org/ldf-celebrates-60th-anniversary-brown-v-board-education/significance-doll-test/

[9] Fiske, S. T., Cuddy, A. J., Glick, P., & Xu, J. (2002). A model of (often mixed) stereotype content: Competence and warmth respectively follow from perceived status and competition. *Journal of Personality and Social Psychology,*82, 878-902.

[10] http://pluralism.org/document/the-williamsburg-charter/

[11] In France, a "deeply corrupt church and a deeply corrupt state…united in their coercive repression of all dissent," culminated in the bloody French Revolution of 1789, along with the Jacobin slogan to "strangle the last king with the guts of the last priest." (Guinness' *The Case for Civility* at p. 37).

[12] Guinness, O. (2008). *The case for civility and why our future depends on it.* New York, NY: HarperCollins Publishers at p. 48.

[13] *Id.* at p. 39.

[14] *Id.* at p. 64.

[15] *Id.* at p. 66.

[16] *Id.* at p. 67.

[17] *Id.* at pp. 68-69.

[18] *Id.* at p. 186.

[19] *Id.* at pp. 98-101.

[20] *Id.* at pp. 93-94.

[21] *Id.* at p. 103.

[22] *Id.* at pp. 78-80.

[23] *Id.* at pp. 111-112.

[24] *Id.* pp. 120.

[25] *Id.* at p. 123. "The liberal passion for tolerance all of a sudden becomes intolerant, and the liberal dream of diversity ends in conformism and uniformity through the rise of political correctness."

[26] 506 U.S. 390.

[27] Guinness, *supra* at p. 149.

[28] *Id.* at pp. 140-141.

[29] Graham, J., Haidt, J., Koleva, S., Motyle, M., Iyer, R., Wojcik, S., & Ditto, P.H. (2013). Moral foundations theory: The pragmatic validity of moral pluralism. *Advances in Experimental Social Psychology, 47,* 55-130.

[30] Martin, N.G., Eaves, L.J., Heath, A.C., Jardine, R., Feingold, L.M. & Eysenck, H.J. (1986). Transmission of social attitudes. *Proceedings of the National Academy of Sciences, 15,* 4364-68.

[31] Oxley, D.R., Smith, K.B., Alford, J.R., Hibbing, M.V., Miller, J.., Scalora, M., Hatemi, P.K., & Hibbing, J.R. (2008). Political attitudes vary with physiological traits. *Science, 321,* 1667-1670. Also at https://experts.nebraska.edu/en/publications/political-attitudes-vary-with-physiological-traits

[32] Koleva, S.P., Graham, J., Iyer, R., Ditto, H., Haidt, J. (2012). Tracing the threads: how five moral concerns (especially Purity) help explain culture war attitudes. *Journal of Research in Personality, 46,* 184-94.

[33] Dunlop, W.L., Walker, L.J., & Matsuba, M.K. (2013). The development of moral motivation across the adult lifespan. *European Journal of Developmental Psychology, 10,* 285-300.

[34] Haidt, J. (2008). *The righteous mind: Why good people are divided by politics and religion.* New York, NY: Pantheon Books.

[35] The moral roots of liberals and conservatives. TED Talks, March 2008. https://www.ted.com/talks/jonathan_haidt_on_the_moral_mind?language=en; The righteous mind: Why liberals and conservatives can't get along. Knowledge at Wharton, July 1, 2013. https://www.youtube.com/watch?v=qN42ZLwNFBY

---

[36] Haidt, *supra* at p. 102.

[37] Fishkin, J., Keniston, K., & McKinnon, C. (1973). Moral reasoning and political ideology. *Journal of personality and Social Psychology, 27*, 109-119.

[38] Sowell, T. (2002). *A conflict of visions: The ideological origins of political struggles*. New York, NY: Basic Books.

[39] This theory can seem to be counterintuitive, since liberals are often accused of supporting government regulation while conservatives are considered to be more *laissez-faire*.

[40] Frimer, J.A., Biesanz, J.C., Walker, L.J. & MacKinlay, C.W. (2013). Liberals and conservatives rely on common moral foundations when making moral judgments about influential people. *Journal of Personality and Social Psychology 104*(6), 1040-1059.

[41] *Id.* at p. 1048.

[42] *Id.* at p. 1052.

[43] Haidt, *supra* at p. 271.

[44] Even tiny and trivial power advantages can change how people think and act—and usually for the worse. In Sutton, R.J. (2007) *The No Asshole Rule.*

[45] https://www.theguardian.com/world/commentisfree/2019/mar/20/eco-fascism-is-undergoing-a-revival-in-the-fetid-culture-of-the-extreme-right

[46] https://eesc.columbia.edu/courses/v1003/readings/Pentagon.pdf

Section Three
Power, Privilege and Antisocial Pathology

It is beyond our power to explain either the prosperity of the wicked or the affliction of the righteous.

The Talmud

*

This disposition to admire, and almost to worship, the rich and the powerful, and to despise, or, at least, to neglect persons of poor and mean condition, though necessary both to establish and to maintain the distinction of ranks and the order of society, is, at the same time, the great and most universal cause of the corruption of our moral sentiments.

Adam Smith
The Theory of Moral Sentiments, 1759

*

All for ourselves, and nothing for other people, seems, in every age of the world, to have been the vile maxim of the masters of mankind.

Adam Smith
The Wealth of Nations, 1776

*

...some of the drivers for antisocial strategies and behaviors are new contexts of large groups (of non-reciprocating strangers) and opportunities for control over vast resources

Paul Gilbert and Jaskaran Basran[1]

*

There is little a man can do to alter the fact that his special talents are very common or exceedingly rare. A good mind or a fine voice, a beautiful face or a skillful hand, a ready wit or an attractive personality are in a large measure as independent of a person's efforts as the opportunities or the experiences he has had. In all these instances, the value which a person's capacities or services have for us and for which he is recompensed has little relation to anything that we can call moral merit or "deserts."

Friedrich Hayek[2]

We cannot understand how a society made up of mostly good people can go bad without a basic understanding of how power and privilege affect both behavior and worldview. *Why Assholes Rule the World*[3] analyzed the dynamic of how the (seemingly innocuous) dictates of efficiency and productivity can encourage certain forms of antisocial behavior, and, as these types of individuals rise in the organizational ranks, these characteristics begin to infect the culture. We probably know this intuitively: People who occupy positions of power have more ability to influence the dominant values and worldview. Higher status members of a group are looked to as role models, and so they have more influence on how individuals become socialized. Research in neuroscience expands this phenomenon beyond role model mirroring by finding that culture itself affects the behavior of those within it by activating latent genetic triggers.[4]

From an evolutionary standpoint, the division of labor and corresponding formation of status hierarchies initially helped to organize increasingly complex societies, but (like the cooperation/competition dichotomy) it also had a negative side. As nomadic human tribes began to settle into more permanent communities, the generally egalitarian ways of the tribe were replaced with greater division of labor and more hierarchical social structures. This allowed people to develop higher level skills, often connected with quantification: weights, measures, math, money. Larger populations also led to different forms of personal interaction. When one could be dealing with strangers every day (as opposed to mostly familiar people), new behaviors of image management and manipulation arose. The settling of humans into larger communities (towns and cities) accompanied the development of trade, mercantilism, and consumerism. By moving to another town, one could instantly gain status with visual displays of material wealth (clothing, home, objects), although one also lost previously established social connections. These higher population density and more impersonal and competitive environments tended to increase emotions like envy and social comparison.

Organizational culture is often attributed to the character of its leadership. Studies on leadership styles have identified prosocial leaders (sometimes called "servant leaders")[5] who focus on the welfare of those they lead, promote fairness and compassion, and exhibit insightful empathy,[6] and antisocial leaders, who tend to be socially divisive and seek to privilege their own group (social dominance).[7] Antisocial leaders focus attention on external threats, promote competitiveness rather than cooperation, and aggravate inter-group conflict.[8] Although prosocial leadership is important to fostering a moral organizational culture, the corruption of such culture often involves a more complex interplay between those in charge and their "followership." Particularly in our highly competitive and individualistic culture, we are prone to choose leaders who portray themselves as "masters-of-the-universe" types, as well as place them on a pedestal of power and privilege that is unwarranted by either facts or justice.[9]

Individual Privilege: I am Better than You

Today, we see that a preoccupation with self-image also seems to have a good side and a bad side. So-called "self-esteem" can encourage us to improve skills and attempt challenging projects, as well as bolster our psychic integrity in an increasingly impersonal world. However, it can also segue into narcissism, or the belief that we are somehow more special and deserving than anyone else. In *Why Assholes Rule the World,* we analyzed how narcissism can be quite helpful in the acquisition of power: narcissists do not have the same reservations as most of us with respect to relentless self-promotion and bragging about accomplishments, they make great first impressions, and are masters at networking.[10] Groups are more likely to attribute higher social rank to narcissistic individuals,[11] and narcissists are more likely to be selected as leaders because they display confidence (often found to be unrealistic overconfidence).[12] One study suggests that social rank itself influences self-image, with social advantage creating confidence, which then leads to the appearance of higher competence, which then perpetuates social advantage.[13] The ultimate result is a system of self-perpetuating privilege under the guise of meritocracy.

The increasing size and concentration of organizations means that those who rise to the top have even more power over more people and resources than in the past. Consequently, such positions tend to attract the sort of individuals who crave power. This is compounded by the extreme (and increasing) dispersion of wages and income between those at the top and everyone else. Thus, positions at the top also tend to attract individuals who are motivated by greed as well as power. This trend of merged mega-organizations along with increasing concentration of wealth and power of those at the top has created a society that is not so much divided between the haves and the have-nots, but between the have-mores and everyone else. As socio-economic inequality has become more extreme across the globe, researchers have recently begun to take an interest in identifying psychological/behavioral differences between the powerful/privileged and the rest of us.

Paul Piff is a professor of psychological science at the University of California who has conducted significant research on relationships between wealth, class, entitlement, narcissism, and antisocial behavior. Professor Piff conducted a number of experiments that tested the relationship between social class, wealth and unethical behavior. In every one of Piff's tests, there was a direct correlation between higher social class and unethical behavior. The specific outcome of Piff's experiments are summarized below:[14]

> The experimenters "coded" vehicle types for indication of social rank and wealth and then stationed observers at an intersection with four-way stop signs. Drivers of "higher status" vehicles were more likely to cut off other vehicles and less likely to yield the right of way to pedestrians on a crosswalk.

A self-reported social class was assigned to participants using the MacArthur scale of subjective social-economic status (SES), and then the participants were asked to make decisions in eight different hypothetical scenarios. Participants with higher SES scores were more likely to make unethical decisions, even after controlling for sex, age, and ethnicity.

Participants were asked to rate their position in the socioeconomic hierarchy relative to people at the very top and the very bottom (based on money, education, and type of job). The experimenters then left a jar of individually wrapped candies out, informing the participants that the candies were for children in another laboratory, but they could take some if they wanted. Participants who ranked themselves higher took more candy than those who ranked themselves lower.

Participants' social status was determined using the MacArthur SES scale, and then they participated in a hypothetical salary negotiation with a "job candidate." In this situation, the job was slated to be eliminated, and the participants could decide whether to tell the "job candidate" the truth or not. As part of the exercise, participants were also asked whether they believed it is justified and moral to be greedy. The researchers' statistical tests found that higher social class was negatively associated with the probability of telling the job candidate the truth and positively associated with favorable attitudes toward greed. Moreover, a favorable attitude toward greed itself was negatively associated with the probability of telling the truth.

Participants were first tested for measures of social class and attitudes toward greed, and then engaged in a game of chance. In this game, computerized die rolls were predetermined to sum up

> to 12, but participants were told to report the sum of their "die rolls," with higher rolls increasing their chance to receive a cash prize. As hypothesized, higher social class and more favorable attitudes toward greed predicted a higher probability of cheating (i.e., misreporting their actual totals).
>
> In another experiment, participants were "primed" with positive attitudes toward greed (the type of greed-is-good propaganda many of us are familiar with). In "unprimed" individuals, upper-class participants exhibited more unethical behavior. However, there was little difference between upper class and lower-class participants who had been "primed" for greed: In this case, both upper and lower class participants exhibited higher levels of unethical behavior. This last experiment is more troublesome, because it suggests that greed, selfishness, and unethical behavior can be inculcated in persons who might not otherwise behave in such a manner.

Professor Piff suggests a number of possible explanations for these findings. Because upper-class individuals have abundant resources and elevated rank, they enjoy greater freedom and independence. This ability to have greater control over their lives and reduced exposure to external influences gives rise to more self-focused patterns of cognition and behavior. That is, there are social identity effects connected with class just as there are for race, ethnicity, and national origin.[15] Upper class individuals are more likely to attribute success to individual effort while lower class individuals are more sensitive to context and situational factors such as opportunity, prejudice, and the economic structure of society.[16] Piff argues that all of these effects tend to make upper-class individuals less cognizant of the feelings and rights of others, making them more prone to unethical behavior.

Alternatively, lower class individuals might at first seem to be more prone to unethical behavior given that they live in environments characterized by fewer resources, greater uncertainty, and more threats to survival. This expectation was demonstrated in the 1983 movie *Trading Places.* In a perversion of Professor Piff's experiments, a group of wealthy Wall Street-style traders set up an "experiment" where they arrange to put a homeless street hustler (played by Eddie Murphy) in the place of a wealthy brokerage executive (played by Dan Aykroyd). There are a couple of scenes in the early part of the set-up where we see Murphy becoming more responsible and Aykroyd becoming more willing to bend and break the rules. However, we never find out conclusively whether success is more the result of inherent personal traits or environmental influence, because Murphy and Aykroyd figure out the game and manage to turn the tables on the bettors. Meanwhile, in the world of real social science, there is an emerging body of research that suggests—in spite of chronic stressors which might drive lower class individuals to prioritize their own needs over others—that they actually tend to be more engaged with the needs of others, possibly because they are more acutely aware of their own interdependence.[17]

Piff has conducted additional studies finding that lower class individuals are more generous. Citing nationwide surveys of charitable contributions, persons earning less than $25,000 per year gave 4.2% of their income to charity, while households making over $100,00 contributed only 2.7%.[18] Piff's experiments confirmed the prediction that lower class participants were more generous to strangers than upper class participants. He also found that egalitarian values (the well-being of others is prioritized the same as self-interest) mediate the relationship between social class and prosocial trust behavior, and compassion moderates the relationship between social class and prosocial helping behavior.[19] This gives us hope that egalitarianism and compassion can be encouraged independently of social class or other antisocial personality traits.

Jennifer Stellar (then a Ph.D. student and now a professor of psychology at the University of Toronto) found physiological differences between responses of lower and upper class individuals. That is, there were measurable neurochemical changes above and beyond specific observable behaviors. In this experiment, the participants viewed an advertisement for St. Jude's hospital that depicted children undergoing chemotherapy while their distraught parents attempted to comfort them. Rather than observing behavior, Stellar measured autonomic reactions such as facial expressions and slowing heart rates, and found that lower social class individuals had much greater physiological responses.

Some researchers even used their own relationships with money as the foundation for experimental research. Kathleen Vohs, a Ph.D. psychologist, became interested in the "psychology of money" when she noted behavioral changes in herself after leaving a low-paid junior faculty position for a faculty spot in a business school where she received a fivefold increase in salary. Professor Vohs' research has corroborated Professor Piff's research in finding that money (even simply "priming" subjects for money) can make people antisocial. Not that the wealthier subjects become malicious or even unethical, rather they tend to lose interest in others, becoming more focused on instrumental objectives (getting things done) instead of caring about people as individuals.[20]

Professor Piff has also looked at the effect of social class on narcissism and entitlement.[21] He places this work in the context of other research that documents increasing narcissism in general.[22] Piff measured narcissism using the forced-choice version of the Narcissistic Personality Inventory (NPI), a "well validated, reliable, and widely used instrument for assessing subclinical narcissism." Social class was determined by the student's parents' annual salary and total household income. As with his prior experiments, social class was positively associated with higher NPI scores, as well as scores on a Me-Versus-Other scale. Piff proposes that entitlement—along with social class—contributes to increased narcissism. Additional experiments showed that narcissism can be reduced by "priming" for egalitarianism. This is the flip side of Piff's prior studies that suggested "priming" for greed increased unethical behavior.

Other researchers explored nuances between behavior that was "unethical" versus behavior that was "selfish," and found that higher class tended to correlate with selfishness, but lower class individuals were more likely to be "unethical" if the behavior was performed to benefit others.[23] An example of this is when a street-level bureaucrat bends or circumvents rules to help a client or fellow citizen, often because the bureaucrat may believe strict application of the rules will result in an unfair outcome. This line of research suggests that how social class impacted results depended on feelings of power (which made subjects more unethical) versus feelings of status. Thus, someone who breaks the rules (i.e., behaves unethically) is not necessarily motivated by selfishness. This research suggests that antisocial behavior itself comes in different varieties and is accompanied by different motivating factors.

Hierarchical social structures also have effects on group behavior independent of individual personalities. As both businesses and governments have grown in size, hierarchical chains of command were adopted in order to improve both efficiency and accountability. Yet, more recent research has found that hierarchies—particularly steeper ones—create adverse effects on group functioning. Hierarchies tend to reduce diversity in thinking and often result in groupthink, a process (driven almost entirely by high-ranking individuals) that encourages conformity.[24] Hierarchies also can operate to inhibit the robust exchange of ideas, depriving the group of its creative and problem-solving potential.[25]

An individual's position in a hierarchy can affect not only behavior, but also the perception of reality. Persons in roles with less control and autonomy tend to under-rate their own performance, while those in positions of higher rank tend to over-rate their skills and competence, creating a situation of both subjective and objective inequality which has negative effects on morale.[26] This explains why so many workers acquiesce to subsistence wages as well as unsafe and/or humiliating working conditions, because they have been inculcated in the belief that they are inferior. Steeper hierarchies also operate to increase intra-group competition and thwart cooperative behavior.[27] While no study has found that hierarchies *cause* corruption, research suggests that steeper hierarchies aggravate existing corruption, which then becomes difficult to remedy when those in higher ranks become corrupted.[28]

The big unanswered question in research on privilege and selfishness is which is the cause and which is the effect. Do people who are naturally selfish and narcissistic rise to positions of power because they are motivated to do so more than those who are less opportunistic? Or is it more a case of individuals who arrive in places where position is justified on the basis of individual achievement, money is everywhere, and others respond to them with deference—which then alters one's mental processes to view others as either aids or obstacles to one's own ambitions. As with most of what we learn about behavior, the answer is probably a little bit of both. The over-privileged selfish asshole is a result of a combination of personality characteristics influencing individual behavioral choices and status hierarchies impacting propensities to entitlement.

This line of research has a number of practical implications. It suggests that we should approach individuals of high status with critical objectivity (if not automatic suspicion) rather than automatic deference. It also suggests that behavior and personality can be shaped by both one's location in power and status hierarchies as well as by broader cultural forces. Whether people in general are going to be predisposed to supportive and trusting relationships or to exploitative relationships can depend on factors such as the distribution of resources, and whether social environments are perceived as threatening.[29] That is, the problem is not so much that the high and mighty have attained their position through unethical means as that the precarity of everyone else causes us to be more suspicious of those who are more likely to be our allies.

Another important finding from the research is that individual attitudes and behavior can be changed by the influence of prevailing cultural values. If people are presented with arguments why cooperation and egalitarianism are good for everyone, they will be inclined to behave accordingly. Conversely, if they are presented with arguments that greed and selfishness are good, they will be inclined to so behave. Because individual behavior can be influenced by cultural messages, it is important that these messages reflect who we want us to be. We will address the issue of antisocial messaging and media complicity more fully in Part IV, Section Four.

Group Privilege: "We" are Better than "Them."

Entitlement is the individual belief that one is deserving of special treatment or deference based on who one is or the position one occupies. Privilege is the group version of entitlement—the dominant (or allegedly "superior") group enjoys unearned (and often unacknowledged) benefits that are not enjoyed by society at large. In the preceding section, we looked at how us-versus-them dichotomies create social divisions. These us-versus-them divisions become even more destructive of the social fabric when they are accompanied by superior/inferior relations. This is the case where one groups sets itself up as the superior, or dominant group. This group may or may not constitute a numerical majority. An example of both is the position of Whites in the United States (a majority, although a decreasing one) and Whites in South Africa (a minority).

Dr. Jim Sedanius (Harvard) and Dr. Felicia Pratto (University of Connecticut) have identified a psychological phenomenon they call social dominance orientation.[30] Social dominance orientation can refer to the belief that one's own group is superior (Whites versus Blacks, men versus women), or that some groups are superior to others generally. Dominant groups often become so not because they are more skilled or better-liked, but because they control resources. As this control over resources becomes institutionalized, it extends to opportunity and influence. That is, access to jobs and positions of power are controlled by individuals in the socially dominant group. Individuals in "inferior" groups may be restricted by law, such as lacking the right to vote, the right to own property, or being segregated in less desirable areas. Alternatively, "inferior" groups may be granted formal legal equality—where they theoretically have access to the same resources as the dominant group—yet this theoretical equality rarely results in actual equality.

The reason that even legal equality does not result in equal opportunity for disadvantaged groups is that dominant groups write the laws and structure systems that are suited to the dominant group's way of being and to accommodate their worldviews.[31] There are a number of psychological, psycho-social and logistical processes that serve to keep inferiorized groups from attaining equality. First, members of subordinated groups are less likely to have the personal connections to organizations and networks of power and influence. Second is the phenomenon of social category norms. When we think generically about persons who are judges, executives, presidents, doctors or other positions of earned privilege, we tend to envision a White man, even when we might personally know a woman or minority who occupies one of these professions. Conversely, when we think generically about a single parent, we tend to envision a Black woman. Indeed, the media (which is mostly under the ownership of the dominant group) often reinforces these stereotyped images. Third, the very notion of hierarchy itself (specifically the maintenance of group dominance) tends to be favored by dominant groups, while subordinate groups tend to be more egalitarian. As a practical matter, subordinated groups also tend to have lower political participation,[32] which then creates a feedback loop where the unresponsiveness of the system to their needs leads to greater disaffection and alienation.

Because the dominant group has the power to define norms, including who and what is meritorious or worthy, they are able to create hierarchy-perpetuating myths that justify the status quo: Blacks are lazy or violent, women are too emotional to make rational decisions, people are poor because they don't apply themselves (either through hard work or the acquisition of skills). The system is essentially set up to favor the dominant group, and when the dominant group (as a matter of statistics and not necessarily all individuals) is more successful, this further justifies claims of superiority. Occasionally, when a member of a subordinated group attains a position of power, this is proclaimed as proof that the system is fair. What often is left unsaid is that these individuals have accommodated themselves to the dominant culture. Some of them find they have become strangers in their own communities, even abandoning their neighborhoods and families of origin once they have gained their place in the dominant society.[33]

Socially constructed relationships of superiority and inferiority are almost never seen as such, but rather simply accepted as the way things are. Researchers have found that people are generally blind to their own privilege.[34] This is because dominant groups are culturally "normalized," while subordinate groups are defined and described as "other." People tend to focus on how Blacks, women, Latinos, Asians, LGBTQ, Muslims, etc. are "different," rather than how Whites, men, cisgender heterosexuals, and Christians are privileged. Because people are blind to their own privilege and more aware of underprivileged difference, those who occupy so-called "intersectional" identities tend to identify with their underprivileged category more so than their privileged ones. That is, a man who is Black, gay or disabled will see his Blackness, gayness or disability before he will view his maleness. A White woman will see herself through a gendered lens before she will see her own Whiteness. We view ourselves in our relationship to the dominant group—either in or out—and not as complex individuals with multiple identities.

Persons who occupy privileged statuses enjoy what some have termed the "luxury of obliviousness."[35] This manifests as a form of attention non-reciprocity: e.g., minorities pay more attention to Whites and women pay more attention to men. When subordinated groups call attention to themselves (protests, parades, advocating for anti-discrimination legislation or diversity programs), members of privileged groups can feel put upon because they have been forced to pay attention—a disturbance of their obliviousness. When subordinated groups attempt to carve out safe spaces for themselves, or simply to be seen and heard, the dominant group resents the attention and accuses these "others" of seeking special treatment. Dominant groups complain of being "sick and tired" of hearing about privilege and oppression, which they allege happens "all the time."[36]

Systems of privilege are essentially about power and control, as well as the justification of injustice, and thus they are designed to be self-perpetuating. Racism arose around the same time as economic systems that relied on colonization and slavery.[37] Male violence against women is an assertion of sexual control. Men even challenge each other's manhood with disparaging terms used to denigrate gays and women (e.g., "fag" or "pussy").[38] White men who are not racist or sexist themselves will blame individual racists and sexists rather than seeing how everyone contributes to the problem by acquiescing to it.[39] Indeed, even well-meaning "diversity" programs are often marginalized—a member of a subordinate group with little real power is put in charge and the program is compartmentalized and under-funded—which creates a "feel-good" exercise that does little to address real change.[40] Because the act of confronting privilege itself creates conflict, it is usually avoided until the situation of marginalized groups becomes intolerable or outrage is ignited by a critical event. "An oppressive system often seems stable only because it limits our lives and imaginations so thoroughly that we can't see anything else."[41]

Dominant social norms can also have an adverse effect on members who purportedly belong to the dominant group. The idealized person in contemporary society is not only White and male, but must also be brave, dependable, logical, critical, but most of all, rich and powerful. When working and lower class White men fall short of this ideal, they attempt to bolster psychic survival by emphasizing their Whiteness and maleness.[42] This is aggravated when they work in a system that views them as disposable at the same time "others" (minorities and women) are gaining or asserting rights in the workplace.[43] In a global economy, when more people of all races and genders are becoming increasingly precariatized—where psychosocial injury is added on top of economic anxieties—everyone begins to view everyone else as a competitor for ever-fewer resources (jobs, opportunity, recognition).

Ironically, the concept of privilege itself has developed into a form of pathology. Instead of objectively analyzing social harm caused by systemic hierarchies, the accusation of "privilege" (or failing to check it) has become weaponized as an argument against one's opponents. It is becoming almost *de rigueur* for politicians (including those from families with generations of inherited wealth) to present themselves to voters as "regular" people against accusations of out-of-touch privilege—they appear at state fairs eating corn dogs and fried catfish, in hard hats at factories, or standing in a field with a family farmer. Yet, in spite of an apparent need to display connection with "regular" people, the growth of inequality increases year after year.

In *The Perils of Privilege,*[44] Phoebe Maltz Bovy argues that discussions about privilege—which initially started as attempts to address real injustice—have morphed into accusations against those we disagree with for failing to "check their privilege." Thus, the concept of privilege can now be applied not only to every White person or male, but to individuals who may occupy positions that we might consider to be middle class or "bourgeoisie." Bovy suggests that the problem is not so much with the privilege framework itself as a media appetite for "privilege content," which drives audience numbers.[45] Bovy's premise is that instead of helping us address real problems of injustice, the discussion about privilege has instead aggravated the war of all against all.

The accusation of privilege carries with it the implication that the offender has benefited from some kind of unearned advantage. Yet, someone born with one form of social privilege may nonetheless be subject to struggles and disadvantages which are not readily apparent. It is not difficult to imagine a working-class White man—who has been working harder for less for decades, who may have been laid off and had to take a lower-paying job, and who is inferiorized at work every day—being resentful at the implication of privilege. Although the White working-class man is not subject to inferiorization ***because of*** his race or gender, the frustration and angst are no less real. In a world that glamorizes material success, along with the propaganda of meritocracy, one must constantly defend against the perception that one is a loser.

In such a world, it seems that everyone else has some advantage that you do not. White men regard women and minorities as being "advantaged" by affirmative action. Conversely, women and minorities regard White men as having a combination of historical legacy advantage as well as cultural advantage. Others are advantaged due to wealth, social connections, or access to "gatekeeping" pathways through elite institutions or corporate hierarchies. There is a sense that everyone is looking upward in comparison, but no one is reaching downward to offer a hand up. But more troublesome is the destruction of general social trust that prevents us from reaching out to those around us with whom we may have more in common than we realize.

Notes

[1] Gilbert, P. & Basran, J. (2019, 25 June). The evolution of prosocial and antisocial competitive behavior and the emergence of prosocial and antisocial leadership styles. *Frontiers in Psychology, 10,* Article 610 at p. 14.

[2] Hayek, F. A. (1960). *The constitution of liberty.* Chicago, IL: University of Chicago Press.

[3] VanHettinga, B. (2019).

[4] Conway, C.C., & Slavitch, G.M. (2017). Behavior genetics of prosocial behavior. In P. Gilbert, Ed., *Compassion: Concepts, research and applications.* London: Routledge; May, A. (2011). Experience-dependent structural plasticity in the adult human brain. *Trends in Cognitive Science, 15,* 475-482.

[5] Spears, L.C. (2010). Character and servant leadership: Ten characteristics of effective, caring leaders. *Journal of Virtual Leadership, 1,* 25-30.

[6] Gilbert, P. (2017). *Compassion: Concepts, research and applications.* London: Routledge.

[7] Gilbert, P. & Basran, J. (2019, June). The evolution of prosocial and antisocial competitive behavior and the emergence of prosocial and antisocial leadership styles. *Frontiers in Psychology*, 10, 1-19.

[8] *Id. at* p. 8.

[9] Lipman-Bluman, J. (2005). *The allure of toxic leaders: Why we follow destructive bosses and corrupt politicians—and how we can survive them.* New York, NY: Oxford University Press.

[10] VanHettinga, *supra* at p. 346.

[11] Brunell, A.B., Gentry, W.A., Campbell, W.K., Hoffman, B.J., Kuhnert, K.W., & DeMarree, K.G. (2008). Leader emergence: The case of the narcissistic leader. *Personality and Social Psychology Bulletin, 34,* 1673-1676.

[12] Camerer, C.F., & Lovallo, D. (1999). Overconfidence and excess entry: An experimental approach. *American Economic Review, 89,* 306-318; Von Rueden, C., & van Vugt, M. (2015). Leadership in small scale societies: Some implications for theory, research, and practice. *The Leadership Quarterly, 26,* 978-990.

---

[13] Belmi, P., & Neale, M. (2019). The social advantage of miscalibrated individuals: The relationship between social class and overconfidence and its implications for class-based inequality. *Journal of Personality and Social Psychology: Interpersonal Relations and Group Processes.* American Psychological Association. Study cites articles finding that the majority of individuals who work at elite and prestigious firms tend to come from elite educational institutions and high-earning entrepreneurs come from highly educated and wealthier families.

.

[14] Piff, P.K., Stancato, D.M., Côté, S., Mendoza-Denton, R., & Keltner, D. (2012, March 13). Higher social class predicts increased unethical behavior. *Proceedings of the National Academy of Sciences, 109*(11), 4086-4091. www.pnas.org/cgi/doi/10.1073/pnas.1118373109.

[15] Kraus, M.W., Piff, P.K., & Keltner, D. (2009). Social class, the sense of control, and social explanation. *Journal of Personality and Social Psychology, 97,* 992-1004; Stephens, N.M., Markus, H.R., & Townsend, S. M. (2007). Choice as an act of meaning: The case of social class. *Journal of Personality and Social Psychology, 93,* 814-830.

[16] Kluegel, J.R., & Smith, E.R. (1986). *Beliefs about inequality: Americans' views of what is and what ought to be.* Hawthorne, NY: Aldine de Gruyter.

[17] Argyle, M. (1994). *The psychology of social class.* London, England: Routledge.

[18] Greve, F. (2009, May 23). America's poor are its most generous. *The Seattle Times;* Johnston, D.C. (2005, December 19). Study shows the superrich are not the most generous. *The New York Times.*

[19] Piff, P.K., Kraus, M.W., Côté, S., & Cheng, B.H. (2010). Having less, giving more: The influence of social class on prosocial behavior. *Journal of Personality and Social Psychology, 99*(5), 771-784.

[20] Miller, L. (2012, 29 June). The money-empathy gap. http://nymag.com/news/features/money-brain-2012-7/

[21] Piff, P. K. (2014). Wealth and the inflated self: Class, entitlement, and narcissism. *Personality and Social Psychology Bulletin, 40*(1), 34-43.

[22] Twenge, J.M. (2006). *Generation me: Why today's young Americans are more confident, assertive, entitled—and more miserable than ever before.* New York, NY: Free Press.

---

[23] Dubois, D., Rucker, D.D., & Galinksy, A.D. (2015). Social class, power, and selfishness: When and why upper and lower class individuals behave unethically. *Journal of Personal Social Psychology, 108*(3), 436-49.

[24] Anderson, C., Keltner, D., & John, O.P. (2003). Emotional convergence between people over time. *Journal of Personality and Social Psychology, 84,* 1054-1068.

[25] Tost, L.P., Gino, F., & Larrick, R.P. (2013). When power makes other speechless: the negative impact of leader power on team performance. *Academic Management Journal, 56,* 1465-1486.

[26] Sande, G.N., Ellard, J.H., & Ross, M. (1986). Effect of arbitrarily assigned status labels on self-perceptions and social perceptions: The mere position effect. *Journal of Personality and Social Psychology, 50,* 684-689.

[27] Anderson, C., & Brown, C.E. (2010). The functions and dysfunctions of hierarchy. *Research in Organizational Behavior,* 30, 55-89.

[28] *Id.*

[29] Cohen, D. (2001). Cultural variation: Considerations and implications. *Psychological Bulletin, 127,* 451-471.

[30] Pratto, F., Sidanius, J., Sallworth, L.M., & Malle, B. (1994). Social dominance orientation: A personality variable predicting social and political attitudes. *Journal of Personality and Social Psychology 67*(4), 741-763, at p. 752, *see also* Sidanius, J., & Pratto, F. (2012). Social dominance theory. In P.A.M. Van Lange, A.W. Kruglanski, & E.T. Higgins, (Eds) *Handbook of Theories of Social Psychology, Vol II* at pp. 418-438. Thousand Oaks, CA: Sage Publications, Inc.

[31] Sidanius, J., & Pratto, F. (1999). *Social dominance: An intergroup theory of social hierarchy and oppression.* New York, NY: Cambridge University Press; Pratto, F. (1999). The puzzle of continuing group inequality: Piecing together psychological, social, and cultural forces in social dominance theory. In M.P. Zanna (Ed.) *Advances in Experimental Social Psychology* (Vol. 31, pp. 191-263). San Diego, CA: Academic Press.

[32] Krauss, M. (2015, October). The inequality of politics: Social class rank and political participation. *Institute for Research on Labor and Employment,* University of California Working paper #120-15. http://irle.berkeley.edu/files/2015/The-Inequality-of-Politics.pdf

[33] Goffman, E. (1963). *Stigma.* Englewood Cliffs, NJ: Prentice Hall.

[34] Pratto, F., & Stewart, A.L. (2012). Group dominance and the half-blindness of privilege. *Journal of Social Issues, 68*(1), 28-45.

[35] Johnson, A.G. (2018). *Privilege, power and difference.* New York, NY: McGraw-Hill Education.

[36] *Id.* at p. 103.

[37] *Id.* at p. 36.

[38] *Id.* at p. 54

[39] *Id.* at p. 67.

[40] *Id.* at p. 102. "Most organizational failures in the area of diversity result not from being run by mean-spirited bigots...but from poorly dealing with issues of privilege." *Id.* at p. 58.

[41] *Id.* at p. 109.

[42] Coston, B.M., & Kimmel, M. (2012). Seeing privilege where it isn't: Marginalized masculinities and the intersectionality of privilege. *Journal of Social Issues, 68*(1), 97-111.

[43] Pyke, K.D. (1996). Class-based masculinities: The interdependence of gender, class, and interpersonal power. *Gender and Society, 10*(5), 527-549.

[44] Bovy, P.M. (2017). *The perils of privilege: Why injustice can't be solved by accusing others of advantage.* New York, NY: Saint Martin's Press.

[45] Bovy, P.M. (2017, March 6). The perils of privilege. *The New Republic.* https://newrepublic.com/article/140985/perils-privilege-phoebe-maltz-bovy-book-excerpt

Section 4
Obeying Orders: When Good People Go Bad

Human Behavior is always subject to situation forces. This context is embedded within a larger macrocosmic one, often a particular power system that is designed to maintain itself. Traditional analyses by most people, including those in legal, religious, and medical institutions focus on the actors as the sole causal agent. Consequently, they minimize or disregard the impact of situational variables and systemic determinants that shape behavioral outcomes and transform actors.

Phillip Zimbardo[1]

When most of us think of evil, what often comes to mind is a specific individual, usually one of a number of historical authoritarian dictators like Adolph Hitler, Joseph Stalin, Saddam Hussein and the like. If we are religious, we might vision evil as an abstract personification which we call the devil, Satan, Lucifer, etc. "Evil" is thus explained as the act of a bad person, or (the religious view) the work of the devil, who has come to "possess" a possibly otherwise good person. In a modern, rationalized society, most of us know that human beings operate along a spectrum of prosocial and antisocial orientation and behavior. While we may not divide people into "saints" and "sinners," we tend to discuss such things in terms of specific personality traits like narcissism, anti-social personality disorder, sociopathy and psychopathy.

The inhumanity of the Nazi regime, particularly its drive to ethnic cleansing and genocide of Jews, prompted some researchers who study behavior to ask the question how such a thing could happen. Certainly, there were individuals in power with obvious sociopathic traits (at least in hindsight). But individuals generally do not rise to power in modern societies by the simple assertion of social dominance (or bullying their way to the top).[2] At its most innocuous level is the acquiescence to (or failure to resist) the rise of evil leaders. As the leader gains power, a more troublesome issue is why otherwise good people then facilitate evil acts in the name of serving an evil system? This is especially problematic when there is no evidence of direct threat or coercion. The underlying question is whether all of us might be capable of evil given the right circumstances.

Who Was John Demjanjuk?

In the late 1980s, my husband and I lived in Cleveland, Ohio, specifically on the East side of town in a neighborhood located at the intersection of Jewish, Polish and Italian communities. During that time, the local news media (*Cleveland Plain Dealer)* was preoccupied by the story of one John Demjanjuk, a Ukrainian immigrant who lived in the area for decades and had recently been convicted of Nazi war crimes. Demjanjuk had purportedly served as the ruthless former Nazi prison guard at Treblinka known as "Ivan the Terrible." The neighborhood was divided into pro-Demjanjuk (mainly Poles) and anti-Demjanjuk (mainly Jews) camps, while most of the rest of us were in disbelief that such a seemingly normal person and quintessential family man could have committed such atrocities.

According to records, Demjanjuk was born in 1920 to a disabled Ukrainian veteran of World War I. Records further indicate that Demjanjuk was drafted into the Soviet Red Army in 1941. He was wounded in combat with the Germans, but patched up and sent back to the front lines, where he was captured in 1942. Here, the record of Demjanjuk becomes murkier. Demjanjuk alleged that he spent some time doing heavy labor in prisoner-of-war camps until he met up with and joined a group of Ukrainian soldiers. Demjanjuk admitted that he sometimes fought with the Germans against the Soviets, depending upon the exigency of the situation, but had never developed true loyalties to either side.

The next time Demjanjuk appears in the record is at an American-operated displaced persons camp in 1945. While at one of the refugee camps, Demjanjuk met the woman who would become his wife and mother to his children. Demjanjuk told American authorities that he would be executed if he returned to Ukraine because he had refused to fight for the Nazis. During his stay at the camps, Demjanjuk also worked as a truck driver for the U.S. Army.

Demjanjuk came to the United States in 1952 and became a naturalized citizen in 1958. During this time, he worked as an assembly line mechanic at the Ford Motor Company plant and raised two children. According to neighbors, he was a model citizen, regularly attending Saint Vladimir Ukrainian Orthodox Church, spending his spare time repairing the neighbors' cars and the neighbors' children's bicycles. Demjanjuk retired from his job at Ford and otherwise led a quiet and uneventful life.

The war crimes charges against Demjanjuk were instigated by the former Soviet Union, and not the United States. The Soviet war crimes authorities produced a document purporting to be an identification card from the Trawniki training camp, where Nazis were instructed in the logistics of mass executions. This evidence was bolstered by statements of Treblinka survivors obtained by the U.S. Justice Department. The survivors identified Demjanjuk as Ivan the Terrible, a guard known to torture Jewish inmates and who was responsible for the extermination of over 900,000 Jews. Demjanjuk was stripped of his US citizenship in 1981 and deported to Israel to stand trial, although Israel did not formally charge Demjanjuk with war crimes until 1986. Following a trial, Demjanjuk was convicted in 1988 and sentenced to death. Demjanjuk spent six years in an Israeli prison until a new batch of apparently exculpatory documents was released following the collapse of the Soviet Union in 1991. The new evidence obtained by his lawyers cast sufficient doubt on his identification to overturn the conviction.

Demjanjuk returned to the United States and his family in 1993. His citizenship was reinstated in 1998. For awhile, it seemed that Demjanjuk's ordeal as an accused Nazi war criminal was over, but then new evidence and accusations came to light. In 2000, the Justice Department's Nazi-hunting unit re-opened the case, alleging that new documentary evidence positively identified Demjanjuk as a guard at the Sobibor prison camp and had independently corroborated his training at Trawniki. Demjanjuk's citizenship was again revoked, and he was deported to Germany to stand trial in 2009. At that time, he was eighty-nine years old and in failing health.

During all this time, Demjanjuk maintained his innocence, claiming he was the victim of mistaken identity and prosecutorial overzealousness. At the second trial, a lot of the same evidence was introduced, including the Nazi identification card which Demjanjuk's attorneys argued was a forgery. All of the eyewitnesses who had previously testified against Demjanjuk (i.e., identified him as Ivan the Terrible) were now deceased. However, the documentary evidence of his time at Sobibor and training at Trawniki was more conclusive. After a trial that lasted 18 months, in May of 2011 Demjanjuk was again convicted of being an accessory to over 28,000 deaths at Sobibor. This time, he was sentenced to five years in prison, but allowed to remain in a nursing home while his appeal was pending.

Demjanjuk's advanced age and failing health prompted both practical and humanitarian concerns about prosecuting otherwise law-abiding individuals for crimes committed during a war that had ended some 65 years ago. One of Demjanjuk's attorneys made the argument that most of the accused Nazi guards were lower-ranking privates and draftees—essentially "nobodies" in the Nazi chain of command—whose only function was to patrol the perimeter of concentration camps. Alternatively, the purpose of the war crimes trials was to send a message to the world that such behavior would not be tolerated and subject to appropriate consequences.

Demjanjuk died in a German nursing home at the age of 91. Although he had been temporarily freed to appeal his second conviction, he was not permitted to return to his family in the United States. His family and friends in Cleveland are adamant to this day that it is unthinkable that Demjanjuk did was he was accused of. Although Demjanjuk had been convicted in a legitimate court of law, many among those who knew him personally do not believe his guilt has been proven beyond a reasonable doubt.

Perhaps a more disturbing question than whether Demjanjuk is guilty or innocent is whether it is possible that both sides are correct. That is, was Demjanjuk essentially a decent, hard-working family man who had somehow been induced to perform atrocities against other human beings? If the answer to this question is affirmative, does it also not suggest that any of us might be capable of such acts under similar circumstances?

Obedience and Authority

As children growing up, we are taught—even conditioned—to obey. Obedience to parents, then teachers, then bosses---and ultimately, obedience to God—is usually framed as a behavioral and moral virtue. The problem with the obedience-as-a-virtue worldview is that it presumes the authority to whom we owe obedience is thoughtful, benevolent, and has the best interest of ourselves and the group in mind when issuing orders. Parents tell us to look both ways before crossing the street, teachers urge us to do our homework, bosses instruct us on how to do a better job, and God teaches us how to live as moral human beings. But what happens when we are ordered to do something bad—like, for instance, exploiting, torturing, or killing other humans? We may be deeply conflicted at the Hobson's choice between our internal moral standards and our behavioral conditioning of obedience.

A researcher in social psychology named Stanley Milgram (1933-1984) became famous for a series of experiments on obedience and authority that he conducted in the early 1960s. Milgram's parents were Jews who emigrated to America during World War I, so he took a keen interest in the history of the Nazi Holocaust and subsequent Nuremberg Trials of Nazi war criminals. As a researcher, he wanted to find answers, and he was particularly troubled by how many Holocaust perpetrators attempted to defend themselves by arguing that they were only following orders. Milgram wanted to know if it was possible that people could commit atrocities based on "following orders" without being in some way complicit themselves.

With this backdrop, Milgram designed his now famous experiments on obedience and authority. He recruited his participants through a newspaper advertisement, offering to pay

$4.00 (plus 50 cents for carfare) for one hour of time. In 1961, the hourly minimum wage had just been increased to $1.15, so adjusted for inflation, $4.00 in 1961 would have been worth about $33.00 today. Milgram's participants were all men, although he selected them to represent a range of age, education, and occupation. Some 37.5% were "skilled and unskilled" blue collar workers, another 40% were from sales, business, and white- collar occupations, and 22.5% were considered professionals. Ages ranged from 20 to 50 years (prime working-age adults).

The participants were told that the purpose of the experiment was to study the effects of punishment on learning. One participant would be assigned the role of "teacher" and another would be assigned to be the "learner," with roles to be determined by random drawing. However, unbeknownst to the real participants, their "partner" was one of Milgram's assistants, and the drawing was rigged so that the "partner" would always end up as the learner and the participant would be the teacher. A third individual represented the "researcher," and was the person who had ostensible authority over the study.

The partner-learner was then (in the presence of the participant-teacher) strapped to a machine that was designed to deliver an electric shock. Before the experiment started, the participant "teacher" was subjected to a 45-volt shock, purportedly to demonstrate the degree of real pain that would be administered. The participant "teacher" was then led into an adjoining room where he could no longer see the "learner," but could hear what was going on in the room. The participant was instructed to administer a series of simple memory tasks to read to the "learner." If the "learner" made a mistake, the participant was instructed to deliver an electric shock. Moreover, these shocks were to be increased by 15 volts each time the "learner" made a mistake.

The machine that was used in the experiments was calibrated to deliver a wide range of shocks: slight (15 to 60 volts), moderate (75 to 120 volts), strong (135 to 180 volts), very strong (195 to 240 volts), intense (255 to 300 volts), extremely intense (315 to 360 volts), severe/dangerous (375 to 420 volts) and fatal (435 and 450 volts). All of these shock levels were marked on the machine used by the participants, so there was no ambiguity about the level of "punishment." Before the experiment started, Milgram and his colleagues predicted that 15% of participants would defect (quit the experiment) at 75 volts, 86% would defect at 210 volts, 96% would defect at 300 volts, and only a "pathological fringe" (less than 1%) would remain to deliver the full 450 volt shock. The "learner," of course, received no such shocks, but had prepared an audio recording of pre-scripted sounds for each purported "shock" delivered by the participant. At first, the learner would say nothing, then grunt quietly, then louder, then gradually segue into screaming, begging for the experiment to stop, hysterical cries of "let me out of here," then finally falling silent at the highest voltages. During the experiment, the person in the role of the researcher (who was sitting behind the participant at the controls) would urge the participant to continue, emphasizing the necessity of finishing the experiment.

To Milgram's own surprise, none of the participants defected until the 300 volt level, at which point only 12.5% abandoned the experiment. Most of the rest continued to the end, with 65% staying to deliver the full 450 volts. Some of the participants were visibly uncomfortable, and a few questioned the "researcher" about who was responsible if any harm came to the "learner." Milgram also found variations on willingness to continue the shocks. Participants' willingness to administer increasing shocks decreased when the teacher had to physically place the learner's hand on a shock plate, suggesting that physical distance (or out of sight) might operate to decrease sensitivity to the pain of another. Another variation involved physical surroundings: When the experiment took place in a non-descript office building rather than in Yale's traditional hallowed halls, the willingness to deliver the maximum shock dropped to 47.5%, suggesting that an aura of prestige induced a higher level of obedience. The highest shock level participation rate dropped even further to 2.5% when the participants could determine the level of shock themselves, rather than having it dictated as part of the experiment.

Milgram published a paper on his experiments in the October 1963 *Journal of Abnormal and Social Psychology,* claiming that he had found a possible explanation for the Holocaust. Milgram expanded his findings into a full book, the 1974 *Obedience to*

Authority: An Experimental View, which became a bestseller. Today, the Milgram experiments are a foundational classic for students of psychology, and are often part of sociology curriculum as well. Milgram's theory has been used to explain American military atrocities in Vietnam, and more recently at the Abu Ghraib prison in Iraq.

An Australian investigative journalist named Gina Perry did not believe that records of Milgram's experiments told the whole story.[3] She reviewed archives of Milgram's research and followed up with some of the surviving participants. Indeed, some of them expressed doubts about the reality they were observing, alleging that the voice responses of the "learner" seemed to be coming from a loudspeaker high on a wall rather than the location where the learner was purported to be. Others claimed that the individuals posing as the head "researchers" did not always stick to the script, but resorted to bullying and harassment to enforce obedience. Moreover, Milgram altered the variables in each round, conducting some 24 different scenarios (location, number of other learners and teachers, behavior of the authority figure, etc), making it difficult to parse cause and effect.

Perry also charges Milgram with confirmation bias: that is, he attributed willingness to continue increasing shocks solely to obedience and not to other possible motives, such as general social conformity or a willingness to help science. Yet, Milgram certainly had no personal motive to find a scientific reason to absolve the guilt of Nazi perpetrators as a case of "just following orders." The biggest criticism of Milgram's experiments was that the participants were not properly debriefed when the experiment concluded, causing some of them anger, distress, and mental anguish. One participant reported checking the death notices in the New Haven paper for two weeks following the experiment. Although the Milgram experiments were one of the most famous in psychology, they forced the research establishment to institute changes in procedures involving the ethical treatment of participants, along with requirements for more rigorous methodologies.

More recent attempts have been made to replicate (as nearly as possible) Milgram's experiment under more modernized research guidelines. A study done in 2009 by Jerry Burger at Santa Clara University,[4] and a 2017 study by researchers in Poland[5] basically corroborate Milgram's findings. In both of these studies, the maximum amount of shock was limited. In neither of these modern re-creations were any of the fake "shocks" fatal. Participants were told on more than one occasion that they could withdraw from the experiment at any time (an option not given to Milgram's participants). This provision was also included in a written, signed consent form. In Burger's experiment, 70% made it past the 150 volt mark. In the Polish experiment, 90% were willing to give the highest level shock (a ten—the Milgram experiment had 30 levels). Additionally, participants were deliberately selected who were determined to be "psychologically healthy." That is, they were not individuals who had identifiable psychopathic tendencies.

Although Milgram's experiments had ethical and methodological shortcomings, nearly every subsequent experiment has basically confirmed his original findings. This is particularly disturbing, since we can imagine how much these effects would be exaggerated if the "punishment" was to be meted out on an individual who belonged to a demonized out-group, and/or the participant was out-group intolerant. Such a situation would also likely be worse if the participants (those administering the punishment) were not psychologically healthy, but had latent sociopathic tendencies. In other words, a generalized willingness to obey would make things bad enough, and if the one obeying the orders had anti-social tendencies or pathologies of his own, Milgram's phenomenon would be greatly increased.

Perhaps the biggest contribution of Milgram's experiment is that it expanded the study of bad behavior beyond the explanation of individual hereditary traits, temperament and personal pathologies. That is, the bad behavior of others (orders or threat), environmental exigencies (i.e. survival) and even cultural expectations and ideologies can all impact behavioral choices. This is not a simplistic matter of excusing bad behavior because "the devil made me do it," but a recognition of the more complex impact of social relationships on behavioral choices.

Social Roles and Expectations

Following up on Milgram's experiment, in 1971 a group of psychologists at Stanford University led by Phillip Zimbardo set up a mock prison setting in the basement of Stanford's psychology department.[6] The researchers were prison reform advocates, and they wanted to have a better understanding of how much prisoner problem behavior was attributed to the prisoners themselves and how much was a result of the prison environment. Their theory was that behavior is influenced as much by situational roles (guards versus inmates, prison regulations, etc.) as it is by individual personality types.

In the Stanford prison experiment, the participants were also all male and somewhat more homogeneous than the participants in Milgram's experiment. Zimbardo recruited college students from all across the United States, subjecting them to a battery of tests to ensure that the students were mentally and physically normal, healthy and well-adjusted. The students were then randomly assigned to play the part of either prisoner or guard. Zimbardo expected the students to fall into stereotypical roles, behaving in a way that was required rather than using their own independent judgment (analogous to the Milgram experiments on obedience). Although the experiment was planned to last two weeks, it had to be terminated by the sixth day because the ensuing behavioral changes were so swift, extreme and unanticipated.

Zimbardo's experiment was different in that it analyzed behavior changes in both those who were giving orders and those who were expected to obey. Zimbardo made every attempt to make the prison scenario as realistic as possible, to help participants get into their roles rather than thinking that the activity was only an "experimental" exercise. The Palo Alto police even helped lend realism to the experiment by actually "arresting" the students selected to be prisoners, reading them their rights, taking their mug shots, and leading them to their cells. The "guards" were given military-style uniforms, wood batons, and mirrored sunglasses (to prevent eye contact). The "prisoners" were dressed in cheap smocks, not allowed to even have underwear, and wore a small chain around their ankles. During their stay in the converted Stanford basement facility, the "prisoners" slept on basic mattresses, were given subsistence food, and were to be addressed and identified by their assigned numbers only.

The guards were given no specific instructions other than to run the prison and keep order as they saw fit. Very quickly, the guards began to subject the prisoners to various forms of minor punishment and humiliation. The exertion of control was manifested mainly during the "prisoner counts" that were done at the beginning of every shift. The prisoners were ordered to memorize a list of rules and then repeat them back quickly, sing silly songs, count backwards, and do any number of seemingly innocuous activities that had no purpose. If these acts were not performed to the satisfaction of the guards (based on completely arbitrary and ever-changing standards), the prisoners were punished with exercise. Each night, the prisoners were roused out of bed for a 2:00 am shift change and prisoner count, which meant that they never received a good night's sleep. The guards were especially brutal with the prisoners when they were alone (toilet runs) or during late night and early morning shifts, when the guards believed they were not being observed or recorded. Moreover, the abuse escalated every day, even though the prisoners were mostly nonresistant.

As some of the prisoners began to show signs of distress, they organized a mass revolt on the second day. The guards broke up the riot using fire extinguishers, and then really began to crack down. Daily roll call became an exercise in ritual humiliation, mattresses were confiscated, forced exercise and physical punishment became more common, and access to toilet facilities was now a privilege instead of a right. Punishment took the form of forced exercise, the loss of some comfort or privilege, scrubbing toilets with their hands, or spending time in a solitary closet space both prisoners and guards called "the Hole." The guards also instituted a form of divide and conquer: When one prisoner went on a hunger strike in protest, the guards would punish the other prisoners, with the expectation that the other prisoners would turn against the offender and enforce compliance. Indeed, the protesting prisoner was viewed by his fellows as a troublemaker rather than an ally.

Observing this behavior, Zimbardo began to wonder if the pre-experiment psychological screenings had missed some latent pathologies. In part to resemble activity in a real prison and in part to keep the participants minimally sane, the experimenters arranged for outside visits with friends and family. However, the possibility of visitors became another way the guards exercised control by deciding who could or could not have visitors. During the mock prison "visits," Zimbardo also expressed surprise at how compliant parents, friends and girlfriends were with the rules, even when they had questions about the welfare of their "prisoner" loved one based on observed physical and behavioral changes.

At the very beginning of the experiment, all participants were told that they were free to leave at any time. Although two of the prisoners had to be removed because they were showing signs of psychological disintegration, none of the prisoners even considered leaving the experiment early. The first prisoner to break down was an anti-war activist who had actually wanted to be assigned to the role of prisoner, since he anticipated that his activism would likely lead to jail time in real life. In a later debriefing, one of the guards remarked that "we (the guards) were as much as prisoner as they were…We were both crushed by the situation of oppressiveness, but we guards had the illusion of freedom." This guard also alluded to all of them being "slaves to the money," with the prisoners also being slaves the guards. Given that these were college students and "the money" was payment (although good, it was not life-changing) for only two weeks of participation, one can only imagine the effect if "the money" was dependent on a livelihood.

In some respects, Zimbardo's experiment was a success, in that it had created a sense of reality around the prison experience. In debriefings at the end of the experiment, almost everyone said they had stopped thinking about the experience as an experiment and had internalized their roles. The prisoners began to focus inwardly on their own survival, in essence "hiding themselves," which thwarted any sense of solidarity or strategic group action against their oppression. One of the guards admitted to intentionally shutting off his feelings toward the prisoners, losing all sympathy and respect for them in order to perform his duties in keeping order. When Zimbardo declared an early end to the experiment, another guard said he was both glad and shocked, because some of the other guards seemed to be enjoying it. Even Zimbardo himself confesses to being "caught up" in his role as the prison superintendent, which distorted his judgment. He admits that the need to terminate the experiment should have been apparent as soon as "the second normal, heathy participant suffered an emotional breakdown."[7]

While the Stanford experiment was going on, Zimbardo's fiancé (who would later become his wife) received her Ph.D. in social psychology. On the sixth day of an experiment that was supposed to last two weeks, Zimbardo's fiancé was brought in as another researcher, to interview both the guards and the prisoners. Although she had heard about the experiment, she was unaware of the details. When she witnessed one of the prisoner "counts" and how the prisoners were treated during bathroom visits, she confronted Zimbardo and convinced him to terminate the experiment. Nearly one-third of the guards had begun to show signs of overt sadism. Conversely, the prisoners had become "institutionalized," unable to assert their own humanity in response to the injustices against them.

In retrospect, Zimbardo remarks that—even with its early termination—the experiment had proven his theory. If anything, situational stressors as an inducement to sociopathic behavior are even more powerful than Zimbardo initially realized. First, all of the participants were students who came of age in the culture of the late 1960s and early 1970s, with its emphasis on rebellion and the rejection of authority and conformity. This suggests that these effects would be magnified in today's more authoritarian culture. Second, the prisoners were college students who literally had done nothing to deserve what they were experiencing, which suggests that guilt-induced submissive behavior might be aggravated among actual offenders. Third, Zimbardo himself acknowledges how even someone with his education, training and experience can succumb to these effects: "In the past week, I had gradually morphed into a Prison Authority Figure…I became one of *them*—the authority figure…that I have opposed, even detested, all my life—the high-status, authoritarian, overbearing boss man."[8] Finally, to some degree the induced effects extended to others who were not part of the experiment, either as prisoners, guards, or researchers. Although at least 50 other "outside" people had visited the experiment while it was going on, only Zimbardo's future wife raised concerns about what was happening.

Like the Milgram experiments, the ethics of the Stanford prison experiment were later called into question. Today, such experiments are subject to the oversight of Institutional Review Boards, who are highly conscious of potential physical or psychological harm to participants. Others argue that "real" prisons are subject to laws, regulations, and even Constitutional mandates against cruel and unusual punishment, so such a scenario is not likely in the non-experimental real world. However, what the experiment demonstrated is how the behavior of even normal, decent people can be changed (even radically so) based on situational exigencies and social expectations. Perhaps more chilling than the emergent sadism of the guards was the total acquiescence of the prisoners, who seemed to regard themselves as less than human once stripped of all semblance of individuality and dignity. In essence, participants on both sides abandoned their internal moral compass, with the outcome-determining manifestation depending upon which side of the hierarchical power divide they found themselves.

Zimbardo's research as a prison reform advocate led to him being called as an expert witness for one of the soldiers charged in the Abu Ghraib scandal. We will cover Abu Ghraib (and Zimbardo's analysis of it) in the following section. For now, Zimbardo has identified for us some of the specific mechanisms which lead to dehumanizing behavior. Perhaps the most effective ways of discouraging persons from seeing someone as human is to establish processes of anonymizing (prisoners given numbers) and deindividuation (which reduces personal accountability). When the "other" is dehumanized, they are believed to be without the same feelings, thoughts, values, and purpose in life as "we" have. "Dehumanized relationships are objectifying, analytical, and empty of emotional or empathic content."[9]

A second factor is our need, as social beings, to be part of the in-group. Because of this, authorities can command total obedience not simply through conventional punishments and rewards, but by means of offering acceptance coupled with the threat of rejection.[10]

An environmental factor—which has been backed up by other research—was the distorted time perspective created by long shifts and lack of sleep. "Endless routines and undifferentiated daily activities create a seeming circularity of time."[11]

What can we conclude from this research? It might be easy to say that human beings are either inherently evil or inherently weak. That is, even good people can be easily induced to harm others if they are simply told (or even simply expected) to do so by someone in apparent authority. Most of us would likely argue that we ourselves would do no such thing, that we would be the exception to the rule. Zimbardo suggests that his own experience refutes this comforting illusion. The findings from Milgram's obedience experiments and the Stanford prison experiment are even more troublesome when analyzed in the context of a corrupt leadership or a corrupt system. As more bad people attain positions of power, there are more bad orders to be followed and more perverted ideologies to justify them, resulting in more bad deeds committed by otherwise good people. The choice to obey or resist itself becomes even more problematic when most of the good people occupy power-subordinate positions.

Notes

[1] Zimbardo, P. (2007). *The Lucifer effect.* New York, NY: Random House Publishing Group at p. 445.

[2] Some of these dynamics are discussed in *Why Assholes Rule the World,* VanHettinga (2019).

[3] Perry, G. (2012). *Behind the shock machine: The untold story of the notorious Milgram psychology experiments.* New York, NY: The New Press.

[4] Burger, J. (2009). Replicating Milgram: Would people still obey today? *Am. Psychol. 64*(1), 1-11.

[5] Dolinski, D., Grzyb, T., Folwarczny, M., Grzybala, P.,, Krzyszycha, K., Martynowska, K. & Trojanowski, J. (2017). *Would you deliver an electric shock in 2015? Obedience in the experimental paradigm developed by Stanley Milgram in the 50 years following the original studies.* http://bw.swps.edu.pl/info/article/SWPS11d3b474ae9645478a524865bd640207/Would+You+Deliver+an+Electric+Shock+in+2015%253F+Obedience+in+the+Experimental+Paradigm+Developed+by+Stanley+Milgram+in+the+50+Years+Following+the+Original+Studies

[6] Zimbardo, P.G., Haney, C., Banks, W.C., & Jaffe, D. (1973, April 8). The mind is a formidable jailer: A Pirandelian prison. *The New York Times Magazine.* See also Zimbardo, P.G. (1971). The power and pathology of imprisonment. *Congressional Record.* (Serial No., 15, October 25, 1971). Hearings before Subcommittee No, 3 of the Committee on the Judiciary, House of Representatives, Ninety-Second Congress, *First Session on Corrections, Part II, Prisons, Prison Reform and Prisoner's Rights: California.* Washington, D.C.: U.S. Government Printing Office.

[7] Zimbardo, P. (2007). *Supra* at p. 179.

[8] *Id.* at p. 180.

[9] *Id.* at pp. 222-223. At the lower end of the dehumanization scale, this is how many of us are viewed in our workplaces—as fungible inputs that can be used up, discarded, exchanged or replaced, and whose only purpose is to serve the accumulation of (someone else's) profit.

[10] Zimbardo, P. (2007). *Supra* at p. 259.

[11] *Id.* at p. 244.

Section 5
Administrative Evil: When Systems Go Bad

The common characteristic of administrative evil is that ordinary people within their normal professional and administrative roles, can engage in acts of evil without being aware that they are doing anything wrong.

Guy Adams

One can make the argument that systems or institutions cannot *ipso facto* be evil, because—unlike individuals—systems are amoral constructs that are incapable of forming evil intent. However, systems can operate to facilitate evil, even when their purpose may be wholly innocuous or even benevolent. This can occur through several pathways. One is when antisocial (or sociopathological) individuals occupy leadership positions or otherwise gain control over institutions, thereby manipulating them to serve an ulterior agenda. Another way that systems or institutions can become dysfunctional is when they grow so large and diffuse that most of the individuals living and working within them are only aware of their own narrow functional role, so few are able to see the bigger picture. A third form of dysfunction occurs when certain values operate to override others, e.g., when efficiency (or profit) is pursued above all else such that collateral damage is either not measured nor causally connected with the institution's activities.

Max Weber (1864-1920) was a German sociologist and political scientist, who, along with Woodrow Wilson, is known as an important founder in the modern field of public administration. Weber is also known for being an architect of the bureaucratic model of organization. Weber's lifespan occurred during a period of history when the size of organizations—both in business and government—was expanding significantly. In business, the mom-and-pop family farms and businesses were being replaced by the modern corporation, which presented challenges in how to manage work in these larger and more dispersed organizations. During this time the national government was expanding more slowly, but it was run by a form of "spoils" system, where elected officials appointed their supporters and cronies to civil service jobs. Weber developed his "theory of bureaucracy" as a way to manage large organizations (both business and government) through a hierarchical system of rules, meritocracy, impersonal authority and political neutrality. That is, rationalized structures were designed to replace fallible (and potentially corrupt) human judgment. The objective was to impose efficiency and control as well as to eliminate favoritism and cronyism, resulting in institutions that were better able to serve their purpose (public service or profit). Weber, predicted that "the future belonged to bureaucratization…[or] domination through knowledge."

In his later years, Weber changed his opinion about the benefits of bureaucratic structures. The irony is that bureaucracy was supposed to create a rational "scientific" system of neutral rules and professionalism. Rules that applied equally to everyone and assignment to tasks or positions based on expertise were intended to eliminate favoritism and cronyism. Yet, hyper-rationalized systems often produced irrational results. A focus on quantity and efficiency tended to overlook considerations of quality. People had to serve the system rather than exercise their independent judgment, which alienated them from their work. At work, bureaucratization created "specialists without spirit," which then carried over to home and community life, creating "hedonists without heart." According to Weber, bureaucracy had the potential to trap individuals in an iron cage, where they can see no way out of serving a system that is serving neither them nor the rest of society in return.[1]

Post-Weberian writers complain of a rationalized technocracy, with its sole focus on efficiency and control at the expense of other values, especially the loss of any kind of moral foundations. George Ritzer has named this process *McDonaldization:*[2] Professional McDoctors and McLawyers continue to provide high levels of technical expertise, but they have lost their higher functions as healers, counselors and advocates for justice. Today, professionals also largely serve corporations or government agencies rather than operating as independents, and so have adopted these mindsets. For non-professional workers, dead-end, meaningless *Bullshit Jobs*[3] have replaced purposeful work that binds people to their community. On the home front, fast food has replaced the gathering of family and friends for meals. Pornography has replaced sex. "Likes" and "followers" have replaced genuine friendships. This goes beyond Guinness' complaints about banishing religion from the public square, but rather suggests that we have lost our moral compass entirely and do not even realize it.

In the field of public administration, well-meaning researchers are expanding their attention to ethics and corruption. However, such research tends to focus on either individual personality characteristics or rules of control. A recent meta-analytic review of ethics research found seven primary factors that impact ethical behavior in public service.[4] Greed and egocentrism are personality characteristics that originate within the individual. The desire to maintain a positive self-image (self-view and self-justification) are internal psychological processes that individuals may use to justify unethical behavior. Monitoring and moral reminders are internal rules, procedures, and customs that an organization can develop to reduce unethical behavior. The seventh—social influences—operates outside both the individual and the organization, to include the effects of the broader social culture. These broader social influences—which are the least definable and understood—can alter individual behavior in either direction (either ethical or unethical).

Not surprisingly, a meta-analysis of 26 independent experiments found a significant positive effect of greed on individual unethical behavior.[5] However, even greed is not necessarily a fixed character trait, but can be influenced by the environment: Greed can be triggered by perceptions of unfair treatment[6] and even the mere presence of abundant wealth without any input-to-output (i.e. fairness) inequities.[7] It is not difficult to imagine the temptation presented to a newly-elected congressperson when confronted by armies of lobbyists in $4,000 suits paying for $500 lunches to gain his or her ear. Greed-based unethical behavior can thus be triggered in individuals either to restore fairness/balance the equities, or to maintain egoic "standards" in an environment of extreme wealth.

In addition to greed, egocentrism was another phenomenon that research has established a positive correlation with unethical behavior. Egocentrism is the extent to which individuals define themselves by their unique traits and independence from others. These individuals often fit the economist's definition of the utility maximizer (the rational *homo economicus)* whose main objective is to maximize their own benefits or position while having no concern about the effects their actions have on others. Such individuals are less likely to question whether their behavior violates social norms and have less stringent moral standards.[8]

Our personalities are shaped by our position within social hierarchies as much as they are by inherited behaviors and social conditioning. Whether we ourselves are members of an in-group or an out-group, we generally attempt to emulate the behaviors and mannerisms of the in-group. Social identity theory predicts that individuals will abide by rules that provide them an opportunity to enhance their in-group standing. Because individuals want to identify with the in-group, unethical behavior is more likely if persons in the organization observe unethical behavior from a member of an in-group versus an outgroup.[9] In addition to approval from in-groups, most people also desire to maintain a positive self-concept. Thus they will be motivated to create the impression that they are good and ethical persons, and such intrinsic motivation can serve as a check on unethical behavior.[10] Social identity theory also predicts that individuals will do the right thing if it is also valued by the in-group (or by those in the hierarchy with the power to mete out reward or punishment).[11]

Organizations can reduce the likelihood of unethical behavior through systems of monitoring and moral reminders. In the case of public agencies, monitoring often takes the form of transparency, or making agency information (especially where it concerns finance and budgets) available to the public. Moral reminders usually take the form of codes of conduct and formalized ethics training. Yet codes of conduct and training are not panaceas: while such "moral reminder" systems have increased significantly in both public and private organizations, unethical conduct continues to be a problem. Even the infamous Enron had had an ethics code and other aspects of a formal program—including banners proclaiming "Respect" and

"Integrity" prominently displayed in the Enron lobby as late as October of 2001.[12]

Ironically, individuals may also rationalize unethical behavior that is based on prosocial motivation, particularly if it also creates benefits for others.[13] For example, some international college students who have grown up in more communitarian cultures have trouble understanding the concept of cheating, because in their view giving someone an answer on a test is regarded as helping a friend. Such behavior is the essence of cronyism, which is based on a (usually) prosocial concept of reciprocal obligation, but also violates rules on hiring and meritocracy. This also happens when street level bureaucrats or case managers deliberately circumvent rules in order to help their clients because, in their opinion, application of the rules would result in unfair outcomes.[14]

These researchers admit that experiments performed in controlled laboratory settings, while helpful to establish cause-and-effect relationships, are nonetheless inadequate to capture the complexities of reality in the "field." They advocate for future research to establish causal connection between leadership and unethical behavior of followers, particularly the effect of corrupt politicians on career civil servants. However, keeping corruption out of public administration involves more than selecting the right individuals (screened for traits such as greed and egocentrism) or exercising control by means of rules and ethical codes. As we saw in the Stanford prison experiments, the situation, or environment can create moral hazard. Indeed, some research suggests that bureaucratic structure itself can facilitate evil, creating situations where professional civil servants perpetrate evil in the course of performing their duties.

Administrative Evil

Professors Guy Adams (University of Missouri) and Danny Balfour (Grand Valley State University, MI) have written extensively on what they call "administrative evil."[15] Where Zimbardo focused his research on the pressures that drive otherwise good people to do bad things, Adams and Balfour examine how ordinary people facilitate evil by simply fulfilling their occupational roles. In this situation, individuals are not directly engaging in bad behavior, but facilitate evil acts in the process of doing their routine jobs and serving the system. Adams and Balfour argue that at some (indeterminate) point one can no longer ignore the evil consequences, thus giving rise to a duty to act. Once the evil is "unmasked," individuals can no longer justifiably plead ignorance and hide behind the "just doing my job" excuse. When morally responsible persons become aware of bad acts or bad outcomes, they are now obligated to question their continued support of the system.

Adams and Balfour define "evil" as something that causes real harm to real people who do not deserve it, or creates unjust outcomes that involve pain and suffering. The basic premise of their argument is that often such evil is "masked," or unseen. Because modern organizations are characterized by division of labor, role specialization and compartmentalization, where responsibility is ambiguous or diffused, individuals are often unaware of the remote consequences of their actions. That is, well-intentioned individuals employed in a bureaucratic organization can participate in harmful activity while being completely unaware of it (or perhaps, willfully blind to it). Adams and Balfour describe how "ordinary Germans fulfilling ordinary roles" may have unknowingly participated in Holocaust atrocities: for example, employees of the German Rail Authority transporting Jews to death camps.

Administrative evil is easier to identity from a distance and in hindsight—when it occurred in another time and place. Like many others who have studied systemic evil, Adams and Balfour cite the Nazi Holocaust as the most frequently used case example. Here, we have a totalitarian state which was maintained by terror (SS and Gestapo) and propaganda as well as by more legitimate activities of legislation and public administration. They argue that the large-scale killing of innocent human beings could not have been accomplished by the actions of those who planned the overt acts, but were made possible by the complicity of an army of professional civil servants, public administrators and municipal authorities who were only doing their jobs. Even the notorious SS officers carried out their duties within a framework of responsibility and following rules.

Administrative evil does not necessarily involve death or genocide, but can operate to subvert democratic values. In the American liberal democracy, the attention is focused on civil liberties, voting, procedural fairness (i.e., due process) and evidence-based (technical-rational) policy formulation. Adams and Balfour argue that the combination of technical rationality and cultural individualism thwart the development of a "public service ethics."[16] We view ourselves as independent "free" agents, but the reality is that we spend the majority of our lives "navigating bureaucratic structures, manipulating and being manipulated by others."[17] Democracy itself is subverted when governing is dictated by technocratic experts and not "the people."

Adams and Balfour argue that some of the evil of Nazi Germany was assimilated into the United States in exchange for technical expertise. Mittelbau-Dora was a slave labor factory and subcamp of Buchenwald, responsible for manufacturing the V-2 rocket and other munitions. Slavic people, like Jews, were considered as subhuman, and provided most of the shop floor labor in the beginning, although they were later joined by Jews and political prisoners. It is estimated that around 20,000 Mittelbau workers died due to a combination of unclean conditions, inadequate rations, beatings, and intentional killings. Mittelbau was liberated by U.S. troops in 1945, and the U.S. made a deal with some of the engineers and scientists who provided the technical expertise behind Nazi rocket science.

The most well-known of these scientists, Werner von Braun and Arthur Rudolph, were secretly brought into the United States through Operation Overcast and Operation Paperclip. Von Braun had formerly served as the technical director of the Nazi V-2 rocket program. He had visited the Mittelwork slave labor manufacturing facility at least a dozen times, so it is hard to believe that he had no idea what was going on. As they had done to the slave labor in Mittelbau, these former Nazi scientists and engineers were put to good use in serving the Saturn V program, a primary component of the Apollo mission, including the first moon landing in 1969. Von Braun was made director of the newly created Marshall Space Flight Center in 1960, and he went on to become a well-known public figure in American history. Conversely, Rudolph later voluntarily left the US in 1984, after signing an admission of guilt before the Office of Special Investigations. Although the U.S. Army classified much of von Braun's Nazi history, von Braun eventually admitted he had been a member of the National Socialist Party, with the justification that it was both a career necessity and a "nominal" part of his professional identity. Adams and Balfour argue that "in the narrow pursuit of technical superiority, [the United States] made a Faustian bargain with administrative evil; we now find that evil sullying our nation's single greatest technical achievement, the moon landing."[18]

In the next example of administrative evil, Adams and Balfour move us away from Nazis, but we remain with the American space program. Fast forward to the January 28, 1986 space shuttle Challenger explosion. Here, we find the analogy to evil somewhat more tenuous. Certainly, seven blameless astronauts lost their lives, but surely a technical malfunction—no matter how tragic the outcome—should not be considered evil. However, what Adams and Balfour argue is that it was not the malfunction itself, but the fact that the O-ring problem was preventable. Indeed, two NASA contractors had recommended against launching.

Adams and Balfour argue that NASA directors had a pattern and practice of containing potentially serious problems. After the Apollo program was discontinued, NASA had been decentralized. Now there were three space centers: Johnson (Houston, TX), Marshall (Huntsville, AL) and Kennedy (Cape Canaveral, Florida). This split aggravated competition and divisions between the three centers in an environment where resources were unstable and declining. Although the original German scientists were long gone from the space program, they had passed along a "defensive" organizational culture, which had now grown autocratic and "persecutory." Dr. William Lucas, the director of Marshall since 1974, was known to criticize performance in open meetings and demanded absolute personal loyalty. Engineers were expected to stay on top of every technical detail and to meet every deadline. Everyone was on notice that under no circumstances would Marshall be responsible for delaying a launch. Because perfection is nearly impossible, employees were in the habit of covering mistakes and telling management what it wanted to hear. Thus, it was inevitable that a technical malfunction would be allowed to happen because no one would speak out about potential problems.

Administrative evil is not limited to governments and public administration. Indeed, the modern corporation—with its narrow and short-term focus on profit maximization—is likely to be even more susceptible to administrative evil. We are familiar with cases where a corporation made a rational decision to continue an activity that was dangerous, toxic, or carcinogenic because fixing the problem would cost more than paying off the occasional lawsuit. These types of calculations often include assigning value to a human life, which is then measured against various risk algorithms and corporate balance sheets. One can well imagine that, in the closed-door meetings that decide such things, concerns may be raised about costs and bad publicity, but it is unlikely that anyone thinks to address the obvious moral issues.

One of the most infamous recent business cases of administrative evil was the boom and collapse of Enron. We can easily place the blame on the executives who were found guilty of securities fraud and other criminal conduct involving dishonesty and moral turpitude: Ken Lay, Jeff Skilling and Andy Fastow.[19] However, these executives did not work alone, as Enron was comprised of a small army of accountants, traders and other employees. Perhaps Enron employees should have done more—both to investigate the illegal activity, and/or take steps to stop it. Yet, it is not clear at what point a duty to investigate or take action arises, and this moral duty is likely attenuated based on an individual's position and distance from the sources of power.[20]

In a more chilling turn, Adams and Balfour then raise the issue of what they call "surplus populations." Surplus populations are defined as populations that can find no viable role in the society in which they are domiciled.[21] They argue that history presents many examples of people who are "rendered permanently superfluous [and] eventually condemned to segregated precincts of the living dead or are exterminated outright."[22] This process is grounded in the moral purity foundation, where those who are "not us" are cut off from their traditional livelihoods and forced into ghettoized neighborhoods or reservations, where they are then accused of being freeloaders. When the neighborhoods themselves become run-down or crime-invested, the moral purity foundation is activated; the neighborhoods are described as blighted, and the people therein compared to vermin. The next step is "eliminationist" programs that are designed to address the problems created by surplus populations and ghettoization. These programs operate along a continuum, with the most innocuous likely being gentrification and the most egregious genocide.

Many of us like to believe that genocide could never happen in the United States. Although there is our shameful history of slavery, the treatment of Indigenous populations, and internment of Japanese-Americans during World War II, we like to think that we have learned our lesson and such atrocities are not going to happen here again. Yet today we see increasing migration of populations due to both geopolitical conflict and climate change. As people are forced to move in search of subsistence and safety, they create pressure on native populations, especially those who are already precariatized themselves. This pressure then manifests as eliminationist policies; e.g., the building of walls to keep people out and deportation. "In this era of increasingly ideological and polarized politics and unwanted surplus populations, public administration should not be taught, practiced or theorized about without considering the psychological, organizational, and societal dynamics that can lead public servants to confound the public interest with acts of dehumanization and destruction."[23]

Adams and Balfour argue that administrative evil arises in part due to a lack of historical consciousness, or denial of the past. If something has failed in the past it is because it was not sufficiently rational. The proposed solution then, is "more and better planning, and more efficient, controlled systems that will preclude messy aberrations… The lack of historical consciousness is virtually an open invitation to administrative evil… The linking of technical rationality and morality not only leads to frustration with failed solutions to social problems; it also can set the stage for administrative evil because rational programming in human affairs inevitably entails some degree of dehumanization and often involves restrictions on the political rights of those affected."[24] In the technocratic mind, we could possibly solve our crime and drug "problems" by allowing police to search everyone, everywhere and seize anything without the need for warrants or probable cause. We can solve the problem of hate speech and disinformation by censoring it. That is, abandon Constitutional rights and freedoms in exchange for control and social order.

The ultimate shortcoming in a modern technocratic society is the abandonment of the language of evil, as it is incompatible with the scientific-analytic mind. Professionalization, or legitimacy from specialized knowledge, is disconnected from context, particularly larger ethical social concerns. Trends toward "reinventing" government so that it operates more like a business, along with the outsourcing of public functions, have served to disconnect ethical theory from practice,[25] as well as subvert democratic processes. We do not speak of evil, therefore we do not see it unless and until its effects are so egregious that we can no longer ignore it. The extreme version of masked administrative evil is a moral inversion, in which something evil is redefined as something good—a process we will cover more fully in Part IV. In today's "culture of technical rationality [that] has analytically narrowed the processes by which public policy is formulated and implemented,"[26] Adams and Balfour propose that moral inversions are more likely.

The System Responds: Mental Health Courts in Florida

One of the biggest footprints of rationality over the past several decades has been the cult of austerity. Austerity as public policy probably had its origins in the Reagan era, beginning with the 1978 California anti-tax Proposition 13. The fundamental premise of austerity is to do more with less.[27] Although early proponents of austerity were primarily concerned with reducing deficits and shrinking the public sphere, austerity grew into a favored panacea for almost any situation. While the concept of austerity may initially appeal to a certain logic, one need only conduct a thought experiment about what the compounding effect of "doing more with less" year after year, would look like. Indeed, many of us are experiencing this in our workplaces, and we are paying the price in the form of exhaustion, burnout, frayed relationships, and decreased trust. This generalized austerity became even more acute during the so-called Great Recession (officially in America December 2007 to June 2009).

As a member of the Florida Bar (now inactive) during the post-Great Recession period, I was privy to much lamentation about lack of funding for the courts and its impact on the administration of justice. Ironically, austerity policies arose around the same time period as tough-on-crime policies; i.e. stringent sentencing guidelines for non-violent drug offenses and "three strikes and you're out" laws. The result of this was that caseloads for public attorneys in the criminal justice systems of many states were becoming unsustainable. In addition to the right to a speedy trial, the U.S. Constitution requires the state to provide "competent" legal representation for indigent persons charged with a criminal offense. The National Legal Aid and Defender Society says that 150 felony cases per attorney per year is the upper limit for an attorney to adequately handle a felony representation. Yet, in many jurisdictions, public defenders are being assigned upwards of 500-800 cases, in some instances as high as 1,600.[28] This results in so-called "meet-and-greet" guilty pleas in which the attorney has barely gotten to know the client, let alone investigate the case. In Florida (as in other states), public defenders protested in the state legislature about the need for increased funding. One Florida Supreme Court opinion went so far as to call the situation "unconstitutional."[29]

In 2006, before the Great Recession, a former Florida Chief Justice of the Supreme Court ordered a study on mental health in the Florida justice system. The study found that 61% of the 2.8 million Floridians with serious mental health issues received no treatment.[30] Over 140,000 persons with mental health issues were arrested every year, with many of them cycling in and out of the criminal justice system. That is, these persons were being housed in jails and prisons, yet not receiving the kind of care needed to address their underlying problems. Although the "normal" prison population was stabilizing in Florida, someone figured out that it would cost $10 billion to accommodate mentally ill inmates over the next 10 years (primarily costs of building new prisons). So…some smart people had the idea to create specialized mental-illness courts, whose purpose would be to get the kind of help for mentally ill defendants that would allow them to stay out of the criminal justice system.

Broward county established one of the first of such courts in the country.[31] These courts would involve a forensic psychologist as well as specially trained judges, prosecution and defense attorneys. Mentally ill defendants would also have access to a benefits specialist, who would help them with both treatment and subsistence issues like housing. Other Florida counties began training police officers in crisis intervention. As data on these new programs came in, there was a dramatic reduction in both arrests and recidivism rates: Recidivism for misdemeanors was down from 72% to 20%, and for felonies went down to 25%. The $10,000 cost averages for these new programs also compared favorably to the cost for about three months of jail time and one month in an inpatient mental health facility.[32]

This example shows that a rationalized technocratic system can and will do the right thing when continuing business as usual becomes too costly or obviously dysfunctional. However, where was the moral outcry about the propriety of jailing mentally ill people? We have seen from the Stanford prison experiments that such environments aggravate mental health issues, even among otherwise mentally healthy persons. Yes, there was likely a small group of mental health and prisoner rights advocates pushing for change, but nothing was done until the capacity of the system itself was nearly overwhelmed. The good news is that "the system" can eventually respond appropriately, once conditions are bad enough and persons in power become advocates for change. The bad news, however, is that there will be much human suffering—particularly among the powerless and voiceless in society—in the absence of demand for change based on moral—and not efficiency—grounds.

<u>The System on Trial: Abu Ghraib</u>

Here we will revisit the work of Phillip Zimbardo, the chief researcher in the Stanford prison experiment. Because Zimbardo was known for his work on the psychological effects of prison environments, he was asked to serve as an expert witness at the military trial of the NCO in charge of the night shift at the Abu Ghraib Central Prison in Iraq. Zimbardo agreed to analyze the mistreatment of detainees at Abu Ghraib in the context of his previous Stanford prison research. Zimbardo says he did this not so much because he believed the low-level guards should escape punishment for what they did, but because he wanted the world to understand the effects that such environments have on behavior—and that the "system" was as much to blame as the guards.

Zimbardo's argument for the defense was that the guards were "good apples who had become soured over time by powerful situational forces."[33] Zimbardo argues that, in general (that is, even in contexts other than prisons), we focus too much on the "bad apple" view of individual disposition while ignoring the poisonous "bad barrel" environment. If we are going to punish the perpetrators, we should also punish the "barrel makers"—the power elite working behind the scenes that create the toxic conditions for the rest of us. "As the interests of these diverse power-brokers coalesce, they come to define our reality…Systems create hierarchies of dominance with influence and communication going down—rarely up the line,"[34] in the form of propaganda. The propaganda campaign often begins with creating a stereotyped and dehumanized characterization of persons the elite desires to eliminate (or scapegoat to distract scrutiny of their own actions). This "other" is thus presented as "a fundamental threat to our cherished values and beliefs…[and with] fear notched up and the enemy threat imminent, reasonable people act irrationally, independent people act in mindless conformity, and peaceful people act as warriors."[35]

When the Abu Ghraib photos were first released, Zimbardo had flashbacks to the Stanford prison experiment some thirty years ago. He was struck by the seemingly shameless playfulness of the soldiers and the sexually humiliating games. He also noted other similarities: the worst abuses were perpetrated on the night shift, the prisoners were hooded (in the SPE, they had bags over their heads) to disorient them; what started out as nakedness and humiliation morphed into stress positions and coerced exercise, and eventually sexual and physical assaults. The prison itself was unclean and in disrepair: there was no running water, insufficient cleaning supplies, the port-a-potties had backed up, trash, mold and rodents were everywhere. Adding to this unwholesome environment was that Abu Ghraib had formerly been a place of torture under the rule of Saddam Hussein.

When Zimbardo was asked to testify as an expert on behalf of one of the soldiers, the first thing he did was determine whether the individual had preexisting pathology. Zimbardo's soldier had joined the Army in 1984, and his record was generally good. Psychological tests indicated an average IQ, with no indication of sadistic or pathological tendencies. The solder did have a tendency for neatness and order, which may have made him more likely to be triggered by the chaos and filth at Abu Ghraib. Zimbardo also believed he was susceptible to burnout due to emotional exhaustion.[36]

Zimbardo next addresses the situation. He did not merely take the word of the soldier he was testifying for, but examined the official record. The "official record," however, is comprised of a number of separate reports prepared by separate entities. The official military investigation concluded that, unlike the "Code Red" order given in the movie *A Few Good Men*, investigators found no evidence of military orders or even general policy that encouraged soldiers to torture or humiliate the detainees. In this report, there were 94 confirmed cases of detainee abuse in Iraq and Afghanistan, but the blame was placed entirely on the unauthorized actions of a few individuals.

Another report (the so-called Fay-Jones report)[37] blamed the failure of command oversight. This resulted from a combination of leadership failure and jurisdictional ambiguity, particularly between the CIA interrogators and the military MPs. The Fay-Jones report found even more egregious behavior than that depicted in the infamous photos, including confirmation that a loaded gun was kept in the interrogation room and some of the detainees (not those in the photos) died in custody. The Fay-Jones report also extended culpability beyond the MP guards to military intelligence officers and analysts, interpreters and translators, and even medics (mainly for failure to report obvious abuse).

Zimbardo then analyzes the command structure and surrounding environment, not just of the military MPs, but of the CIA interrogators and the intelligence infrastructure, and even the Iraqi prison guards. Detainees in Tier 1A were considered terrorists, terrorist sympathizers or insurgents as opposed to the "regular" prisoners housed elsewhere in the facility. For a period of several months, military intelligence personnel and private contract interrogators encouraged the MPs to "soften up" the prisoners designated as terrorists. The Fay report found that the purpose of the sexually staged "trophy photos" was for use as threats to aid in interrogation.[38] According to Zimbardo, the bored and stressed night shift MPs were given implicit permission to do what they did, which—in a recreation of the dynamics of the Stanford prison experiment—opened the door to "ever more scenes of creative evil."[39]

The formal commanding officer at Abu Ghraib was Brigadier General Janis Karpinski. Karpinski's command jurisdiction covered three large jails and seventeen prisons in Iraq, so she was hardly ever seen at Abu Ghraib. Moreover, Abu Ghraib was a designated "special site," so prisoners who were targeted for interrogation were not under Karpinski's direct chain of command. As a woman who was mostly absent and only nominally in charge, Karpinski did not receive the same respect as a man in the same rank and position. Subordinates did not always obey her orders, which led to a breakdown in discipline. Karpinski later recounted that two superior officers told her they were going to "take the gloves off" while interrogating suspected insurgents, but she continued to report positive conditions at Abu Ghraib. Karpinski was eventually suspended from duty, officially reprimanded and removed from her command.[40]

Additional reports suggested the complicity of higher-ups. A report by an independent panel led by James Schlesinger[41] found over 300 alleged instances of abuse, with 121 of these confirmed. Five detainee deaths were attributed to interrogation, and another two dozen detainee deaths were still under investigation at the time of the report. The Schlesinger report identifies many systemic and structural contributors to detainee abuse—it even references Zimbardo's Stanford prison experiment—yet it stops short of blaming anyone at the highest levels. At the end of the Abu Ghraib investigation, 150 individuals faced disciplinary action. However, only 79 were court-martialed (with 54 found guilty), and only 5 officers were criminally charged. According to Zimbardo, it was obvious that the military's intention was to place the blame almost entirely on the unauthorized behavior of low-level rogue soldiers who were then publicly punished, essentially whitewashing the higher-level evil that contributed to it.[42]

Zimbardo then looks at yet a third report that was prepared by Human Rights Watch (HRW).[43] Above Karpinski in the military chain of command was Lt. General Ricardo Sanchez and Major General Geoffrey Miller, who the HRW alleges "knew or should have known" about what was going on at Guantanamo and Abu Ghraib. Sanchez did eventually (verbally) accept responsibility for Abu Ghraib, but the only consequence was a forced early retirement (with no loss of pay). Other Army documents obtained by the ACLU revealed that senior government officials were aware of detainee abuse in Iraq and Afghanistan long before the Abu Ghraib scandal. Moreover, they were also aware that the chronic stress of living in a war zone with "elusive enemies and asymmetrical warfare" often induce soldiers to commit crimes against civilians.[44]

As part of his "expert" investigation, in addition to reviewing as many independent reports as he could get his hands on, Zimbardo also interviewed other soldiers and interrogators. At some point, soldiers were ordered to kill males identified as terrorists or insurgents and then cover up shooting deaths of civilians. However, it was nearly impossible to identify "terrorists." Many detainees were brought in by Iraqi police, who were either rounding up everyone in areas where there was insurgent activity, or rounding up everyone they had a grudge against. One interrogator estimated that only 2% of the detainees were actually dangerous.[45] Another interrogator expressed frustration, particularly with the civilian bosses, for creating pressure to get information from detainees (who mostly didn't know anything). Consequently, this frustration was often taken out on (mostly) innocent detainees. There were descriptions of burnings and beatings of people in their homes, and detainees being kept on ice to the point of hypothermia. An interrogator named Lagouranis told Zimbardo he felt disconnected from what he was doing (something Zimbardo calls moral disengagement). When Lagouranis couldn't take it anymore, he sent reports along with photos and sworn detainee statements up the chain of command, but he never heard from anyone.

Because the CIA and intelligence community who were involved in detainee interrogations were just as culpable as the MP guards, Zimbardo follows the culpability all the way up the chain of command to CIA Director George Tenet and Secretary of Defense Donald Rumsfeld. Under Tenet's direction, CIA operatives were permitted to use waterboarding and other feigned methods of suffocation, stress positions, light and noise bombardment, sleep deprivation, and purposeful inducement of depression. So-called "target" detainees were kept completely isolated and frequently moved between various secret locations. Several MPs report finding detainees dead after being "interrogated," whose bodies were then packed on ice by the CIA and delivered to local taxi drivers. All evidence of the dead detainees' existence was destroyed. To this day, many detainees remain unaccounted for. Even the names of the medics who handled the bodies are unidentified.

According to the HRW report, Secretary of Defense Rumsfeld approved interrogation techniques that violated the Geneva Convention and the Convention against Torture. He also approved hiding detainees from the International Red Cross. Like General Sanchez, Rumsfeld also verbally admitted to responsibility, but without consequences. However, Zimbardo's charges do not stop at Secretary Rumsfeld or CIA Director Tenet. Zimbardo argues that blame for evil acts or outcomes should properly be placed to those who have the power to design and maintain the system, although he admits that identifying responsible individuals is more difficult in bigger and more diffuse systems.[46] In the case of the Stanford prison experiment, the ultimate blame would rest with Zimbardo himself. In the case of Abu Ghraib, Zimbardo carries the blame all the way up to Vice-President Dick Cheney and President George Bush.

Zimbardo cites the now infamous "torture memos," drafted by Bush's attorney Alberto Gonzales. One such memo argued that the Geneva Convention limitations were obsolete due to the need to obtain information quickly. Another memo attempts to constrict the definition of torture, which included higher burdens of proof and expanded potential defenses. The memos also made the argument that a previous anti-torture statute was an unconstitutional infringement on executive power. One legal scholar noted that "the memos read like the advice of a mob lawyer to a mafia don."[47] A former chief of staff for Secretary of State Colin Powell claimed that there was a "visible audit trail" from Cheney down through Rumsfeld and the commanders in the field that "suggested" ways for getting the intelligence that the higher-ups were demanding.[48] Bush himself attempted to replace the 1996 War Crimes Act with a new "Military Commissions Act" that would deprive anyone the system designated as an "unlawful enemy combatant" of any rights or remedies under either the Uniform Code of Military Justice or civilian law. In addition to these indictments of culpability at the highest levels, Zimbardo also notes the effect of ubiquitous propaganda surrounding the "War on Terror," along with its relentless, color-coded warnings that kept citizens in a constant state of fear and anxiety.

Zimbardo suggests that, just as the perpetrators in both the Stanford prison experiment and Abu Ghraib were not necessarily evil or psychopathic individuals, the whistleblowers (Zimbardo calls them "heroes") who bring evil out from the darkness and/or resist it are not necessarily extraordinarily brave or virtuous. He praises his fiancée (now wife) for ending the Stanford prison experiment; Joe Darby, the soldier who exposed the Abu Ghraib photos; the Christians who helped Jews escape from the Nazis, and even Rosa Parks, as examples of otherwise ordinary people who stepped up and confronted evil.

While Zimbardo suggests that a heroic individual (or small group of individuals) can confront an evil system, he also argues that efforts to inculcate moral character in individuals may be ineffectual against social and systemic pressures that drive bad behavior. The biggest problem in addressing administrative evil is that we tend to limit our thinking about "evil" to individual antisocial personalities or bad acts. Our technocratic enforcement mechanisms are also designed to address evil in the same manner—it is easier to prove who did what than to attempt to connect evil outcomes to situations or systems with diffused lines of authority and responsibility.

Modern research on organizational dynamics provides us with a better understanding of institutional pressures on individual behavior. We have also learned more about feedback effects between organizational dysfunction and individual personality defects.[49] That is, the combination of certain (generally negative) character types in positions of power can increase the likelihood of organizational evil. It also presents us the question of moral responsibility, particularly with respect to those who are lower in the hierarchy or have little power to change things. Such theories suggest that we can avoid being complicit by either calling out the bad behavior, leaving the organization, or both. However, filing formal complaints may result in nothing being done, except perhaps that we ourselves will be punished. We can leave a corrupt organization, but the corruption is likely to continue. Thus, we may be confronted with the choice between actions that keep our conscience clean at great personal cost but may do nothing to change things, or going along to get along.

Most people recognize that there is something very wrong with our society today, although they may be unable to articulate precisely what or why. In addition to difficulty in articulating the problem, we may feel powerless to change the system based on individual effort alone. However, each of us has some capacity for moral agency. Collectively, we have greater power and opportunity to change things, yet the challenge here is finding ways to name and discuss exactly what is wrong in a productive way. Those who are not religious may balk at discussions about “evil” as being too exaggerated, metaphysical, or off-putting. Conversely, framing our current problems in technocratic policy or management terms while ignoring moral implications trivializes the damage being done to our common humanity. Yet, our future may very well depend on how we address this issue.

Notes

---

[1] See Maley, T. (2004). Max Weber and the iron cage of technology. *Bulletin of Science, Technology & Society.* https://journals.sagepub.com/doi/abs/10.1177/0270467604263181?journalCode=bsta

[2] Ritzer, G. (2008). *The McDonaldization of society.* Thousand Oaks, CA: Pine Forge Press/Sage Publications.

[3] Graeber, D. (2018). *Bullshit Jobs: A Theory.* New York, NY: Simon & Schuster.

[4] Belle, N., & Cantarelli, P. (2017). What causes unethical behavior? A meta-analysis to set an agenda for public administration research. *Public Administration Review, 77*(3), 327-339.

[5] *Id.* at p. 332.

[6] Yam, K.C., Reynolds, S.J., & Hirsh, J.B. (2014). The hungry thief: Physiological deprivation and its effects on unethical behavior. *Organizational Behavior and Human Decision Processes, 125*(2), 123-33.

[7] Gino, F., & Pierce, L. (2009). The abundance effect: Unethical behavior in the presence of wealth. *Organizational Behavior and Human Decision Processes, 109*(2), 142-55.

[8] Fomer, C., Reinders, P., & De Cremer, D. (2012). Bad for me or bad for us? Interpersonal orientations and the impact of losses on unethical behavior. *Personality and Social Psychology Bulletin, 38*(6), 760-71.

[9] Gino, F., Ayal, S., & Ariely, D. (2013). Self-serving altruism? The lure of unethical actions that benefit others. *Journal of Economic Behavior & Organization 93,* 285-92.

[10] Mazar, N., Amir, O., & Ariely, D. (2008). The dishonesty of honest people: A theory of self-concept maintenance. *Journal of Marketing Research, 45*(6), 633-44.

[11] Gino, F., Ayal, S., & Ariely, D. (2009). Contagion and differentiation in unethical behavior: The effect of one bad apple on the barrel. *Psychological Science, 20*(3), 393-98.

---

[12] Swartz, M. & Watkins, S. (2003). *Power failure: The Inside story of the collapse of Enron.* New York: Doubleday.

[13] Gino, Ayal, & Ariely, D. (2013). *Supra.*

[14] Bozeman, B., & Su, X. (2015). Public service motivation concepts and theory: A critique. *Public Administration Review, 75*(5), 700-10; also Perry, J., & Vandenabeele, W. (2015). Public service motivation research: Achievements, challenges, and future directions. *Public Administration Review, 75*(5), 692-99.

[15] Adams, G., & Balfour, D. (2014). *Unmasking administrative evil.* New York, NY: M.E. Sharpe.

[16] *Id.* at p. 172.

[17] *Id.* at pp. 172-173.

[18] *Id.* at p. 105.

[19] Many of Houston's elites still stand by Lay, claiming that he was an honorable person caught up in a corrupt situation. However, Lay deliberately locked Enron employees out of selling their Enron stock for a year, all the while the stock's value was tanking and Lay and his wife were dumping their own shares. Lay was found guilty on six counts of fraud and conspiracy, but his conviction was overturned when he died of a heart attack prior to sentencing.

[20] Reed, George. (2012, April 11). Leading questions, leadership, ethics, and administrative evil. *Sage Journals 8*(2), 187-198. http://journals.sagepub.com/doi/abs/10.1177/1742715011429589?journalCode=leaa.

[21] Adams & Balfour, *supra* at p. 144.

[22] Quoting from Rubenstein, R.L. (1983). *The age of triage: Fear and hope in an overcrowded world.* Boston, MA: Beacon.

[23] Adams & Balfour, *supra* at p. 72.

[24] *Id* .at p. 141.

[25] Adams, G., & Balfour, D. (2010). Market-based government and the decline of organizational ethics. *Administration & Society, 42*(6), 615-37.

---

[26] Adams & Balfour. (2014). *Supra* at p. xxi.

[27] The irony of austerity is that it is promoted as the appropriate solution for budget deficits and low economic growth, yet, those most likely touting austerity as the answer for everyone else are least likely themselves to be subject to it.

[28] Mandel, R. G. (2009). The appointment of counsel to indigent defendants is not enough: Budget cuts render the right to counsel virtually meaningless. *The Florida Bar Journal, 83*(4). https://www.floridabar.org/the-florida-bar-journal/the-appointment-of-counsel-to-indigent-defendants-is-not-enough-budget-cuts-render-the-right-to-counsel-virtually-meaningless/

[29] Public Defender Eleventh Judicial Circuit of Florida, et al. vs. State of Florida, et al. (May 23, 2013). Found at http://caselaw.findlaw.com/fl-supreme-court/1632060.html.

[30] Blankenship, G. (2019, August 28). AGs round table focuses on mental health in the criminal justice system. *The Florida Bar News.* https://www.floridabar.org/the-florida-bar-news/ashley-moody/

[31] *Id.*

[32] *Id.*

[33] Zimbardo, P. (2007). *The Lucifer effect.* New York, NY: Penguin Random House LLC.

[34] *Id.* at p. 10.

[35] *Id.* p. 11.

[36] *Id.* at pp. 337-345.

[37] This report was spearheaded by Major General George Fay. Full report is available at https://www.thetorturedatabase.org/document/fay-report-investigation-205th-military-intelligence-brigades-activites-abu-ghraib

[38] Zimbardo, *supra* at p. 358.

[39] *Id. at* p. 366

[40] *Id.* at pp. 335-337.

[41] Full Report found at http://pdf.prisonexp.org/SchlesingerReport.pdf

[42] Zimbardo, *supra* at 391.

[43] The Road to Abu Ghraib (2004). https://www.hrw.org/reports/2004/usa0604/

[44] Zimbardo, *supra* at p. 417.

[45] *Id. at* p. 419.

[46] *Id.* at p. 226.

[47] Lewis, Anthony. (2004, June 17). Making torture legal. *The Washington Post.*

[48] Zimbardo, *supra* at p. 433.

[49] The intersection of certain antisocial personality traits in positions of power and dysfunctional culture is explored in depth in VanHettinga, B. (2019). *Why Assholes Rule the World.*

Part III

How Societies Become Evil

Introduction to Ponerology

Wherever a society has become enslaved to others or to the rule of an overly-privileged native class, psychology is the first discipline to suffer from censorship and incursion on the part of an administrative body which starts claiming the last word as to what represents scientific truth.

Dr. Andrew Lobaszewsky

Perhaps there is no historical personification of evil as infamous as Adolph Hitler. Not close behind is Joseph Stalin. While history books tend to focus on individuals in power—their individual personality exceptionalism and defects—neither Hitler nor Stalin would have been able to cause the harm that they did if they had been acting alone. We can perhaps understand that they might have surrounded themselves with a handful of cronies who were willing to do their bidding in exchange for power. We might also expect that some individuals were bullied into bad behavior, perhaps performing inhumane acts under threat of being tortured or killed themselves. The big question then is how many bad guys does it take (as a percentage of the total population) before no one else can stop them? The more complex and interesting question is why the rest of society fails to resist and even acquiesces as obviously evil individuals begin to exert greater control and influence.

In 1934, Hitler had signed a non-aggression treaty with Poland as one of his first foreign policy initiatives. Yet, in direct contradiction to the treaty, German troops invaded Poland some five years later. Poland remained under German occupation until the end of World War II in 1945, although it was at various times "partitioned" between Germany and Stalinist Russia, subsequently falling under the domination of the post-war communist Soviet Union. During the Nazi war occupation, some 6 million (noncombat) Poles were killed, about half of them Jews. In addition to ethnic cleansing of Jews and other ethnic minorities, the Nazis' objective was to completely eradicate Polish culture, and they destroyed Polish schools, universities, libraries, laboratories and museums. Members of the Polish intellectual elite were executed.

After years of enduring Nazi atrocities, some Poles initially welcomed the post-war Soviets. This was more true of some ethnic subpopulations (e.g., Ukrainians) and Polish peasants, who received land after it was taken from the large land-owning kulaks and redistributed. While the Soviets never declared outright war on Poland, Poland was never free and independent while under Soviet domination. The Soviets re-opened the schools and universities that had been shut down by the Nazis, but these institutions were placed under the control of Soviet supervisors, who imposed the teaching of Russian language and literature as well as Soviet ideology. Rather than sending in troops, the Soviets controlled the Polish population primarily through the state security apparatus. They also imposed more subtle control by undermining the authority of the Catholic Church, which occupied an important place in Poland's culture and self-identification.

After Stalin's death in 1953, political prisoners were freed, but Poland experienced an ongoing cycle of repression, resistance, and reform. Reforms were usually precipitated by protests and strikes, followed by increased authoritarian rule, with grievances alternately arising from workers, students, or citizens unhappy with prices and inflation. Poles began to reassert their cultural identity with the election of the first Polish Pope in 1978 (Karol Wojtyla, Pope John Paul II) and the birth of the Solidarity movement in 1980. However, Poland was not entirely independent until the fall of the Soviet Union in 1989.

Dr. Andrew Lobaczewsky was a psychiatrist—a member of the Polish intellectual elite-- who studied and lived in Poland during its occupation by the Nazis and then as a subject of the communist former Soviet Union. Lobaczewsky managed to continue his studies during the Nazi occupation and graduated from the last class to receive an education uninfluenced by Soviet ideology. His training covered the causes and diagnoses of individual psychopathology. Yet, Lobaszewsky and some of his colleagues had a bigger question: Could psychopathology infect entire societies? Neither Hitler nor Stalin could have exterminated the millions that are attributable to their regimes alone. Since most typical Germans or Russians were not evil people themselves, why did an entire nation support the Nazi (or Soviet) agenda? Lobaszewsky wanted to better understand the relationship between individual psychopathy and social evil.

Lobaczewsky describes, as a university student, being herded under threat to back-room indoctrination lectures. Professors were replaced, and knowledge was re-written practically overnight. The students discovered that the persons replacing their university professors often had only attended high school, and these individuals were appointed to bombard the students with "naïve, presumptuous paralogistics and a pathological view of human reality."[1] As Lobaczewsky was conducting his studies, he observed the emptying of the library and destruction of the "old knowledge." He noted how academics denounced findings and conclusions from their own previous research almost overnight, in order to accommodate the new "party line" and maintain their social positions. He describes the challenges of dealing with his own fears and maintaining objectivity while studying psychopathic individuals and living under authoritarian rule.

Lobaczewsky soon observed changes in the thought patterns and worldview of his friends and colleagues. Lobaczewsky and some of his colleagues were aware enough to be concerned with similar changes even in themselves, which they termed "personality disintegration." They also recognized that some individuals were more susceptible to the indoctrinating messages than others. The individuals who were more easily subjected to so-called "transpersonification" came from all social groups and various religions, but the one unifying characteristic was that they seemed to be persons of "lower talent." Unfortunately, Lobaczewsky does not expressly define what constitutes "talent," but apparently these individuals were more susceptible to messages from apparent authorities without questioning their factual and logical basis.

As their "world of psychological reality and moral values seemed suspended," Lobaczewsky and a small group of his colleagues vowed to understand what was happening to them as well as to the rest of society. In their pursuit of a scientific explanation, Lobaczewsky and a small group of colleagues attempted to understand everything they could about antisocial behavior both at the individual (moral evil) and macrosocial (psychobiological evil) levels. As they tried to collect information that would help them to understand, they discovered that entire libraries had been emptied of knowledge about psychopathology. The group of colleagues at first studied themselves, since their usual sources of reference had been destroyed. The rest of their work had to be conducted in secret and in isolation, connected only by an intermittent (and often unreliable) system of hand-carried messages. Lobaczewsky himself spent many years conducting detailed tests and observations in an undisclosed location in Poland, "far away from active political and cultural centers…."[2]

As most of us know, stereotypically evil dictators like Hitler[3] and Stalin did not act alone. Any search for names of individuals convicted of war crimes, crimes against humanity, and genocide turns up hundreds of names from many different countries, including the United States. These are not all Nazis or backward third-world dictators. Even two catholic priests have been convicted of crimes against humanity (one a Croatian Nazi collaborator, the other a Rwandan). It is hard to believe that every one of these individuals was an evil person. Yet, there is adequate evidence to suggest that they participated in evil acts. So, along with Lobaszewsky, we ask what could cause otherwise normal and decent people to commit acts of atrocity against other human beings.

Lobaczewsky's work was not without sacrifice. The scattered researchers faced many "material and academic problems," due to the underground nature of their work. Lobaczewsky collected data for this work while also "earning a difficult living," because it would have been impossible for him to enjoy the life of an esteemed academic or man of science in the society in which he found himself. More than the material and logistical hardships was the constant necessity to "keep both abhorrence and fear under control," as the researchers had to interview psychopathic prisoners while living through Nazi or Soviet atrocities. Scientific curiosity became their ally against "the natural, moralizing reflexes of revulsion, and other painful emotions that the phenomenon provokes in any normal person when it deprives him of his joy of life and personal safety, ruining his future and that of his nation."[4]

When the Soviets took over Poland after World War II, the study of genetics and psychopathy was forbidden. Thus, Lobaczewsky and his colleagues continued to work in secret. Many of them remained anonymous even to each other, and they developed a way to communicate their research through an underground messaging system. In this manner, if any one of them had been caught, he would have been unable to share the names of the others—similar to the way some terrorist groups operate today.

The ultimate objective of Dr. Lobaczewsky and his unknown colleagues was to not only just understand psychopathic behavior, but to document the process of how an entire society becomes infected by it. Dr. Lobaczewsky terms this science ***ponerology***, and the process ***ponerogenesis.*** While some may argue that Lobaczewsky's observations were made during a unique historical period, his descriptions of the degradation of society has implications for our society today. Indeed, Lobaczewsky writes in 2005 (three years before his death and less than a year after the creation of the US Department of Homeland Security), that "the overt system of suppression I had so recently escaped was just as prevalent, though more covert, in the United States."[5]

According to Dr. Lobaczewsky's theory, all advanced societies experience a periodicity between so-called "normal" times and a ***hysteroidal*** high point. Normal times are occasionally also described as "happy" or good times, although the surface fun and glamour often obscure real problems, particularly corruption and extreme inequality. Historical examples of this include the Gilded Age (called Belle Epoque in Europe) which preceded World War I, and the "Roaring Twenties" decade in the United States which was quickly followed by the Great Depression. More recently, the period between the end of World War II (1945) and approximately the middle 1970s represented a period of American ascendency as a world superpower, general prosperity along with a burgeoning middle class, and historically low levels of inequality. These so-called "good times" were not limited to the United States, with the same period being called "trente glorieuses" in France, "Wirtschaft swunder" in Germany and "miracolo economico" in Italy. Yet, the post-war boom also included a Europe still divided by an Iron

Curtain, along with nascent civil rights and feminist movements that would demand greater justice and equality.

Hysteroidal cycles tend to be particularly extreme in hedonistic societies, who focus on immediate gratifications at the expense of long-term consequences. This is in part due to collective denial, where "people have the tendency to escape into ignorance or naïve doctrines…[and] some feel contempt for suffering persons."[6] In the introduction to Dr. Lobaczewsky's work, his descriptive analysis of Nazi and Soviet-occupied Poland is compared to what is happening in our society (primarily in the United States) today by Laura Knight-Jadczyk, the editor who oversaw the publication of Lobaczewsky's work:

> "On a personal level, our lives are steadily deteriorating. The air we breathe and the water we drink is polluted almost beyond endurance…Stress and tension have become an accepted part of life and can be shown to have killed more people than the cigarettes that some people still smoke to relieve it…Combined with wars, insurrections, and political purges, multiplied millions of people across the globe are without adequate food or shelter due to political actions…At the social level, hatred, envy, greed and strife multiply exponentially…"

Perhaps the most disturbing conclusion of Lobaczewsky's work is that the dominance of a small minority can "normalize" evil and infect an entire society. This is particularly so when psychopathic (or characteropathic) persons gain control over the institutions that influence culture; e.g., media, governments, businesses, universities and academic think tanks.

Lobaczewsky had nearly as much challenge with getting the reconstructed work published as he did to compile it. The first manuscript was hastily thrown into a furnace when he received warning of an impending search only minutes before. A second copy was given to an American tourist to be delivered to the Vatican, but Lobaczewsky was unable to follow up on its whereabouts. Lobaczewsky left Poland before it was liberated and came to the

United States, where he recreated the work from memory, and had it translated into English in 1984. He even enlisted the assistance of fellow Polish ex-pat Zbigniew Brzezinski, the former National Security Advisor to President Carter. Brzezinski was initially supportive, but later mysteriously lost interest. Lobaczewsky was unable to get the work published by traditional publishers, who told him his work was "too political" for psychological editors and "too psychopathological" for political editors.

Convinced of the importance of his work, Lobaszewsky finally got it published in 2005. Although his research was conducted decades earlier, in a totally different historical period and culture, in the introduction to his work, Lobaszewsky writes, "the overt system of suppression I had so recently escaped was just as prevalent, though more covert, in the United States." Lobaszewsky calls his research an inquiry into the general laws of the origin of macrosocial evil, or ***ponerology***. Lobaczewsky's "evil" is not about individual psychopaths or bad acts, but rather about how large numbers of "good" or normal people can be co-opted by evil systems.

Lobaszewsky proposes that macrosocial evil occurs by a complex process. It begins with individual psychopathy, which itself exists along a continuum. While the expression of individual psychopathy can range from serial killers to street robbers to robber barons, the main diagnostic similarity is lack of empathy. These individuals are incapable of understanding the emotions or needs of others. Their relationships are instrumental, that is, they decide whether or not to pursue a relationship based solely on how it will benefit them by fulfilling their own needs or promoting an agenda. They also tend to crave power over others, and the more intelligent ones can be quite skilled in attaining positions of institutional power.

Lobaszewsky alleges that such individuals comprise, at most, some 6% of the total population. They rise to power and are able to influence "normal" society through the intersection of what Lobaszewsky terms a ponerization process and a high point in what he terms a hysteroidal cycle. The ***hysteroidal cycle*** begins when a society abandons its ability to use common sense or to think critically during so-called "good times." The blissfully ignorant good times are then followed by "bad times," which leads to a longing for (sometimes not entirely accurate) past greatness and a search for scapegoats. Ponerization occurs when deviant worldviews become integrated into popular culture and normalized. The final stage is what Lobaszewsky terms ***pathocracy***. This is when pychopathological individuals have become firmly entrenched into the ruling elites. Because common people are prone to identify with the emperor, "the rest of society adopts a characteropathic worldview."[7]

According to Lobaszewsky, truly psychopathological persons comprise approximately 6% of the population, with some variation among different societies. They are then able to enlist the assistance of another approximately 12% of the population, who Lobaszewsky labels as "characteropathological." Characteropathological individuals are those who have latent character defects or personality disorders (which may be activated by real injustices of the dominant society) not amounting to a diagnostic pathology. Thus, ponerologic, or evil societies can be established and run by less than 20% of the total population.

Lobaszewsky warns against the temptation to simplify complex matters by identifying a single cause or perpetrator. Indeed, the "oversimplification of reality" is a primary weapon of political propaganda.[8] Many would like to think of evil society as being the result of a single dictator. A typical explanation goes like this: bad guy rises to power—either legally by election (deception) or illegally by coup (force)—and then terrorizes the population into submission. The reality is that these people are able to seize and hold power because they have the assistance of others. In the case of a coup, the dictator accomplishes this through the assistance of legitimate military officers. In the case of a psychopathological or characteropathological individual who is elected, not only do voters ignore the pathologies, they might even view them as leadership assets.

What Lobaczewsky's research has done is expand the concept of evil beyond individuals to include organizations and even entire societies. That is, what happens when the bad guys gain such control over social institutions that they are able to affect how many of us think and view the world? In Part III we will follow Lobaczewsky's analysis of the process by which sociopathic individuals gain control over a society, infecting its culture and corrupting the morals of the majority of people within it. While most of the history of Nazism was written by looking at the past, with a focus on individual leaders, military tactics and politics, Lobaszewsky gives us a real-time view of what was happening to ordinary people and how their thinking and behavior was changed. We will also look at how these processes are manifesting in contemporary American life, because, although the operational details vary depending on specific time, place and culture, many of Lobaczewsky's documented patterns are quite recognizable.

Notes

[1] Lobaczewsky, A.M. (1998). *Political ponerology: A science on the nature of evil adjusted for political purposes. Red Pill Press* at p. 33. Full document PDF at http://www.survivorshandbook.com/wp-content/articles/political-ponerology.pdf.

[2] *Id.* at p. 28.

[3] Hitler was democratically elected in 1933. Although he did not receive a majority of votes, the 43.9% of the vote he did receive was sufficient in Germany's parliamentary (multi-party) Reichstag. The politics surrounding Hitler's rise to power are complex (including some questionably extra-constitutional gamesmanship), but—like Trump—he (or the Nazi party) had significant popular support.

[4] Lobaczewsky, *supra* at p. 37.

[5] *Id.* at p. 31.

[6] *Id.* at p. 40.

[7] *Id.* at p. 108.

[8] *Id.* at p. 71

Section 1
Individual Psychopathy

The presence or absence of conscience is a deep human division, arguably more significant than intelligence, race, or even gender.

Laura Knight Jadczyk in the preface to ***Ponerology***

In this section, we are going to introduce the psychopath. Contrary to what many people might think, psychopaths are not all serial killers, rapists or bank robbers, although some of them are. While prison populations contain a higher percentage of psychopaths than the general population, not all prisoners are necessarily psychopaths and not all psychopaths become involved with the criminal justice system. There is a behavioral continuum of psychopathy, sociopathy, and antisocial personality disorder, with many overlapping behavioral traits. A diagnosis of psychopathy will usually include sufficient criteria for a concurrent diagnosis of antisocial personality disorder. The psychopaths who avoid entanglement with the criminal justice or mental health system might actually be more dangerous to the rest of us, because they are able to function in normal society and may indeed even be successful in it. Such individuals who manifest "sub clinical psychopathic traits" between a pathological personality disorder and normal personality traits are "more likely (than normal people) to engage in manipulative and antisocial behavior."[1]

Psychopaths are generally defined as being "without conscience and incapable of empathy, guilt, or loyalty to anyone but themselves."[2] There is significant overlap between the characteristics of psychopaths and personality traits such as dominance, entitlement, and narcissism. The really dangerous psychopaths are not the serial killers who usually end up in prison, but those who have higher-level social skills and intelligence, particularly the ability to manipulate and deceive others (sometimes referred to as Machiavellianism). These higher-functioning psychopaths can appear to be charming and "normal," but their ultimate objective is to gain trust and work their way into positions of power, at the same time they are premeditating selfish or antisocial objectives.

A truly malevolent character has been identified in more modern times. This so-called "Dark Triad" is comprised of narcissism, Machiavellianism, and psychopathy.[3] The Dark Triad individual is particularly dangerous because he (usually a "he," but not absolutely) combines the self-absorption of the narcissist and the cunning of the Machiavellian with a total lack of regard for the human rights of anyone else. Dark Triad personalities have been found to be correlated with rude and provocative comments online as well as a behavior called "trolling," which involves a combination of aggression and deceptiveness.[4] Although online trolls may sometimes target specific individuals or groups, their primary motivation is to gain negative power and influence by creating hateful discourse and social conflict.[5] In essence, a Dark Triad psychopath enjoys making all the rest of us more like themselves.

According to Lobaczewsky, the foundation of human evil is individual psychopathy, which he asserts is due to an organic abnormality (the disease model) which is found in only a small fraction of the population. Psychopathic individuals—because they are either born this way or suffer some kind of brain injury or chemical imbalance—have no capacity for empathy. At some point, such individuals discover that they do not experience the same concern for others, i.e., moral sentiments, as everyone else, and they tend to deal with this in one of two ways. They sometimes attempt to hide this fact and behave as if they have "normal" feelings of empathy (the insincere). Alternatively, recognizing that their lack of conscience gives them a secret advantage, they use this to fulfill their own ambition and desires. Harm to society occurs when these individuals obtain positions of power, from which their worldviews (i.e., greed is good, people perform only under threat of punishment, winner-take-all systems motivate productivity, certain groups are inherently inferior, empathy is for the weak, etc.) infect the rest of society.

Lobaszewsky spends a good portion of his book discussing the origins of psychopathology—particularly the forms that lead to ***ponerogenesis***. Most cases of psychopathy are caused by acquired deviations—either inherited defects or the result of brain tissue damage. Lobaszewsky provides a lengthy description of the origins of psychopathology or characteropathy in individuals, even identifying particular areas of the brain with specific behaviors. For example, damage to the frontal areas of the cerebral cortex—a "rather frequent" occurrence due to conditions at birth as well as later injury—creates character disorders without affecting memory, associative capacity or instinctive reactivity. In countries with highly developed medical care, Lobaszewsky estimates that 5-7% of children have brain tissue lesions which negatively impact academics or behavior; i.e., about 6% of the general population is psychopathic.[6] Left untreated, these negative character deformations grow over time.

Clinical cases have also corroborated Lobaczewsky's findings that psychopathy can be induced in otherwise normal persons by injuries to the brain, specifically the prefrontal cortex. In 1848, Phineas Gage was working as a railroad construction foreman when a tamping rod was accidentally dynamited completely through his head, taking part of his prefrontal cortex with it. (Lobaczewsky may even have been aware of this case). Amazingly, Gage walked away and sought medical assistance, greeting the doctor by saying "here is business enough for you." Although Gage lived another 11 years, his personality was changed forever. While Gage had been a considerate and decent person before the accident, afterward he become irritable, dishonest, and unable to control his impulses.

Lobaszewsky suggests that not all forms of mental illness are equally harmful. Neurotics, for example, tend to experience excessive guilt over actions which are easily forgiven. Although neurotics are capable of true love, they have difficulty expressing it. They also find it difficult to achieve their personal goals. Thus, neurotics tend to create more trouble for themselves than they do for others. Schizoidal types are hypersensitive and distrustful. Typically pessimistic about human nature in general, schizoids usually do not target individual victims. However, they can cause harm at the macrosocial level if they "invent great doctrines that are put to paper" and their "disturbingly divisive works" are spread among the populations. Lobaszewsky places the 19th century economist Karl Marx in this category.

In modern times, the Diagnostic and Statistical Manual is a reference used by mental health professionals in the diagnosis of mental disorders. It has undergone many changes as research developed, and at various times there have been overlaps, ambiguities, and disagreements between what the mental health community terms anti-social personality disorder, borderline personality disorder, sociopathy, psychopathy, Machiavellianism, and malignant narcissism. There were attempts to differentiate whether a particular characteristic was inherited or produced by environment, whether the behavior involved unregulated emotions or lack of emotion, variations in IQ level, propensity to commit crimes, and even the degree to which any of these represented separate and distinct disorders.[7] For example, studies find that the prevalence of narcissistic personality disorder is 6%; antisocial personality disorder is around 4%; and both have overlapping criteria with psychopathy.

According to Lobaszewsky, the most socially harmful diagnosis is essential psychopathy, which affects about ½ of 1% of the population. Genetically, psychopathy works similar to color-blindness, but it affects both sexes. However, it manifests stronger in men, suggesting (but inconclusive) that it is inherited through the X chromosome. Lobaczewsky asserts that psychopathy is not connected with personality disorders generally, with the exception of antisocial personality disorder. Lobaszewsky also asserts his belief that most people are good. The small minority of humans who lack empathy is due to identifiable neuropsychiatric (i.e., organic) disorders, and thus our response should not be to cast blame, but rather to prevent these individuals from harming the rest of us, specifically by preventing them from attaining positions of power and authority.

Lobaszewsky's review of research available at that time, found three consistent qualities of psychopaths: (1) an absence of a sense of guilt for anti-social actions,[8] (2) an inability to love others, and (3) the pursuit of relationships solely to satisfy one's own desires.[9] Psychopaths view normal human emotions such as trust, love and caring for others as weaknesses to be exploited.[10] In the 1930s, the American psychiatrist Dr. Hervey Cleckley developed a checklist of over 100 behavioral, emotional, interpersonal, and lifestyle traits that had been observed in criminal populations. Cleckley's list was subsequently consolidated into a 20-item checklist by the Canadian psychologist, Dr. Robert Hare.[11]

Dr. Hare's diagnostic checklist is as follows:

1.Glibness/superficial charm
2. Egocentricity/grandiose sense of self-worth
3. Proneness to boredom/low frustration tolerance
4. Pathological lying and deception/gaslighting
5. Conning/lack of sincerity
6. Lack of remorse or guilt
7. Shallow affect
8. Callous/lack of empathy
9. Parasitic lifestyle
10. Poor behavioral controls
11. Promiscuous sexual behavior
12. Early behavioral problems
13. Lack of realistic long-term goals
14. Impulsivity
15. Irresponsibility
16. Failure to accept responsibility for own actions
17. Many short-term marital relationships
18. Juvenile delinquency
19. Revocation of conditional release
20. Criminal versatility

To determine if a diagnosis of psychopathy applies, an individual is assigned a rating of 0 (trait is definitely not present), 1 (information is insufficient or inconclusive), or 2 (trait is definitely present) for each criteria. Ideally, behavioral information is collected over a period of time (to reflect longstanding and stable traits) rather than a clinical snapshot. Scores are tallied, with scores over 30 receiving the diagnosis of psychopathy, although some researchers will make this diagnosis with a score of 25. The average score among the general population is 5 (surprise, we're not all saints!), but for the prison population the average score for males is 22 and for females it is 19. After decades of research bolstering its validity, Dr. Hare's list, known as the PCL-R, has become the "gold standard" for identifying psychopathic personalities.[12]

Modern researchers on psychopathy estimate that only 1% of the general population can be identified as psychopaths (as opposed to Lobaszewsky's 6%). Hare's research has also found an almost three to one ratio of psychopathic prevalence between males and females. Moreover, studies of differences between identical and fraternal twins have found that psychopathy has a hereditability rate of over 50%.[13] Thus, most of the core symptoms can be traced to hereditability, while research has not been able to confirm any link between psychopathy and dysfunctional childhood (independent of genetic factors). Thus, modern research also confirms Lobaszewsky's "disease model" of psychopathy, (i.e., the psychopath is not to blame for his condition).

More recent research has also identified brain structure differences connected to bad behavior. For example, psychopaths are more likely to have an oddly shaped corpus callosum, the bridge that connects the brain's hemispheres. This could possibly explain their lack of emotion as well as aggression, because the two sides of the brain cannot perform their normal regulatory functions.[14] Psychopaths process emotionally-charged language in the temporal lobe area of the brain, where non-psychopaths process emotional language in the paralimbic midbrain. Psychopaths have also been found to have less gray matter, as well as less connectivity between the prefrontal cortex and amygdala (which negatively impacts their reasoning).

Other research suggests that psychopaths have a malfunctioning amygdala. The amygdala is a structure deep within the limbic mid-brain that is responsible for more primitive functions such as the startle reaction, fight or flight, and fear generally. The amygdala is also responsible for moral fear associated with punishment, and it is much less active in psychopaths. This lack of fear, or reactivity to the environment, may also be responsible for lack of a conscience.[15] That is, because the psychopath does not experience the normal association between fear and punishment, they are immune to such efforts at socialization.

Borderlines (what Lobaszewsky terms characteropaths) have significantly smaller right parietal lobes.[16] However, borderline manifests as a continuum, with some borderlines having greater ability to control their negative emotions. Other research has found that those who inherit borderline traits may not develop into a clinical diagnosis unless they are also exposed to a dysfunctional childhood.[17] Pathological lying (as a problem behavior unto itself unconnected with any specific disorder) was found to be connected to a larger mass of prefrontal white matter than that found either in normal individuals or even those with antisocial personality disorder without a history of pathological lying.[18]

Modern research has also established connections between behavioral and personality disorders with the way our brain cells communicate with each other.[19] Behavioral neuroscience research has been supplemented by genetics—specifically in the genes that regulate neurotransmitters. Neurochemicals such as serotonin are released in response to stimuli and then bind to receptors which transmit further instructions that affect behavior or emotions. Researchers have been able to track genetic markers for serotonin activity, which plays a critical role in mood and temperament disorders such as depression, anxiety, bipolar disorder, and borderline personality disorder. New theories also suggest a role for so-called "mirror neurons" in the formation of empathy.[20] Mirror neurons, found in the premotor and inferior parietal cortex, are unique to humans. These neurons are triggered when performing an activity as well as when viewing another person performing the same activity. The firing of mirror neurons explains why many of us feel sad when see someone crying, even if we don't know the reason.

Studies of these nature-nurture feedback loops also explain why some children who experience childhood trauma or are raised in dysfunctional families grow up to be dysfunctional themselves, while others grow up to be relatively normal. A British study that followed twins born over a period of three years (1994-1996) looked at differences between identical twins (who share 100% of their DNA) and fraternal twins (who share only 50% of their DNA), as compared to their environments growing up.[21] Out of 3,687 pairs of twins, 187 pairs (about 5%) were identified with extreme psychopathic traits, while another 177 pairs (about 4.8%) were found to display antisocial behavior not amounting to full-blown psychopathy. In the psychopathic twins, the researchers found that 81% of antisocial behavior could be traced to genetics. However, in the "merely" antisocial twins, only 30% of their bad behavior could be traced to genetic hereditability. That is, there are some people who are simply "born to be bad" regardless of whether they are raised in a loving or an abusive home. Others are born with a genetic "switch," or a vulnerability to turning out bad if they are raised in the wrong environment or exposed to specific triggers.

The main difference between Lobaszewsky's earlier research and Dr. Hare's more recent work is that Lobaszewsky treated psychopathy as a disease rather than a personality disorder. Lobaszewsky's subject sample pool was comprised of some 5,000 psychotic, neurotic and healthy patients who "came from all circles of Polish society [and] represented various moral, social, and political attitudes." One thing that Lobaszewsky's subjects had in common was that they lived in a "large industrial center characterized by poor working conditions and substantial air pollution."[22] From this group, Lobaszewsky selected 384 individuals whose behavior had "seriously hurt others." Lobaczewsky estimates that 14% to 16% of his subjects (54-61 individuals) did not previously exhibit any psychopathological factors which could have influenced their behavior, although he admits that lack of diagnosis does not *ipso facto* establish lack of disease.

Like Lobaszewsky, Dr. Hare has done a lot of research into criminal psychology. Dr. Hare more modestly estimates the percentage of psychopaths in the general population as closer to 1%. However, he also states that approximately another 10% fall into a gray area, where they have sufficient psychopathic features to warrant concern, but not enough to be termed "psychopathic."[23] Like Lobaczewsky, Dr. Hare also estimates that the percentage of psychopaths is higher in prison populations (about 15%). The main distinguishing characteristic of psychopaths is that their criminal behavior is instrumental—that is, cold, calculated and cunning—as opposed to the reactive, emotional actions of non-psychopathic criminals.

Dr. Hare argues that psychopaths represent a higher form of deviance than an antisocial personality, who may also be motivated by greed, egocentrism, and an ends-justify-the-means regardless of cost ethos. Drs. Hare and Babiak[24] differentiate a psychopath from a more garden-variety antisocial by their inability to tell the truth, to share, to be modest, or to accept blame. While non-psychopathic individuals might exhibit these behaviors at various times, what distinguishes a psychopath is that these behaviors are universal and immutable. A psychopath is incapable of sharing because he cannot see others as equals with legitimate claims to resources. A psychopath not only refuses to accept blame, but will actively create evidence that others are to blame. Like the socially dominant individual, the psychopath attributes love and status to himself but never to others. He views himself as worthy and important, while others are unworthy and insignificant. Like the malignant narcissist, the psychopath exhibits a sense of entitlement and total lack of consideration for the needs of others.

Although psychopaths fail to develop what most of us would call a conscience, they are nevertheless aware of society's expectations. Psychopaths also come in variants, or subtypes, depending on their primary modus operandi: manipulators (primary modus operandi is deceit) and bullies (primary modus operandi is coercion, abuse, humiliation and aggression).[25] Many psychopaths use both types of operational behavior by manipulating others to abuse or bully those lower in the hierarchy.[26] Dr. Hare also suggests that psychopathy may manifest differently between males and females. Males tend to adopt the "macho" male gender role and will use intimidation and aggression to achieve their desires. Females tend to adopt the passive, warm and nurturing gender stereotype to get what they want, although they are able to break out of the gender stereotype and become as cold-blooded and violent as males.[27] Thus, the different manifestations of psychopathic behavior between men and women may be due as much to cultural stereotyping as it is to gender-differentiated psychopathic typologies.

To a psychopath, truth itself is transactional and is adapted to the moment: A psychopath speaks power to truth rather than the other way round. A psychopath will not simply lie to achieve an objective, but lies constantly for the excitement of it. Moreover, the true psychopath will be unconcerned if the lie is so obvious that everyone knows it is a lie. The psychopathic liar is differentiated from persons in occupations such as sales or politics, where hedging the truth is to be expected, because most people in these professions are capable of being honest in other contexts (i.e., with friends and family). A psychopath is a pathological liar and a well-skilled one.

Dr. Hare does not believe that psychopathy is a "disease" of mental illness, but rather a personality disorder. He also warns against labeling someone a psychopath on the basis of personality or behavior characteristics without a full expert evaluation. Which leads to the question whether or not the rest of us would be able to recognize a psychopath. While there is no definitive checklist for laypersons to identify a psychopath, Dr. Hare provides some clues which strongly suggest someone might be a psychopath: behavior that is superficial, grandiose, deceitful, impulsive and irresponsible; the individual lacks remorse and empathy; the individual does not accept responsibility for his actions; and the individual generally has a history of antisocial behavior and run-ins with the legal system.

Other psychologists have also given us some clues to help us identify socio- and psychopaths. Martha Stout[28] notes that socio/psychopaths are more easily able to advance through hierarchies because they are unencumbered by concern tor legal consequences or moral doubt. They are easily able to "steamroll over groups who are dependent and voiceless," and they "have a special talent for whipping up other people's hatred and sense of deprivation." David Shapiro[29] describes psychopaths as being ruled by impulse and an attention that is focused on immediate opportunities and frustrations. The psychopath is driven by a perpetual need to "win" in the moment and "dominate." Thus, the modern psychopath is defined by the three consistent qualities of (1) absence of conscience, (2) inability to empathize or bond deeply with others, and (3) impulsiveness.

According to Lobaszewsky, early in their lives, psychopaths recognize that they do not have the same emotions as others, particularly empathy. Psychopaths lack what most of us would call a conscience. When confronted with the harm their behavior has caused, they will typically either deny, minimize, or even blame the victim. Many higher-functioning psychopaths become adept at hiding this by learning how to mimic facial expressions and behavior. Although psychopaths are incapable of incorporating the worldview of normal persons, many of them try.

Psychopaths exhibit wide variation with respect to intelligence, resources, and ambition. Just as in normal populations, the intelligence level of psychopathic individuals varies, although it is on average lower than in normal individuals. Psychopaths may excel in certain activities, but they generally manifest no "technical or craftsmen talents." That is, a psychopath can excel only in "those sciences which do not require a correct humanistic world view or practical skills." One skill that psychopaths do possess is the ability to "...recognize each other in a crowd as early as childhood, and they develop an awareness of the existence of other individuals similar to them."[30]

An individual psychopath's history often involves frequent changes in residence, a string of random and disconnected jobs without any discernable long-term career, and a series of short-term romantic relationships. Because their own lives are characterized by constant turmoil, the psychopath has learned to function smoothly in chaotic environments. Such an individual is often favored as an employee in organizations undergoing rapid change or internal chaos. Psychopaths thrive in fast-paced environments where change is constant, and no one is concerned about keeping track of the past. This correlates with Lobaczewsky's ponerized society, in which parts of the past are deliberately erased from the public record. It is also consistent with research that finds increased risk of workplace mobbing in organizations undergoing transition.[31]

The common denominator of psychopaths, regardless of specific modus operandi or level of intelligence is a lack of empathy. Lobaczewsky estimates that this type of person comprises only about 6% of the world's population, but they have a profound effect on the rest of us. While the extremely violent sociopaths are dealt with through a formal legal system, such systems are generally ineffective against the nonviolent varieties, especially those who are clever enough to find ways to circumvent the law—or even are the ones writing the laws. While many of us may envision psychopaths as serial killers, they can also be a highly successful businessman or politician. Psychopathic behavior thus manifests along a continuum, and less serious dysfunctions do not necessarily result in illegal behavior. Lobaszewsky proposes that psychopaths who have intelligence and resources—or who have done a good job in developing their tangential skills—can actually be quite successful. This is especially so in occupations that require extroverted and assertive personalities, along with the good fortune of access to material means:

> "...if you are born at the right time, with some access to family fortune and you have a special talent for whipping up other people's hatred and sense of deprivation, you can arrange to kill large numbers of unsuspecting people. With enough money, you can accomplish this from far away, and you can sit back safely and watch in satisfaction....What differentiates a sociopath who lives off the labors of others from one who occasionally robs convenience stores, or from one who is a contemporary robber baron—or what makes the difference between an ordinary bully and a sociopathic murderer—is nothing more than social status, drive, intellect, blood lust, or simple opportunity."[32]

As psychopaths come to recognize that they are different from normal people, they begin to develop skills connected to their undamaged functions. Some of these compensatory skills then become overdeveloped. Because psychopaths do not experience the self-doubts and second-guessing that often accompany more critical thinking, these individuals can appear to others as commanding and decisive. Consequently, these individuals develop a reputation as being decisive, assertive, efficient, and effective, thus insuring their rise in the organizational (or social) hierarchy. These individuals then interpret their ability to make oversimplified split-second decisions—where more normal people experience conflict and self-doubt—as a form of superior ability. When large numbers of "normal" people also attribute superior ability to such individuals, it further perpetuates their egocentricity and belief in their own genius.[33]

What ultimately makes psychopaths more dangerous than those with related personality disorders is that the rest of us often do not recognize a psychopath, particularly a higher-functioning one. This ability to operate undetected was recognized in an early work on psychopathy by Dr. Hervey Cleckley, the 1976 *Mask of Sanity.* These individuals can appear to have superficial charm and high intelligence, and they often succeed in business or professional activities. Many of them do not display overt mental disorder and have learned how to avoid technically breaking the law. They are often particularly effective with deceit because they are unconcerned with whether their deceit will be discovered. In the business world, their impulsivity can appear as decisiveness, a trait which is sought for leadership positions. Because the rest of us regard a conscience as innate to the human condition, we cannot imagine someone being without it—which the psychopath is able to exploit to his own advantage.

Lobaszewsky argues that some amount of egotism may be necessary to help the individual overcome life's difficulties and protect the personality from neurotic disintegration. This egotism becomes pathological when individuals believe they must force others in the social group, and if possibly entire nations, to feel and think like themselves. As psychopaths are often acutely aware of their differences from others, they may at first attempt to hide them (the so-called "mask of sanity"). However, the psychopath is incapable of questioning his motivations or being critical of his behavior.[34] The psychopath thus maintains the illusion of his own reality by means of extreme psychological repression of evidence to the contrary, which is further compounded by the psychopath's skills at manipulation and deceit.

How Normal Individuals Become Psychologically Deformed

One need not be born a psychopath to develop psychopathic behavior. Lobaczewsky describes how an evil individual can affect others in his environment. While not everyone who comes in contact with a psychopath will become psychopathic themselves, they may experience detrimental effects to personality and behavior. According to Lobaszewsky, the behavior of a psychopath can "traumatize the minds and feelings of normal people, gradually diminishing the ability to use common sense."[35] As we now know from more modern research, these effects are aggravated when the victims are young people: Children raised in dysfunctional homes are more likely to suffer abnormal development, which can lead to character deformation in adulthood.

Lobaszewsky differentiates "essential" (i.e., hereditary) psychopathy from a lesser defect he terms characteropathy. This can best be described as environmental impact on hereditary personality traits, or what Lobaszewsky describes as the interdependence of someone's personality and his or her life circumstances. That is, someone with a characteropathic defect may still function normally, so long as that individual was raised (or is now living in) a normal environment. The earliest influences are those of immediate family, but the impact of external influences continues throughout the life of the individual. Thus, an individual is a combination of his own genetic characteristics, impact and habits of family, then later influences of peers, schoolmates and neighbors. This environmental influence increases in scope throughout one's life, expanding to include the state of development of the whole society.[36]

Characteropathic abnormality may be latent and only expressed when the individual is exposed to a dysfunctional environment. For example, a child raised in an abusive home will develop hypervigilance and other protective and avoidant behaviors. While these adaptations may indeed help the child survive the dysfunctional environment, the same behavior as an adult can seem abnormal, where the individual may be described as anxious and neurotic. A characteropathological individual may be raised in a psychologically healthy family, but then later be adversely influenced by peers (e.g., falling in with the "wrong crowd").

Characteropathological activation need not necessarily be solely caused by interaction with deviant individuals. When society (or significant portions of it) also becomes dysfunctional, it can have a negative impact on individual psychology and behavior. Lobaszewsky argues that individuals can become pathological when the society does not provide opportunities to express their individual talents, skills and gifts. Lobaszewsky found instances of characteropathological behavior in persons who were underemployed; that is, they are "forced [by circumstances] to exercise functions which do not make full use of [his or her] talents."

Most of my own research has revolved around the dysfunctions of our labor market, specifically underemployment. Just as we see higher rates of obesity among the poor and food insecure than among those with more than enough money to stay well-fed, the labor market exhibits a schizoid dichotomy between some employees working so many hours they barely have anything resembling a human social life while others are involuntarily un- and under-employed. There is also the paradox of the working poor (working full- time or near full-time and yet struggling to maintain subsistence), and overeducation-underemployment—educated and experienced individuals who must by necessity take lower quality employment—while politicians continually tout the need to produce more workforce skills.[37] However, instead of revolutionary discontent (a reasonable reaction to the reality of labor status), underemployment in the United States instead tends to produce anxiety and depression. This is another example of the fundamental attribution error, in which underemployed individuals blame their own shortcomings rather than the fact that there is not a sufficient number of decent jobs to assimilate the increasing educational and skill levels of the population. It is not difficult to imagine such conditions aggravating characteropathy.

Psychopathy in Organizations

Where most of us are likely to personally experience the negative effects of a psychopath is in our workplaces. Indeed, large organizations are microcosms of society, and can be subject to ponerization perhaps even more easily. According to Dr. Hare, psychopaths are attracted to environments which provide opportunities for them to manipulate their way to the top: "Like all predators, psychopaths go where the action is, which to them means positions, occupations, professions, and organizations that afford them the opportunity to obtain power, control, status, and possessions, and to engage in exploitative interpersonal relationships."[38]

Dr. Hare's more recent research on psychopaths in the workplace corroborates the special abilities of psychopaths—particularly high-functioning ones—to get ahead in modern society. We have seen that certain characteristics of psychopaths actually facilitate their ability to succeed, particularly in contexts where self-promotion and image management help one to stand out from the crowd, and rewards are determined by narrow productivity/bottom line metrics that may be easy to manipulate. Some psychopathic traits make job candidates attractive due to a combination of personal charisma, social manipulation, and an ability to deceive. They also possess characteristics associated with leadership such as taking charge, making decisions, and motivating others to do what you want them to do. In psychopaths, these can be "well-packaged forms of coercion, domination, and manipulation."[39]

Modern business rewards social skills generally associated with leadership such as charisma, extroversion, risk-taking, assertiveness and self-confidence. Risk-taking is expected of leaders in times of crisis, but it can sometimes be hard to draw the line between risk-taking and foolhardiness, because there are situations where it may truly be risker to do nothing. What differentiates a psychopath is that risks are taken to satisfy personal needs for thrill-seeking and are not part of a calculated and coherent strategy. More so than "regular" persons, psychopaths can keep their emotions under control and remain calm in a crisis, an ability which is also associated with leadership. Where a non-psychopath must possess an ability to manage and control emotions, the psychopath does not experience emotions, so there is no need to control them. This means that the psychopath has more energy to deal with the task at hand, further bolstering the appearance of leadership skill. In essence, a psychopath does not experience self-doubt, and "displays few, if any, of the idiosyncrasies, foibles, and neuroses that make the rest of us unique,"[40] but perhaps less suited to high-stress and dispassionate organizational leadership.

In a society that is increasingly impersonal and transactional, the ability to manage one's public image; i.e., "branding," can have significantly more impact on personal success than actual skills, talent, knowledge or work history. In the area of impression management and manipulation, psychopaths are masters: "A talented corporate fraudster easily comes across to executives as an ambitious, enthusiastic player. Competence and loyalty, two critical business values, are often assumed (i.e., without requirement of actual proof). To coworkers and peers, the psychopath comes across as a likable person, perhaps a bit narcissistic or manipulative, but friendly, open, and honest nonetheless."[41] Although all new employees attempt to make a good impression and may, to some extent, be putting on an "act," the difference with the psychopath is that their entire agenda revolves around deceit and manipulation. Dr. Hare warns that it is often difficult to tell when someone has crossed the line between normal impression management and predatory deception.[42]

According to Dr. Hare, most psychopaths start out in an organization being liked by their bosses and co-workers. As they manipulate and build their network, they gain power within the organization, both formal and informal. Psychopaths form alliances with individuals who possess personality traits such as narcissism, assertiveness and dominance, because these individuals are usually found in positions of power.[43] In the beginning, the psychopath is able to secure sufficient loyalty that he can operate unchallenged, imposing his own agenda onto the organization. Once in power, such individuals can be difficult to remove, as "Those with power and authority rarely give it up willingly, even in service of the greater good of the organization….These individuals may feel threatened by the erosion of their own positions, and can sabotage the transition by virtue of their sense of entitlement."[44]

When psychopathic individuals achieve positions where they can impose their own agenda, it can negatively impact organizational culture, rendering it toxic for normal people. Eventually some individuals begin to see the psychopath's dark side. Someone might either confront the psychopath or bring his behavior to the attention of higher-ups. By this time, the psychopath has established himself with the organization's hierarchy and is able to turn complaints against the complainant. This serves as a chilling effect on other employees, who decide it is not worth their own reputation to challenge the psychopath.[45] In such a manner, the psychopath is able to build a career that leads to increasingly higher-level positions within the organization, sometimes even deposing those who helped them rise. Dr. Hare suggests in his studies of corporate psychopaths that most of them are still enjoying successful careers in their original organizations, and most of the rest were able to move up to larger jobs in other companies. This scenario is more likely in organizations undergoing chaotic change, where power structures can shift almost overnight, with negative consequences for the corporate culture.[46] For normal people, sometimes the best (or only) course of action to protect oneself is to simply leave. However, as normal people abandon an organization that is being taken over by psychopaths or other anti-socials, there are decreased countervailing cultural norms to help reverse the condition.

It is difficult to spot the high-functioning psychopath because they have an unusual ability to read others—identifying someone's likes, dislikes, motives, needs and vulnerabilities—and finding the right buttons to push to get what they want.[47] Psychopaths are known for a behavior known as "gaslighting," a process whereby they convince someone else to doubt their own thoughts, knowledge, and even their own reality. Their level of deceptiveness goes beyond an aggressive salesperson trying to close a deal or a politician trying to get votes, but "cynical, facile lying…[is] an integral, systemic part of their personality."[48] However, notwithstanding the negative effects on the workforce in general, the psychopath's demeanor of confidence and strength appeals to organizations who are struggling with change or in a state of chaos. "Egocentricity, callousness, and insensitivity suddenly become acceptable trade-offs in order to get the talents and skills needed to survive in an accelerated, dispassionate business world."[49]

Recent studies on leadership have identified the so-called corporate psychopath. While most studies estimate that less than 1% of the general population is psychopathic, this proportion has been estimated to rise to 10% among corporate executives, who are attracted to thrill-seeking, extreme risk taking, and money. While researchers of corporate psychopathology admit there are logistical difficulties in collecting data and more work is needed, they have found that business school students are significantly higher in narcissism,[50] are less cooperative, are 50% more likely to engage in cheating,[51] and value empathy the least.[52] At the same time, these individuals are also rated high on traits such as assertiveness, competence, order, achievement-striving and self-discipline.[53] So-called "successful" corporate psychopaths are described as charming and ambitious, while at the same time described as manipulative, self-serving, opportunistic, and ruthless.[54] Other research supports the proposition that psychopathic managers often rise rapidly to positions of power. In addition to an ever-accelerating pace of change and chaotic environments, organizational features that facilitate psychopathic empowerment are reward systems that value profits and stock prices above all else, the strict control that leaders have over information, and the cultural ideal of the charismatic leader.[55] Thus, the research suggests that these individuals have obvious advantages in climbing corporate hierarchies, notwithstanding their otherwise antisocial tendencies.

Dr. Hare also proposes that the increasing size of organizations, along with increased competitiveness and constant change, have created an environment wherein psychopaths thrive, since "psychopaths are more attracted to work for businesses that offer fast-paced, high-risk, high-profit environments."[56] The corporate psychopath survives and thrives in a large company. Bigger companies, especially those undergoing change, provide the best opportunity for psychopaths to rise to power. Constant change, which often frustrates the rest of us, is attractive to psychopaths since it presents new relationship potentials to manipulate. The main tactic of the psychopath at work is to manipulate communication networks to enhance their own reputation and disparage others, to create conflict and rivalry, and to spread disinformation.[57] Moreover, the constant turmoil prevents the development of long-term bonding and trust among the rest of the employees, making it easier for the psychopath to manipulate them. Thus, the psychopath is better able to operate unimpeded by others who are not specifically recruited to become either a "pawn, patron or patsy" and are able to observe the psychopath objectively.[58]

Dr. Hare further argues that the abandonment of the psychological contract at work has increased the likelihood of psychopaths assuming power. Between the 1940s and 1970s, employees could expect a long and stable career, with reciprocal loyalties between the organization and its employees. The new business model mandates that organizations must be flexible and willing to change constantly in order to survive. No one expects (or should expect) any semblance of safety and security, as there is a constant urge for reinventing, reenergizing and rebuilding. Employees are no longer loyal, since anyone's skills can become obsolete, no matter how long it took to acquire them. In this new business order, organizations are constantly looking for new "entrepreneurial" employees, who are often younger and less experienced.

"Entrepreneurial" organizations are also attractive to psychopaths because they present opportunities of increased freedom to act unconstrained by longstanding rules and policies. Entrepreneurial organizations are more tolerant of risk—indeed, they often encourage it—which has particular appeal to a psychopath. These organizations also present opportunity in the form of fluid leadership or management positions, which allows a psychopath to exert power over people and resources, to delegate most of their real work to underlings (freeing them to build and manipulate networks), and to obtain larger-than-average salaries.[59] Thus, large and entrepreneurial organizations (which are idolized by our media and culture) both appeal to psychopaths and prefer certain of their behavioral characteristics.

While most of us are more concerned about street crime—murderers, rapists and armed robbers—statistically we are more likely to be harmed by the white-collar criminal. Almost 30% of case filings in U.S. District Courts involve business crimes, which rob citizens of between $40 and $200 billion per year. This compares to about $4 billion per year that is stolen by way of burglary, muggings and vandalized property. Instead of killing individuals, the corporate raider eliminates companies through mergers and acquisitions; the executive eradicates worker's livelihoods through layoffs and downsizing. Citing reports from the World Health Organization, a study by Polish researchers at the Warsaw School of Economics found that the current business environment predisposes individuals with pathological personality features to hold the highest posts within organizations, with the most common behavioral manifestations being bullying, mobbing, sexual harassment, and "political behaviors."[60] One writer has argued that psychopaths represent the "new man that is being produced by the evolutionary pressures of modern life."[61]

Another line of studies has examined what is called the "Dark Triad" of narcissism, psychopathy and Machiavellianism. Machiavellianism is named after a 16th century Italian politician, whose works *The Art of War* (1521) and *The Prince* (1532) advocated for the employment of cunning and duplicity in promoting one's goals, agenda and career.[62] A well-known Machiavellian quote is that, "It is better to be feared than loved if one cannot be both." An interesting debate arose in the May 2017 *CPA Journal* between one set of researchers (both who possessed PhDs and CPAs)[63] who argued that Dark Triad traits were associated with financial fraud and such traits should be included in calculations of risk, and a second set of researchers (a psychiatrist and a CPA),[64] who argued that there was no way to quantify a "financial fraud personality type." The Dark Triad team presented evidence that investment banks in particular had been deliberately recruiting Dark Triad types (using psychometric testing) because of their positive traits connected with persuasiveness, strategic thinking, and willingness to take risks, suggesting that measurement of the personality scales had not only been adequately verified, they were being used to identify these individuals for positive selection. The opponents argued that "our most creative, interesting, and profitable clients are frequently those who are building business empires," and to discourage such behavior would eliminate such companies as Apple, Google and Facebook (as well as Enron, which they characterized as "very creative"). Evidently, there are people who believe that the "benefits" of Dark Triad personalities outweigh their destructiveness.

Dr. Hare references the documentary *The Corporation,* which analyzes organizational bad behavior in the context of the diagnostic criteria for psychopathy. Dr. Hare caveats that there is nothing inherent in corporations that leads to psychopathic behavior, but suggests that corporate culture and behavior can indeed be deemed psychopathic in some instances. Just as not all criminals are psychopaths, not all corporations engage in psychopathic behavior. Again, Dr. Hare admonishes against untrained attempts to diagnose either individuals or organizations. However, just as Lobaszewsky argues that a few psychopathic individuals can infect an entire society, Dr. Hare implies that bad behavior can extend beyond individuals acting alone and result in both organizationally-condoned bad behavior and dysfunctional culture.[65]

Psychopaths and Society

Most of us can readily imagine how a psychopath can infect an organization. Indeed, some of us may have actually experienced this. A bigger question is whether this same dynamic can apply to an entire national—or even global—culture. This is the essence of

Lobaczewsky's study of ponerization. When a critical mass of psychopaths attain social positions where they can influence popular culture and the foundation of individual worldviews, the society adapts itself accordingly. While such processes may be driven by psychopaths, they are also aided and abetted by purportedly normal people. These are people who, perhaps like John Demjanjuk, or the participants in the Milgram experiments, would not normally engage in behavior involving the torture of other humans, but who have been indoctrinated to believe that such behavior is now perfectly acceptable, and maybe even justified.

Where Lobaszewsky's genius is most salient is when he probes further into how social systems can operate to deform emotional functioning in otherwise normal (or only minimally abnormal) individuals. Lobaczewsky describes a form of feedback loop in which increasingly pathological individuals obtain influence on society, which results in increasingly pathological social structures. It begins with the acceptance of harmful behaviors that are not yet considered pathological by the opinion of the social environment.[66] Positions of power are at first filled by characteropathic individuals with higher developed skills (usually involving manipulation and subterfuge). From here begins a process of harmful negative selection, where critically-thinking people are replaced by persons with lesser brains, more subservience, and sometimes discreet psychological deviations of their own.[67] Characteropathic individuals are gradually replaced by more psychopathological individuals, i.e., those with inherited deviations. These individuals then solidify their control over society through methods of authoritarianism, oppression, and fear. The complexities of this process, which Lobaszewsky terms ***ponerization,*** will be explored in the following section.

Ponerization is more likely to occur in societies which Lobaszewsky describes as "psychologically ignorant."[68] According to Lobaszewsky, the wide variance in human intellect is actually a good thing, because it allows societies to be highly creative and complex.[69] Research suggests that our reasoning faculties continue to develop throughout adult life, reaching their peak only when "our hair starts greying and the drive of instinct, emotion, and habit begins to abate."[70] This basic emotional intelligence, or what is sometimes termed "common sense," is widely distributed within society and often recognized in individuals whose intellectual talent may be otherwise average.[71] Although Lobaczewsky never terms it as such, he suggests that ponerization is more likely to occur in societies where a large percentage of citizens lack the capacity for critical thinking.

Ponerization is also more likely to occur in societies where large numbers of individuals feel excluded and unable to reach their full potential, as well as in highly unequal societies. This has negative implications for the unacknowledged shadow of underemployment,[72] along with frustration of opportunity and economic mobility. It is not surprising that individuals and groups who are subject to genuine social injustices are receptive to messages that address their grievances and promise a solution. An observant and cunning psychopath with a desire for power is thus able to exploit these grievances for his own ends by co-opting others into a mission purportedly based on justice. Compounding this process is the fact that psychopathic individuals tend to seek positions of power and authority, most often in politics and commerce.

We have seen that psychopaths thrive in a materialistic "success at any cost" culture. Where a psychopath becomes particularly dangerous to society as a whole (as opposed to individual victims) is when they become obsessed with conforming others to their own worldview. In essence, the psychopath defines his own lack of empathy as "normal" and empathy as "abnormal." In his explanation of the rise of Nazi Germany, Lobaszewsky argues that, "Common people are prone to identify with the emperor" (the just world and status quo biases)[73] and adopt the leader's characteropathology. The power of paranoid minds is that they easily enslave less critical minds, e.g. people with other kinds of psychological deficiencies.[74] This phenomenon is aggravated when the regime gains control over media and other forms of propaganda, where "slogans take on the power of arguments and real data are subjected to subconscious selection."[75] The ultimate result is a "web or continuum of mutual conditioning…[an] interlocking structure [in which] one kind of evil feeds and opens doors for others,"[76] The state itself, when "fed for a generation on pathologically altered psychological material," exhibits pathological characteristics similar to that of individuals, namely an inability to use common sense and lack of critical thinking. Harking back to the Milgram experiments, in such conditions even "honorably trained army officers perform inhuman orders."[77]

Even today, psychopathy has no known cure. It is nonresponsive to behavioral modification or even religious conversion. Although medical science has learned a lot about structural and neurochemical markers, we don't know enough to fix it. However, Lobaszewsky proposes that the humane response is not to punish such people, but to learn to identify them and prevent them from attaining societal positions where they could determine the fate of other people. Because Lobaszewsky views psychopathy as a disease, to punish someone for the random misfortune of being born this way is itself a form of pathology. In a word of hope, Lobaszewsky argues that human instinct is naturally coded to control anyone who is harmful to the individual or to the group. This suggests that when psychopaths rise to power, it is a result of dysfunctional (rather than natural) causes. Indeed, Lobaszewsky views the rise of pathocratic society as a cyclical phenomenon, which is eventually replaced when normal people take back control.

In the following section, we will review Lobaszewsky's description of the ponerization process, along with an analysis of how this phenomenon is playing out in our early 21st century world.

Notes

[1] Stevens, G.W., Dueling, J.K., & Armenakis, A. (2012). Successful psychopaths: Are they unethical decision-makers and why? *Journal of Business Ethics,* 105, 139-149.

[2] Babiak, P., & Hare, R.D. (2006). *Snakes in suits.* New York, NY: HarperCollins Publishers, Inc.

[3] Some mental health professionals have proposed an even more malevolent Dark Tetrad, which also includes sadism.

[4] Buckels, E.E., Trapnell, P.D., & Paulhus, D.L. (2014). Trolls just want to have fun. *Personality and Individual Differences, 67,* 97-102.

[5] Craker, N., & March, E. (2016). The dark side of Facebook: The Dark Tetrad, negative social potency, and trolling behaviors. *Personality and Individual Differences, 102,* 79-84.

[6] Lobaszewsky, A. (1998). *Ponerology: A science on the nature of evil adjusted for political purposes.* Red Pill Press, at p. 105. Full document PDF at http://www.survivorshandbook.com/wp-content/articles/political-ponerology.pdf.

[7] A full discussion of the complexity of these issues will not be attempted here. Our primary focus is on psychopathy, specifically the lack of empathy, which is consistent with both Lobaszewsky's work and modern mental health definitions.

[8] Lobaszewsky, *supra* at p. 131.

[9] *Id.* at p. 132.

[10] *Id.* at p. 145.

[11] Hare, R.D. (1998). *Without Conscience: The disturbing world of the psychopaths among us.* New York, NY: Guildford Press. Dr. Hare is one of today's leading researchers on psychopathy.

[12] See *The Clinical and Forensic Assessment of Psychopathy, A Practitioner's Guide.*

[13] Willerman, L., Loehlin, J., & Horn, J. (1992). An adoption and cross-fostering study of the MMPI psychopathic deviate scale. *Behavior Genetics, 22*, 515-529. Also Lyons et al. (1995). Differential heritability of adult and juvenile antisocial traits. *Archives of General Psychiatry, 52,* 906-915.

[14] Raine, A., & Yang, Y. (2006). The neuroanatomical bases of psychopathy: A review of brain imaging findings. In *Handbook of Psychopathy*, Christopher Patrick, Ed. New York, NY: Guilford Press, pp. 278-95.

[15] Blair, R.J. (2003). Neurobiological basis of psychopathy. *British Journal of Psychiatry, 182,* 5-7.

[16] Irle, E., Lange, C., & Sachsse, U. (2005). Reduced size and abnormal asymmetry of parietal cortex in women with borderline personality disorder. *Biological Psychiatry, 57,* 173-82.

[17] Posner, M.I., et al. (2003). An approach to psychobiology of personality disorders. *Development and Psychopathology 15*(4), 1093-1106.

[18] Yang, Y. (2005). Prefrontal white matter in pathological liars. *British Journal of Psychiatry, 187,* 320-25.

[19] Oakley, B. (2007). *Evil genes: Why Rome fell, Hitler rose, Enron failed, and my sister stole my mother's boyfriend.* Amherst, NY: Prometheus Books.

[20] Blakeslee, S. (2006, January 10). Cells that read minds. *New York Times.* Also, Blair, R.J. & Perschardt, K.S. (2002). Empathy: A unitary circuit or a set of dissociable neuro-cognitive systems. *Behavioral and Brain Sciences, 25,* 42-43.

[21] Viding, E., et al. (2005). Evidence of substantial genetic risk for psychopathy in 7-year-olds. *Journal of Child Psychology and Psychiatry, 46*(6), 592-97.

[22] Unfortunately, Lobaszewsky did not pursue the question whether such conditions were more conducive to psychopathy than cleaner, healthier environments.

[23] Lobaszewsky, *supra* at p. 177.

[24] Babiak & Hare, *supra*, at pp. 250-270.

[25] *Id.* at pp. 185-188.

[26] *Id.* at p. 190.

---

[27] *Id*. at p. 102.

[28] Stout, M. (2005). *The sociopath next door.* New York, NY: Broadway Books/Random House, Inc.

[29] Shapiro, D. (1999). *Neurotic styles.* Basic Books/Perseus Books Group.

[30] Lobaszewsky, *supra,* at p. 127.

[31] Duffy, M., & Sperry, L. (2012*). Mobbing: Causes, consequences, and solutions.* New York, NY: Oxford University Press.

[32] Quote by Laura Knight-Jadczyk, attributed to Dr. Martha Stout, author of *The sociopath next door: The ruthless versus the rest of us.*

[33] Lobaszewsky, *supra* at pp. 113-114.

[34] *Id*. at p. 147.

[35] Id. at p. 106.

[36] Id at p. 72.

[37] Vanhettinga, B. (2018). *The Great Jobs Deception.* Also, Professional Reserve Armies: Underemployment and Labor Degradation in Professional Occupations. (Doctoral Dissertation, February 2015).

[38] Babiak & Hare, *supra* at p. 97.

[39] *Id.* at p. xi.

[40] *Id.* at p. 216.

[41] *Id*. at p. 123.

[42] *Id*. at p. 127.

[43] *Id*. at p. 131.

[44] *Id*. at pp. 162-163.

[45] *Id*. at p. 139.

---

[46] *Id.* at pp. 140-141.

[47] *Id.* at p. 37.

[48] *Id.* at p. 51.

[49] *Id.* at p. xii.

[50] Westerman, J.W., Bergman, J.Z., Berman, S.M., & Daly, J.P. (2011). Are universities creating millennial narcissistic employees? An examination of narcissism in business students and its implications. *Journal of Management Education, 36*(1), 5-32.

[51] Brown, T.A., Sautter, J.A., Littvay, L., Sautter, A.C., & Bearnes, B. (2010). Ethics and personality: Empathy and narcissism as moderators of ethical decision making in business students. *Journal of Education for Business, 85*(2), 203-208.

[52] Holt, S., & Marquez, J. (2012). Empathy in leadership: Appropriate or misplaced? An empirical study on a topic that is asking for attention. *Journal of Business Ethics, 105,* 95-105.

[53] Mullens-Sweatt, S.N., Glover, N.G., Derefinko, K.J., Miller, J.D., & Widiger, T. A. (2010). *Journal of Research in Personality, 44*(4), *554-558.*

[54] Boddy, C.R. (2005). The implications of corporate psychopaths for business and society: An initial examination and a call to arms. *Australasian Journal of Business and Behavioural Sciences, 1*(2), 30-40.

[55] Gudmundsson, A., & Southey, G. (2011). Leadership and the rise of the corporate psychopath: What can business schools do about the 'snakes inside'? *e-Journal of Social and Behavioral Research in Business, 2*(2), 18-27.

[56] Babiak & Hare, *supra* at p. xiii.

[57] *Id.* at p. 129.

[58] *Id.* at p. 127.

[59] *Id.* at p. 164.

[60] Wojtczuk-Turek, A., & Turek, D. (2011) Executive psychopaths: Abusive behavior of the management. Edukacja Ekonomistów i Menedżerów. https://www.researchgate.net/profile/Dariusz_Turek/publication/275637711_Executive_Psychopaths_Abusive_Behaviour_of_the_Management/links/55488c720cf2b0cf7aceceb0/Executive-Psychopaths-Abusive-Behaviour-of-the-Management.pdf

Harrington, A. (1973). *Psychopaths.* New York, NY: Simon & Schuster.

[62] Both of these works are often on the reading lists of students attending elite institutions of higher education which groom them for higher-level positions in business and government.

[63] Sridhar Ramamoorti and Barry Jay Epstein.

[64] Jeffrey Borenstine and Arthur J. Radin.

[65] Babiak & Hare, *supra* at p. 95.

[66] Lobaczewsky, *supra* at p. 102.

[67] *Id.* at p. 107.

[68] *Id.* at p. 48.

[69] *Id.* at p. 65.

[70] *Id.* at p. 63.

[71] *Id.* at p. 64.

[72] VanHettinga, B. (2018). *The Great Jobs Deception.*

[73] Just world theory and system justification biases are more thoroughly analyzed in *Why Assholes Rule the World,* VanHettinga (2019).

[74] Lobaszewsky, *supra* at p. 110.

[75] *Id.* at p. 108.

[76] *Id.* at p. 101.

[77] *Id.* at p. 109.

Section 2
The Hysteroidal Cycle and Ponerogenic Process

"Society is not an organism subordinating every cell to the good of the whole; neither is it a colony of insects, where the collective instinct acts like a dictator. However, it should also avoid being a compendium of egocentric individuals linked purely by economic interests and legal and formal organizations....Isolating an individuals' personal interest as if it were at war with collective interests is pure speculation which radically oversimplifies real conditions...[and] asking questions based on such schemes is logically defective..."

Dr. Andrew Lobaczewsky

Although all societies can be said to contain one or more cultures, the culture that is dominant at any specific time period is subject to cyclical effects. In discussing the genesis of evil, Lobaczewsky describes what he calls a ***hysteroidal cycle***. It is difficult to define this precisely, but one might consider it a periodicity of progress and decline. According to Lobaczewsky, the potential for evil to infect an entire society depends on the intersection of a peak in this hysteroidal cycle with ponerogenic processes that are operating within the society, culminating in the establishment of a pathocracy (sociopathic leadership). Moreover, Lobaczewsky suggests that the ability to thwart any one of these phenomena from taking firm root in a society can avoid the emergence of another Nazi Germany or Soviet Russia.

In order to help us understand Lobaczewsky's concept, we will analyze the meaning of the word ***hysteria.*** Hysteria as a term of psychological science has changed meanings over the years, and it may very well have had a somewhat different meaning when

Lobaczewsky was engaged in his studies and research. During the Freudian period (approximately 1885-1930), hysteria was a (generally disparaging) patriarchal term connected with the female menstrual cycle. In modern mental health science, hysteria is a neurotic disorder of psychological dissociation, or a process in which memories, feelings, perceptions and ideas are lost to conscious awareness. It is a complex neurosis in which psychological distress manifests as physical symptoms (e.g., blindness, paralysis, amnesia) that have no know medical cause. It has also been associated with histrionic personality disorder, or personalities that are self-centered, attention-seeking, and operate on high drama and emotion rather than fact and logic.

Modern psychology no longer recognizes hysteria as a single definite condition. Indeed, the word has expanded beyond mental health terminology to indicate a state of uncontrollable emotion or excitement, which is often applied to groups (e.g., mass hysteria) as well as individuals. In Lobaczewsky's work, the hysteroidal cycle is associated with a loss of ability to think critically and deal with complexity among the general population. As society devolves, it begins to "strangle the capacity for individual and societal consciousness."[1] The "good times" eventually degenerate into hedonism, ignorance, lust of power, a narrowing of worldview, and an increase in egotism, all of which result in an evil society.[2]

The cycle begins with good, or happy times. However, these so-called "good times" usually involve benefits and privileges for one group that is rooted in injustice to another group.[3] In order to keep the peace during these "good times," the privileged classes learn to "repress from their field of consciousness" the idea that they are benefitting from injustice. They teach their children to disparage the "moral and mental values" of those who they "over-advantage."[4] Lobaczewsky also alludes to a "formative deficiency of character that is a perennial sickness of societies, especially the privileged elites,"[5] foreshadowing the work of Professor Paul Piff on the connection between social class and selfishness.

The cycle of happy, peaceful times leads to a narrowing of worldview and an increase in egoism. "When communities lose the capacity for psychological reason and moral criticism, the processes of the generation of evil are intensified…until everything reverts to 'bad times.'"[6] The loss of critical thinking skills in the general population--along with a generalized hopelessness, confusion, and other features of cultural disintegration—then paves the way for "pathological plotters, snake-charmers" and others who rise to power, which accelerates the social degeneration.[7] Fortunately, the "bad times" contains the seeds of its own destruction, as the "suffering, effort, and mental activity during times of imminent bitterness lead to a progressive, generally heightened, regeneration of lost values," and eventually, resistance in both thought and action.[8] Normal, prosocial people eventually regain control, good times return in due course, and the cycle begins again.

Ponerogenic Processes

According to Lobaczewsky, each society contains a small but active minority of persons with "deviant worldviews." This deviance is caused by internal psychological anomalies or by longer-term influence of a dysfunctional environment. The pathological individual may have dreams and idealism similar to those of normal people, including the desire to reform the world to their liking. The psychopath is motivated by "the pursuit of immediate attractions, moments of pleasure, and temporary feelings of power,"[9] and he is incapable of understanding the prosocial motives of others. Consequently, the main objective of pathological deviants is to create a world where their way of experiencing and perceiving reality would dominate—they would not be "forced" to submit to laws and customs which to them are incomprehensible.[10] To psychopaths, a social structure dominated by normal persons is viewed as oppressive.[11]

While the psychopathic minority is always among us, their way of thinking gains influence as the rest of society becomes hysteroidal. Lobaszewsky describes what he calls "conversive thinking," which becomes highly contagious and spreads during "happy times." Although Lobaczewsky does not precisely define conversive (sometimes he calls it conversion) thinking, he alludes to a lack of reason and logic. This defect in reasoning serves to reduce the ability of the population at large to detect and divert pathological individuals and processes. As an antidote to conversive thinking, Lobaczewsky suggests educating people in the "art of proper reasoning," or what we today might call critical thinking. Lobaczewsky thus suggests that so long as a sufficient percentage of the population is so fortified, there will be sufficient resistance to the incorporation of pathological worldviews.

Pathological individuals are often able to utilize ideology (which in itself may not be pathological in its original form) to impose their own pathologies on the worldview of the rest of society.[12] It starts with indoctrination of a smaller group or groups. The persons recruited may have lesser pathologies of their own, or might be "naïve rebels or people who have suffered injustice."[13] Thus the message may also resonate with normal people who have truly been treated unfairly. Indeed, social injustice is often a precursor to a radicalized worldview.

A subset of deviant yet articulate individuals learns to promote an ideology with a natural (i.e., pre-existing) following. Lobaczewsky calls these individuals "spellbinders," because they can create cult-like followings who have lost the capacity to perceive the individual's underlying pathology.[14] While ideologies do not necessarily need spellbinders for their propagation, a spellbinder usually needs to start with a foundational ideology—even if the ideology is later perverted for other purposes. The spellbinder convinces his followers of his own exceptionalism, and some are even messianic.[15] A typical modus operandi of the spellbinder is to shower his followers with attention and favors, while demonizing outsiders. As the spellbinder gathers those who are sympathetic to his message, others who maintain their "healthy critical faculties" attempt to counteract the spellbinder's messages. This process results in a polarization of social attitudes,[16] which, even without underlying psychopathology can be harmful to social coherence.

Lobaczewsky alleges that even individuals with high intelligence might not be immune to a spellbinder,[17] and commonsense resistance might include "feelings of helplessness."[18] Lobaszewsky proposes that in a healthy society, there are enough critically thinking people around to minimize the damage of a spellbinder. That is, the spellbinder may have a following, but they are considered a fringe group rather than mainstream. However, in societies where there is a high degree of "social injustice, cultural backwardness, or intellectually limited rulers," spellbinders can lead entire societies to "large-scale human tragedy."[19]

As spellbinder-type leaders gain control over larger followings (both in number of individual members and number of different groups), the next stage of the process involves the formation and growth of these ponerogenic associations. These groups may be called gangs, cliques, mobs, or mafia, and they frequently aspire to political power. All ponerogenic groups lose the capacity to view their own behavior as pathological and instead interpret it as heroic. However, in order to spread their particular ideology, they must find a way for their positions to be accepted by the broader group of normal people.

What follows the genesis and proliferation of ponerogenic groups is what Lobaczewsky terms a "secondary ponerization process." Primary ideologies, which may have been founded upon genuine social injustice or other higher social values, are gradually re-written and adopted to functions and goals other than the original ones.[20] The group splinters into factions—one who incorporates the more valuable elements of the original ideology (what Lobaczewsky terms the "critical-corrective") and another who interprets the original ideology through their own psychological deficiencies (what Lobaczewsky terms "pathological acceptance").[21] Indeed, the "greater and truer" the original ideology, the longer its ponerogenic metamorphosis can be disguised from outside criticism.[22] Lobaczewsky cites the example of early communists, who would not have favored a centralized, top-down government, but the original ideology was subsumed to State corporatism.[23]

The original leadership (including the spellbinders) is gradually taken over by more pathological leaders, who often arise from powerful elites, which then serve to give the organization more mainstream credibility. Under the second generation of leadership, the organization's members are increasingly scrutinized and tested for ideological purity. Anyone expressing doubt or raising legitimate questions is subject to condemnation.[24] A ponerized organization may even turn against its original members and throw them out. As more normal people are being assimilated, individuals with inherited (rather than characteropathic) deviations progressively take over the leadership and inspirational positions. The original ideology becomes repackaged, and the organization splits into factions divided between the more normal members and the pathological ones. A group of psychopathic individuals may even end up steering the leader, which Lobaszewsky asserts happened to Hitler.[25] The leader himself eventually realizes that if he does not fulfill his assigned role he will be killed.

As more organizations become taken over by pathological elites, they gain greater power to frame worldviews and set political agendas. In essence, one form of evil serves to open the door to others. However, Lobaczewsky argues that whether this takeover of organizations by pathocrats impacts society at large is also affected by socio-economic conditions, aggregate intellectual functioning, and collective moral values. That is, the takeover by pathocrats is not inevitable so long as "good" society maintains some control over macrosocial agendas. The implication is that a society characterized by extreme inequities in power and wealth, decreased critical thinking ability, and increasing social polarization and incivility will more likely be disposed to takeover by pathocrats than a society that is functioning more healthfully.

Lobaczewsky's own analysis is that the world is now dominated by countries who have "destroyed the structural forms worked out by history and replaced them with social systems inimical to creative functioning [i.e., bureaucracies]… systems which can only survive by means of force."[26] Contemporary social hysterization is identified by the destruction of social connection and sense of moral duty, the distraction of the population over trivial matters to the exclusion of real problem-solving, and the paralysis of government. As ponerogenic processes encompass an entire nation, or even just its ruling elite, opposition from normal people is stifled—either by means of censorship, exclusion, or physical compulsion.[27] In Lobaszewsky's prediction, the next phase is going to be "marked by wars, revolutions and the fall of empires."[28]

Contemporary Signs of Hysterization

While Lobaczewsky has described ponerogenesis in broad, general terms, he also acknowledges that such phenomenon "has its own characteristic process of genesis."[29] The seeds of ponerization exist in every society (as we have seen in our analysis of human nature), but the manifestation and logistical process of how this occurs can take many forms, depending on socio-historical context and culture. Lobaczewsky even warns that attempting to parse whether the moral failings of society or individual pathologies come first is only "academic speculation."[30] Rather, it is the confluence and feedback effects of both that ultimately create macrosocial evil. In this subsection, we will apply Lobaczewsky's generalized criteria to what we are observing to be happening in American (and even global) society today (2020).

According to Lobaszewsky, an early indication of social ponerization is failure of the legal system to contain the harm caused by some individuals or entities. Only 30 of Lobaszewsky's subjects were punished by the law, which Lobaczewsky describes as "harsh." Some of these subjects who had also harmed others either escaped punishment or committed acts which were not punishable under current law. This failure of the legal system to contain the harm caused by some individuals is an indication of societal ponerization. In essence, the unpunished harm-doers were "...protected by a political system which is in itself a ponerogenic derivate."[31] An example from our modern times is the system's failure to punish any of the executives and officers of financial entities responsible for the 2007 mortgage market crash and ensuing worldwide recession. Indeed, these entities have emerged larger and wealthier while the rest of the country struggles to recover, suggesting that economic ponerization is alive and well in the United States. We are also seeing increasing failure to punish companies that pollute the environment or subject workers to hazardous conditions, bolstered by propaganda that such activities are necessary to promote economic growth.

Excess of Egotism

One sign of social ponerization is an increase in egotism, along with decreasing "links of moral duty and social networks."[32] Lobaczewsky describes egoism as an attitude that attributes excessive value to one's own traits, skills, knowledge, habits and worldview.[33] Egotism is probably something distinct from what we call narcissism today, although it has similar manifestations. "When three 'egos' govern, egoism, egotism, and egocentrism, the feeling of social links and responsibility toward others disappear, and the society in question splinters into groups ever more hostile to each other."[34] Even nations can be egotistic, especially when they attempt to force other nations to be and act as they do, since they are incapable (or perhaps unwilling) to understand other cultures and values.[35] Pathological egotism results when an individual (or a group or a nation) succeeds in repressing any consciousness of his (or its) own shortcomings or ability to be self-critical.[36]

While narcissism (a personality trait) may not be precisely the same thing as Lobaczewsky's egotism (a psychiatric term), they both involve a preoccupation with self which tends to include a disregard of others. Researchers have documented an increase in narcissism between 1950 and 2013 by analyzing best-selling non-fiction book titles for narcissistic content. The idea was that book sales were a better indicator of true motives than surveys, which might have been influenced by a social desirability bias.[37] Research on leadership suggests that a combination of narcissistic traits and cultural reward of narcissistic behavior contribute to narcissists' rise to power.

Narcissistic traits—even among non-narcissists—can be quite helpful in the pursuit of personal success, because they are often associated with leadership. One study found that narcissists perform well when interviewing for CEO positions because they are perceived as being charismatic and visionary.[38] Other studies have found a positive correlation between narcissism and strategic dynamism—the ballyhoo of the masters-of-the-universe types about the benefits of disruption and constant change—which tends to leave most everyone else confused and disoriented.[39] Moreover, in a hypercompetitive, winner-take-all society, some degree of narcissistic self-promotion may be necessary in the competition for decent employment, or even to insure that oneself is simply seen and heard in a noisy world.

Researchers have documented an increase in narcissism—both in the number of persons manifesting the personality trait and as a social phenomenon.[40] Narcissists are often associated with arrogance and selfishness, but it is often more about concern with image. Thus, narcissists can be friendly and charming when attempting to make a good impression, but can become hostile when their carefully crafted self-image is threatened.[41] These researchers blame a constellation of modern influences rather than an increase in hereditary narcissists, which include an emphasis on developing self-esteem that neglects social responsibility, a cult of celebrity, easy credit along with a culture that encourages competitive consumption, social media that encourages the display of flashy, glamorized images and shallow connections, and the need for constant self-promotion in a hypercompetitive labor market. In addition to all the ways society pushes individuals into narcissistic behavior, there is also a form of cultural narcissism.[42] Cultural narcissism arises as a normal ego defense to preserve psychic survival in an increasingly impersonal and bureaucratized society. It also is the result of a society that tells us we can have everything if we only "fix" ourselves. This (sometimes neurotic) preoccupation with the self conveniently redirects our energy, attention, and criticism away from the system.

Wasted Talent

Lobaczewsky asserts that, "The creation of a fair social structure continues to be a basic precondition for social order and the liberation of creative values."[43] In early 21st century America, society is perhaps the least fair in those places where most of us earn our livelihoods. More and more of us are finding out that a college education is no guarantee of a good job—or even of a minimally decent one. We are finding out that a large percentage of individuals receiving public assistance are not some mythical "welfare queen"—or even those who are unable to work due to illness or disability—but people with jobs.

In describing his observations of contemporary America, Lobaczewsky writes, "A highly talented individual in the USA finds it ever more difficult to fight his way through to self-realization and a socially creative position. Universities, politics, and businesses ever more frequently demonstrate a united front of relative untalented persons and even incompetent persons. The word 'overeducated' is heard more and more often."[44] When an individual is deprived of opportunity to make full use of his talents, he may feel cheated. "Revolutionary and radical ideas find fertile soil" in such downwardly adjusted individuals, who may then come to believe that the only fix for an unfair world is power.[45]

Full disclosure alert—I have done a lot of research on underemployment, more specifically the "overeducated" form of underemployment. Because I have kept up with the (somewhat sporadic) academic literature on this topic as well as completed a doctoral dissertation, I am more aware of the pernicious (and generally unacknowledged) effects of underemployment than most others. There was some renewed public interest in overeducation-underemployment following the Great Recession. News stories would feature new college graduates working as waitstaff or baristas, or alternatively, laid off executives who now had to work for millennial managers (if they could find work at all) at significantly reduced pay. What we didn't hear about, however, was a study by the Federal Reserve Bank of New York that was quietly released in early 2014.[46] While most of the mainstream media treated underemployment as an artifact of the Great Recession, the Federal Reserve study corroborated what most of the academic literature had been documenting: that is, persons with college degrees working in jobs that do not require them has remained at a fairly uniform rate of 33% over the past two decades. Moreover, job quality in general has been declining, with most jobs paying less, offering less security, fewer benefits and fewer avenues to upward mobility.

In my own research, I looked at underemployment among professionals in the STEM (science, technology, engineering, and math), health care, legal and academic professions.[47] Survey respondents were "screened" for a minimum of a four-year college degree (many of them also had post-graduate and professional degrees) and membership in one of 28 specific occupational categories. In addition to their education, some 58% of respondents had also passed some form of state professional licensing certification, and 42% maintained membership in at least one professional organization. That is, these were not the sort of uneducated and unskilled individuals the skills shortage alarmists are always complaining about. Additionally, their education was more professional-occupation-specific than a generalized liberal arts or business degree.

The study participants came from 46 of the 50 US states plus the District of Columbia, and they were asked about underemployment over the course of their career. This was to ensure that the study would document under-employment among people other than recent graduates, as well as time periods other than in a post-Great Recession economy (where under-employment is likely to be higher). Moreover, underemployment itself was defined narrowly: respondents were deemed underemployed only if they could find no full-time work that required their highest level of education (other forms of underemployment identified in the literature were not included). From this broad sample, narrow definitional construct, and longitudinal question format, the respondents had a 60% probability of experiencing underemployment at some point over their professional careers. Also corroborating the majority of prior research, underemployment appears to have structural features (it is embedded in how our labor markets work) above and beyond situations involving recent graduates and recessionary economic cycles.

The interviewees in my own study described a variety of forms of labor degradation in professional markets. In the case of an information technology (IT) professional, he had difficulty making ends meet as he scrambled with other overqualified IT job-seekers for short-term impermanent gigs that had no future. At the same time, the IT workers had to continually upgrade their credentials to cover perennially changing systems and platforms—usually at their own expense. STEM workers in general noted the irony of outsourcing along with the liberalization of H1-B visas, with many of them having to train their cheaper foreign replacements. A similar situation described the job market for college instructors: permanent, full-time positions were replaced with part-time and low paying adjunct positions. On top of being low-paid (PhDs working literally in poverty) and unpredictable (assignments were awarded only for a semester), adjunct gigs offered no opportunities for professional development or for accessing the resources of the institution generally. The legal profession was characterized more by a poverty in the midst of plenty syndrome: While the lawyers who "defaulted" to opening a solo practice were not technically underemployed (they were still practicing law), they struggled to survive financially, often blaming law schools for producing "too many" lawyers. These new lawyers found themselves in the paradoxical position of competing with "too many" other lawyers, while at the same time there was substantial unmet demand for legal services from people who could not afford it.

What this study (as well as the many other studies that provided its foundation) suggested was a system that is inefficient and out of balance. Yet, so long as a few are making fortunes, no one (except underemployed individuals) seems troubled by this. Indeed, we are not even measuring underemployment. In the eyes of the US Bureau of Labor Statistics (BLS), anyone who works a few hours per week, or works without pay in a family-owned business more than 15 hours in a week is considered fully employed. Also considered fully employed is someone with a college degree (or higher) working in a job that does not require it. The BLS has recently added the categories of involuntary part-time (which tripled between 1970 and 1990) and discouraged worker (neither currently working or looking for work, but want to work and have looked for work within the past 12 months). There are no measurements for overeducation, and even the involuntary part-time and discouraged numbers are not included in the "official" unemployment rate. As most of the studies that looked at underemployment found, we are not even measuring all of the various ways our labor market is not working for workers.

Disconnection of the Privileged from Everyone Else

Lobaczewsky argues that the narrowing worldview and increase in egotism that begins the hysteroidal process generally originates (or is found to be stronger) among the privileged elites.[48] According to Lobaczewsky, the vast majority of the "average" population "generally accepts its modest social position" so long as they are guaranteed an "equitable way of life."[49] This is one of the few times where Lobaczewsky alludes to basic fairness as a precondition for a good society. As we have previously discussed in situations of underemployment, when large numbers of individuals are unable to express their talents or are otherwise prevented from earning a livelihood commensurate with their abilities, it sows the seeds of social discord.

Lobaczewsky here describes what he terms "upwardly adjusted" individuals, who represent the flip side of underemployment. These individuals may find themselves in high level positions because of their connection to power and social privilege, yet find that "their talents and skills are not sufficient to fully perform their duties…[so] In fear of being discovered as incompetent, they begin to direct attacks against anyone with greater talent or skill, removing them from appropriate posts and playing an active role in degrading their social and professional adjustment."[50] Thus Lobaczewsky has described the dynamic of the workplace bully asshole.[51] He then goes on to predict that such individuals favor "whip-cracking, totalitarian governments" in order to protect their positions.[52] Here, we also see the beginnings of authoritarianism.

The conjunction of downwardly adjusted (underemployed) persons with upwardly adjusted (unearned privilege) persons results in a waste of society's human capital as well as generalized feelings of injustice. In the United States, employment is considered to be an individual issue that is determined by the neutral operation of "markets" and meritocratic principles. The issue of systemic underemployment is almost never addressed except in obscure academic articles. Conversely, upwardly adjusted individuals become "contemptuous of their supposed inferiors in a way highly reminiscent of czarist Russia…"[53] Lobaczewsky warns that addressing the matters of upward and downward adjustments in employment as a strictly private matter is "dangerously naïve,"[54] suggesting that these situations are caused as much by social structures as by individual personalities. It is also obvious how the dynamics of these downward and upward "adjustments" unrelated to merit have contributed to exaggerated economic polarization as well.

Most of us have heard about increasing inequality—a phenomenon that likely began in the late 1970s—but has become so extreme that even the mainstream media broadcasts an occasional story or article addressing it. The kind of inequality we are talking about here is not the same thing as a neighbor with a larger home or fancier car. It is also not about people who are paid more perhaps because they work more hours or have higher-level skills (i.e., doctors, lawyers or engineers). The new inequality represents extremes way beyond the normal variations of human effort, talent, and skills. If today's inequality is represented by a graphical representation of a six-foot man, the median household income would be found at the top of the man's shoe toe. Households earning $100,000 per year (in the top 20%) would be found around the man's ankles, at about a height of four inches. At the top of the man's head would be found households earning $1.5 million, nowhere near the range of multimillionaires and billionaires. To represent this level, one would need to ascend a skyscraper, from which height the bottom 99% would be almost invisible.[55]

The concentration of wealth is something that has occurred historically. In the comprehensively documented *Capital in the Twenty-First Century,*[56] Thomas Piketty argues that such concentration occurs whenever the rates of return to capital exceed the average rate of economic growth. Since the essence of capitalism is the extraction of wealth (from labor or from the environment), it almost always enjoys rates of increase higher than the rest of us. This has also been facilitated by legalized tax avoidance schemes perpetrated by the super-wealthy—who also have an inordinate influence on our legal and political systems.[57]

However, the process of extreme concentration has been aggravated by technological developments and new forms of winner-take-all markets. Winner-take-all markets are usually associated with the sports and entertainment industries, when recording and media distribution technologies allowed national and even global audiences access to the "best" performers, which crowded out opportunities for lesser-known artists, actors and minor sports leagues to earn a living. Winner-take-all markets are also created when early success in a new endeavor permits a company (or a small group of companies) to capture venture capital, market share, supply chains, and media attention, which they then use to grow bigger and/or buy out competitors. Early advantages are further amplified by so-called "network effects," which increase a firm's value the more people use its infrastructure. For example, Facebook captures information about its users, which increases its value because this allows it to better predict buying behavior. Google actually "learns" as people search with it, perfecting its algorithms and adding to its stores of information.

These new forms of leverage and networked markets have allowed huge concentrations of wealth and/or market share to be built up quickly, rather than through more traditional accumulations over time. Robert Frank documented the lives of these "new rich," concluding that their lives were so different from the rest of us they occupy a different country—a place he calls *Richistan.*[58] Many of the über-rich claim to be "regular" people, as they shuttle aboard private jets between 30,000 square foot homes, 200-foot yachts, and a posh resort or club where the entrance fees range in the six figures. Many of them are "new rich," in that they did not inherit wealth, but created fortunes by founding a company (Bill Gates, Sheldon Adelson, Michael Dell), or were high-level stakeholders in a company that was sold in an IPO or to someone bigger and wealthier (key employees at Microsoft and Google whose stock made them millionaires). Others took a percentage of the huge sums of money they moved around for Wall Street and other über-rich (hedge-fund managers). Another group is comprised of the "salaried rich;" i.e., the executives in corporate C-suites.

Other than sharing opulent lifestyles, these new rich differ from the old rich in that most of them got rich quickly, becoming millionaires and billionaires in their 20s and 30s rather than after a lifetime of building a business or working their way up. Many of them continue to work, putting in as many hours as most of the rest of us. The new rich dealmaker might be dressed in his shorts at a beachfront resort, but he is also putting in 18-hour days tethered to electronic devices, tracking deals and giving orders. Many of them are generous, and giving to charity—just like building a fortune—becomes another competitive event. The dark side is that many of them are also deeply in debt. As huge wealth has boomed, the bar for being regarded as wealthy has been raised considerably. Frank describes one fellow standing on his 100-foot yacht (which he had been proud of at one time) dwarfed by other yachts two and three times its size and calling it a "dinghy." Some of the yachts are so big they can't even berth in the regular marina, instead having to park in shipyards occupied by freighters, oil tankers and aircraft carriers (and hence require secondary yachts to get back and forth).

Although the rest of us can hardly imagine such lifestyles, Frank tells us the wealth divisions in Richistan are as acute as they are anywhere, "creating a new kind of upper-class warfare between the haves and the have-mores."[59] Frank also argues that these new rich have created a form of plutonomy,[60] with job growth for personal servants (butlers and nannies) and sales of luxury items (Gulfstream jets, Bentleys, Rolex, Cartier and Patek Phillippe watches), while retailers who serve the middle and working class are struggling. Indeed, spending by the rich has been propping up the US economy, making the overall performance numbers look good even while the middle and working classes fall behind. The real problem is not simply that the rich have so much, but that they are driving the standards for everyone else. Unlike the wealth itself, the race to keep up has trickled down to the (mostly upper) middle class, where everyone is working harder, taking on more debt, spending less time with family and friends, and sleeping less.

Extreme concentrations of wealth create real social and economic distortions beyond matters of simple fairness. In a plutonomy, where productive output is focused on luxury goods, the things that everyone else needs don't get built or produced. For example, when builders are focused on larger and more luxurious homes, it becomes ever harder for a middle-class family to find a modest, affordable home in a safe neighborhood. When even the wealthy (what Frank calls "lower Richistan") are anxious about money, it tends to erode a spirit of generosity. In the urgency to maintain or increase one's own position, those who are able to do so (generally those in the top 20%) engage in a form of opportunity hoarding, which creates barriers to social mobility.[61] Moreover, researchers have found that humans have a need for a shared reality, or an "experience of connection to other people's inner states."[62] This is one reason many of us start a conversation with strangers by talking about the weather—it is the one thing where we're all in it together. According to research, shared reality is a necessary foundation for empathy and finding common ground. However, when the very rich experience the world so differently than all the rest of us, it thwarts the formation of a shared reality.

The wealth distribution in the United States today also presents a threat to democracy above and beyond obvious issues of fairness and "us-versus-them" polarization. In addition to contributing to a war-of-all-against-all dynamic generally, the increasing wealth gap threatens to re-create the class society of old Europe—a form of society over which Americans fought a revolution. When we learn about our own political history, we are taught that politics is the result of a majoritarian pluralism or interest group pluralism. That is, everyone has a say, but what actually gets done depends on how many people want the same thing (the majority), or the outcome of conflict and concessions between various groups.

However, a recent study has cast serious doubt on this model, presenting evidence that the United States today politically works more like an oligarchy. In this study, the researchers selected policy choices that had a clear dichotomy between the preferences of elites with the preferences of the majority, and then compared them to policy outcomes.[63] The full study is worth a read, but the bottom line is that when the preferences of elites (wealthy individuals) and net interest-group alignments (Chambers of Commerce and business groups versus grass-roots or popularly supported organizations like AARP) are held constant, the preferences of the general public have virtually no effect on policy. The authors summarize by stating, "When the preferences of economic elites and the stands of organized interest groups are controlled for, the preferences of the average American appear to have only a miniscule, near-zero, statistically non-significant impact upon public policy."

This scenario presents us with a situation where we have groups who not just look, live and think differently, but experience two separate realities. The wealthy occupy positions of power—political, economic, and cultural—and so largely define what reality should look like for the rest of us. This creates a form of cognitive dissonance, which leads to a form of cognitive debilitation that

Lobaczewsky argues is a precursor to a ponerized society. As the rest of us suffer from cognitive dissonance, the wealthy experience a lack of empathy that is more situational than a result of personal pathology. When money is literally everywhere, there is no reason anyone should not be successful: It's only a matter of working a little harder, positioning oneself within a network of opportunities, or finding the right deal—and then you can always borrow money until the next venture pays off. The idea that anyone has to struggle for daily subsistence is totally foreign.

Decline of Civility and the Rage of the Masses

Serious students of American history are aware that—behind all the rhetoric of freedom and individual rights—the founding fathers had some very anti-democratic concerns. Checks and balances split among three separate and co-equal branches of government were built into the new system as much to thwart control by the masses as it was to prevent accumulation of power in general. As men of aristocratic means, the founders were concerned about government being taken over by the "passions" of the masses (which is one of the reasons property rights are enshrined in our Constitutional jurisprudence). The potential for tyranny of the majority was a favorite topic of many writers of early American history, as well as the founders themselves.[64] Although elitist, there are rational reasons to be skeptical of direct popular rule. Without a minimum guarantee of specific rights, a government that was subject to direct popular rule was susceptible to tyranny of the majority. That is, the dominant group would strip the civil rights of everyone else in order to insure its continued dominance. So, while a divided government was created to prevent the concentration of power, the Bill of Rights was created to protect the fundamental political and civic rights of minorities.[65]

A corollary to concern about tyranny of the majority was the potential for a political split into warring factions, where a divided government would find itself unable to function. In this dynamic, as the masses become increasingly frustrated and agitated, many of them lose the ability to think critically or conduct civil discourse—in essence compromising their ability to solve the problems creating their frustration to begin with. What happens here is that the urge to suppress the rights of the "other" results in the suppression of the rights of everyone. This problem of factions appears to be what we are experiencing today. It is sometimes defined as Republicans versus Democrats, red versus blue, left versus right, or liberal versus conservative. Because neither side/party has a permanent majority, electoral results tend to swing back and forth, and elections are becoming more polarized, hostile, and expensive.[66] The result of this is that there is less and less tolerance for viewpoints different than one's own, and less ability to compromise for the good of the whole. We see the effects of this with the inability of the U.S. Congress to function in anything approaching a normal and productive manner, as well as Supreme Court decisions split along predictable ideological lines. We also see it in increasing incivility, and this is not just occurring among the working and lower middle classes: Civility issues are often the topic in the rarified environments of State Bar Boards and academia.[67]

The American founders' concern with tyranny of the majority in conjunction with a hystericized society was also noted by Lobaczewsky, who lamented "...the emotionalism dominating individual, collective and political life...[and] the mania for taking offense at the drop of a hat [that] provokes constant retaliation, taking advantage of hyper-irritability and hypo-criticality on the part of others...."[68] It seems that one can't have a rational conversation anymore because someone will be extremely offended. This is not a matter of rudeness, but the need to discuss difficult issues (or confront inconvenient truths) in a civilized manner if we are ever going to resolve them.

As a personal example, there is a website I occasionally visit because—in a post-truth world—the site presents a broad range of *reasonably* reliable news articles from both mainstream and alternative media. Although the site is left-leaning and appeals to Democrats, it is by no means radical left, revolutionary, or anarchist. However, it does tend to serve—as many sites like it do on both the right and the left—as an ideological echo chamber and promoter of groupthink. Although my usual interaction with this site is "read only," one day there appeared a thread that argued any women who did not vote for Hillary Clinton voted against their own interest and were essentially traitors to their gender.

Against my better judgment (and intending to appeal to reason as well as mutual dislike of Trump), I submitted a response stating that, while I did not vote for Clinton, I did vote for another woman who was on the ballot. A lot of people are completely unaware of independent and third-party candidates because it requires more effort and an open mind to learn about them [this part I did *not* state in my post]. I further argued that—as insincere as it was—Trump's message captured the angst of people who have been working harder for less for decades, who live in the middle heartland of "flyover" country, and who view their representatives as being indifferent to their lives and out of touch with their concerns. I suggested that the Democrats may have missed the boat on how much voters viewed Clinton as a system insider, and that they ignored this popular disaffection at their own peril.

From some of the responses to this post, one would have assumed that my sole vote for a third-party candidate was more responsible for the election of Trump than Vladimir Putin. I could not tell if these people were rabid Clinton supporters, rabid Democrats, or rabid feminists. Even a vote for Bernie Sanders (another old white man and sometimes Independent) would not have been sufficiently "pure" to satisfy some of them. More chilling than the linguistic blue streak was the suggestion that people like me should not be allowed to vote. Moreover, this type of reaction was not limited to a few hotheads visiting one site. Shortly after my own experience, Hillary Clinton's book *What Happened* was released. Apparently, Clinton suggested in her book that Sanders' primary challenge was partly responsible for her electoral loss to Trump. The Twitterverse lit up with invective from supporters on both sides, which even some Democrats labeled as "Trumpian."

Of course, the Republicans are just as guilty of similar behavior. It may be more worrisome that many on the extreme right carry handguns and assault weapons, but neither major party nor supporters of a specific candidate has a monopoly on intolerance and abusiveness. One difference is that the right has always been more unified than the left. Research suggests that (statistically) individuals on the right also tend to be more authoritarian, willing to "follow the leader" and support whoever is in charge, regardless of what the leader is actually doing. Thus, the right tends to cluster in homogeneous groups who engage in groupthink and demonize everyone in the "outgroup," which increases the degree of internal cohesion.

Conversely, individuals on the left are more likely to question their own leaders as well as those on the right. While the left has a broader range of positions and apparent greater ability among its members to think independently, many of its members tend to either argue over trivial differences or focus on a narrow and specific issue of concern. Although various groups on the left can and do work together when an issue is deemed to be important enough, these coalitions tend to be ad hoc rather than unified fronts. Unfortunately, both the right and the left seem to have lost the ability to find a broader common ground, fracturing the polity into nearly equal perennially warring camps. Just like crossing the street, we can be faced with threats to our civil liberties and our personal dignity from both the right and the left.

During the 2016 election, I heard both Republicans and Democrats, in moments of candor, tell me that they had to "hold their nose" to vote for their own candidate—and only because the alternative would be much worse. While average citizens are lamenting the candidate choices of their own party yet voting for them anyway, the parties themselves contain factious groups who accuse others within their own party of insufficient ideological purity. People become embroiled in arguments about which candidate is more unlikeable/untrustworthy/crooked/asshole rather than questioning why the system provides so little in the way of acceptable choices. As a society, we have become extremely intolerant of trivial differences and minor annoyances, while at the same time we are expansively tolerant of a system that no longer serves most of us. In essence, we have become an example of Dr. Lobaczewsky's hysteroidal society.

In this section, we looked at contemporary trends that more or less fit into Lobaszewsky's model of ponerization. However, according to Lobaczewsky, a truly evil regime arises through a combination of a hysteroidal high point and the establishment of a pathocracy, which we will look at in the following section. As a practical matter, it may be difficult to precisely distinguish the cause-and-effect dynamic. In a hystericized society—where the average person is frustrated and angry but doesn't understand why, and where most people have abandoned critical thinking—--it is easier for antisocial and malevolent persons to attain positions of power. At the same time, if a few of the more clever Machiavellian types manipulate their way into power positions where they can exert influence on either public policy or popular culture, they are able to reform society in their own image. We have seen this in the past, when persons who were otherwise decent supported eliminationist programs. We see it today in the promotion of everyone-for-himself, greed-is-good ideologies by persons who we might not identity as psychopaths. In the next section, we will make the case that we have also established a pathocracy, even if only a rudimentary one.

Notes

[1] Lobaczewsky, A.M. (1998). *Political ponerology: A science on the nature of evil adjusted for political purposes.* Red Pill Press, at p. 86.

[2] *Id.* p. 89.

[3] *Id.* p. 86.

[4] *Id.* at p. 176.

[5] *Id. at* p. 89.

[6] *Id.* at p. 86.

[7] *Id.* at pp. 86-87.

[8] *Id.* at p. 87.

[9] *Id* at p. 131.

[10] *Id.* at p. 139.

[11] *Id.* at p. 140.

[12] *Id.*

[13] *Id.* at p. 134.

[14] *Id.* at p. 158.

[15] *Id.* at p. 155.

[16] *Id.* at p. 156.

[17] *Id.* at p. 157.

[18] *Id.* at p. 156.

[19] *Id.* at p. 156.

[20] *Id.* at pp. 165-167.

[21] *Id.* at p. 187.

[22] *Id.* at p. 167.

[23] *Id.* at p. 166.

[24] *Id.* at p. 171.

[25] *Id.*at p. 163.

[26] *Id.* at p. 81.

[27] *Id.* at p. 173.

[28] *Id.* at p. 174.

[29] *Id.* at p. 183.

[30] *Id.* at p. 141.

[31] *Id.* at p. 99.

[32] *Id.* at p. 174.

[33] *Id.* at p. 145.

[34] *Id.* at p. 177.

[35] *Id.* at p. 146.

[36] *Id.* at p. 147.

[37] Kopelman, R. & Rovenpor, J. (2017, Feb 23). Research spotlight: Societal narcissism—history, measurement, implications. https://openforest.net/research-spotlight-societal-narcissism-history-measurement-implications/. See also Mullins, L.S., & Kopelman, R.E. (1984). The best seller as an indicator of societal narcissism: Is there a trend? *The Public Opinion Quarterly, 48,* 720-730.

[38] Hogan, R., & Kaiser, R.B. (2005). What we know about leadership, *Review of General Psychology 9*(2), 169-180.

---

[39] Chatterjee, A., & Hambrick, D.C. (2007). It's all about me: Narcissistic chief executive officers and their effects on company strategy and performance. *Administrative Science Quarterly, 52,* 351-386.

[40] Twenge, J., & Campbell, K. (2009). *The narcissism epidemic.* New York, NY: Free Press.

[41] A detailed discussion of narcissistic behavior as well as its effects can be found in VanHettinga, B. (2019). *Why assholes rule the world.*

[42] Lasch, C. (1979). *The culture of narcissism.* New York, NY: Norton & Company.

[43] Lobaczewsky (1998). *Supra* at p. 78.

[44] *Id.* at p. 92.

[45] *Id.* at p. 75.

[46] Abel, J.R., Deitz, R, & Su, Y. (2014). Are recent college graduates finding good jobs? *Current Issues in Economics and Finance 20*(1), 1-8. Retrieved from: http://www.newyorkfed.org/research/current_issues/ci20-1.html.

[47] VanHettinga, B. (2018). *The great jobs deception.* Also doctoral dissertation (2015): Professional reserve armies: Underemployment and labor degradation in professional occupations. http://search.proquest.com/docview/1655360861.

[48] Lobaczewsky (1998). *Supra* at p. 89.

[49] *Id.* at p. 77.

[50] *Id.* at p. 75-76.

[51] For more about workplace bullying and assholes in general, see *Why Assholes Rule the World* (VanHettinga, 2019).

[52] Lobaczewsky (1998). *Supra* at p. 76.

[53] *Id.* at p. 91.

[54] *Id.* at p. 76.

[55] Payne, K. (2017). *The broken ladder: How inequality affects the way we think, live, and die.* New York, NY: Penguin Random House LLC.

---

[56] Piketty, T. (2014). *Capital in the twenty-first century.* Printed in India by Gopsons Papers Ltd. Translated by Arthur Goldhammer.

[57] Saez, E., & Zucman, G. (2019). *The triumph of injustice: How the rich dodge taxes and how to make them pay.* New York, NY: W.W. Norton & Co.

[58] Frank, R. (2007). *Richistan.* Crown Publishers/Random House, Inc.

[59] *Id.* at p. 7.

[60] The concept of plutonomy, or an economy in which the majority of growth is generated and consumed by a wealthy few, was first proposed by a group of Citibank analysts in describing the economic impact of their wealthy clientele: Kapur Ajay, Niall Macleod, Narendra Singh: "Plutonomy: Buying Luxury, Explaining Global Imbalances," Citigroup, Equity Strategy, Industry Note: October 16, 2005 at https://delong.typepad.com/plutonomy-1.pdf; Kapur Ajay, Niall Macleod, Narendra Singh: "Revisiting Plutonomy: The Rich Getting Richer", Citigroup, Equity Strategy, Industry Note: March 5, 2006 at https://delong.typepad.com/plutonomy-2.pdf; Kapur Ajay et al.: "The Plutonomy Symposium – Rising Tides Lifting Yachts", Citigroup, Equity Strategy, The Global Investigator, September 29, 2006 at https://delong.typepad.com/plutonomy-3.pdf.

[61] Reeves, R.V. (2017). *Dream hoarders: How the American upper middle class is leaving everyone else in the dust, why that is a problem, and what to do about it.* Washington, D.C.: The Brookings Institution.

[62] Echterhoff, G., Higgins, E. T., & Levine, J.M. (2009). Shared reality: Experiencing commonality with others' inner states about the world. *Perspectives on Psychological Science 4*(5), 496-521.

[63] Gilens, M. & Page, B. (2014). Testing theories of American politics: Elites, interest groups and average citizens. *Perspective on Politics, 12*(3), 564-581. American Political Science Association. https://scholar.princeton.edu/sites/default/files/mgilens/files/gilens_and_page_2014_-testing_theories_of_american_politics.doc.pdf

[64] James Madison, *Federalist Papers #10* (1788); Alexis de Tocqueville, *Democracy in America.* (1835-1840); John Stuart Mill, *On Liberty* (1859).

[65] At that time, the concern was for "minorities" based on political views, religious beliefs, national origin, and—of importance to the founders—property

ownership. Similar protections based on race and gender did not arrive until nearly (or—in the case of women—over) a century later.

[66] For an analysis of this phenomenon in the context of contemporary America, please see the Frontline documentary *America's Great Divide* at https://www.youtube.com/watch?v=SnMBYMOTwEs

[67] Twale, D., & Deluca, B. (2008). *Faculty incivility: The rise of the academic bully culture and what to do about it.* San Francisco, CA: Jossey-Bass.

[68] Lobaczewsky. (1998). *Supra* at p. 91.

Section 3
Pathocracy

Whenever a society contains serious social problems, there will also be some group of sensible people striving to improve the social situation by means of energetic reforms, so as to eliminate the cause of social tension...[However], elimination of social injustice and reconstruction of the country's morals and civilization could deprive a pathocracy of any chance to take over. Such reformers and moralists must therefore be consistently neutralized by means of liberal or conservative positions and appropriately suggestive catchwords and paramoralisms; if necessary, the best among them has to be murdered.

Dr. Andrew Lobaszewsky[1]

*

Trump...may be the inevitable stigmata of mankind's evolutionary unfitness...He is a distillation, mouthpiece, and terrifying living embodiment of all the worst in human nature and social delusion. If you were assigned the task of punishing humanity for its original sins, you could do no better than invent a Donald Trump and give him extraordinary power over the world's future.

Dr. Allen Frances[2]

Lobaszewsky defines pathocracy as a "system of government created when a small pathological minority takes control over a society of normal people."[3] It can be inferred that a full-blown pathocracy involves more than a psychopath (or even a group of them) in positions of power, but rather occurs when the pathocrats' worldview comes to be accepted by the more-or-less "normal" society at large. In the first part of this section, we will work through Lobaszewsky's descriptions of how pathocracies form and develop. In the second part, we will analyze factors that suggest pathocratic phenomena we are seeing today.

How Pathocracy Begins

Pathocracies are generally rooted in forms of social injustice. During stable, or "happy" times, the welfare of the majority or dominant group may be dependent upon injustice to other individuals, groups, or nations. As cultural myths develop to justify the injustices, society loses its capacity to challenge them. Even those who are subjected to the injustice find it difficult to express their grievances, lacking any kind of language or framing that makes sense to everyone else. Over time, the ability to dig deeper and question anything among the population at large decreases, and society as a whole begins to develop a simplistic and simplified worldview. These simplified worldviews—even if they might make no logical sense upon objective scrutiny—come to be accepted as truth. Over time, a "schizoidally impoverished psychological worldview does not stand out as odd" and, in such a society, pathological individuals are easily able to impose their own worldview upon others using "relatively controlled pathological egotism and the exceptional tenacity derived from their persistent nature."[4]

When a psychologically normal person achieves high office, a typical reaction is to doubt one's ability to meet the demands and to seek the assistance of others. This is in contrast to psychopathic individuals, who dream of power from an early age. In addition to the hereditary psychopaths, the characteropathic individual who may be discriminated against in some way by society also develops a desire for power, which operates as an overcompensation for feelings of humiliation.[5] Some individuals who are merely predisposed to psychopathy may be redirected toward more prosocial behavior if they are positively influenced by socializing organizations. However, "[P]sychopathic individuals generally stay away from social organizations characterized by reason and ethical discipline.... [They hold a] Utopian dream of a world where they are in power and all those other, 'normal people,' are forced into servitude."[6]

According to Lobaczewsky, only about 6% of the population "constitutes the active structure of the new rulership." About twice this many (12%) have managed to warp their personalities to meet the demands of the new reality. Lobaszewsky alleges that this second group tends to be "on average, weaker, more sickly, and less vital."[7] Pathocrats believe it is only a matter of indoctrination—perhaps combined with varying degrees of force and terror—to achieve a state where those "other" people accept the pathocrats' view of reality.[8] The 6% (the pathocratic elites who set the new standards) constitute the new nobility and the 12% (those who are not part of building the system, but who serve it in exchange for some personal benefit) constitute the new bourgeoisie. However, some among these 12% occasionally experience "conflicts of conscience" and act as intermediaries between the "oppositional society" and the pathocratic elites. "Normal people see them as persons they can approach, generally without being subjected to pathological arrogance."[9]

Pathocrats are able to take over the will of normal persons by means of "humiliating and arrogant techniques, brutal paramoralizations [which] deaden the thought processes and self-defense capabilities of the normal person."[10] As pathocrats begin to take over society and impose their own social norms, personality development is impoverished, particularly regarding the more subtle values widely accepted in society (e.g., respect, empathy, civility). Even normal people lose respect for their "own organism," failing to take care of themselves. This is often manifested as workaholism, which is encouraged in the ponerized society.[11] The children of pathocratic parents may be "normalized" by interaction with peers at school, which "rescues the society of normal people from deeper deformations in personality development."[12] However, this normalizing effect is reduced if the children of pathocrats are kept segregated; i.e., in elite private schools, country clubs, and gated communities.

The Role of Ideology

Pathocrats are non-ideological in the sense that they can take the form of fascists, communists, or capitalists, because their only objective is power, or the ability to impose their will and worldview on everyone else. While pathocracy has no distinctive ideology of its own, it often borrows from existing ideologies, particularly those that are based on some form of social injustice or psychological injury (defeat in a prior war or threats to one's way of life or identity). Pathocracy tends to "hide in one of the ideologies characteristic of the respective culture and era,"[13] although the ideology itself does not constitute its essence.[14]

A pathocracy may be founded upon an ideology that was originally socially dynamic and creative. Lobaszewsky warns that it may be difficult to differentiate between normal people who genuinely support an ideology and pathocrats who merely adopt it for their own malicious purposes. While an ideology may contain elements of truth and social progress, it can become perverted when taken over by pathocrats (Lobaczewsky suggests this is what happened to communism). "Every great ideology thus contains danger, especially for small minds. Therefore, every great social movement and its ideology can become a host upon which some pathocracy initiates its parasitic life."[15] Because pathocrats have the ability to "mesmerize" the masses of normal people, ideological followers eventually lose the capacity for critical analysis of the ideology's premises as well as self-critical control over their behavior.

Over time, the original ideology, which may have attempted to address complex social problems, becomes dominated by an oversimplified worldview. This is especially likely if the simplified worldview is framed around easily available data and appeals to individuals who are "insufficiently critical, frustrated as a result of downward social adjustment, culturally neglected, or characterized by some psychological deficiencies of their own."[16] As this process intensifies, more psychologically aberrant individuals become attracted to the ideology, who in turn further "vulgarize and pervert" the original.[17]

In the rest of society, interpretation of this oversimplified worldview tends to break down into three segments. One branch rejects the ideology, either on the basis of personal motivations or moral objections. A second branch (which Lobaszewsky terms "critically-corrective") incorporates those elements of the ideology which might be true or have societal value and disregards its obvious errors. A third branch Lobaszewsky terms "pathological acceptance," which is "manifested by individuals with psychological deficiencies of their own…personality malformations, or who have been injured by social injustice."[18] As the pathocracy matures, it builds "an extensive and active indoctrination system….with suitably refurbished ideology….for the purpose of pathologizing the thought processes of individuals and society."[19]

Eventually, the split in the ideology's adherents reaches a "point of no return," in which a group of pathocrats clashes with the original founders for control of ideological dogma and direction. Lobaszewsky alleges that Nazism had passed this point of no return, but the inevitable ideological confrontation was avoided by the Allied invasion.[20] In essence, as evil as it was, Hitler's Nazified Germany had not yet reached its apex of evil. So, Lobaczewsky tells us what such an ideology-based pathologized system might look like: "If such a movement triumphs by revolutionary means and in the name of freedom, the welfare of the people, and social justice this only brings about further transformation of a governmental system thus created into a macrosocial pathological phenomenon. Within this system, the common man is blamed for *not* having been born a psychopath, and is considered good for nothing except hard work, fighting and dying to protect a system of government he can neither sufficiently comprehend nor ever consider to be his own."[21]

<u>How Pathocracy Develops and Evolves</u>

How do we ascertain if (or when) a pathocracy has begun? Lobaczewsky tells us the process is lengthy, and its origin is difficult to pinpoint precisely. Pathocracy is more likely to arise in nations which are already experiencing some forms of ponerization: "Pathocracy will always find a positive response if some independent country is [in] an advanced state of hysterization, or if a small privileged class oppresses and exploits other citizens keeping them backward and in the dark."[22] It also tends to arise "…where an over-egoistical ruling class defends its position by means of naively moralizing doctrines, where injustice is rampant, or where intensification of the hysteria level stifles the operation of common sense."[23] As with other phenomenon we have analyzed herein, ponerization/pathocracy becomes a self-reinforcing feedback loop, in which "Evil in the world…constitutes a continuum: one kind opens the door to another, irrespective of its qualitative essence or the ideological slogans cloaking it.[24]

As pathocracy takes root, only those who will serve the system are put in charge. Because these individuals are often incompetent, those who are doing the actual work have their patience tested by having to explain what they do to those who "manage" them. At some point, the people who supported the original ideology realize that the game has changed. Normal people begin to push back and resist the system. When the pathocratic minority's grip on power is threatened, they "employ any and all methods of terror and exterminatory policies against individuals known for their patriotic feelings and military training…[while] Individuals lacking the natural feeling of being linked to normal society become irreplaceable."[25]

As the psychopaths "climb up the organizational ladder, [and] gain influence, [they] almost involuntarily bend the contents of the entire group to their own way of experiencing reality and to the goals derived from their deviant nature."[26] Once in positions of power and influence, pathocrats develop a form of doublespeak, in which the same words will have two meanings—one for initiates and one for everyone else. Others create new names with suggestive effects on others (i.e., "dog whistles") outside the immediate scope of the system's rule, but who nonetheless accept such things uncritically.[27]

As the pathological social structure eventually covers the entire country, it creates a new privileged class who feels permanently threatened by the majority of normal people. Anything which threatens pathocratic rule becomes deeply immoral,[28] and survival of the system becomes a moral imperative. "Thus, the biological, psychological, moral, and economic destruction of the majority of normal people becomes, for the pathocrats, a biological necessity."[29] The new class may even purge its own leaders if it views their behavior as jeopardizing the system. Moreover, the masses must be "distracted" from attempts to re-establish normal society, and "educated and channeled in the direction of imperialist strivings."[30]

"After a typical pathocratic structure has been formed, the population is effectively divided or polarized between pathocrats (and characteropaths who opt to serve them) and normal (prosocial) people. In early pathocracies, social control is maintained by treating dissidents as mentally abnormal, or otherwise marginalizing them."[31] In order to appear normal (as in not be perceived as a threat to the system) "...people from every social group...suddenly start changing their personality and world view. Decent Christians and patriots just yesterday, they now espouse the new ideology and behave contemptuously to anyone still adhering to the old values."[32] As pathocrats gain control over the system from the top, the pathology "spreads downward until it reaches every village and every human individual."[33]

Besides infecting the rest of normal society, ***a pathocracy creates the means to perpetuate itself by conferring great personal advantages to descendants of pathocrats***, since they have been "reared to allegiance since infancy....People with knowledge and skills are allowed to get things up and running, but once programs or facilities are operational, the pathocrats take over, "which then often leads to technical and financial ruin."[34] A full-fledged pathocracy is established when there is a second upheaval in which the transitional leadership is purged as being insufficiently loyal. ***Prior to this final purge, there is ever-increasing social control***.[35]

Religious systems—those institutions that we would normally expect to serve as a bulwark of morality against the forces of evil—are not immune from ponerization. Indeed, Lobaszewsky suggests that religion may even be more susceptible to ponerizing influence because of a tendency to revert to simplistic moralizations. People gravitate to faith during times of change and threat; i.e., at a point in their lives when their moral judgment is more likely to be perverted. As we saw in Part II, religion can become a form of social identity which divides people into "us" and "them," often losing its more universal pro-social messages. "The religious idea then becomes both a justification for using force and sadism against nonbelievers [and] heretics.... Something which was to be originally an aid in the comprehension of God's truth now scourges nations with the sword of imperialism."[36]

Religion is also employed strategically by pathocrats (who may not even be true believers themselves) in order to gain and maintain power. "Protecting their own faith and social position will then cause them to employ violent means against anyone daring to criticize or bring about liberalization."[37] Anyone challenging the pathocracy will be labeled as "evil" or "sinful" and dealt with harshly. In some cases, religious institutions themselves may be forced to become involved in what are usually "political" matters in order to protect their own existence.[38] In other cases, religious leaders make a conscious decision to take advantage of secular ponerization, particularly if they can co-opt it to their own ends.[39]

Effects on Individuals

According to Lobaczewsky, "...a person raised in a normal man's system is accustomed since childhood to seeing economic and ideological problems in the foreground, possibly also the results of social injustice."[40] Those environmental, economic, and ideological motivations that influence the formation of an individual personality also operate as modifying factors in how an individual responds to pathocracy.[41] Younger generations, who grow up under pathocratic rule, are more likely to succumb to "worldview impoverishment and rigidification of personality" than older generations who grew up in a normal society.[42]

Lobaczewsky also again references "talent," which seems to suggest an ability to think critically and beyond convenient simplifications. Lobaczewsky's person of "talent" finds it harder to reconcile himself to pathocratic reality, and thus is more likely to resist. But "talent" alone does not predict who supports and who opposes the pathocracy, as gifted and talented people sometimes join the pathocracy while some simple and uneducated people criticize it. However, Lobaszewsky asserts that those with the *highest* intelligence levels are unable to find meaning within the system. Although these critically-thinking individuals can sometimes find ways to use their superior mentality to be useful to others, the waste of their talents "spells eventual catastrophe for any social system."[43]

At some point during or when a pathocracy becomes established, the rest of society experiences psychological decomposition. However, this is not the same thing as becoming psychopathic (or buying into the pathocracy) oneself. When people are confronted with the fact of having been under the "traumatizing influence of a macrosocial pathological phenomenon, regardless of whether they were followers or opponents thereof....[they] suffer an inevitable shock and react with opposition, protest, and disintegration of their human personality."[44] The society as a whole will experience rising rates of anxiety, neuroses and depression. "[A]lmost every normal person carries within him some neurotic response of varying intensity. After all, ***neurosis is human nature's normal response to being subjugated to a pathological system***."[45] In a pathocratic state, even normal people develop a form of chronic neurosis, as one must constantly control one's emotions in order to avoid provoking a vindictive regime.[46] When people have lived under pathocratic rule for years, anyone who attempts to help them back to normality should expect resistance, as people may be "protecting their livelihoods and positions as well as defending their personalities from a vexatious disintegration."[47]

Individuals attempting to resist or challenge the pathocracy can expect to face opposition from the pathocrats. When pathocrats are in the process of gaining control, they find ways to weaken the population through subtle means, often by creating conditions of poverty and hardship, which limits the possibility of subversive activities on the part of normal people.[48] In American society today, the majority of us are experiencing stagnating wages, unstable jobs, rising costs of living, and austerity being touted as public policy. Our labor market is characterized by some people working so many hours they barely have a life, while others struggle to find sufficient work to provide basic subsistence. Research has shown that prolonged austerity produces negative cognitive effects as well as distraction with survival issues and demoralization.[49] When the majority of people are working harder for less, year after year, and often find themselves either overworked (workaholism and exhaustion) or underemployed (shame and humiliation), few have the energy and resources to organize an effective resistance.

During the "initial shock" following pathocratic establishment, social links between normal people fade. Many people end up joining the system out of necessity, and "pretend to represent [it's] more reasonable adherents."[50] As the pathocrats gain power and a resistance begins to coalesce, the pathocrats (who by now control the majority of mass media) find ways to demonize the resistance and question its morality. Opposition society is subjected to poverty, harassment, and curtailment of human freedoms.[51] However, over time the majority of normal society begins to develop a form of psychological immunization, creates an informal communications network, and slowly starts to rebuild social bonds and reciprocal trust. Lobaszewsky identifies this stage as a "separation between the pathocrats and the society of normal people."[52] When normal people regain their psychological faculties and mutual trust, they begin to "wake up" to the fact of the pathocracy's evil and to see past its manipulations.

Do We Have an American Pathocracy in the Early 21st Century?

Pathocracies tend to be identified after the fact—in times and places not our own. Pathocratic rulers are identified as such when they systematically murder large numbers of their own citizens and/or loot and plunder the resources of their own people. Hitler is a textbook case example. Others are associated with post-revolutionary communist dictatorships: Joseph Stalin, Slobodan Milosevic (the infamous "Butcher of the Balkans") and China's former Chairman Mao Zedong. Mao showed evidence of both borderline personality disorder and psychopathy, which were compounded by an addiction to barbiturates.[53] Indeed, several students of psycho-history have suggested that Mao was likely not ideologically predisposed toward communism; rather it offered him a way to express his appetites, sadism and vindictiveness under cover of an "unchecked Communist political party that gained followers through its unabashed idealism and ability to provide the poor and working classes revenge against those they worked for, owed money to, or were simply jealous of."[54]

Lobaszewsky tells us that one sure sign of pathocracy is "the figure of an autocratic ruler whose mental mediocrity and infantile personality...open[s] the door to the ponerogenesis."[55] This leads to the obvious next question, which is whether Donald Trump is a psychopath. A number of writers have certainly identified Trump as the quintessential asshole,[56] as well as the poster child for narcissistic personality disorder. Trump's personal history also suggests a pattern of antisocial behavior—bullying (beginning in childhood, but used often in adulthood to silence critics and bury negative information), disregard of the legal system (including tax and labor laws), media manipulation, serial marriages, and a propensity for blatant untruthfulness.[57] Perhaps the most telling example comes from Michael Wolff, who was allowed intimate access to the Trump White House during the first nine months of Trump's presidency. Wolff reports that Trump was incapable of understanding government employees. Trump once remarked, "Why would anyone want to be a government employee? They max out at what? Two hundred grand? Tops."[58] Thus, we have evidence that human beings who deliberately seek out careers in public service— and are not solely focused on personal gain—are incomprehensible to Trump.

Trump's mental state has also been a subject of much debate in the mental health community, and the debate involves an apparent conflict in professional ethical standards. On one side are mental health professionals who subscribe to the so-called Goldwater Rule, which prohibits a diagnosis of someone you have not personally examined. On the other side are mental health professionals who believe that their professional code of conduct requires them to warn about potential harm to the public (e.g., if a patient threatened to kill someone, they are required to warn the intended victim notwithstanding their duty to maintain patient confidentiality). These professionals formed an advocacy group called Duty to Warn,[59] and they allege over 53,000 people have signed their petition to remove Trump pursuant to the 25th Amendment.[60]

A group in the Duty to Warn camp produced a book entitled *The Dangerous Case of Donald Trump,*[61] and the primary diagnosis was malignant narcissism, along with various other forms of anti-social pathology. Trump's psychopathology was even corroborated by his own niece, who herself has a doctorate in clinical psychology.[62] While the message of the Duty to Warn group is that Trump is dangerous because of what he can do as President, Yale medical school psychiatrist Robert Lifton also suggested the possibility of ponerization, which he termed ***creeping malignant normality***: "Under a malignantly narcissistic leader, alternate facts, conspiracy theories, racism, science denial and delegitimization of the press become not only acceptable but also the new normal. If we do not confront this evil, it will consume us."[63]

At least one psychologist has come out with a definitive diagnosis of psychopathy.[64] Dr. Vincent Greenwood is Executive Director of the Washington Center for cognitive therapy. Dr. Greenwood begins by stating that newer (i.e. post-DSM) diagnostic criteria are less subjective and more quantifiable, which gives them a higher degree of validity than in the days of the Goldwater Rule. He also argues that many of his own colleagues place too much emphasis on the clinical interview, which—as we now know—can be subverted by a psychopath who is a master of impression management. For information to be sufficient to support a valid diagnosis, it ideally should come from a variety of sources over a long period of time, in order to provide evidence of persistency and pervasiveness. Fortunately for Dr. Greenwood, there is an abundance of archival information on Trump, including 63 biographies, 13 autobiographies, hundreds of interviews from print, radio and television, over 17,000 tweets since Trump announced his candidacy, along with voluminous court records and details of financial dealings that were dug up by investigative reporters.

Dr. Greenwood then subjects this huge amount of information to a process of coding and quantification; i.e., number of lies, lawsuits, threats, grandiose statements, etc. He then uses this data to work through Dr. Hare's 20-item PCL-R checklist. Trump scores a "2" on 15 items, a "1" on two items (early behavior problems and juvenile delinquency) and a "0" on three items (parasitic lifestyle, lack of realistic long-term goals, and revocation of conditional release), giving Trump a total score of 32, which places him squarely in "moderate to severe" psychopath territory.

In *Why Assholes Rule the World,* we found that the consensus among academics who study assholes (yes, such a thing exists) is that Donald Trump (who was not President at the time of the writings) is the quintessential example of asshole personality and behavior. Many in the mental health community landed on the diagnosis of either narcissistic personality disorder and/or malignant narcissism during the early years of Trump's presidency (using a methodology similar to Dr. Greenwood's, but not as exhaustive). Regardless of whatever diagnosis or label one attaches to Trump, he is definitely not someone who will concern himself with the welfare of others, particularly people who he deems to be inferior (which is practically everyone). However, the salient question in determining whether or not a pathocracy has been established is not whether a specific individual is a psychopath, but whether a psychopathic worldview has infected the society at large.

Dr. Allen Frances is among the psychiatric experts who deny that Trump has a narcissistic personality disorder. While Trump may be the poster child for narcissism, he does not have narcissistic personality disorder because he is not troubled by it. Indeed, he has benefited from it, which suggests some level of societal ponerization (i.e., narcissistic bullies are rewarded). Dr Frances continues with this broader concern by suggesting that, more troubling than Trump himself is the fact that enough of the rest of us elected him. Dr. Frances believes that, "…Trump is a mirror of the American soul, a surface symptom of our deeper societal disease."[65] That is, a President Trump is not causing ponerization, he is the result of it. Pointing a finger at Trump or labeling him crazy only avoids the critical self—and societal—examination as to what led to popular fascination with Trump and his ascent to power in the first place.

Dr. Frances admits he is "perplexed" by how many Americans could be so gullible. Even if Trump said all the right things (particularly about the loss of jobs and the destruction of communities), how could people believe that Trump—with his history of looking out for no one but himself and flaunting the law—would do anything to help others, let alone serve the "losers" who work hard and receive little? According to Dr. Frances, Trump "succeeded in mobilizing and exacerbating the denial, fears, and resentments (and sometimes also the hate, paranoia, racism and misogyny) of people whose needs had been ignored by other politicians. People left out of the American dream were willing to accept Trump's simple and wrong solutions to complex problems."[66] Indeed, some Trump supporters exhibit an almost messianic devotion, notwithstanding his history of traditionally immoral behavior.[67] Dr. Frances admits that he too might have been "snookered by Trump—but for the grace of my unearned easy life."[68] We have to give Dr. Frances credit for acknowledging the pernicious effects of the struggle to keep body, family, dignity, sanity and soul intact in today's environment on our ability to think critically.

There is evidence to suggest that Trump has also had a ponerizing effect. In addition to his own behaviors, Trump has given others permission (if not encouragement) to engage in lack of self-restraint, unrepressed expressions of anger, delusions of grandeur and other natural indulgences of our darker natures. We have seen that Trump has energized hate-filled alt-right and neo-Nazi groups—a fairly obvious sign of pathocratic ponerization. He has also instigated violence against journalists who dare to tell the truth. On a more anecdotal note, friends who are schoolteachers report increased bullying in their classrooms, where children are purportedly emboldened to abuse others because they are emulating the actions of the President.

Trump has had a definite effect on an increase in anti-social behavior, and he may indeed have pathological characteristics. However, a single individual—no matter how dysfunctional—does not constitute a pathocracy. Whether or not Trump's particular pathology has infected society as a whole is more ambiguous. In the examples here, we can make the argument that fringe hate groups and schoolyard bullies do not represent society as a whole. Moreover, there are a lot of people who oppose Trump and are working to remove him from office—sooner or later—which indicates that there still exists a segment of society that will not tolerate manipulativeness, untruthfulness, bullying, and obvious corruption.

At the same time, we should not minimize the danger of Trump. We are dealing with someone whose primary motivation is domination and power (followed by greed). We now know that Trump has engaged (or allowed) the assistance of persons and organizations outside the United States to affect his election in 2016, and is doing so again in 2020. He has appointed cronies whose only qualification is loyalty to Trump to head agencies responsible for national security, public health, and safety (covered in more detail in our introduction to Part 4). Trump has also removed both expertise and institutional memory by firing (or making it easier to remove) advisors, technical experts, and public servants with decades of experience. Even the staid and nonpartisan American Society for Public Administration has publicly taken the position that Trump has so "weaponized" bad public management that democratic stability is under threat.[69]

As the 2020 election was imminent (and most of the polls indicating that Trump was going to lose), Trump engaged his cabal of cronies in various machinations for a possible illegitimate takeover, instigating efforts to suppress votes,[70] deliberately dismantling the post office to thwart the surge in mail-in voting during a pandemic,[71] and ramming a questionably qualified Supreme Court Justice through barely a week before the election—a justice who has made no secret she intends to "participate" in rulings on election challenges.[72] In addition to blatant attempts to "steal" a second term (which could have resulted in unconstitutional additional terms plus the installation of a permanent Trump family dynasty), Trump has been using authoritarian tactics to suppress dissent.[73]

Analogous to the rise of Hitler, Trump would not be able to exercise the power that he does without the assistance of others. During the 2016 elections, many Republicans voiced concern about the potential of a President Trump.[74] Some of these individuals, including Lindsey Graham and Ted Cruz, are now supportive of Trump and have assisted in his attempts to power-grab. Perhaps they are focused on maximizing their own position in the hierarchy, perhaps they share Trump's insatiable drive for power and domination, or perhaps they are salivating at the prospect of one-party rule. The correlation of such behavior with Lobaszewsky's description of people abandoning their prior moral stance for personal gain or expediency is obvious. Although we can point to ponerization within the Republican party, there are a number of well-known Republicans who do not support the re-election of Trump.[75] Moreover, there are Republican groups—like Republican Voters Against Trump[76] and the Lincoln Project[77]—who actively oppose Trump, suggesting that ponerization has not infected the entire Republican party.

More salient to whether ponerization has infected society beyond specific individuals, institutions, or political parties is how it has affected the thinking and behavior of regular people. Dr. Allen Frances points to ponerizing influences (he does not use this term) that have been operating longer than Trump's appearance on the political scene. He cites the work of Theodore Adorno on the authoritarian personality, stating that authoritarianism, along with the tendency to blame others, cynicism, and subscribe to conspiracy theories, is "fairly common in the American character."[78] Dr. Frances blames the use of new technologies for creating the paradox of overwork and underemployment: "Advancing technology has either enslaved workers even more or replaced them altogether."[79] In addition to our work life, there has been a pattern of ponerizing influences affecting various other of our social institutions for several decades. We will examine the plethora of non-Trump-related ponerizing phenomena in Part IV.

In a modern democracy, early-stage ponerization is not likely to occur in the context of a term-limited elective office—where it will likely be derailed by democratic processes. In the fictional *House of Cards,* (Season 5, Episode 8, Chapter 60), we see President Frank Underwood (an undisputed psychopath) attending a strange "retreat" in the middle of the woods—an event that is "invitation only" for wealthy and powerful white men. During the series, Frank has already demonstrated that he is able to manipulate the system and override the voice of popular criticism, but he usually manages to prevail by a razor-thin margin (which gives the show its almost addictive tension). Frank is at this event because he recognizes that, even as President of the United States, these are the people who truly have power precisely because they are accountable to no one but themselves. We can thank our American founding fathers for creating a government that at least strives to answer to the will of "the people" on most occasions. However, this is not to suggest that such a system is immune from ponerization if enough of the rest of society becomes so.

Where many of us may be experiencing mini-pathocracies—regardless of who is president—is in our workplaces. While a narcissistic psychopath may seek the celebrity and public attention that high office confers, the more goal-directed and calculating pathocrats will find ways to acquire power removed from public scrutiny in places and positions that allow them to manipulate opinion and frame cultural reality. Places where we are more likely to find a modern pathocracy include multinational corporations (who are often able to avoid regulation by any single nation), the corporate media giants, the state-corporate military alliance, corporate-funded think tanks, global financial empires (the World Bank, The International Monetary Fund, the International Finance Corporation), and globe-spanning organizations generally, with their expansionary imperatives, constant search for cheap and compliant labor, drive for efficiency/expropriation at the expense of everything else, and lack of allegiance to any nation or people.

The individuals who occupy the top positions in these institutions are virtually unknown to the public, but they have a huge influence on the development of policy agendas as well as the everyday information presented to the rest of us. Not surprisingly, these individuals are almost always members of the social and economic elites, and so are motivated to preserve the system and defend it from challenges. As such, their objective is to not only convince the rest of us how great everything is (in essence, denying our own reality), but to inculcate a sense of powerlessness to do anything to change things. Since these are people who have no qualms about exploiting the earth, the labor and knowledge of others, and anything else they turn their attention to, they will also have no qualms about squelching resistance. Although a pathocratic regime may at first prefer to use softer means of control through manipulation and propaganda, it will not hesitate to use violence and murder if necessary if it believes it is threatened or overt opposition intensifies.

How Do People Thwart, End, and Recover from a Pathocracy?

Ponerogenesis is a cycle, and every pathocracy contains the seeds of its own destruction. The pathocracy itself destroys the society that it rules by corroding its values and wasting human talent. Additionally, there will always be a source of resistance: "Every country within the scope of this macrosocial phenomenon contains a large majority of normal people living and suffering there who will never accept pathocracy; their protest against it derives from the depths of their own souls and their human nature."[80] The time comes when the common masses of people want to live like human beings again and the system can no longer resist. This does not come about as a great counter-revolution, but rather "a more or less stormy process of regeneration will instead ensue."[81]

The ability to resist pathocracy depends on many factors, including "prosperity and its equitable distribution, the society's educational level (especially that of the poorer classes), the proportion of participation of individuals who are primitive or have various deviations, and the current phase of the hysteroidal cycle."[82] Ironically, the exercise of keeping one's body and soul together, as well as maintaining one's own sanity and decency during pathocratic rule, stimulates the population of normal people into critical thinking and psychological hardening. During times of brutal confrontation with evil, human capacity for critical analysis, and "apperceptive and moral sensitivity" become better developed.[83] "Under altered conditions of both material and moral limitations, an existential resourcefulness emerges which is prepared to overcome many difficulties. A new network of the society of normal people is also created for self-help and mutual assistance…"[84]

Lobaczewsky proposes that a healing society is built upon social bonds formed across diverse groups. As ordinary people struggle to survive in a pathocracy, they begin to see the things they have in common where they may have formerly focused on their differences. "Those of the highest mental culture, simple ordinary people, intellectuals, headwork specialists, factory workers, and peasants [are] joined by the common protest of their human nature against the domination of para-human experiential and governmental methods. These links engender interpersonal understanding and fellow-feeling among people and social groups formerly divided by economic differences and social traditions."[85]

Lobaczewsky suggests that people recovering from pathocracy will generally not look to legal solutions, especially since legal systems tend to be "geared toward maintaining law and order" and "punitive repression." He argues that the law (which is more evolved in Europe than in the U.S.) is "rather outdated everywhere and insufficiently congruent with bio-psychological reality."[86] Moreover, "pathocracy knows how to take advantage of the weaknesses of such a legalistic manner of thinking."[87] Rather, Lobaczewsky suggests that societies recovering from pathocracy will return to respect for "education and intellectual values. New social and moral values also appear and may prove to be permanent."[88]

Lobaszewsky argues that healing from pathocracy must also include forgiveness for the pathocrats. Indeed, any approach to dealing with pathocracy must come from a place of reason and understanding in order to control our "instinctive vindictive reflexes [and] the tendency to impose moralizing interpretations upon psychopathological phenomenon."[89] Indeed, punishing the pathocrats may only create the foundation for a future generation of pathocracy. Only an act of mercy can "break the age-old chain of the ponerogenic cycles."[90]

Lobaczewsky proposes that normal people are more likely to prevent the rise of evil when they have themselves been provided with the resources and abilities to think critically. On a more mundane level, people are better able to resist when they are not chronically distracted and exhausted. Persons who interact with a psychopath often report feeling drained, confused, anxious, and may experience deteriorating health after prolonged exposure.[91] This suggests that this ability to enervate normal people may partially explain acquiescence and lack of resistance to pathocratic control.

Lobaszewsky's proposed "cure" is an "improved social system" in which the population as a whole is "… endowed with a better comprehension of self, other people, and the complex interdependencies of social life."[92] In such a society, Lobaszewsky advocates that individuals should be "more independent of the various circumstances of life,"[93] suggesting that systems might be more vulnerable to corruption if people believe they are dependent on them. He further argues that, unless the individual develops a "healthy critical faculty," he may become fixated on the unfairness of the world and come to believe that the only way to achieve justice is through the struggle for power. "Revolutionary and radical ideas find fertile soil among such [downwardly adjusted] people."[94]

Lobaszewsky's recommendations revolve around the need for understanding of psychological processes among the various professions and institutions that run society. He also recommends establishment of a "logocracy," or a new system that would allow "normals" to peacefully coexist with "pathologicals." In such a system, the pathologicals are not punished (Lobaszewsky views them through the disease model rather than moral blame), but are nonetheless prevented from harming the rest of society. In Lobaszewsky's ideal system, decisions are made based on scientific knowledge and methodology rather than impulsive reactions and revenge. He also recommends development of the "science" of ponerology, or the study of evil in the context of systems processes. There are genuine issues of what and how to measure, as pathocrats are able to traumatize people in ways that may not be readily detectible (i.e., not involve physical injury).

Lobaszewsky's further recommends that everyone—not just mental health professionals, but professionals in other science disciplines, political science, law, education, and even linguistics—should be trained to recognize the processes of ponerization. Indeed, language itself can be used to create mass misconceptions and even delusions, as well as create cynicism and distrust which subverts collaborative capacity—especially the collaborative capacity needed to challenge the pathocracy itself. Activists who challenge unjust systems are often ineffective because they lack a complete understanding of pathological manipulations and may be unable to identify the real (as opposed to the nominal) sources of power.

Removal of pathocracy does not mean that one returns to the *status quo ante*. Lobaszewsky suggests that we should take advantage of toppled pathocracies as learning opportunities, identifying the underlying pathologies and tactics to determine what went wrong and how. As we have seen, pathocracy itself is often born out of social injustice. ***When normal society awakens to the pathocracy, it also becomes conscious of the injustice which may have precipitated it.*** Thus, the process by which a pathocracy becomes established and then eventually collapses has likely created so much social change that, as a practical matter, the "old" ways will no longer work either: "Whenever old social systems created by historical processes have been almost totally destroyed by the introduction of state capitalism and the development of pathocracy, that nation's social and psychological structure has been obliterated. The replacement is a psychological structure reaching into every corner of a country, causing all areas of life to degenerate and become unproductive. Under such conditions, it proves unfeasible to reconstruct a social system based on outdated traditions and the unrealistic expectations that such a structure does exist."[95] Thus, the renewed society that is born out of pathocracy will likely look very different from the pathocracy as well as whatever came before it.

From all of this, we can distill a few strategies to either prevent or mitigate the formation of a pathocracy:

- Ensure that the majority of people—and even minorities of significant numbers—do not feel excluded from society.

- Treat mental health as a public health good and provide appropriate resources for it. This includes "hardening" the population to resist pathological domination. Lobaszewsky credits his own training in being able to continue his work through Nazi and Soviet occupations.

- Ensure that most people have sufficient and independent means of subsistence and self-improvement.

- Train people in the art of critical thinking, encourage critical analysis, and seek out evidence-based frameworks that avoid simplistic solutions to complex problems.

- Develop broadly inclusive and deliberative policy-formulation and conflict resolution structures where people can be heard, where they are unafraid to express legitimate grievances, and where dialogue is encouraged without posing an existential threat to its participants.

Some have criticized Lobaszewsky because his own division of society into "normal" and "pathologicals" not only creates another form of "us versus them" division, it too can be subject to perversion. Which means that there should be another way of looking at evil to serve as a counterpoint to the technocratic operation of a logocracy. But we should heed Lobaszewsky's advice to apply our understanding of human behavior to the operations of our social systems. Lobaszewsky's bottom line is that "Power should be in the hands of normal people."[96]

Notes

[1] Lobaczewsky, A.M. (1998). *Political Ponerology: A science on the nature of evil adjusted for political purposes.* Red Pill Press at p. 218.

[2] Frances, A. *Twilight of American Sanity: A psychiatrist analyses the age of Trump.* New York, NY: HarperCollins Publishers at p. 177.

[3] Lobaczewsky, (1998). *Supra* at p. 193.

[4] *Id.* at p. 184.

[5] *Id.*

[6] *Id.* at p. 190.

[7] *Id.* at p. 224.

[8] *Id.* at p. 231.

[9] *Id.* at p. 225.

[10] *Id.* at p. 236.

[11] *Id.* at p. 232.

[12] *Id.* at p. 234.

[13] *Id.* at p. 184.

[14] *Id.* at p. 194.

[15] *Id.* at p. 201.

[16] *Id.* at p. 185.

[17] *Id.* at p. 187.

[18] *Id.* at p. 187.

[19] *Id.* at p. 195.

[20] *Id.* at p. 200.

[21] *Id.* at p. 192.

[22] *Id.* at p. 280.

[23] *Id.* at p. 217.

[24] *Id.* at p. 280.

[25] *Id.* at p. 195.

[26] *Id.* at p. 192.

[27] *Id.* at p. 205.

[28] *Id.*at p. 205.

[29] *Id.* at p. 207.

[30] *Id.* at p. 209.

[31] *Id.* at p. 265.

[32] *Id.* at p. 214.

[33] *Id.* at p. 215.

[34] *Id.* at p. 198.

[35] *Id.* at p. 220.

[36] *Id.*at p. 271.

[37] *Id.* at p. 272.

[38] *Id.* at p. 277.

[39] *Id.* at p. 275.

[40] *Id.* at p. 226.

[41] *Id.* at p. 237.

[42] *Id.* at p. 250.

[43] *Id.* at p. 238.

[44] *Id.* at p. 285.

[45] *Id.* at p. 283.

[46] *Id.* at p. 251.

[47] *Id.* at p. 286.

[48] *Id.* at p. 209.

[49] The British Psychological Society. (2013, Sept.). *Austerity Psychology.* https://thepsychologist.bps.or.uk/volume-26/edition-9/austerity-psychology. *See also* Psychologists Against Austerity. (2015). *The psychological impact of austerity.* Briefing paper, School of Psychology, University of East London. https://psychagainstausterity.filed.workplress.com/2015/03/paa-briefing-paper.pdf

[50] Lobaczewsky, *supra* at p. 226.

[51] *Id.* at p. 225.

[52] *Id.* at p. 196.

[53] Terrill, R. (1999). *Mao: A biography. Stanford, CA: Stanford University Press.*

[54] Oakley, B. (2007). *Evil genes: Why Rome fell, Hitler rose, Enron failed, and my sister stole my mother's boyfriend.* Amherst, NY: Prometheus Books, p. 250. Oakley also argues that Mao could have risen to power in a capitalist business environment or even as a leader of a religious cult, but not likely in American government, with its independent judiciary, two-party system, and media scrutiny, which would have thwarted his complete control. However, Mao to this day enjoys a "benevolent" image in China, where knowledge of his dysfunctional character and "active role in the deaths of millions [has] been suppressed in China through the self-serving dictates of his successors." (p. 251).

[55] Lobaczewsky, *supra* at p. 213.

[56] Sutton, R.J. (2007). *The no asshole rule.* New York, NY: Business Plus/Hatchette Book Group, USA; James, A. (2016). *Assholes: A theory of Donald Trump.* New York, NY: Doubleday/Penguin Random House.

[57] For a full history of Donald Trump, see Johnston, David C. (2016). *The making of Donald Trump.* Brooklyn, NY: Melville House Publishing.

[58] Wolff, M. (2018). *Fire and fury: Inside the Trump White House.* New York, NY: Henry Holt & Company at p. 94.

[59] https://www.theatlantic.com/politics/archive/2018/01/bandy-lee/550193/ See also https://www.adutytowarn.org/

[60] Amendment XXV sets forth the process of executive succession in the event of the Presidents' removal, death, resignation, or "inability to discharge the powers and duties of his office."

[61] Lee, B.X. (2018). *The dangerous case of Donald Trump.* Download full PDF here (you will need to sign up): https://iebooks.xyz/books-en-2019-13524#spread010420

[62] Trump, M. L. (2020). *Too much and never enough: How my family created the world's most dangerous man.* New York, NY: Simon & Schuster.

[63] https://www.usatoday.com/story/opinion/2017/05/04/trump-malignant-narcissistic-disorder-psychiatry-column/101243584/

[64] Greenwood, V. (27 May 2020). A duty to differentially diagnose: The substance behind the assertion the President has a serious psychiatric condition. https://medium.com/@vgwcct/a-duty-to-differentially-diagnose-the-validity-underpinning-the-diagnosis-of-the-president-371354142a02

[65] https://www.statnews.com/2017/09/06/donald-trump-mental-illness-diagnosis/

[66] Lobaszewsky, *supra* at p. 114.

[67] In America today, there are a number of evangelical pastors preaching that Donald Trump is the harbinger of the second coming of Christ. https://rewire.news/article/2017/07/24/meet-group-right-wing-christians-believe-president-trump-chosen-god/. These stories illustrate contemporary

ponerization (disconnection from reality and total lack of critical thinking) more than anything I (or anyone else) could possibly make up.

[68] Lobaszewsky, *supra* at p. 114.

[69] https://www.govexec.com/federal-news/2020/10/open-letter-trump-administration-management/169394/

[70] https://fivethirtyeight.com/features/five-ways-trump-and-gop-officials-are-undermining-the-election-process/; https://www.buzzfeednews.com/article/clarissajanlim/trump-republicans-confuse-voters; https://news.berkeley.edu/2020/09/29/stacking-the-deck-how-the-gop-works-to-suppress-minority-voting/

[71] https://www.precinctreporter.com/2020/08/20/trump-efforts-to-dismantle-post-office/; https://www.theguardian.com/us-news/2020/aug/13/donald-trump-usps-post-office-election-funding

[72] https://www.cnn.com/2020/10/09/politics/barrett-recuse-presidential-election/index.html

[73] https://www.washingtonpost.com/politics/more-federal-agents-dispatched-to-portland-as-protests-rise-in-other-cities/2020/07/27/20a717be-d03c-11ea-8d32-1ebf4e9d8e0d_story.html; https://www.npr.org/2020/06/01/867532070/trumps-unannounced-church-visit-angers-church-officials

[74] https://time.com/4325178/donald-trump-republican-support/

[75] https://www.axios.com/republicans-not-voting-for-trump-in-2020-9e2f02fa-0f36-418d-bedd-ed53181dd99c.html

[76] https://rvat.org/

[77] https://lincolnproject.us/

[78] Frances, *supra* at p. 127.

[79] *Id.* at p. 225.

[80] Lobaszewsky, *supra* at p. 253.

[81] *Id.* at pp. 226-227.

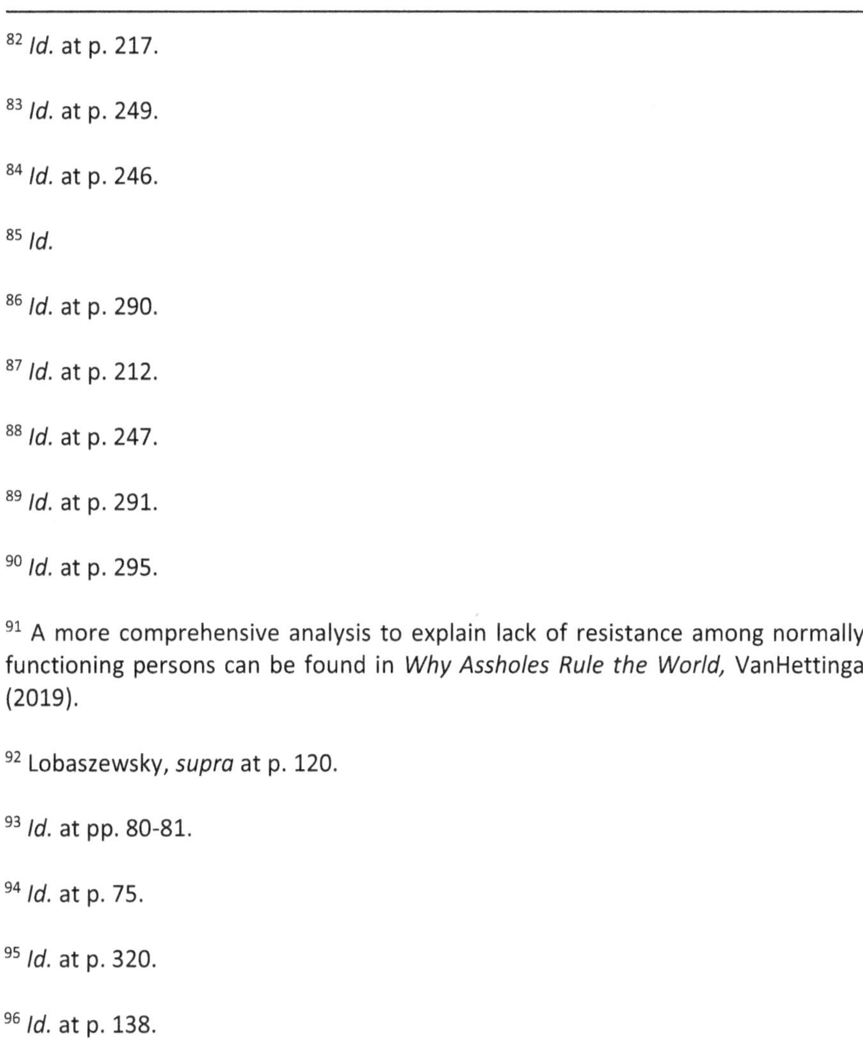

[82] *Id.* at p. 217.

[83] *Id.* at p. 249.

[84] *Id.* at p. 246.

[85] *Id.*

[86] *Id.* at p. 290.

[87] *Id.* at p. 212.

[88] *Id.* at p. 247.

[89] *Id.* at p. 291.

[90] *Id.* at p. 295.

[91] A more comprehensive analysis to explain lack of resistance among normally functioning persons can be found in *Why Assholes Rule the World,* VanHettinga (2019).

[92] Lobaszewsky, *supra* at p. 120.

[93] *Id.* at pp. 80-81.

[94] *Id.* at p. 75.

[95] *Id.* at p. 320.

[96] *Id.* at p. 138.

Part IV

How Ponerization and Pathocracy Manifest Today

Introduction to Part IV
How Ponerization and Pathocracy Manifest Today

Government is instituted for the common good; for the protection, safety, prosperity, and happiness of the people; and not for profit, honor, or private interest of any one man, family, or class of men; therefore, the people alone have an incontestable, unalienable, and indefeasible right to institute government; and to reform, alter, or totally change the same, when their protection, safety, prosperity, and happiness require it.

John Adams

*

The more liberal pathocrats would not be averse to giving such a society a certain minimum of economic prosperity in order to reduce the irritation level, but their own corruption and inability to administer the economy prevents them from doing so.

Dr. Andrew Lobaczewsky

*

The country I live in today uses the same civic, patriotic, and historical language to describe itself, the same symbols and iconography, the same national myths, but only the shell remains...The words "consent of the governed" have become an empty phrase...The government, stripped of any real sovereignty, provides little more than technical expertise for elites and corporations that lack moral restraints and a concept of the common good. America has become a façade. It has become the greatest illusion in a culture of illusions.

Chris Hedges[1]

At this point, we have covered the fundamentals of Lobaczewsky's ponerization, but may still lack a clear understanding of such concepts. More importantly, how can we recognize nascent evil in time to correct it? Like former Supreme Court Justice Potter Stewart's infamous observation about pornography, most of us think we "know it when we see it." Yet such things tend to develop over time and not appear as sudden, discrete phenomenon. Ponerization processes are difficult to precisely define, which exacerbates the task of finding a solution. Moreover, ponerization is not a one-size-fits-all phenomenon, but will take different forms in different cultures and historical contexts. Most of us know what happened in Nazi Germany and Stalinist Russia, and we do not believe that such things will happen here.

As we read Lobaczewsky's account of Nazi and Soviet domination of Poland, we can imagine ponerization manifesting at the level of national politics. Perhaps the most flagrant and unambiguous evidence of both a ponerized society and nascent (if not full-blown) pathocracy is the current Trump administration. We are beginning to see and hear words which were born during the fall of the Roman Empire: kleptocracy, kratocracy, and kakistocracy. In a kleptocracy, government leaders exploit their own people and plunder the national resources of their own territory in order to extend their own personal wealth and political power. In a kratocracy, power can be seized by means of coercion, social persuasion, or deceptive cunning. The kratocrat can thus appear to be legitimate. A kakistocracy occurs when the government is run by the least qualified and/or most unscrupulous citizens. Kakistocracies are often associated with cronyism, nepotism, and hereditary aristocracies. In all of these cases, the regime maintains power through the manipulation of reality: kleptocrats must distract citizens from their corruption, kratocrats must distract citizens from their illegitimate power, and kakistocrats must distract citizens from their ineptitude. This distraction is often perpetrated through the manipulative use of ideology (which the leaders may or may not actually support), attacking their rivals, or starting foreign wars.

Once unthinkable in the United States, Trump presents a real threat of subverting democracy in order to maintain his position (i.e., establish an unconstitutional dictatorship). Although there have been ongoing attempts by incumbents to push elections in their favor for decades (primarily through legal means such as campaign advertising propaganda and legislative gerrymandering), we are now seeing the influence of foreign governments (including those who are hostile to the interests of the United States), and illegal dismantling of the infrastructure of democracy (e.g., the selective closure of polling places) as well as essential government services (the United States Postal Service) to prevent or discourage people from exercising their right to vote.

Out in the streets we are witnessing a form of Rodney King redux, where Black people are being shot and beaten by the police with apparent impunity. When citizens (both Black and White) take to the streets in protest, Trump is sending unidentified armed federal forces to "keep order." In more normal times, the internal intervention of federal forces was activated only upon the request of state officials, usually in response to labor strikes or generalized urban riots. Today, federal agents without apparent jurisdiction (BORTAC) are being deployed into urban areas in direct contradiction to the requests of state governors to keep the feds out and let the states handle their own problems. Trump is not only sending in questionably legitimate federal forces, he is also urging his supporters to take to the streets as armed citizen vigilantes. So, now in addition to local police shooting unarmed Black people and federal agents beating peaceful protesters, we are seeing Americans shooting each other. When a bipartisan group (the Transition Integrity Project) of retired military officers, political strategists and law professors "war-gamed" various models of potential electoral outcomes, nearly every result included some combination of election uncertainty, mass protests, unending legal battles, constitutional crises, and literally blood in the streets.[2]

Trump is a master of media manipulation, the quintessential narcissist who was able to create a public image as a successful businessman and celebrity game-show host. Although information about Trump's unsavory history was available, it was primarily in the hands of independent filmmakers and investigative journalists, but seldom if ever appeared in the mainstream media prior to Trump's election. The release of the 1991 movie *Trump—What's the Deal?*[3] was suppressed for decades because Trump threatened to sue any broadcaster or distributor who dared to publish it. Although the movie exhibits an obvious "indie" quality, it reveals what people who know the "real" Donald Trump think about him, which is contrary to his deliberately manipulated public persona. One journalist covering Trump says he "talks a good game, but lacks character." Actor Christopher Reeve characterizes Trump fever as "the American dream gone berserk."

Tony Schwartz is the co-author of Trump's 1987 *Art of the Deal,* which catapulted Trump onto the national stage, paving his way to fame and fortune as the host of *Celebrity Apprentice.* With no experience in government service, Trump's strategic use of the media—along with his celebrity name-recognition—allowed him to run for President.[4] In July of 2016—when a Trump Presidency was beginning to look like it might be possible—Schwartz had a *mea culpa* interview with the *New York Times,* where he disclosed the deception in *The Art of the Deal* and warned of real negative consequences for the country should Trump become President.[5]

David Cay Johnston is an investigative journalist who has been covering Trump since Trump's casino days in the 1980s. In *The Making of Donald Trump,* Johnston not only exposes the corruption of Trump's Atlantic City casino empire (which collapsed in multiple bankruptcies), along with its Mafia connections, but the whole seamy history behind the Trump family fortune. [6] Long before he became President, Trump had a history of avoiding legal (contractual and statutory) obligations, using and abusing the legal process to bully anyone who threatened to thwart his agenda, particularly through lawsuits designed to suppress unfavorable—but true—publicity. The story continued as Trump transitioned into the White House—where some people were hoping (almost against hope itself) that Trump would transcend his baser nature and grow into at least a minimally Presidential character. In Michael Wolff's *Fire and Fury,*[7] we see the same chaos, manipulation, cronyism, and incompetence in the Trump White House that has characterized the rest of Trump's life history.

Now that the cat was out of the bag, the never-ending parade of persons who revolved through Trump's regime began to write their own tell-all accounts of ever-escalating corruption. John

Bolton, former national security advisor and U.S. Ambassador to the United Nations, alleges that he knew from direct observation that Trump actively sought the intervention of various foreign governments to aid him in his re-election, that Trump offered personal favors to dictators, and that Trump demonstrated gross ignorance around the geography and history of countries he was dealing with.[8] Bolton also alleges that Trump suggested he was going to serve more than 2 terms. Bolton chastises the Democrats for not only failing to remove Trump by impeachment, but for limiting the impeachment inquiry to "only" Ukraine.

Michael Cohen, former Trump attorney and confidante, has pled guilty to five counts of tax evasion, one count of making false statements to a financial institution, one count of willfully causing an unlawful corporate contribution, and one count of making an excessive campaign contribution at the request of a candidate (surprise, it was Trump). Cohen's tell-all book *Disloyal*[9] exposes not only the lying, corruption and manipulation of Trump, but also how Cohen himself fell under Trump's "spell" and lost his moral compass. Cohen also corroborates Bolton's statement that Trump is planning to execute some extra-legal maneuver to keep himself in power indefinitely. In his testimony before the House Oversight Committee in February of 2019, Cohen made a chilling statement that removing Trump from the White House—whether he was impeached or lost an election—would be both unpleasant and dangerous.

The whole story of Trump's corruption (and how it is adversely affecting the rest of us) is still being written, and it is likely that through all the scandals, impeachment hearings and investigations (Trump has been firing Inspectors General right and left), we have only seen the tip of the iceberg of Trump's malfeasance.[10] In addition to corruption and evidence of psychopathology, Trump is also incompetent. This is not only with respect to his current mishandling of the coronavirus pandemic,[11] but his apparent disregard for expertise, science, or even the rudiments of data-driven decision-making.[12] Trump instead prefers to make decisions based on mood and instinct (i.e., his gut).[13] This has resulted in Trump appointing cronies to positions of power whose only criteria for qualification is uncritical loyalty to Trump.

Moreover, Trump's appointments seldom last, creating turmoil and chaos in the federal government (which some suggest might be intentional). Trump's cabinet has broken the record for turnover of personnel.[14]

Trump's appointments are worse than people who are merely unqualified, rather he selects individuals who are blatantly hostile to the agencies they are appointed to lead.[15] In a now (in)famous blooper during a 2011 primary debate, former Texas Governor Rick Perry announced he would eliminate three government agencies: Commerce, Education, and one whose name he forgot—the Department of Energy![16] Trump appointed Perry to head the Energy department at the same time Perry was also on the Board of Energy Transfer Partners, a partner in the Dakota Access Pipeline. Betsy Devos, Trump's Education Secretary,[17] heir to family fortune and product of private schools, is intent on privatizing American education primarily by destroying the public version of it.[18] Devos is also the sister of Eric Prince, founder of the private military contract firm Blackwater. Although Prince sold his interest in Blackwater in 2010, and the company has changed its name several times, Blackwater received more than $174 million of government funds under the Obama administration.[19] While Blackwater's fortunes are harder to track during the Bush administration, It was definitely involved in operations in Iraq and Afghanistan, and likely also received hundreds of millions in taxpayer dollars.[20] Thus we have our own version of hereditary imperialists, who direct public money into their own pockets while depriving same to services that benefit the ordinary citizen.

Much of Trump's success can be attributed to the fact that he is a master of media manipulation as well as "branding," a reality-distorting practice we will cover more fully in Section 4. The American people were both dazzled by Trump's self-created aura of celebrity and success as well as (in many cases, quite legitimately) fed up with the status quo—which made them susceptible to Trump's message of populist angst. While Trump made the usual (basically prosocial, but generally insincere) campaign promises to do something about jobs and revitalize communities, he was also adept at tapping into the darker emotions of fear and hate, particularly expressed as racism, misogyny and xenophobia. Yet, anyone who knew the "real" Trump would have realized he had no intentions of doing anything for anyone other than himself—especially for all the "losers" who have to work for a living.

Although some on the left portray Trump as a right-wing ideologue, Trump apparently has no real ideology other than his own self-interest. While covering the first 90 days of the Trump White House, Michael Wolff reports that Trump had no real objection to people having health insurance; rather his hatred and jealousy of former President Obama drove the campaign to "repeal and replace" the Affordable Care Act, for which he needed the assistance of the real anti-ACA ideologues to do.[21] The insider accounts of both David Johnston and Michael Wolff also suggest a ponerized relationship between Trump and the Republican party, where it is difficult to determine which one is using the other to serve his (or its) own agenda—which is primarily about holding onto power. The one thing we can know for certain is that neither of them intend to serve the nation as a whole, nor the majority of average American citizens.

Because America under a Trump administration provides new and never-ending examples of ponerization on a daily basis, we will not engage in an exhaustive coverage of Trump administration incompetence and corruption. We also don't want to become bogged down in the analysis of specific personalities,[22] since our main premise here is the dysfunction of systems and not individual psychopathy or antisocial personality disorders. Rather, we want to examine harder-to-discern and harder-to-define phenomena that have been going on for some time—and likely set the stage for the ascension of Trump, along with his ensuing disastrous Presidency and threat of incipient fascism in the United States of America. Our argument is that a Trump Presidency was not an aberration that spontaneously appeared in a vacuum. Ponerization is a process—not a person or a discrete event—and there have been incremental, pre-existing elements of it in American society for at least the past four decades. The signs may have been subtle, but they were there.

Even before Trump, one did not need to search long and hard to find any number of authors and thinkers making the argument that society is going straight to hell in a handbasket. We are seeing similar concerns coming not just from the American political right and left, but from an international perspective as well. Moreover, these are not the opinions of conspiracy theorists, social outcasts and demagogues, but of well-educated individuals who occupy relatively high-status positions. What differentiates some of this from what we might label as hysteria itself (or even simply sensationalism for the purpose of sales and marketing) is that there seems to be a general agreement that something is terribly wrong. While the focus might shift (e.g., the right tends to focus on loss of freedom, the left tends to focus on loss of democracy and/or compassion, psychologists focus on alienation and personality disorders, economists focus on the widening wealth gap, sociologists focus on loss of community and trust, and religious leaders focus on loss of morality and connection with God), at some root level the various analyses corroborate each other. They also describe reality as many of us are actually experiencing it, rather than the feel-good glamorized hype we are fed by the establishment entertainment industry.

Perhaps one way to help us understand ponerization is to look at how a corrupted culture affects our thinking and emotions—which ultimately affects our behavior. We like to believe we are self-directed beings who make conscious decisions about what we do. And at the conscious level we might be right. But at the subconscious level, we are driven by biological imperatives of physical survival, psychological coherence, and ego identity. When any (or all) of these are threatened, our behavior may be subconsciously driven in a direction we don't consciously intend to go. In a world where we are constantly presented with distractions and demands for our attention, we are more likely to be unaware of these negative influences.

In this part, we are going to look at the degradation of society with respect to how we earn our livelihoods, the effects of extreme inequality, the erosion of operational democracy, the distortion of truth in mass information, and how all of this has affected our ability to address these problems because we seem to have lost any sense of social cohesion or capacity to think critically:

In Section One, we examine the degradation of our work lives and how we earn our livelihoods. Most of us know we have been working harder for less for decades. We are alternately working too many hours, or our work (and income) is unpredictable. We can hardly hope to find meaning in our work, which often presents us more pressing challenges of survival. For many of us, our work lives have produced precariatization—a form of powerlessness not amounting to poverty that reduces our sense of personal agency, which then infects the rest of our lives as well. We have little time or energy to educate ourselves about what is happening to us as well as to the larger society, and even less time to participate in the duties of citizenship.

In Section Two, we analyze inequality—i.e., the extent to which it is not natural as well as the extent to which we have been propagandized to accept it. Here, we will look at the research of the French economist Thomas Piketty to gain a historical perspective on inequality, as well as other structures and institutions that contribute to it. We also visit the research of the American epidemiologists Richard Wilson and Kate Pickett, who exhaustively describe (backed by multi-disciplinary research) the ponerizing (they do ***not*** use this term) effects of inequality, particularly in the United States.

In Section Three, we look at ponerization in our democratic institutions. Even in a purported "government by the people," the power of responsible citizens can be eroded by more subtle methods. Since many of us have abandoned the active practice of citizenship (either through exhaustion, distraction, or futility), there is less resistance or pushback when democratic institutions are threatened. Pathocrats in a modern democracy will not usurp power by force, but rather gradually assume it through manipulation and ***reproduction,*** where a pathocratic (i.e., undemocratic) worldview will become normalized. Once believed to be unthinkable, we now see the real possibility of fascist-style totalitarianism and a Soviet-style rigged election emerging in the United States.

In Section Four, we examine the ponerizing influence of our media and information systems, beginning with consolidation and corporatization that has been going on for over four decades. Here, a technocratic elite has enshrined the worldview of neoliberal economics (with its values of efficiency, self-interest, and exploitation) into our political, academic, and cultural institutions. The drive to efficiency (and profits) has resulted in massive industry consolidation, as well as an emphasis on both "scale" and sensationalism. As budgets for real journalism have been slashed, media outlets and platforms compete for attention (i.e., traffic and the advertising dollars that follow). In the competition for public attention, we are bombarded with "infotainment," but the sound-bite sensationalist stories do little to help us understand our complex contemporary problems

While fewer resources are available to investigate and fact-check, media decisions are made based on marketing messages and behavioral science findings that play to emotions rather than logic. Tactics from behavioral science—which are usually directed at our baser instincts—are deployed to capture attention rather than to inform us. The goal of the so-called information industry is to either titillate us with trivia or trigger our hostilities toward some "other" of our fellow humans, destroying both empathy and critical thinking. Increasingly, the drive to capture audiences has resulted in an explosion of misinformation and so-called "fake news." This phenomenon has not only aggravated polarization, but has created a society where people literally occupy alternate realities. The phenomenon of false information combined with the pathocratic worldview of everyone-for-himself and society as a war-of-all-against-all thus takes root into the population at large.

In the final Section Five, we analyze how ponerizing influences have affected our ability to think rationally and how we relate to each other—which has negative implications for our collective ability to solve the problems before us. There is evidence to suggest that we may be descending into a new dark age, where scientific reasoning is condemned and truth is deliberately obfuscated. Elites, who are positioned to seize opportunity in the disruption that they create, demand that the rest of us—whose lives are turned upside down and social fabric torn asunder—embrace the chaos with the same celebratory zeal. Religious fundamentalists of all persuasions (Christians, Muslims, and Jews) increasingly feel that their way of life is existentially threatened. Even among the non-religious, generalized feelings of resentment, alienation and rootlessness create a form or populist romanticism that disparages logic. This is juxtaposed against a technocratic elite, who rule society based on amoral algorithmic dictate. We are witnessing a form or moral inversion, the foundation of "greed is good" ideology. There is even evidence that the personalities of basically decent people can literally be changed—and not for the better.

Notes

[1] Hedges, C. (2009). *Empire of illusion: The end of literacy and the triumph of spectacle.* New York, NY: Nation Books at pp. 142-143.

[2] You can download the full report here: https://paxsims.files.wordpress.com/2020/08/preventing-a-disrupted-presidential-election-and-transition-8-3-20.pdf

---

[3] https://www.youtube.com/watch?v=5UO3nn7awUk

[4] Trump had previously proposed himself as the running mate for former President George H.W. Bush (41), then ran briefly on the Reform Party ticket in 2000. Trump switched to the Democratic Party in 2001, then became an Independent in 2009 before changing back to Republican in 2012.

[5] Mayer, J. (2016, July 25). Donald Trump's ghostwriter tells all. *The New York Times.* https://www.newyorker.com/magazine/2016/07/25/donald-trumps-ghostwriter-tells-all#

[6] Johnston, David C. (2016). *The making of Donald Trump.* Brooklyn, NY: Melville House Publishing.

[7] Wolff, M. (2018). *Fire and fury: Inside the Trump White House.* New York, NY: Holt and Company.

[8] Bolton, J. (2020). *The room where it happened: A White House memoir.* New York, NY: Simon & Schuster.

[9] Cohen, M. (2020). *Disloyal: A memoir: The true story of the former personal attorney to Donald J. Trump.*

[10] https://www.globalwitness.org/en/campaigns/corruption-and-money-laundering/trump-deals/,
https://www.washingtonpost.com/opinions/2020/05/20/trump-just-said-corrupt-part-out-loud/
https://prospect.org/power/mapping-corruption-donald-trump-executive-branch/
https://www.usatoday.com/story/opinion/2020/05/18/michael-flynn-case-tests-justice-system-independence-column/5204400002/,
https://projects.thestar.com/donald-trump-fact-check/,
https://www.washingtonpost.com/news/fact-checker/ and on, and on and on *ad infinitum.*

[11] A story which is still unfolding and will not be addressed herein.

[12] https://www.scientificamerican.com/article/a-year-of-trump-science-is-a-major-casualty-in-the-new-politics-of-disruption/;
https://www.scientificamerican.com/article/leading-scientists-urge-voters-to-dump-trump/

[13] https://www.cnn.com/2018/11/28/opinions/trump-decision-making-gut-instinct-ghitis/index.html

[14] https://time.com/5625699/trump-cabinet-acosta/, https://www.brookings.edu/research/tracking-turnover-in-the-trump-administration/, https://thehill.com/homenews/administration/476083-rapid-turnover-shapes-trumps-government, https://www.politico.com/story/2019/07/16/trump-cabinet-turnover-1416134

[15] https://www.cnn.com/2016/12/10/opinions/government-is-the-problem-jacobs/index.html

[16] https://abcnews.go.com/Politics/rick-perry-forgot-agency-lead/story?id=44163625

[17] Unlike Perry, who left the administration in December 2019, and many other of Trump's now-departed cabinet, DeVos remained during the majority of her appointed term, tendering her letter of resignation on January 7, following the armed insurrection at the U.S. Capitol on January 6th. DeVos' letter can be viewed here: https://www.washingtonpost.com/context/betsy-devos-resignation-letter/cfd93504-2353-4ac3-8e71-155446242dda/

[18] https://www.americanprogress.org/issues/education-k-12/news/2018/04/18/449811/prince-devos-plan-privatize-american-institutions/, https://educationvotes.nea.org/2019/03/22/devos/, https://populardemocracy.org/news-and-publications/5-reasons-billionaire-gop-donor-and-public-school-privatizer-betsy-devos, https://thehill.com/blogs/pundits-blog/education/318948-beware-of-trump-and-devos-grand-plan-to-privatize-public

[19] https://www.thenation.com/article/archive/us-still-paying-blackwater-millions/

[20] https://www.cbsnews.com/news/making-sense-of-the-blackwater-connection/

[21] Wolff, M. (2018). *Fire and fury: Inside the Trump White House.* New York, NY: Holt and Company, at pp. 164-165.

[22] Covered more fully in *Why Assholes Rule the World* (2019).

Section One
Our Livelihoods: Work Isn't Working for Us

The property which every man has in his own labour, as it is the original foundation of all other property, so it is the most sacred and inviolable.

Adam Smith,
The Wealth of Nations

*

Downsizing, reorganization, bubbles bursting, unions busted, quickly outdated skills and transfers of jobs abroad create not just fear, but an economy of fear, a system of control whose power feeds on uncertainty, yet a system, that, according to its analysts, is eminently rational.

Sheldon Wolin[1]

*

Those in the precariat have lives dominated by insecurity, uncertainty, debt and humiliation. They are denizens rather than citizens, losing cultural, civil, social, political and economic rights built up over generations. ***The precariat is the first class in history expected to labour and work at a lower level than the schooling it typically acquires****...The state and the politicians in control want those in the precariat to feel small and inadequate, to blame themselves rather than the structures producing inequality and precariatarization.*

Guy Standing[2]

*

Resignation to oppression and incompetence without a viable choice has become a way of life for far too many workers.

Richard Werre[3]

*

Hell is a collection of individuals who are spending the bulk of their time working on a task they don't like and are not especially good at.

David Graeber[4]

*

The road to fascism and dictatorship is paved with failures of economic policy to serve the needs of the general public.

Tim Wu[5]

The place where most of us have experienced ponerization/pathocracy on a daily, ongoing and personal basis has been in our workplaces. Sociopaths are not simply in charge of our workplaces, they are writing the rules of the workplace—rules that minimize or ignore real biological needs for safety, predictability. meaning, and community. Our contemporary workplaces are driven by heightened risk and insecurity, constant change, and lack of meaning. At the same time, our culture demands that we maintain a relentlessly cheerful demeanor and optimistic outlook, because to do otherwise—or question the benefits of progress as they are delivered by the system—brands one as either a "loser" or "un-American."

In January 1990, a group comprised of over one hundred theologians, ethicists and development practitioners met in Oxford, England to discuss contemporary economic issues within the context of their Christian faith tradition. In the ensuing Oxford Declaration on Christian Faith and Economics,[6] the authors propose that the purpose of work is first, to satisfy human needs, and second, to serve God in the preservation of creation. Because work is central to God's intention for humanity, is has intrinsic value. At the same time, humans are warned to guard against over-valuing work, especially if the work itself impedes God's purpose. In our society today, the corporatocracy often presents us a false choice between destruction of "jobs" or destruction of the environment. We fail to challenge the assumption that corporate "jobs" are the only form of human work.

According to the Oxford theologians, in an idealized world there would be a proper balance between work and leisure. Work would be sufficient to provide for our physical needs as well as give us a purpose in God's greater plan. However, we are confronted with the oxymoronic "working poor," whose jobs do not pay enough for minimally decent subsistence, as well as lack of meaning. Working for "the man" takes us away from the real work of caring for our families and being engaged in our communities. Work should not consume us, but rather should allow us opportunity to develop and use our God-given ability to the fullest, as well as sufficient time for the enjoyment of nature, worship (communion with God) and fellowship with other humans.

Yet, the reality for most of us is quite the opposite. Many of us are either overworked or underemployed. Workers with higher-level skills often work upwards of 50 or 60 hours per week, especially if they are covering for former co-workers who have been laid off or downsized. Alternatively, other workers (usually those with lower-level skills and education) tend to work at part-time and low-wage jobs, often stringing together a number of such jobs in order to make ends meet. Workers at both ends of the skills and education spectrum also deal with increasing commutes, juggle with day care and other family management issues (i.e., work-life balance), and worry about whether or not they will have a job tomorrow.

Workplace angst is more than anecdotal or the subject of opinion pieces on a slow news day. In March of 2016, the American Psychological Association (APA) Center for Organizational Excellence conducted its sixth survey of working Americans, selected from participants in previous Harris Poll surveys.[7] Keep in mind that in March 2016, the economy was some six or seven years past the "official" Great Recession and not yet under the nightmare of a Trump Presidency. Although the main focus of the survey was employer health and well-being programs, it captured other forms of workplace angst. Less than half of survey respondents said that their employer supports employee well-being, and 33% reported being "chronically stressed" on the job. The employees who reported being stressed attributed the stress to low salaries, lack of opportunity for advancement, and lack of opportunity for participation in decision-making. A similar survey in 2018 tended to focus on workload and vacation time issues.[8] However, even though 80% of respondents reported being in good physical and mental health, there were still significant levels of workplace stress: low salaries (49%), lack of opportunities for advancement (46%), heavy workload (42%), unrealistic job expectations (39%), long hours (39%), job insecurity (37%), and lack of participation in decision-making (37%).

Lobaczewsky identifies one symptom of ponerization (where normal people have internalized pathological thinking and worldview) as a lack of respect for one's own organism.[9] In the workplace, this manifests as workaholism, lack of sleep, failure to use even the limited vacation days one receives as an American worker, failure to eat regular, balanced and healthy meals, and other lifestyle behaviors that end up making us sick. But we are afraid to do anything that suggests we are less than 100% committed to a "job" that could disappear instantly. This dysfunction has been documented by Jeffrey Pfeffer in his recent *Dying for a Paycheck*, where he makes the argument that companies regularly permit—if not encourage—management practices that sicken or kill their employees.[10] Employee use of anti-anxiety and anti-depression medication is on the rise, as is workplace-related suicide.[11]

Even as (relatively) long ago as the 1980s, I was able to discern a growing gap between the cost of housing and wages. I moved frequently, as relocations in search of better wages in one place led to huge increases in rent, and relocations in search of affordable housing led to correspondingly lower wages, leaving one in the same precarious position. Managing the disconnect between wages and housing costs often required living far from one's place of employment, which then entailed increased commuting time and costs, further eroding one's quality of life. I have also worked as a volunteer at various organizations serving the homeless and hungry, and can confirm that many people who are homeless and hungry are not necessarily jobless.

A 2018 study by the Center on Budget and Policy Priorities found that 74% of individuals receiving SNAP assistance (formerly called food stamps) worked at least sporadically. Although participation in SNAP is usually short-term for non-disabled adults, over a third of them continue to work while receiving SNAP benefits.[12] A 2019 survey by the Federal Reserve found that almost 40% of working Americans could not come up with $400 to meet an unexpected emergency.[13] We cling to the belief that people are poor or homeless because they are mentally ill, addicted to drugs or alcohol, or just plain lazy, because to acknowledge that jobs don't pay people enough to live or support a family would require a more difficult mental reckoning.

Jessica Bruder spent a year following a group of "work campers," mainly middle-aged and older folks who traveled the country living in run-down campers or converted pickups in search of seasonal work—Amazon warehouses for holiday delivery, campground maintenance work in the summer, and the fall beet harvest in North Dakota.[14] Workers were sometimes outside in 100 degree heat for hours without water or shade. If they became injured, they were quickly patched up and sent back to physically demanding work. During the summers, they were able to camp for two weeks free in national parks, which sometimes involved lying to park rangers. Most other places involved a similar constant alert for police, due to local ordinances that criminalize homelessness and otherwise prioritize property over people. Bruder proposes that work campers represent the perfect form of "plug and play labor…transforming trailer parks into ephemeral company towns that empty out when the jobs are gone."[15] They are ideal workers because they aren't around long enough to unionize and demand very little in benefits.

Even establishment economists have begun to realize that something is wrong with the job market. In November of 2019—***before*** the economy was suffering effects from the COVID-19 pandemic, a group of economists developed a new measurement they call the Job Quality Index (JQI).[16] The JQI measures weekly incomes in 180 sectors of the American economy, and then calculates the number of jobs that are above or below the mean. A JQI of 100 means that there is an equal distribution of high quality and low quality jobs. A JQI that is less than 100 means that there are more low quality jobs than high quality jobs. While the researchers note that, historically, low quality jobs have always outnumbered high quality jobs, over the past three decades the JQI dropped from 94.9 in 1990 to 79.0 in July of 2019.

US Private Sector Job Quality, 1990-2020

Charts and more at https://www.jobqualityindex.com/

The JQI researchers argue that the current focus on job counts and unemployment rates does not produce an accurate picture of the economy. The JQI data also corroborates findings from a longitudinal study in Australia,[17] as well as finding from a 2014 US study that the quality of jobs (in terms of both pay and hours) taken by underemployed college graduates had also declined.[18] Moreover, current data fails to explain the erosion of the so-called Phillips Curve, or a traditionally-accepted relationship between inflation and lower unemployment levels. That is, if unemployment is low, then wages should be going up and not stagnating. As the focus of the JQI is on a combination of income and hours (and whether or not the job pays enough to support a worker or a worker's family), it does not even take into consideration the less measurable forms of labor degradation and dysfunction that we will address below.

Precariatization: Institutionalized Insecurity

It is only because of a (often maligned) social safety net that our poverty rate is not higher. Rather, in most modern industrialized knowledge economies, the problem is one of precariatization rather than absolute poverty. The British economist Guy Standing has coined the term "precariat" to define a growing new social class.[19] The precariat is comprised of persons quite diverse in age, race, ethnicity, national origin, income and education, but they all share a condition characterized by unstable labor, lack of identity, and erosion of citizenship rights.

Standing identifies seven distinct classes that make up the current global economy. At the top is a plutocracy, a small group of super-citizens with enormous wealth ("mostly ill gotten") along with vast informal power and influence. Plutocrats have no national loyalties and often maintain citizenship/passports of convenience from several countries. Below the plutocracy is an elite, comprised of persons who occupy positions of power at the national level. The elite operates to rig the rules of the game in their favor and generally serves either their own interest or the interests of the plutocracy (who they hope to join). Plutocrats and elites constitute the effective global ruling class. They are known colloquially as the "one percent," although Standing asserts their numbers are fewer than this.

Immediately below the ruling class is the salariat. The salariat is a shrinking group of persons with high-wage jobs and stable income connected to high-status positions in corporations or large state bureaucracies. The salariat enjoys robust labor benefits such as health care, stock ownership, guaranteed retirement income and/or golden parachutes. Alongside but somewhat below the salariat is a smaller but growing group that Standing calls proficians. Proficians are technical experts who often work as self-employed consultants and independent contractors (software engineers, stock traders, attorneys, medical and technical specialists). This group earns high incomes, but "lives on the edge of burn-out and constant exposure to moral hazards." The proficians are also growing in both political and cultural influence, promoting an ethos of rugged individualism and "excessive opportunism." The salariat and proficians constitute what we used to call the middle (or upper middle) class, although many of the salariat live in fear of falling into the precariat. Conversely, the proficians are "essentially entrepreneurs selling themselves" to the highest bidder.

Below the proficians are the old-style proletariat, a rapidly shrinking group that still enjoys the disappearing protection of collective bargaining agreements and pensions. The old proletariat is what was once known as the middle class (in America) or the working class (in Europe). This group is not only shrinking in numbers but also in rights and ability to influence the rules of the system. Below the old-style proletariat is the precariat, the fastest growing yet still unformed group who we will describe more fully next. At the very bottom (below the precariat) is a permanent underclass of persons who have been "effectively expelled from society, lack agency and play no active role in the economic system beyond casting fear on those inside it."

Standing's precariat is comprised of three subgroups, but their unifying feature is labor that is insecure and unstable. They have little loyalty to either the state or the corporatocracy, having little in the way of guaranteed rights. The precariat is suspicious of old-style laborism and generally uninterested in the mechanics of citizenship or even collaborative rebellion, instead tending to follow an "everyone for himself" approach to economic survival. The first subgroup is those who have dropped out of the old working class. This group "tends to relate their sense of deprivation and frustration to a lost past," and they are susceptible to messages from the far right. The second group consists of immigrants and minorities, who have traditionally experienced no sense of real belonging within the "system" and are often subject to discrimination. The third group is the overeducated and underemployed—those who experience both a sense of relative deprivation and status frustration. These are folks who might have ended up as proficians if they had either been able to access the right opportunity or had been willing to squelch their own moral values in order to serve the system. This group tends to be receptive to messages from the far left. In spite of these potentially polarizing differences, the unifying feature of the precariat is a sense that their voices are not heard and generalized disconnection from the political and economic system.

Standing suggests that unifying the interests of the precariat may hold the key to making the system more responsive to human needs. However, this group has extremely low levels of trust in traditional institutions (both business and government), having been abandoned by a system that no longer serves most of us. The precariatized mind is under constant stress, because it has no way of predicting the best way to allocate time or even attempt to plan for the future. Consequently, its primary emotion is fear. This generalized anxiety serves the system because it keeps the precariat suspicious of institutions that facilitate collective action. It also makes it easier to manipulate emotions and influence worldview—a subject we will cover in more depth in Section Four of this part. Yet, Standing also believes that the precariat is also less likely to suffer from the "false consciousness" that the answer to insecurity is more corporate jobs.

Cult of Workaholism

Our labor history has been characterized by a pattern where new forms of working arise because they benefit corporate elites at the expense of all the rest of us, yet these new forms of work are ballyhooed as paragons of productivity. Early industrialists perfected the breakdown of craft work into the discrete, repetitive tasks of the factory assembly line, disconnecting the worker from control over the work. Giant retailers like Walmart and fast-food outlets perfected the "just-in-time" scheduling of part-time hourly work, which increased the unpredictability and complexity of managing family life as well as family budgets. Today, the so-called gig economy was created by tech startups—backed by Wall Street—and the Silicon Valley model has become our new work model of success. It has been worshipfully referred to by former President George W. Bush as the "ownership society" and by former President Barack Obama as "Startup America." Yet Silicon Valley has greatly aggravated the wage-housing disconnect, as well as a culture of unhealthy workaholism.

Antonio Garcia-Martinez in *Chaos Monkeys,*[20] David Lyons in *Lab Rats,*[21] and Corey Pein in *Live Work Work Work Die*[22] describe the realities of living and working in Silicon Valley. While Garcia-Martinez focuses more on the finance logistics and economics, Lyons and Pein focus more on the culture. All describe a frantic workaholic existence in an area of skyrocketing rents. While increasing rents are common everywhere, this is aggravated in Silicon Valley by the hordes of "techie colonizers" who descend on the area and are able to "pay through the nose to live in concrete garages without bathrooms."[23] Garcia-Martinez managed to snag a tidy sum by selling his startup to Facebook. This allowed him to purchase a sailboat, which he could dock in a marina for $700 per month—a fraction of typical rents in the area. Pein describes a similar experience of frequent moving in search of a balance between location/commute, cost, and tolerability. Pein ends up in a tent which he rents from a woman who works as an intellectual property attorney. Although Pein's landlady has an undergraduate degree from Yale, a law degree, and a full-time professional job, she can only make ends meet by renting out both the second bedroom in her small apartment and a small space under a tent in her backyard.

The workaholism in Silicon Valley is driven by the illusion that "anyone" can get rich. However, both Garcia Martinez and Pein report the reality that most people are going to crash and burn. "For every Zuckerberg there's one hundred guys who basically got fired from their startups."[24] Tech companies are able to "exploit a variety of well-honed managerial tactics" to expropriate tech talent and feed the insatiable appetite of Wall Street.[25] Employees are kept in constant fear of layoff through tactics such as stack ranking and scrum procedures which operate to turn even creative entrepreneurs into wage labor. The companies present themselves as hip startups offering fun work and perks such as onsite catering and game rooms, but such distractions are often no more than thinly disguised wage theft. No one protests because the carrot of striking it rich always dangles enticingly near yet out-of-reach. Better yet, the slaving coders are hostile to the concept of solidarity, because everyone believes that he is going to be the next tech billionaire.[26]

On a preliminary visit to Facebook (which ultimately absorbed his interest in a startup), Garcia-Martinez describes overhearing an employee in the men's room frantically typing code while sitting on the commode. He also noticed that there were two big buckets of disposable toothbrushes and small tubes of toothpaste—which actually got used judging by the wrappers in the trash. The provision of basic comforts—catered meals, game areas and even nap rooms—gave the appearance of employer generosity and concern for employee wellbeing, but instead were calculated means of insuring that employees practically lived at the workplace. Which indeed some of them did. Pein describes how some Yahoo employees were able to "camp out" in the company conference rooms to avoid the extravagant rents in the area.[27] Garcia- Martinez, whose time in the Valley was longer as he launched a start-up, strategized a buy-out, and ended up working for Facebook, laments missing out on his daughter's childhood.

Although workaholism is most prevalent in the United States, it also exists in other developed countries. In Japan, they even have a word—*karoshi*—which literally means death from overworking. This malady affects primarily mid and upper-level executives, who often work sixteen to nineteen-hour days only to die prematurely from strokes, heart attacks, and other stress related illnesses. Workaholism can also segue into an addictive perfectionism, which then bleeds into other aspects of our lives. So-called "goal pursuit" means that we track the number of our steps rather than walk to get some fresh air and exercise or even enjoy the outdoors.[28] At work we strive for the next promotion, the next big client, the next million bucks, even when we have more than enough to meet our needs (and even our reasonable wants). On social media, we jockey to get more views, likes, shares, and re-tweets. Our lives thus become a series of scorekeeping drills disconnected from any sense of higher meaning or purpose.

Underemployment and the Fallacy of the Knowledge Economy

One can argue that the flip side of overwork is underemployment. A logical assumption is that both overwork and underemployment could be remedied simply by creating more jobs; i.e., hiring the underemployed to help out the overworked. Of course, this also assumes that workforce policy even tangentially considers the well-being of workers as a worthy objective. By now, must of us know this is certainly not the case here. Such wholesale abandonment of concern for the great majority of the citizenry without corresponding popular uprising is a fairly obvious sign of ponerization.

Underemployment is a subject I am intimately familiar with, both in terms of personal experience as well as it being the subject of my doctoral dissertation.[29] I wrote my first paper on underemployment as an undergraduate during the Reagan years. In this early paper, I looked at patterns that were already obvious: the baby boom generation was entering mid-career at the same time there was massive corporate downsizing, the emergence of the so-called "service" economy, globalization, diminishing returns to education, and the myth of unlimited opportunity. At that time, I was also working in a family-owned retail specialty store. A co-worker presented the classic case of overeducated underemployment, as she had completed a Masters degree in geology in Brazil, and was fluent in German and Portuguese as well as her native English.

At the time of this early paper, Teresa Sullivan's *Marginal Workers, Marginal Jobs* was the primary foundational study on underemployment.[30] Sullivan parsed underemployment into four broad categories: unemployment (the extreme, total version), inadequate wages, involuntary part-time, and overeducation. We have briefly discussed the poverty and involuntary part-time (particularly the gig economy) versions, so now we will turn to the overeducation version, which was the subject of my own research. By the time of my dissertation study, there were three other full-length books that had been written about the subject: Russell Rumberger's *Overeducation in the U.S. Labor Market,*[31] David Livingstone's *The Education-Jobs Gap,*[32] and the more recent *Underemployment: Psychological, Economic and Social Challenges* [33] by Douglas Maynard and David Feldman. Over these several decades, there had also been sporadic research among academics, who approached the issue from a variety of disciplines and frameworks: economics, psychology, sociology, "industrial relations," and behavioral science.

There was a resurgence of popular interest in overeducation following the 2007-2009 Great Recession, with articles appearing weekly featuring baristas with college degrees or laid off executives working at Walmart. When the number of involuntary part-time workers tripled between 1970 and 1990,[34] the Bureau of Labor Statistics (BLS) began measuring involuntary part-time and so-called "discouraged" workers, yet it continued to report the official unemployment rate expressed as a percent of persons not working but looking for work compared to the persons who are working. The number of persons who are considered (by the BLS) to be fully employed are those who work as little as one hour per week, or even work for free in a family-owned business more than 15 hours per week. Although the sporadic academic research that exists suggests that overeducation is an ongoing and serious problem, the BLS does not measure either overeducation or overqualification.

In my own study, I surveyed 596 pre-qualified individuals from 28 specifically defined occupations in the STEM (science, technology, engineering and math), health care, legal and academic professions residing in 46 states plus the District of Columbia (a national cross-section). These individuals had to have a minimum of a four-year degree with a specific professional focus (i.e., not a general liberal arts or business degree). Many of them had additional post-graduate and professional credentials and licenses. The respondents were asked about both underemployment—which was as narrowly defined as permitted by the literature—and work satisfaction. Moreover, respondents were asked about underemployment over their career rather than the usual snapshot-in-time during a post-Great Recession economy. This longitudinal focus was intended to "correct" for documented higher rates of underemployment both in the early phases of one's career and during economic recessions. In my study, I urged a conservative interpretation due primarily to possible effects of self-selection bias. The end result was that my sample pool of credentialed professionals indicated a 60% probability of being underemployed at some point during their career.

The main purpose of my study was to counter the argument of the skills shortage alarmists—those who argue that we only need to get the workforce trained and everyone will have a great job. While I do not oppose training and education (how could I have so many letters after my own name and be anti-education?), all the workforce training in the world will not solve the problem of inadequate jobs. Here in the United States, we have an entirely employer-driven political ideology focused on the necessity of maintaining global competitiveness, with its primary objective to externalize the cost of training onto individual workers or taxpayers as a whole. Politicians everywhere were making public statements parroting complaints from their business constituents about skills shortages, yet skills surplus in the form of under-employment was not even being measured. Moreover, the concurrence of skills shortages and stagnating wages defies every rule of classical economics—another phenomenon that no one was questioning. While I was collecting data for my own study, the Federal Reserve quietly released a report that its own research had found ***a fairly uniform underemployment rate of 33% over the past two decades,***[35] a study which—unsurprisingly—never made the nightly news or mainstream media headlines.

What my own research uncovered was not so much armies of people with graduate degrees working in restaurant and retail jobs, but rather a complex form of labor degradation that is more difficult to describe and quantify. For example, academics with Ph.D. degrees were still working in academia, but more of them were working as low-paid, part-time contingent adjunct faculty. Some of these highly educated persons were living in near poverty, but their students also suffered diminished quality of educational life from this failure of institutional support for their instructors. Adjuncts—who often had the same level of education and experience as the tenured faculty--were never fully integrated into the institution, had no research budget to further their own careers, and often had no office or space to meet with and advise students. Likewise, law school graduates who were unable to secure legal employment were also able to practice law by opening their own solo law practices. However, here we see the phenomenon of poverty in the midst of plenty, with the law graduates complaining that the system produced too many lawyers while at the same time low and moderate income persons could not afford to hire an attorney.

The Meaninglessness of Work

So far, we have described a work economy that is comprised of an underclass surplus population, a larger and growing precariat that includes gig workers and independent consultants, a sizeable cohort of overeducated and underemployed, and a smaller (but also growing) group of proficians and technocrats who, although they receive better pay, are subject to extreme forms of workaholism and cutthroat competition. Somewhere in the middle are people who have jobs where they are paid reasonably decently and they actually enjoy the work. But here too, we see less obvious signs of discontent. David Kusnet's *Love the Work, Hate the Job*[36] and Richard Werre's *I Love My Work But I Hate My Job*[37] attempt to explain this phenomenon. Kuznet follows employees in the Seattle, Washington area who work for Microsoft, Boeing, Kaiser Aluminum and Northwest Hospital. He primarily lays the blame on globalization and constant cost-cutting, which operates to thwart workers from doing their best. Werre—an addiction counselor—focuses more on the indignities and "unrecognized trauma" suffered by inferiorized employees attempting to "do what is right" in toxic workplace environments.

David Graeber describes yet an even more dysfunctional, but hard to describe work relationship that he calls *Bullshit Jobs*.[38] The paradox of bullshit jobs is that they usually pay decently (sometimes quite well) and generally do not involve overwork, yet Graeber documents that persons occupying these jobs report feeling frustrated and unfulfilled. This frustration is often accompanied by guilt, because the occupant of a bullshit job probably knows others who are either overworked, underemployed, or struggling to make ends meet. Thus, there is also a sense of feeling trapped.

Graeber makes a distinction between garden-variety "shit jobs," which tend to be blue collar and pay by the hour, and "bullshit jobs," which tend to be white collar and salaried.[39] Although bullshit jobs often correlate with hierarchical bureaucratization, they are not confined to the public sector, since "bureaucracies" can exist in private, government, and non-profit organizations. Graeber divides these job types into flunkies (exist only to make someone else look or feel important), goons (apply force to keep others under control), duct tapers (assigned to clean up the predictable mess or problems that the organization creates; e.g., many tech support and customer service positions), box tickers (who create the illusion that the organization is actually accomplishing something), and taskmasters (the typical person occupying a managerial or administrative position whose only purpose is to assign and evaluate the work of others who are capable of doing these things for themselves).

Compared to the precariatized jobs or gig work done by most of us, Graeber's so-called bullshit jobs are often better in terms of pay, prestige and reasonable work hours. Yet, the people who work in these jobs report a non-descript malaise. Sometimes this can be traced to a lack of meaning, sometimes to boredom, but often to other emotions that are harder to capture. Some complain that they always have to "look busy" even when there is nothing to do (a combination of forced pretense and social uselessness). Others struggled with feelings of emptiness or worthlessness—an "agonizing disparity between the outward respect they received from society (as a consequence of some important-sounding corporate title) and the knowledge of what they actually did."[40]

One fellow had an apparently ideal job, making huge amounts of money producing reports for pharmaceutical marketing. He spends his free time on medical research to eliminate tuberculosis in third world countries. The fellow comments how "the amount of workplace aggression and stress is inversely related to the importance of the work."[41] Others reported "minor acts of sadism."[42] While the meaningful work always seemed to happen in a more collaborative and congenial atmosphere, there usually wasn't anyone willing to pay for it. Many of us may have experienced this phenomenon in our volunteer work. We perform our paid jobs to meet our basic material needs but perform a volunteer side gig to give us meaning and purpose.

Graeber argues that the social value of work is inversely related to its economic value—that is, the more the work itself benefits others, the less one is likely to be paid for it.[43] Nurses, garbage collectors, cooks and mechanics serve an obvious purpose. Less obvious, but also serving a social purpose are artists and musicians. Graeber proposes that the disappearance of these persons would be "immediate and catastrophic" for society. We are seeing this now in the midst of the COVID-19 epidemic, where "essential" workers are not just the health care and medical folks, but grocery store workers, delivery drivers and other positions that are low paid, unglamorous and (in normal times) unappreciated.[44] Conversely, the rest of us might hardly notice the disappearance of CEOs, private equity traders, PR researchers, legal consultants and telemarketers.[45] Ironically, in an era of downsizing and layoffs, it is the people at the bottom—"the ones who are actually making, maintaining, fixing or transporting things"—who are most likely to be laid off.[46]

Graeber acknowledges the problem of measuring something as subjective as social value. However, he cites a 2017 paper by a group of American economists who attempted to determine social value by measuring externalities (social costs) and spillover effects (social benefits).[47] The study found that the most valuable workers were medical researchers, who add $9 of overall value to society for each $1 of compensation. The least valuable were those who worked in the financial sector, who subtract $1.80 from society for each $1 of compensation. The net positive occupations (in descending order) were researchers, schoolteachers and engineers. The net negative occupations (in ascending order) were financial sector, managers, advertising/marketing, and lawyers. Consultants and IT professionals netted out at zero. Of course, the study does not even address the various street-level persons who keep things running or care for the rest of us—mechanics, nursing and home health aids, child care, truck and delivery drivers, restaurant workers—that most of us would indeed miss if they disappeared. Thus, the paradox of work is that most people want to earn enough money to have at least a modestly comfortable lifestyle while at the same time making a positive contribution to the world, but the way work is organized today creates an inverse relation between these two objectives.[48]

According to Graeber, the bullshitization of jobs came about as jobs in industry and agriculture were replaced by service jobs. This was compounded by the rise of finance capital and the so-called knowledge economy and technocratic "symbolic analysts." Graeber argues that financialization and bullshitization arose in the corporate sector, but then expanded into universities and hospitals, where the values of the so-called "learning" and "caring" professions were also transformed into neoliberal, technocratic institutions run by the professional-managerial class.[49] Graeber describes the financial sector itself as a "scam of sorts" with the "overwhelming bulk of its profits com[ing] from colluding with government to create, and then to trade and manipulate, various forms of debt."[50] Moreover, corporate lobbyists and financial consultants, who "seem responsible for a disproportionately large share of the harm done in the world" tend to be surrounded by "yes-men and propagandists" who convince them (as well as everyone else) that they are important and what they do is valued.[51]

One obvious question is how can bullshit jobs proliferate in a capitalist system that is purportedly driven by demands for efficiency. Graeber proposes that bullshit jobs serve the system in a number of ways. First, in a system that is generally hell-bent on destroying real jobs that support people, the creation of bullshit jobs serves as a pressure release valve on unemployment. Graeber references statements from former President Barack Obama in explaining why he "bucked the preferences of the electorate and insisted on maintaining a private, for-profit health insurance system." In one word, the answer is jobs—the jobs of those millions of paper-pushers in the private insurance industry.[52] This suggests that both the corporatocracy and those in the political class basically admit that the "system" would not produce enough jobs to keep everyone employed without the backstop of bullshit jobs.

Another explanation for the proliferation of bullshit jobs is the pursuit of power. The ambitious recognize that power and prestige grow with the number of people over which one has authority, so the creation of bullshit jobs is a feature of personal empire-building. Closely connected to power is parasitism—the impetus to drive resources into one's own pocket—sometimes called rent-seeking by economists. Graeber's examples are the practices of financial entities who take a small "cut" every time money is moved, or a team of attorneys who "keep the battle over a huge estate alive for a lifetime," suggesting that there is much profit to be made by employing an army of paperwork drones, even highly paid ones.[53] Indeed, many bullshit jobs involve the creation of highly complex "bullshit" reports, metrics and software algorithms, which then serve to cover up the fact that the masters-of-the-universe had no clue what their underlings actually did.[54]

Graeber also argues that bullshit jobs play a role in creating inequality by funneling the output of productive workers in the lower quintiles into the bullshit jobs of the upper quintile, operating as a form of "managerial feudalism[55] [which] has produced a similar infatuation with hierarchy for its own sake."[56] Thus, we experience the paradox of a "seemingly endless accrual of layer upon layer of unnecessary administrative and managerial positions, resulting from the aggressive application of market principles…"[57] In other words, an Orwellian justification of inefficiency.

Ponerized Cultural Attitudes Toward Work and Workers

Graeber makes the potentially revolutionary argument that paid labor is unnatural. He documents the history of paid work, beginning in the European Middle Ages, when English peasant families in the Middle Ages "turned their children out" at the age of 7 to perform service in the households of the better-off. Here, the young people either learned a trade or adopted the "manners" of the upper classes. These periods of unpaid indenture were temporary, lasting either a specified number of years or until one had sufficient skills and/or property to support oneself and start a family. Thus, paid labor for others was a phase one passed through on the path to adulthood and self-sufficiency.

Here in America, before the industrial Revolution, most people owned their own labor—working on family farms or as self-employed craftsmen and small shopkeepers. Beginning in the early 1800s, society gradually became organized around factories and offices that were separate from the home. Over a few generations, paid work began to replace self-provisioning and solo entrepreneurialism. This resulted in the increasing bifurcation of workplaces as places of production and homes as places of consumption. Over a few generations, lifetime paid employment became the norm and not the exception.

Today we are seeing new theories that traditional jobs may be becoming obsolete. Those of us who are old enough may remember all of those rosy predictions about how technological advances would allow people to support themselves working only 15 or 20 hours per week. In our current workaholic culture, these predictions seem quaint, if not unrealistically optimistic. It seems that the promise of new forms of work has both a bright side (we will no longer be indentured to the corporatocracy for our livelihoods) as well as a dark side (the loss of security and predictability has created a dog-eat-dog, winner-take-all society). The bright side is presented by Taylor Pearson's *The End of Jobs: Money, Meaning and Freedom Without the 9 to 5,* the dark side is presented by Standing's *Precariat* and Graeber's *Bullshit Jobs,* and a sort of both-sider-ism is presented by any number of the proliferating books about the gig economy.

Graeber describes a form of ideological ponerization that is undefinable and unmeasurable, although he does present evidence to support it. We developed our perverted attitudes toward work (particularly workaholism) as the Protestant work ethic was born and nurtured concurrently with the Industrial Revolution. In order to wrest the new armies of industrial workers away from the work in their own homes, farms and shops, it was necessary to inculcate an attitude that such work was somehow more virtuous. Those who did not leave their homes to toil for "the man" were labeled as lazy never-do-wells who would never be deserving of the good life.

What happens today is the collective shaming of anyone who is not traditionally employed, even if (as is usually the case) it is no fault of their own. Thus, the value of any job—even a bullshit job—cannot be questioned. The world of work involves a constant trade-off between doing something that is either personally fulfilling or socially useful for a large part of our day, or doing whatever we have to in exchange for subsistence and some modicum of social respect. We are caught in a paradox of basing our self-worth and dignity on what we do for a living while at the same time hating it.[58] I will leave it to psychiatrists and psychologists to explain the effects of cognitive dissonance, system justification,[59] surplus powerlessness,[60] and (possible) latent self-loathing created by such a condition.[61]

This dysfunctional relationship with work creates an ungenerous and judgmental attitude that then plays out in systems of means testing for public benefits. These systems are based on the presumption that people hate work, and so they are designed to require a huge amount of work (and costs) to detect fraud and waste. Yet, studies in the UK indicate that only 1.6% of means tested payments are the result of either cheating or honest mistakes, while 60% of persons eligible for unemployment benefits do not receive them. Graeber asserts that such systems are part of a "vast apparatus that exists to maintain the illusion that people are naturally lazy and don't really want to work."[62] The system is designed to "make the process of providing [applicants] with the means of continued existence as confusing, time, consuming, and humiliating as possible," while agency employees are engaged in "a kind of horrific combination of box ticking, and duct taping, making up for the inefficiencies of a system of caregiving intentionally designed not to work."[63]

In his examination of perverted attitudes toward work, Graeber found an underlying philosophy that if work was gratifying in any way at all, no one should be paid for it. The bottom line of this worldview is that everyone must do something that makes them miserable in exchange for subsistence. Doing work that you like, or work that is socially useful, should be done on an unpaid voluntary basis. This explains the intense hostility toward schoolteachers who strike for smaller classes, higher pay, or even more money for their classrooms. It also explains why the managers and administrators who occupy the bullshit jobs in such a system resent those beneath them who may be engaged in more meaningful work, and then proceed to deliberately make the underlings' lives miserable.

Dysfunctional attitudes and relations toward work are deeper and broader than those described by Graeber's bullshit jobs. In *The Corrosion of Character,*[64] Richard Sennett describes the "culture of Davos," where those at the top celebrate the ability to abandon the past and accept fragmentation in order to pursue opportunity. However, while the wealthy and powerful are creating a world where they can "position themselves in a network of opportunities," the systems they create are destructive for those lower in the social order who simply want to play by the rules.[65] While the masters of the universe know that the majority do not live comfortably in the disorder they have created, they are unable (or unwilling) to do anything to change the fate of those who are left behind.[66] Indeed, we are seeing the irony of billionaires—who created fortunes based in part on their ability to predict the future—preparing for the apocalypse of system collapse.[67]

Silicon Valley—the source of a new aristocracy that is creating our new relations with work—is ballyhooed as a meritocracy, where literally "anyone" with talent and hard work can become rich. Yet, the masters (as well as most of the denizens) of today's Silicon Valley are Whiter and more male-dominated than it was in the 1980s. Pein describes a culture of "tech bros" who mostly look, talk, and think alike. He divides them into three character types: creatives with a flair who he calls clowns, the majority of hard working types who he calls drones, and the "binge-drinking gym rats" he calls bullies. The bullies are more likely to be successful due to a combination of "bullshitting skills" and the ability to "emulate the coked-up machismo of their overlords."[68] Garcia- Martinez describes a subtle form of discrimination under the rubric of "cultural fit," where females (who could potentially "buzzkill the weekly happy hour") and persons from more self-effacing cultures (Chinese or Indian), along with the scrappy kid from a small local college "without the glib sheen of effortless superiority you get out of Harvard or Stanford" do not stand a chance.[69] "…anyone who claims the Valley is meritocratic is someone who has profited vastly from it via nonmeritocratic means like happenstance, membership in a privileged cohort, or some concealed act of absolute skulduggery."[70]

The wholesale embracement of disruption and social chaos buttressed by a culture of workaholism that is characteristic of the Silicon Valley-Wall Street cabal has even created a new form of religion called Singularitariansim. The founder of this movement is the software engineer and antidemocracy agitator Curtis Guy Yarvin. Yarvin preaches his gospel under the online name of Mencius Moldbug. The objective of Singularitarianism is to create a society run by an "aristocracy of brains," unimpeded by "small-minded normie meddlers."[71] This school of thought believes that democracy and pluralism pose a threat to their vision of techno-feudalism, and proposes that dissidents should have no other option but to become a refugee from society (i.e., surplus population).[72] Here we see the beginnings of a new philosophy of eugenics, where the sacrifice of human beings conveniently labeled as "losers" becomes not only acceptable, but necessary. Singularitarian philosophy is not limited to a small group of fringe individuals, but has been embraced by the likes of Google co-founder Larry Page, Peter Thiel and other masters-of-the-techie-universe.[73] These are the folks who eagerly anticipate the creation of an artificial superintelligence that will rule the rest of us, or alternatively, the establishment of space colonies—where they can go to escape the hordes of humanity who have been left behind on a dying planet.

Most people have internalized the moral values of the workplace as it has been defined by cultural elites: workaholism is a virtue, greed is good, human beings are expendable, chaos and disruption are to be embraced, your value as a human being is entirely dependent on that which the corporatocracy confers, and those who rise in the hierarchy are somehow superior to the rest of us. We do not think to question the dysfunction, precariatization, alienation (from not only our work, but also from each other and even ourselves), and generalized angst that the system creates in our own lives, instead attempting to distort ourselves to accommodate it. While our primary concern for ponerization might be focused on politics, the foundation of ponerizing influences in modern American society can be traced to relationships with our work.

Notes

[1] Wolin, S. (2008). *Democracy, Inc: Managed democracy and the specter of inverted totalitarianism.* Princeton, NJ: Princeton University Press at p. 67.

[2] Standing, G. (2016). *The precariat: The new dangerous class.*

[3] Werre, R. (2004). *I love my work, but I hate my job.* Lincoln, NE: iUniverse, Inc.

[4] Graeber, D. (2018). *Bullshit jobs: A theory.* New York, NY: Simon & Schuster.

[5] Wu, T. (2018). *The curse of bigness: Antitrust in the New Gilded Age.* (2018). New York, NY: Columbia Global Reports.

[6] The Oxford Declaration. (April-June 1990). *Transformation, 7*(2), 7-18.

[7] http://www.apaexcellence.org/assets/general/2016-work-and-wellbeing-survey-results.pdf?_ga=1.59334189.1847309124.1466619764

[8] http://www.apaexcellence.org/assets/general/2018-work-and-wellbeing-survey-results.pdf?_ga=2.266489934.1119012920.1590348937-1805864100.1590348937

[9] Lobaczewsky, A.M. (1998). *Political ponerology: A science on the nature of evil adjusted for political purposes. Red Pill Press* at p. 232. Full document PDF at http://www.survivorshandbook.com/wp-content/articles/political-ponerology.pdf.

[10] Pfeffer, J. (2018). *Dying for a paycheck: How modern management harms employee health and company performance—and what we can do about it.* New York, NY: HarperCollins.

[11] https://www.theatlantic.com/health/archive/2015/03/workplace-suicides-are-on-the-rise/387916/

[12] https://www.cbpp.org/research/food-assistance/most-working-age-snap-participants-work-but-often-in-unstable-jobs

[13] https://abcnews.go.com/US/10-americans-struggle-cover-400-emergency-expense-federal/story?id=63253846. Full report can be found here: https://www.federalreserve.gov/publications/files/2018-report-economic-well-being-us-households-201905.pdf

[14] Bruder, J. (2017). *Nomadland: Surviving America in the 21st century.* New York, NY: W.W. Norton & Company.

[15] *Id.* at p. 58.

[16] Alpert, D., Ferry, J., Hockett, R.C., & Khaleghi, A. (2019, November). The U.S. private sector job quality index. Cornell Law School, Jack G. Clark Program on the Law and Regulation of Financial Institutions and Markets. https://d3n8a8pro7vhmx.cloudfront.net/prosperousamerica/pages/5467/attach

ments/original/1573727821/U.S._Private_Sector_Job_Quailty_Index_White_Paper.pdf?1573727821

[17] McGuiness, S., & Wooden, M. (2009). Overskilling, job insecurity, and career mobility. *Industrial Relations, 48*(2), 265-286. As workers are cyclically laid off and then rehired in subsequent jobs of diminishing quality, they often eventually exit the workforce altogether.

[18] Able, J.R., Deitz, R., & Su, Y. (2014). Are recent college graduates finding good jobs? *Current Issues in Economics and Finance 20*(1), 1-8.

[19] Standing, G. (2011). *The precariat: The new dangerous class.* London: Bloomsbury Academic Publishing. Read the entire book here: https://www.hse.ru/data/2013/01/28/1304836059/Standing.%20The_Precariat_The_New_Dangerous_Class__-Bloomsbury_USA(2011).pdf

[20] Garcia-Martinez, A. (2016). *Chaos monkeys: Obscene fortune and random failure in Silicon Valley.* New York, NY: HarperCollins Publishers.

[21] Lyons, D. (2018). *Lab rats: How Silicon Valley made work miserable for the rest of us.* New York, NY: Hatchette Books.

[22] Pein, C. (2017). *Live work work work die: A journey into the savage heart of Silicon Valley.* New York, NY: Metropolitan Books/Henry Holt & Company.

[23] *Id.* at pp. 52-53.

[24] *Id.* at p. 73.

[25] *Id.* at p. 77.

[26] As early as 1776, Adam Smith noted the "conceit every man has in his own abilities...and the absurd presumption of his own good fortune" in *The Wealth of Nations.*

[27] Pein, *supra* at p. 53.

[28] Alter, A. (2017). *Irresistible: The rise of addictive technology and the business of keeping us hooked.* New York, NY: Penguin Press.

[29] VanHettinga, B. (2015). Professional reserve armies: Underemployment and labor degradation in professional occupations. http://search.proquest.com/docview/1655360861. This study was then re-

formatted into a book for general (i.e., non-academic) audiences: *The great jobs deception: Why more workforce education will not solve the problem of inadequate jobs.* (2018).

[30] Sullivan, T. (1978). *Marginal workers, marginal jobs: The underutilization of American workers.* Austin, TX: University of Texas Press.

[31] Rumberger, R.W. (1981). *Overeducation in the U.S. labor market.* New York, NY: Praeger.

[32] Livingstone, D. W. (1999). *The education-jobs gap: Underemployment or economic democracy.* Toronto, Ontario: Garamond Press.

[33] Maynard, D.C., & Feldman, D.C. (2011). *Underemployment: Psychological, economic and social challenges.* New York, NY: Springer Science+Business Media, LLC.

[34] Stratton, L.S. (1991, August). Reexamining involuntary part-time employment. University of Arizona Discussion Paper 92-2. UC Berkeley and NBER. Also, Tilly, C. (1991). Reasons for the continuing growth of part-time employment. *Monthly Labor Review, 118*(10), 19-26.

[35] Abel, J.R., Deitz, R., & Su, Y. (2014). Are recent college graduates finding good jobs? *Current Issues in Economics and Finance, 20*(1), 1-8.

[36] Kusnet, D. (2008). *Love the work, hate the job: Why America's best workers are unhappier than ever.* Hoboken, NJ: John Wiley and Sons, Inc.

[37] Werre, R. (2004). *I love my work but I hate my job.* Lincoln, NE: iUniverse, Inc.

[38] Graeber, D. (2018). *Bullshit jobs: A theory.* New York, NY: Simon & Schuster.

[39] *Id.* at p. 15.

[40] *Id.* at p. 125.

[41] *Id.* at p. 118.

[42] *Id.* at p. 119.
[43] *Id.* at p. 196.

[44] Robertson, C., & Gebeloff, R. (2020, April 18). How millions of women became the most essential workers in America. *The New York Times.*

https://www.nytimes.com/2020/04/18/us/coronavirus-women-essential-workers.html "...being essential does not at all mean being well compensated or even noticed."

[45] Graeber, *supra* at p. xxi.

[46] *Id.* at p. 18.

[47] Lockwood, B.B., Nathanson, C.G., & Weyl, E.G. (2017, October). Taxation and the allocation of talent. *Journal of Political Economy, 125*(5), 1635-82.

[48] Graeber, *supra* at p. 207.

[49] *Id.* at pp. 266-269.

[50] *Id.* at p. 151.

[51] *Id.* at p. 12.

[52] *Id.* at p. 157.

[53] *Id.* at p. 167.

[54] *Id.* at pp. 171-172.

[55] *Id.* at p. 175.

[56] *Id.* at p. 182.

[57] *Id.* at p. 189.

[58] *Id.* at p. 241.

[59] Jost, J.T., Banaji, M.R., & Nosek, B.A. (2004). A decade of system justification theory: Accumulated evidence of the conscious and unconscious bolstering of the status quo. *Political Psychology, 25*(6), 881-919.

[60] Lerner, M. (1991). *Surplus powerlessness: The psychodynamics of everyday life.* Atlantic Highlands, NJ: Humanities Press International, Inc.

[61] These issues are addressed in more detail in VanHettinga, B. (2019). *Why Assholes Rule the World.*

---

https://www.amazon.com/Assholes-Rule-World-Brynne-VanHettinga/dp/1732285640/ref=sr_1_1?dchild=1&keywords=Why+Assholes+Rule+the+World&qid=1587411962&s=books&sr=1-1

[62] Graeber, *supra* at p. 273.

[63] *Id.* at p. 273-274.

[64] Sennett, R. (1998). *The corrosion of character: The personal consequences of work in the new capitalism.* New York, NY: W.W. Norton & Company.

[65] *Id.* at pp. 62-63.

[66] *Id.* at p. 147.

[67] Osnos, E. (2017, January 20). Doomsday prep for the super-rich. *The New Yorker.* https://www.newyorker.com/magazine/2017/01/30/doomsday-prep-for-the-super-rich

[68] Pein, *supra* at pp. 24-27.

[69] Garcia-Martinez, *supra* at p. 220.

[70] *Id.* at p. 229.

[71] Pein, *supra* at p. 211.

[72] *Id.* at p. 276.

[73] *Id.* at p. 282.

Section 2
The Economy: Extreme Inequality Harms More Than Our Bank Accounts

...concentrating capital and rulership in one place always leads to degeneration. Capital must be subject to the authority of fairness.

Dr. Andrew Lobaszewsky[1]

*

An elite whose philosophy is embedded in a materialistic arms race, driven by predominant Darwinian notions, and in total disregard of any moral sentiments tends to create societies that are socially fragmented and politically unstable.

Willy Munyoki Mutunga[2]

*

Among the oldest methods to maintain control are belief systems that portray wealth and power in the hands of a few as natural and inevitable.

Robert Reich[3]

*

Equality of opportunity alone cannot fashion a moral order. The principle must be embedded in a larger context of social justice.

Philip Selznick[4]

*

Indeed, whether such extreme inequality is or is not sustainable depends not only on the effectiveness of the repressive apparatus but also, and perhaps primarily, on the effectiveness of the apparatus of justification.

Thomas Piketty[5]

*

MarketWorlders claim they are powerless to do anything that will fix structural inequality. Yet, the system under which MarketWorld has thrived in recent decades is not a naturally occurring phenomenon...
MarketWorlders are debtors who need society's mercy and not saviors who need its followership.

Anand Ghiridharadas[6]

*

When one is accustomed to privilege, equality feels like oppression.

Origin Unknown

Here in America, we tend to think of equality as a legal issue. Everyone has equal rights under the law, and the concept of "everyone" has generally expanded from property-owning white males, to all white males, to African American males, to all women, to LGBTQ individuals. The premise is that the removal of legal impediments and restrictions creates equal opportunity. Legal equality purportedly solves the problem of caste (social class, race, gender, or origin) by removing prejudicial systemic obstacles while maintaining the legitimacy of unequal outcomes based on individual merit.

For the most part, our concept of legal equality is applied to specifically defined groups (i.e., race, gender and other categories that constitutional law defines as "suspect class"). This derives from some of our founding fathers' concerns about factionalism, or the possibility that an excluded minority would be rendered impotent and alienated while the successful majority is "tempted to tyranny."[7] "A 'mechanical' majority—a faction large enough, cohesive enough, and enduring enough to shut out or negate minority views—threatens both community and democracy."[8] These classical views of equality were not intended to erase differences in talent, achievement, contribution or even inherited wealth or good luck, but rather establish the right to be regarded with equal human dignity and moral value.

As Philip Selznick argues in *The Moral Commonwealth,*[9] legal equality is not sufficient to guarantee what he terms the "covenant" of moral equality. The premise of moral equality has both a religious and a secular manifestation. In religious traditions, this amounts to equal worth in the eyes of God. In the secular tradition, it means that all persons have an equal right to be seen and heard, especially on matters that affect the well-being of the whole. While this does not necessarily mean that individuals should be guaranteed equal outcomes, it does require that inequalities not be so extreme as to essentially exclude persons from participation in the community.

Opponents of egalitarianism (especially if it is socially enforced) argue that it has the effect of thwarting individual autonomy and expression, subverting the drive for achievement, inefficiently allocating labor, and wasting human talent. This view portrays the egalitarian world as one of drab sameness, where everyone lives in identical housing, wears the same clothing, does the same type of work, and even engages in the same forms of recreation. Selznick also argues that a certain degree of elitism is necessary in complex advanced societies, with its need for advanced skills in multiple areas of expertise.[10] Equality as it relates to civic and social cohesion is something that is thus more nuanced (and less easier to measure) than a guarantee of equal economic outcomes.

To illustrate this principle, let us imagine a physician (medical doctor) and a janitor. For purposes of our comparison, these individuals should be members of the same race and gender (unfortunately, such distinctions still make a difference). Even the most egalitarian among us would likely agree that the physician should be paid more due to a higher skill level and longer years of education and training. We would also likely defer to the physician's opinions on matters of health and medicine (e.g., policy proposals regarding the current coronavirus pandemic). But do we give the same deference to the janitor on matters of cleaning and sanitation? Now imagine that these individuals are appearing before a governing body—a legislative committee or a city council—to testify as concerned citizens about a matter that is outside the expertise of either of them (e.g., a local zoning change or state regulation). The ideal of moral equality requires that both of them be given equal consideration of viewpoint. Yet, in practical reality (assuming their respective occupations are known to the members of the governing body), which one do you believe is more likely to be heard?

Many of us might think that—as long as we have legal equality (i.e., certain groups are not officially stigmatized)—differences between individuals are the result of normal and "natural" phenomena (meritocracy, markets) and do not indicate any form of broader social dysfunction. Indeed, this may be true in a hypothetical sense, yet research on social dominance orientation[11] describes a self-perpetuating system where previously subordinated (but now legally "equal") groups continue to struggle due to legacy effects of past discrimination: they do not have the same access to networks of power and privilege, and they have been subjected to ubiquitous messaging about their own inferiority. In a culture of meritocracy, these individuals subconsciously accept the worldview of the dominant system, even at the cost of their own self-identity.[12]

While overt discrimination against individuals based on group membership (race, ethnicity, gender, religion and national origin) are now illegal, these groups continue to be subject to (often subconscious) negative judgments. These judgments may not even necessarily be based specifically on so-called "out-group" membership, but some combination of income, occupation, and status. Because women and racial minorities continue to earn less, it is difficult to parse out that which is due to occupational tracking (inducements to pursue lower status jobs and discouragement of pursuing higher status occupations), generalized status differentials, or actual discrimination. There is also the confounding effect of whether the work itself is devalued because of who generally does it (i.e., is child care and development actually "worth" more to the future of society, but low-paying because it is work usually done by women?).[13]

In 2009, the Pew research Center conducted a study of household incomes sorted by religion.[14] Ironically, in a nation that is majority Christian, a higher percentage of Jewish (46%) and Hindu (43%) households earn over $100,000. Fewer (21%) mainline Protestant churchgoers earn over $100,000 (behind orthodox and Buddhists) and only 13% of Evangelical churchgoers do so. However, Black Protestant churchgoers have the lowest percentage (8%) of incomes over $100,000. This suggests that inequality is multi-faceted, most likely connected to race and other outgroup status, but also based on more complex and difficult to measure factors.

From here forward, we are going to be looking at inequality based on income and wealth and not race, gender, religion, or other group affiliation. While discrimination (either conscious or subconscious) may impact economic outcomes, our argument here is that inequality itself can have detrimental effects independent of outgroup discrimination. You may recall our discussion about the difference between mean and median in Part I, Section One, where we looked at how averages can be misleading.

Here we will start with the proposition that a certain amount of income inequality is normal. We are going to be looking at charts and graphs, because a visual demonstration is easier to understand for most folks than lines of mathematical expressions.

As in most natural systems, measurable characteristics are distributed by a mathematical representation of a bell-shaped (or "normal") curve. In a normal distribution, the majority of individuals are found around the middle (the peak), with a small number of outliers on both the high and low tails. A normal distribution can have different values for what statisticians term variance (sigma). A distribution with a small variance will have a high and narrow peak (more individuals are closer to the mean), while a distribution with a large variance will have a lower, less defined peak and a greater difference between individuals at the low and high ends. This is illustrated in Figure 1. This normal-shaped distribution holds for many measurable human characteristics such as height, weight, IQ, and number of ridges in a fingerprint.

Figure 1: Normal Distribution Curves

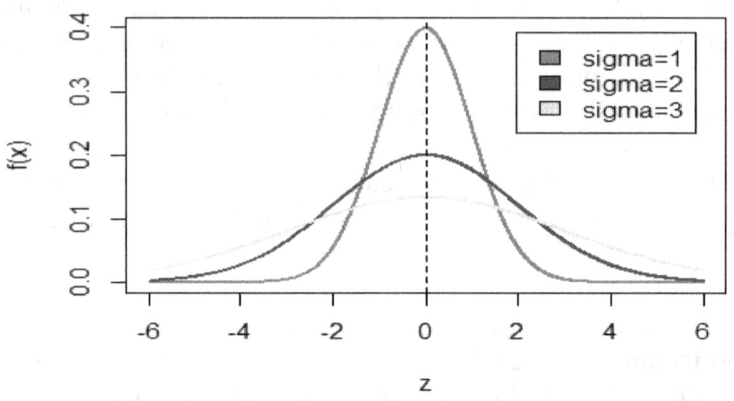

<u>The Level of Inequality Now is Neither Natural nor Normal</u>

Perhaps the most effective graphic illustration of income distribution in the United States is from Keith Payne's (2017) *The Broken Ladder.* Income distribution in the U.S. is represented by the height of a six-foot man. The median income falls at about the top of the toe on the man's shoes. Households earning $100,000 per year (those in the top 20%) would be represented by a height of about four inches. The top 1% (earnings between $300,000 and $400,000) fall around the man's knees. A slim line rises to the man's head, where we find the top 0.1%, with earnings at $1.5 million. To represent the really huge fortunes, we would need to extend the line to the top of a skyscraper.[15]

Now we will look at data on the distribution of household income ranges from 2018.[16] We first reproduce the data as a bar chart in Figure 2. Here we can see that around the middle (household incomes between $35,000 and $99,999), the curve looks something like the middle of a normal bell curve. However, we see that the overall pattern is definitely anything but "normal:" the lower tail actually curves upward toward the lower income ranges. There is an upward spike for income range $100,000 to $149,000, which then drops for the next higher range, only to rise again for household incomes over $200,000. This is easier to see in the line graph, produced from the same data in Figure 3. Because the tails at both ends curve upward, this suggests that more people are dropping into lower income ranges and/or being pushed upward than what we would see in a more "normal," or natural situation.

Figure 2: Household Income Distribution by Percentage

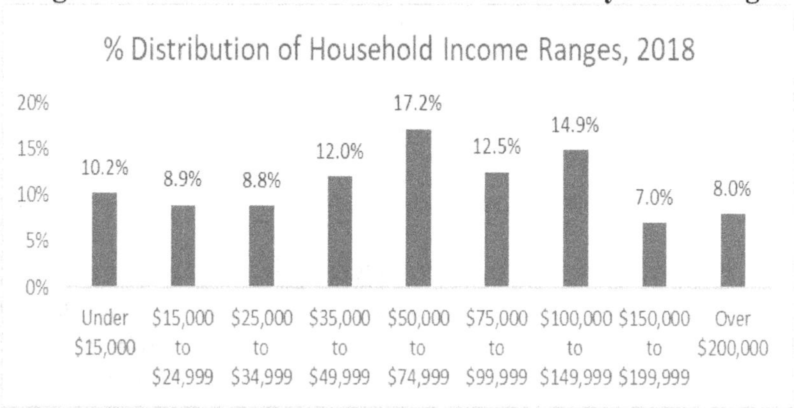

Figure 3: Household Income Distribution Curve

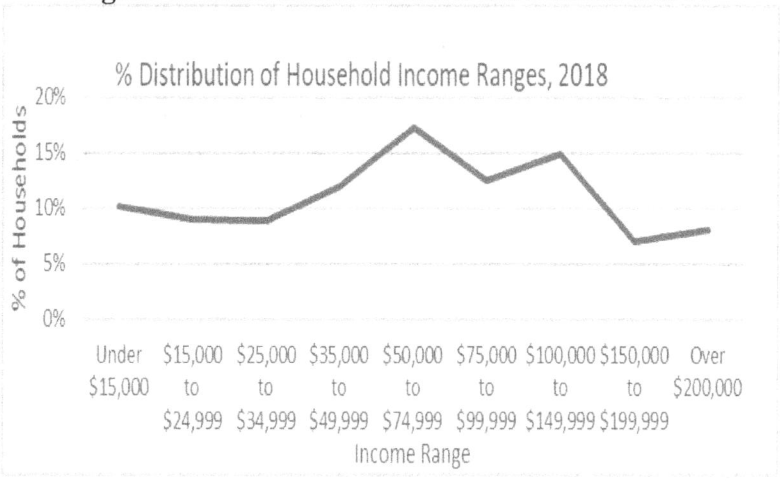

Beginning in the 1980s, a group of radical economists proposed what they termed "segmented" labor markets, or a split between good jobs and bad jobs. This was even before most economists noticed that so-called "middle class" jobs were disappearing. As the segmented market model developed and was tested against empirical data, its predictability outperformed more traditional economic models of the labor market.[17] By the 1990s, even mainstream economists acknowledged the bifurcation between good jobs and bad jobs, along with the hollowing out of the middle.[18] This phenomenon was first attributed to the shift from manufacturing (these jobs had mostly moved overseas in search of cheap labor) to an economy that was split into low-paid (and low-skill) "service" jobs and high-paid (high skill) "knowledge" jobs. Other researchers found that income polarization was not only occurring between demographic groups, but even among white men, "traditionally the most privileged and secure group."[19]

Inequality would be more acceptable if it was accompanied by high social mobility. That is, so long as everyone has more or less the same chances to end up either rich, poor, or somewhere in the middle, there is no foul when individuals experience unequal outcomes. However, in spite of the American promise of equal opportunity and Horatio Alger mythologies, the United States has the lowest rate of mobility among the eight wealthy Western democracies.[20] Indeed, the more extreme inequality is, the less opportunity there is for upward mobility, a relationship known as the Gatsby curve.[21] This phenomenon is actually easy to intuit: wealthy families are not only able to provide the best education, they are more likely to provide their children with competitive advantages such as intensive tutoring and test-preparation, as well as having access to networks of privilege and gatekeepers (e.g., alumni of prestige universities, country club co-members, friendships with high-ranking individuals, etc.)

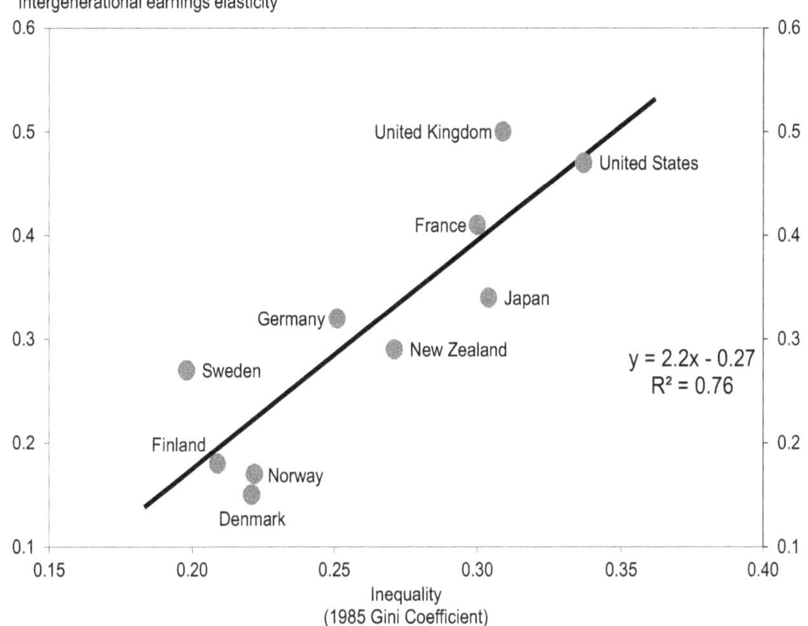

Source: Corak (2011), OECD, CEA estimates

A study by a pair of Italian economists challenges the argument that socio-economic advantage dissipates over a few generations. They examined tax records in Florence, Italy between 1427 and 2011, comparing surnames, occupations, earnings and wealth.[22] In spite of huge historical changes over the ensuing six centuries,[23] the richest families of Florence in 1427 are still the richest families there today, and the authors identified a form of professional dynastization (families of lawyers, bankers, doctors and goldsmiths). A similar study of England over the period 1170 to 2012 found that the inheritability of social status (along with weatlh) persists for centuries.[24] America was supposed to be the land of opportunity, where people were purportedly free of the old strictures and systems of inherited privilege. Yet, the evidence (based on a 2014 empirical review by four prominent economists)[25] suggests that intergenerational mobility is lower in the US than in other developed countries.

A bigger question than the inequality itself is whether or not people deem it acceptable at the level it is. In 2005, Michael Norton (Harvard Business School) and Daniel Ariely (Duke University Dept of Psychology) queried a nationally representative, random sample of 5,522 respondents drawn from a panel of over one million Americans.[26] The respondents were instructed to state their preference of income distribution assuming they would randomly be assigned to a quintile. Respondents had three choices: a purely equal distribution (each quintile received 20% of income), a distribution modeled on Sweden (there is some inequality), and a distribution model based on the U.S. (where the top quintile receives 84% of the income, the second quintile receives 11%, and everyone else gets to split the remaining 5%).

Most of the respondents (47%) preferred the Swedish distribution. A sizeable minority (43%) preferred the purely equal distribution. Only 10% preferred the U.S. distribution. When preferences were solely between the U.S. and Swedish distributions, the Swedish distribution was preferred 92% to 8%, a choice that was consistent across a wide range of income levels, men and women, and even Democrats and Republicans. Although Americans have a greater tolerance for inequality than citizens of other Western democracies, they nonetheless would prefer to live in a less unequal society. Norton and Ariely also asked their respondents to estimate the actual amount of inequality compared to what they considered ideal, and found that Americans drastically underestimate the level of inequality in their own country.

The Mechanics of Concentration

Accumulations of capital in the economic sense did not become a phenomenon of interest until approximately the middle 15th century, with the beginnings of banking and mercantile (trading) companies. Most of us know that wealthy families and individuals have existed as far back as Egyptian and Chinese dynasties, as well as what we know of biblical times. Yet, these accumulations of weatlh were not associated so much with "growth"as they were with control over people and territories. While the lifestyles of these ancient wealthy individuals might seem simple to us today, they typically had larger dwelling places, more servants (or slaves) and ate better food.

The association of accumulations of capital with economic growth did not develop until the beginnings of industrialization around the middle of the 19th century, along with the ascendance of the nation-state and the concept of GDP. Many consider the Scottish political economist and philosopher Adam Smith to be the father of modern economics. Smith was an extraordinary thinker, who attempted to explain the complexity of the new phenomena relating to wages, growth and capital accumulation—all without the benefit of modern computing capacity. Unlike modern economists (who primarily focus on mathematical models), Smith incorporated observations about human behavior. Smith also concerned himself with moral issues involved in economies, adressing the importance of the well-being of workers,[27] as well as the moral hazard created by cabals of "merchants and master-manufacturers."[28] However, Smith's tangential writings on the beneficial operation of self-interest have been the primary focus of the enshrinement of his theories in modern economic thought.

Smith went to great pains attempting to formulate a distinction between "productive" and "unproductive" labor, as well as "unproductive consumption" and "productive" use of capital. He theorized that over the long run, increasing capital accumulation would cause profits to decline,[29] and there was a natural limit to growth. Smith also acknowledged potential negative behavioral effects when profits become too high (as in the case of monopolies), when "sober virtue" is replaced by "superfluous and expensive luxury."[30] Smith proposed the theory that "primitive accumulations" of capital allowed the division of labor, and it is this division of labor (and not capital accumulation itself) which is the primary driver of growth and prosperity. That is, as people were able to accumulate a greater variety of goods to fulfill their needs, they were better able to concentrate on the activities and interests which better suited them.

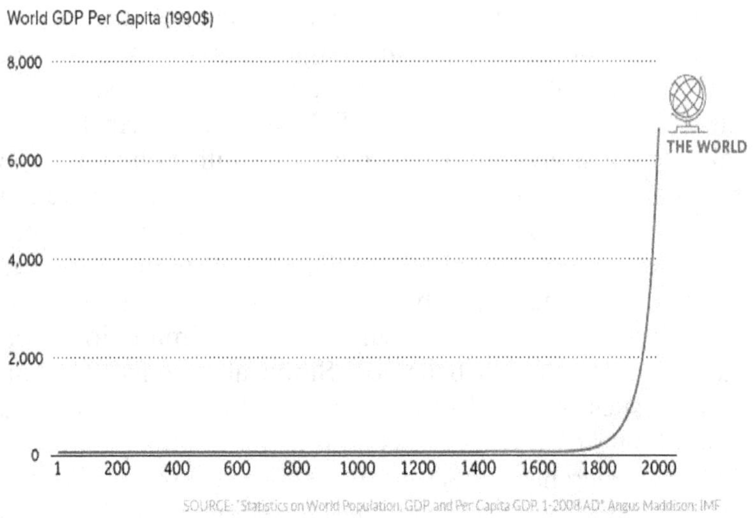

One of the mythologies that arose around Smith's theories was that capital accumulation automatically results in demand for productive labor. That is, allowing the rich to get richer will create jobs—a phenomenon which empirical evidence has since disproved—yet the mythology continues. As the phenomenon of capital accumulation became more familiar, later economists—most notably Karl Marx—suggested that such accumulations were often accompanied by expropriation rather than the saving of the surplus of one's own labor. Examples of expropriation unnconnected to war and conquest are the English enclosure system (where peasants were driven off the land which provided them subsistence), the removal of indigenous people by expansionary empires (and later by corporations), along with early forms of indenture and industrialization, where people everywhere were forced to either sell their labor for subsistence or submit to slavery. Marx was also one of the earliest economists to propose a formal principle of capital accumulation. That is, as profits decreased with increasing levels of accumulation, capital would ravage the globe for "untrammeled accumulation," seeking to exploit, extract and expropriate everything in its path, driving people from their land and homes, who are then "whipped, branded, and tortured by laws grotesquely terrible, into the discipline necessary for the wage system."[31]

As we have seen, inequality has been around nearly as long as human history and is not something that has suddenly appeared. The most comprehensive analysis of historical inequality is the French economist Thomas Piketty's 2014 *Capital in the Twenty-First Century.*[32] Using historical data, Piketty traces the ebb and flow of inequality beginning in pre-industrial Europe (1700). But the story is more than about just numbers—Piketty places his economic data in a broader historical context. Piketty's primary argument is that inequality is not simply an economics issue, or even a result of the natural operation of markets or mathematics. Rather inequality is driven by relations of power and domination between social groups. Moreover, these relations impact (quite differentially) each person's perception of what is and what is not fair.[33]

As Piketty began his post-doctoral career, he was initially flattered to accept a position at a university in the U.S. However, he returned to his native France after only three years. While Piketty found the American economists to be very smart, they didn't seem to fully understand economic problems on a broader level beyond abstract mathematical theorems.[34] Moreover, "Intellectual and political debate about the distribution of wealth has long been based on an abundance of prejudice and a paucity of fact."[35] So Piketty's goal was a comprehensive understanding of "the conditions under which such concentrated wealth can emerge, persist, vanish, and perhaps reappear."[36]

In analyzing the phenomenon of inequality, Piketty's nutshell finding is that huge fortunes are created whenever the rate of return to "capital" (r) is greater than overall economic growth (g). This formula suggests that increasing the rate of growth (provided that the rate of return to capital remains unchanged) can reduce the level of inequality. Yet, we have seen that economic growth can happen concurrently with increasing inequality, on the presumption that the rate of return to capital must be outpacing it. Obviously, the connection between growth, capital accumulations, wages, and inequality is more complex than even a 600-plus-page study (not including the raw data that Piketty and others make available through the World Inequality Database)[37] is able to cover. A more salient question is whether such a state is "natural" or not.

Piketty used Simon Kuznet's pioneering work on the evolution of income inequality in the US between 1913 and 1948, and expanded the methodology to a much longer historical period and globally. Kuznet's work generally supported the prevailing notion that growth was the rising tide that lifts all boats. This data was initially limited to time periods and countries that collected income tax (for most countries, this began between 1910 and 1920, but as early as 1880 in Japan and Germany). Piketty incorporated both income tax and estate tax, along with World Top Incomes Data. He also strived to parse out how much wealth is inherited versus the result of personal savings. Advances in computer technology, statistics, and a longer passage of time between the "shocks" of two World Wars allowed Piketty to build on previous research and construct a bigger picture.

Piketty also reviews the literature of Western Europe (quoting authors such as Honoré de Balzac and Jane Austen), and notes a plethora of stories and advice to marry into a family of inherited wealth, since it was a better guarantee of acquiring a fortune than even such occupational pursuits as law and medicine. Piketty also provides a comprehensive discussion of the differences between the production of labor and income from capital. In feudal societies, "property" income came from owning land and charging others a fee or tax to either use it or protect it. During and after the industrial revolution, "property" came to be defined more by man-made things like factories and machinery. Beginning in the latter part of the 19th century, "property" was increasingly defined in terms of money—not only having it, but earning income by making it available to others.

Based on an exhaustive analysis of historical data, Piketty proposes that the distribution of income from capital has always been more unequal than the distribution of income from labor: the upper 10% of the labor income distribution generally captures 25-30% of the total income received by labor, where the upper 10% of the capital income distribution has historically held more than 50% of total wealth.[38] Although Piketty acknowledges that "income from labor is not always equitably distributed,"[39] it is the extreme inequalities of capital that create the extreme inequalities of income and wealth rather than the (more natural) inequalities associated with labor. Citing a survey conducted by the Federal Reserve, in the United States the bottom 50% of the population owns just 2% of national wealth, while the top 10% of the population owns 72% of national wealth.[40] Moreover, the share of income from capital rises as one rises up the income hierarchy: the income share of capital for the top 9% is 20%, while the top centile (.01%) receives 60% of its income from capital.[41]

In spite of inequality being primarily driven by capital accumulation, wage inequality is contributing to a growing portion of it. Wage inequality is "relatively new [and] was largely created by the United States over the past few decades."[42] Piketty attributes this to what he terms a "hypermeritocratic society,"[43] or what some other economists have termed "winner-take-all" markets.[44] As a result, the United States has broken the historical record for inequality of income from labor, including past societies where skill differentials were much greater (i.e., the elites were able to read and write where most people could not).

Piketty's data shows that there have been historical periods of general "growth" where wages did not also rise. Working wages over the first half of the 19th century stagnated at levels that were inferior to the levels of prior centuries. Beginning in the 1840s, industrial profits grew while labor wages stagnated. The period between 1870-1914 witnessed entrenched and spiralizing inequality. However, Piketty was particularly interested in the period between 1945 to 1975. This period saw the rise of what Piketty terms a "patrimonial (propertied) middle class,"[45] along with a drastic reduction in the wealth share of the upper centile. This period was transformational: it represented the heyday of the American middle class as well as American global ascendance. This phenomenon was not limited to the United States, being also described in glowing terms by the French (Trente Glorieuses), the Germans (Wirtschaft Swunder), and the Italians (Miracolo Economico).

According to Piketty, the primary forces that reduce, or compress, inequalities are the diffusion of knowledge and investment in training and skills. These things are also correlated with economic growth—which suggests an alternate pathway by which growth correlates with lower inequality levels. The post-war economic golden age was also the golden age of American education.[46] The launch of Sputnik—a relatively simple radio satellite—by the Soviet Union in 1957, galvanized a frightened and jingoistic nation to commit larger investments in public education. The Higher Education Act was passed In 1965, which created the federal Pell grant program and federal guarantee of student loans. These programs allowed working and middle class students ways to pay for college, which was previously the domain of wealthy elites. This was also a period where civil rights were expanding, and women and minorities were entering both colleges and the workforce in greater numbers. At the same time, the world was witnessing a "technological convergence," as previously undeveloped countries adopted the modes of production, skills and education levels of rich countries. This suggests that the extremes of inequality can be reduced through universal education, which ideally leads to the "triumph of human capital over financial capital and real estate."[47]

Below is a chart of marginal tax rates from 1913 (when the income tax was passed) to 2013, plotted against unemployment rates (annual averages). While the obvious message is that unemployment does not fall (indeed it appears to increase, or at least becomes more volatile), it is also obvious that during the time period of the American golden age (1945-1975), marginal tax rates were higher. Also, the period immediately preceding the Great Depression followed a drastic drop in the marginal tax rate. You can draw your own conclusions.

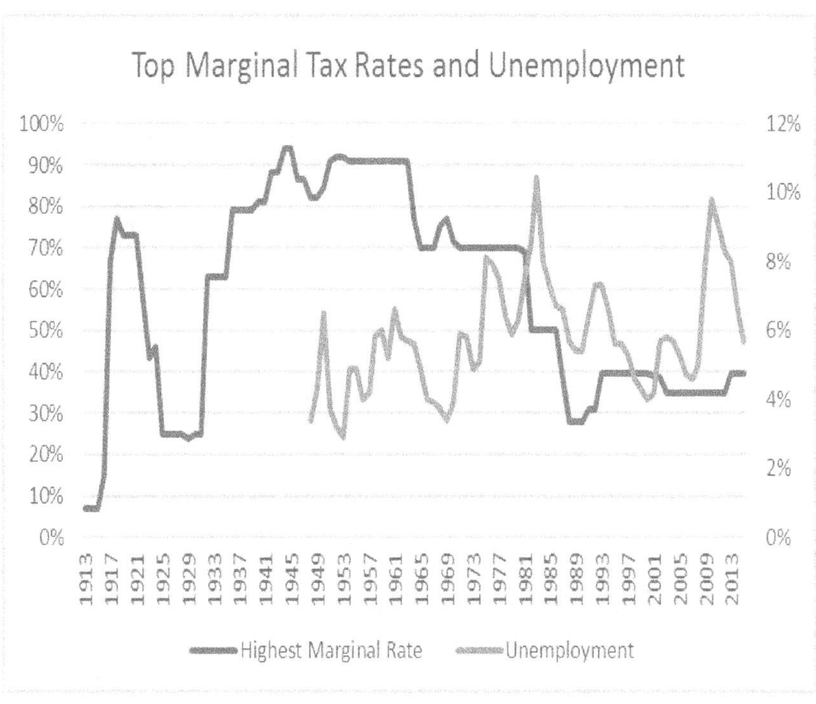

It is no surprise that manipulation of the tax system has served to perpetuate the accumulation of fortunes. Income from capital gains has historically been taxed at lower rates than the highest marginal rates taxed on income from wages. The estate tax—even more so than the income tax—was specifically designed to *prevent* the accumulation of hereditary fortunes. However, a review of the history of both the gift tax and the estate tax indicates the highly volatile (i.e., political) nature of these things. The gift tax was repealed in 1926, only to be re-instituted in 1932. The amount of income exempt from estate tax has risen over the years, although the top rates have fluctuated. The 2017 Tax Cuts and Jobs Act doubled the amount of the estate tax exemption from $5,490,000 to $11,180,000 (double these for married couples). Although 99.98% of us will never have to even think about paying the estate tax, we have been conditioned by propaganda to view the world through the eyes of the oligarchy.

Piketty also addresses the economic collapse predicted by Marx that has obviously not happened. Marx predicted that capital wealth would become so concentrated (bigger capitalists would merge or buy out smaller ones, becoming ever larger themselves) that its returns would start to diminish, which would lead to violent conflict among the capitalists. Alternatively, as capital's share of national income increased while wages stagnated, the workers would revolt. In either scenario, no system would be able to sustain a stable political economy. According to Piketty, we have avoided the Marxian apocalypse due to a combination of economic growth and the diffusion of knowledge. Most modern countries have also succeeded in reducing inequality through a system of progressive taxation. Without controls, "capitalism automatically generates arbitrary and unsustainable inequalities that radically undermine the meritocratic values on which democratic societies are based."[48] There is also a propensity among both economists and statisticians (as well as politicians) to focus on happy endings rather than the end-of-society-as-we-know-it scenarios.

Today, eight billionaires have as much wealth as the bottom half of humanity (3.6 billion people). Six of these billionaires control tech empires: Bill Gates, Mark Zuckerberg, Jeff Bezos, Larry Ellison (Oracle), Michael Bloomberg and Carlos Slim (Telmex). The other two are the investor Warren Buffet and Amancio Ortega, founder of the retailer Zara. Instead of public discussions and popular concern about this, we are instead bombarded with dire warnings about threats to freedom any time an effort is made to reverse huge accumulations—even though for most of us such changes would be irrelevant. Indeed, the threats to freedom and opportunity for the rest of us is most likely to ***come from*** the existence of these huge fortunes. These threats to our democratic institutions will be more fully explored in the rest of this section.

Extreme Inequality Threatens Democracy, Social Cohesion, and Moral Virtue

The negative effects of extreme inequality are more than just economic ones. With economic dominance also comes political dominance. When a small percentage of overly privileged individuals exerts an inordinate influence on the rest of society, particularly politics and culture, it threatens to undermine the principles of democracy, or government "by the people." We briefly visited the study of Martin Gilens and Benjamin Page[49] in Part III Section 2, which documented how legislation was responsive to the demands of elites and contrary to the interests of the public at large—a situation which most of us have been aware of intuitively for decades. This becomes a self-reinforcing feedback loop: As more people believe that their voices are unheard, they disconnect from the system (e.g., lower voter participation), which results in the system becoming ever less accountable to the wishes of the people.

Much has been written about the undue influence of money in politics, as well as the negative fallout from the Supreme Court decision in *Citizens' United.*[50] I could quote a whole book worth of statistics on this issue alone, but will summarize by saying that the evidence overwhelmingly confirms that campaign contributions—as well as participation in party politics at the highest levels—primarily come from high-income individuals, corporations, or their funded "non-profit" think tanks. It is not just who gets elected, but also what issues appear on legislative and policy agendas that are orchestrated by well-paid lobbyists who answer only to the highest bidder and not to the people. It is no surprise then, that our rights as workers and citizens have been eroded along with our paychecks.

We will cover the decline of democratic institutions more fully in Section Three of this Part, and the influence of the oligarchy on our media and culture more fully in Section Four. Here we will state that establishment discourse on inequality has generally been to justify it with arguments about meritocracy, the impersonal operation of markets, or inevitable consequences of globalization and advances in technology. By now we are aware that markets—just like governments, media and even religion—are socially created institutions. Fortunately, we are seeing more economists (mostly Europeans like Thomas Piketty, but increasingly including Americans) coming out with research that challenges the establishment orthodoxy.

We are also starting to recognize that extreme inequality, particularly that which is created by winner-take-all markets, results in a form of moral hazard. When both the rewards of "winning" and the costs of "losing" are ever greater, there is more incentive to win at any cost—including by means of unethical or illegal activity. We discussed the ponerizing effects of extreme inequality briefly in Part III, Section 2, and have seen how winner-take-all "markets" and the lifestyles of Robert Frank's "Richistanis" create an additional form of us-versus-them above and beyond the usual divisions of race, politics, and other forms of tribalism. As the "winners" gain more control over the institutions that affect our popular culture, these attitudes (greed, selfishness, ruthlessness in pursuit of self-interest, and lack of empathy) become normalized.

Returning to our previous discussion about whether happiness correlates with income, psychology researchers tracking happiness in America between 1972 and 2008 found that it tracked more closely with levels of inequality than it did with levels of absolute income.[51] This effect was noted not just among the poor, but nearly everyone in the middle, with only the happiness of the wealthiest 20% being unaffected. However, inequality can affect the quality of life of the rich as well, keeping them on a never-ending treadmill of social comparison and wanting more.[52] But what rising inequality does most of all is make more of us distrustful and cynical.

Perhaps not surprisingly, a pair of epidemiologists[53] (and not economists) have thoroughly documented the correlation of inequality with social ills ranging from mental and physical health, drug and alcohol addiction, out-of-wedlock teenage births, violence, involvement with the criminal justice system, and even something as seemingly unrelated as obesity. As epidemiologists, their role is not so much to document inequality, but to trace the cause of diseases in populations. They document their findings with exhaustive citations to peer-reviewed research in medical science, psychiatry and psychology, sociology, and neuroscience. The interesting thing about their findings is that these negative effects increase for everyone in the relevant population, not just those at the bottom.

The Wilson and Pickett findings are consistent with our previously cited study by American economists, who found a high correlation between lower social mobility and higher incidents of inequality.[54] Other correlations were found between levels of inequality and segregation, the quality of K-12 schools (including higher local tax rates), levels of social capital (including religious participation), and family structure. The interesting thing here is that these things also negatively affected persons who were not members of the disfavored group: Whites in areas with large African-American populations were adversely affected, as were two-parent families living in areas with high rates of single parents. Even something as seemingly unrelated as lengthier commute time has a negative correlation with social mobility.

Wilson and Pickett suggest that extreme inequality undermines social trust and cohesion, which operates to increase the overall level of stress, pessimism, and cynicism. Reviews of studies in developed countries document a substantial rise in incidents of anxiety and depression. Ironically, these increases in anxiety have been accompanied by increases in narcissism. Wilson and Pickett theorize that we have become overly concerned with our perceived social status, and as a consequence many of us have developed a "self-promoting, insecure egotism, which is easily mistaken for high self-esteem."[55] We view social status as a marker of ability—of superiority or inferiority. Thus, we are constantly managing the impressions of our social status, under constant tension between the opposites of shame and pride, having to create and re-create our social identity with each encounter in an increasingly mobile and impersonal society. This shifting anxiety can easily segue into violence if we perceive that our very worth as a human being is challenged when others look down on and disrespect us.

Wilkinson and Pickett lament the sentiments among many Americans, who expressed a desire for a society less focused on greed and more centered on values, community and family; while at the same time accusing their fellow Americans of becoming increasingly atomized, selfish and irresponsible.[56] Increasing inequality increases status competition, which results in defensive self-promotion and thwarts the building of solidarity. It appears that many of us have lost faith in the possibility of collectively building a better society, confirming the loss of our moral commonwealth which we described in Part I, Section 2.

There is also a darker side to inequality than its detrimental effects on democratic governance, civic engagement, and social cohesion. Our American concept of liberty historically grew out of the desire to be free from subservience to feudal nobility, yet today we appear to be in greater danger of subservience to plutocracy. As we learned in Part II, Section 3, power and privilege can exert antisocial behavioral effects at the individual level.[57] Social and economic inequality represents the systemic manifestation of privilege and entitlement at the level of society as a whole. It also contains forms of dysfunction which feed into ponerization (e.g., domination and subjugation). Thus, it is not difficult to imagine how a highly unequal society can devolve—a phenomenon we are unfortunately witnessing today.

Notes

---

[1] Lobaczewsky, A.M. (1998). *Political Ponerology: A science on the nature of evil adjusted for political purposes.* Red Pill Press at p. 240.

[2] Mutunga, W.M. (2014). Inequality and the moral crisis of the elite. *Development, 57*(3-4), at p. 340.

[3] Reich, R.B. (2020). *The system: Who rigged it, how we fix it.* New York, NY: Alfred A Knopf.

[4] Selznick P. (1992). *The moral commonwealth. Social theory and the promise of community.* Berkeley, CA: University of California Press at p. 494.

[5] Piketty, T. (2014). *Capital in the twenty-first century.* Printed in India by Gopsons Papers Ltd, at p. 264.

[6] Giridharadas, A. (2018). *Winners take all: The elite charade of changing the world.* New York, NY: Alfred Knopf at p. 261.

[7] Selznick, *supra* at p. 505.

[8] *Id.* at p. 504.

[9] *Id.* at pp. 492-498.

[10] *Id.* at pp. 498-501.

[11] Sidanius, J., & Pratto, F. (2012). Social dominance theory. In P.A.M. Van Lange, A.W. Kruglanski, & E.T. Higgins (Eds.) *Handbook of Theories of Social Psychology, Vol II* at p. 418-438. Thousand Oaks, CA: Sage Publications, Inc.

[12] Sidanius, J., Pratto, F., & Rabinowitz, J. (1994). Gender, ethnic status, ingroup attachment and social dominance orientation. *Journal of Cross-Cultural Psychology 25,* 194-216.

[13] Early feminist studies found that in the US, the majority of physicians and engineers—traditionally high-paying occupations—were held by men. Yet in the former Soviet Union, where these occupations were much lower paid, women comprised at least half of physicians and engineers. So, assuming that physicians and engineers perform the same "value" of contribution to society, wages are lower when women do the same work. We see this even today: women do the

majority of cooking—both in the home and as cooks in workplaces—but the majority of high-paid celebrity chefs are men.

[14] https://www.pewforum.org/2009/01/30/income-distribution-within-us-religious-groups/

[15] Payne, K. (2017). *The broken ladder: How inequality affects the way we think, live, and die.* New York, NY: Viking/Penguin Random House, LLC

[16] https://www.statista.com/statistics/203183/percentage-distribution-of-household-income-in-the-us/

[17] Dickens, W.T., & Lang, K. (1988). The re-emergence of the segmented labor market theory. *American Economic Review, 78*(2), 129-134.

[18] Ilg, R.E., & Haugen, S.E. (2000). Earnings and employment trends in the 1990s. *Monthly Labor Review 123*(3), 21-33. www.bls.gov/opub/mlr/2000/03/art2full.pdf. See also Kalleberg, A.L. (2011). *Good jobs, bad jobs: The rise of polarized and precarious employment systems in the United States, 1970s to 2000s.* New York, NY: Russell Sage Foundation; and Kalleberg, A.L., Reskin, B., and Hudson, K. (2000). Bad jobs in America: Standard and nonstandard employment relations and job quality in the United States. *American Sociological Review 65*(4), 256-278.

[19] Morris, M., & Western, B. (1999). Inequality in earnings at the close of the twentieth century. *Annual Review of Sociology, 25*(1), 623-657 at p. 623.

[20] Wilkinson, R., & Pickett, K. (2009). *The spirit level: Why greater equality makes societies stronger.* New York, NY: Bloomsbury Press at pp. 159-160. This fact was also confirmed by Thomas Piketty's exhaustive data in the 2014 *Capital in the Twenty-First Century.*

[21] Krueger, A. (2012, January 12). The rise and consequences of inequality. Presentation made to the Center for American Progress. www.americanprogress.org/events/2012/01/12/17181/the-rise-and-consequence-of-inequality

[22] Barone, G., & Mocetti, S. (2016) "Intergenerational mobility in the very long run: Florence 1427-2011", Bank of Italy working papers, 1060. https://voxeu.org/article/what-s-your-surname-intergenerational-mobility-over-six-centuries.

[23] Florence at one time was the capital of an independent city-state, which was incorporated into the nation of Italy in 1861. It subsequently experienced the turmoil of two world wars and the Mussolini dictatorship.

[24] Clark, G., & Cummins, N. (2014, 15 November). Surnames and social mobility in England, 1170-2012. *Human Nature, 25*, 517-537. https://link.springer.com/article/10.1007/s12110-014-9219-y

[25] Raj Chetty and Nathaniel Hendren of Harvard University, Patrick Kline and Emmanuel Sa**ez** of University of California Berkeley. https://voxeu.org/article/where-land-opportunity-intergenerational-mobility-us

[26] Norton, M.I., & Ariely, D. (2011). Building a better America—one wealth quintile at a time. *Perspectives on Psychological Science 6*(1), 9-12. Full study (with charts) available here: https://eee.uci.edu/12f/69260/home/Perspectives+on+Psychological+Science-2011-Norton-9-12.pdf

[27] "The liberal reward of labour, as it encourages the propagation, so it increases the industry of the common people...Servants, labourers and workmen of different kinds, make up the far greater part of every great political society. But what improves the circumstances of the greater part can never be regarded as an inconveniency to the whole." From *Wealth of Nations* at pp. 78-81.

[28] "Our merchants and master-manufacturers complain much of the bad effects of high wages in raising the price, and thereby lessening the sale of their goods both at home and abroad. They say nothing concerning the bad effects of high profits. They are silent with regard to the pernicious effects of their own gains. They complain only of those of other people." From *Wealth of Nations* at pp. 136-137. Also, "Whenever the legislature attempts to regulate the differences between masters and their workmen, its counsellors are always the masters. When the regulation, therefore, is in favor of the workmen, it is always just and equitable; but it is sometimes otherwise when in favor of the masters." From *Wealth of Nations* at p. 195.

[29] Smith, A. (1776). *The wealth of nations* at pp. 87-89.

[30] *Id.* at p. 578.

[31] Marx, K. (1867). *Capital: A critique of political economy* at p. 2129. The general law of capitalist accumulation proposes that, initially, accumulations of capital will cause a rise in wages. However, as more people enter the wage system (or

are forced to work for wages because their traditional livelihoods have been destroyed or rendered impracticable), the stock of capital will no longer be sufficient to adequately employ everyone, and wages will fall. Although Marxist theories are generally disparaged in the United States, there is empirical evidence even today that supports some of his theories.

[32] Piketty, T. (2014). *Capital in the twenty-first century.* Printed in India by Gopson's Papers Ltd.

[33] *Id.* at p. 2.

[34] "...the discipline of economics has yet to get over its childish passion for mathematics and for purely theoretical and often highly ideological speculation, at the expense of historical research and collaboration with the other social sciences." (Piketty, *supra* at p. 32).

[35] Piketty, *supra* at p. 2.

[36] *Id.* at p. 262.

[37] https://wid.world/

[38] Piketty, *supra* at p. 244.

[39] *Id.* at p. 241.

[40] *Id.* at p. 257.

[41] *Id.* at p. 281.

[42] *Id.* at p. 264.

[43] *Id.* at p. 265.

[44] Cook, P.J., & Frank, R.H. (1995). *The winner-take all society: Why the few at the top get so much more than the rest of us.* New York, NY: Penguin Books USA, Inc.

[45] Piketty, *supra.*

[46] https://higheredbybaylis.net/wp/the-golden-age-of-american-higher-education/

[47] Piketty, *supra* at p. 21.

---

[48] *Id.* at p. 1.

[49] Gilens, M., & Page, B. (2014). Testing theories of American politics: Elites, interest groups and average citizens. American Political Science Association *Perspectives on Politics, 12*(3), 564-581. Retrieved from: https://scholar.princeton.edu/sites/default/files/mgilens/files/gilens_and_page_2014_-testing_theories_of_american_politics.doc.pdf

[50] *Citizens United v. Federal Election Commission*, 558 U.S. 310, 130 S. Ct. 876, 175 L. Ed. 2d 753 (2010).

[51] Oishi, S., Kesebir, S., & Diener, E. (2011). Income inequality and happiness. *Psychological Science,* 22, 1095-1100.

[52] Frank, R.H. (2001). *Luxury fever: Why money fails to satisfy in an era of excess.* New York, NY: Simon & Schuster.

[53] Richard Wilkinson & Kate Pickett. (2009). *The spirit level: Why greater equality makes societies stronger.* New York, NY: Bloomsbury Press.

[54] https://voxeu.org/article/where-land-opportunity-intergenerational-mobility-us

[55] Wilson & Pickett, *supra* at p. 36.

[56] *Id.* at p. 4.

[57] These dynamics are more fully analyzed and described in *Why Assholes Rule the World.* VanHettinga (2019).

Section 3
The Government: Democracy Under Siege

The prospect of domination of the nation's scholars by Federal employment, project allocations, and the power of money is ever present and is gravely to be regarded.

Yet, in holding scientific research and discovery in respect, as we should, we must also be alert to the equal and opposite danger that public policy could itself become the captive of a scientific-technological elite.

Dwight D. Eisenhower[1]

*

The oppressed are allowed once every few years to decide which particular representatives of the oppressing class are to represent and oppress them.

Karl Marx

*

Corporate economic power became the basis of economic power on which the state relied, as its own ambitions, like those of giant corporations, became more expansive, more global, and, at intervals, more bellicose. Together, the state and corporation became the main sponsors and coordinators of the powers represented by science and technology.... Those powers are also the means of inventing and disseminating a culture that taught consumers to welcome change and private pleasures while accepting political passivity.

Sheldon Wolin[2]

*

Our government is supposed to respond to the will of the majority while protecting the rights of the minority. Instead, we have the tyranny of the minority. That tyranny is super-wealthy, politically powerful, and dangerously out of touch with the American people.

NM Senator Tom Udall[3]

*

We say, for instance, "What are we going to do about the problem of X?" as if "we" were society as a whole, somehow acting on ourselves, but, in fact, unless we happen to be part of that roughly 3 percent to 5 percent of the population whose views actually do affect policy makers, this is all a game of make-believe; we are identifying with our rulers when, in fact, we're the ones being ruled.

David Graeber[4]

Our American history is replete with evidence that we tend to distrust the concentration of power. More ambiguous is whether or not we have faith in the wisdom of the common people.[5] Many no longer view government as a collection of "us," instead relating to government as a "them" of technocratic elites. We vilify our public servants in the form of bureaucrat bashing, which then serves to negatively impact policy implementation,[6] as well as erodes a general motivation to choose a career or occupation in public service.[7] The notion of "community service" is something we impose on criminal offenders, not an aspiration.

At the same time, most of us recognize that government serves legitimate functions, particularly in the delivery of what are known as "public goods"—those things required of a civilized society but which are unsuitable for delivery by profit-motivated enterprise. Typical examples are national defense, schools, courts and law enforcement, multijurisdictional connective infrastructures (e.g., nationwide mail delivery, interstate highways, and an argument can be made for the internet), and public parks. Most of us also want some form of social safety net, either based on the sympathetic notion that sometimes random bad stuff happens, or the more practical calculation that the existence too many desperate and hopeless people is the foundation of revolution.

Today, our distrust of government is at an all-time high and there is plenty of reason for it. There are allegations (some based on real evidence, some based on conspiracy theories) that the "system" is rigged against the common people. In *Why Assholes Rule the World* (2019), I analyzed the dynamic of how positions of power both attract antisocial personalities as well as aggravate pre-existing negative personality characteristics, a phenomenon we also looked at here in Part II, Section Three. If government is indeed going to "go bad," this will likely manifest at the highest levels of power, and not necessarily among the ranks of the street-level public servants—the ones who are likely to be members of one or more of our own communities (neighborhood, church, school).

Lobaczewsky does not discuss government in terms of political science, as his emphasis is on social psychology and not politics. While we don't really know what form of government Lobaszewsky prefers, we can infer that Lobaczewsky prefers democracy or other forms of self-rule, based on his obvious abhorrence to top-down totalitarian regimes (whether Nazi fascists or Soviet communists). However, Lobaszewsky does suggest that democratic forms of government are not alone enough to prevent ponerization. According to Lobaczewsky, a democratic form of government will be effective so long as (1) the country has a historical tradition of it, (2) the social structure is well-developed, and (3) the aggregate level of education is adequate. "A democracy composed of individuals of inadequate psychological knowledge can devolve."[8]

As Lobaczewsky has suggested, "democracy" in practice is more than a collection of purportedly democratic systems and institutions, but also relies on the operation of unwritten rules and social norms. Here in the United States, we more or less take democracy for granted. However, democracy means more than the opportunity to vote, but implies a greater agency with respect to the conditions of one's everyday life. As we have seen in the preceding Section One, for many of us our livelihoods require that we spend the greater portion of our days in a place that is tantamount to a dictatorship. The fact that we can vote for a mayor, the city council, a Senator, or even the President seems to have little effect on the precariatization and powerlessness of our working life. Yet, this powerlessness with respect to our livelihood expands into the rest of our lives as well, as the system (or those who run and benefit from it) has found ways to provide the appearance of democracy without corresponding power to the people.

Destruction of Social Norms and Threats to Democracy

In *How Democracies Die,* Harvard professors of government Steven Levitsky and Daniel Ziblatt make the case that democracy is in danger of being destroyed by a weakening of traditional institutions (e.g., the press) and the erosion of long-standing political norms.[9] The professors argue that current threats to democracy are presented in the forms of political extremism, along with changing rules of the game under the guise of some public good but with the objective of either favoring incumbents or disadvantaging the opposition. While some polarization is necessary in a healthy democracy (the loyal opposition who keeps those in power honest and accountable), when it becomes extreme (i.e., worldviews are not just different, but mutually exclusive), toleration is absent and common ground becomes nearly impossible to find.[10] We are also seeing the erosion of democratic practices and procedures in the form of redistricting (to protect incumbents) and stringent voter ID laws (along with exaggerated claims of voter fraud).

Levitsky and Ziblatt argue that, in addition to the above threats from polarization and tinkering with the system, democracy is being undermined by the destruction of social norms that informally governed political behavior in the past. Two of these norms—mutual toleration and forbearance—are "fundamental to a functioning democracy."[11] Toleration requires that one recognize the legitimacy of the opposition and its right to compete for power. Forbearance is refrainment from the maximum exercise of legal power, respecting the spirit as well as the letter of the law.[12] "U.S. presidents, congressional leaders, and Supreme Court justices enjoy a range of powers that, if deployed without restraint could undermine the system."[13] While each branch of government (Executive, Congress and the Supreme Court) has both the right and the duty to check the power of the others, they also must "routinely underuse" that power in order to allow the government to function.[14]

Levitsky and Ziblatt then document the expansion of executive authority over the 20th century. Even with this expansion, the unilateral exercise of presidential power was the exception (exercised only in times of war) rather than the rule. They cite the example of Roosevelt's attempt to "pack" the Supreme Court at the height of his popularity, which was successfully resisted by opposition within and without his own party. The authors argue that critical dysfunctions did not occur in the past not just because the founding fathers had created a system of checks and balances, but because prevailing norms discouraged those in powerful positions from exercising the full legal extent of their powers. They term these prevailing norms "guardrails," which operated to preserve democratic functioning. However, these guardrails began to come down during the Civil Rights era. Levitsky and Ziblatt suggest that this was due to both increasing polarization as well as the reality that the "norms" were created in a culture that was white and male, which increasingly viewed itself as under threat.

Levitsky and Ziblatt trace the beginning of hyper-partisan polarization to the 1994 "Gingrich revolution," when the Republicans gained their first House majority in 40 years. Gingrich fomented a strategy of absolute refusal to compromise, which Levitsky and Ziblatt allege was a reflection of more generalized popular discontent.[15] This "politics as warfare" strategy only got worse after Gingrich left Congress in 1999. Tom Delay, the new House Majority leader, created a culture of non-compromise and norm-breaking as routine, allegedly at one point saying, "If it [isn't] illegal, do it."[16] Dysfunction in Congress only got worse over each successive election: During the last Congress of the George Bush (43rd) presidency, the number of filibusters (139) broke the record.[17] Raising the debt limit—a long-standing bipartisan practice which had been done 78 times between 1960 and 2011 under both Republican and Democratic presidents—now became all-out war, with a new crop of Tea Party congressional representatives using the debt limit to hold congress hostage, threatening to bring the whole system down if they had to.[18] This extreme polarization was inflamed by partisan media outlets (mainly on the right), some who were controlled by wealthy individuals with their own agenda and had only ties of convenience to the traditional Republican party.[19]

Levitsky and Ziblatt suggest that this hyper-partisanship was not so much directed by the political parties as it was an expression of "status anxiety," which emerges when a group's social status, identity, and sense of belonging are threatened. Challenges to group dominance (white and male privilege) were accompanied by economic anxieties as well: "For many Americans, the economic changes of the last few decades have brought decreased job security, longer working hours, fewer prospects for upward mobility, and consequently, a growth in social resentment."[20] This generalized sense among previously privileged groups of declining economic prospects, declining majority status, and that "the other" is gaining when one's own group is losing, creates further social cleavages and aggravates intense animosities. "…[P]oliticians from Newt Gingrich to Donald Trump learned that in a polarized society, treating rivals as enemies can be useful—and that the pursuit of politics as warfare can be appealing to those who fear they have much to lose."[21]

Authoritarianism

In America, we pride ourselves on being one of the first post-enlightenment societies which was founded on the principles of democracy. While it was true that only property-owning white men were allowed to have a voice in self-governance, the idea that ordinary people could govern themselves was actually quite radical for its day. As students learning about American history, we are presented a story arc of democratic ideals being expanded—first to include all white men (even those who had to work for subsistence rather than being supported by property or the labor of others), then all races of men, and finally to women. Yet, current threats to our democracy are coming as much from us as they are from over-ambitious political leaders driving through the guardrails.

Post-World War II researchers attempting to understand the rise of Hitler and fascism identified something they called the "authoritarian personality."[22] The focus was not so much on the dictator himself as it was on a critical mass of persons in the general population with a predisposition to favor conformity, obedience and defense of the status quo. Authoritarians tend to be unwilling to critically question conventional beliefs and generally have a black-and-white view of right and wrong. Later research has found that authoritarianism is highly correlated with both religious fundamentalism and a "law-and-order" view of the world as being a dangerous place.[23] Authoritarians also have a tendency to project their own feelings of inadequacy, fear, and rage onto a scapegoated group.[24] Authoritarianism within the population tends to increase during times of rapid change, particularly when the existing social order is being threatened.

Based on their research as political scientists, Levitsky and Ziblatt identify a set of four behavioral signs of authoritarianism: (1) rejection of democratic rules of the game (e.g., undermining the legitimacy of elections, willingness to violate the Constitution), (2) denial of legitimacy of political opponents (e.g., claiming your opponent is a threat to national security or prevailing way of life), (3) toleration or encouragement of violence against opponents, and (4) readiness to curtail civil liberties of opponents, especially the media. The professors further state that even before his inauguration, Trump "tested positive on all four measures on our litmus test for autocrats,"[25] which was followed by "clear authoritarian instincts during his first year in office."[26] They document how Trump attempted to insure that the heads of the FBI, the CIA and the National Security Agency would all be loyal to him, apparently to protect him from investigation into alleged connections between Trump's campaign and Russia. Without some element of forbearance (especially the ability to control one's own appetites and lust for power), it is not difficult to image the threat posed by a president with the authority to pardon himself.

The impulse to fascism is not an aberration unique to the personality of Donald Trump, but appears to be baked into a certain segment of American society. That is, Theodore Adorno's authoritarian personality is as much part and parcel of the American character as the more publicized jingoistic claims of freedom, democracy, and equality. In 1980, Bertram Gross, a professor of political science at Hunter University, wrote a book about American-style *Friendly Fascism.*[27] At that time, the suggestion of fascism in

America was practically heretical. However, Gross made the argument that fascism was the inexorable result of "...more concentrated, unscrupulous, repressive, and militaristic control by a Big Business-Big Government partnership to preserve the privileges of the ultra-rich, the corporate overseers, and the brass in the military and civilian order."[28] Gross termed the cabal of transnational corporations—that were able to operate outside the legal constraints of any one nation—the "Golden International." The objective of this new power structure was the expansion of empire based on the political economy of capitalism. The corporate and military alliance gained control of the media, political parties, and even the machinery of democracy, as it sought clever new ways of ruling and fooling the people. Part of this strategy involved appeals to a false patriotism, which was incited by stressing the danger of an external enemy (at that time, "the enemy" was the former Soviet Union, which morphed into Islamic terrorists after 9-11-01, and more recently, immigrants along the U.S.-Mexico border) and suppressing dissent at home in the name of law and order.

Other scholars have identified a religiously-based form of friendly fascism, which is found primarily in the American South (the so-called "Bible Belt.") Also called the "tyranny of Puritanism," or "apple pie authoritarianism," this version of fascism is "friendly" because it relies on the peer pressure of small-town conformism rather than the brute force of subjugation.[29] This friendlier version of fascism is a "persistent, structural, and regular phenomenon deeply rooted in the collective 'psyche' and 'spirits'" of Southern evangelicalism, which is characterized by "sadistic intolerance to cultural otherness." This form of control is operationalized by criminalizing all conduct that is deemed "sinful," along with onerous punishments typically disproportionate to the social harm of the activity. Additionally, this "sinfulness" (i.e., evil) is automatically attributed to religious, ethnic, or political "others." Thus, the punitive and arbitrary institutionalized behavioral controls of theocratic Islam and Evangelical Christian fundamentalism in some respects converge. This tendency to describe the "other" as sinful also has implications for racist stereotypes; i.e., the violent and/or hypersexualized Black man.

Evangelical-style fascism is also often associated with anti-science and anti-intellectualism, another sign of ponerization. Intellectualism is disparaged as an instrument of the elites. There is a legitimate argument that supports some form of populist challenge to hyper-rationalized managerialism, which has resulted in the degradation of both working and family life for the majority (see Section 1 of this Part). Unfortunately, this usually expands to rejection of all forms of science, knowledge, or attempts to make responsible decisions (including those that affect public policy) on the basis of data or sound science. This corresponds with the authoritarian's need to view the world in overly simplistic good-versus-evil terms.

The real threat of authoritarianism is that it is anti-democratic. A 2017 survey of voters sponsored by the Democracy Fund measured popular support for democracy.[30] The good news is that the majority of Americans continue to support democracy, or at least are opposed to authoritarianism. The bad news is that only a slim majority (54%) were consistently pro-democracy across the survey's five measures: preferences for a strong leader, army rule, having a democratic political system, living in a country that is governed democratically, and the desirability of democracy over other kinds of government. The authors acknowledge that there was some definitional ambiguity. What "democracy" looks like may not be the same across all individuals. As another example, "support for a strong leader," has obvious anti-democratic implications, but it also might be a rational reaction to the real perception that our gridlocked government (particularly at the national level) is unable to carry out its duties. Ironically, support for a strong leader has fallen since 2011, and the authors suggest a possible explanation that "Donald Trump has personified authoritarian leadership in a way many Americans found distasteful."[31]

More troubling findings are that support for army rule has increased steadily over the past 20 years, and nearly a quarter favor a "strong leader" who wouldn't be bothered with answering to Congress or even elections. Although support for a "strong leader" has fluctuated based on party affiliation (stronger for Democrats between 2006 and 2017, but now stronger for Republicans), the highest support for authoritarian leadership overall (both strong leader and army rule) comes from individuals who are "disaffected, disengaged from politics, deeply distrustful of experts, culturally conservative, and have negative views toward racial minorities."[32] Most troubling is that the Unites States has become an outlier among other western democracies with an 18% support for army rule (where most other western democracies range from 3% to 9%).

Paradoxically, support for democracy is strongest among those who are consistently liberal or consistently conservative, possibly because they are more likely to be engaged with the political system. However, authoritarianism is still higher among the consistent conservatives. The one generally consistent finding was that support for democracy was lowest among the least educated and the least politically engaged,[33] which might imply that individuals who are already disengaged from politics may believe that they have little to lose. Notwithstanding a greater support for democracy among the better-educated, a surprising 17% of respondents with a four-year Bachelors' degree or higher said that democracy was "not always preferable" as a form of government.[34] Perhaps the most troubling facet of authoritarianism is the willingness to sacrifice one's own civil liberties for the purpose of controlling some demonized "other."

Disturbed by the increasing boldness and violence of the white nationalist movement, Clemson University political scientist Steven V. Miller took measures of white outgroup intolerance (with outgroups being defined as everyone from criminals, drug addicts, heavy drinkers, emotionally unstable, Muslims, members of a different race, members of a different religion, and people who speak a different language) and anti-democratic attitudes.[35] Miller's theory is that typical Americans do not generally support the lofty and normative ideals of democracy as propounded by our founders, but rather it is simply assumed that Americans value democracy for its own sake. Operational democracy—which promises the guarantee of equal opportunity of access to power, politics, and collective rule regardless of race, religion, national origin, or economic status—itself can be seen as problematic when a dominant group perceives it is threatened. Indeed, Miller's regressions have found a positive correlation between white outgroup intolerance and lack of support for democracy (Miller's study also found the same correlation with lower levels of education). According to Miller, the problem is bigger than a matter of racism, but rather suggests that researchers need to "start asking the hard questions about support for democracy in the United States we would otherwise ask in Pakistan or Venezuela."

Miller's findings were confirmed in a more recent (January 2020) survey conducted by Larry Bartels at Vanderbilt University.[36] Although Americans will state they are pro-democracy in the abstract, this support breaks down when questions are asked more specifically. Surveys originally designed for use in Latin America found that 23-26% of Americans would favor a military coup "when there is a lot of crime" or "a lot of corruption." Only 73% of Americans believed that government should not interfere with journalists or news organizations. Although anti-democratic sentiments are higher among persons with less education and those living in rural areas, anti-democratic sentiments are not exclusive to those whose "lives are circumscribed by apathy, ignorance, provincialism and social or physical distance from the centers of intellectual activity." However, the factor with the highest correlation to anti-democratic sentiment was "ethnic antagonism," or what we might also term racism or tribalism. Bartels is careful to explain that correlation does not necessarily imply causation, and there are certainly other factors (political cynicism, economic and cultural conservatism, and anti-intellectualism) that also contribute to anti-democratic sentiment. This ethnic and racial antagonism is fueled by a "bellicose, partisan media" advocating lawlessness by "patriotic Americans" in pursuit of political ends.

Managed Democracy and Inverted Totalitarianism

American national pride is often based on the idea that we are the world's pre-eminent democracy. Indeed, the American nation was born out of the ideals of the Enlightenment. What most of us are not taught in our history classes is that our founders had varying degrees of democratic sympathies. The founders were elites—men of property who believed that affairs of state could not be trusted to the common people. Antidemocratic sentiments were the basis of our constitutional checks and balances—not only to restrain the power of those at the top, but to prevent the "passion of the mob" from overrunning rational governing.

Indeed, the motivation for forming a central government that was superior to the original Articles of Confederation (which was more like a treaty that loosely bound the semi-sovereign and autonomous states than a unifying constitution), was to quell an uprising of farmers and debtors in Massachusetts.[37] National power, which had authority over the individual states and local governments, was formed to insure the protection of "property" and privilege against a politically mobilized population.[38] The Constitutional Convention itself was kept secret until its conclusion, and it was highly contentious. The Bill of Rights was added later (some two years after the ratification of the original Constitution) in order to placate those who had concerns about the power of a central government to infringe individual liberties.

Sheldon Wolin, a political philosopher and former Professor Emeritus at Princeton University,[39] quotes from the writings of James Madison, particularly in *The Federalist* No. 10, to illustrate how and why the founders enshrined the principles of expansionism and protection of private property. According to Madison, the main source of factionalism was the "different and unequal abilities in acquiring property" and the "different degrees of accumulation."[40] The sanctity of property (and its unequal distribution) extended even to the ownership of other human beings. Unknown to the founders at that time, the issue of slavery would create extreme factionalism that would nearly fracture their new nation.

In addition to property, the founders also articulated justification for the imperative of territorial expansion: As the jurisdictional territory incorporated a greater variety of parties and interests, it would be more difficult for the common people to discover their common interests and act in unison with them.[41] This expansionary imperative was later given the term "frontier" and associated with economic opportunity. The promise of the frontier gradually redirected popular energy away from political involvement and toward economic opportunism, and it transformed the ethos of "all men are created equal" into the ethos of competition.[42]

The theory that the "people" are not fit to govern themselves has been most thoroughly developed by the political scientist Thomas Dye in his serially updated *Irony of Democracy.* Like the founders, Dye argues that if we allow the people to govern themselves, the majority would trample the rights of minorities (racial, religious, national origin, political), and we probably wouldn't even enjoy freedom of speech. Thus, a certain degree of elitism was deliberately built into the system, which Dye also argues has become detrimental to society at large today.

There is a distinct difference between the regular folk and elites regarding relationships to power. Elites—perhaps subconsciously sensing that their elevated position is not due solely to their own merit and deserts—view power as a means to keep everyone else in their place. Wolin proposes that—unlike Lobaszewsky's pathocrat who craves power over others—"the people" only want enough power to be able to control their own lives: "A would-be demos is drawn to democracy not because ordinary people expect to rule, but because, in theory, democracy legitimates the expression of widely felt and usually deep-seated grievances, the possibility that those who have only numbers can use them to offset the power of wealth, formal education, and managerial experience."[43]

The opposite of democracy is totalitarianism. Wolin defines totalitarianism as "an attempt to realize an ideological, idealized conception of a society as a systematically ordered whole, where…family, churches, education, intellectual and cultural life, economy…politics…are premeditatedly, even forcibly if necessary, coordinated to support and further the purposes of the regime."[44] Our historical model of totalitarianism is usually framed around a ruthless and charismatic leader (e.g., Hitler, Stalin, Saddam Hussein) in which the totality of a society's institutions, practices and culture are dictated from the top. The traditional totalitarian regime thus involves a single bad guy in the highest government leadership position, aided by a cadre of cronies and sycophants. The implication is that a traditional totalitarian regime can be removed by getting rid of the person at the top.

Notwithstanding real concerns about President Trump, it is not likely that we are going to see the installment of a traditional dictatorship in the United States.[45] The usual argument is that we live in a democracy, and the system has sufficient checks and balances to prevent a dictatorship from being established (i.e., we will find ways to get rid of someone in high political office who shows signs of dictatorial tendencies, or we will otherwise find legal or political ways to thwart an authoritarian agenda). But what if our democratic processes have already been subverted—not so much by a powerful individual, but by subtle systemic changes that we have failed to recognize? More paradoxically, can totalitarianism exist within a democratic system?

Professor Wolin has coined the term ***inverted totalitarianism*** to describe a system with totalitarian features that nonetheless exists within a purported democracy. Inverted totalitarianism occurs when corporate power expands beyond the barriers of purely economic activity and merges into a globalizing co-partnership with the state.[46] In an inverted totalitarian state, the leader is a product of the system and not its architect, and the system itself is designed to survive serial leadership replacements.[47] Indeed, Wolin describes something that looks a lot like what Lobaczewsky's ponerized society would look like today rather than what existed in the first half of the last century.[48]

Inverted totalitarianism is the ultimate Orwellian double-speak, a purported democracy that keeps everyone in line through subtle means of manipulation and propaganda. Wolin cites the example of professing the sanctity of the rule of law while imprisoning and torturing humans without due process.[49] An example for today would be professing the sanctity of democracy while enacting measures—stringent voter identification rules, gerrymandering, poll-closings—to disenfranchise citizens. It also manifests at the global level as a pro-democracy propaganda campaign to justify expansionism (e.g., the imposition of controlled or manipulated elections designed to legitimize a foreign leader who will be amenable to your own regime's agenda, i.e., a puppet). Thus, such a system relies on illusion, and so must gain control over mass media and the shaping of political discourse and popular culture.

Inverted totalitarianism gains power not so much by direct control of government, but by exploiting the resources of the state and by combining with other forms of power. In the United States, one way this has been accomplished is by the commingling of religion and politics.[50] Religion—with its dynamic of hope and triumphalism—has been co-opted to reproduce American exceptionalism as well as fuel the dynamic of Superpower (which we will cover next). Evangelism (or rather, Christian fundamentalism) serves the corporate state by promoting the mythos of limitlessness and the focus of hope on the future,[51] the sort of thinking that is also promoted by Prosperity Gospel. The other—and probably stronger and longer-enduring—unholy alliance is with the corporation. Indeed, it is probably the corporate ethos that drives inverted totalitarianism more than any specific political ideology other than the economic primacy of the market: "The ethos of the twenty-first-century corporation is an antipolitical culture of competition rather than cooperation, of aggrandizement, of besting rivals, and of leaving behind disrupted careers and damaged communities."[52]

Wolin argues that today's "inverted" form of totalitarianism is combined with a phenomenon he terms "Superpower," or the projection of power outwards. Wolin quotes extensively from a *National Security Strategy* statement dated September 9, 2002. The statement is full of self-congratulatory hubris and jingoistic expansionism, proclaiming that the United States has a duty to "extend the benefits of freedom across the globe," particularly with respect to free trade and free markets. But "...freedom is granted conditionally and performance is accountable to the power that makes freedom possible....The freedoms being dangled before the unfree are, in reality, disguised power."[53] Superpower is "...indeterminate, impatient with restraints, and careless of boundaries as it strives to develop the capability of imposing its will at a time and place of its own choosing. It represents the antithesis of constitutional power."[54] Another synonym for Superpower is Empire.

Empire is built on the backs and sacrifice of the common people while it enriches and empowers war-mongering elites. The common people go along with their own exploitation in service to Empire because they are exhorted to identity with it. In America, Empire is privatized, so it enriches government-connected members of the corporatocracy. In addition to well-known companies like Lockheed Martin, Boeing, General Dynamics, and Northrop

Grumman, others have been able to tap into the public treasury due to connections with high-ranking officials (e.g., Halliburton and former Vice-President Dick Cheney; Erik Prince and Blackwater). Conversely, those who pay for Empire with their blood, limbs, bodies, and futures are left to languish. Although the poverty and homelessness rates of U.S. veterans are lower than in the general population, it is shameful that it exists at all. Moreover, veterans suffer from higher rates of physical and mental disabilities—including suicide—than the population in general.[55] Empire, or Superpower, thus embodies the twin evils of domination outward and exploitation inward, greatly enriching and empowering a minority of elites who externalize the costs of their actions onto others—all of which is justified by patriotic propaganda.

Wolin became concerned about the erosion of democratic principles during the Bush (43rd) administration. The main focus of his analysis here is the pretext for the invasion of Iraq (the distortion of facts to support an agenda), the expansion of executive powers which were justified by a seemingly global and permanent war on terror, and the ensuing construction of the surveillance state. However, Wolin does not allege that Iraq war issues served as the foundation for inverted totalitarianism. Rather, such action was necessary because the external "threats" that formerly allowed those in power to manipulate the fears of the general population—Hitler and World War II, Korea, the "Red" scare, Vietnam, the Cold War—had more or less either been resolved or had faded from immediacy.

The War on Terror created a permanent war and perpetual emergency, which serves the system by normalizing repression. The Patriot Act, with its "inroads into personal liberties and the reduced power of the courts to check overly zealous officials is first accepted by the public as a practical response to terrorism." However, the "normalizing of deviation" (the increasing militarization of police and internal activation of the National Guard to quell legitimate protests) is thrown back on the public, who the system alleges purportedly demand harsher sentences, safer streets and no coddling of prisoners.[56] Protests against the Iraq war must be contained because they also might "embolden anticorporate elements," presenting a dual threat to the expansion and totalization of Superpower.[57] Dissent is also neutralized by the corporate media's unflattering portrayal of populist protests: those protesting the Iraq war are labeled as unpatriotic; Tea Party protestors are labeled as racists; and Occupy Wall Street protestors are labeled as slackers. Analyses of anyone's actual grievances are minimized or over-simplified.

Superpower has a double-edged function: It provides its citizens a source of national pride, feeding the need for common belonging (tribalism) as well as evidence that the system is working for all citizens, because "we're number one." It also serves as a soft warning: with our infrastructure and technology we know who you are, where you are, and what you are doing. We also have the power to take anyone out who presents a threat to us. But even this veiled threat is not necessary among a citizenry who has been socialized not to think critically or question anything outside their immediate range of concerns.

Wolin argues a connection between the growth of Superpower, the decline of democracy, and concentration of media ownership: "American rulers prefer to manage the population as would a corporate CEO, manipulatively, alternatively soothing and dismissive, relying on the powerful resources of mass communication and the techniques of the advertising and public opinion industries."[58] A media oligopoly serves multiple functions: distraction, misinformation, and the trivializing of dissent. It also operates to inculcate a way of relating to the world through passive observation, and provides us with images and stories of intimate celebrity glamor, sanitized war, military triumphalism, and a booming economy. A nationalist and patriotic propaganda thus need not be promoted by the government itself. Moreover, by promoting "...a myth of national unity, consensus, that obscures real cleavages in order to substitute synthetic ones...[this] manufactured divisiveness complements the politics of gridlock and induces apathy."[59]

In addition to Superpower, inverted totalitarianism is accomplished by means of what Wolin terms ***managed democracy***. Managed democracy is a system that has surface features of a democracy, but in which real democracy (in the form of citizen engagement and empowerment) is actually suppressed. Just as the

American founders established checks and balances to constrain the "power of the people," the management of democracy works by containing actual democratic processes to discrete political matters (e.g., voting), but not allowing the same to apply to social, cultural, and especially economic relationships, which would destabilize the inequalities of power that are embedded therein.[60] "The paradox is that while in the abstract the demos has the authority of electing, it lacks effective power to control or set the terms of actual elections, including the regulation of campaign finance, television ads, and debate formats. Instead we have the phenomenon of highly managed elections controlled by those who use the resources and know-how of economic organizations to manipulate the capture of authority."[61]

Wolin's "managed democracy" can control the population at large through manipulations that alternate between creating fear or engendering apathy. The "mobilization" of society is useful only when it serves the system, otherwise it is better to keep people apathetic lest they attempt to challenge it. The purpose of fear is obviously to generate popular acquiescence to restraints on freedoms. Apathy is induced when people are encouraged to be cynical of politics and to distrust government.[62] "While the war on terrorism induces feelings of helplessness and a natural tendency to look toward government, the domestic message [is that] the citizenry should distrust its own elected government, thereby denying themselves that very instrument that democracy is supposed to make available to them."[63]

In the United States, loss of popular power has resulted not so much from actions of the traditional political state—where, under traditional totalitarianism, opposition is eliminated by force— but has been driven by technocratic rationalization, an attribute of the modern corporate state. In such a scenario, totalizing forces tend to come from economics rather than politics, through the promotion of "integration, rationalization, concentrated wealth, and a faith that virtually any problem—from health care to political crises, even faith itself—could be managed, that is, subjected to control, predictability, and cost-effectiveness..."[64] The management of democracy has been made possible by the same ethos that created scientific management and bureaucracy.

As both the size of corporations and government agencies grew during the early part of the twentieth century, it created a new form of organization, “with its emphasis upon expansion, dynamic leadership, and risk taking, [which] contrasted with constitutional authority, with its emphasis upon restraint…checks and balances.”[65] The new organization also produced a “new cult figure…the executive who is trained and certified in the ways of power—organizing, administering and exploiting.”[66] This new form of socialization—bureaucracy—"has made life predictable and even boring while reviving, in a new form, the war of all against all. Our over-organized society, in which large-scale organizations predominate but have lost the capacity to command allegiance, in some respects more nearly approximates a condition of universal animosity than did primitive capitalism….People no longer dream of overcoming difficulties but merely of surviving them.”[67]

Both the corporate state and the concept of managed democracy are governed by a “managerial” ethos: extreme competition, ruthlessness, intolerance of criticism from subordinates, and an entitlement mentality that demands huge bonuses—even when these are detrimental to the organization (or nation)—replacing the “indifference to material perquisites supposedly characteristic of traditional elites.”[68] Wolin argues that the biggest clash between Superpower elitism and anti-Superpower democracy is in the domain of education. Elites view education as the sole source of legitimization, rather than elections or democracy. The system has thus constructed a technocratic meritocracy in which a class of “Supercitizens” receives a privatized (and lavishly endowed) education that prepares them for positions in the ruling elite, while everyone else is funneled into publicly-subsidized (struggling and under-funded) education that is designed to give them the requisite technical skills to serve the system, but not the critical thinking skills to challenge it.[69]

The elite institutions that produce the next generation of rulers also produce “authorities,” or individuals who shape public opinion, policy, and culture in a way that is consistent with system objectives.[70] The corporatocracy has found ways to infect its own values into nearly all the important institutions that govern our lives. As the media becomes increasingly concentrated into a few corporate oligopolies, the general public has fewer venues of thought that would challenge not just the corporatocracy itself, but ask why such concentration was dangerous. At the same time, anti-trust enforcement has been reduced to practically nothing, being exercised only at the prospect of increased prices or price-fixing collusion. There have been some independent complaints about the concentration of the media and its potential threat to democracy,[71] but of course one will never hear of such things in the mainstream popular media. The vast wealth of the corporatocracy allows it not only to control the media, but to control other sources of information—information which is used to shape the worldview of those who ascend to positions of power who don't already subscribe to the "approved" worldview.

Managed Justice

The ability of the corporatocracy to exert an outsized effect on law and policy goes beyond a simple quid-pro-quo payment for legislative sponsorship or favorable court decision, but involves a calculated and generally unseen influence on our judges and legislatures. As a former practicing attorney who represented employees in discrimination and other workplace rights cases, I was privy to witnessing the transformation of the federal judiciary from a justice-for-all orientation to a pro-corporate one. Following passage of the Civil Rights (1964), Equal Employment Opportunity (1964), Age Discrimination in Employment (1967), and Environmental Protection (1970) Acts, the federal courts were the forum of choice for those looking to assert their rights (or remedy violations) under the new laws.[72] It was axiomatic among attorneys that if you represented a minority, a woman, an employee, or most any other person(s) with little power against an organization, you were encouraged to find a way to get into federal court. There were also legal reasons other than "forum shopping" to prefer federal over state courts, such as broader definitions and larger or expanded damage awards.

But sometime between the 1980s and 1990s, things began to shift. Federal Judges were becoming increasingly hostile to worker rights/employment/discrimination and environmental cases. By the middle 1990s, attorneys who represented employees (or any plaintiffs asserting rights or claims against corporate interests) were urged to take the case to state court—even if your ultimate award was lower or reduced by state-level "tort reform."[73] Ironically, corporate defendants found new and clever ways to have state cases "removed" to federal court. Thus the period beginning in the middle to latter 1980s through the present saw a perfect storm of individual federal judges becoming more hostile, unfavorable Supreme Court decisions, and pro-corporate legislation, prompting some commentators to remark that our system of "justice" was becoming outright unfair.[74]

In 1976, a corporate-funded think tank called The Law and Economics Center was established at George Mason University which provided education and "training" to federal judges. The Law and Economics Center sponsored an all-expense paid junket for judges to attend a two-to-three-week seminar—located in a Florida resort-style accommodation as an added incentive—where participants were lectured by academic economists. The main focus of these lectures was to imbue the judges in the language of economics as well as the concept that justice always comes at a cost—a cost which they were duty bound (although there is no Constitutional requirement for this) to consider when ruling on the legal questions brought before them.

Obviously, the "justice" parameter usually involves the rights of some lesser "other" (employees, minorities, consumers, the environment), while the cost parameter almost invariably involves a corporate interest. You can guess which one is likely to be given priority. Although even some liberal judges said they found the training useful (the late Supreme Court Justice Ruth Bader Ginsburg said she appreciated an understanding of regression analyses), the program was shut down in 1999 due to the fact that many of the corporate funders (AT&T, Chase Bank, Exxon, IBM, ITT, Merrill Lynch and numerous others) also had cases pending before some of the participating judges.

A recent study has corroborated a correlation between the Law and Economics Center training classes and the anti-people attitude that gradually came to dominate the federal courts. The researchers in this study cross-referenced judicial decisions in some 380,000 federal district court cases and 1 million criminal sentences, and found a distinct difference between decision outcomes of judges who attended the corporate economics course and those who did not.[75] This "anti-justice" and "pro-cost" bias extended beyond economics-based cases (employment, civil rights, consumer, and environmental law), but also impacted criminal sentencing. Moreover, this bias was not limited only to those judges actually attending the training, but had "diffused throughout the judiciary," affecting judges who were colleagues of attendees.

Judges are not the only ones subject to the indoctrinating influence of the corporatocracy. The Kennedy School of Government at Harvard University has been conducting a bipartisan "educational and preparatory program" for newly elected members of the House of Representatives since 1972.[76] The ostensible purposes of the program are to develop a modicum of expertise in such policy topics as the federal budget, foreign affairs, and congressional reform as well as to develop a sense of collegiality and civility in a neutral environment. However, like the training session for judges,[77] the Harvard program is developed in collaboration with The American Enterprise Institute and the Center for Strategic and International Studies. As such, it receives a large part of its funding from the corporatocracy, either directly or indirectly through Harvard endowments.

In a small sign of hope, some of the 2018 newly elected House members (most of them women and/or minorities) are taking part in an "alternative" orientation session, with a focus on challenging, rather than accommodating, the system.[78] One of the new members who did attend the Harvard program reports that attendees were subjected to speeches from corporate CEOs and lobbyists from companies like Johnson & Johnson, Boeing, and General Motors. One of the "highlights" was Gary Cohn, former economic advisor to President Trump and former president/CEO of Goldman Sachs, who told the attendees that they were in "way over [your] head" and that they "don't know how the game is played." The inference being that it is the corporate elites who tell the lawmakers what to do and not the people who elected them.

Managed Obedience

At least one clinical psychologist has integrated the concepts of Lobaczewsky's pathological use of psychology, loss of reasoning power among the general population associated with hysterization, and the propaganda of Wolin's inverted totalitarianism. David Ferraro begins with the observation that, "...the ideas of the ruling class are in every epoch the ruling ideas," and then argues how modern positive psychology and mindfulness practices are used "as a method of pacification and obedience, for the promotion of personal narcissism and consumerism, and in service of crypto-fascist and militaristic functions."[79] Although mindfulness is based on a Buddhist philosophy of calming the mind in order to make better use of it or to connect on a higher spiritual level, the secular use of these techniques is aimed at the suppression of critical thinking. The basic premise is to focus on the positive, ignore the negative, and concentrate only on the present. The secular objective is to eliminate context and history (a technique that invariably favors the oppressors over the oppressed) as well as to teach a form of self-pacification that does not question or challenge the circumstances creating the distress.

Positive psychology was initially used as a form of soft discipline for the unemployed, underemployed, and others suffering the angst of modern life. The way out of your suffering is not to attempt to understand how you got there, but to reframe your reality into something that you can live with cheerfully. In the old Nazi and Soviet-style regimes, simple obedience was generally sufficient. The new regime not only demands compliance, but also love and approval. As psychological attention becomes increasingly narrowed to the self and the immediate present,[80] one is conditioned to ignore a pathocratic unfreedom in exchange for "the narcissistic satisfaction of small, 'novel' rewards, rather like the dog biscuits of classical behaviorism."[81] Ferraro then describes how the military is making use of positive psychology to help harden soldiers to witnessing death and mutilation—not only of their comrades and enemies, but also their own—as well as the stomach to participate in torture (patriotically reframed as "enhanced interrogation"). In such manner, "psychoanalytic practice has aligned itself with the implementation of normative functions...the agent of the 'positive' and 'authentic' is not only a cop, but also a military commander combined with a marketing guru, whose 'spiritual' prattle betrays its hollow opposite at every turn."[82]

Wolin's inverted totalitarianism suggests that our society is governed by the dictates of both Superpower and managerial technocracy. The problem is that this system benefits a minority of the world's population and either does nothing for or actually harms everyone else. However, the system is designed to maintain itself through reproduction, where the leaders and cultural influencers are chosen and groomed to uphold the standards of competitiveness, aggression, and control of the population. This minority who the system does benefit needs to ensure that everyone else does not decide to change things. Most of those who run the system (former White House occupant excepted) would prefer not to send jackbooted soldiers and militarized police into cities to terrorize their own citizens into submission, instead preferring to keep people under control with the softer tactics of distraction, illusion and propaganda. But the system is also designed to ensure that everyone knows the consequences if they do not know and keep their place.

Thus we have seen that, while "we the people" participate in democracy primarily through the elective process, the way the system actually works (how and which candidates are presented to us, what issues arise on the policy agenda) is highly managed by those in power. Our voices are co-opted in ways that are more subtle than outright censorship, which makes these techniques much more difficult to identify and challenge. The members of these power elites, even if the majority of them are not brutal or completely anti-social, have developed an ethos of entitlement: they are above the same laws and rules that apply to everyone else. Their assertion of power over our worldview begins with keeping us economically precariatized. As more of us become distracted with economic and psychological (ego) survival, we lose any sense of solidarity with others who are in the same position. This is accompanied by demonization of those who can be conveniently scapegoated, which facilitates appeals to authoritarianism. The ultimate objective is to make us believe that we are unworthy of anything but hard work and obedience.

Notes

---

[1] From President Eisenhower's farewell address, January 17, 1961. For entire transcript, visit https://www.ourdocuments.gov/doc.php?flash=false&doc=90&page=transcript

[2] Wolin, S. (2008). *Democracy, Inc.: Managed democracy and the specter of inverted totalitarianism.* Princeton, NJ: Princeton University Press at p. *xxiii.*

[3] From Senator Udall's farewell speech to Congress, December 8, 2020. https://www.c-span.org/video/?507077-8/senator-tom-udall-farewell-speech

[4] Graeber, D. (2018). *Bullshit jobs: A theory.* New York, NY: Simon & Schuster at p. 270.

[5] Please see any edition of Thomas Dye's *Irony of Democracy,* which is updated every year or two. Dye developed the political model called elite theory, which proposes that (1) society is divided into the few who have power and the many who do not, (2) the few who govern are not typical of the masses who are governed, (3) elites share consensus on the basic values of the social system and the preservation thereof, (4) public policy is set by, and reflects the demands of, prevailing elites and is imposed downward on the masses and (5) the masses are relatively apathetic and exert little direct influence on elites and their policies. The ultimate "irony of democracy" is that if you permit the demos, or "the people," to rule, you won't have a democracy, but something more like tyranny of the majority or authoritarianism. However, Dye does not make the argument that elite rule is necessarily good for the rest of us either.

[6] Garrett, R.S., Thurber, J.A., Fritschler, A.L., & Rosenbloom, D. (2006, March). Assessing the impact of bureaucracy bashing by electoral campaigns. *Public Administration Review, 66*(2), 228-240.

[7] Ferdus, J., & Shahan, A.F. (2012). Bureaucrat bashing and public service motivation: A case for the civil service of Bangladesh. *International Journal of Public Administration, 35*(4), 272-284.

[8] Lobaczewsky, A.M. (1998). *Political ponerology: A science on the nature of evil adjusted for political purposes. Red Pill Press* at p. 77. Full document PDF at http://www.survivorshandbook.com/wp-content/articles/political-ponerology.pdf.

[9] Levitsky, S., & Ziblatt, D. (2018) *How democracies die.* New York, NY: Crown Publishing Group/Penguin Random House, LLC. These two professors are not the only ones concerned about the erosion of democracy. In 2018, at least three other books have been released dealing with the same subject: David Runcimen's *How Democracy Ends* (declaring democracy an "endangered political philosophy"); Steve Zolno's *Death of Democracy,* and Benjamin Carter Hett's *The Death of Democracy: Hitler's Rise to Power and Downfall of the Weimar Republic* (which revisits the events of Nazi Germany). Prior to the 2018 releases, we also see Ryszard Legutko's *Demon in Democracy: Totalitarian Temptations in Free Societies* (argues that liberal democracies share similar worldviews as communist totalitarian states and exert similar controls by more subtle methods); Robert Reich's *Beyond Outrage: What Has Gone Wrong with Our Economy and Our Democracy and How to Fix It;* Barrie Edward's (2012) *Death of Democracy* (fictional account of an investigative political journalist covering a presidential election); and Noreena Hertz's (2003) *Silent Takeover: Global Capitalism and the Death of Democracy.*

[10] Levitsky & Ziblatt at p. 115.

[11] *Id.* at p. 102.

[12] *Id.* at p. 114.

[13] *Id.* at p. 127.

[14] *Id.* at p. 126.

[15] *Id.* at p. 149.

[16] *Id.* at p. 151.

[17] *Id.* at p. 153.

[18] *Id.* at p. 165.

[19] *Id.*at p. 172, 222-223.

[20] *Id.* at p. 228.

[21] *Id.* at p. 174.

[22] Adorno, T., Frenkel-Brunswik, E., Levinson, D., & Sanford, N. (1950). *The authoritarian personality.*

---

[23] Sibley, C.G., Wilson, M.S., & Duckett, J. (2007). Effects of dangerous and competitive worldviews on right-wing authoritarianism and social dominance orientation over a five-month period. *Political Psychology, 28*(3), 357-371.

[24] Altemeyer, B. (1981). *Right-wing authoritarianism.* Winnipeg: University of Manitoba Press. See also *The authoritarian specter.* Cambridge, MA: Harvard University Press.

[25] Levitsky & Ziblatt at p. 61.

[26] *Id.* at p. 177.

[27] Gross, B. (1980). *Friendly fascism: The new face of power in America.* South End Press.

[28] *Id.* at p. 161.

[29] Zafirovski, M. (2006). Toward friendly fascism? American conservatism in the 21st century. *Quarterly Journal of Ideology, Vol 29*(1 and 2).

[30] Drutman, L., Diamond, L., & Goldman, J. (2018, March). Follow the leader: Exploring American support for democracy and authoritarianism. Democracy Fund Voter Study Group. https://www.voterstudygroup.org/publications/2017-voter-survey/follow-the-leader

[31] *Id.* at p. 13.

[32] *Id.* at p. 3.

[33] *Id.* at p. 14.

[34] *Id.*

[35] Miller, S. (2017, Aug 18). Outgroup intolerance and support for democracy: An analysis of white Americans in the World Values Survey. http://svmiller.com/blog/2017/08/usa-intolerance-xenophobia-racism-strong-leader-democracy-trump/. See also https://www.nbcnews.com/think/opinion/trump-effect-new-study-connects-white-american-intolerance-support-authoritarianism-ncna877886

[36] Bartels, L. (2020, July 10). Ethnic antagonism erodes Republican's commitment to democracy. https://www.pnas.org/content/117/37/22752

[37] Shays' Rebellion, 1786-1787.

[38] Wolin, S. (2008). *Democracy, Inc.: Managed democracy and the specter of inverted totalitarianism.* Princeton, NJ: Princeton University Press at p. 255.

[39] Dr. Wolin died on October 21, 2015, so we don't know his thoughts on a Trump presidency.

[40] Wolin, *supra* at p. 279.

[41] *Id.* at p. 230.

[42] *Id.* at p. 232.

[43] *Id.* at p. 255.

[44] *Id.*

[45] Although we came very close to losing democracy on January 6, 2021, an event that occurred as I was doing final editing on this book, I have concluded that the current level of hysterization and ponerization in American society is even higher than I believed it was when I started this book in late 2019.

[46] *Id.* at p. 238.

[47] *Id.* at p. 44.

[48] "...concentrating capital and rulership in one place *always* leads to degeneration. Capital must be subject to the authority of fairness." Lobaczewsky at p. 240.

[49] Wolin, supra at p. 46.

[50] *Id.* at p. xxi.

[51] *Id.* at pp. 116-117. The same phenomena apply to Muslim religious extremism that fuels terrorism.

[52] *Id.* at p. 138.

[53] *Id.* at p. 85-86

[54] *Id.* at p. xxi.

---

[55] https://www.apa.org/monitor/2020/01/ce-corner-suicide

[56] *Id.* at p. 215.

[57] *Id.* at p. 205.

[58] *Id.* at p. 107.

[59] *Id.* at p. 204.

[60] *Id.* at p. 213.

[61] *Id.* at p. 149.

[62] *Id.* at p. 110.

[63] *Id.*

[64] *Id.* at p. 47.

[65] *Id.* at p. 222.

[66] *Id.*

[67] Lasch, C. (1979). *The culture of narcissism.* New York, NY: W.W. Norton & Company, Inc.

[68] Wolin, supra at p. 145.

[69] *Id.* at p. 161.

[70] *Id.* at p. 163.

[71] Baker, C.E., & Sinha, D. (2009). *Media concentration and democracy: Why ownership matters.* Cambridge, MA: Cambridge University Press.

[72] The Americans with Disabilities Act (1990) had similar goals of social justice and inclusion, but it came about **after** the federal courts had been corporatized. An attorney who represented employees told me straight up that he did not accept ADA cases because the literal language of the law (along with unfavorable interpretational rulings) makes it almost impossible for employees to win.

---

[73] Another legislative agenda that was driven by pro-corporate groups like the Chamber of Commerce and the American Legislative Exchange Council (ALEC) and not the people.

[74] Samuels, D., & Bannon, A. (2017, January 24). Big money's other casualty: Fair courts. *The American Prospect.* https://prospect.org/article/big-money%e2%80%99s-other-casualty-fair-courts

[75] Ash, E., Chen, D.L., & Naidu, S. (2018, October 22). Ideas have consequences: The impact of law and economics on American justice. http://elliottash.com/wp-content/uploads/2018/08/ash-chen-naidu-2018-07-15.pdf

[76] https://iop.harvard.edu/get-inspired/bipartisan-program-newly-elected-members-congress

[77] In the opinion of this author, the stated objectives of these programs are worthwhile—no new judge or Congressperson assumes the position knowing everything they need to know to do their job. The problem with these programs is their unstated (and unacknowledged) pro-corporate bias.

[78] https://www.rollcall.com/news/politics/progressives-crash-historic-harvard-bipartisanship-forum-for-new-members

[79] Ferraro, D. (2015, Aug/Sept). The jargon of authenticity. *Arena Magazine* (Fitzroy, Vic). *137,* 26-29. https://search.informit.com.au/documentSummary;dn=504398662375205;res=IELAPA

[80] One need only look to Twitter, Snapchat and other forms of social media to witness this dynamic.

[81] Ferraro, *supra* at p. 27.

[82] *Id.* at p. 29.

Section 4
The Media: Fake News and Manufactured Reality

A popular Government, without popular information, or the means of acquiring it, is but a Prologue to a Farce or a Tragedy...And a people who mean to be their own Governors, must arm themselves with the power which knowledge gives.

James Madison, 1822

*

There was no point in seeking to convert the intellectuals....For the man in the street, arguments must therefore be crude, clear and forcible, and appeals to emotions and instincts, not the intellect. Truth was unimportant and entirely subordinate to tactics and psychology.

Joseph Goebbels

*

Freedom of the press is guaranteed only to those who own one.

A.J. Liebling, 1960

*

Whatever changes platform companies make, and whatever innovations fact checkers and other journalists put in place, those who want to deceive will adapt to them. Misinformation is not like a plumbing problem you fix. It is a social condition, like crime, that you must constantly monitor and adjust to.

Tom Rosenstiel[1]

As 2016 came to a close, Oxford Dictionaries chose "post-truth" as the word of the year,[2] defining it as "relating to or denoting circumstances in which objective facts are less influential in shaping public opinion than appeals to emotion and personal belief." In a world that is increasingly subject to alternative facts and fake news, Lobaczewsky's description of events in Nazi/Soviet dominated Poland seems eerily prescient: "During the good times, people progressively lose sight of the need for profound reflection, introspection, knowledge of others, and an understanding of life's complicated laws."[3] The people who enjoy the benefits of the good times lose the capacity to understand suffering because it takes too much mental energy. "…[The] search for truth becomes uncomfortable because it reveals inconvenient facts…", so people revert to taking the "easy way out and blaming the victim…[This] unconscious elimination of data which are, or appear to be, inexpedient gradually turns into habit, and then becomes a custom accepted by society at large."[4] Anyone who questions the orthodoxy is labeled as a troublemaker, and a "cult of power" replaces the capacity for critical thought.[5] Here in America, we had a recent former President who lied so often that it no longer was "news." Fact-checkers and journalists estimate that Trump made over 22,247 false statements since his inauguration.[6] This does not, of course, count the lies and misinformation promulgated by Trump during his previous "careers" as a real estate developer and television reality show host. But Trump's lies as President—which are not so easily dismissed as celebrity fluff—have had a more devasting effect on the welfare of Americans.

Perhaps a valid question is what exactly constitutes a "lie." Throughout history, printed and broadcast media have been able to manipulate factual information either by framing it in a biased or one-sided manner, or only presenting select parts of it. Media can also control information simply by decisions about what to publish or not publish. Those of us who can recall an earlier era of newspapers may remember the general tone of jingoistic optimism—which also ironically preached against the censored propaganda of our enemies in the former Soviet Union. That is, we can nevertheless have a distorted view of reality even when presented with information that is factually truthful. Lobaczewsky describes what he terms "conversive thinking," or deliberate selection and substitution of information that is calculated to avoid "the crux of the matter," along with "the reflex assumption that every speaker is lying..."[7] The truth becomes irrelevant because people don't know how to respond to it.

Corporatized Information

However, long before "fake news" entered the popular lexicon, a more insidious media trend had been taking place for decades. The mass (*aka* mainstream) media has increasingly been consolidated into fewer large megacorporations. According to the Media Reform Information Center, in 1983, some 50 corporations controlled the majority of news media outlets; by 2000, this number had fallen to six. This consolidation was the result of deregulation and gradual erosion of prior legislation that regarded the media as a public good. It began in the Reagan administration with increases in the number of television stations a single entity was allowed to own, followed by the elimination of the Fairness Doctrine, which required outlets to cover contrasting views. This trend continued in the Clinton administration with the Telecommunications Act of 1996, which further aggravated media consolidation and reduced media accountability to the public.

GateHouse Media is the nation's largest newspaper conglomerate, owning hundreds of daily and weekly newspapers in 44 states. GateHouse itself is owned by New Media Investment Group, which is owned by a Wall Street hedge fund, Fortress Investment Group. In December 2017, Fortress was taken over by SoftBank Group, a Japanese corporation that also owns Sprint. Then, in November 2019, the New Media/Fortress/SoftBank empire grew even larger when it merged with Gannett, Inc., the owner of *USA Today*. In addition to *USA Today,* the merger added another 100 plus dailies and 1,000 weekly newspapers. Today, ***one in five American daily newspapers*** are owned by this über-conglomerate, with its ties to Wall street, technology, and fossil fuel industries. Jim Hightower, a syndicated columnist, author, and former editor, laments how his formerly beloved *Austin-American Statesman* has become "an ever-thinner, ever-pricier paper...filled with chopped-up wire copy and extraneous features from faraway...regurgitat[ing] corporate press releases as 'news'...[and] shamelessly act[ing] as a PR agent for Big Tech and other corporate powers."[8]

It is no surprise that media consolidation has resulted in a pro-corporate bias. This can possibly explain why we never see stories about why our work life sucks or hear about research that corroborates how corporate jobs are failing us. A recent study by Gregory Martin of Stanford Graduate School of Business and Joshua McCrain of Emory University[9] analyzed changes in both content and viewership of 743 local news stations during a period they were being acquired by Sinclair Broadcast Group. The authors of this study found that—when compared to other stations within the same designated media market area—the Sinclair-acquired stations had substantial increases in coverage of national news at the expense of local news, a "significant rightward shift in the ideological slant of coverage," and a small decrease in viewership. The authors conclude that this shift has "negative implications for accountability of local elected officials and mass polarization." Another potential downside is that the reduction of local news coverage also erodes a sense of community.

Other corporate-driven changes in the media landscape have involved a combination of profit motive and neoliberal-style cost-cutting which has reduced the number of stories produced by professional journalists. Yes, journalism is a profession, and it (at least it used to) operates by a code of ethics. The four main tenets of professional journalism are (1) seek truth and report it, (2) minimize harm, (3) act independently (i.e., avoid conflicts of interest), and (4) be accountable and transparent, to include exposing unethical conduct within your own organization.[10] It doesn't take rocket science to see how such a code of ethics is completely incompatible with corporate imperatives. Moreover, paying someone to investigate a story, track down witnesses, find subject matter experts, and delve into a deeper analysis of complex issues not only costs money, it isn't sufficiently responsive to the 24-hour news cycle, where one always has to be ahead of the competition on the next breaking story.

In her exposé of the influence of big money in politics, Jane Mayer also sets out in detail how wealthy interests have captured the public policy agenda over decades by gradually taking over centers of influence—not just media, but universities and non-profit think tanks.[11] Most notoriously the Koch brothers, but also other wealthy individuals such as John Olin, Richard Mellon Scaife, and the Mercer family didn't merely want to win elections, they "wanted to change how Americans thought."[12] In their war of information, it was not enough to merely line the campaign coffers of legislators, but they intended to win the hearts and minds of the general public. This was accomplished by establishing "beachheads" in academia and law, as well as cloaking huge sums of money in complex non-profit organizations—which also shielded their vast fortunes from taxes while they created narratives which convinced ordinary people to vote against their own interests.[13]

So, even before the Internet, we already had a mass media with a corporate bias and a propensity for quick and shallow stories that were cheap to produce. There was also incentive to sensationalize stories to attract audiences and feed advertising with images of wealth and glamor—which serves the dual purpose of generating advertising dollars as well as convincing the masses that the lifestyles of the rich and famous were attainable (keeping their noses to the grindstone and the system unchallenged). This was on top of the influence of dark money, which was likely behind the creation and promotion of the winner-take-all, greed-is-good, everyone-for-himself ideology that seemed to be everywhere during the 1980s and 1990s (and still exists today). Yet, for all the hype, spin, sensationalism,[14] and ulterior dark and selfish agendas, most mainstream media outlets did not generally make up stories that had no basis in fact whatsoever.

The Human Behavioral Factor

There is an inclination to attribute today's explosion of fake news to technology—the Internet and social media platforms like Facebook and Twitter. However, it is not necessarily the technology itself, but the fact that most of us are hard-wired to make decisions based on shared group-level narratives and not fact-based logic.[15] While bots and algorithms help to make a story "go viral," news (both real and fake) is often spread by celebrities and media accounts with high numbers of followers; i.e., through shallow diffusion chains of perceived credibility.[16] A study on Twitter found that real people generally shared fake news stories (sometimes without even reading them) coming from a small group of sites, some which were run by individuals who had the technical knowledge to grow large audiences around inflammatory content.[17]

Historically, we have known of false or blatantly slanted information being put out by more traditional print media—usually in the form of advertising or political propaganda. We also seem to recall that most people regarded these things with skepticism. Citizens of former Soviet block countries would tell foreign visitors that they only read the paper for weather and sports, because they knew the state-sponsored "news" could not be trusted. Here in America, most people also regard advertising copy (even that which does not amount to outright scam or fraud) with some degree of skepticism, assuming the content contains some hyperbole and exaggeration. Yet, today's outrageously fake stories seem to be accepted as truth more readily than yesterday's advertising puffery or blatantly slanted political propaganda.

There are two primary motivations for the creation of fake news. The first is old-fashioned greed. Since social media platforms—as well as many webpages and blogs—derive income from traffic, they are incentivized to generate traffic by any means short of illegal behavior. Internet traffic is generated by a combination of both code, algorithms (e.g., SEO) and behaviorally-based capture of attention. This is done first, by tech platform companies' anonymous collection of aggregated user data, which allows content creators to target very specific audiences. These new sorting algorithms—which can determine not only how someone votes, but what they buy, how often they go to church, and even how many and what kind of pets they have—are embraced enthusiastically by both politicians and advertisers, who are willing to pay for targeted user data. This ability to micro-target narrow, niche audiences is used by both political parties, and was deployed successfully by the Russians in the 2016 election.[18]

In a world where people are literally drowning in information—in essence suffering from a collective attention deficit disorder—messages are increasingly tailored to trigger emotional reactions in order to get attention. A 2012 study of Twitter messages that had "gone viral" found that the main drivers of so-called "virality" were competition for user attention and social network structure.[19] Thus, one motivator of fake information (in the form of sensationalized headlines) is to attract revenue-producing traffic (e.g., "clickbait"). The second type of fake news motivation can range anywhere from the most obvious (vote for/against so-and-so), to a more generalized creation of doubt and distrust[20]—which is a lot of what happened in the 2016 election.

The PEW Research Center conducted a number of (admittedly unscientific) surveys about online misinformation. A survey of 1,002 Americans in December 2016 found that some 64% believed that so-called fake news stories created a great deal of confusion about basic facts or current events.[21] People also admitted to sharing fake news—23% overall, with 14% admitting to sharing a story they knew was false and another 16% saying they had shared a story they later found out to be false. The PEW Research Center conducted another survey between July 2 and August 7, 2017, where they asked 1,116 media and technology experts[22] whether they thought the information environment would improve or not.[23] A slight majority (51%) believed that the quality of online information would not improve.

Among the pessimists in the PEW survey, the biggest barrier to improvement is not technology, but human nature. This group argues that humans are by nature selfish, tribal, lazy, and gullible. At least one study has found that negative false information is shared "faster, farther, deeper and more broadly than truth," and while bots facilitate the spread of fake news, it is more likely to be spread by humans.[24] Moreover, psychologically, Americans are increasingly starved for time, bombarded with messages for attention, and in search of some form of community. Messages are targeted to niche audiences designed to stand out from the "noise," mainly by means of some form of manipulative, emotional trigger. Because people are inclined to pay more attention to messages from their own social circles, they spread these messages among themselves, creating an echo chamber or "filter bubble," which avoids questioning or challenging the original information. Thus, there is no incentive to search for the truth (which takes time and effort), and people prefer to have their own views validated rather than challenged.

Another barrier to an improved information environment is that the platforms who spread (but do not necessarily themselves create) fake news are primarily incentivized by profit. Their bottom line is boosted by the promotion of sensationalist click-bait stories that "go viral," without regard for either the truth or the public interest in general. The PEW pessimists lamented that there simply was little to no public demand for truth, although some in this group suggested that there might be a "small market" for reliable information (i.e., users who would be willing to pay a premium to receive fake-news-filtered content). However, this would further divide the population into "elites" who can pay for quality information and the "masses" marinating in fake news and chaos.[25]

The PEW pessimists also had little faith in proposed technical solutions, which they argued would either endanger the "dwindling privacy rights" of the population or, alternatively, present threats to free speech. Between October 2017 and September 2018, Facebook disabled over 2.8 billion "fake" accounts, many of them bots that were also connected with outright scams.[26] It is not difficult to see how an overzealous platform like Facebook—even pursuant to a well-intentioned objective—can operate to silence legitimate speech that may not fit some algorithmic parameter. There is often a fine line between "fringe" viewpoints (which should not be censored in a free society) and intent to deceive or defraud. Moreover, efforts by social media platforms to determine the source and veracity of content require them to delve deeply into a user's networks and online behavior—presenting an obvious threat to privacy (which the platforms apparently have little reservation in violating anyway).

Organizations who advocate for freedom of speech and press have also expressed concern about the potential for even well-meaning efforts to control misinformation to infringe free expression.[27] While technology can help identify botnets and "fake" social media accounts, an overreliance on algorithms or artificial intelligence to "root out" untrustworthy information can result in legitimate information being blocked. As Americans, we are instinctively distrustful of government censorship. However, the thought of such broad power of control in the hands of companies like Facebook, Google or Twitter should concern us even more.

Information can be manipulated in ways other than direct dissemination of untruthful stories when it is controlled by a small group of giant media platforms (Google, Apple, Facebook, Amazon) who make proprietary decisions about how information is handled—and how it is monetized. Although these platforms appear to us as being democratic and "grass roots," they nonetheless are corporate—and—unlike government—have no mandate or even tradition to operate in the public interest.

The Technology Factor

Each time a new form of media distribution is introduced, there are corresponding concerns about information being manipulated. In 1925, *Harper's* magazine ran an article entitled "Fake News and the Public," which warned about the "mischief" that could be created by the Associated Press, with its centralized news production and globe-spanning telegraph wires that could send information around the world five times before anyone could verify the truth of it.[28] Along with a popular backlash against the sensationalist "yellow journalism" reporting styles spread by the Hearst and Pulitzer empires of the late 1800s, this new perceived threat was met with efforts to "professionalize" journalism and focus on impartiality in reporting.[29]

Some of us remember when television first came out (i.e., it was the "new" communication technology). Most of the early shows were trivialized fluff aimed at the lowest common denominator, and the television device earned the pejorative nickname "the boob tube." This concern was as much about the medium itself as it was about the content. The visual and graphic nature of television was more likely to appeal to sensation rather than reason, as print media purportedly does. Yet, television also brought us knowledge about other cultures (e.g., *National Geographic*), brought us along with science explorers such as Jacques Cousteau and Margaret Mead, and allowed the nation to share momentous and historical events (e.g., the Apollo 11 moon landing on July 16, 1969 and the Watergate hearings during the summer of 1974).

Many of us remember that there has historically been a credibility divide even in traditional print media sources. Newspapers were categorized as either serious news outlets who employed real journalists, or "tabloid," which was characterized by salacious stories about celebrities and more sensationalized content. Except for the occasional defamation suit, many people regarded the tabloids as harmless, mainly because most people did not take them seriously (i.e., they were more like entertainment than news). In the world of television news, instead of the medium bifurcating into sources of "serious" stories and sources of popular celebrity fluff, the news itself became blurred into something called "infotainment"—a form of sensationalized presentation of purportedly factual stories. Yet, the divide between mainstream (i.e., establishment) and popular media does not necessarily mean that the established media has a monopoly on the truth, notwithstanding it's greater investigative resources. Ironically, the term "muckraker" was used during the period of corporate ascendance (1890s to 1920s) to describe popular journalists (e.g. Ida Tarbell and Upton Sinclair) who exposed corruption among the high and mighty, as well as the activities of corporations that harmed the public interest.

As the mass media became more corporatized, popular discontent—or even a simple desire to see and hear more about one's own community rather than stories involving elite interests and lifestyles—continued seeking an outlet. Developments in technology allowed more grassroots outlets to sprout up, primarily in the online environment. Anyone with an internet connection and a laptop could start a blog, a podcast, or an online newsletter. This increase in sources of "news" has the potential to democratize information because one no longer has to be wealthy—or a corporate conglomerate—to "own" a media outlet.

However, although the new media landscape has created a plethora of outlets, platforms and voices, the number of traditional journalists has declined from around 55,000 in 2000 to around 33,000 in 2015.[30] Thus, while there is more information giving us a greater diversity of voices and opinion, there is almost no way a random consumer (without an investigative infrastructure) can determine whether such information is true or not. Fact and source-checking every bit and byte of information online would simply take too much time.

One issue presented by technology-driven media is anonymity and lack of transparency. There is almost no way for a user untrained in cyber-tracing protocol to locate the source, let alone do much to actually investigate the facts. Newspapers are required to identify their editorial boards as well as their owners. They are also subject to defamation lawsuits for publishing blatantly false information. Bloggers can also usually be identified, even those who post under pseudonyms (although this might require some cyber-sleuthing). However, it is easy to create anonymous accounts on social media, as well as to make the account's source extremely difficult to trace. Although anonymity can be a good thing because it allows oppressed peoples (e.g., citizens of authoritarian regimes like China or overworked and underpaid employees) a safe forum to express legitimate grievances, it can also create obstacles to finding the truth.

There is also something different about the *way* we consume information through our screens and devices today. Steve Jobs, Chris Anderson (former editor of *Wired)*, and Evan Williams (founder of Twitter and Blogger) each at one time told journalist Nick Bilton that they limited the amount of time their own children were able to use technology in the home. Some of us recall similar candid interviews with former tobacco executives, who told journalists that they never smoked themselves and also prohibited their own children from doing so. In the words of Adam Alter, these tech billionaires were simply "following the cardinal rule of drug dealing: never get high on your own supply."[31] Even more interesting is what it says about the rest of us. Rather than being outraged that these people are selling us (and our children) things that they know are harmful, we are idolizing them as models of success.

These new technologies subject us to new forms of communication comprised of limited and easily digestible "sound bites," and new forms of media which are designed to be addictive. In addition to our general condition of being overworked and overwhelmed (which we covered in the previous Section One), it becomes more and more difficult for us to discern not only simple truthfulness, but hidden agendas and intent to deceive. The exercise of our free will and critical thinking processes require ever more of our increasingly depleted energy. We cannot completely blame ourselves for lacking willpower and self-regulation when huge amounts of resources are deployed to break it.

While technology *ipso facto* does not create fake news, it does allow the spreading of information—whether right or wrong—on a much larger and faster scale than in the past. Fake news can be inadvertently spread when social media users do not take the time to analyze or critique information before sharing it. More than 6 million tweets were linked to fake and conspiracy news publishers in the month before the 2016 election, and many of these accounts were still "active" in 2018.[32] In addition to hundreds of thousands of ignorant users re-posting, sharing, re-tweeting and otherwise spreading with a single click, there are now sophisticated botnets that can make a false piece of information appear to be more popular or widely accepted than it actually is. This creates what researchers call the ***false consensus effect,*** or the perception that a large number of others share a belief in a particular fact or worldview.[33]

Facebook's own investigation of "hacking" during the 2016 election found that, between June 2015 and May 2017, some 3,000 Facebook ads were purchased by "inauthentic accounts" which were "likely operated out of Russia."[34] Many of the questionable ads did not focus specifically on the 2016 election, yet they served to "amplif[y] divisive social and political messages across the ideological spectrum."[35] In July 2018, Facebook told Congress that it had taken down 32 pages/accounts that it had determined to be "fake," including accounts that had been coordinated across other social media platforms. Although Facebook said it could not determine the source, it noted that some of the tactics were "similar to those employed by the Kremlin-linked Internet Research Agency."

The minority of respondents (49%) in the 2017 PEW survey who believed that the information environment would improve had a greater faith in oversight actions by platforms like Facebook and Twitter, technical solutions (algorithmic filters, crowdsourcing, and even blockchain), in conjunction with an increased commitment to education in "information literacy." Both researchers and civic-minded citizens have made honorable attempts to reign in fake news. A number of independent fact-check sites (Media Bias/FactCheck,

Politifact, Snopes, and FactCheck.org,) employ the old-fashion way of investigation and verification of facts.

Newer, more high-tech ways of combatting false information use algorithms designed to detect fake news (which is often itself generated by algorithms). On the technology battlefront, a group of computer science researchers at the Indiana University Network Science Institute has developed tools that can identify Twitter accounts that are automated bots (Botometer), and even identify accounts that are spreading or fact-checking a claim (Hoaxy).[36] These algorithms analyze both content (including linguistic style used to express rumors) and network propagation dynamics (the strength of social networks, the participation of botnets, etc).[37] These researchers encourage social media users to run stories through both a fact-checker and a bot detector before sharing and spreading misinformation.

Another of PEW's internet studies found that 67% of Facebook users and 71% of Twitter users get most of their news from these platforms.[38] Recent court rulings have found First Amendment implications when elected officials block or ban critics from their personal accounts, on the theory that such accounts constitute a "limited public forum."[39] We know how easy it is for an elected official to simply declare any unfavorable information as "fake news" and demand its removal. Alternatively, requiring privately-owned platforms to determine truthfulness and police information posted by users also opens the door to private censorship. The fake-news detection advocates argue that their intent is not to impose a system of censorship, but rather to encourage users of social media to at least run information through the "checkers" before spreading it in cyberspace.

To its credit, Facebook has taken steps to address its own part in the spread of misinformation. In addition to disabling accounts that it determines to be "fake" or bots, it now works with a global network of internationally certified fact checkers.[40] A February 2019 study concluded that Facebook's actions had reduced user's exposure to fake news between the 2016 and 2018 elections. The PEW optimists argued that a combination of self-regulation by tech platforms, legal requirements to disclose sources (and who is funding them), human and AI fact-checking and bot detection, in conjunction with expanded education on media and digital literacies, could go a long way to solving the problem of the spread of misinformation.

Just as television changed the form of information delivery as much as its content, social media platforms themselves can influence both the form and manner in which information is shared. An analysis of activity on Twitter, which tends to promote discourse that is "simple, impetuous…denigrating, and dehumanizing,"[41] found there was a total disconnect between message quality (truthfulness) and whether or not it "goes viral."[42] The Twitter researchers found that virality was based more on social network structures and competition for attention rather than quality/truthfulness or even general appeal. This suggests that drivers of information ubiquity (i.e., virality) depend primarily on access to both technical resources and self-interest.

Moreover, in the technology arms race—just like corruption in general—the bad guys always seem to be one step ahead: "As existing channels become more regulated, new unregulated channels will continue to emerge."[43] In addition to inadvertent spreading of false information, there are now "news businesses" who actually develop and spread fake news for profit. A Belgian company called Media Vibes SNC even markets an app that allows users to generate and spread their own fake news.[44] This suggests that there is a demand side for misinformation as much as a supply-side driven by ulterior motive.

The Human Hard-Wiring (Neurological) Factor

Distortion of the truth was born in the world of advertising and public relations, particularly when Edward Bernays (1891-1995, a nephew of Sigmund Freud) developed ways to combine the knowledge of psychoanalysis, behaviorism, and group psychology to manipulate public opinion. This "engineering of consent" (aka propaganda) has been used successfully by corporations to make us buy things we don't need (and sometimes don't even really want), as well as by political parties and candidates.[45] Early researchers in this dark science of persuasion discovered that people could be subconsciously motivated by appealing to primitive emotions such as greed, fear/survival, and quest for power (status). Fake news is designed to appeal to these baser emotions.

In 2019, some $240.68 billion was spent on advertising in the US, and this has been projected to increase to $263.05 billion in 2020.[46] Analogous to the exploding expenditures on political races, an ever-increasing spend of advertising dollars becomes ever-more necessary to be heard above all the noise. Branded logos and messages increasingly occupy every square inch of space and every moment of distracted attention. At the same time money becomes more concentrated into fewer hands, so does the ability to be heard. Ironically, huge national branding campaigns tend to give us narrower views of reality: only about 5,000 people around the world create the "look" of 90% of what Americans buy.[47]

The entire purpose of branding is to short circuit critical thinking and logic. Marketers use sophisticated neuroscience research to locate emotional triggers to which they can then target their messages. Marketers target not only the "usual" triggers of fear and greed, but areas of the brain associated with self-image and cultural identity. Today, the objective of branding is to create branded emotional connections that instill "loyalty beyond reason,"[48] as well as to generate trust through appearances of social proof—which is facilitated by social media. When branding is successful, it not only circumvents our logic, but even our own experience: In *Obsessive Branding Disorder* (2008), Lucas Conley recounts how Pepsi has been winning blind taste tests for over thirty years, but when consumers can see the labels, Coke wins over 75% of the time.[49]

Branding has become such a ubiquitous way of life we are now exhorted to brand ourselves. Tom Peters, a management consultant guru urges us to think of ourselves as "Me, Inc." or "The Brand Called You."[50] Today, one cannot attend any kind of job search or resume-writing service which does not attempt to help you develop your "brand." The usual advice is to find something that makes you unique or memorable and target all of your messaging to this quality. In essence, you must create an image of yourself that conforms to the dictates of the market. Conley argues that there is a "sinister inverse" to the idea of branding people—it both transforms human beings who are created by God into commodities for sale, while personifying fictitious (and soulless) corporations.[51]

More recently, this science of psychological manipulation has been used to create "buzzwords" (sometimes also called "dog whistles"). Buzzwords are linguistic emotional triggers that are designed to short-circuit higher-level thinking, disguise prejudice or self-interest, or to amplify political differences rather than attempt to solve them.[52] Other researchers have identified endorsement of a "pseudo-profound bullshit" (their own words), or a belief in false statements that are couched in randomly selected buzzwords (e.g., "we are in the midst of a self-aware blossoming of being that will align us with the nexus itself").[53] Participants who were most likely to believe that such statements are profound tend to be conservative generally, endorse neoliberal economics, and tend to give credibility to any information that is related to hazards (a negative/threat/fear-based bias).[54]

Perhaps of more concern than the manipulation of information in pursuit of an ulterior agenda has been our (collective) increasing inability to discern it. For example, a story about Candidate X having an extramarital affair or catering to cronies is not *ipso facto* unbelievable. Most of us will figure out that such information is likely coming from opposition Candidate Y, and it may or may not be true (i.e., it could have legitimately turned up in opposition research). Conversely, a story about Candidate X running a child sex slave ring from the back of a restaurant (where the activity could have been detected by patrons, neighbors, and/or the authorities) strains credulity, yet people who don't like Candidate X may actually believe it. So, we ask not just the question why people believe fake news, but why anyone believes anything that is patently incredible.

Some have suggested that there has been a "dumbing down" of the general population.[55] This has been attributed to either disinvestments in public education due to neoliberal austerity ideology, or a deliberate agenda of keeping the middle and working classes ignorant of civics (how "the system" works) and lacking critical thinking skills. The result has been an anti-science backlash, which applies not just to scientific facts, but to the process of scientific inquiry itself. Real knowledge or expertise is deemed elitist, while opinions of celebrities, big corporations, or botnets that can capture large audiences create an alternate reality because they also create the illusion of widespread acceptance.[56] Other researchers argue that declining trust in science (particularly among conservatives) is part of a larger trend of declining social capital, which has led to declining trust in others generally.[57]

In June of 2020, the Pew Research Center conducted a survey to explore the extent that people are likely to believe misinformation about the COVID-19 pandemic.[58] A majority (71%) of American adults are at least tangentially familiar with an uncorroborated conspiracy theory that the pandemic was intentionally perpetrated by unidentified "powerful people." One source of this story is a pseudo-documentary titled "Plandemic," based on a video created by a Ph.D.-level virologist named Judy Mikovitz. Although this video has since been debunked by multiple fact-checkers,[59] it nonetheless went "viral" (no pun intended) on social media. According to the Pew survey, people who rely primarily on national news outlets are 68% likely to believe the story is probably or definitely **not** true. Conversely, people who receive their news primarily from social media are 44% likely to believe the story is at least probably true. Some 57% of people who receive the majority of COVID-19 news from Trump and the White House believe the story is true. However, the real tragedy is that—in the middle of a pandemic when real information is vital to keeping people safe—some 38% of Americans say it is difficult to determine what information is true. Moreover, the pandemic—a situation which we are all in together—has not made Americans feel more connected.

Some research on cognitive processing suggests that most people will adjust an initially incorrect judgment when presented with corrected information. However, the degree to which people adjust their attitudes after being presented with correct information depends on the level of their cognitive ability. Even after express disconfirmation of false information, individuals who had lower cognitive ability retained more residual bias toward the false information.[60] This lower-cognitive-ability-bias was consistent after the researchers controlled for right-wing authoritarianism and need for closure. This also corroborates Lobaczewsky's findings that "lower ability" individuals were more susceptible to spellbinders, conversive thinking, and general disregard for the truth, especially if discernment required additional effort.

However, correction, or presenting truthful information to counteract false information, is not always effective. The repetition of misinformation—even for the purpose of refuting it—can operate to reinforce the original false story. In addition to lower ability, cognitive science has identified other reasons why false information may be difficult to correct by simple exposure to the truth. If new (truthful) information challenges an individual's worldview, belief in the false information may actually increase. The researchers who observed this phenomenon suggest that issuing corrections will only be effective if they also address challenges to worldview (i.e., they affirm the self-worth of the recipients).[61] Other studies have looked at how juries respond when they are instructed to disregard information in reaching a verdict (improper evidence or inflammatory pretrial publicity), and found that juries are more likely to be able to do so if they are given a reason to doubt the misinformation—or at least a reason why it was disseminated in the first place—otherwise, a routine instruction to disregard will have no effect.[62]

Other research suggests that social pressure can help to prevent the spread of misinformation because some people will want to avoid embarrassment or preserve their reputation, although this may have limited effect.[63] For so-called peer pressure to be effective, a critical mass of one's peers must be sufficiently grounded in reality that they themselves are able to disavow misinformation. The real threat posed by fake news plus reproduction across social platforms is that it can create networks of individuals in so-called "filter bubbles" who are disconnected from reality. These filter bubbles, or echo chambers, are obvious sources of polarization. In extreme cases, these individuals can come to regard inflammatory and hateful misinformation as fact, which drives its consumers to create scapegoats, normalize prejudice, and even lead to violence.

A number of academics and journalism professionals are sponsoring discussion forums to devise strategic approaches to deal with misinformation—particularly misinformation that is harmful to society.[64] Among their recommendations: (1) Bring more conservatives into the discussion, as misinformation is mainly (but not exclusively) a pathology of the right. This theory supposes that challenges to misinformation are more likely to be accepted if they originate from the same side of the partisan divide; (2) Encourage collaboration between behavioral science researchers and journalists, to include making research easily available to journalists;[65] (3) Find ways to strengthen and support sources of high-quality factual information that are not completely reliant on market mechanisms; and (4) Support and strengthen local reporting. This can mean allowing local news outlets to operate as non-profits, or encouraging partnerships with local colleges and universities.

In this section we have seen what amounts to ponerization of media and information, but we have also seen that there are a lot of smart people concerned about the problem of fake news and actively trying to fix it. This contrasts with the problems of our work life and our livelihoods—which most of us can barely even articulate because we don't see a mass public discussion about things such as underemployment, precariatization, and meaningless work. These subjects seldom appear outside of academia or a few rogue writers—and we certainly aren't going to hear about them from the corporate media.

In *Obsessive Branding Disorder,* Conley argues that "branding has devolved into a disorder that corrodes the nature of identity" and "the world is cheapened when everyone sees it with a marketer's eye."[66] When reality seldom (if ever) lives up to the marketing hype, it breeds cynicism and distrust. Paradoxically, as "we become more isolated and self-conscious, [we become] more prone to rely on brands for status."[67] Conley suggests that the way to combat marketing messages at the individual level is to first, pause, and then analyze whether the message is being targeted to impulsive emotional triggers. At the level of society, Conley exhorts us to "realign our culture" and "reclaim control…community…our public spaces, our core principles, and our future."[68] While this is excellent advice, it also presumes that a critical mass of persons actually cares enough to operationalize it.

In a world where "post-truth" and "fake news" seem to be everywhere, it is not difficult to see how these things can contribute to both fragmentation of our identities and social breakdown. Information is viewed with skepticism or outright distrust. Conversations about difficult issues become impossible, as insecure and anxious individuals would rather cling to a false worldview than analyze the facts—which themselves may be subject to dispute. According to the fake-news researchers, "A large share of the populace is living in an epistemic space that has abandoned conventional criteria of evidence, internal consistency, and fact seeking [such that] public discourse can no longer be examined through the lens of misinformation that can be debunked but as an alternative reality that is shared by millions."[69] When large segments of the population are literally living in separate mental realities, the potential for misunderstanding and even hostility increases exponentially.

Notes

[1] Tom Rosenstiel is the director of the American Press Institute and a senior fellow at the Brookings Institution. As quoted in The Pew Research Center report *The Future of Truth and Misinformation Online,* October 19, 2017. http://www.pewinternet.org/2017/10/19/the-future-of-truth-and-misinformation-online

[2] https://en.oxforddictionaries.com/word-of-the-year/word-of-the-year-2016

[3] Lobaszewsky, A. (1998). *Ponerology: A science on the nature of evil adjusted for political purposes.* Red Pill Press, at p. 85. Full document PDF at http://www.survivorshandbook.com/wp-content/articles/political-ponerology.pdf.

[4] *Id.*

[5] *Id.* at p. 83.

[6] https://www.inputmag.com/culture/fact-checkers-cant-keep-up-with-trumps-growing-lie-count-25k; https://www.theguardian.com/us-news/2020/jul/13/donald-trump-20000-false-or-misleading-claims; plus numerous articles in *The New York Times* and *The Washington Post* throughout the summer and fall of 2020.

[7] Lobaczewsky, *supra* at p. 91.

[8] Hightower, J. (2020, January). Wall Street is savaging local journalism. *The Hightower Lowdown.*

[9] Martin, G.J., & McCrain, J. (2019). Local news and national politics. *American Political Science Review 113*(2), 372-384.

[10] From the Society of Professional Journalists at https://www.spj.org/ethicscode.asp

[11] Mayer, J. (2016). *Dark money: The hidden history of the billionaires behind the rise of the radical right.* New York, NY: Anchor books, a division of Penguin random House LLC.

[12] Mayer, *supra* at p. 461.

---

[13] Mayer, *supra* at p. 462-463. The billionaire Warren Buffet called this elaborate wealth defense infrastructure "the charitable-industrial complex."

[14] Sometime in the 1980s, media workers coined the term "If it bleeds it leads." That is, a story about murder or a gory accident was more likely to bring viewers/readers than a story about neighbors helping others in the community.

[15] Sloman, S. & Fernback, P. (2017). *The knowledge illusion: Why we never think alone.* New York, NY: Penguin.

[16] Goel, Sharad et al., (2015). The structural virality of online diffusion. *Management Science, 62*(1), 180-196.

[17] Grinberg, N., Friedland, L., Joseph, K., et al. (2019, January 25). Fake news on Twitter during the 2016 presidential election. *Science, 363*(6425), 374-78.

[18] Frenkel, S. (2018, October 11). Facebook tackles rising threat of Americans aping Russian schemes to deceive. *The New York Times.* https://www.nytimes.com/2018/10/11/technology/fake-news-online-disinformation.html

[19] Weng, L., Flammini, A., Vespignani, A., & Menczer, F. (2012). Competition among memes in a world with limited attention. *Scientific Reports, 2,* 335.

[20] The creation of doubt around climate change science (https://www.skepticalscience.com/) and denial that smoking is unhealthy (https://www.theatlantic.com/politics/archive/2016/05/low-tar-cigarettes/481116/) are examples of this. *See also* Oreskes, N., & Conway, E.M. (2010). *Merchants of doubt: how a handful of scientists obscured the truth on issues from tobacco smoke to global warming.*

[21] https://www.journalism.org/2016/12/15/many-americans-believe-fake-news-is-sowing-confusion/

[22] A partial list of self-identified participants can be found here: https://www.pewresearch.org/internet/2017/10/19/the-future-of-truth-and-misinformation-online-about-this-canvassing-of-experts/

[23] Full report here: https://www.pewresearch.org/internet/2017/10/19/the-future-of-truth-and-misinformation-online/

---

[24] Vosoughi, S., Roy, D., & Aral, S. (2018). The spread of false news online. *Science, 359,* 1146-1151 at p. 1147. "Humans, not robots, are more likely to spread [fake news]", at p. 1150.

[25] This is true even in my own research. Most peer-reviewed studies are hidden behind paywalls, available only to academics or institutional paid subscribers. Thus, part of my mission is to bring some of this research to light—particularly studies that address why most of us have been working harder for less. Studies addressing the dysfunctions in our job market are sporadic and fragmented, so it is likely even those of us who study such things don't know as much as we should (particularly about how to fix it). The fundamental problem is that those who control the vast majority of resources don't want the rest of us to know the truth about anything that could challenge them.

[26] Facebook (2019, February 24). Community standards enforcement report at https://transparency.facebook.com/community-standards-enforcement#fake-accounts

[27] Pen America. (2019, March 13). *Truth on the ballot: Fraudulent news, the midterm elections, and prospects for 2020.* Get report at: https://pen.org/truth-on-the-ballot-fraudulent-news/

[28] McKernon, E. (1925). Fake news and the public: How the press combats rumor, the market rigger, and the propagandist. *Harper's Magazine.* https://harpers.org/archive/1925/10/fake-news-and-the-public/

[29] Schudson, M. (2001). The objectivity norm in American journalism. *Journalism, 2*(2), 149-170.

[30] Painter, J. (2017). New players and the search to be different. In J. Painter et al. (Eds) *Something old, something new: Digital media and the coverage of climate change* (pp. 8-23). Reuters Institute for the Study of Journalism.

[31] Alter, A. (2017). *Irresistible: The rise of addictive technology and the business of keeping us hooked.* New York, NY: Penguin Press.

[32] Hindman, M., & Barash, V. (2018, October 4). Disinformation, 'fake news' and influence campaigns on Twitter. Knight Foundation. https://www.knightfoundation.org/reports/disinformation-fake-news-and-influence-campgains-on-twitter

[33] Krueger, J., & Zeiger, J.S. (1993). Social categorization and the truly false consensus effect. *Journal of Personality and Social Psychology, 65,* 670-680.

---

[34] Weedon, J., Nuland, W., & Stamos, A. (2017, April 27). An update on information operations on Facebook. Facebook Newsroom. https://Newsroom.fb.com/mews/2017/09/information-operations-update/

[35] Stamos, A. (2017, September 6. An update on information operations on Facebook. Facebook Newsroom. https://about.fb.com/news/2017/09/information-operations-update/

[36] https://www.aace.org/review/interview-with-the-creators-of-hoaxy-from-indiana-university/?cli_action=1589387296.84

[37] Figueira, A. & Oliveira, L. (2017). The current state of fake news: Challenges and opportunities. *Procedia Computer Science, 121,* 817-825.

[38] Shearer, E., & Matsa, E. (2018, September 2018). News use across social media platforms. Pew Research Center. https://www.journalism.org/2018/09/10/news-use-across-social-media-platforms-2018/ This suggests that people are getting news in the form of sound bites and factoids that—even if true—are completely removed from context and analysis. That is, just like fast food, information is being "dumbed down" for fast consumption.

[39] *Knight First Amendment Institute et al. v. Trump*, No. 18-1691-cv (2nd Cir 2019).

[40] Lyons, T. (2018, June 14). Hard questions: What's Facebook's strategy for stopping false news? https://about.fb.com/news/2018/05/hard-questions-false-news/.

[41] Ott, B.L. (2017). The age of Twitter: Donald J. Trump and the politics of debasement. *Critical Studies in Media Communication, 34,* 59-68 at p. 60.

[42] Weng, L., Flammini, A., Vespignani, A., & Menczer F. (2012). Competition among memes in a world with limited attention. *Scientific Reports, 2,* 335.

[43] Not unlike the perennial, yet futile attempts at campaign finance regulation. https://books2read.com/u/mleqoB

[44] Figueira & Oliveira (2017), *supra.*

[45] *Id.* at pp. 166-168.

[46] https://www.statista.com/statistics/272314/advertising-spending-in-the-us/

[47] Conley, L. (2008). *Obsessive branding disorder.* New York NY: Public Affairs.

---

[48] *Id.*

[49] *Id.* at p. 156.

[50] *Id.* at p. 179.

[51] *Id.* at p. 184.

[52] *Id.* at p. 169.

[53] Pfattheicher, S., & Schindler, S. (2016). Misperceiving bullshit as profound is associated with favorable views of Cruz, Rubio, Trump and conservatism. *PLOS ONE, 11,* e0153419. http://dx.doi.org/10.1371/journal.pone.0153419

[54] Hibbing, J.R., Smith, K.B., & Alford, J.R. (2014). Differences in negativity bias underlie variations in political ideology. *Behavioral and Brain Sciences, 37,* 297-350.

[55] Haupt, W. (2018, November 26). The dumbing down of America (Op-Ed). https://www.thecentersquare.com/national/op-ed-the-dumbing-down-of-america/article_61f64000-f181-11e8-a22e-6bd70b62cd6c.html

[56] Lewandowsky, S., Ullrich, K.H.E., Cook, J. (2017). Beyond misinformation: Understanding and coping with the post-truth era. *Journal of Applied Research in Memory and Cognition, 6*(4), 353-369.

[57] *Id.*

[58] Mitchell, A., Jurkowitz, M., Baxter Oliphant, J., & Shearer, E. (2020, June). Three months in, many Americans see exaggeration, conspiracy theories and partisanship in COVID-19 news. Pew Research Center. https://www.journalism.org/2020/06/29/most-americans-have-heard-of-the-conspiracy-theory-that-the-covid-19-outbreak-was-planned-and-about-one-third-of-those-aware-of-it-say-it-might-be-true/

[59] https://www.sciencemag.org/news/2020/05/fact-checking-judy-mikovits-controversial-virologist-attacking-anthony-fauci-viral

[60] De keersmaeker, J. & Roets, A. (2017). 'Fake news': Incorrect, but hard to correct. The role of cognitive ability on the impact of false information on social impressions. *Intelligence, 65,* 107-110.

[61] Nyhan, B., & Reifler, J. (2011). When corrections fail: The persistence of political misperceptions. *Political Behavior, 32,* 303-330.

[62] Fein, S., McClosky, A.L., & Tomlinson, T.M. (1997). Can the jury disregard the information? The use of suspicion to reduce the prejudicial effects of pretrial publicity and inadmissible testimony. *Personality and Social Psychology Bulletin, 23,* 1215-1226.

[63] Schwartz, N., Sanna, L.J., Skurnik, I., & Yoon, C. (2007). Metacognitive experiences and the intricacies of setting people straight: Implications for debiasing public information campaigns. *Advances in Experimental Social Psychology, 39,* 127-61.

[64] Baum, M., Lazer, D. & Mele, N. (2017, February 17-18). Combating fake news: An agenda for research and action. Conference sponsored by Harvard Kennedy School Shorenstein Center on Media, Politics and Public Policy. https://shorensteincenter.org/combating-fake-news-agenda-for-research/

[65] Too much of valuable research is "hidden" behind the paywalls of obscure academic journals.

[66] Conley (2008), *supra* at p. 199.

[67] *Id.*

[68] *Id.* at p. 200.

[69] Lewandowsky, S., Ecker, U.K.H., & Cook, J. (2017). Beyond misinformation: Understanding and coping with the "post-truth" era. *Journal of Applied Research in Memory and Cognition, 6,* 353-369.

Section 5
Generalized Signs of Hystericized Thinking

"...our almost ubiquitous use of substances risks turning us into a sick society. Expecting quick chemical fixes generalizes easily into expecting quick political fixes...We must gradually withdraw from our unprecedented substance dependency if we are to become a mature society that can shed its denial and face reality as it is."

Dr. Allen Frances
Twilight of American Sanity

*

One achievement of neoliberalism was a degree of linguistic hegemony in capturing the language of political, social, and economic discourse, extending into cultural discourse as well. A challenge today is to recapture the language, so as to create an imagined desirable future. This is nothing less than reviving the very idea of the future, which has been lost in the neoliberal dystopia of endless consumerism and electronic bread-and-circus plebeian existence.

Guy Standing[1]

*

When a citizenry no longer feels that it can find justice through the organs of power, when it feels that the organs of power are the enemies of freedom and economic advancement, it makes war on those organs....The longer citizens are locked out of and abused by systems of power the more these systems become targets.

Chris Hedges[2]

*

The anxious class faces equally serious challenges, for its problems are not only cultural and psychological but sharply material…economic developments [have] rendered the underclass (some 20 or 30 million people) superfluous, while the anxious class has become marginally relevant...We are becoming a society of what has been called "advanced insecurity." The anger and fear generated by acute economic anxiety are easily displaced onto "welfare queens" and illegal immigrants.

From *Habits of the Heart*[3]

*

Powerlessness can pave the road to the acceptance of tyranny.[4]

*

People in the reality-based community believe that solutions emerge from judicious study of discernable reality. That's not the way the world works anymore. We're an empire now and we create our own reality."[5]

*

Trump acted at once the emperor and the boy who said the emperor had no clothes, ripping the illusory cover of decency off the system, forcing everyone to stare at its obscene nature.

Masha Gesen[6]

Ordinary people in the aggregate know intuitively that something is wrong with the way we are going, even if they are unable to articulate it. The American Psychological Society has been conducting annual "stress in America" surveys since 2008. In the very first survey—which was done in the middle of the Great Recession—the top three sources of stress were money, the economy and work.[7] Some 33% of women and 27% of men reported experiencing extreme stress, with physical and emotional symptoms that negatively affected their lives. In the 2017 survey, while money (62%) and work (61%) continue to be major sources of stress, concern about the future of America was highest (63%). The survey also found that the gender gap had widened, with women, as well as Black and Hispanic men, experiencing significantly higher stress.

This sense that things are not right transcends concerns about one's own individual life circumstances: In developing a measure of what they term "zeitgeist," or collectively shared ideas about the world, researchers found a sense of pessimism about the way things are going even as respondents reported satisfaction with their own personal situation.[8] The rapid change which has created fortunes for a few along with chaos and anxiety for the many is predicted to intensify. Klaus Schwab, head of the World Economic Forum, predicts change of even greater scale, scope and complexity in the future: "We stand at the brink of a technological revolution that will fundamentally alter the way we live, work, and relate to one another." In the new millennium, many people are already "disillusioned and fearful…with a pervasive sense of dissatisfaction and unfairness."[9] There is a collective sense that the world is going to hell in a handbasket that only aggravates increasing personal distress.

Today, we are living in a schizoid paradox. Our institutions are governed by a form of hyper-technical rationality that has abandoned moral logic. At the same time, the masses of global citizens—perhaps in protest against the loss of something that is fundamental to humanity—have abandoned the capacity to think critically and logically. This is more than a simple return to faith and religion in troubled times—although this may play a part in it—but a form of romanticism that denies evidence-based reality. This denial is aggravated by the social fracturing caused by extremes of inequality: The anti-science worldview is anti-elitism cloaked in religious "us versus them" righteousness.

The psychotherapist Jeremy Shapiro notes a "striking parallel" between science denial and disorders such as depression, anxiety, antisocial personality disorder, and the type of dichotomous "black and white" thinking typically associated with authoritarianism.[10] So-called "science denialism" is not simply rejection of science based on a conflict with faith teachings, like the historical conflict between the 16th century astronomer Galileo and the Catholic church regarding a heliocentric solar system. Rather, science denial itself has devolved into a form of pseudoscience,[11] which one researcher has argued uses "deviant criteria of assent to distort the scientific process."[12] This type of thinking will harp on a factor where science is not absolutely 100% certain, and choose to deny something that is not only 97% likely, but ignore the empirical evidence of experience as well.

The Right and the Left Agree: We Are in Trouble

Jonah Goldberg is a writer at the American Enterprise Institute who is mainly known for his best-selling *Liberal Fascism* (2008). In his more recent (2018) *Suicide of the West,* Goldberg describes the problem as an abandonment of the ideals of the Enlightenment—particularly traditional conservative values such as natural rights, limited government, and the importance of tradition that values ideas and personal character.[13] Goldberg blames the decay of society on what he calls "romanticism," or a desire to return to some pre-modern natural state. He portrays the common man as somehow yearning to abandon technological progress as well as rejecting logic and science as a way of understanding the world. Goldberg is certainly correct in that there has been a "dumbing down" of society—which also fits into Lobaczewsky's portrayal of a simplified worldview because cognitive complexity requires too much effort. What he doesn't address, however, is that much of this is a backlash against a technocratic society that is leaving many people behind. This specific issue will be addressed by other thinkers later in this section.

Goldberg's ideal society is based on a Lockean philosophy that promotes pluralism, meritocracy, and tolerance.[14] In Goldberg's view, the current resurgence of tribalism, populism and nationalism threatens social stability as well as freedom. He is also correct in this respect, as an increasing "us-versus-them" mentality makes people more willing to curtail civil liberties—the quintessentially authoritarian (and illogical) act of stripping away rights that apply to everyone because one wants to keep "the other" under control. Goldberg further argues that Enlightenment values of Institutional pluralism—along with plurality of meaning and identity—operated to constrain abuses by both traditional elites and the state. The American form of limited government in particular is successful because—in rejecting the illusion of the perfectibility of human nature—its goal was to direct natural impulses into productive behavior rather than attempt to suppress or control them.[15]

Goldberg presents us a historical account of the evolution of thought regarding human nature as well as its impact on social institutions.[16] According to Goldberg, modern institutions such as civil society and capitalist economies are not "natural," and it is only by happy accident that they emerged from Enlightenment ideals. Instead, Goldberg argues that modern society is corrupted by romanticism, which is characterized by man's more "natural" proclivities to nationalism (which he differentiates from patriotism) and tribalism. Goldberg acknowledges that the romanticist might have legitimate grievances: he recognizes that modern life is somehow out-of-balance, inauthentic or oppressive, and that the system itself (including the elites who run it) is corrupt.[17] Like many on the right who have legitimate concerns about loss of civil liberties, Goldberg also seems to ignore the possibility that giant multinational corporations create freedom-stultifying bureaucracies, economic dependence, and cultural corruption as much as any state. Yet, his detailed account is worth reading because it also describes the process of Lobaczewsky's moral inversion in modern terms that more of us might find relevant.

Goldberg suggests that there is a connection between nationalism, racial essentialism, and tribal superiority, where the creation of collective mythologies and the elevation of passion with no limiting principles ultimately results in statism or some form of socialism.[18] While tribalism is natural, manufactured tribalism is "the heart of aristocracy and the soul of identity politics."[19] Goldberg blames the left for inflaming social divisions through the identity politics of diversity (although he acknowledges some of this was necessary during the civil rights era), which then created a backlash on the right: "[T]the perceived reality for millions of white, Christian Americans is that their institutional shelters, personal and national, are being razed one by one."[20] Trump was then able to successfully tap into white angst over diversity initiatives as well as frustration with unfulfilled political promises to "fix" immigration.[21] Goldberg thus seems to suggest that people on both sides had legitimate grievances, but the reaction of institutions—as well as politicians like Trump—was to aggravate differences rather than attempt to find mutually acceptable resolutions.

The danger of populism is that, like nationalism, it elevates the abstraction of the group, heroically defined as "the people," over the individual. However one defines "the people" almost invariably ends up excluding someone.[22] In America, the first populists were farmers and residents of rural communities as the country was experiencing rapid transitioning to industrialization and urbanization. Populism also tends to arise during times of significant change and be driven by people who the system has failed in some way:[23] "...whenever you try to replace well-established cultural norms and traditions with an abstract new system, you do not open the door to a new utopia; you open the door to human nature's darker impulses."[24]

Populism thus captures feelings of resentment, alienation and rootlessness, as well as demonization of the "new order,"[25] whether it be industrialists, technocrats, or Wall Street financial players. According to Goldberg, populism becomes more dangerous when the people voluntarily cede power to the state in order to "cure" social alienation, which absolves all the rest of us from the responsibility to repair our own broken emotional, psychological and social lives.[26] Goldberg argues that the objective of the left is for the State to replace the bonds of family and the source of meaning in our lives, in essence, reducing an entire nation into tribalism—which eventually demands a strong leader and devolves into autocratic socialism.[27]

In presenting evidence for his diagnosis, Goldberg cites many of the symptoms we have covered herein: a decline of support for the basic rights that define a liberal democracy, particularly among young people;[28] an overuse of social media that "drown[s us] in information but starv[es us] for knowledge;"[29] and icons of popular culture (Rebel Without a Cause, Batman, Breaking Bad, Dexter) who—even as they commit evil acts—achieve cult hero status because they represent the romantic ideal of abandoning social norms and following your own inner direction.[30] He cites Harvard sociologist Robert Putnam (author of *Bowling Alone),* who grudgingly acknowledges a correlation between increased diversity (as expressed in tribalism and identity politics) and community breakdown.[31] Goldberg admits that the economy (i.e., capitalism as practiced) has been failing many working Americans, but the answer is not to abandon a system that has generated prosperity for many Americans in the past.[32]

Goldberg is a conservative who thinks for himself, so he has expressed many of the same concerns about a Trump presidency as those on the left. Trump—who at various times has switched between the Republican, Democrat, and Reform parties—is not a proponent of traditional conservative values. Indeed, Trump's only "values" are winning and dominance, which are neither moral nor intellectually serious.[33] Goldberg asserts that Trump is a "thoroughly romantic figure" because he puts his faith almost entirely "in his own instincts," which are driven by "insecurities and megalomania."[34] Goldberg honestly admits that he at one time truly believed that the authoritarian threat would come from the left and not from the right.[35] He also acknowledges (as does the psychiatrist Dr. Allen Frances) that Trump himself is not the cause of our social ills, but rather a symptom of a darker disease that is infecting society as a whole.[36]

On the left we have Chris Hedges, an American journalist and Presbyterian minister (Harvard Divinity School). Hedges is a former foreign correspondent for the *New York Times,* where he was an early critic of the war in Iraq. He has written numerous books dealing with wars, rebellion and revolt around the world, as well as decline of the American empire. Although Hedges is typically associated with the left, he sued the Obama administration in 2012, claiming the National Defense Authorization Act was unconstitutional. Where Goldberg predicted that fascism would come from the left, in *American Fascists: The Christian Right and the War on America* (2007), Hedges' (a Christian minister himself) prediction was that it would come from the right—specifically from Christian fundamentalists. Where Goldberg describes the problem as an abandonment of Enlightenment rationality in a return to romantic tribalism, Hedges describes the problem as an abandonment of reality in favor of illusion.

The American working class is fed "glamorous crumbs" from images of unimaginable wealth and impossible physical beauty by talk and entertainment shows, reality television and glossy magazines—places where people like themselves are invisible.[37] This "[m]oral nihilism of celebrity culture [encourages] a dark voyeurism into other people's humiliation, pain, weakness and betrayal."[38] The format of television is predictable and formulaic—it "provides a mass, virtual experience that colors the way many people speak and interact with one another…[including] a false sense of intimacy with our elite."[39] The effect of modern entertainment is to inculcate a passive acceptance of what the corporate state is doing to us: "Magical thinking is the currency not only of celebrity culture, but also of totalitarian culture….The fantasy of celebrity culture is not designed simply to entertain. It is designed to keep us from fighting back….reality shows like *Big Brother* and *Survivor* glamorize the intrusiveness of the surveillance state"[40]

In researching the degradation of popular culture, Hedges spent time observing behind-the-scenes operations of professional wrestling and the adult pornography industries. The objective of celebrity, glamor and entertainment is obviously to keep the masses distracted so they don't (most of them, anyway) start questioning why their own lives don't seem to be working. But the content of the entertainment itself has a less obvious purpose: the normalization (and even glamorization) of physical violence, aggression, and objectification. Even pornography is no longer only about sex, but about degradation and humiliation. It primarily appeals—as it always has—to men looking for sexual gratification and release. But the more modern version, with its depiction of women being raped, degraded, and sometimes even tortured, now provides a different kind of satisfaction for men who are now competing with women for work in a world where there seems to be fewer rewards and avenues to upward mobility. Hedges argues that the influence of this newer-style pornography was graphically depicted in the infamous photos of the prisoners at Abu Ghraib. The hostility of those who have been left behind by the system is thus conveniently redirected to images of abuse against those even lower in the hierarchy.

As in Lobaczewsky's hystericized society, where logic and harder critical thinking have been abandoned, Hedges argues that the educational establishment itself has been complicit in the loss of our higher intellectual facilities, instead turning out technocratically trained but obedient individuals whose primary function is to manage and maintain the corporate state. "The elite universities disdain honest intellectual inquiry, which is by its nature distrustful of authority, fiercely independent, and often subversive."[41] The people who are in charge "...the ones in Congress...Wall Street...and [at] prestigious universities and business schools—do not have the capacity to fix our financial mess"[42] because they have no ability—or inclination— to question the fundamentals of the system. Indeed, the individuals presiding over the mortgage collapse that precipitated the Great Recession hailed from the ranks of elite prep schools, Yale and Harvard.

Hedges proceeds to expose the dark side of positive pop psychology, which is a major manufacturer of illusion. He interviews researchers who explain that positive psychology can create positive results, but it can also be used for purposes of coercion and manipulation.[43] Hedges alludes to the use of psychiatric/psychological research by the military and intelligence agencies to develop techniques of interrogation and control.[44] One management professor explained that "All organizations exist to eliminate deviance," admitting that sometimes this operated to eliminate positive as well as negative deviance.[45] In the corporate world, where control is paramount, cult-like features of positive psychology have been adapted to create peer pressure in order to destabilize an individual's sense of self, as well as the use of manipulation and total control of the social environment in order to ensure compliance and conformity.[46] "Positive psychology, like celebrity culture, the relentless drive to consume, and the diversionary appeals of mass entertainment, feeds off the unhappiness that comes from isolation and the loss of community. The corporate teaching that we can find happiness through conformity to corporate culture is a cruel trick, for it is corporate culture that stokes and feeds the great malaise and disconnect of the culture of illusion."[47]

The objective of this effort is to keep the citizenry from questioning the cost of military expansionism and empire as our own infrastructure crumbles and our communities decay.[48] Quoting Albert Einstein, Hedges argues that it is "extremely difficult and [even] in most cases quite impossible" for average citizens to formulate rational decisions or objective conclusions about their political rights and their place in society when "private capitalists inevitably control, directly or indirectly, the main sources of information."[49] Indeed, journalists themselves have become celebrities, where their cozy relations to the rich and powerful violate their professional public duty as journalists to root out and report the truth.[50]

As Hedges was writing in 2009—before anyone could know that Donald Trump would be President—he warned that growing civil unrest would result in the corporate state escalating measures of internal control.[51] Hedges alleges that this had already begun with the expansion of the surveillance state and a policy of perpetual "war on terror." Hedges was already predicting the emergence of radicalism from the right—specifically the Christian right—as increasing personal and economic despair would create a crisis of faith.[52] As Americans, perhaps our most ironic illusion is one of individualism, when the reality is that the majority of us readily and without question "submit…to the tyranny of the corporate state."[53]

Ironically, individual citizens are torn between a desire to stay informed about current events (a prerequisite of responsible citizenship) and the reality that information may be deliberately manipulated or false (so-called "fake news"). There is also a growing realization that news consumption produces feelings of anxiety and helplessness. Anecdotally, many people say they have to take occasional self-imposed periods of abstention from news and social media to maintain their sanity—or even just to get a good night's sleep. In addition to anxiety, many of us are also experiencing a schizoid sense that all the mass of information we receive is contrary to the everyday reality we observe in our own lives. Many of us are chronically exhausted from managing constant change and dealing with insecurity, uncertain about the truth, and barely able to make decisions about what is best for our own lives, let alone develop the cognitive capacity to diagnose and solve broader social ills. So, most of us (understandably) take the path of least resistance. Which is, of course, right where they want us.

Anger, Angst, and Anomie

At the same time as a large proportion of the population has abandoned critical thinking and questioning, there is an increasing level of hostility and generalized anxiety that struggles to find an object. As we have seen in Section Two of this part, increasing inequality reduces levels of public trust, sense of community, and empathy. Yet, there seems to be an additional level of generalized angst and anxiety above and beyond the pathologies created by inequality and precariatization. People may choose to either abandon hope for the future (nihilism) or seek refuge and solace in their faith traditions. In a ponerized (or hysteroidal) environment, this return to faith—instead of promoting the hopeful and helpful prosocial messages of its prophets—becomes perverted into an ever-more extreme form of us-versus-them division and breeding ground for authoritarianism.

In *The Age of Anger,*[54] Pankaj Mishra describes the contemporary mood as one of ***ressentiment.*** The concept of ressentiment was first proposed by Friedrich Nietzsche to describe an intense mix of envy, humiliation and powerlessness that is buried within the psyche rather than expressed openly. Ressentiment is a "characteristic phenomenon of modern societies founded on the principle of equality...where formal equality between individuals coexists with massive differences in power, education, status, and property ownership."[55] The foundation of ressentiment is a "suspicion—potentially lethal among the hundreds of millions of people condemned to superfluousness—that the present order, [whether] democratic or authoritarian—is built upon force and fraud."[56] Ressentiment is the unsurprising result of broken promises of endless economic expansion, increasing isolation, the abandonment of the ideals of social democracy, and the rise of "globalized technocratic elites," who have created a system "where grossly unequal distributions of wealth and power have created humiliating new hierarchies."[57] According to Mishra, the irony of ressentiment is that it manifests similarly in groups who normally view each other as opposites: marginalized blue-collar Christian fundamentalists in the American Rust and Bible Belts as well as young Muslims. Both groups see their traditional way of life being destroyed, and thus "push a narrative of victimhood and heroic struggle between the faithful and the unfaithful, the authentic and the inauthentic…[where] their blogs, YouTube videos,…and conspiracy theories mirror each other."[58]

Mishra is Indian, but he is thoroughly familiar (more so than most Americans are today) with the historical development of Western intellectual writers. Mishra's argument is that a rationalized, technocratic society has abandoned romanticism. In using the term "romanticism refers to the writings of Jean-Jacques Rousseau, particularly as Rousseau captured the "basic psychological outlook of those who perceive themselves as abandoned or pushed behind"[59] during periods of rapid change. Mishra proposes that individual liberty is threatened in a society driven by commerce, competitiveness and *amour propre*—which Rousseau defines as self-esteem that depends on the opinions of others. Mishra also accuses many intellectuals of being driven by amour propre, because they gain status by "provid[ing] literary and moral cover to the unjust and the powerful, entrench[ing] inequality [along with] the suffering and violence it breeds."[60] Thus, those who have the intellectual resources to question the system are too often co-opted by it.

Although Mishra argues that ressentiment is a global phenomenon, a large part of his analysis focuses on religious fundamentalism, particularly in Muslim cultures. He wanted to understand how young people could be both "seduced by modernity" while searching for "salvation by faith and tradition," along with the "need for authority, hierarchy, obedience and subjection."[61] He tells the story of a young Syrian who grew up in a lower middle-class neighborhood in the old city of Aleppo. The boy watched as the construction of highways and high-rises fractured his old neighborhood, disrupting the daily routines of his family and neighbors. This experience motivated him to earn a Masters degree in urban planning from a university in Hamburg, where his thesis proposed replacing massive impersonal modern structures with more human-friendly courtyard homes and small-scale marketplaces. This young man never became a design guru for advocates of sustainable communities, but he did become infamous for the destruction of one of the world's largest modern (and symbolic) structures. The man's name was Mohammed Atta.

Mishra's argument is that Muslim hostility toward the West is about more than religion. He describes Iran under the former Shah in the 1950s and 1960s. At this time, Iran was considered a model of progress among Islamic majority countries. More people had access to Western-style education, women were gaining more equal rights, and the country experienced both economic growth and secularization under the Shah. However, in spite of all the apparent progress, not all Iranians loved the Shah. The Shah, who had taken over leadership from his deposed and exiled father, was subject to at least two unsuccessful assassination attempts as well as attempted coups. He also gradually lost support from the Shi'a clergy as well as the traditional class of merchants known as bazaari.

Many Iranians under the Shah's regime were uprooted from villages and crowded into urban slums, where there was neither work nor adequate housing for them. Mishra coined the term "Westoxification" to describe this process. But popular complaints were not so much about the modernization itself as that it was a form of hypocrisy: The promise of increasing opportunity and material wealth simply did not materialize for the masses, whose lives were turned upside down but who received no corresponding benefit. It is in such context and background that Iran witnessed the rise of Ayatollah Khomeini.

Mishra draws an analogy between the social conditions that created Islamic fundamentalism with those that existed in Germany prior to and during the rise of Hitler, those that existed in India upon the election of the anti-Muslim authoritarian Narendra Modi, and those in the United States at the election of Donald Trump. "Many more billions of individuals, struggling to find a place in the world, or defeated by the whole grueling process, and resigned to failure, boost their self-esteem through identification with the greatness of their country."[62] Alternatively, they "seek self-esteem through a sense of belonging to a group defined by ethnicity, religion, race or common culture.

Mass media, popular culture and demagogues fulfil and manipulate their need for psychological dependency, and fill up their imaginative lives with a range of virtual enemies."[63] In explaining the popular appeal of Modi (which could equally apply to Trump), Mishra describes a demagogue who "positioned himself in the gap that a democracy dominated by a liberal elite had opened between itself and ambitious, lower-middle class Hindus (substitute Christians in the case of Trump)….[The] "poorly educated, underprivileged laggards—people brought up on Ayn Randian clichés of ambition, iron willpower and striving…[then come to identify] with an apparently ruthless strongman and uninhibited loudmouth…Modi's angry voters mirror many electorates around the world—people gratified rather than appalled by trash-talk and the slaughter of old conventions."[64]

Mishra has provided us a multicultural understanding of nationalism, tribalism and religious fundamentalism as it exists in a globalized world where international travel and instant global communication should facilitate inter-cultural understanding and tolerance: "Globalization, while promoting integration among shrewd elites, incites political and cultural sectarianism everywhere else, especially among people forced against their will into universal competition….Even those who are mercifully employed and anchored find their subjection to economic necessity harder to bear in a climate where mediating forces and buffers (churches, guilds, trade unions, local government) between the individual and an impersonal economic order are absent or greatly diminished."[65] This angst manifests as what Freud once termed the narcissism of small difference, growing movements supporting formal and informal secessionism, and the development of darker philosophies such as nihilism and anarchism.

Mishra also lends support to Lobaczewsky's description of ponerization through the lens of social justice and basic fairness (or rather lack thereof). He describes the development of a "destructive instinct in a society whose political arrangements fail to accommodate the growing aspirations to justice and equality of the masses....[while] ruling groups become evil to the point that the accumulated hatred of the victims breaks the impasse through violence."[66] Mishra describes our age as one of "soft despotism" that tends to exist in "atomized societies devoted to the pursuit of wealth" and rampant individualism.[67] In such societies, rights and liberties are destroyed as much from below (by democratic means) as they are from above (by totalitarian means). His analysis thus provides us a real-time explanation for the rise of psychopaths to positions of power by means of democratic elections.

Moral Inversion

Lobaczewsky warns us against taking a moralistic view of human behavior, as it "poisons the human soul and deprives us of our capacity to understand reality more objectively."[68] Indeed, he even goes so far as to claim that a "unilaterally moral interpretation of the origins of evil" is itself immoral. Thus presents a paradox, where the moral issue of evil must be addressed in ways other than moralizing. This paradoxical phenomenon was also addressed by the Austro-Hungarian historian, philosopher, and political economist Karl Polanyi (1886-1964), who described the phenomenon as one of moral inversion. While Lobaczewsky's studies focused on individual psychological effects, Polanyi wanted to understand how totalitarianism (and the dehumanization and violence associated with it) came to be rationalized.

According to Polanyi, human behavior is motivated by appetites and passions. Appetites are lower-level drives which we typically associate with basic instincts such as hunger and sex. The objective of appetites is the benefit of the individual organism, and the satisfaction of appetite consumes its object (there is only so much food or mates to go around), creating scarcity. Passions are higher-level drives with objectives outside the individual and are what separate humans from animals. Unlike appetites which consume its object, mental passions perpetuate themselves in their gratification. There is a somewhat amorphous distinction between intellectual and moral passions, although both require reasoning processes. Intellectual passions revolve around achievements, arts, and sciences, while moral passions almost always involve the broader society: justice, truth, equality, and freedom.[69] Unlike the appetites, which are focused on the self, the moral passions often involve self-sacrifice and self-transcendence. However, while the appetites operate automatically, mental passions are learned, which means that they can be subverted or misdirected.

Polanyi traces the roots of moral inversion to the rise of science and rationality during the Enlightenment. The new knowledge created a mechanistic view of the world, as well as a sense of dynamism and unlimited improvement. The scientific method was then applied to the study of the social order, which in turn created a materialist and utilitarian view of politics. Freedom itself came to be viewed in individualistic terms rather than as a function of membership in a community with reciprocal obligations. This reductive view of the human person and materialist view of the social order produced a cynicism in which politics is viewed as a perennial conflict over survival, power, and dominance. Appeals to humanity's lower nature were considered "good," because such nature is authentic and untainted by artificial social convention. Increasingly, people came to distrust government and view society itself as a form of corruption. As material welfare is elevated to the ultimate social objective, other values (intellectual passions/science and moral passions/liberty) are subordinated, devalued, and suppressed.

Moral inversion is not a one-time event or even a linear process, but rather a series of cascading inversions resulting from inter-related, overlapping, and mutually reinforcing cultural developments. It is, like Lobaczewsky's ponerization, a complex process with feedback effects. Polanyi argues that totalitarian violence should be viewed as a perversion rather than an abandonment of morality. Totalitarianism results from the inability to reconcile skepticism (the search for absolutely impersonal knowledge) and religion (the utopian passion for social perfection).[70]

This passion for absolutely impersonal knowledge along with a corresponding passion for social perfection leads to the abandonment of traditional moral values. Personal discomfort with the new reality becomes magnified into a wholesale suspicion of authority and social distrust, culminating in a form of nihilism. Popular attitudes are expressed through a cynical distrust of politics, which people believe is motivated by greed and fear and only responsive to force. However, moral passions that have nowhere to go because there is no longer a self-transcending obligation to a larger society do not disappear. These passions are instead separated from their original objectives, and replaced with new objectives of power and wealth, which then acquire a form of moral sanctity.[71] In essence, moral passions are diverted back into appetites, which are now bolstered by moralizing logic and become unrestrained.

An apt demonstration of this phenomenon in our modern times is the growth of Prosperity Gospel thinking. So-called "Prosperity Gospel" is an offshoot of Evangelical Protestantism, although it is not specifically affiliated with a particular Christian denomination. The crux of Prosperity Gospel is a narrow interpretation of select Bible verses that are taken out of the Bible's broader context: Mark10:30 (what you give to God, you will receive back a hundredfold in this lifetime), James 4:2 (you have not because you ask not), and Mark 11:23 (if you have enough faith, you will be able to cast a mountain into the sea). Prosperity Gospel says that God wants you to be rich, wealth and good health are a sign of God's favor, you only need to ask God with faith to receive whatever you want, and giving generously is a profession of your faith that God will provide. Prosperity Gospel thus turns the traditional notion of obedience to God (or higher spiritual values) on its head, instead proclaiming that good fortune is simply a matter of petition, prayer and faith, essentially making God a high-powered concierge who will fulfill all of our desires so long as we ask and believe.

Prosperity Gospel was born in the USA, as it is more adaptable to individualistic cultures. There are also cultural and behavioral roots which facilitate adherence to prosperity gospel thinking that have nothing to do with religion. In *Twilight of American Sanity*, Dr. Allen Frances explains how our limbic system, which is responsible for emotions such as fear, anger and pleasure often overrides our cortex, which governs our ability to think logically.[72] Our limbic system had survival value in a primitive world of scarcity, but in order to function in modern society, humans must learn to control the impulse for immediate gratification. Natural selection has also created an "optimism bias," which "promotes the triumph of hope over experience."[73] Like the limbic system, an optimism bias can serve a survival function in a challenging environment. However, an over-developed optimism bias, combined with a culture of American exceptionalism, can result in a dangerous tendency to both blind us to reality and to underestimate risk, harm and costs.

Prosperity Gospel is thus designed to tap into both a natural optimism bias as well as specific features of American culture. Early Protestant settlers to America were known for their work ethic, which created a general prosperity and also took on a form of morality. Writers and thinkers of the day from Adam Smith and Alexis de Tocqueville[74] to Max Weber[75] reinforced popular narratives that correlated moral superiority with capitalism, American exceptionalism, and God. Wealth was seen as a sign of both hard work and God's grace. The so-called "Protestant work ethic" was only the first version of a new spiritual worldview that morphed traditional religious doctrine with an increasingly individualistic/narcissistic culture and American dream ideology.

A recent study[76] that attempted to identify who constitutes the believers of Prosperity Gospel found that there was no correlation with income. Proposed explanations for this are that prosperity gospel offers both hope to the poor (assuming they can overcome the self-blame for their own condition) and moralistic justification for the rich. While the followers of prosperity gospel come from all income groups, its leaders are almost always quite wealthy. These charismatic "preachers" have been able to capture national and even international audiences by strategic use of media, while building empires of economic and political power (not unlike Lobaczewsky's spellbinders). The extreme wealth of these megachurch leaders has led to criticism that prosperity gospel is just another con game to get people to hand over money in exchange for false hope. These criticisms have also come from other Christian leaders who argue that Prosperity Gospel perverts the real message of Jesus, including Pope Francis and even more mainstream evangelicals.[77]

The one factor that correlates with Prosperity Gospel adherence—or at least certain of its tenets—is less education. While not directly correlated with being a member of a prosperity movement (some of this has morphed into more general self-help advocacy such as *Think and Grow Rich, The Secret, The Four Spiritual Laws of Prosperity, The Prosperity Bible, The Dynamic Laws of Prosperity, The Law of Attraction,* and a multitude of other books unconnected with a specific church), those with less education are more likely to agree that material wealth is a sign of God's blessing and that poverty is a sign of God's disgrace.[78] Moreover, in order for faith to manifest, it must be clear of doubt, questioning and uncertainties. We can already see that Prosperity Gospel represents a form of Lobaczewsky's ponerization in that it requires complete faith amounting to suspension of critical thinking.

However, the real danger of Prosperity Gospel is not that it creates false hope, but that it reduces all social problems to questions of individual faith, which absolves anyone of responsibility to do anything. If you are sick, it is because you have not asked God to heal you, or, alternatively, you don't believe God ***can*** heal you. If you are poor, again it is because of your lack of faith (whereas in the old days it was because you were lazy). There is no critical inquiry into other possible causes, such as environmental toxins or exploitative labor markets, which leaves such things unchallenged.[79] But perhaps the most insidious effect is that Prosperity Gospel operates to create a lack of empathy and solidarity with human suffering. It subverts the real teachings of Jesus to "do unto others," to serve the poor, and to love your neighbor. The goodness of "faith" is used to justify behaviors like greed and hubris, that once—in times past—were considered sinful.

Transpersonification and Chaos

One obvious question is why don't more good people resist? As we have seen in the case of Hitler, Stalin and other dictators, the takeover by pathocrats—at least in the early stages—is fragmented and incremental. It is possible that by the time most people realize what is happening, the pathocracy has attained sufficient power to suppress dissent by force or law. Yet, the dynamics of pathocratic takeover are more complex than the mass of good people living their lives in ignorant bliss until they realize it is too late. Just as we cannot understand evil by looking at individuals without also looking at systems and culture, we also cannot fully understand pathocracy by analyzing politics and culture without also looking at what is happening to individual thinking patterns. As the pathocratic worldview grows to dominate popular culture, some people undergo what Lobaszewsky terms "transpersonification." This can take various forms of psychopathology, including actual changes in personality.

Perhaps the best example of transpersonification can be seen in the 2015 documentary *The Brainwashing of My Dad.*[80] In this documentary, which was funded by a kickstarter campaign, non-professional film-maker and ordinary person Jen Senko documents changes in her father's personality beginning in the 1980s. Senko's father, Frank, took a new job where he was unable to carpool with his usual group. Because he was now commuting alone, he started listening to right-wing talk shows. Frank started out as a lukewarm (and essentially apolitical) Democrat who was ultimately transformed into a rabid Republican. This transformation was more than a change of political views or party based on deliberative reasoning, but involved transformation from a loving, community-minded family man to a raging, hate-filled ideologue.

Senko's film was more about the effects of media propaganda than psycho-social explanations for personality changes. That is, we understand the right-wing agenda as the subversion of both critical thinking and solidarity, but we don't really understand why some people are more susceptible to such influences while others are able to resist. According to Lobaszewsky, a "normally resistant" person is better able to survive disintegration than someone who allows their mind to be filled with "pathological propaganda material without sufficient controls."[81] In the course of producing *The Brainwashing of My Dad,* Senko found others that were noting the same phenomenon.[82] Even my own sister admits that she indulged in these programs when she had to drive some distance alone, usually over the wee hours of the night or early morning. Sis says she did not necessarily agree with the programming, but it did a good job of keeping her awake and aroused (without having to stop for coffee)—suggesting that it tapped into the neurological system of adrenaline and endorphins. Even a former Fox News anchor refers to a disorder he calls "Foxycontin," and suggests ways to resist "tribal hate media."[83]

Here in the United States, politically polarizing influences arise primarily from the political right.[84] It is probably no coincidence that the right generally represents the position of the global oligarchy and the corporatocracy. However, we have seen manipulative propaganda operate in other countries (e.g., the former Soviet Union, Cuba and Venezuela) coming from the left (usually also from those in positions of economic and political privilege). Unfortunately, in a nothing-succeeds-like-success, if-you-can't-beat-them-join-them response, some on the left are now adopting the tactics of sensationalist fake news that "goes viral."[85]

Perhaps the most disturbing finding is the identification of what one group of researchers has termed the "need for chaos."[86] While the generation and spread of hostile fake news is often performed for partisan purposes, these researchers have identified a group of persons whose only motivation is to increase hostility generally. This motivation has been correlated with a desire to "burn down" the entire established political order—regardless of political party or affiliation. It has also been correlated with feelings of social exclusion, status frustration, and extreme discontent with the workings of democracy. In America, some 40% of persons agree to some extent with statements about "burning down" political and social institutions, which—although this is not most people—represents a significant minority. These researchers also conclude that the prevalence of a psychological desire for chaos is consistent with rising inequality.

This inchoate nihilism has been suggested as a reason why political polling "missed" so much of Trump support—twice. Yes, the 2020 polls accurately predicted a Biden win, but it was nowhere near the landslide their data was indicating. Trump received 10 million more votes in 2020, notwithstanding the (quite public) defection of many people who voted for him in 2016. The non-partisan political pollster FiveThirtyEight has propounded a theory that there is a sizeable minority who voted for Trump who are not necessarily Republicans, conservatives, pro-America patriots, or even Trump cultists, but "socially disconnected" and politically disengaged individuals who simply do not participate in polls or surveys.[87] Indeed, some 60% of white voters without social connections favored Trump, compared to 46% of white voters who were socially connected. One theory proposes that these are individuals who actually want to see institutions fail (or alternatively, Armageddon) and are hoping that Trump will destroy them. The unfortunate consequence is that these people have such diminished sentiments of any form of community that it is nearly impossible for the rest of us to ascertain what they think or how they feel about anything.

Lobaszewsky asserts that some form of neuroticism is a normal reaction to a ponerized society. As more and more of us can no longer deny the failures of society, we want answers—which sometimes means that we are also in search of scapegoats. Data-driven decision-making is abandoned because anything that requires thought and analysis is deemed too elitist. Instead of offering hope and inculcating a sense of communal solidarity, our faith traditions are perverted into a moralizing form of further division. Here in America, where the ponerizing messages suggest a winner-take-all, everyone-for-himself, war-of-all-against-all ethos, the outcome is that more people begin to view each other as adversaries. Which serves the system up to a point, as the masses are too distracted and fragmented to plan and coordinate a collective resistance. The irony is that even some of the pathocrats realize that there needs to be some minimum number of prosocial people who are willing to keep society functioning in some semblance of normality. The question is what happens when too many of us simply abandon the effort to confront dysfunction, as well as any hope of making a difference.

Notes

[1] Standing, G. (2014, May). Published as O precariado e a luta de classes. *Revista Critica d Ciẽncias Sociais, 103,* 9-24.

[2] Hedges, C. (2015). *The wages of rebellion.* New York, NY: Nation Books/ Perseus Books Company.

[3] Bellah, R.N., Madsen, R., Sullivan, W.M., Swidler, A., & Tipton, S.W. (2008). *Habits of the heart.* Berkeley, CA: University of California Press at p. xxxviii.

[4] Sindic, D., Barreto, M., & Costa-Lopez, R. (2014). Power and identity: The multiple facets of a complex relationship. In Sindic, Barreto and Costa-Lopes (Eds.), *Power and Identity* at p. 8. Current Issues in Social Psychology Series. London: Psychology Press. A series of case studies by various authors that examines the ways that the powerful define the identities of the powerless, and ways that the powerless can challenge this.

[5] Statement recorded by journalist Ron Suskin in 2004 from a "senior ranking official working for former President George W. Bush," many believe to have been Karl Rove.

[6] Gessen, M. (2020). *Surviving autocracy.* New York, NY: Riverhead Books/Penguin Random House, LLC at p. 46.

[7] https://www.apa.org/news/press/releases/2008/10/stress-in-america.pdf

[8] Van der Bles, A.M., Postmas, T., & Meijer, R.R. (2015). Understanding collective discontents: A psychological approach to measuring Zeitgeist. *PLOS ONE.* Available through Creative Commons: https://journals.plos.org/plosone/article?id=10.1371/journal.pone.0130100

[9] Schwab, K. (2016, January 14). The fourth industrial revolution: What it means, how to respond. World Economic Forum. https://www.weforum.org/agenda/2016/01the-fourth-industrial-revolution-what-it-means-and-how-to-respond

[10] https://theconversation.com/the-thinking-error-at-the-root-of-science-denial-96099

---

[11] Hansson, S.O. (2017). Science denial as a form of pseudoscience. *Studies in History and Philosophy of Science, Part A, 63,* 39-47. https://www.sciencedirect.com/science/article/abs/pii/S0039368116300681

[12] Hansson, *Id.*

[13] Goldberg, J. (2018). *Suicide of the West: How the rebirth of tribalism, populism, nationalism, and identity politics is destroying American democracy.* New York, NY: Crown Publishing Group/Penguin Random House.

[13] *Id.* at p. 61.

[14] *Id.* at p. 130.

[15] *Id.* at p. 153.

[17] *Id.* at p. 249.

[18] *Id.* at p. 313.

[19] *Id.* at p. 61.

[20] *Id.* at p. 233.

[21] *Id.* at p. 322.

[22] *Id.* at p. 293.

[23] *Id.* at p. 294.

[24] *Id.* at p. 231.

[25] *Id.* at p. 295.

[26] *Id.* at p. 304.

[27] *Id.* at p. 307.

[28] *Id.* at p. 283.

[29] *Id.* at p. 335.

---

[30] *Id.* at p. 257.
[31] *Id.* at p. 319.

[32] *Id.* at p. 307.

[33] *Id.* at p. 288.

[34] *Id.* at p. 290.

[35] *Id.* at p. 345.

[36] "It is easy to point at Donald Trump and say the American body politic is rotting from the head down. But the real rot is systemic. The shadow government of the new class has fortified itself against democratic accountability and is sawing off the ladder to success beneath it." Goldberg at p. 208.

[37] Hedges, C. (2009). *Empire of illusion.* New York, NY: Nation Books at p. 26.

[38] *Id.* at p. 30.

[39] *Id.* at p. 45.

[40] *Id.* at p. 38-39.

[41] *Id.* at p. 89.

[42] *Id.* at p. 111.

[43] *Id.* at p. 124.

[44] *Id.* at p. 128.

[45] *Id.*

[46] *Id.* at p. 135.

[47] *Id.* at p. 138.

[48] *Id.* at p. 144.

[49] *Id.* at p. 164.

[50] *Id.* at p. 169.
[51] *Id.* at p. 177.

[52] *Id.* at pp. 183-184.

[53] *Id.* at p. 182.

[54] Mishra, P. (2017). *The age of anger: History of the present.* New York, NY: Farrar, Straus and Giroux.

[55] *Id.* at p. 333.

[56] *Id.* at p. 346.

[57] *Id.* at p. 13.

[58] *Id.* at p. 80.

[59] *Id.* at p. 112.

[60] *Id.* at p. 106.

[61] *Id.* at p. 113.

[62] *Id.* at p. 267.

[63] *Id.* at p. 269-270.

[64] *Id.* at p. 271.

[65] *Id.* at pp. 333-334.

[66] *Id.* at p. 319.

[67] *Id.* at p. 269.

[68] Lobaczewsky, A.M. (1998). *Political ponerology: A science on the nature of evil adjusted for political purposes.* Red Pill Press at p. 149.

[69] Polanyi, K. (1958). *Personal knowledge: Towards a post-critical philosophy.* New York, NY: Harper and Row.

[70] Polanyi, K. (1951). *The logic of liberty: Reflections and rejoinders.* London: Routledge and Kegan Paul. Also, Yeager, D.M. (2002). Confronting the Minotaur: Moral inversion and Polanyi's moral philosophy. *Tradition and Discovery, 29*(1), 22-48.

[71] Polanyi, K. (1958). *Supra.* Chapter Six, "Intellectual Passions."

[72] Frances, A. (2017). *Twilight of American sanity: A psychiatrist analyzes the age of Trump.* New York, NY: HarperCollins Publishers at p. 63.

[73] *Id.* at p. 73.

[74] De Tocqueville, A. (1831). *Democracy in America..*

[75] Weber, M. (1905). *The protestant ethic and the spirit of capitalism.* London/New York, NY: Routledge Classics (1992).

[76] Koch, B.A. (2014). Who are the prosperity gospel adherents? *Journal of Ideology 36,* 1-46.

[77] Spadaro, A., & Figueroa, M. (2018, July 18). The prosperity gospel: Dangerous and different. *La Civiltà Cattolica. https://laciviltacattolica.com/the-prosperity-gospel-dangerous-and-different/*

[78] Koch, B.A. (2014). *Supra* at p. 25.

[79] "...the poor who are fascinated by this pseudo-Gospel remain dazzled in a socio-political emptiness that easily allows other forces to shape their world, making them innocuous and defenseless." Spadaro & Figueroa, *supra.*

[80] See movie trailer at https://www.youtube.com/watch?v=Qh3TeTxgNVo

[81] Lobaszewsky, *supra* at pp. 235-236.

[82] https://nymag.com/intelligencer/2019/04/i-gathered-stories-of-people-transformed-by-fox-news.html

[83] https://www.frontpagelive.com/2020/01/01/ex-fox-anchor-explains-how-to-start-deprogramming-your-fox-brainwashed-friends-and-relatives/

---

[84] https://www.wgbh.org/news/2017/03/15/politics-government/major-new-study-shows-political-polarization-mainly-right-wing. See also Benkler, Y., Faris, R., Roberts, H., & Zuckerman, E. (2017, March 3). Study: Breitbart-led right wing media ecosystem altered broader media agenda. https://www.cjr.org/analysis/breitbart-media-trump-harvard-study.php

[85] https://www.theatlantic.com/politics/archive/2017/07/liberal-fever-swamps/530736/

[86] Peterson, M.B., Osmundsen, M., & Arceneaux, K. (May 2020). A "need for chaos" and the sharing of hostile political rumors in advanced democracies. Download full article at https://psyarxiv.com/6m4ts/?fbclid=IwAR25DFJIHEMx4CEqbAyQWopz-x87PRqQL3ZifecDFHIHx8y0OnDkFD2CcoY

[87] Cox, D. (2020, November 24). Could social alienation among some Trump supporters help explain why polls underestimated Trump again? https://fivethirtyeight.com/features/could-social-alienation-among-some-trump-supporters-help-explain-why-polls-underestimated-trump-again/ More partisan groups have labeled these loners the "hidden deplorables."

Part V

Is A Good Society Possible?

Interlude

It was not desirable that the proles should have strong political feelings. All that was required of them was a primitive patriotism which could be appealed to whenever it was necessary to make them accept longer working hours or shorter rations. And even when they became discontented, as they sometimes did, their discontent led nowhere, because, being without general ideas, they could only focus it on petty specific grievances.

George Orwell, *1984*

*

How concerned should we be that a president who assails essential institutions and traditions of democracy has found millions of followers willing to endorse significant violations of democratic norms, including resort to force in pursuit of political ends, lawlessness…and casting doubt on the legitimacy of elections? The simple answer is that no one knows.

Larry M. Bartels[1]

The intention was to have this book finished by July of 2020. This obviously did not happen. As everyone is now aware, we have been beset by a global pandemic—a virus that spreads without direct contact, and with human carriers who may be asymptomatic. While other developed countries have been able to get the spread of the virus under control (at least, in between the spikes and surges), the United States has not. Throughout February and early March, the Trump administration and its lackeys were making public pronouncements that the virus was nothing to worry about—either it was a "hoax," or it would "all go away."

The purported motivation behind this was that Trump was concerned about having to shut down the economy in order to contain the virus. Such a mandated shutdown would then result in an economic recession that would adversely affect his prospects for re-election. And with Trump, self-interest always comes before public interest or even duty. An alternative theory was that a psychopathic Trump actually relished the thought of chaos and large numbers of people dying (including his own supporters, who were being tested to prove their loyalty). At the same time the Trump administration was attempting to convince the public that the danger of the virus was being exaggerated by the "liberal media," wealthy insiders (specifically, two billionaire Senators from Georgia) were quietly dumping stocks in resort and hospitality industries while buying up stock in internet communication and online delivery platforms.

When the pandemic was officially recognized to be a problem around the middle of March, schools and most businesses not deemed "essential" were either shut down completely or allowed to open during limited hours. As the weather warmed and summer approached, restrictions were loosened: Although life did not return to pre-pandemic "normal," people were allowed to gather in small groups, and restaurants could serve people outside. But another dark side of American culture was about to burst through and replace the pandemic as the top news of the day.

The United States has a history of official violence against its own civilians—particularly outgroups—beginning with the occasional round-up of escaped slaves, to the forced removal and migration of Native Americans, to quelling legitimate labor protests, and then in response to generalized urban riots. This combination of brutal authoritarianism (control) and racism sometimes resulted in police shootings of unarmed citizens, Black men being disproportionate victims of these events. In July of 2013, a group of activists formed Black Lives Matter, a movement dedicated to calling out the deaths of unarmed Blacks at the hands of police.

On May 25, 2020—as the country was coming to terms with the "new normal" of the pandemic—George Floyd, a Black man who had lost his job as a bar security guard due to the pandemic, attempted to make a purchase at a neighborhood convenience store in Minneapolis. The store employee thought the $20 bill Floyd had presented looked odd, so the employee (politely) asked Floyd to wait while he called the police to check whether the $20 was counterfeit. Floyd (politely) agreed to wait outside the store. Although Floyd had a criminal record, there is no evidence that he had been involved with the criminal justice system since 2013, when he became involved with various ministries of helping: meal delivery, drug rehabilitation, and job placement services. When the police arrived at the store, they surrounded Floyd (who was unarmed), and forced him on the ground while handcuffing him. One of the officers drew a gun on Floyd, but did not shoot him. Rather, another officer kept his knee on Floyd's neck for 8 minutes and 46 seconds. During this time, Floyd begged for his life, his last words being "I can't breathe." During the final two minutes of his life, Floyd was motionless and had no pulse.[2] Like the Rodney King incident nearly 30 years ago, Floyd's abuse at the hands of the police was captured by the cell phone video of a bystander, in addition to public surveillance cameras.

The news of Floyd's death not surprisingly resulted in protests by Black Lives Matter (BLM) groups. At that time, BLM social media was already ablaze with outrage over earlier police killings of Ahmaud Arbery and Breonna Taylor. However, either because people were on edge due to the pandemic, or simply paying more attention to the news, the Floyd protests were much larger than previous BLM protests—multi-city events that included many more of both White and Black people. Unlike the Rodney King riots, the multi-racial BLM protests were generally peaceful—more like demonstrations (some events had formal programs with speakers, entertainers, and ministers offering prayer). There were some "troublemakers" during these protests—individuals who came out at night (often when the main event was over) who took advantage of the chaos and police distraction to loot and vandalize. A number of city hall officials determined that most of the "troublemakers" were from out-of-town (where the protestors were usually locals), and likely unconnected with the main protests.

The saga of George Floyd and resulting BLM protests was further inflamed by counter-protests from White Nationalist and Neo-Nazi groups. These groups had always been around, but they had more or less operated under the radar. Until, that is, Trump latched onto their racist rhetoric (whether Trump actually believes it or is simply adopting it as a form of popularity boosting and branding strategy will be left for other analysts) and gave these hate groups permission to come out. In August 2017, there was a white supremacist "Unite the Right" rally in Charlottesville, Virginia, which turned much more violent than any of the BLM protests. Although Trump did not exactly endorse the neo-Nazi groups, he did nothing to condemn them. Now that BLM protests were gaining numbers and audiences, they were increasingly met with "counterprotests" from violent white supremacist groups. So, in the middle of a deadly pandemic we had one group of folks—basically armed with signs and megaphones—raging about their people being murdered by an authoritarian state, and another group of folks—much better armed with assault rifles and other military gear—raging about their lost social dominance and threats to their way of life.[3]

An almost forgotten event that also occurred over the Summer of 2020 was the appointment of Louis DeJoy as Postmaster General. Under DeJoy, who was widely viewed as a Trump lackey, people began to experience noticeable delays in mail delivery. Postal delivery drivers' hours and routes were being curtailed, and postal machinery was found being dismantled. Now, DeJoy is a "businessman," so he may likely subscribe to the pare-expenses-to-the-bone philosophy that is typical of the private sector, and all the dismantling was simply part of a massive cost-cutting exercise. But more worrisome was the prospect that DeJoy was deliberately screwing up the postal service in order to thwart the delivery of mail-in ballots during the election. Most pundits were predicting that more Democrats would be voting by mail, since many Republicans (especially those who only listened to Trump and right-wing media) continued to downplay the virus. Indeed, one study estimates that between 25,000 and 50,000 ballots arrived too late to be counted due to USPS performance problems. Although the USPS is facing a flurry of litigation over DeJoy's actions, due to unexpired terms of Trump-appointed individuals on the USPS Board of Governors the earliest DeJoy could be removed is October of 2022.[4]

But wait, there's more! In the middle of a raging pandemic, raging racial unrest, and generalized rage about everything, soon-to-be former President Donald Trump literally attempted to steal the election by preventing the counting of legitimate votes—all the while shouting and shrieking that the election was "rigged." Trump inflamed his already radicalized base with demands that they take action to "stop the steal"—a message which was relentlessly posted and reposted on social and right wing media. The "cause" was taken up by a hodgepodge of Trump allies in positions of power (state attorneys general and congressional representatives in both state and federal houses) and Trump's "base." The "base" is comprised of the usual white supremacist and neo-Nazi groups, as well as a new group of delusionals calling themselves Q-Anon. Q-Anon followers believe that a cabal of elites are Satan-worshipping pedophiles embedded within the "deep state" who are running a global child sex-trafficking ring. The "Q" conspiracy also incorporates re-packaged anti-Semitic blood libel and similar accusations from the Nazi era. Although the "Q" conspiracy originated independently of Trump, at some point, they incorporated the belief that Trump was waging a secret war against the evil elite pedophile ring and the deep state. Although Trump himself does not subscribe to the "Q" conspiracy, he is nonetheless more than willing to use it for his own purposes.

In the November elections, there were more than the usual number of absentee, (i.e., mail-in) ballots, primarily the result of pandemic-related voter accommodations. Although all of the states have (varying) rules to deal with absentee ballots, not all of them were set up to efficiently handle the increased load. Thus, it took several days to receive election results from some states. As the votes were counted, initial results shifted in favor of Joe Biden—again, something that was predicted to happen by most political scientists and pollsters. When it became clear that Trump lost, he began a campaign to overturn the results. It started with demands for recounts, which are allowed under the law and were done—over and again multiple times in some of the swing states. When the recounts did not change the results, Trump sycophants began to file legal challenges in both state and federal courts. Most of these cases were dismissed on basic procedural grounds such as lack of evidence, lack of standing, or failure to state a claim, case, or controversy.[5] Some judges called these suits what they were—attempts to disenfranchise millions of votes and thwart the will of the people.

Trump—as he had done during his entire term of Presidency—took to Twitter with his unhinged, raging conspiracy theories—which were then re-tweeted among his cult-like following. Trump's "base" was more than happy to externalize his rage, storming state capital buildings armed with assault weapons and even plotting to kidnap, torture, and possibly murder state Governors. There was speculation circulating that Trump would attempt an illegal coup—either to cling to the power necessary to stoke his narcissistic supply, or to avoid the litany of indictments that have lined up from a lifetime of grift, thievery and corruption. In early January, 2021, an audiotape surfaced in which we unmistakably hear Trump attempt to bully and browbeat the Georgia Secretary of State to "find" him another 11,780 votes. Brad Raffensperger (a Republican) held his ground and maintained his honor, notwithstanding Trump's barely veiled mob-boss-style threats and subsequent real threats of violence by Trump supporters against Raffensperger and his family.[6]

The unhingery around delusional claims of election fraud came to a bloody boil on January 6th, the day designated by the Constitution for the electoral votes to be "counted" by a joint session of Congress. This is traditionally a purely ceremonial exercise which allows newly elected members of Congress a low-key opportunity to acclimate and longer-term members a chance to reconnect as they begin a new session. But, prior to the ceremony, Trump held a rally (which had been preceded by a massive social media campaign) designed to whip his deliberately gathered base into a hateful frenzy. At the urging of Trump (and his sycophants in positions of power), the mob headed to the Capitol building, where they easily breached a (deliberately) inadequate perimeter of Capitol police.

ProPublica, a nonpartisan investigative journalist organization, obtained over 500 individual video recordings that were taken within and during the Capitol invasion, and has made these available to the public, arranged by digital time-stamp.[7] Several in the mob appeared to have military training. A few individuals were captured on video with zip-tie hand cuffs, apparently intent on taking hostages. While some of the mob appeared to be intent on mission and purpose, others wandered around taking cell-phone videos of the interior of the Capitol, almost like an ordinary tourist would. Indeed, a strange phenomenon was the plethora of video being recorded, some of which was subsequently uploaded to right-wing media platforms (which is where ProPublica—and most likely also the FBI—obtained it). In some of the video, we can overhear people calling for the "death" of Vice-President Pence (a gallows with a noose had been erected outside), Speaker of the House Pelosi and others. Although the national guard was late in coming (again, this appears to be by prior planning and design), the mob was eventually cleared from the Capitol building. Congress was able to finish its business of counting the electoral votes, but not until 3:30 a.m., because Trump supporters in Congress continued to make objections which had no chance of changing the outcome.

The Capitol invasion resulted in the death of both police officers and insurrectionists, theft of government items that potentially implicated national security, and property damage to the Capitol itself. The District of Columbia issued a 6 p.m. curfew that night, and the entire city was essentially in lockdown mode through the Biden inauguration on January 20th. Many of the Trump insurrectionists—who were identified from the same videos that some of them conveniently provided—were subsequently arrested and/or found themselves on the "do not fly" list that normally applies to foreign terrorists. In a perhaps too-little-too-late move, social media platforms (primarily Twitter and Facebook) banned both Trump and any reference to "stop the steal." So, we had our first taste of what private censorship looks like. Fortunately, no violence marred the inauguration of President Biden and Vice-President Kamala Harris (herself a source of angst to patriarchal white supremacists), thankfully due to increased security and tight vetting of the national guard personnel assigned to inauguration duty.

One might perhaps breathe a sigh of relief that the United States has (much too narrowly) avoided becoming a fascist dictatorship. Pathocracy averted! While still-functioning democratic processes barely avoided a Hitler-esque style dictatorship, the specter of fascism is alive and well in the United States of the early twenty-first century. The certified election results and official swearing-in of President Biden do not signal a permanent calm, but more like a temporary relief. It is like living in Florida during hurricane season, anxiously watching the projected path of the storm, then breathing a sigh of relief when the storm goes elsewhere—all the while knowing that the same drill of boarding up, watching warily, and potential evacuation will be repeated again and again.

Radicalized Trump supporters have not gone away, and—according to our own counterterrorism agencies—continue to present a clear and present danger.[8] Trump continues to have a sizeable minority of supporters. The more extreme versions parade the streets wearing military camouflage and carrying assault weapons. Alternatively, they take to social media, threatening death to government officials for any number of grievances, both real and imagined. The less rageful ones travel freely and run about in public places mindless of facial covering or maintaining distance, in essence weaponizing the coronavirus.

Trump has also made statements about another Presidential run in 2024 or returning to politics in some capacity. Which will be interesting to see, given the plethora of criminal indictments that are likely to be forthcoming. Some of these originated prior to Trump's presidency: tax and bank fraud, rape and sexual assault, campaign finance violations, with likely new charges involving bribery, extortion, sedition and perhaps treason. Now that we are literally embroiled in a war-of-all-against-all, even Charles Koch—one of the billionaire oligarchs who has pushed the greed-is-good ethos, climate change denialism, and other propaganda to keep the rabble inflamed and unorganized so the rich can get ever richer—is now admitting that he "screwed up."[9]

Yes, this is the United States of America in January of 2021 Although the extreme dysfunction has manifested in the past year—particularly as it relates to the impulses of racial violence, fascism, elitism, and ignorance—it did not come upon us suddenly. The earliest sign might have been former President Eisenhower's warning about the military-industrial complex (with its suggestion of totalitarianism and empire), which was documented in much more elaborate detail by Sheldon Wolin's Superpower some forty years later. In 2015—before anyone could even imagine a President Donald Trump—the words of Chris Hedges in his *Wages of Rebellion* were eerily prescient:

> *Any revolutionary movement that builds a mass following will have to contend with state-orchestrated vilification and vigilante violence...*
> *These reactionary movements while defining themselves as the guardians of patriotism and the Christian faith, will draw on the deep reserves of racial hostility....Scratch the surface of the survivalist cult in the United States and you expose terrified white supremacists.*
>
> * * *
>
> *The breakdown of American society will trigger a popular backlash, which we glimpsed in the Occupy movement, but it will also energize the traditional armed vigilante groups that embrace a version of American fascism that uses Christian and national symbols. The longer we remain in a state of political paralysis, dominated by a corporate elite that refuses to respond to the growing misery and governed by an ineffectual liberal elite, the more the rage of the white male underclass—whose economic status often replicates that of poor blacks—will find expression through violence. If it remains true to the American tradition, this violence will not be directed at the power elite but will single out minorities, dissidents, activists, radicals, and scapegoats....The impoverishment of a working class and the snuffing out of hope and opportunity always produce angry mobs ready to kill and be killed.*

Yet, for all of the prescient warnings, it is difficult to fully recognize the ponerization that is in front of you. Even as I was writing this book based on the more subtle warnings of academic and journalistic research that had been produced within the past several decades, the exploding evidence before me suggested a much higher level and broader diffusion of ponerization than I had been prepared to identify when I started this book. Indeed, one need search no farther than the daily news over the past four years to find more than sufficient evidence of hysteroidal high-point and significant social pathology.

Anti-democratic sentiment is not only on the rise in America, but in other western democracies as well. In America, popular angst might be attributed to the decline of empire. Yet this seething rage against institutions, anti-intellectualism, and the rise of nationalism, nativism and demonization of social and cultural diversity are manifesting across the globe. Europeans have also expressed alarm at the resentments stirred up by "status anxieties…floods of refugees (many who have been displaced by some combination of climate change, political instability, or war), economic uncertainty and stagnation, [and] alienation from the large, anonymous institutions" that comprise the global power structure.[10] This suggests that American hegemony—which once was touted for exporting the ideals of democracy—is now exporting a newer version of authoritarianism.

The paradox of American-style moral/religious authoritarianism is that it exists alongside a "licentious libertinism" in economic matters. This phenomenon is possibly a remnant of the mythology of the American frontier. It could also be a deliberate result of elite propaganda that frames the pursuit of individual wealth as the path to national greatness. The rubes are thus convinced that allowing their purported "superiors" to amass huge fortunes—even if this means their own children will have constrained opportunities—is tantamount to patriotic duty. If working people are frustrated, it is easy to point to a scapegoat—someone (or a group of someones) who may be lower in the hierarchy but who might be on the verge of gaining rights or making their voices heard.

Gross' *Friendly Fascism* also predicted a "powerful extractive process that would siphon income and wealth upward." Gross predicted that the collective treasure of American productivity would increasingly be directed toward military expansionism (and into the coffers of privateering contractors) and away from programs that served the needs of people at home (foreshadowing Wolin's *Inverted Totalitarianism* by almost three decades). Beginning in the late 1970s and 1980s, the system also set out to crush the labor movement—which not only provided better wages and benefits for workers, it also gave them an avenue into power structures that wrote the laws and determined policy outcomes. Which for most of us meant both working harder for less and a reduction of our agency in the public square.

This phenomenon has helped to create the extreme and growing inequality that we are witnessing today, and which we discussed in more detail in Part IV, Section 2. However, the problem of extreme inequality has moved out of esoteric academic studies and is actually starting to be addressed in popular culture. In 2013, three dystopian feature films were produced in which the main theme revolved around a wealthy or elite class that lived off the labors of the majority of society—who they kept oppressed through some combination of force, physical separation, and ideological habit. An early example was the movie *Elysium*, in which the ultrarich have established a luxury spa-like colony on a distant space station, while the masses of humanity struggle to survive on an overpopulated and polluted Earth.

Elysium came out around the same time as the first installment in the blockbuster trilogy *Hunger Games. Hunger Games* is based on a 2008 eponymous novel by Susan Collins. Here, a dominant minority residing in the national capital is maintained by the labor of 12 outlying districts. Every year, there is a "competition" in which each district presents two of its young people in a contest to the death until there is only one survivor. The winner's district then enjoys some of the largess of the nation as a whole for one year—until the next contest. The better-off districts (those closer to the capital) devote resources to the training and preparation of their own contestants. It is not hard to see the analogy to the modern job market (justification of deserts) and hypercompetitive winner-take-all globalized economy in some of the scenes.

Also appearing in 2013 (a good year for this type of thing), we have *The Snowpiercer,* a Korean/Czech allegory of class division. The Snowpiercer is the name of a train that contains what is left of humanity on an Earth that appears to be frozen and devoid of life. The train circles the earth once a year, and is powered by a seeming perpetual motion machine. The people on the train occupy specific cars which represent their position in society, with the cars toward the rear of the train representing the lower orders (with correspondingly impoverished existence). As one moves up toward the engine room (which the culture imbues with religious overtones of "great" and "eternal"), both material conditions and status improve. Higher status persons are free to travel to "lower level" cars, but never in the opposite direction. So, of course, the main plotline involves a revolution from below. We follow our revolutionaries up through the various cars, as they break through both physical barriers and security apparatus that have been set up to contain them. When they finally reach the "great engine" room, it is occupied by one man. They also discover the true source of its eternal energy—their own children.

Within the past year, Netflix has come out with several dystopian series based on obvious class barriers. *Three Percent (3%)* is a Brazilian-produced story about a wealthy "Offshore" society that holds an annual event called the "Process." Society on the mainland is impoverished, and although the Offshore does not brutally "police" it, the society is nonetheless controlled. Citizens of the poor society are allowed (and encouraged, but not expressly required) to participate in the Process when they become 20 years of age. The Process is designed so that only 3% of participants will succeed, and thus be allowed to migrate and live in the Offshore. Again, we see some analogy to modern job market competition (ambiguity, randomness, and outright cheating). We also see that the great Offshore is not all it's cracked up to be, as well as the inevitable story conflict involving a resistance.

An even darker and more dystopian Netflix series (still in production) is *The Barrier.* Here we see a definitely unfriendly fascism as well as a pandemic (the show's premise had been established before the current actual pandemic). *The Barrier* takes place in Spain (subtitles) after there has been some sort of war. An authoritarian government has been installed to deal with the pandemic (and possibly is an artifact of the prior war). The elites reside behind a barrier in Madrid, and the obviously poorer rabble who reside outside the barrier are allowed inside to serve the elites, but only after an elaborate documentation and disinfecting process (the purity motive is obvious). The main story line involves one of the elite ministers (who seems like he is basically a decent person) with a prior personal connection to the matriarch of a family on the other side. The individuals reconnect with each other while attempting to trace children who have been mysteriously "disappeared." These children (from the wrong side of the divide) are being used as guinea pigs in research to develop a vaccine by none other than the minister's physician wife—who herself is gunning for a power position. Here we also see the same recurring subthemes of resistance and repression.

The consistent themes running through these futurist dystopias are: (1) hierarchical class divisions not based on any identifiable merit other than being at the right place at the right time; (2) the separation of castes/classes by means of both physical barriers, security forces, and ideological mythologies; and (3) honorable resistance and justifiable rebellion among the lower castes/classes. Although we see members of the elites in these stories who are obvious "bad guys" and unlikeable characters, we also see others among the elites who are merely doing their job and serving the system (i.e., they are not necessarily "bad" people themselves). We also see the folks in the "resistance" communities deal with their own dark sides. These allegorical depictions in many ways represent how our current society extracts wealth from the working masses today and (sometimes literally) eats the future of their children tomorrow, all in order to serve a system that only benefits the minority who run things.

Perhaps these stories leave out matters of faith in order to discuss a moral issue without "preaching." Yet, our faith traditions have an important role to play in confronting the social degradation produced by extremes of inequality. It is unfortunate that Christian evangelicalism in the United States is often associated with the promulgation of ignorance, along with "friendly" fascism that results from a system that is designed to keep certain people in their (much more undesirable) place. To the secular community, religion often appears to serve as righteous justification for tribalism, racism, and xenophobia. Yet, religious teachings can also serve to moderate the worst impulses of "othering:" A 2019 survey of Trump voters sponsored by the Cato Institute found that those who attended church regularly had more favorable views of ethnic, racial, and religious minorities, as well as greater concern for racial equity.[11] Moreover, the moral wisdom of faith communities has played many a historical role in fighting macrosocial evil in the past: establishment of an Underground Railroad to help slaves escape into free territory; the harboring and hiding of Jews during Nazism, the role of Southern Christian churches in supporting the civil rights movement, and today in promoting a faith-based concept of "stewardship" by caring for the Earth and combating climate change.

However, the most salient role that I envision for our faith communities is to expose the moral inversion of our culture's worship of greed and selfishness. If—like the Earth itself—other people—including all those who are different from us—are also part of God's creation, then their purpose is not for us to use and abuse for our own enrichment, egoic gratification, or other selfish purposes. We can make all of the rational arguments in the world (from social scientists, economists, psychologists, public health researchers and epidemiologists) about how extreme inequality can only produce a dysfunctional society. But we also need a moral argument.

Notes

---

[1] Bartels, L.M. (2020, July 10). Ethnic antagonism erodes Republicans' commitment to democracy. https://www.pnas.org/content/117/37/22752

[2] Floyd's official autopsy ruled his death a homicide: cardiopulmonary arrest caused by subdual and restraint.

[3] https://acleddata.com/2020/08/31/us-crisis-monitor-releases-full-data-for-summer-2020/

[4] https://slate.com/business/2020/12/louis-dejoy-postmaster-general-biden-postal-service.html

[5] Full disclosure: Some of these cases were so egregiously meritless, I have filed disciplinary complaints with the State Bar of Texas and the District of Columbia Bar.

[6] https://thehill.com/homenews/state-watch/526222-georgia-secretary-of-state-says-graham-other-republicans-have-pressured

[7] https://projects.propublica.org/parler-capitol-videos/

[8] https://www.justice.gov/opa/video/acting-us-attorney-michael-sherwin-district-columbia-and-fbi-washington-field-office-adic; https://www.csis.org/analysis/escalating-terrorism-problem-united-states; https://news.yahoo.com/attack-on-us-capitol-was-the-beginning-of-an-american-insurgency-counterterrorism-experts-warn-100000381.html

[9] https://www.independent.co.uk/news/world/americas/us-politics/charles-koch-koch-brothers-trump-mess-b1722749.html

[10] Kroes, R. (June 2017). Signs of fascism rising: A European Americanist looks at recent political trends in the U.S. and Europe. *Society 54*(3), 218-225. https://www.researchgate.net/publication/318168117_Signs_of_Fascism_Rising_A_European_Americanist_Looks_at_Recent_Political_Trends_in_the_US_and_Europe

[11]https://www.cato.org/publications/public-opinion-brief/religious-trump-voters-how-faith-moderates-attitudes-about

Section 1
What Will Be the Future?

"It was the best of times, it was the worst of times, it was the age of wisdom, it was the age of foolishness, it was the epoch of belief, it was the epoch of incredulity, it was the season of Light, it was the season of Darkness, it was the spring of hope, it was the winter of despair, we had everything before us, we had nothing before us, we were all going direct to Heaven, we were all going direct the other way.

Charles Dickens
A Tale of Two Cities, 1859

*

There are two possible scenarios for our next half-century—our species will either come together or tear itself apart. Our biological makeup and social structures are completely compatible with either result. We have "bad angel" genes and institutions that propel us to greed, competition, aggression, and shortsighted decision-making. But we also have "better angel" genes that promote altruism, sharing, responsibility, and rational decision-making...The contingencies of history are often precariously balanced and very evenly matched, the results of the endgame uncertain and unpredictable.

Allen Frances, M.D.
Twilight of American Sanity, 2017

*

Blessed are the meek, for they shall inherit the earth.
Matthew 5:5

Minding and managing our own personal morality is important. Indeed—as so many of our faith traditions teach us—it is the foundation, the basic building block so to speak, of a good society. But simply working on ourselves so that we can be (or become) good people will not alone guarantee a good society. A truckload of solid bricks does not necessarily guarantee a sound structure. As we have seen herein, social institutions can take on a character of their own, independent of the people operating within them. Culture is something that all of us collectively co-create, whether consciously or not. In order that our efforts to build a good society be fruitful, we must first view ourselves as part of a larger whole and not as isolated individuals with interests totally independent of and disconnected from the collective.

There are modern techno-rational and religious/spiritual thinkers who—like Dr. Lobaszewsky in 1940s Poland— have discerned a connection between the individual dark side and macrosocial evil. Dr. Allen Frances is a medically-trained psychiatrist who served as lead advisor in the development of the Diagnostic and Statistical Manual. In *Twilight of American Sanity,* Dr Frances argues that the election of Donald Trump—"a mirror of the American soul"—is a symptom of a greater social sickness.[1] On the spiritual side, we have Dr. Dan Matthews. Dr. Matthews was trained as a chiropractor, but after he had a near death experience, he began incorporating revealed divine healing modalities in service of his patients, as well as speaking about healing and spiritual topics. He speaks of the current period of time (September 2015 through September 2021) as being the "exodus of a downfall world", and argues that Trump "became president for the purpose of being the catalyst to purge the downfall world."[2] So we have examples of both medical science and New Age spiritualism conveying the same message: Purging ourselves of Trump (or any individual bad guy/psychopath/fascist/dictator) will not resolve the underlying social pathologies that put him there. If such an antisocial individual can attain the pinnacle of success by appealing to our baser nature, then we have to find ways to control our baser natures—preferably without the imposition of authoritarianism.

In Steve Taylor's *The Fall* (which we covered in Part II, Section 1), he hopefully suggests that there is evidence of an emergent trans-Fall society. Taylor argues that the beginning of trans-Fall thinking and relationships can be found in the Hindu Upanishads, along with practices such as meditation, which were intended to re-connect humans with creation. Taylor argues that most people attempt to alleviate their inherent psychological discord by reducing the symptoms, which results in either chasing wealth and power or constant busyness and distraction.[3] He then discusses the teachings of Jesus—who Taylor describes as "trans-egoic (as was the Buddha)—proclaiming that "The Kingdom of Heaven is within you." Here we see the beginnings of moral teachings promoting "the kind of intense compassion which can only come through transcending the separate sense of self."[4] Thus, religious teachings had a major part to play in early efforts to override dominator culture and psychology.

According to Taylor, a "second wave" of trans-fall evolution occurred during the Enlightenment—a period of intellectual, philosophical, and scientific progress occurring roughly between the latter eighteenth through the nineteenth centuries:

> *For almost 6,000 years people—at least those in the fallen world—had taken slavery for granted. It was seen as inevitable, even ordained by the gods....In the same way, it has always been taken for granted that some human beings were born superior to others, and entitled to special rights and privileges. Members of the aristocracy saw peasants as little more than animals, and kings believed they had a divine right to rule over their subjects. But toward the end of the eighteenth century a new concept of democracy began to spread, based on the idea that all human beings were born equal and entitled to the same rights. And alongside this, there was a realization that if the great majority of people did not have the equal rights they were entitled to, it was because they were being oppressed by an unfair social system.*[5]

Enlightenment philosophy was based on reason, logic (including understanding of the world through scientific methodology and not religious mysticism), and challenge of authority, including religious authority. While the Enlightenment ushered in an era of unprecedented technological advancement as well as modern democracies, its technocratic dictates of efficiency and logic have also contributed to the phenomenon of human separation. In our modern era, we have seen the new concept of "meritocracy" and hierarchical bureaucratic systems (which operate to push many people behind) replace the divine right of kings and a self-justified "natural order" of superiority and inferiority. Thus, we see throughout history that both religion and technocratic rationality have at various times contributed to human advancement and prosocial cultures, or increased dominator culture and inter-group hostility. Which means that we are not going to solve our current crisis by choosing between either scientific logic or spiritual teachings/religion, but will need to identify and incorporate the helpful elements of both.

Biblical End Times

If you are the sort of person who subscribes to the concept of the end times, specifically the biblically described apocalypse, it is not difficult to presume that our current dysfunctional, socially degraded, rage-filled, and delusional global pandemic times aptly fit the prediction. On the other hand, the "end times" have been predicted so often throughout history that one wonders how anyone—religious or otherwise—could give such predictions credence. Human evil and fallibility—not to mention geophysical events like earthquakes, floods, fires, and even pandemics—have been around for millennia. So, as bad as things may seem to us now, such things are not new, and humanity has survived the same or worse.

The Jewish Essene sect believed the uprising against the Romans in the years 66-70 was the final end-time battle. This was followed by numerous declarations of end times by various Christian bishops, monks, and historians through the first Christian millennium. The turn of each millennium itself (the years 1000 and 2000)[6] saw increased predictions of end times, as did events such as the Black Death which spread across Europe from 1290 to 1335.

Pope Innocent III predicted the world would end 666 years after the rise of Islam (i.e., in the year 1284). In his 1501 *Book of Prophecies,* Christopher Columbus predicted that the world would end in 1658. With the secular developments of math and astronomy, new astrological and numerically-based predictions of the end times began to be promulgated

The number of end times predictions throughout the nineteenth and twentieth centuries are too numerous to cite here. Many of them involved the founding of Christian offshoot churches and sects, but these end-times predictions were not limited to Christians. The Muslim Louis Farrakhan believed the 1991 Gulf War was the sign of Armageddon. The secular astrologer Jean Dixon predicted mass destruction in conjunction with a planetary alignment on February 4, 1962 (many such predictions were associated with the appearance of comets, eclipses, blood moons, or other astrological phenomenon). A big one was based on the end of the Mayan calendar on December 21, 2012. Dixon is now predicting the end will come in 2020. (If you are reading this, the prophecy obviously didn't come to pass). Unfortunately, not all of these things were simply predictions that never came true and forgotten, but some of them ended human lives. Perhaps the most infamous of these is the mass murder-suicide of the People's Temple cult led by the "Reverend" Jim Jones in Jonestown, Guyana in 1978.

The big question is why people continue to believe in end times prophesies even when none of them have come true in the past. One theory is that religious people have a need to feel "special"—that they have been given knowledge that is not available to the rest of the world. Another explanation is that it is a psychological defense mechanism when the world is viewed as threatening, or perhaps a reaction in the face of unmanageable change. Thus, such beliefs tend to surge during periods of war, disease, and social upheavals. In the current pandemic, a group of evangelical scholars felt it was necessary to pronounce that these are ***not*** the end times and urge faith over fear.[7] Yet a third explanation is that people are enervated by despair at the magnitude of the evil around them. Because they believe they are powerless to change it, the idea that God will end it all for them presents a sick form of psychological or spiritual comfort.

Before we indulge in our own hypothetical future scenarios, we will return to our Abrahamic scriptures for a description of events signifying the apocalypse, or so-called end times. This is found in the Book of Revelation, the last book in the Bible. The events depicted herein were purportedly revealed to the disciple John as the "testimony of Jesus" revealed through an angel.[8] John was instructed by the angel not to "seal up the words of the prophesy of this book, for the time is near."[9] Most modern religious scholars say that the events described are allegorical or symbolic rather than literal, and that its purpose was to give hope to early Christians living under the threat of persecution by the Roman Empire. However, it is also easy to see how these allegorical descriptions can be broadly interpreted to apply to a variety of noteworthy events.

In this vision, God holds a book containing seven seals, and the message is that God's plan will not be executed until all of the seals are opened or revealed. The first four seals involve horses of various symbolic colors: a white horse ridden by Christ, a red horse signifying the persecution of followers of the gospel, a black horse signifying grief, a pale horse ridden by Death, signifying judgment against the world. The fifth seal signifies the souls of those slain for the word of God seeking vengeance. When the sixth seal is opened, there is a great earthquake, the sun is 'blackened," and the moon becomes "like blood." (Rev. Chapter 6). Four angels then appear to "seal" with a mark on the forehead the 144,000 saints, 12,000 from each of the 12 tribes of Israel (Rev. Chapter 7). When the seventh seal is opened, there is one-half hour of silence, followed by seven angels blowing seven trumpets, bringing all manner of death and destruction to the inhabitants of Earth (Rev. Chapter 8 to 11). There is reference to the "great whore and the beast" as well as to "Babylon," which many scholars believe is reference to a great imperial power in opposition to God (i.e., Rome).

In Rev. Chapters 12 to 20, John has a second vision, which revolves around a symbolic battle between Christ and Satan. These visions begin when seven angels pour out seven bowls of God's wrath. Babylon is destroyed, there is rejoicing in heaven, and a white horse again comes forth symbolizing the Word of God. An angel binds Satan with a "great chain" and throws him into a "bottomless pit," where Satan remains for a thousand years. When the thousand years have ended, Satan is released, where he again "deceives the nations at the four corners of the earth." The dead are released from Hades and are then "judged according to what they had done."[10] Chapter 21 describes a "new heaven," a "new earth," and a "new Jerusalem," where the temple has been replaced by the Lord God Almighty....and the city has no need of sun or moon to shine on it, for the glory of God is its light..." The Church itself is not mentioned at all in the description of the Tribulation, suggesting that it will be gone or removed beforehand.

Upon reading the violent and destructive language of both Old and New Testament prophecies, it is not difficult to see how these can be manipulated for ponerological purposes. As we have seen with end-times prophesies, there have also been fraudulent Messiahs: They can appear among Jews claiming to be the original, among Christians claiming to be the second coming of Christ, or among Muslims claiming to be the Madhi.[11] As we have also learned herein, such individuals—who are capable of tapping into the very deepest roots of believers' moral foundations and faith teachings—can foment all manner of evil acts, up to and including murder, political coup, genocide, and war.

Here we would like to give credit to Dr. Robert Leonhard in conjunction with the Johns Hopkins University. Dr. Leonhard is a retired Army Lieutenant Colonel, author of several war strategy books, creator of war games, and Bible teacher. In May of 2010, Dr. Leonhard prepared a comparative analysis of apocalyptic predictions for purposes of national security risk assessment.[12] Dr. Leonhard argues that U.S. foreign policy planning should take into account the end times philosophies among the various faith traditions because these apocalyptic predictions provide the reasoning which underlies so much of the conflict in the Middle East. As the book of Revelation attempted to address the existential concerns of the nascent Christian church vis à vis the Roman Empire, Dr. Leonhard looks at how the three Abrahamic religions interpret God's promise to "make you into a great nation." Although the focus of Dr. Leonhard's analysis is the origins of geopolitical turmoil in the Middle East rather than an analysis of scriptural prophesy, he argues that U.S. foreign policy planners need to understand the fundamental beliefs around end-times prophesy if they hope to be effective.

The sacred texts of the three Abrahamic faiths—Judaism, Christianity, and Islam—all describe a future "Golden Age," where there is literally peace on earth, prosperity for all, and the reign of righteousness and justice. For Jews, this Golden Age is ushered in by the as-yet-to-arrive Messiah. For Christians, the Golden Age arrives at the return of Christ. For Jews and Christians, this Golden Age will last a millennium, or a thousand years.[13] For Muslims, the Golden Age arrives with the Mahdi—the final and greatest Caliph—who will rule for only seven years before the final judgment. However, there is a split among believers of all faiths as to whether humanity brings about the Golden Age through its own efforts to bring peace on Earth or whether only God's intervention can do this. If God's intervention is necessary, the faith question then becomes what can believers do to hasten the arrival of the Golden Age.

According to Dr. Leonhard, Jewish eschatology was instrumental to the foundation of the State of Israel and the Zionist movement. This certainly contains the elements of the return of a scattered peoples to an ancestral homeland. Reformed Jews tend to believe that the purpose of Israel is not to restore the Jewish nation under a descendant of David, but rather to create a religious community unified under God. Thus, Jews are split between those who view the expansion of the Jewish state (a form of dominance and empire) as necessary to speed the arrival of the Anointed One, and those who object to the Jewish occupation of territories that do not belong to them.[14]

For Christians, there is a split in whether Christ will return before the Millennium or after it. That is, will Christ's return usher in the Golden Age, which will then be followed by the Final Judgment, or will Christ return after humans have somehow achieved the ideals of God's kingdom only to perform the Final Judgment. Premillennials believe that even if humans work toward the good, they will never be able to eradicate evil— possibly as a consequence of original sin—thus, only Jesus will be able to bring about the Golden Age. Conversely, postmillennials tend to be optimists who believe that humans—with the help of Christ working through the church—will gradually improve the world by eliminating wars, crime, poverty and disease. Thus, premillennials are more likely to subscribe to literal interpretations of the apocalyptic prophesies, tend to be members of more fundamentalist and orthodox denominations, and support authoritarian-style governance; while postmillennials are more likely to seek goals that benefit everyone as well as focus on the model of Christ as peacemaker.

Christianity evolved from a "despised and persecuted cult" after its merger with the Roman establishment, turning its "ambitions toward universal rule in the name of Christ." Dr. Leonhard suggests that "some Christians were ready and willing to support Roman repressive policies against Jews, motivated in part by the Gospel narratives that laid at least part of the blame for the crucifixion at the feet of the Jewish people, and in part by the need to mollify Rome."[15] Indeed, the notion of how the "righteous" will return to destroy the evil establishment has varying interpretations depending on whether the particular interpreter identifies with the "establishment" or views himself as a subject or victim of it.

Although the United States of America was nowhere near existence at the time of scriptural prophecies, Dr. Leonhard argues that American fundamentalist, premillennial worldviews have substituted it for the biblical "promised land." This image of America as a God-founded "shining city on a hill" has been reinforced by our cultural and political mythologies. The fundamentalist thus fears the loss of American sovereignty and views the threat of an international order the same as a Zionist views threats to Israeli territory. Christians themselves are split between the belief that Christians have replaced Jews as God's chosen people, and Christian Zionists who believe that Palestine must be returned to the Jews so that the end times can occur.

Islamic eschatology revolves around a Final Judgment in which Allah will split humanity into sinners (who will be punished) and the faithful (who will be blessed). Prior to the Final Judgment, al-Mahdi al-Muntadhar, the Anointed One (the Mahdi) will reign following a cataclysmic battle. Jesus too will return, in order to demonstrate to both Jews and Christians that they have erred, although they will not necessarily be punished. The Mahdi will be a descendant of Muhammad as well as share his name. Under Mahdi rule, there will be peace, justice and prosperity in the world.

Previously lost copies of the Torah and Gospels as well as the original Ark of the Covenant will be found and made available for all to see.

Some Muslims believe that the end-times will occur when the Mahdi sets up his headquarters in Jerusalem, following the conquest of Africa, Turkey, Syria and Lebanon. This brand of fundamentalist Islam views the liberation of Palestine as a key factor in the end times, and anticipates that it will be violent. This suggests that if the Palestinian government is legitimized among the majority of the world's nations, this may reduce some of the tensions around this specific conflict. However, many fundamentalists will continue to view themselves as victims of "repeated humiliation at the hand of the Byzantine West."[16]

Dr. Leonhard argues that, although Islam was subjected to disruptions, it did not experience anything at the scale of the Jewish Diaspora or the Christian wars of the 16th and 17th centuries. However, the Arab-Israeli War of 1967 was a "cataclysmic event" for Muslims. This is when we see a shift of Islam from a previously peaceful religion that co-existed with the state to "a system of thought that could accommodate perpetual warfare."[17] Like their counterpart Jews and Christians, Muslims who focus on eschatological teachings also believe that actions of the faithful can affect the timing of the apocalypse. However, like the majority of Jews and Christians, most mainstream Muslims focus on practical aspects of right living rather than a predicted apocalypse.

According to Dr. Leonhard, most moderate interpreters of Biblical prophesies do not believe they are intended to be taken literally, nor are they descriptions of either future events or the end times specifically (i.e., they are allegorical). However, fundamentalists of all faiths tend to believe that these are literal predictions, although there is no indication of when these events are supposed to happen.[18] Ironically, a serious threat to global peace may come from eschatological interpretations of the Abrahamic Covenant, or the fulfillment of God's promise that Abraham's descendants would become a "great nation" that would dominate the Earth. That is, although the individual religious prophets speak a gospel of peace and brotherhood, there is an inherent conflict in exactly who among Jews, Christians, and Muslims is intended to comprise God's promised "great nation" and what believers should be doing to achieve this.

Dr. Leonhard also makes that observation that, "believers in those nations, states, and religious groups that face foreign domination, marginalization, or failure tend toward a fundamentalist interpretation of prophecies…[Because] the status quo is neither acceptable nor likely to improve…the prospect of a dramatic, divine visitation is welcome."[19] Here, Dr. Leonhard corroborates the observations of Pankaj Mishra that fundamentalist radicalization is not so much the product of specific faith teachings as it is the interpretational choice of people who are left or pushed behind, subjected to domination, and rendered irrelevant and superfluous. Rather than condemning any particular faith, Leonhard argues that the more reasonable elements of all faiths adopt a "more moderate and optimistic way of interpreting prophecy."[20]

The Dangerous Combination of Authoritarianism and Social Dominance Orientation

This subject is covered in much greater depth and detail in *Why Assholes Rule the World,* but it merits a brief description here. Scholars became interested in the phenomenon of authoritarianism after World War II, as they attempted to understand the rise of dictators like Hitler and Stalin. Researchers identified a specific "authoritarian personality," which was characterized by submission to authority, uncritical acceptance of conventional beliefs, a lack of creativity, and a simplistic, black-and-white view of right and wrong. Authoritarianism is also characterized by a propensity to project one's own feelings of inadequacy upon a scapegoated "other," and calls for social control directed toward this "other." Moreover, research on outgroup intolerance suggests that authoritarianism is incompatible with the democratic values of individualism and difference, equal access to opportunity and power, balancing majoritarian decision-making against minority rights, and expectations of robust debate and challenges to those in power. Authoritarian tendencies tend to increase during periods when the existing social order is undergoing rapid change, particularly if one's own position in the social hierarchy is challenged (or perceived to be).

Behavioral researchers subsequently identified a related, but distinct personality they call Social Dominance Orientation, or SDO. Dr. Jim Sidanius of Harvard University and Dr. Felicia Pratto of the University of Connecticut have been the primary pioneers of SDO research. Social Dominance Orientation (SDO) theory was developed as a way to measure individual differences in the acceptance of hierarchical social relationships. High social dominance orientation (SDO) is associated with racism, ethnic prejudice, sexism, nationalism, cultural elitism, and meritocracy (rewards are appropriately distributed based on deservingness). SDO is also positively correlated with political conservatism and authoritarianism, and is negatively correlated with empathy, altruism and communality, even after controlling for gender differences.[21]

The degree of SDO within a society can be estimated by measuring how the society directs its resources. A society that directs more resources to military and law enforcement is likely to have higher average SDO scores (as well as more SDO individuals) than a society that directs more resources to education and human services. While both authoritarian and SDO individuals are more likely to be found on the political right,[22] there are some distinguishing features. Authoritarians may behave prosocially towards those within their own group, where an SDO is constantly in search of advantage and domination. Authoritarians are also likely to be motivated by some moral calculus (however misguided it may be) of right and wrong, while SDOs are motived almost exclusively by self-interest.

The biggest threat to social ponerization is the combination of SDO leaders and authoritarian followers. Bob Altemeyer, one of the better-known researchers on authoritarianism, conducted studies of authoritarian traits in connection with the Global Change Game. The Global Change Game is a sophisticated simulation of the earth's future over 40 years, a group exercise which was designed by Dr. Altemeyer's son to raise environmental awareness in high school students.[23] In this game, participants are randomly assigned to different regions on a world map and charged with solving world problems such as poverty, overpopulation, and environmental degradation. In a 1994 experiment, Dr. Altemeyer compared game outcomes where the participants scored high on right wing authoritarianism (RWA) versus a game where the participants scored low on RWA. The future world created by the low RWAs was relatively peaceful, although it was not immune from disease and starvation. Conversely, the game played by high RWA participants ended in nuclear war and human annihilation.

When Dr. Altemeyer heard about the research on SDO, he ran another set of experiments with the Global Change Game in 1998.[24] In the first test, the participants all had high scores for RWA, but low scores for SDO. The second test involved individuals who scored high on both RWA and SDO—all of them men. In the RWA-only game, the world did not devolve into war, but the individuals were unable to work outside their own group to solve bigger problems, and 1.9 billion people died of starvation and disease. In the RWA-SDO game, fewer people died (1.3 billion), although the game facilitators believed that nuclear war was imminent and did not occur only because the time for the game had run out. One behavioral difference that was noted was that in the RWA-only game, the participants stayed within their own groups to solve problems, while the RWA-SDOs were busy making deals with other elites. While the wheeling and dealing brought resources to their own regions, none of these partnerships ever became permanent, and—while actual war was only declared once—there was more frequent bullying and aggressive posturing.

The real danger of authoritarian-SDO combinations is that it opens the door to totalitarian dictatorship. As individuals, high RWA-SDOs are "among the most prejudiced persons in society. Furthermore, they seem to combine the worst elements of each kind of personality, being power-hungry, unsupportive of equality, manipulative, and amoral, as social dominators are in general, while also being religiously ethnocentric and dogmatic, as right-wing authoritarians tend to be."[25] The RWA-SDO dynamic begins when the SDO leader gains favor with authoritarian followers by exerting power over groups their followers fear, dislike or envy. There is little resistance when the low-status group is attacked, but the dictator-to-be almost always escalates the assertion of power over others. He convinces followers of the need to voluntarily surrender their own freedoms by presenting a false choice between totalitarianism or anarchy. Only too late do the authoritarian followers discover they have lost all power to challenge their now-dictator.

A Tale of Two Futures

We are now going to take an imaginary journey into the future. As with all such predictions, it is based on trends we are seeing now and patterns we have seen in the past, but it represents only one possibility among millions of potential probabilities. We will attempt to be realistic, although some may recognize themes that tend to recur in dystopian futuristic fiction as well as those that arose in research on authoritarianism.

In this imagined future, society will become so internally fractured that the nation-state as a political unit will be more or less obsolete. We base this premise on a pattern that began with the breakup of the former Soviet Union, the Brexit referendum, a proliferation of separatist movements around the globe (e.g., Kosovo's declaration of independence from Serbia in 2008), and approximately 40-50 identified separatist or secession movements here in the U.S., including extreme and violent white nationalism.[26] Indeed, as I am writing this, we are in the middle of an attempted coup by supporters of soon-to-be-former President Donald Trump. Some have even speculated that there is no longer a "United" States of America, with some pundits asserting that the United States today is simply too big and too diverse to govern effectively as a unified democracy.[27]

Also in this imagined future, the problems we are seeing today—particularly climate change, population growth, and resource depletion—will continue apace, further aggravating social and political unrest. Large numbers of people or territory will be essentially ungovernable, so political units will revolve around something more like city-states dominated by one major metropolitan area, or regional semi-states. There will be only one group who exercises control on a global scale, and that is corporate and wealthy elites. This group will also have control over the majority of organized armed forces (training, personnel and weapons) because it will be the only group who can afford to pay for it. However, the main interest of this group is in managing resources and preserving their own wealth, so they are at least tangentially interested in keeping things peaceful. They generally abstain from interference in local affairs and local rule, and do not threaten or use force unless they believe their own interests are threatened.

The primary cultural division between human beings may not necessarily be race, gender, or nationality (although these will still exist to some degree), but between those who dwell in global cities (what are now known as places like New York, Washington, D.C., Los Angeles, Tokyo, London, Paris, Singapore, etc.) and those who reside in the more scattered and less developed rest of the planet. Life in the cities will be more comfortable and "modern," as they will have more resources for education and technological development. Life in the outlying areas will be less materially comfortable and less technologically developed. People in these areas will generally be engaged in subsistence activities, small industry, or "Main Street," hometown providers of services like accountants, attorneys, physicians, and pharmacists. The folks who provide these professional services will earn less than their counterparts in the global cities, but they will feel more embedded in their communities.

The global governance structure will be run by a shifting and tenuous alliance between the major city-states and the corporatocracy. Problems such as global climate change and resource depletion will likely be addressed in an ad hoc, piecemeal manner, which may postpone, but not prevent, the inevitable. However, residents of the global cities will lead lives that are relatively comfortable, mainly because they expropriate what they need from the rest of the planet. It is very expensive to live in these places, and only those who have the proper identification are allowed in. However, many people seek entry and citizenship, because the global cities are perceived as a gateway to better opportunity and the good life. Because these places are nodes of power, wealth, opportunity, and control, they tend to attract psychopathic and characteropathic individuals.

As climate change renders the environment increasingly harsh, polluted, and unpredictable, the global cities begin a process of building climate-controlled domes around themselves—which obviously requires more resources from the rest of the planet. The global cities maintain control over huge agricultural, mining, and energy production operations located in other places to supply their material needs. Some of these facilities have similar domes and some do not, but all of them are secured by a military perimeter with restricted access. Most of the leaders in the global cities recognize, but do not publicly acknowledge, that the finite and dwindling supply of resources will eventually result in unmanageable conflict, but—in spite of huge amounts of data and state-of-the-art computing infrastructure—they have no way to accurately predict when or where.

The denizens of the global cities are, for the most part, highly educated. A few of them have knowledge of human history (which has been carefully crafted to justify the existing system), but most of them are financial and legal technocrats. Because these elites still have need for personal services, colonies of server-class persons are "allowed" to live within the domed cities, although they are required to live in inferior segregated areas. While there is no specific legally-sanctioned race-based segregation, most of the individuals living in the server-class colonies are different (racially, ethnically, linguistically) from the majority residents. Which, as we know from our understanding of "otherness," justifies their inferior status.

The cities are generally governed by a purportedly benevolent authoritarianism. So long as everyone keeps their place and obeys the rules, there is peace. However, everyone is required to carry an identification card with them at all times. These IDs contain varying restrictions where citizens can go (including the forms of transportation they are allowed to use), with those living in the server-class colonies having the most restrictions and those in the top leadership positions having no restrictions. There is ostensible "freedom of speech" in that people can generally say or write anything they want; however, access to an oligopoly of major communication systems is limited to "approved" content. These communication platforms are owned by wealthy private citizens, and so are not directly controlled by government. Rather, the owners of these and other oligopolistic industries are the ones who run the global government—deciding who is qualified to hold office and what policy issues are salient. In theory, dissent is allowed, but it has no access to means of broad-based dissemination.

Extraterritorial relationships primarily involve the other domed cities, where the leaders enter into agreements (and sometimes military confrontation) over resources located elsewhere. The cities co-exist with each other (and trade resources) through a constantly shifting series of negotiated agreements. Cities will align with other cities to acquire one form of resource, and then align against them to acquire something else. Occasionally, the cities will expand their external holdings by displacing the residents who live outside of them. It is easier (i.e., costs less in the form of material resources) to force the subsistence populations to abandon their communities than to confront another militarized outpost. While most city leaders do what they can to avoid a war with another city, most of them expect a major war to be inevitable. Although there is an uneasy peace, most of the cities take steps (e.g., appropriate resources) to be prepared for war.

The cultural division between those who live in the global cities and those who don't will be defined by ostensibly meritocratic terms such as the "elect" versus the "uncultured," although—like it is today—where one ends up in society will be mostly determined by where one starts out. It will also depend on whether one accepts the fundamental premises of the dominant social order. That is, there will be those who dwell outside the global cities because they have chosen to do so, in addition to those who have been involuntarily cast out.

Outside of the domed cities lives an underclass that populates what is left (i.e., not owned by the oligopolist farms and energy production facilities that serve the cities or unruined by environmental degradation) of small towns and rural areas. Many of these communities are comprised of indigenous populations or pre-existing religious communities such as the Amish, who continued to live in traditional ways as the rest of the world industrialized and developed. Other communities are comprised of what we would call hippies, new agers, or survivalists—individuals who once participated in modern lifestyles, but deliberately chose to live in a more simple, earth-friendly fashion or to be free from servitude to the corporate state. A third group is comprised of exiles from the cities—individuals who could not conform to the dictates of their assigned productive function or were otherwise perceived as a threat to the status quo. Because these individuals generally do not possess the self-provisioning and cooperative survival skills of the self-selected groups, they roam the land in search of whatever they can take.

Although cooperator-types and dominator-types both reside in the global cities and the "outlands," the cooperator-dominator conflict is more likely to be apparent in the outlands because the global cities are managed technocracies. Thus, there are those living in the outlands (especially those from traditional and earth-friendly cultures) who have figured out how to live cooperatively with each other and peacefully with their neighbors. However, there is small-scale violence in the outlands, as those who have been outcast from one of the cities, or whose livelihood is displaced by climate or other disruptions, find themselves rootless, frustrated, and desperate. Because they have not developed cooperative skills, they spend a large part of their lives either fighting each other or attempting to seize resources from the self-provisioning communities.

Like our world today, there are good ways and bad ways for this story to end. In one scenario, the outland communities are increasingly squeezed by the expansionary cities, raided by the marauding city outcasts, or surrendering ground to environmental exhaustion or ruin. In the best-case scenario, refugees from the outlands arrive at one of the cities and offer their services in exchange for protection and citizenship. They may find like-minded prosocials who have power and authority within the system and to whom they can successfully preach the gospel of cooperative behavior as the key to survival. But this may be difficult to do, since the mindset in the cities is a rationalized, technocratic, and possibly Machiavellian ethos of looking out for oneself and mistrust of everyone else. As the domed cities themselves run out of places to acquire more resources, they turn on each other. In the end, it becomes the proverbial war of all against all.

In an alternative future, people both within and without the global cities make the decision to build intentional communities that are self-sustaining. These communities will look and operate differently, but they will generally be based on a concept of individual and collective self-provisioning that is do-able by people of modest means. In the outland areas, for example, people will have a garden in their own back yard as well as participate in a larger community farm, which can produce food to be sold outside the community. Individuals in the cities may form work cooperatives, where they share space, knowledge, and other resources. In both places, individuals may have a rooftop solar panel, but also be connected to a sustainable energy electric cooperative. In this way, individuals in the cities develop cooperative skills and communitarian worldviews, and they may then ascend to positions where they can exercise power on a global scale. In the outland areas, individuals develop skills and build resources for the community; establishing small, cooperatively-owned manufacturing facilities, which further strengthens their economic viability.

These new communities are deliberately designed to be of human scale—that is, people can easily get to their places of work, worship, education (which is continuous over one's lifetime), and recreation without need of an automobile. They are governed as pure democracies, in that every resident has a voice in decisions that affect the community. People maintain individual control over their own small private domain, while having an equal voice in the collective governance and production activities. Everyone contributes and everyone shares. People look out for each other, celebrate with each other, mourn with each other. While unique talents and skills are recognized and appreciated, no one is considered superior or inferior to another in a general sense. Anti-social behavior is rare, and when it does occur, it is humanely discouraged.

Gradually, more of these communities take root. As they gain viability, they find ways to connect with each other (internet, joint town halls, resurrected rail and bus lines) to share expertise and ideas, as well as to trade goods and services. True alliances (which are not based solely on instrumental practicality) are forged between a few of the global cities and portions of the outlands. At some point, a collection of these communities becomes a regional presence. As the success and sustainability of these communities becomes more obvious, the cooperative model spreads. In essence, people build a new way of living from the ground up— rather than directly confront (or attempt to overthrow) a corrupted system—which other good and decent people then self-select into.

So, which of these scenarios is more likely? The answer is that anyone's guess is as good as anyone else's guess. However, looking at the way things are going today (in early 2021), the first scenario seems more likely.

Notes

[1] Frances, A. (2017). *Twilight of American sanity: A psychiatrist analyzes the age of Trump.* New York, NY: Harper Collins Publishers.

[2] As reported in interview with *The Edge,* May 2019.

[3] Taylor obviously favors the Buddhist teachings on how to address human suffering. However, he does not reconcile the caste system with his own characterization of the "fallen" manifestations of patriarchy and inequality.

[4] Taylor, S. (2005). *The fall: The insanity of the ego in human history and the dawning of a new era.* New York, NY: O-Books/John Hunt Publishing, Ltd. at p. 271.

[5] Taylor, *supra* at p. 282-283.

---

[6] The first millennium was a popular end times date of Christian Popes. A quatrain from the astrologer-physician Nostradmus (1503-1566) is said to have predicted the end of the world in July of 1999.

[7] https://www.foxnews.com/us/coronavirus-end-times-revelation-christian-scholars

[8] Rev. 1: 1-2.

[9] Rev: 22: 10.

[10] Rev. Chapter 20.

[11] Al-Mahdi al-Muntadhar, or the Awaited One.

[12] Leonhard, R. (2010, May). Visions of Apocalypse: What Jews, Christians, and Muslims believe about the end times, and how those beliefs affect our world. The Johns Hopkins University Applied Physics Laboratory. https://www.jhuapl.edu/Content/documents/ApocalypseVision.pdf

[13] Revelation 20: 6.

[14] Dr. Leonhard's paper has a much fuller discussion of the differences between various Jewish religious groups as well as the various Israeli political parties.

[15] Leonhard, *supra* at p. 91.

[16] *Id.* at p. 120.

[17] *Id.* at p. 104.

[18] Jesus tells his apostles that "this generation will not pass away until all these things have taken place." Matthew 24: 34, suggesting the signs of the end of the age were coming in the near future, yet, "But about that day and hour no one knows, neither the angels of heaven, nor the Son (Jesus himself), but only the Father (God)." Matthew 24: 36.

[19] Leonhard, *supra* at p. 122.

[20] *Id.* at p. 122.

---

[21] Pratto, F., Sidanius, J., Sallworth, L.M., & Malle, B. (1994). Social dominance orientation: A personality variable predicting social and political attitudes. *Journal of Personality and Social Psychology 67*(4), 741-763, at p. 752.

[22] Benjamin, A.J., Jr. (2014). Chasing the elusive left-wing authoritarian: An examination of Altemeyer's right-wing authoritarians and left-wing authoritarianism scales. *National Social Science Journal, 43*(1), 7-13.

[23] Altemeyer, B. (2003). What happens when authoritarians inherit the earth? A simulation. *Analysis of Social Issues and Public Policy, 3*(1), 161-169. https://www.researchgate.net/publication/227524227_What_Happen_Happens_When_Authoritarians_Inherit_the_Earth_A_Simulation

[24] *Id.*

[25] Altemeyer, B. (2004). Highly dominating, highly authoritarian personalities. *The Journal of Social Psychology, 144*(4), 421-448. Also available online at https://www.tandfonline.com/action/showCitFormats?doi=10.3200%2FSOCP.144.4.421-448

[26] Many of these extreme white nationalist groups (e.g., the American Nazi Party, the Aryan Brotherhood, Patriot Front, as well as the newer Proud Boys and Atomwaffen and the older Ku Klux Klan) have begun to merge into larger organizations that are better able to spread their malevolent ideology. Some of these groups have been identified by the FBI and other counterterrorism agencies as internal terrorist threats.

[27] *National Review.* (May 14, 2018). Of course America's too big to govern. https://www.nationalreview.com/2018/05/america-too-big-to-govern-needs-federalism/Independent Institute. (October 31, 2016). Is America too big to be free? https://www.independent.org/news/article.asp?id=8911 *New York Magazine (November 14, 2018). Maybe it's time for America to split up.* https://nymag.com/intelligencer/2018/11/maybe-its-time-for-america-to-split-up.html. *The New Republic* (September 1, 2020). Could the United States break up? https://newrepublic.com/article/159172/united-states-break-up

Section 2
What Are We to Do?

...we have to be willing to travel without knowing where we are going. We need faith to do what seems right without being sure of the effect that it will have...we have to move away from how social life is organized now and toward the certainty that alternatives are possible, even if we have no clear idea of what those are, or have never experienced them ourselves.

Allan G. Johnson[1]

*

Optimism is a political act. Those who benefit from the status quo are perfectly happy for us to think nothing is going to get any better. In fact, these days, cynicism is obedience.

Alex Steffen[2]

*

It is a remarkable paradox that, at the pinnacle of human material and technical achievement, we find ourselves anxiety-ridden, prone to depression, worried about how others see us, unsure of our friendships, driven to consume and with little or no community life...
We talk as if our lives were a constant battle for psychological survival, struggling against stress and emotional exhaustion, but the truth is that the luxury and extravagance of our lives is so great that it threatens the planet.

Richard Wilkinson & Kate Pickett[3]

*

Do nothing from selfish ambition or conceit, but in humility regard others as better than yourselves. Look not to your own interests, but to the interests of others.

Philippians 2: 3-4

*

"The survival of the species now depends on the development of an environment of hope.
We must contain the rage within us. . . .
We must reverse the process of frustration and despair.
We must no longer tolerate the gradual erosion of the public space, the diminution of our self-pride and the deterioration of mutual relationships of trust."

Willard Gaylin
The Rage Within

It is almost obligatory when presenting an analysis of a problem that one concludes on a hopeful note with proposed solutions. So, I will propose some suggestions, with the caveat that these are not presented as absolute solutions. First, I do not possess the necessary hubris to think that I—or any single individual, no matter how learned, sincere, or moral—have all the right answers. Second, is the very real concern whether there is a sufficient critical mass of humanity who actually gives a flying freak about what happens to everyone else, so long as their own needs are met. That is, how many of us actually care about the collective "we," and will it be enough? This does not even factor in the group of folks who are actively anticipating the end of humanity, either as a form of religious reckoning or driven by pessimism and despair.

In this final section we first ask the necessary question: what will be our future? Even assuming our individual better natures prevail within the majority of us, if antisocial personalities are in charge of our institutions and defining our reality (Lobaszewsky's pathocrats), the outcome could be catastrophic. We can easily imagine a world governed by a greed-is-good, everyone-for-himself dominator ethos as the definition of success, because in some sense we are already living in it. The culmination of such a world is an inevitable war of all against all, with its potential annihilation of humanity and destruction of a habitable planet.

We have seen that most of us operate along a continuum of prosocial and antisocial behavior. We have also seen that our own individual propensities can be affected by an immediate situation or our cultural environment. Since we obviously can do little to change basic human nature, the challenge for us, therefore, is to design social systems (governments, economies, etc.) that operate to encourage our better angels and not our evil (or antisocial) propensities. Our religious and faith traditions typically are designed to do this, but they can serve to divide people into the us-versus-them dichotomy of believers and nonbelievers. Rationalized technocracy (or bureaucracy) was introduced to solve the problem of fallible human judgment and inefficiency, but it, too has been found to have undesirable dehumanizing effects on behavior. So, in our final section we will look at some practical suggestions on how we can begin to construct a good society.

We have learned how both competitive and cooperative behavior had survival value for early human communities. We have also learned how we are hard-wired to divide the world into "us" (which encourages cooperation) and "them" (which encourages competition). Research in neuroscience has provided us evidence that propensity to anti-social behavior may be hereditary as well as environmentally induced—with most of us falling along a continuum, where our propensity to behave either pro-socially or anti-socially may be triggered by specific environments or situations. This is compounded by variations in the ability to self-regulate, which is also partially genetically determined. What this means is that simply telling people to "behave," even when it is backed by laws, ethical codes, or scriptural mandates, is not going to work for everyone.

We have seen how moral philosophies, ethical codes and religion have developed, primarily with the intent to promote prosocial behavior. However, these well-intentioned belief-systems-coupled-with-behavioral-rules aimed to encourage our better natures can also serve to divide us. Our moral zealotry may result in our viewing the "other" as an existential threat, or even as evil. Thus, it seems like all of us carry within us the capacity (triggered by circumstance) to be our neighbor's savior, an avenging angel, or a murderous brute. As the old saying goes, one person's terrorist is another person's freedom fighter.

As complex as our behavior is at the individual level, it becomes even more so when we live and behave in groups. While early hunter-gathering tribes developed behavioral strategies to manage the necessities of physical survival, the modern human who inhabits today's impersonal and technocratic society is more likely to be concerned with psychic survival. Many of us must learn to get along with people who are not members of our tribe. Indeed, there is now a major worldview rift between persons who live in small, rural communities (where most everyone is like them, and they generally encounter only people they know) and those who live in large, urbanized areas (where they are likely to run into a complete stranger nearly every day). That is, it is increasingly more difficult to even agree on the rules about how we are to live with each other and resolve our differences civilly.

Yet, in spite of the diversity and complexity of the modern world, most of the people we run across in our day-to-day lives are decent: A neighbor who helps with yard and housework when we are ill or injured, the folks at church who bring food and comfort when we have lost a loved one, a co-worker who covers a shift when we have to deal with a family emergency, a driver who stops and lets other drivers enter a roadway or make a turn in heavy traffic, the good Samaritan at the grocery store who steps up and pays the balance when the shopper in front of them is short on money. Most of the time, these acts of kindness involve one of "us," but many times they cross the lines of race, religion, and other ways we define ourselves as different.

For all these small acts of kindness and decency, we may often feel like the world is going to hell in a handbasket. While good people are all around us, the worst of humanity seems to have the upper hand—they occupy positions of power—not just political power, but possession of the majority of the world's resources—along with the influence to define our collective reality. Dr.

Lobaszewsky's ponerization theory seems to be on full display in early 21st century America. A similar phenomenon was addressed in *Why Assholes Rule the World,*[4] which developed a model of how antisocial behaviors such as dominance, narcissism, and entitlement combined with hierarchical power structures actually serve such individuals in attaining positions of power. In a feedback loop similar to Lobaszewsky's ponerization process, once such individuals attain positions of power and privilege, they are able to exert a disproportionate effect on society by serving as role models, rewriting the rules (or abandoning rules altogether), and infecting the culture.

The Possibility of Hope

As the world seems to become less predictable, our own survival becomes ever more tenuous, and the "bad guys" (sociopaths and pathocrats) gain wealth, power, and privilege—along with greater ability to impact present and future events—our faith in a benevolent, God-promised future is shaken. During troubled times such as these, Christians throughout the ages have taken comfort in the promises contained in the New Testament: Jesus' promise that the "meek shall inherit the earth" suggests that evil will not prevail forever. That is, we can look forward to a future (even if it is long after we ourselves are gone from this present lifetime) when the earth will be managed by people who appropriately care for it and each other—the way God intended.

In our language today, meekness is tantamount to weakness. That is, a meek person is one who submits his or her own will to the will of another. We can presume that in the Bible, this was intended to refer to the will of God and not the dictates of whatever malignant pathocrat happens to be in charge. Obviously, the Bible has been translated across many languages over many centuries, so there might be a different interpretation. What exactly does the word "meek" mean? There are Biblical references to meekness also found in Psalm 37:11. Biblical persons who were considered meek include the heroic and strong personalities of Abraham, David, Moses, and Jesus, so Biblical meekness does not refer to someone who will simply go along to get along. Linguistically, the Hebrew origin of the word is anav, or humble. In the Bible, characteristics of meekness include patience, slowness to anger, not "fretting" when evil prevails, and poverty (either material or "in spirit"). Some translators have described meekness as "strength under control." That is, a meek person is anything but weak, but uses his or her strength in service to God and not in service to self. Perhaps the best single-word definition is humility.

Most of us can agree that the people who are in charge of things today—everyone from Donald Trump to the U.S. Congress to corporate CEOs who command wealth and resources that rival many smaller nation states—are anything but humble. This is aggravated by a culture that idolizes greed and self-promotion. The masters-of-the-universe have captured the conversation about what it means to be a "winner." In this manner, they attempt to convince all the rest of us that the only way to be successful or to get what we want from life is to become like them. However, many of us do not want to see a dog-eat-dog, winner-take-all, everyone-for-himself world, even if that means we are labeled as "losers." It is not just human beings who are being used up and thrown out, but the earth itself is subject to the same destructive forces. For many of us, the question is not so much who is going to win and who is going to lose, but whether or not there will be anything left for anyone—meek or otherwise—to inherit.

It is not beyond imagination to foresee a future in which we pass a tipping point where—instead of merely elevating antisocial individuals to positions of power as we seem to be doing today—one actually has to become sociopathic simply to survive in the corrupted culture. Like Lobaczewsky's pathocrats, those in positions of power view anyone who challenges their winner-take-all everyone-for-himself ethos as an intolerable existential threat. Thus, those who advocate for a more compassionate worldview and adopt humble lifestyles are labeled as deviants (tree-huggers, socialists, etc.) and marginalized. Young people growing up in such an environment may know of no other way of life. Eventually, the elders—who remember what it was like in a more "normal" society—themselves die off.

Staid and stuffy academia is now turning its analytic attention to the phenomenon of asshole behavior. Academic contributors to the theory of assholes[5] (a subset of sociopathic behaviors) themselves have differing predictions. Sutton[6] argues that an asshole's rise to the top is inevitably a short-term phenomenon. This is because an asshole rises to power through superficial support (people ally themselves with the asshole to gain something for themselves rather than genuine loyalty), or on the backs of others, thereby accumulating a list of enemies who are biding their time for revenge. This scenario presumes that there are prosocial persons working in opposition who have either sufficient numbers or sufficient power to challenge the assholes.

Conversely, James[7] argues that assholes assume that there will always be a sufficient number of cooperative others willing to subsume their own self-interest to the goals of collective survival. This fallacy allows assholes the comfort of believing that their actions will not lead to social collapse, because someone else will be able and willing to pick up the pieces and fix things. However, when the asshole population reaches a tipping point, cooperative people may decide their choices are to either join the assholes or withdraw. "Joining" the assholes takes on increasing utility as the payoff becomes greater. This is aggravated by winner-take-all markets and a popular media that glamorizes the lifestyles of the rich and famous (as well as sensationalizing their asshole behavior). Consequently, the non-asshole population increasingly withdraws from cooperative civic life, because keeping the assholes in check will simply become too exhausting.

Lobaszewsky also asserts that the rule of pathocrats cannot last forever: "The achievement of absolute domination by pathocrats in the government of a country cannot be permanent since large sectors of the society become disaffected by such rule and eventually find some way of toppling it."[8] According to Lobaszewsky, once people get over the "initial shock" of an established pathocracy, they eventually develop a form of psychological immunization and slowly start to rebuild social bonds and reciprocal trust.[9] Although Lobaszewsky also warns of the likelihood of good, or "normal" people withdrawing, he seems to view pathocracy as a cyclical phenomenon, rather than a permanent end state.

The good news from research is that the model of *homo economicus,* or the theory that all behavior is based on self-interest, is incomplete. There is a significant number of people who are prosocial, or altruistic. Moreover, research supports the benefits of having a prosocial person in charge. For example, a study of grocery store employees found that those who had agreeable leaders perceived their workplace to be more fair, just, and ethical,[10] which has positive implications for workplace engagement and morale. Moreover, the negative interpersonal consequences of power can be eliminated or reversed when powerholders are prosocially-oriented[11] and/or possess a higher moral identity (i.e., they are less likely to engage in actions that benefit the self at the expense of others because moral values are central to their self-concept).[12]

Follow-up research to the Milgram experiments (Part II, Section 4) also offers us a basis for optimism. In several variants of Burger's reproduction of Milgram's electroshock experiment, there were suggestions of ways to thwart blind obedience. In one scenario, two experimenters of equal status could not agree on the level of shock to give, so no shocks were given past the point of disagreement. This suggests that the fomentation of disagreement among individuals in charge can lead to indecision, thus circumventing evil dictates. In another scenario, two of the "teachers" were actually accomplices. As instructed, these accomplices refused to obey orders beyond a certain shock level, and 36 of the 40 "real" participants joined them in disobedience. So, if we find ourselves caught in an oppressive system, resistance may ***not*** be futile. Indeed, it may even be necessary, since all it may take is a handful of dissenters to break the bonds of obedience to a corrupted culture and inhumane orders.

One interesting study suggests the possibility of a truly altruistic personality[13]—in essence, an anti-psychopath. As you may recall from Part II, Section One, individuals who seek status (rather than dominance) may engage in prosocial behavior because it enhances their reputation within the group. Prior explanations for prosocial behavior fell into two camps: sincere altruism[14] (i.e., unconditional generosity) and strategic altruism[15] (generosity calculated to earn the approval of peers). Additional research divided people into the underlying motivations of egoist (who seek to maximize their own gain), competitors (who seek to maximize their relative advantage over others), and prosocials (who seek to maximize joint gain and equality of outcomes between themselves and others).

Respondents in this study were asked about their charitable giving as well as their desires for status and approval. The researchers controlled for variables such as gender, race, age, income, education and even the strength of religious beliefs. They also surveyed users of Freecycle, an online platform that facilitates the exchange of "free" goods, where direct reciprocity is not allowed (so it is not a "barter" agent). The Freecycle platform was chosen because a lot of people use it and most of the giving is anonymous. The researchers found that individuals who donated more to charity as well as those who gave more items to the Freecycle community scored lower on desire for status. Conversely, individuals who took more items through Freecycle reported a greater desire for social status. So, although some people may "do good" for social approval or other reasons of self-interest, there is also a significant cohort of persons who are sincerely motivated to help others with no ulterior motive of status-seeking or social impression management.

Finally, we have the promise from scripture that the "meek" shall inherit the earth. While what this means as a practical matter—as well as who exactly are the "meek"—is subject to interpretation, it is probably safe to assume that the Earth's Creator did not intend for its inheritors to be either assholes or pathocrats. Perhaps the biggest practical concern is whether or not there will be anything left of Earth to inherit. In the past, ruling dictators/pathocrats may have killed individuals and made life unpleasant for the masses, but they did not possess the wherewithal to destroy the world. In 2021, we are confronted by a multitude of potentially destructive events that could not only destroy most of organic life, but even the Earth itself: global climate change, nuclear and biological warfare, the destruction of ecosystems, and a finite food and water supply that must support an exponentially growing and desperate population.

We return to the concept of free will, a concept which, "after 2,500 years of sustained study, we still don't know how free will arises, whether it is a biological or psychological phenomenon, whether it can be explained in terms of physical laws, or whether it is irreducibly mysterious…[yet the concept of free will] allows us to be blamed, judged, and punished."[16] Scott Peck argues that any exertion of power over us negates our free will—whether that force be imposed by another human, by a situation or environment, or even by God himself. Thus, in order to permit humanity the ability to exercise free will, God has deliberately forsaken the use of force to "punish" humanity, but rather has "painfully and terribly chosen never to use it," voluntarily rendering Himself "impotent to prevent the atrocities we commit upon one another."[17]

The spiritual dilemma here is that, as some faithful believe, if God is ultimately in control, the bad guys are not going to win in the long run, and all the rest of us have to do is pray and wait for God to stop them. Alternatively (the cynical view) God has given us free will, thus we are free to destroy ourselves (the Earth and each other) and God—who is limited by neither space nor time—will simply send this failed experiment back to the cosmic drawing board. In such a scenario, the theological question then becomes whether the good people actually inherit what is left of the Earth or are assimilated into the "Kingdom of God," or heaven.

Christians who pride themselves on faith assert that God would not leave us with the hollow promise of a scorched and ruined Earth. In the extreme version of this worldview, good people do not have to do anything (except perhaps to pray) because God—via some as-yet-undetermined *deus ex machina*—will insure the Earth's survival. Some of us may not have the faith—or the patience—to wait for God. Others of us believe God intends that we prove our worthiness to inherit by good stewardship of creation. If we fail to stop the destruction of Earth and every living thing upon it, then God will be spared the necessity of punishing us for it. Yet, those of us who believe we are at least partly responsible for the welfare of creation find it difficult to see how we can change the current course on which we seem to be headed.

Thus we are faced with both a practical and a spiritual, or philosophical question. The biggest practical question is what, exactly, are we to do about preventing sociopaths and pathocrats from destroying civil society and maybe even all life as we know it? For believers of all religious denominations, the big question is to what extent those of us who care about the welfare of earth and other beings are supposed to "turn the other cheek" when the powerful seize, corrupt, exploit and destroy creation while we wait for God to step in and fix things, and to what extent are we supposed to actively resist. Even non-believers struggle with the question of when to acquiesce and/or ignore and when to confront macrosocial evil.

In a world ruled by pathocrats, what, realistically, ***can*** any of the rest of us do? We may have immediate concerns for survival or more tangential concerns for our sanity and/or our humanity. We may be either ignorant of the operation of social power structures or discouraged by our own lowly place in it, doubting our ability to make a significant difference. Some may engage in symbolic acts of resistance, while others may segregate themselves into cooperative communities on the fringes of society or even isolation. When pathocrats rule, how do the rest of us restore and establish a decent society? In more succinct terms, is there any hope?

Some Practical Suggestions

Lobaszewsky's own prescription for recovering from pathocracy is to (1) promote the truth, because it is the ultimate healer, (2) forgiveness, (3) the avoidance of oversimplifying ideologies, especially those that distort reality, and (4) building "psychological immunity" among the population, which he describes as an understanding of our own mental functioning. Lobaszewsky further argues that Nuremberg-style trials of legal retribution are insufficient if they focus solely on the acts of individual "war criminals" without also thoroughly exposing the psychopathology of the system.

Lobaczewsky also warns against taking a moralizing position to combat ponerizing influences, as opposed to a scientific (or rational) one. The reason is that an extension of pathological egoism is paramoralism, or moralization to such an extreme that it circumvents common sense, "sometimes leading to acceptance or approval of behavior that is openly pathological."[18] Lobaszewsky thus describes a phenomenon similar to Professor Haidt's description of "blind" morality that we covered in Part II, Section 2. Under the wrong influence, this egoistic hyper-moralization can lead to thought-terrorization, in which a "pathologically hypersensitive censor lives within the citizens themselves."[19] This eliminates much of the need for more traditional forms of externally imposed censorship, which tends to serve dictators and pathocracies.

Identify and Screen for Prosocial and Antisocial Personalities. Behavioral research has suggested ways that we can identify prosocial and antisocial personality traits. This research thus suggests a radically simple solution to pathocracy: Select leaders who are prosocial. Yet there are obvious logistical problems with this. Paradoxically, the people who most of us would likely want to lead us are the least likely to seek out positions of power. We complain of this often in our lack of real political choices, as the good people who truly desire to serve either do not have the resources to wage a winning campaign or, once elected, they become disaffected with (or corrupted by) the system.

James Perry, our professor at the School of Public and Environmental Affairs at Indiana University is the founder of Public Service Motivation (PSM) theory, which we discussed in the Introduction. As PSM research expanded, it explored ways to help public servants overcome the limitations of technocratic bureaucracies by seeing their role in a larger social enterprise. After some three decades of research on PSM, Perry and others have come up with practical suggestions for attracting, selecting, and retaining pro-social individuals to public service:[20]

- Screen for value-congruence the same way you screen for knowledge, skills and abilities.
- Project an organizational image (both generally and in the recruiting process) emphasizing organization mission and values, particularly that the organization values PSM.

- Develop procedures to screen in candidates with PSM and screen out candidates that are primarily motivated by self-interest. At least one study found that offering a lower wage can be effective for this purpose,[21] which also makes this a logical strategy in an environment of fiscal austerity.

- Develop onboarding, orientation, and mentoring programs that are designed to create a stronger public service ethos.

- Create a supportive work environment that nurtures PSM. Some research has suggested that daily stress and strain can undermine PSM and employee engagement.[22]

- Leverage relationships between employees and service beneficiaries or constituents so employees can directly connect with how their work benefits others. "Public work, work that makes things of value and importance in cooperation with others is the taproot of American democracy. Linking everyday work to democracy gives work larger meaning and makes citizenship serious."[23]

- Develop and promote leaders who can articulate the organization's mission and vision, and who can communicate and model PSM values.

Another practical implication affects how our leaders are selected. This goes beyond how we decide who to vote for, but implicates the process by which our political candidates are presented to us for selection. Many people believe that most politicians are corrupt. However, even if this is true, the question then becomes whether it is the choice of a political career that determines corruption, or the nature of politicians themselves. It would seem that the choice of a career in public service (where salaries tend to be lower for professional and managerial positions) would indicate a pro-social orientation. It also seems that politicians come with a wide range of personality traits. We can probably surmise that some people enter politics for selfish (possibly positioning themselves for a high-paid job in the private sector) or narcissistic purposes, while others choose politics because they genuinely want to make a difference. Yet, even prosocially motivated political wanna-bes may become corrupted after they have occupied positions of power for some period of time

Rather than blaming the nature of "politics" or of specific individuals, Paul Piff's research (Part II, Section 3) suggests that what makes politicians corrupt is their place among the privileged in society. Indeed, some modicum of this privilege may even be necessary in order for someone to achieve a prominent place in national politics. It is extremely difficult for anyone without either substantial personal wealth and/or connections with elite networks to even entertain the possibility of becoming a President, Senator, Cabinet Secretary, or Supreme Court Justice. Perhaps a system that screens out all but the wealthy and privileged to occupy the highest positions of power is the basis of corruption rather than "politics" more generally. Again, we cannot judge individuals until we have given the same level of scrutiny to the system.

While we may have some choice in electing our public leaders, we often have little or no choice in selecting our work bosses. Even in those situations where we do have a choice, how do we know who is "prosocial" and who is not? As a practical matter, we may not be able to require every candidate running for office to submit to Professor Perry's PSM test. On top of this, people are more likely to rate themselves as being morally superior or more prosocial than others.[24] It also does not address the situation in which people knowingly choose a psychopath to lead them, which is likely to happen in a ponerized society.

Build Inclusive Forums for Public Discussion and Decision-Making. Fortunately, we are seeing innovation in this area, mainly at the level of local governments. Perhaps my next book will be about the resurrection of town halls, "designing our future" and other exercises designed to encourage public engagement in civic affairs. The public administration community is also promoting ways to encourage citizen participation in public budgeting, although there is still a long way to go in this.[25] The idea is that there will be more "buy-in" from citizens if they feel they have had an opportunity to be heard and participate in the decision. This is balanced by the practical considerations that public inclusion requires more time and resources to identify stakeholders and educate them about the issues so that their participation is meaningful. Which is made even more difficult when working people are already overworked, exhausted and stressed, and the government entity itself is struggling with understaffing and underfunding.

Diversity and inclusion are more than just ways to make governance "look like" your citizens or give the appearance of fairness. Getting multiple points of view allows everyone to examine problems in a broader perspective, as well as avoids the danger of groupthink (which can lead to pathocracy). Here too, well-intentioned programs can present logistical land mines, and we are still learning about what works and what doesn't.[26] Like all inclusive and democratic processes, these will likely be slower and less efficient than the more traditional top-down, command and control systems we are accustomed to. As necessary as these exercises may be, none of it will be easy in an era characterized by constrained resources and high levels of public distrust and cynicism.

Perhaps the most obvious route to increasing democracy is to make voting easier for all citizens. Here we have seen progress in the form of expanded early voting and absentee ballots in most states, but we have also seen efforts to effectively disenfranchise certain groups of people by means of strict voter ID legislation, district gerrymandering and other forms of protecting incumbents against popular challenge. This may be easier to address because voter participation is something that is relatively easy to measure (as opposed to a more amorphous "engagement"). We will never be able to build a sense of community if too many people disconnect from this most basic form of civic engagement.

My last proposal on this topic is to make the following information easily accessible to the public, preferably in searchable, online format:

- The source of all campaign donations over a certain amount for all candidates for public office.

- The sources of ***primary*** financing for groups engaged in political activity. This is not so much about tracing every small donor, but to expose so-called "astroturf" organizations who purport to be on the side of the "people," but are actually funded by wealthy individuals and corporations. The dark money needs to be exposed to sunshine.

- A list of visitors to every federal and state member of congress, including identification of their employers and/or lobbying firm. This will allow voters to know who has the legislator's ear.

- A list of proponents and opponents of legislative bills and proposed agency rules.

Minimize or Dismantle Hierarchical Power Structures. Another proven way we can reduce antisocial behavior is to design our organizations and institutions to be less hierarchical and more democratic. Research has shown that a democratic leadership style is more effective: the group is more cooperative, constructive, cohesive, and stable. Individuals are less apathetic and aggressive than when leaders use a more autocratic style.[27] Moreover, new theories of leadership make the argument against dividing social groups into "leaders" and "followers," instead proposing that followers should not view themselves as passive recipients of the leader's orders, but collaborators in a common objective.[28] Flatter hierarchies generally reduce "us versus them" divisions and hostilities, but for this strategy to work, there must be an explicit objective to reduce power distance. However, as we have seen, getting anyone to give up power (particularly sociopaths and psychopaths who crave it) can be problematic.

Develop Prosocial Cultural Norms. Another way we might be able to influence the behavior of those in charge is through the establishment of cultural norms that encourage prosocial behavior. Some of us may recall an older concept of *noblesse oblige.* This is the notion that those who occupy positions of power or status (whether through birth or appointment), were expected to be socially responsible and generous toward those lower in the hierarchy (i.e., exhibit behavior fitting a "gentleman.").[29] Power expectations research has shown that when people expect the powerful to behave more politely or more rudely, a person's behavior will be affected accordingly.[30] That is, people behave in a manner consistent with cognitive role constructs (Zimbardo's Stanford prison experiment is an example).

As a society, we can define prosocial role models for occupations of power. Alternatively, we can punish leaders who violate prosocial norms. Studies of small-scale egalitarianism suggest that the behavior of social dominants can be actively controlled through censure, ostracism, or other punitive action.[31] In other experiments, leader behavior that was self-aggrandizing and/or deviated from fairness norms elicited retaliatory "leveling" punishment from the other participants.[32] However, these suggestions presume that the rest of us are willing and able to collectively reward or punish our leaders rather than emulate them.

Some writers have suggested that our culture is narcissistic.[33] This is not so much a result of individual narcissists, and not necessarily even the evil variety (i.e., malignant narcissism). Rather, it manifests in our jingoistic optimism and irrational exuberance, as well as a general focus on image over substance—which has become particularly more acute with the explosion of social media. Twenge & Campbell[34] suggest channeling narcissistic impulses into philanthropy rather than attempting to eliminate them. A number of educational and charitable institutions are already doing this—naming a building or a program after a generous donor and/or generating positive media coverage. Such a strategy appeals to the narcissistic desire to "look good" while making it easier for a narcissist to get attention by doing good rather than hurting others. This type of strategy may work for other kinds of pathologies as well.

Eliminate extremes of economic and social inequality. In Part IV, Section Two, we visited the work of epidemiologists Richard Wilkinson and Kate Pickett as they demonstrated (with evidence) how current levels of inequality in the U.S. are causing real harm to "we the people." We also saw how the majority of us have no idea how extreme and unnatural the current level of inequality is. So, there first needs to be a lot of public education and discussion on this issue. Organizations like the Economic Policy Institute have been advocating for incremental-type actions like increasing the minimum wage and a more progressive tax code, both which have a surprising amount of public support.

However, this will be politically difficult when our political infrastructure and major media are dominated by an oligarchy. There is hope for this, but it will depend on finding ways to talk about this issue that can move people past both centuries of entrenched propaganda and their own insecurities, so it is likely going to take more time than we would like. More than just a matter of law and economics, I personally would like to see us abandon our cultural infatuation with the wealthy and privileged. They are not better than us, and they are not good for "us." And we need to treat them accordingly.

Promote Critical Thinking Skills. This obviously begins with education. Which implicates a larger argument about investment in public goods. But we also have to look beyond the corporatized model where students are imbued with technical skills and indoctrinated to become "productive workers" while the concept of broader citizenship is ignored. Education must be about more than basic skills and "job readiness," but the ability to think through and analyze problems in an increasingly complex and unpredictable environment. It also means a level of skill diffusion that is universal, rather than reserved for a select few of chosen elites.

Encourage Empathy. In *The Empathy Gap,* J.D. Trout proposes that our "competence as citizens depends on accurately understanding and depicting the lives of others;" [35] i.e., empathy. Trout alleges that only rarely will one find a culture that completely lacks empathy, but it is "common to find a culture whose most powerful members typify a disdain for empathy."[36] Particularly in the West, we are prone to the fundamental attribution error which blames people for their own condition (a blame-the-victim mentality) rather than examining broader cultural, social, and economic factors.[37] Trout describes how "merchants and marketers" spend huge sums on behavior science research to subconsciously control our behavior—usually to our own detriment—yet we howl with indignation when some regulation is proposed with the intent to make us behave in ways that benefit everyone.[38] Empathy is necessary because it "is alert to the humiliation and indignity of being treated differently for reasons that are morally irrelevant (such as race or class), ...[it] propels us to envision lost hopes and prospects [and] serves as a kind of political sentinel, announcing the unfair or harsh conditions" that cause undeserved human suffering.[39]

Trout further argues that lack of empathy renders us too quick to judge the decisions made by others without consideration of the context. All human decisions—including our own—are subject to natural and entrenched biases of availability, base rate, overconfidence, hindsight, anchoring, and status quo (which Trout defines and describes). All of these biases impact our ability to exert self-control, i.e., free will. As a practical manifestation, we tend to "not see" the work of volunteers, and thus underestimate the degree to which society is not fulfilling its duty to its own people. Because we have "grown comfortable with this goodwill,...it subsidizes an attitude of civic neglect."[40] Moreover, the typical member of Congress is so "socially distanced" from not only the poor, but even the more modest "regular folks" in their district that they discount huge amounts of suffering when formulating policies."[41]

Moderate extreme individualism. Here in the United States, we have been subject to a history and culture that elevates the individual above the commonwealth. While this has had an upside for us in the development of individual rights and appropriate skepticism of concentrated power, it has left a hole in our soul when it comes to community. Decades of propaganda have conditioned us to fear "collectivism" (sometimes called communism). We imagine a dystopian future where we will all look alike, live in the same types of places, and our identities will be subsumed into a Borg-like hive. Yet this same fear prevents us from forging the common bonds to challenge those things that actually do oppress us—working harder for less at meaningless jobs, failing to exercise our civil rights (free speech or voting) because we believe we will not be heard and nothing we do or say will make a difference. Although the proper balance between autonomy and community may be different for each individual, we will never be able to determine where that is until we start to talk to each other. We might be surprised at how many others are also seeking greater community.

Identify and Discourage Harmful Spread of Disinformation. In my opinion, this possibly presents a greater source of ponerization in our society than individual psychopaths. It is more than a simple matter of making bad decisions because one has bad information, but it creates bubbles of alternate realities, which makes efforts at finding common ground practically impossible. It also tends to lead to personality disintegration. A large part of this problem is the profit-oriented nature of media outlets, where the drive for attention (and advertising revenue) determines the type of content at the expense of not only quality but often even the truth itself.

We looked at efforts to root out disinformation in Part IV, Section Four. While it is encouraging to see that smart folks in academic, journalist, and technology communities are concerned about this and brainstorming solutions, it presents a genuine problem in a society that also values freedom of speech and personal privacy. An overly zealous campaign to eliminate "fake news" itself can segue into ponerization. Moreover, although fact check services and botnet detection technologies are available, they aren't going to work if people do not use them because they ***deliberately choose*** to live in an alternate reality.

Greater Public Dissemination and Incorporation of Psychological Knowledge. Lobaszewsky was a psychiatrist, and so it not surprising that he would view the "cure" for modern evil through the lens of his own training and profession. But some contemporary American psychiatrists have also offered the benefits of their expertise in analyzing contemporary evil. Dr. Bandy Lee, a forensic psychiatrist and Professor of Law and Psychiatry at the Yale School of Medicine, issued plenty of warnings (along with others among her profession) about Trump's psychopathy and the danger such an individual presented in occupying the most powerful position in the world.[42] Dr. Allen Frances' *Twilight of American Sanity*[43] analyzes the Trump phenomenon more in the manner of Lobaszewsky—in the context of a larger societal pathology rather than a sole focus on individual psychopathologies and antisocial characteristics.

In *The Cult of Trump,*[44] Steven Hassan likens the Trump phenomenon to a cult, grounding his analysis in both behavioral science research and his own experience as a former member of the Moon Unification Church (*aka* Moonies). Hassan describes the use of influence and mind control techniques typically used by cult leaders, whose ultimate objective is to "make people dependent and obedient," and also addresses how Trump was aided in this by a "vast and mutually supportive right wing media machine."[45] For those of us who have read these books, the horrifying incidents and events over the past four years—including the near loss of our democracy to an authoritarian psychopath and enraged, lawless mob—have nonetheless not been particularly surprising. Which suggests that more of us may need to be paying attention to these things.

Here I am specifically recommending the establishment of multidisciplinary task forces and work groups. Mental health professionals can advise journalists and policymakers about ways to manage the effects of disinformation, who in turn can be advised by constitutional lawyers on how to do this without running afoul of the First Amendment. Public health, community groups, and economists can explore ways to design livelihoods that actually work for workers and serve communities. Behavioral health professionals and faith leaders can work together to design effective ways to increase empathy. That is, professional expertise and research needs to be expanded beyond the limited silo of a single occupational specialty. Moreover, original research itself needs to be made freely available to journalists as well as the general public, and not hidden behind obscure academic paywalls which are only accessible to the wealthy and those with institutional connections.

We have seen throughout our journey here how all of these things are interconnected. Reducing economic inequality won't happen until we find ways to have inclusive public discourse and real democratic decision-making. Critical thinking skills will be in short supply as long as quality education is dependent on unequal economic opportunity. Empathy won't happen unless there are safe spaces free of hierarchical status divisions where people can learn to understand each other. And we will never be able to find and forge common ground as long as a large section of the population is living in an alternate epistemic reality.

Include the Teachings of Both Science and Faith in Discussions of Evil. Lobaszewsky warns us that we should not resort to moralizing or moral argument in discussions of macrosocial evil, as this may cloud our logic and capacity for critical thinking. But science, the same as religion, can itself become too dependent on presumed and/or unchallenged "authority." That is, the two different frameworks can serve both as checks and balances on each other as well as a source of expansionary thinking. This means that even the language we now use to describe and discuss evil—whether in religious terms of "original sin," or the technocratic terms of behaviorism—may possibly evolve into something workable to both.

M. Scott Peck, M.D., is an American psychiatrist (1936-2005), who is probably best known for his 1978 book, *The Road Less Traveled.* After years of dabbling in Buddhism, Islam, and various other religious mysticisms, Peck committed to Christianity in 1980. In 1984, Peck co-founded the Foundation for Community Encouragement, an educational non-profit dedicated to teaching the principles of community. In 1983, Dr. Peck came out with another book, *People of the Lie,* wherein he advocates—as we do here—for greater cooperation between the scientific and religious communities in the analysis of evil. Peck argues that the scientific method tends to be too analytic and "reductionist," reducing problems to small pieces so they can be better examined, which results in missing the bigger picture.

Peck defines evil not so much as a "sinful" act itself, but as the failure to acknowledge it and engage in the appropriate self-reflection to change. At the individual level, this manifests as a form of malignant narcissism. According to Peck, this is something different than Lobaszewsky's psychopath, who is biologically incapable of experiencing empathy. Rather, the offender is acutely concerned with outward appearances of moral purity. They project their own evil into the world, often in the form of scapegoating. As life events begin to reveal their own shortcomings, they double down on "hating and destroying life—usually in the name of righteousness." They engage in extraordinary efforts to conceal their own imperfections. These lies are intended to deceive themselves as much as they are intended to deceive others, because they "cannot or will not tolerate the pain of self-reproach."[46]

Peck explains the spiritual dimension of malignant narcissism as an "unsubmitted will." Peck alleges that an unsubmitted will was demonstrated in the Biblical stories about Satan, and that of Cain and Abel. People who are "evil" under this theory are "extraordinarily willful" and possess a "remarkable power" in their attempts to control others.[47] Like psychopaths, the malignant narcissist also "seems to lack empathy." The malignant narcissist also "needs victims to sacrifice to their narcissism," which also "permits them to ignore the humanity of their victims."[48]

Peck addresses group, or institutional-level evil, and argues that this is even more dangerous than individual evil. He notes that we are "living in the Age of the Institution." While only a century earlier, the majority of Americans were self-employed, today, the majority of us today depend on organizations for our livelihood and subsistence. In a group or institutional setting, "responsibility becomes diffuse," making it easier to deflect blame. As institutions grow ever larger, it becomes more and more difficult to sometimes differentiate between those who are giving orders and those who are following them. Peck's increasingly large institutions thus become "faceless" and "soulless."[49]

Peck's "institutional evil" demonstrative example is when U.S. troops killed between five and six hundred unarmed residents of the village of My Lai, Vietnam in 1968. Here, Peck engages in an analysis similar to that of Zimbardo's study of what happened at Abu Ghraib (Part II, Section 5). Although it was individuals who gave the orders and pulled the triggers, Peck argues that one has to take into account the general immaturity of the soldiers as well as the conditions of constant stress. Moreover, "the military organization and its group dynamics do everything to make it just about as painful and difficult and unnatural as possible for the solder to exercise independence of judgment or practice disobedience."[50] Peck also suggests that evil is more likely to be perpetrated under conditions of ignorance: "At least 95 percent of the men going off to risk their very lives did not even have the slightest idea what the war was about, [and] Department of Defense civilians who directed the war [had an] atrocious ignorance of Vietnamese history."[51]

However, Peck argues that an evil greater than the massacre of the village itself was the subsequent attempts to cover it up. He accuses officials in the Johnson administration as being "lazy and self-satisfied. They, like most more ordinary individuals, had little taste for intellectual confusion—nor for the effort involved in maintaining a posture of constant self-doubt and criticism.... Ordinarily, if our noses are rubbed in the evidence, we can tolerate the painful narcissistic injury involved, admit our need for change, and correct our outlook. But as is the case with certain individuals, the narcissism of whole nations may at times exceed the normal bounds. When this happens, the nation—instead of readjusting in light of the evidence—sets about attempting to destroy the evidence."[52] Thus, "evil," according to Peck, results from a confluence of laziness, ignorance, narcissism, and unwillingness to face the truth.

Finally, Peck provides a counter to Lobaszewsky's argument that one must set moral judgment aside when attempting to resolve an immoral problem. He proposes that Jesus' admonishment to "Judge not, that ye be not judged" (Matthew 7:1) has been misinterpreted. The following verses ask us to first examine ourselves ("Why do you see the speck in your neighbor's eye, but do not notice the log in your own eye?") before we judge others. We must also examine the purpose of our judgment. If our intent is to heal or to prevent harm, then judgment may indeed be appropriate. If our intent is to enhance our own self-esteem, pride, or vengeance, then judgment is wrong.[53] Thus, while we must be mindful that it is a characteristic of evil to label others as evil (deflection, projection, and distraction), there are times when we ***must*** exercise our moral judgment. Peck rhetorically asks us whether we would have addressed Hitler with a tolerant attitude of "I'm OK; you're OK."[54]

Upon review of our list of practical suggestions, we come to the realization that they are impracticable to implement when pathocrats are already in charge. Even Professor Perry's suggestions presume that prosocial individuals are in positions of sufficient authority to implement them. The collective enforcement of social norms may be ineffective in an authoritarian environment, and the norms themselves may have been corrupted when ruling sociopaths have had sufficient opportunity to influence the culture. Peck suggests that it is a good idea to develop a "psychology of evil" that is grounded in behavioral science, but at the same time we should not be solely dependent upon it. It must be balanced with the moral compass of our faith teachings.

And so we return to one of the primary arguments made here: We need to bring matters of faith—including its instructions on morality, good and evil—back into the public square. We have seen herein how religious fundamentalism (Christian, Muslim, and Zionist) arose in protest against the secular techno-rationalized state. Yet, some faith-keepers are prone to both anti-science and authoritarian worldviews that—ironically sometimes even contrary to the teachings of their own faith—are inimical to human welfare. Conversely, technocratic rationality can impose its own form of authoritarianism, claiming to be couched in objective science while it cloaks a malevolent agenda. Thus, we are tasked with finding a balance—a task that we will only be able to accomplish together.

Notes

[1] Johnson, A.G. (2018). *Privilege, power, and difference.* New York, NY: McGraw-Hill Education at p. 111.

[2] April 2010 Interview with *The Sun's* Arnie Cooper about his book *Bright Green: A Worldchanging Guide to a Future That Works.* https://www.thesunmagazine.org/issues/412/the-bright-green-city

[3] Wilkinson, R., & Pickett, K. (2009). *The spirit level: Why greater equality makes societies stronger.* New York, NY" Bloomsbury Press, at p. 3.

[4] VanHettinga (2019).

[5] This theory is expounded upon in *Why Assholes Rule the World.* (2019).

[6] Sutton, R.J. (2007). *The no asshole rule.* New York, NY: Business Plus/Hatchett Book Group USA.

[7] James, A. (2012). *Assholes: A theory.* New York, NY: Doubleday/Random House.

[8] Lobaczewsky, A. M. (1998). *Political ponerology: A science on the nature of evil adjusted for political purposes* at p. 194.

[9] *Id* at p. 196.

[10] Mayer, D.M., Nishii, L.H., Schneider, B., & Goldstein, H. (2007). The precursors and products of justice climates: Group leader antecedents and employee attitudinal consequences. *Personal Psychology, 60,* 929-63.

[11] Côté, S., Kraus, M.W., Cheng, B.H., Oveis, C., van der Löwe, I., Lian, H., & Keltner, D. . (2011). Social power facilitates the effect of prosocial orientation on empathic accuracy. *J. Pers. Soc. Psychol*. 101, 217-232.

[12] Decelies, K.A., et al. (2012). Does power corrupt or enable? When and why power facilitates self-interested behavior. *J. Appl. Psychol*. 97, 681-689.

[13] Willer, R., Feinberg, M., Flynn, F.J., & Simpson, B. (2012). Is generosity sincere or strategic? Altruism versus status-seeking in prosocial behavior. https://www.researchgate.net/publication/268407221_Is_generosity_sincere_or_strategic_Altruism_versus_status_seeking_in_prosocial_behavior.

---

[14] Batson, C.D. (1991). *The altruism question: Towards a social-psychological answer.* Hillsdale, NJ: Lawrence Erlbaum Associates.

[15] Blau, P.M. (1964). *Exchange and power in social life.* New York, NY: John Wiley and Sons.

[16] Trout, J.D. (2009). *The empathy gap: Building bridges to the good life and the good society.* New York, NY: Viking/Penguin Group USA, Inc. at p. 60.

[17] Peck, M.S. (1983). *People of the lie: The hope for healing human evil.* New York, NY: Touchstone/Simon & Schuster.

[18] Lobaszewsky, *supra* at p. 150.

[19] *Id.* at p. 177.

[20] Christensen, R.K., Paarlberg, L., & Perry, J.L. (2017). Public service motivation research: Lessons for practice. *Public Administration Review, 77*(4), 529-542.

[21] Fehrler, S., & & Kosfled, M. (2014). Pro-social missions and worker motivation: An experimental study. *Journal of Economic Behavior and Organization, 100*, 99-110.

[22] Bakker, A.B. (2015). A job demands-resources approach to public service motivation. *Public Administration Review, 75*(5), 723-32.

[23] Boyte, H.C., & Kari, N.N. (1996). *Building America: The democratic promise of public work.* Philadelphia, PA: Temple University Press.

[24] White, J.A., & Plous, S. (1995). Self-enhancement and social responsibility: On caring more, but doing less, than others. *Journal of Applied Social Psychology, 25*, 1297-1318.

[25] Ebdon, C., & Franklin, A.L. (2006, May/June). Citizen participation in budgeting theory. *Public Administration Review,* pp. 437-447. https://www.ca-ilg.org/sites/main/files/file-attachments/budget_linked_resource_1.pdf

[26] Stevens, S.G., Plaut, V.C., & Sanchez-Burks, J. (2008). Unlocking the benefits of diversity: All-inclusive multiculturalism and positive organizational change. *The Journal of Applied Behavioral Science, 44*(1), 116-133.

---

[27] Bass, B.M. (2008). Bass' handbook of leadership: Theory, research and managerial application. New York, NY: Free Press; Lewin, K., & Lippitt, R. (1938). An experimental approach to the study of autocracy and democracy: A preliminary note. *Sociometry, 1,* 292-300.

[28] Rost, C.J. (2008). In R.E. Riggio, I. Chaleff, & J. Lipman-Blumen (Eds.) *The Art of Followership* at pp. 53-64. San Francisco, CA: Jossey Bass.

[29] Fiddick, L., Cummins, D.D., Janicki, M., Lee, S., & Erlich, N. (2013). A cross-cultural study of noblesse oblige in economic decision-making. *Human Nature, 24,* 318-335.

[30] Bargh, J.A., Chen, M., & Burrows, L. (1996). Automaticity of social behavior: Direct effects of trait construct and stereotype activation on action. *Journal of Personality and Social Psychology, 71*(2), 230-44.

[31] Boehm, C. (1999). Hierarchy in the forest: The evolution of egalitarian behavior. Cambridge, MA: Harvard University Press.

[32] Fehr, E., & Fischbacher, U. (2004). Third party punishment and social norms. *Evolution and Human Behavior, 25,* 63-87.

[33] Lasch, C. (1979). *The culture of narcissism.* New York, NY: Norton & Company; Silva, J.M. (2013). *Working class adulthood in an age of uncertainty.* New York, NY: Oxford University Press.

[34] Twenge, J., & Campbell, K. (2009). *The narcissism epidemic.* New York, NY: Free Press.

[35] Trout, J.D. (2009). *The empathy gap: Building bridges to the good life and the good society.* New York, NY: Viking/Penguin Group USA. Inc. at p. 39.

[36] *Id.* at p. 26.

[37] *Id.* at p. 41.

[38] *Id.* at p. 68.

[39] *Id.* at p. 17.

[40] *Id.* at p. 101.

[41] *Id.* at p. 37.

---

[42] Lee, B.X. (2017). *The dangerous case of Donald Trump: 37 psychiatrists and mental health experts assess a president.* New York, NY: St. Martin's Press.

[43] Frances, A. (2017). *Twilight of American sanity: A psychiatrist analyzes the age of Trump.* New York, NY: HarperCollins Publishers.

[44] Hassan, S. (2019). *The cult of Trump: A leading cult expert explains how the president uses mind control.* New York, NY: Free Press.

[45] *Id.* at p. xvi.

[46] Peck, *supra* at pp. 74-75.

[47] *Id.* at pp. 78-79.

[48] *Id.* at p. 136.

[49] *Id.* at p. 251.

[50] *Id.* at p. 224.

[51] *Id.* at p. 249.

[52] *Id.* at p. 241.

[53] *Id.* at p. 256.

[54] *Id.* at p. 255.

Postlude

When fascism comes to America, it will be wrapped in the flag and carrying a cross.

James Waterman Wise (1901-1983)

*

What prepares men for totalitarian domination in the non-totalitarian world is the fact that loneliness, once a borderline experience usually suffered in certain marginal social conditions like old age, has become an everyday experience.

Hannah Arendt

Although Joe Biden and Kamala Harris were sworn into office without incident on January 20th, America is still not at peace. Trump supporters and Q-conspiracists now have their very own representatives in Congress, some who continue to threaten the lives of their colleagues. A sizeable (and vocal) minority—along with the far-right disinformation machine—is still making noise about a "stolen" election (although the precise nature and details of the grievance appear to be shifting). Republicans are now split between those who have abandoned or denounced Trump (and joined Democrats in calling for Trump to be impeached a second time), and those who answer to the rabid and deluded "base." Which now also includes members of Congress. The Trump-affiliated senators and representatives lurch from hypocritical calls for "unity" (they want the rest of us to forgive and forget their attempts to subvert the will of the majority and install a fascist dictator), and shrieking threats to bring perennial impeachments against President Biden or otherwise obstruct anything he attempts to do. Meanwhile, the rest of the country is wondering when the pandemic will be under control as well as attempting to recover from a recession.

We ask ourselves, "Is there a pathocracy in the United States in 2021?" If Trump and his minions had been able to pull off their coup, the answer would be a definite yes. A few more Trump loyalist judges in the right place, a couple of loyalists in swing states election offices who would have been willing to do Trump's bidding (or succumb to his bullying), or if the insurrection mob had burned down the Capitol along with the electoral votes, and we would indeed be subject to a full-blown pathocracy. However, what we are seeing is not exactly what Lobaszewsky was seeing in 1940s Poland.

If I had to describe what we are seeing in the language of Lobaszewsky, I would call it a partial pathocracy, but in a much more hysteroidal society. There are still honorable people in positions of power: judges (including a few who were Trump appointees) who upheld the rule of law; attorneys in the Department of Justice who stood up to Trump; members of the national guard and the capitol police—who at previous times exercised the same force against protesting minorities—did their jobs and protected democracy; and extremely courageous Republican officials in key positions in both state and federal governments—who would not be bullied by threats coming from both Trump and the mob and held onto their honor. Thus, we do not have a full pathocracy because decent people, for the most part, remain in some positions of power. At the same time, we also should not trivialize real threats to our democracy, as well as the continued (and largely unacknowledged) power of the corporatocracy.

However, the mass psychosis we are seeing among the general population is a new kind of pathology. These people are not being coerced into obeying the party line by force or threat. The "mind control" is not coming from an oppressive government, but is a product of privately-owned right wing media and the people themselves (through social media). The Trump phenomenon has been compared to a cult, and more than one mental health professional believes that cult-level deprogramming will be required to bring these people back to reality.

It is probably too easy to blame mass psychosis on "social media." The tech oligopolies (primarily Facebook and Twitter) were not themselves producing disinformation and hateful rhetoric, although they were profiting from it. After the January 6th insurrection, Facebook and Twitter banned Trump (who was still President) as well as content that referenced "stop the steal." Yet, simply banning particular persons or content is probably not an effective way to address the underlying problem (even if it stops the spread). It also presents obvious threats to the concept of free speech and expression.

My own theory is that propagandizing began in the middle 1970s. It was primarily instituted by corporate executives and wealthy individuals, who feared the collective power of working people and were also intent on dismantling labor rights. These individuals had either inherited wealth from previous oligopolies (railroads, oil, telecommunications), were serving the corporatocracy in a high-level capacity, or had founded a company with which they were able to dominate the market (i.e., establish an anti-competitive advantage). The increase of their own fortunes was dependent on disempowering those who had to "earn" their living.

These propertied interests developed a multi-prong strategy which consisted of (1) creating well-endowed foundations, institutions and "think tanks" (e.g., the Heritage Foundation, the American Enterprise Institute) to conduct "studies" demonstrating the benefits of "free enterprise," a term used to cloak deregulatory and anti-worker objectives; (2) capturing the apparatus of government by flooding Congress with well-paid lobbyists, controlling the nomination of the judiciary, and establishing a revolving door between the corporate C-suites and regulatory agencies; and (3) media capture and consolidation, which focused on covering "basic fact" news (i.e., without in-depth analyses), sports and celebrity gossip while deliberately neglecting stories and issues that impacted the lives of working people.

In addition to reframing their own interests in the language of patriotic freedom, the strategy also included ways to keep working people focused on their differences. This included bootstrapping onto divisions inadvertently created by the civil rights movement and "diversity" initiatives, as well as more time-worn tropes against "the liberal establishment" and "socialism" directed at any suggestion of policies or programs in the public interest.[1] These tactics also spread to incorporate fundamentalist religions, perhaps as a way to divert the obvious moral challenges to greed and selfishness. This was accomplished by focusing on single "hot button" moral issues like abortion, which could then be morphed to accommodate broader objectives of cultural and thought control. The right wing disinformation machine thus grew throughout the 1980s and 1990s, gaining the status of corporatized legitimacy while relentlessly tapping into White and working class grievance without ever addressing the fundamental problems.

In addition to gaining control over public policy discussion frameworks and culture, there were also attempts to consolidate political power, primarily on the right. Some of this advantage resulted from the "natural" operation of the electoral college, which tends to shift voting power in favor of small, rural states. An analogous disparity in voting power also exists in the Senate—the "upper" chamber of Congress that approves Presidential cabinet appointments, Supreme Court justices, and holds the power to try Presidential impeachments brought over from the House. An example of this voting power disparity is that each Senator from California represents 19.8 million people, where each Senator from Wyoming only represents some 290,000 people, giving voters in Wyoming over 68 times more "voice" than voters in California. The smaller states who enjoy this disproportionate favorable bias not only tend to be rural versus urban, but also have much lower percentages of non-white and immigrant residents. Thus the "system" is already set up to favor the voices of White privilege and grievance against everyone else.

Yet, many Republicans/White supremacists are not content with these already built-in advantages. For the past several decades they have engaged in a campaign of voter suppression (increasing the stringency of voting requirements aimed at communities who are poorer, non-white, or immigrant) along with reducing the number of polling places in these communities. In addition to voter suppression, they have engaged in gerrymandering—a process of "packing" minorities into discrete districts and "cracking" other districts designed to dilute the minority vote. In spite of all the inherent systemic bias and decades of legal maneuvering to gain an advantage, a lawyer recently admitted on record in an argument before the U.S. Supreme Court that such voting restrictions were necessary because otherwise Republicans would be at a "competitive disadvantage."[2] Here we see the culmination of ponerized thinking appear in Supreme Court arguments: "We" should be allowed to violate the Constitution because "our" rights are superior to everyone else's and winning is everything,

The past four years have thus served as a black mirror which forces us to look into the face of our own evil. In my own case (because I already abhor greed, selfishness, hypocrisy, fascism, and White supremacy) this moment came at the revulsion in witnessing the Trump mob on January 6th removing the American flag from the United States Capitol pole and replacing it with a Trump flag. Although I do not consider myself a jingoistic patriot, I could not help but think about my deceased husband—who literally took bullets in his flesh for the United States of America while serving in the U.S. Marines—and how I was almost grateful that he was no longer alive to witness this travesty because it would have broken his heart. The event triggered my own inner "law and order" authoritarian, demanding punitive justice—up to and including the death penalty (which I normally oppose on moral grounds) for ALL the perpetrators.

At the same time, I also recognize that many in the mob were likely deluded by a combination of Trump's lies and decades of right-wing disinformation. I have since viewed video interviews of former members of so-called "Q-Anon"—a cult-like movement that now seems to have a life of its own independent of either Trump or the Republican party. In the video, "reformed" members of "Q" struggled to explain how and why they came under the spell of delusional conspiracy theories. A few of them did not connect "Q" with White supremacy or fascism until after they had left it (and were able to think clearly). When asked to suggest effective ways to reach others still caught in the delusion, almost all of them expressed something along the lines of compassion and understanding. That is, approaching these individuals as an avenging angel of truth will only drive them further into the conspiracy rabbit-hole rather than help them to see the light—a recommendation that bolsters Lobaczewsky's advice to refrain from moralizing.

Officials in the law enforcement and counter-terrorism communities are now recognizing the danger of radicalized White supremacists, with some saying that we are now in a state of "permanent insurrection." Domestic terrorism, however, cannot be addressed in the same way that we have previously addressed foreign terrorist groups like Al-Qaeda and Isis. Certainly, some in the mob and/or the "Q" cult are motivated by very real fears of existential threat, as well as very real perceptions that "the system" is not working for most of us. As Lobaszewsky admonishes, those of us who found the acts of the January 6th mob despicable must also recognize that it would be more productive for some of them to be subjected to the tough love of deprogramming or other training in socialization rather than the iron rod of legal punishment.

The problem is how to distinguish when we are dealing with intentional criminal acts or psychological sickness. While some of this mob was likely motivated by true evil, it will take time to identify precisely those who should be subject to prosecution and those who should be provided psychological healing. Yet, we must also look beyond what individuals may have done as well as their intent. This event did not happen in a vacuum, and so any determination of individual culpability must also include analyses of sources that create and systems that spread disinformation and exploit psychosocial grievance.

As this book goes to print, a Minneapolis jury found the police officer who killed George Floyd guilty on counts of second degree manslaughter, third and second degree murder.

We stand today at the crossroad that will determine who "We" will be.

Notes

[1] Conason, J. (2003). *Big lies: The right-wing propaganda machine and how it distorts the truth.* New York, NY: Thomas Dunne Books/St. Martin's Press.

[2] https://www.nbcnews.com/politics/elections/supreme-court-gop-attorney-defends-voting-restrictions-saying-they-help-n1259305

Bibliography

Lists all full-length books that are cited herein.
Citations to academic articles and articles in print and online media can be found in the footnotes appearing at the end of each section.
Send questions/comments to: **brynne@thegreatjobsdeception.com**

Adams, G., & Balfour, D. (2014). *Unmasking administrative evil.* New York, NY: M.E. Sharpe.

Alford, C.F. (2001). *Whistleblowers: Broken lives and organization power.* Ithaca, NY: Cornell University Press.

Altemeyer, B. (1981). *Right-wing authoritarianism.* Winnipeg: University of Manitoba Press.

Alter, A. (2017). *Irresistible: The rise of addictive technology and the business of keeping us hooked.* New York, NY: Penguin Press.

Argyle, M. (1994). *The psychology of social class.* London: Routledge.

Babiak, P., & Hare, R.D. (2006). *Snakes in suits.* New York, NY: HarperCollins Publishers, Inc.

Baker, C.E., & Sinha, D. (2009). *Media concentration and democracy: Why ownership matters.* Cambridge, MA: Cambridge University Press.

Batra, R. (1996). *The great American deception: What politicians won't tell you about our economy and your future.* New York, NY: John Wiley & Sons.

Batson, C.D. (1991). *The altruism question: Towards a social-psychological answer.* Hillsdale, NJ: Lawrence Eribaum Associates.

Bellah, R.N., Madsen, R., Sullivan, W.M., Seidler, A., & Tipton, S. W. (Orig. 1985). *Habits of the heart.* Berkeley, CA: University of California Press.

Bellah, R.N., Madsen, R., Sullivan, W.M., Seidler, A., & Tipton, S. W. (1991). *The good society.* New York, NY: Vintage Books/ Random House Inc.

Blau, P.M. (1964). *Exchange and power in social life.* New York, NY: John Wiley and Sons.

Boehm, C. (1999). *Hierarchy in the forest: The evolution of egalitarian behavior.* Cambridge, MA: Harvard University Press.

Bolton, J. (2020). *The room where it happened: A White House memoir.* New York, NY: Simon & Shuster.

Bovy, P.M. (2017). *The perils of privilege: Why injustice can't be solved by accusing others of advantage.* New York, NY: Saint Martin's Press.

Bruder, J. (2017). *Nomadland: Surviving America in the 21st Century.* New York, NY: W.W. Norton & Company.

Case, A., & Deaton, A. (2020). *Deaths of despair and the future of capitalism.* Princeton, NJ: Princeton University Press.

Cohen, M. (2020). *Disloyal: A memoir: The true story of the former personal attorney to Donald J. Trump.*

Conason, J. (2003). *Big lies: The right-wing propaganda machine and how it distorts the truth.* New York, NY: Thomas Dunne Books/St. Martin's Press.

Conley, L. (2008). *Obsessive branding disorder.* New York, NY: Public Affairs.

Cook, P. J., & Frank, R.H. (1995). *The winner-take-all society: Why the few at the top get so much more than the rest of us.* New York, NY: Penguin Books USA, Inc.

Dawkins, R. (1978). *The selfish gene.* London: Paladin.

De Tocqueville, A. (1831). *Democracy in America.*

.

Duesenberry, J.S. (1949). *Income, saving and the theory of consumer behavior.* Cambridge, MA: Harvard University Press.

Duffy, M., & Sperry, L. (2012). *Mobbing: Causes, consequences, and solutions.* New York, NY: Oxford University Press.

Frances, A. (2017). *Twilight of American sanity: A psychiatrist analyzes the age of Trump.* New York, NY: HarperCollins Publishers.

Frank, R.H. (2001). *Luxury fever: Why money fails to satisfy in an era of excess.* New York, NY: Simon & Shuster.

Frank, R. (2007). *Richistan.* New York, NY: Crown Publishers/ Random House, Inc.

Garcia-Martinez, A. (2016). *Chaos monkeys: Obscene fortune and random failure in Silicon Valley.* New York, NY: HarperCollins Publishers.

Gessen, M. (2020). *Surviving autocracy.* New York, NY: Riverhead Books/Penguin Random House LLC.

Giridharadas, A. (2018). *Winners take all: The elite charade of changing the world.* New York, NY: Alfred Knopf.

Goffman, E. (1963). *Stigma.* Englewood Cliffs, NJ: Prentice Hall.

Goldberg, J. (2018). *Suicide of the West: How the rebirth of tribalism, populism, nationalism, and identity politics is destroying American democracy.* New York, NY: Crown Publishing Group/Penguin Random House.

Graber, D. (2018). *Bullshit jobs: A theory.* New York, NY: Simon & Schuster.

Gross, B. (1980). *Friendly fascism: The new face of power in America.* South End Press.

Guinness, O. (2008). *The case for civility and why our future depends on it.* New York, NY: HarperCollins Publishers.

Haidt, J. (2008). *The righteous mind: Why good people are divided by religion and politics.* New York, NY: Pantheon Books.

Hare, R.D. (1998). *Without conscience: The disturbing world of the psychopaths among us.* New York, NY: Guilford Press.

Harrington, A. (1973). *Psychopaths.* New York NY: Simon & Shuster.

Hassan, S. (2019). *The cult of Trump: A leading cult expert explains how the president uses mind control.* New York, NY: Free Press.

Hayek, F. (1960). *The constitution of liberty.* Chicago, IL: University of Chicago Press.

Hedges, C. (2009). *Empire of illusion: The end of literacy and the triumph of spectacle.* New York, NY: Nation Books.

Hedges, C. (2015). *The wages of rebellion.* New York, NY: Nation Books/Perseus Books Company.

James, A. (2012). *Assholes: A theory.* New York, NY: Doubleday/Random House.

James, A. (2016). *Assholes: A theory of Donald Trump.* New York, NY: Doubleday/Penguin Random House.

Johnson, A.G. (2018). *Privilege, power, and difference.* New York, NY: McGraw-Hill Education.

Johnston, D.C. (2016). *The making of Donald Trump.* Brooklyn, NY: Melville House Publishing.

Kluegel, J.R., & Smith, E.R. (1986). *Beliefs about inequality: American views of what is and what ought to be.* Hawthorne, NY: Aldine de Gruyter.

Kohlberg, L. (1980). *The meaning and measurement of moral development.* Worcester, MA: Clark University Press.

Kusnet, D. (2008). *Love the work, hate the job: Why America's best workers are unhappier than ever.* Hoboken, NJ: John Wiley and Sons, Inc.

Lasch, C. (1979). *The culture of narcissism.* New York, NY: Norton & Company.

Lee, B.X. (2018). *The dangerous case of Donald Trump.*

Lemann, N. (2019). *Transaction man: Rise of the deal and decline of the American dream.* New York, NY: Ferrar, Straus & Giroux.

Lerner, M. (1991). *Surplus powerlessness: The psychodynamics of everyday life and the psychology of individual and social transformation.* Atlantic Highlands, NJ: Humanities Press Intern'l.

Levitsky, S., & Ziblatt, D. (2018). *How democracies die.* New York, NY: Crown Publishing Group/Penguin Random House LLC.

Lipman-Bluman, J. (2005). *The allure of toxic leaders: Why we follow destructive bosses and corrupt politicians and how we can survive them.* New York, NY: Oxford University Press.

Livingstone, D.W. (1999). *The education-jobs gap: Underemployment or economic democracy.* Toronto, Ontario: Garamond Press.

Lobaszewsky, A.M. (1998). *Political ponerology: A science on the nature of evil adjusted for political purposes.* Red Pill Press.

Lyons, D. (2018). *Lab rats: How Silicon Valley made work miserable for the rest of us.* New York, NY: Hatchette Books.

Mayer, J. (2016). *Dark money: The hidden history of the billionaires behind the rise of the radical right.* New York, NY: Anchor Books/ Penguin Random House LLC.

Maynard, D.C., & Feldman, D.C. (2011). *Underemployment: Psychological, economic and social challenges.* New York, NY: Springer Science+Business Media, LLC.

Mishra, P. (2017). *The age of anger: History of the present.* New York, NY: Farrar, Straus and Giroux.

Norris, P. (2011). *Democratic deficit: Critical citizens revisited.* New York, NY: Cambridge University Press.

Oakley, B. (2007). *Evil genes: Why Rome fell, Hitler rose, Enron failed, and my sister stole my mother's boyfriend.* Amherst, NY: Prometheus Books.

Payne, K. (2017). *The broken ladder: How inequality affects the way we think, live, and die.* New York, NY: Penguin Random House LLC.

Peck, M.S. (1983). *People of the lie: The hope for healing human evil.* New York, NY: Touchstone/Simon & Shuster.

Pein, C. (2017). *Live work work work die: A journey into the savage heart of Silicon Valley.* New York, NY: Metropolitan Books/Henry Holt & Company.

Perry, G. (2012). *Behind the shock machine: The untold story of the notorious Milgram psychology experiments.* New York, NY: The New Press.

Pfeffer, J. (2018). *Dying for a paycheck: How modern management harms employee health and company performance—and what we can do about it.* New York, NY: HarperCollins.

Piketty, T. (2014). *Capital in the twenty-first century.* Printed in India by Gopsons Papers, Ltd and translated by Arthur Goldhammer.

Polanyi, K. (1951). *The logic of liberty: Reflections and rejoinders.* London: Routledge and Kegan Paul.

Polanyi, K. (1958). *Personal knowledge: Towards a post-critical philosophy.* New York, NY: Harper and Row.

Rawls, J. (1971). *A theory of justice.* Cambridge, MA: Belknap/ Harvard University Press.

Reeves, R.V. (2017). *Dream hoarders: How the American upper middle class is leaving everyone else in the dust, why that is a problem, and what to do about it.* Washington, D.C.: The Brookings Institute.

Reich, R. B. (2020). *The system: Who rigged it, how we fix it.* New York, NY: Alfred A. Knopf.

Ritzer, G. (2008). *The McDonaldization of society.* Thousand Oaks, CA: Pine Forge Press/Sage Publications.

Rumberger, R.W. (1981). *Overeducation in the U.S. labor market.* New York, NY: Praeger.

Sachs, J.D. (2011). *The price of civilization: Reawakening American virtue and prosperity.* New York, NY: Penguin Random House, LLC.

Saez, E., & Zucman, G. (2019). *The triumph of injustice: How the rich dodge taxes and how to make them pay.* New York, NY: W.W. Norton & Company.

Selznick, P. (1992). *The moral commonwealth: Social theory and the promise of community.* Los Angeles, CA: University of California Press.

Sennett, R. (1998). *The corrosion of character: The personal consequences of work in the new capitalism.* New York, NY: W.W. Norton & Company.

Shapiro, D. (1999). *Neurotic styles.* New York NY: Basic Books/ Perseus Books Group.

Shermer, M. (2004). *The science of good and evil.* New York, NY: Henry Holt & Company.

Sloman, S., & Fernback, P. (2017). *The knowledge illusion: Why we never think alone.* New York, NY: Penguin.

Smith, Adam. (1759). *The theory of moral sentiments*

Smith, Adam. (1776). *The wealth of nations.*

Sowell, T. (2002). *A conflict of visions: The ideological origins of political struggles.* New York, NY: Basic Books.

Standing, G. (2011). *The precariat: The new dangerous class.* London: Bloomsbury Publishing.

Stout, M. (2005). *The sociopath next door: The ruthless versus the rest of us.* New York, NY: Broadway Books/Random House, Inc.

Sullivan, T. (1978). *Marginal workers, marginal jobs: The underutilization of American workers.* Austin, TX: University of Texas Press.

Sutton, R.J. (2007). *The no asshole rule.* New York, NY: Business Plus/Hatchette Book Group, U.S.A.

Swartz, M., and Watkins, S. (2003). *Power failure: The inside story of the collapse of Enron.* New York, NY: Doubleday.

Taylor, S. (2005). *The fall: The insanity of the ego in human history and the dawning of a new era.* New York, NY: O-books/John Hunt Publishing, Ltd.

Terrill, R. (1990). *Mao: A biography;* Stanford, CA: Stanford University Press.

Trout, J.D. (2009). *The empathy gap: Building bridges to the good life and the good society.* New York, NY: Viking/Penguin Group USA, Inc.

Trump, M.L. (2020). *Too much and never enough: How my family created the world's most dangerous man.* New York, NY: Simon & Shuster.

Turiel, E. (1983). *The development of social knowledge: Morality and convention.* Cambridge, UK: Cambridge University Press.

Twale, D., & Deluca, B. (2008). *Faculty incivility: The rise of the academic bully culture and what to do about it.* San Francisco, CA: Jossey-Bass.

Twenge, J.M. (2006). *Generation me: Why today's young Americans are more confident, assertive, entitled—and more miserable than ever before.* New York, NY: Free Press.

Twenge, J.M., & Campbell, W.K. (2009). *The narcissism epidemic.* New York, NY: Free Press.

VanHettinga, B. (2019). *Why assholes rule the world.*

Weber, M. (1905). *The protestant ethic and the spirit of capitalism.* London/New York, NY: Routledge Classics (1992).

Werre, R. (2004). *I love my work, but I hate my job.* Lincoln, NE: iUniverse, Inc.

Wilkenson, R., & Pickett, K. (2009). *The spirit level: Why greater equality makes societies stronger.* New York, NY: Bloomsbury Press.

Wolff, M. (2018). *Fire and fury: Inside the Trump White House.* New York, NY: Henry Holt & Company.

Wolin, S. (2008). *Democracy, Inc.: Managed democracy and the specter of inverted totalitarianism.* Princeton, NJ: Princeton University Press.

Wu, T. (2008). *The curse of bigness: Antitrust in the New Gilded Age.* New York, NY: Columbia Global Reports.

Younge, G. (2011). *Who are we—and should it matter in the 21st century*. New York, NY: Nation Books/Perseus.

Zimbardo, P. (2007). *The Lucifer effect.* New York, NY: Random House Publishing Group.

Index

A

A Few Good Men, 201
A Tale of Two Futures, 496
Abrahamic religions, 77, 80, 86, 87, 93, 110, 489
Abu Ghraib, 105, 178, 184, 199, 200, 201, 202, 203, 204, 205, 210, 445, 527
  pornograpy as influence, 445
accumulations of capital
  as defined by Adam Smith, 363
  as drivers of inequality, 367
  associations with economic growth, 363
  Piketty's formula, 365
Adams, Guy, 105, 191, 192, 193, 194, 195, 196, 197
administered state
  as antipolitical, 64
administrative evil, 105, 191, 194, 195, 196, 197, 205, 208
Adorno, Theodore. *See* authoritarian personality
advertising
  and psychology, 425
Age of the Institution. *See* Peck, Dr. Scott
Altemeyer, Bob, 494, 495, 504
altruistic personality, 512
American Fascists: The Christian Right and the War on America, 443
amygdala, 115, 126, 127, 130, 228
Art of the Deal, 314, *See* Schwartz, Tony
asshole behavior
  as a subject of academic study, 510
Atta, Mohammed, 449
authoritarian personality, 386
  and connection with fascism, 493
authoritarianism
  and anti-democratic attitudes, 389
  as threat to democracy, 387

B

Balfour, Danny, 105, 191, 192, 193, 194, 195, 196, 197
Bartels, Larry, 391
Batra, Ravi, 47
Bernays, Edward, 424
Biblical End Times, 486
bio-cultural evolutionary pyramid, 114
Blackwater, 316
Bolton, John, 315
Book of Revelation, 488
Botometer, 423
Bovy, Phoebe Maltz, 164
Bruder, Jessica, 329
  and nomad workers, 329
Buddhism, 77, 78, 79, 80, 88
bullshit jobs
  and inequality, 342
  as empire builders, 342
  as pressure valve for unemployment, 342
Bullshit Jobs, 189, 207, 339
Bush, George
  and Abu Ghraib, 204
buzzwords, 426

C

Capital in the Twenty-First Century, 266, *See* Piketty, Thomas
Center for Strategic and International Studies, 402
Chaos Monkeys, 333
characteropathological activation, 236
characteropathy, 220
  and underemployment, 236
  definition, 220
Cheney, Dick, former VP
  and Abu Ghraib, 204
Christianity, 8, 77, 78, 80, 81, 82, 83, 84, 85, 87, 91, 131, 134
civic virtue, 54, 58
Cleckley, Dr. Hervey, 226
Clinton, Hillary, 271
Cohen, Michael, 315

Collins. Susan. *See* Hunger Games
community
  and commonwealth, 45
  and tradeoff with autonomy, 59
Confucianism, 44, 74, 77, 78, 80
Conley, Lucas. *See* Obsessive Branding Disorder
cooperation
  and economic success, 116
cooperation-competition dichotomy, 111
corporate control of information
  and inability to think critically, 446
corporatocracy, 326, 332, 342, 343, 347, 395, 399, 400, 402, 457
corpus callosum
  and psychopathy, 228
corruption
  institutionalization, 7
  of culture, 7
creeping malignant normality, 291
culture of Davos, 345

D

Dark Triad, 224
de Tocqueville, Alexis, 56
DeJoy, Louis, 470
Demjanjuk, John, 104, 172, 173, 174, 175, 244
democracy, 29, 60
  and connection to happiness, 39
  and decentralized egalitarianism, 57
  and emancipative values, 45
  and political diversity, 62
  as foundation of a good society, 22
  as threat to techno feudalism, 346
  threat from expansion of executive power, 385
  threat from hyper-polarization, 385
Democracy in America, 56
democracy index, 30
Devos, Betsy, 316
Diagnostic and Statistical Manual, 226, 484
disinformation
  and social harm, 524
Disloyal. *See* Cohen, Michael
dominant groups
  and social norms, 164
Draconian
  code and constitution, 117
DSM. *See* Diagnostic and Statistical Manual
Duesenberry, James, 37
Duty to Warn, 291
Dye, Thomas, 392
Dying for a Paycheck. *See* Pfeffer, Jeffrey

E

Easterlin paradox, 34
Easterlin, Richard, 34
eco-fascists, 143, 144, 145
economic democracy, 64
Economic Policy Institute, 522
economic royalism, 59
economic utility, 33
Economist, 30, 48
education
  as remedy for inequality, 367
egotism
  as sign of ponerization, 260
electroshock experiments. *See* Stanley Milgram
Elysium, 477
Empire
  as form of Superpower, 395
End Times prophesies
  and reasons for belief, 487
Enlightenment, 28, 29, 30, 44, 91, 117, 133, 441, 444
  and trans-fall evolution, 486
Enron, 195
equality
  as historical ideal, 354
essential workers
  and bullshit jobs, 340
essentialism. *See* stereotyping
ethnic antagonism
  and anti-democratic sentiment, 391
Etzioni, Amitai, 60
evil
  and human suffering, 75
exodus of a downfall world, 484

F

Facebook
and 2016 election "hack", 422
factionalism, 58, 392
Fairness Doctrine, 413
faith traditions, 23, 74, 489, 507
fake news
and gullibility, 417
and technology, 419
motivated by greed, 416
targeted to emotional triggers, 416
fascism, 15, 317, 386, 443, 539
and religion, 388
as part of American personality, 387
Fay-Jones report, 201
Feldman, David. *See* Underemployment: Psychological, Economic and Social Challenges
Ferraro, David, 403
filter bubbles, 428
Fire and Fury. *See* Wolff, Michael
flatter hierarchies
as mitigation of us-versus-them, 143
flawed democracy, 30
Floyd, George, 468
Foundation for Community Encouragement. *See* Peck, Dr. Scott
Foxycontin, 456
fragmentation, 66, 68, 97, 345, 430
Frances, Dr. Allen, 293, 295, 296, 443, 483, 484, 502, 525, *See* Twilight of American Sanity
Frank, Robert, 267, 268, 296, 456, *See* Richistan
free will
and sin or evil, 94
Friendly Fascism, 387, *See* Gross, Bertram
fuzzy logic, 121, 122, 145

G

Gage, Phineas, 225
Garcia-Martinez, Antonio. *See* Chaos Monkeys
Gatsby curve, 360
Gingrich revolution, 385
Global Change Game, 495
Goldberg, Jonah, 440, 441, 442, 443, 444
Golden Age
of Abrahamic religions, 490
Golden International, 388
Golden Rule, 74, 75, 119, 138
Goldwater Rule, 291, 292
Graeber, David, 207, 339, 340, 341, 342, 343, 344, 345, 351, 352
greed
and unethical behavior, 189
Greenwood, Dr. Vincent, 292, 305
and Trump psychopathy, 292
Gross, Bertam. *See* Friendly Fascism
group dominance
and inferiorization, 161
group privilege, 160
Guinness, Os, 104, 130, 131, 132, 133, 134, 135, 141, 143, 189
and separation of church and state, 132

H

Habits of the Heart, 61, 62, 64, 65, 66, 68
Haidt, Johnathan, 104, 136, 137, 139, 140, 141, 142, 143, 516
happiness, 22, 33, 34, 35, 36, 37, 38, 39, 40, 42, 44, 59, 63, 65, 76, 107, 122, 372
and income, 33
and inequality, 41
and inflation, 39
and unemployment, 39
and work, 40
Happiness Institute, 34, 38
Hare, Dr. Robert, 227, 228, 230, 231, 232, 237, 239, 241, 243, 292
psychopathy checklist, 227
Hassan, Steven
The Cult of Trump, 525
Hedges, Chris, 321, 443, 444, 445, 446, 475
hedonic adaptation, 37
hierarchy
and effects on behavior, 159
Hinduism, 77, 78, 80
historical consciousness

as denial of the past, 196
Hoaxy, 423
homo economicus, 8, 9, 190, 512
House of Cards, 296
How Democracies Die, 384
Human Rights Watch
and report on Abu Ghraib, 203
human suffering
and Hebrew Book of Job, 89
and Islam, 90
and the Four Noble Truths, 88
Hunger Games, 477
hyper-individualism, 24
hysteria, definition, 253
hysteroidal cycle, 218
and "happy times", 254
and destruction of social cohesion, 258
and ideology, 256
and incorporation of deviant worldviews, 255
and seconday ponerogenic processes, 257

I

I Love My Work But I Hate My Job, 339
income inequality
and segmented labor markets, 360
as driver of ponerization, 374
as moral hazard, 371
as threat to democracy, 370
as unnatural distribution, 357
undermines trust and cohesion, 373
individual free will, 23, 75
individual freedom
and civic responsibility, 61
individualism, 5, 8, 28, 56, 57, 59, 62, 65, 66, 68, 93, 193, 331, 523
and utilitarianism, 65
inequality
and American mis-estimates, 362
and American preferences, 362
and civic virtue, 58
and progressive taxation, 369
and threat to democracy, 269
institutional culture, 6
institutionalized inferiority, 30
institutions
and technocratic administration, 63
institutions,, 5, 29, 35, 43, 67, 88, 117, 393
inverted totalitarianism. *See* Wolin, Sheldin
Irony of Democracy. *See* Dye, Thomas
Islam, 77, 80, 84, 85, 86, 87, 90, 92, 487

J

January 6th insurrection, 472
Job Quality Index, 329
Johnston, David Cay, 167, 314, 317, 322
Judaism, 77, 80, 81, 85, 86

K

kakistocracy
definition, 312
Karpinski, General Janis, 202
Kennedy School of Government, 402
King, Rodney, 1, 81, 116, 140, 313, 469
kleptocracy
definition, 312
Knight, Barry, 42, 218
Koch, Charles
admits to "screwing up", 474
Kohlberg
theory of moral development, 126
Kohlberg, Lawrence, 126, 140
kratocracy
definition, 312
Kusnet, David, 339

L

Lab Rats, 333
lack of empathy. *See* psychopathy
Law and Economics Center, 401
Lee, Dr. Bandy, 524
Leonhard, Dr. Robert
and apocalyptic geopolitics, 489
Levitsky, Steven, 384
Liberal Fascism. *See* Goldberg, Jonah
Live Work Work Work Die, 333
Livingstone, David. *See* The Education-Jobs Gap
Lobaczewsky, 225, 230, 233, 235, 244, 245, 251, 253, 254, 255, 256, 257,

258, 259, 260, 261, 262, 264, 265, 270, 271, 273, 277, 282, 284, 285, 288, 298, 299, 312, 328, 383, 394, 403, 412, 428, 440, 441, 445, 450, 452, 454, 455, 510, 515, 539
Lobaczewsky, Dr. Andrew
  Polish Psychiatrist, 214
  thoughts on democracy, 383
  warning against moralization, 451
Love the Work, Hate the Job, 339
luxury of obliviousness, 163
Lyons, David. *See* Lab Rats

M

macrosocial evil, 15, 23, 88, 111, 112, 121, 219, 259, 480, 484, 515, 526
Mahdi
  and Muslim eschatology, 491
  as final Muslim prophet, 490
Malina, Bruce, 7
managed democracy, 391, 397
managed justice, 400
managed obedience, 403
manufactured tribalism
  as cause of social decay, 441
mapping
  and socioeconomic status, 129
  warmth v competence, 129
Marginal Workers, Marginal Jobs, 336
Mask of Sanity, 235, *See* Cleckey, Dr. Hervey
mass psychosis
  as modern ponerization, 536
Matthews, Dr. Dan, 484
Mayer, Jane, 414
Maynard, Douglas. *See* Underemployment: Psychological, Economic and Social Challenges
McDonaldization, 188
media concentration
  as threat to democracy, 399
media consolidation, 413
  and pro-corporate bias, 414
meek shall inherit the earth
  Biblical interpretation, 509
mental health courts in Florida, 197
Milgram, Stanley, 15, 104, 175, 176, 177, 178, 179, 180, 184, 186, 244, 246, 512
Miller, Steven V., 390
Miracolo Economico, 367
Mishra, Pankaj, 447, 448, 449, 450, 451, 493
misinformation
  and cognitive processing, 427
  as source of polarization, 428
Mittelbau
  connection to NASA, 193
moral ambiguities, 120
moral capital, 141
moral commonwealth, 15, 17, 22, 23, 24, 61, 93, 104, 373
moral emotions
  and neuroscience, 119
moral evolution
  and neuroscience, 114
moral foundations, 104, 134, 136, 137, 139, 140, 141, 142, 188, 489
moral inversion, 451
moral reminders, 189, 190
moral systems, 74

N

need for chaos, 457
neuroscience
  and psychopathy, 229
neuroticism
  as normal response to ponerization, 458
nihilism. *See* need for chaos
noblesse oblige, 8, 139, 521

O

obedience
  and authority, 175
Obedience to Authority. *See* Milgram, Stanley
Obsessive Branding Disorder, 425, 429
Occupy Wall Street, 397
oligarchy, 16, 269, 371, 457
Operation Paperclip, 105, 193
original sin
  and secular theory, 108

out-group intolerance
as threat to morality, 122
Overeducation in the U.S. Labor Market, 336
Oxford Declaration on Christian Faith and Economics, 326

P

pathocracy, 16, 220, 253, 273, 281, 284, 285, 286, 287, 288, 289, 290, 293, 298, 301, 516
and ability to resist, 288
and cooptation of religion, 287
and foregiveness of pathocrats, 299
and ideology, 283
and level of hysterization, 285
and paramoralization, 283
and simplified worldview, 284
and social injustice, 282
how to end and recover, 298
perpetuation and social control, 287
PCL-R
psychopathy checklist, 227
Pearson, Taylor. *See* The End of Jobs
Peck, Dr. Scott, 514, *See* The Road Less Traveled
Pein, Corey. *See* Live, Work, Work, Work, Die
People of the Lie. *See* Peck, Dr. Scott
Perry, James L., 9, 178, 208, 316, 323, 516, 518, 529
Perry, Rick, 316
Peters, Tom
as advocate of branding, 425
Pew Research Center
and studies on misinformation, 427
Pfeffer, Jeffrey, 328
Pickett, Kate, 43, 68, 319, 372
Piff, Paul, 104, 154, 156, 157, 158, 254, 518
and experiments with greed, 155
and experiments with social class, 154
Piketty, Thomas, 266, 319, 354, 365, 366, 367, 370, 371, 548
plutocracy, 331, 374
plutonomy, 16, 268
Poland
under Nazis and Soviets, 213
Polanyi, Karl, 451, 452
polarization, 30, 256, 258, 265, 269, 360, 385, 414
political rights
as moral codes, 117
ponerization
and attitudes toward workers, 343
and disconnection of the privileged, 264
and excess of egotism, 260
and failure of legal system, 259
and inequality, 266
and narcissism, 260
and social exclusion, 245
and underemployment, 261
as workaholism, 328
ponerized workplaces, 326
ponerogenesis, 217, 224, 259, 290
ponerology
definition, 217
populism
as source of alienation, 442
Positive and Negative Affect Schedule, 36
positive psychology, 403, 445
postmillennials
and Christian eschatology, 491
post-truth, 412
Pratto, Felicia, 161, 494
precariat. *See* Standing, Guy
precariatization, 319
as institutionalized policy, 331
premillennials
and Christian eschatology, 490
Prince, Eric. *See* Blackwater
privilege
and division of labor, 152
and organizational culture, 153
as role model, 152
professionalism., 64
proficians, 331, 332, 338
proletariat,, 332
ProPublica
video recording of January insurrection, 472
Prosperity Gospel, 8, 395, 453, 454
Protestant work ethic, 454
provisional morality, 122

pseudo-democracy, 16
pseudo-profound bullshit, 426
PSM. *See* Public Service Motivation
psychopath
  and domination, 232
  and hierarchy, 232
  and lack of empathy, 233
  and relation to truth, 231
psychopath.
  definition and traits, 223
psychopathy
  and business sucess, 238
  and Dark Triad, 242
  and Donald Trump, 290
  and impression management, 239
  and leadership, 240
  and organizational toxicity, 239
  and social systems. *See* ponerization
  hereditary or conditioned, 236
  thrives in entrepreneurialism, 242
Public Service Motivation, 9, 516
Putnam, Robert, 76, 443

Q

Q-Anon, 471

R

racism, 2, 291, 293, 494
rational man. *See* homo economicus
rationalization
  as basis of managed democracy, 398
rational-philosophical, 28, 30
religion and the secular state, 91
religious intolerance, 118
  as immoral behavior, 117
ressentiment, 447, *See* Mishra, Pankaj
Rethinking Poverty, 42
riba
  and Islamic law, 93
Richistan, 267, 268
right wing authoritarianism, 495
romanticism
  as abandonment of Enlightenment, 440
  as defense to technocracy, 448
Rudolph, Arthur, 193
Rumberger, Russell. *See* Overeducation in the US Labor Market
Rumsfeld Donald
  and Abu Ghraib, 204
RWA. *See* Right Wing Authoritarianism

S

Saharasia
  and the Fall, 109
salariat., 331
Sapolsky
  Robert, 127, 128, 130, 142, 143
Satisfaction With Life Scale, 35
Schlesinger, James
  and report on Abu Ghraib, 202
Schwab, Klaus, 439
Schwartz, Tony, 314
Science of Good and Evil, 103
SDO, 10, 494, 495, *See* Social Dominance Orientation
Sedanius, Jim, 161
Selznick, Philip. *See* The Moral Commonwealth
Senko, Jen. *See* The Brainwashing of My Dad
Sennett, Richard. *See* The Corrosion of Character
separatist movements
  and empire, 63
Shapiro. Jeremy, 440
shared reality, 46
  as basis of empathy, 268
Shermer, Michael, 103, 111, 112, 114, 116, 118, 119, 121, 122, 145
Singularitarianism, 346
small town
  as moral foundation, 58
social capital, 76
social cohesion, 14, 30, 35, 43, 61, 68, 97
Social Dominance Orientation, 10, 161, 493, 494
social quality model, 35
social value orientation, 10
soft despotism, 451
Sosis, Richard, 141
spellbinder, 256, 257
Standing, Guy, 42, 331, 332, 333

Stanford prison experiment, 15, 104, 180, 184, 185, 199, 200, 202, 204, 205, 521, *See* Phillip Zimbardo
State Bar associations, 11
statistics, 31, 33, 43, 162, 366
status anxiety
as source of polarization, 386
Stellar, Jennifer
neurochemistry and social class, 157
stereotyping, 128, 231
Suicide of the West. *See* Goldberg, Jonah
Sullivan, Teresa. *See Marginal Workers Marginal Jobs*
Superpower, 395, 396, 397, 399, 404, 475
surplus populations, 195, 196

T

Taylor, Steve, 103, 108, 109, 110, 111, 485
Tea Party, 385, 397
Tenet, George, 204
and Abu Ghrai, 204
Texas Bar Journal, 12
The Age of Anger, 447
The American Enterprise Institute, 402
The Barrier, 478
The Brainwashing of My Dad, 456
The Corrosion of Character, 345
The Cult of Trump, 525
The Dangerous Case of Donald Trump, 291
The Education-Jobs Gap, 336
The Empathy Gap, 522
The End of Jobs: Money, Meaning and Freedom Without the 9 to 5, 343
the fall
and original sin, 93
The Fall, 103, 108, 485
The Making of Donald Trump, 314
The Moral Commonwealth, 355
The Perils of Privilege, 164
The Righteous Mind, 136
The Road Less Traveled, 526
The Snowpiercer, 478
The Spirit Level, 68
theocracy, 75, 132, 134
Theory of the Leisure Class, 36
Three Percent (3%), 478
totalitarianism, 393
Trading Places, 157
trans-Fall evolution, 485
Transition Integrity Project, 313
transpersonification, 455
Trente Glorieuses, 367
Trout, J.D., 522, 523
Trump
and narcissism, 293
Trump, Donald
and ponerization, 294
Trump—What's the Deal?, 313
Twilight of American Sanity, 483, 484, 525, *See* Frances, Dr. Allen
tyranny of the majority, 30, 270, 271

U

underemployment, 47, 236, 245, 262, 263, 264, 265, 296, 336, 337, 338, 429
and fallacy of the knowledge economy, 335
and Federal Reserve study, 338
and overeducation, 262
VanHettinga study, 262
Underemployment: Psychological, Economic and Social Challenges, 336
Unite the Right, 470
us-versus-them, 58, 104, 269, 440
and neuroscience, 127
and politics, 135
and religion, 130
and tribalism, 126

V

Veblen, Thorsten, 36
Vohs, Kathleen
psychology of money, 158
von Braun, Werner, 193

W

wage gap, 328
Wages of Rebellion, 475
War on Terror, 205, 396

Weber, Max, 187
Werre, Richard, 339
Westoxification, 449
What Happened. *See* Clinton, Hillary
white outgroup intolerance, 390
Why Assholes Rule the World, 143, 152, 153, 210, 251, 277, 292, 383, 509
Wilkinson, Richard, 43, 68
Williamsburg Charter, 130
Wilson, Richard, 187, 319, 372
Wirtschaft Swunder, 367
Wise, Lois, 9, *See* Perry, James L
Wolff, Michael, 291, 314, 317
Wolin, Sheldin, 392
workaholism
  and Silicon Valley, 334
  as cultural ideal, 333
workplace stress, 327
World Economic Forum, 439
World Inequality Database, 365
World Values Survey, 43, 44

Y

Yarvin, Curtis Guy. *See* Singularitarianism

Z

Ziblatt, Daniel, 384
Zimbardo, Phillip, 15, 104, 105, 180, 182, 183, 184, 199, 202, 203, 204

www.ingramcontent.com/pod-product-compliance
Lightning Source LLC
Chambersburg PA
CBHW070620270326
41926CB00011B/1753

9781732285651